THE Z80 MICROPROCESSOR

Architecture, Interfacing, Programming, and Design

Second Edition

THE Z80 MICROPROCESSOR

Architecture, Interfacing, Programming, and Design

Second Edition

Ramesh S. Gaonkar
STATE UNIVERSITY OF NEW YORK
O.C.C. Campus at Syracuse

Merrill, an imprint of
Macmillan Publishing Company
New York

Maxwell Macmillan Canada
Toronto

Maxwell Macmillan International
New York   Oxford   Singapore   Sidney

Cover Photo: © Ross M. Horowitz Photography

Editor: Dave Garza
Production Editor: Stephen C. Robb
Art Coordinator: Peter A. Robison
Cover Designer: Thomas Mack
Production Buyer: Patricia A. Tonneman

This book was set in Times Roman by Compset, Inc. and was printed and bound by R. R. Donnelley & Sons Company. The cover was printed by Phoenix Color Corp.

Figures 3.4, 3.5, 3.6, 15.17, 15.20, 15.21, 15.22, 15.23, and 18.10 courtesy of Zilog, Inc. Reproduced by permission. © 1991, Zilog, Inc. This material shall not be reproduced without the written consent of Zilog, Inc.

Macmillan Publishing Company
866 Third Avenue
New York, NY 10022

Macmillan Publishing Company is part of the Maxwell Communications Group of Companies.

Maxwell Macmillan Canada, Inc.
1200 Eglinton Avenue East, Suite 200
Don Mills, Ontario M3C 3N1

Library of Congress Cataloging-in-Publication Data
Gaonkar, Ramesh S.
    The Z80 microprocessor : architecture, interfacing, programming,
  and design / by Ramesh Gaonkar.—2nd ed.
      p.   cm.
    Includes index.
    ISBN 0-02-340484-1
    1. Zilog Z-80 (Microprocessor)   I. Title.
  QA76.5.G323   1992
  004.165—dc20
                                                                92-1191
                                                                  CIP

Printing: 2 3 4 5 6 7 8 9   Year: 3 4 5

MERRILL'S INTERNATIONAL SERIES IN ENGINEERING TECHNOLOGY

INTRODUCTION TO ENGINEERING TECHNOLOGY

Pond, *Introduction to Engineering Technology, 2nd Edition*, 0-02-396031-0

ELECTRONICS TECHNOLOGY

Electronics Reference

Adamson, *The Electronics Dictionary for Technicians*, 0-02-300820-2
Berlin, *The Illustrated Electronics Dictionary*, 0-675-20451-8
Reis, *Becoming an Electronics Technician: Securing Your High-Tech Future*, 0-02-399231-X

DC/AC Circuits

Boylestad, *DC/AC: The Basics*, 0-675-20918-8
Boylestad, *Introductory Circuit Analysis, 6th Edition*, 0-675-21181-6
Ciccarelli, *Circuit Modeling: Exercises and Software, 2nd Edition*, 0-02-322455-X
Floyd, *Electric Circuits Fundamentals, 2nd Edition*, 0-675-21408-4
Floyd, *Electronics Fundamentals: Circuits, Devices, and Applications, 2nd Edition*, 0-675-21310-X
Floyd, *Principles of Electric Circuits, 4th Edition*, 0-02-338501-4
Floyd, *Principles of Electric Circuits: Electron Flow Version, 3rd Edition*, 0-02-338531-6
Keown, *PSpice and Circuit Analysis*, 0-675-22135-8
Monssen, *PSpice with Circuit Analysis* 0-675-21376-2
Tocci, *Introduction to Electric Circuit Analysis, 2nd Edition*, 0-675-20002-4

Devices and Linear Circuits

Berlin & Getz, *Fundamentals of Operational Amplifiers and Linear Integrated Circuits*, 0-675-21002-X
Berube, *Electronic Devices and Circuits Using MICRO-CAP II*, 0-02-309160-6
Berube, *Electronic Devices and Circuits Using MICRO-CAP III*, 0-02-309151-7
Bogart, *Electronic Devices and Circuits, 3rd Edition*, 0-02-311701-X
Tocci, *Electronic Devices: Conventional Flow Version, 3rd Edition*, 0-675-21150-6
Floyd, *Electronic Devices, 3rd Edition*, 0-675-22170-6
Floyd, *Electronic Devices: Electron Flow Version*, 0-02-338540-5
Floyd, *Fundamentals of Linear Circuits*, 0-02-338481-6
Schwartz, *Survey of Electronics, 3rd Edition*, 0-675-20162-4
Stanley, *Operational Amplifiers with Linear Integrated Circuits, 2nd Edition*, 0-675-20660-X
Tocci & Oliver, *Fundamentals of Electronic Devices, 4th Edition*, 0-675-21259-6

Digital Electronics

Floyd, *Digital Fundamentals, 4th Edition*, 0-675-21217-0
McCalla, *Digital Logic and Computer Design*, 0-675-21170-0
Reis, *Digital Electronics through Project Analysis* 0-675-21141-7
Tocci, *Fundamentals of Pulse and Digital Circuits, 3rd Edition*, 0-675-20033-4

Microprocessor Technology

Antonakos, *The 68000 Microprocessor: Hardware and Software Principles and Applications, 2nd Edition*, 0-02-303603-6
Antonakos, *The 8088 Microprocessor*, 0-675-22173-0
Brey, *The Advanced Intel Microprocessors*, 0-02-314245-6
Brey, *The Intel Microprocessors: 8086/8088, 80186, 80286, 80386, and 80486: Architecture, Programming, and Interfacing, 2nd Edition*, 0-675-21309-6
Brey, *Microprocessors and Peripherals: Hardware, Software, Interfacing, and Applications, 2nd Edition*, 0-675-20884-X
Gaonkar, *Microprocessor Architecture, Programming, and Applications with the 8085/8080A, 2nd Edition*, 0-675-20675-6
Gaonkar, *The Z80 Microprocessor: Architecture, Interfacing, Programming, and Design, 2nd Edition*, 0-02-340484-1
Goody, *Programming and Interfacing the 8086/8088 Microprocessor: A Product- Development Laboratory Process*, 0-675-21312-6
MacKenzie, *The 8051 Microcontroller*, 0-02-373650-X
Miller, *The 68000 Family of Microprocessors: Architecture, Programming, and Applications, 2nd Edition*, 0-02-381560-4
Quinn, *The 6800 Microprocessor*, 0-675-20515-8
Subbarao, *16/32 Bit Microprocessors: 68000/68010/68020 Software, Hardware, and Design Applications*, 0-675-21119-0

Electronic Communications

Monaco, *Introduction to Microwave Technology*, 0-675-21030-5
Monaco, *Preparing for the FCC Radio-Telephone Operator's License Examination*, 0-675-21313-4
Schoenbeck, *Electronic Communications: Modulation and Transmission, 2nd Edition*, 0-675-21311-8
Young, *Electronic Communication Techniques, 2nd Edition*, 0-675-21045-3
Zanger & Zanger, *Fiber Optics: Communication and Other Applications*, 0-675-20944-7

Microcomputer Servicing

Adamson, *Microcomputer Repair*, 0-02-300825-3
Asser, Stigliano, & Bahrenburg, *Microcomputer Servicing: Practical Systems and Troubleshooting, 2nd Edition*, 0-02-304241-9
Asser, Stigliano, & Bahrenburg, *Microcomputer Theory and Servicing, 2nd Edition*, 0-02-304231-1

Programming

Adamson, *Applied Pascal for Technology*, 0-675-20771-1
Adamson, *Structured BASIC Applied to Technology, 2nd Edition*, 0-02-300827-X
Adamson, *Structured C for Technology*, 0-675-20993-5
Adamson, *Structured C for Technology (with disk)*, 0-675-21289-8
Nashelsky & Boylestad, *BASIC Applied to Circuit Analysis*, 0-675-20161-6

Instrumentation and Measurement

Berlin & Getz, *Principles of Electronic Instrumentation and Measurement*, 0-675-20449-6
Buchla & McLachlan, *Applied Electronic Instrumentation and Measurement*, 0-675-21162-X
Gillies, *Instrumentation and Measurements for Electronic Technicians, 2nd Edition*, 0-02-343051-6

Transform Analysis

Kulathinal, *Transform Analysis and Electronic Networks with Applications*, 0-675-20765-7

Biomedical Equipment Technology

Aston, *Principles of Biomedical Instrumentation and Measurement*, 0-675-20943-9

Mathematics

Monaco, *Essential Mathematics for Electronics Technicians*, 0-675-21172-7
Davis, *Technical Mathematics*, 0-675-20338-4
Davis, *Technical Mathematics with Calculus*, 0-675-20965-X

INDUSTRIAL ELECTRONICS/ INDUSTRIAL TECHNOLOGY

Bateson, *Introduction to Control System Technology, 4th Edition*, 0-02-306463-3
Fuller, *Robotics: Introduction, Programming, and Projects*, 0-675-21078-X
Goetsch, *Industrial Safety: In the Age of High Technology*, 0-02-344207-7
Goetsch, *Industrial Supervision: In the Age of High Technology*, 0-675-22137-4
Horath, *Computer Numerical Control Programming of Machines*, 0-02-357201-9
Hubert, *Electric Machines: Theory, Operation, Applications, Adjustment, and Control*, 0-675-20765-7
Humphries, *Motors and Controls*, 0-675-20235-3
Hutchins, *Introduction to Quality: Management, Assurance, and Control*, 0-675-20896-3
Laviana, *Basic Computer Numerical Control Programming* 0-675-21298-7

Reis, *Electronic Project Design and Fabrication, 2nd Edition*, 0-02-399230-1
Rosenblatt & Friedman, *Direct and Alternating Current Machinery, 2nd Edition*, 0-675-20160-8
Smith, *Statistical Process Control and Quality Improvement*, 0-675-21160-3
Webb, *Programmable Logic Controllers: Principles and Applications, 2nd Edition*, 0-02-424970-X
Webb & Greshock, *Industrial Control Electronics, 2nd Edition*, 0-02-424864-9

MECHANICAL/CIVIL TECHNOLOGY

Keyser, *Materials Science in Engineering, 4th Edition*, 0-675-20401-1
Kraut, *Fluid Mechanics for Technicians*, 0-675-21330-4
Mott, *Applied Fluid Mechanics, 3rd Edition*, 0-675-21026-7
Mott, *Machine Elements in Mechanical Design, 2nd Edition*, 0-675-22289-3
Rolle, *Thermodynamics and Heat Power, 3rd Edition*, 0-675-21016-X
Spiegel & Limbrunner, *Applied Statics and Strength of Materials*, 0-675-21123-9
Wolansky & Akers, *Modern Hydraulics: The Basics at Work*, 0-675-20987-0
Wolf, *Statics and Strength of Materials: A Parallel Approach to Understanding Structures*, 0-675-20622-7

DRAFTING TECHNOLOGY

Cooper, *Introduction to VersaCAD*, 0-675-21164-6
Goetsch & Rickman, *Computer-Aided Drafting with AutoCAD*, 0-675-20915-3
Kirkpatrick & Kirkpatrick, *AutoCAD for Interior Design and Space Planning*, 0-02-364455-9
Kirkpatrick, *The AutoCAD Book: Drawing, Modeling, and Applications, 2nd Edition*, 0-675-22288-5
Lamit and Lloyd, *Drafting for Electronics, 2nd Edition*, 0-02-367342-7
Lamit and Paige, *Computer-Aided Design and Drafting*, 0-675-20475-5
Maruggi, *Technical Graphics: Electronics Worktext, 2nd Edition*, 0-675-21378-9
Maruggi, *The Technology of Drafting*, 0-675-20762-2
Sell, *Basic Technical Drawing*, 0-675-21001-1

TECHNICAL WRITING

Croft, *Getting a Job: Resume Writing, Job Application Letters, and Interview Strategies*, 0-675-20917-X
Panares, *A Handbook of English for Technical Students*, 0-675-20650-2
Pfeiffer, *Proposal Writing: The Art of Friendly Persuasion*, 0-675-20988-9
Pfeiffer, *Technical Writing: A Practical Approach*, 0-675-21221-9
Roze, *Technical Communications: The Practical Craft*, 0-675-20641-3
Weisman, *Basic Technical Writing, 6th Edition*, 0-675-21256-1

To Gaokar, Deodhar, Bhandwalkar, and Khadapkar—
who dedicated their lives to teaching,
devoted their waking moments to helping
others, and who have been my source of
inspiration and guidance.

Preface

This text is intended for microprocessor courses at the undergraduate level in technology, engineering, and computer science. It is a comprehensive treatment of the microprocessor, covering both hardware and software based on the Z80 microprocessor family. The text assumes a course in digital logic as a prerequisite; however, it does not assume a background in programming. This text is also suited for the second level course in curricula where the first level course is based on another microprocessor.

The Z80 microprocessor is widely used in Europe to teach the basic concepts of microprocessor technology. The Z80 is also gaining rapid acceptance in colleges and universities in this country. Before we examine the features of this book, we must answer two critical questions:

(1) In the 1990s, is an 8-bit microprocessor an appropriate device through which to teach the microprocessor concepts? If we consider the worldwide sales volume of microprocessor chips, the answer is a resounding *yes*; 8-bit microprocessors (including single-chip microcontrollers) account for 85% of the total. This question can be better answered by an anology from the auto industry. For transportation, we have trucks, sports cars, family cars, and compact cars. Each serves a different purpose. The 8-bit microprocessors have already established their market in the areas of industrial control, such as machine control, process control, instrumentation, and consumer appliances. The 16- and 32-bit microprocessors are used primarily in computers; they are so powerful that their applications are better suited in such areas as high-speed data processing, CAD/CAM, multi-tasking, and multi-user systems. The 16- and 32-bit microprocessors are less likely to replace 8-bit microprocessors in industrial control applications. In many applications, even 8-bit microprocessors are utilized at less than 50 percent of their capacity. Furthermore, the basic concepts of architecture, programming, and interfacing are easier to teach with the 8-bit than with the 16-bit microprocessor.

(2) Why teach Z80? The second question has several answers. One is that the Z80 is one of the most widely used microprocessors in industrial applications. It has simple architecture and a powerful instruction set that includes the 8085 instruction set (except for two instructions. The Z80 mnemonics are logical and easy to learn. The instruction set includes many powerful concepts of 16-bit microprocessors. In addition, there appears to be a resurgence of interest in the Z80, indicated by the introduction of Z80-compatible microprocessors by major manufacturers such as National Semiconductor, Hitachi, Toshiba, and Zilog itself.

The microprocessor is a general purpose programmable logic device. A thorough understanding of the microprocessor demands the concepts and skills from two different disciplines: hardware concepts from electronics and programming skills from computer science. Hardware is the physical structure of the microprocessor and the programming makes it function—one without the other is meaningless. Therefore, in this text, the contents are presented with an integrated approach to hardware and software in the context of the Z80 microprocessor. It is gratifying to witness such wide acceptance of that approach as used in the first edition of *The Z80 Microprocessor: Architecture, Interfacing, Programming, and Design*. The second edition preserves the same focus and includes additions suggested by reviewers and by faculty who have used the book in their classrooms.

Part I focuses on the microprocessor architecture and interfacing, Part II introduces programming, and Part III integrates the hardware and software concepts from earlier sections to illustrate interfacing and designing microprocessor-based products. Each topic is covered in depth from basic concepts to industrial applications and illustrated by numerous examples with complete schematics. Material is supported with assignments having practical applications.

Part I consists of five chapters that deal with the hardware aspects of the microcomputer as a system, presented with the spiral approach. The material is presented in a format analogous to the view from an airplane that is getting ready to land. As the plane circles, the passenger observes a view without details. As the plane descends, the same view is seen with more details. This approach is preferable because students need to use a microcomputer as a system in their laboratory work in the early stages of a course, without understanding all aspects of the system. Chapter 1 presents an overview of microprocessor-based systems. It presents the 8-bit microprocessor as a programmable device and an embedded controller, rather than a computing device or CPU used in computers. Chapter 2 develops a generalized model of the microprocessor unit and focuses on the basic concepts related to memory and input/output (I/O). Chapter 3 examines the Z80 microprocessor in the context of the hardware and software models developed in Chapter 2. Chapters 4 and 5 are concerned with basic concepts in interfacing memory and I/O.

Part II has six chapters that deal with Z80 instructions, programming techniques, program development, and software development systems. Chapters 6

and 7 are general in nature, serving as an introduction to assembly language programming and assemblers. Chapter 6 now includes the detailed programming
model of the Z80 microprocessor. This will enable faculty members to teach the
programming independently of Part I. Because of easy access to personal computers on college campuses, I have emphasized the use of assemblers to assemble
programs. The remaining chapters include few changes in the content except the
addition of end-of-chapter questions. The contents of Chapters 8 through 11 are
presented in a step-by-step format. A few instructions that can perform a simple
task are selected. Each instruction is reviewed briefly by referring to the instruction set in the appendix. These instructions are then used in writing programs with
explanations of programming techniques and troubleshooting hints. Each illustrative program begins with a problem statement, provides the analysis of the problem, illustrates the program, and explains the programming steps. These chapters
conclude by reviewing all the instructions discussed in those chapters. The contents in Part II are presented in such a way that, in a course with heavy emphasis
on hardware, students can teach themselves assembly language programming if
necessary.

Part III synthesizes the hardware concepts of Part I and software techniques
of Part II. It deals with advanced topics in interfacing memory and I/Os with
numerous industrial and practical examples. Each illustration analyzes the hardware and includes software, and describes how hardware and software work together to accomplish given objectives. Chapters 12 through 16 include various
types of data transfer between the microprocessor and its peripherals, such as
interrupts, interfacing of dynamic memory, I/O with handshake signals using programmable devices, and serial I/O. Chapter 13 has been expanded to include an
additional illustration of interfacing a stepper motor using the 8255. This empha-
sizes the growing importance of the 8255 in the microcomputer industry. Chapter
17 has been substantially revised. Memory design illustrations from Chapter 16
are now included in Chapter 17. In addition, the project—which brings together
all the concepts discussed in the text—has been changed from a single-board microcomputer to a simpler project: the IC Tester. Chapter 18 has been updated to
include the latest 32-bit microprocessors such as the Intel 486, as well as retaining
a brief introduction to 16-bit microprocessors and single-chip microcontrollers.
Finally, the text includes two appendices related to the instruction set. Appendix
A includes the complete set of Z80 instructions explained with illustrative examples in alphabetical order so that students can easily access the instruction set
with a complete explanation of each item. Appendix E has been added to include
explanation of data converters. Appendix F summarizes all the instructions with
flag information for quick reference when writing programs.

A Word to Faculty

This text was based on my teaching experience, my course development efforts,
and my association with industry engineers and programmers. It was an attempt

to share my classroom experiences and my observations of industrial practices. My assumptions and observations of four years ago, outlined in the preface of the first edition, appear to be valid today. They were as follows:

1. It is easier to teach microprocessor concepts with an 8-bit microprocessor than with a 16-bit microprocessor. Because of easy accessibility on college campuses to personal computers, they can be used to develop programs using cross assemblers.
2. Software (instructions) is an integral part of the microprocessor and demands an emphasis equal to that of the hardware.
3. In industry, for the development of microprocessor-based projects, 70 percent of the efforts are devoted to software and 30 percent to hardware.
4. Technology and engineering students tend to be oriented toward hardware and have considerable difficulty in programming.
5. Students have difficulty in understanding mnemonics and realizing the critical importance of flags.

The text meets the objectives of courses with various emphases at the undergraduate level. For a one-semester course with 50 percent hardware and 50 percent software emphasis, the following chapters are recommended: Chapters 1 through 5 for hardware and interfacing lectures, and Chapters 6 through 10 and selected sections of Chapter 11 for software laboratory sessions. For additional interfacing concepts, the initial sections of Chapters 12, 13, and 15 (concepts in introduction to interrupts, programmable I/O devices, and serial I/O) are recommended. If the course is heavily oriented toward hardware, Chapters 1 through 5 and Chapters 12 through 16 are recommended, and necessary programs can be selected from Chapters 6 through 10. Interfacing laboratory sessions can be designed around the illustrations in chapters or assignments given at the end of chapters. If the course is heavily oriented toward software, Chapters 1 through 3 and Chapters 6 through 11 can be used. For a two-semester course, the entire text can be covered. The instructor's manual includes a course design, suggested weekly lecture and laboratory schedule, solutions, and selected figures to produce transparencies.

My courses have evolved since 1988 when the first edition was published. I have started using an assembler and a simulator three weeks into a semester. We spend more time in examining the flag register to observe how flags are affected, and we devote several laboratory periods to examining the relationships between instructions and waveforms on the oscilloscope.

In the last four years, numerous faculty members shared their classroom experiences, concerns, and students' difficulties with me through letters and the feedback questionnaires included in the instructor's manual. They made valuable suggestions for programming problems and interfacing projects. I have made every effort to incorporate those concerns and suggestions in the second edition. In addition, a set of answers to selected assignments is available with the instructor's manual. I appreciate any communication about the text from the reader; please feel free to write or send a message on BITNET.

A Word With Students

The microprocessor is an exciting, challenging, and growing field; it will pervade industry for decades to come. To meet the challenges of this growing technology, you will need to be well conversant with the programmable aspect of the microprocessor. Programming is a process of problem solving and communication in a strange language of mnemonics. Most often, hardware-oriented students find this communication process very difficult. One of the questions frequently asked by a student is, How do I get started in a given programming assignment? One approach to learning programming is to examine various types of programs and imitate them: Begin by studying the illustrative program relevant to an assignment, its flowchart, its analysis, program description, and particularly, the comments. Read the instructions from Appendix A as necessary and pay attention to the flags. This text is written in such a way that simple programming of the microprocessor can be self-taught. Once you master the elementary programming techniques, interfacing and design become exciting and fun.

ACKNOWLEDGMENTS

For all the efforts behind this second edition, I express my sincere appreciation to my family: my wife, Shaila, for her unwavering support and my daughters, Nelima and Vanita, for their good-natured assistance in completing various tasks. I also thank all the faculty members who provided valuable comments and suggestions and my reviewers: Stanley N. Brown, Vincennes University, Vincennes, IN; James A. Cercone, West Virginia Institute of Technology, Montgomery, WV; David G. Delker, Kansas State University, Manhattan, KS; Waldemar Gerassimoff, Milwaukee School of Engineering, Milwaukee, WI; Nazar Karzay, Indiana Vocational Technical College, Evansville, IN; Daniel A. Merkel, Milwaukee Area Technical College, Milwaukee, WI; Michael O'Donnell, Milwaukee School of Engineering, Milwaukee, WI; Robert A. Steker, Waukesha County Technical College, Pewaukee, WI; and Hue V. Tran, Milwaukee School of Engineering, Milwaukee, WI.

I also thank Macmillan Publishing Company staff including editor Dave Garza, production editor Steve Robb, and art coordinator Pete Robison.

Ramesh Gaonkar
Onondaga Community College
Syracuse, NY 13215

Email: RGAONKAR @SUVM

Contents

I
Microprocessor Architecture and Interfacing

Part I of this book is concerned primarily with microprocessor architecture in the context of microprocessor-based products. The microprocessor-based systems are discussed in terms of three components—the microprocessor, memory, and input and output—and their communication process. The role of the programming languages, from the machine language to high-level languages, is presented in the context of the system.

The material is presented in a format similar to the view from an airplane preparing to land. As the plane circles, one observes a view without any details. As the plane descends, one begins to see the same view but with more details. Chapter 1 presents the microprocessor from two points of view: the microprocessor as a programmable embedded device in a product and as an element of a computer system, and how it communicates with memory and I/O. The chapter also discusses the role of assembly language in microprocessor-based products and presents an overview of various types of computers—from large computers to microcomputers—and their applications. Chapter 2 describes a generalized model of a microprocessor-based system and its three components: the microprocessor, memory, and input and output (I/O). Chapters 3, 4, and 5 examine these components in detail and discuss how memory and I/O devices interface with the Z80 microprocessor.

PREREQUISITES

The reader is expected to know the following concepts:

☐ Number systems (binary, octal, and hexadecimal) and their conversions.
☐ Boolean algebra, logic gates, flip-flops, and registers.
☐ Concepts in combinational and sequential logic.

Microprocessors, Microcomputers, and Assembly Language

The microprocessor plays a significant role in the everyday functioning of industrialized societies. The microprocessor can be viewed as a programmable logic device that can be used to control processes or to turn on/off devices. On the other hand, the microprocessor can be viewed as a data processing unit or a computing unit of a computer. The **microprocessor** is a programmable integrated device that has computing and decision making capability similar to that of the central processing unit (CPU) of a computer. Nowadays, the microprocessor is being used in a wide range of products called microprocessor-based products or systems. The microprocessor can be embedded in a larger system, can be a stand alone unit controlling processes, or it can function as the CPU of a computer called a **microcomputer.** This chapter introduces the basic structure of a microprocessor-based product and shows how the same structure is applicable to microcomputers and other large (mini- and mainframe) computers. Later in the chapter, microprocessor applications are presented in the context of the entire spectrum of various computer applications.

The microprocessor communicates and operates in the binary numbers 0 and 1, called

bits. Each microprocessor has a fixed set of instructions in the form of binary patterns called a **machine language.** However, it is difficult for humans to communicate in the language of 0s and 1s. Therefore, the binary instructions are given abbreviated names, called **mnemonics,** which form the **assembly language** for a given microprocessor. This chapter explains both the machine language and the assembly language of the microprocessor known as the Z80. The advantages of assembly language are compared with such English-like languages as BASIC and FORTRAN.

OBJECTIVES

☐ Draw a block diagram of a microprocessor-based system and explain the functions of each component: microprocessor, memory, and I/O, and their lines of communication (the bus).

☐ Explain the terms SSI, MSI, and LSI.

☐ Define the terms *bit, byte, word, instruction, software,* and *hardware.*

☐ Explain the difference between the machine language and the assembly language of a computer.

☐ Explain the terms low-level and high-level languages.

☐ Explain the advantages of an assembly language over high-level languages.

1.1   MICROPROCESSORS

A microprocessor is a multipurpose, *programmable* logic device that reads *binary* instructions from a storage device called *memory,* accepts binary data as *input* and processes data according to those instructions, and provides results as *output.* A typical programmable machine can be represented with three components: microprocessor, memory, and I/O as shown in Figure 1.1. These three components work together or interact with each other to perform a given task; thus, they comprise a system. The physical components of this system are called **hardware.** A set of instructions written for the microprocessor to perform a task is called a **program,** and a group of programs is called **software.** The machine (system) represented in Figure 1.1 can be programmed to turn traffic lights on and off, compute mathematical functions, or keep track of a guidance system. This system may be simple or sophisticated, depending on its applications, and it is recognized by various names depending upon the purpose for which it is designed. The microprocessor applications are classified primarily in two categories: reprogrammable systems and embedded systems. In reprogrammable systems, such as microcomputers, the microprocessor is used for computing and data processing. These systems include general-purpose microprocessors capable of handling large data, mass storage devices (disks), and peripherals such as printers; a Personal Computer (PC) is a typical illustration. In embedded systems, the microprocessor is a part of a final product and is not available for reprogramming to the end user. A copying machine is a typical example of an embedded system. The microprocessors used in these systems are generally categorized as: (1) microcontrollers that include all the components shown in Figure 1.1 on one chip, (2) integrated microprocessors that include various devices (such as timers and various types of I/Os) on a chip, and (3) general-purpose microprocessors with discrete components shown in Figure 1.1. Embedded systems can also be viewed as products that use microprocessors to perform their operations; they are known as microprocessor-based products. Examples include a wide range of products such as washing machines, dishwashers, automobile dashboard controls, traffic light controllers, and automatic testing instruments.

FIGURE 1.1
A Programmable Machine

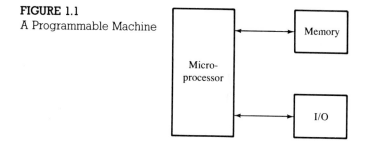

BINARY DIGITS

The microprocessor operates in binary digits, 0 and 1, also known as bits. **Bit** is an abbreviation for the term *binary digit*. These digits are represented in terms of electrical voltages in the machine: generally, 0 represents one voltage level, and 1 represents another. The digits 0 and 1 are also synonymous with low and high, respectively.

Each microprocessor recognizes and processes a group of bits called the **word,** and microprocessors are classified according to their word length. For example, a processor with an 8-bit word is known as an 8-bit microprocessor, and a processor with a 16-bit word is known as a 16-bit microprocessor.

A MICROPROCESSOR AS A PROGRAMMABLE DEVICE

The fact that the microprocessor is programmable means it can be instructed to perform given tasks within its capability. A piano is a programmable machine; it is capable of generating various kinds of tones based on the number of keys it has. A musician selects keys depending upon the musical score printed on a sheet. Similarly, today's microprocessor is designed to understand and execute many binary instructions. It is a multipurpose machine: it can be used to perform various sophisticated computing functions, as well as simple tasks such as turning devices on or off. A programmer can select appropriate instructions and ask the microprocessor to perform various tasks on a given set of data.

The person who designs a piano determines the frequency (tone) for a given key and the scope of the piano music. Similarly, the engineers designing a microprocessor determine a set of tasks the microprocessor should perform and design the necessary logic circuits, and provide the user with a list of the instructions the processor will understand. For example, an instruction for adding two numbers may look like a group of eight binary digits, such as 1000 0000. These instructions are simply a pattern of 0s and 1s. The user (programmer) selects instructions from the list and determines the sequence of execution for a given task. These instructions are entered or stored in a storage device called memory, which can be read by the microprocessor.

MEMORY

Memory is like the pages of a notebook with space for a fixed number of binary numbers on each line. However, these pages are generally made of semiconductor material. Typically, each line is an 8-bit register that can store eight binary bits, and several of these registers are arranged in a sequence called memory. These registers are always grouped together in powers of two. For example, a group of 1024 (2^{10}) 8-bit registers on a semiconductor chip is known as 1K byte of memory; 1K is the closest approximation in thousands. The user writes the necessary instructions and data in memory through an input device (described below), and asks the microprocessor to perform the given task and find an answer. The answer is generally displayed at an output device (described below) or stored in memory.

INPUT/OUTPUT

The user can enter instructions and data into memory through devices such as a keyboard or simple switches. These devices are called **input devices.** The microprocessor reads the instructions from the memory and processes the data according to those instructions. The result can be displayed by a device such as seven-segment LEDs (Light Emitting Diodes) or printed by a printer. These devices are called **output devices.**

MICROPROCESSOR AS A CPU

We can also view the microprocessor as a primary component of a computer. Traditionally, the computer is represented in block diagram as shown in Figure 1.2(a). The block diagram shows that the computer has four components: Memory, Input, Output, and the central processing unit (CPU), which consists of the Arithmetic/Logic Unit (ALU) and Control Unit. The CPU contains various registers to store data, the ALU to perform arithmetic and logical operations, instruction decoders, counters, and control lines. The CPU reads instructions from the memory and performs the tasks specified. It communicates with input/output devices either to accept or to send data. These devices are also known as **peripherals.** The CPU is the primary and central player in communicating with devices such as memory, input, and output. However, the timing of the communication process is controlled by the group of circuits called the control unit.

In the 1960s, the CPU was designed with discrete components on various boards. With the advent of the integrated circuit technology, it became possible to build the CPU on a single chip; this came to be known as a microprocessor, and the traditional block diagram shown in Figure 1.2(a) can be replaced by the block diagram shown in Figure 1.2(b).

1.1.1 Advances in Semiconductor Technology

In the last forty years, semiconductor technology has undergone unprecedented changes. After the invention of the transistor, integrated circuits (ICs) appeared on the scene at the end of the 1950s; an entire circuit consisting of several transistors, diodes, and resistors could be designed on a single chip. In the early 1960s, logic gates known as the 7400 series were commonly available as ICs, and the technology of integrating the circuits of a logic gate on a single chip became known as Small-Scale Integration (SSI). As semiconductor technology advanced, more than 100 gates were fabricated on one chip; this was called Medium-Scale

FIGURE 1.2

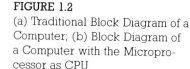

(a) Traditional Block Diagram of a Computer; (b) Block Diagram of a Computer with the Microprocessor as CPU

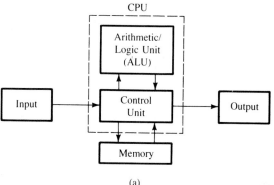

(a)

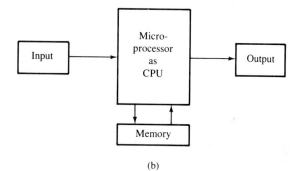

(b)

Integration (MSI). A typical example of MSI is a decade counter (7490). Within a few years, it was possible to fabricate more than 1000 gates on a single chip; this came to be known as Large-Scale Integration (LSI). Now we are in the era of Very-Large-Scale Integration (VLSI) and Super-Large-Scale Integration (SLSI). The lines of demarcation between these different scales of integration are rather ill-defined and arbitrary.

As the technology moved from SSI to LSI, more and more logic circuits were built on one chip, and they could be programmed to do different functions through hard-wired connections. For example, a counter chip can be programmed to count in Hex or decimal by providing logic 0 or 1 through appropriate pin connections. The next step was the idea of providing 0s and 1s through a register. The necessary signal patterns of 0s and 1s were stored in registers and given to the programmable chip at appropriate times; the group of registers used for storage was called memory. Because of the LSI technology, it became possible to build many computing functions and their related timing on a single chip.

The Intel 4004 was the first 4-bit programmable device that was primarily used in calculators. It was designed by Intel Corporation and became known as the 4-bit microprocessor. It was quickly replaced by the 8-bit microprocessor (the

Intel 8008), which was in turn superseded by the Intel 8080. In the mid-1970s, the Intel 8080 was widely used in control applications, and small computers also were designed using the 8080 as the CPU; these computers became known as microcomputers. Within a few years after the emergence of the 8080, the Motorola 6800, the Zilog Z80, and the Intel 8085 microprocessors were developed as improvements over the 8080. The 6800 was designed with a different architecture and the instruction set from the 8080. On the other hand, the 8085 and the Z80 were designed as **upward software compatible** with the 8080; that is, they included all the instructions of the 8080 plus additional instructions. In terms of the instruction set, the 8080 and the 8085 are almost identical; however, the Z80 has a powerful instruction set containing twice as many instruction types as the 8080. As the microprocessors began to acquire more and more computing functions, they were viewed more as CPUs rather than as programmable logic devices. Most microcomputers are now built with 16- and 32-bit microprocessors, and 64-bit microprocessors are also being used in some special-purpose computers. The 8-bit microprocessors are not simply being replaced by more powerful microprocessors, however; each microprocessor has begun to carve a niche for its own applications. The 8-bit microprocessors are being used as programmable logic devices in control applications, and the 16- and 32-bit microprocessors are being used for mathematical computing (number crunching) and data processing applications. Our focus here is in using 8-bit microprocessors as programmable devices.

1.1.2 Organization of a Microprocessor-Based System

Figure 1.3 shows a simplified but formal structure of a microprocessor-based system or a product. Since a microcomputer is one among many microprocessor-based systems, it will have the same structure as shown in Figure 1.3. It includes four components: *microprocessor, input, output,* and *memory* (Read/Write Memory and Read-Only Memory). These components are organized around a common communication path called a **bus.** The entire group of components is also referred to as a system or a microcomputer system, and the components themselves are referred to as sub-systems. At the outset, it is necessary to differentiate between the terms *microprocessor* and *microcomputer* because of the common misuse of these terms in popular literature. The microprocessor is one component of the microcomputer. On the other hand, the microcomputer is a complete computer similar to any other computer, except that the CPU functions of the microcomputer are performed by the microprocessor. Similarly, the term **peripheral** is used for input/output devices. The various components of a microprocessor-based product or a microcomputer are shown in Figure 1.3 and their functions are described in this section.

MICROPROCESSOR

The microprocessor is a semiconductor device consisting of electronic logic circuits manufactured by using either a large-scale (LSI) or very-large-scale integration (VLSI) technique. The microprocessor is capable of performing various com-

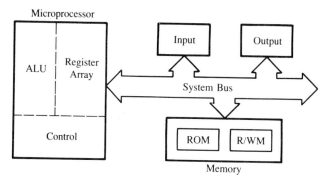

FIGURE 1.3
Microprocessor-Based System with Bus Architecture

puting functions and making decisions to change the sequence of program execution. In large computers, a CPU implemented on one or more circuit boards performs these computing functions. The microprocessor is in many ways similar to the CPU, but includes all the logic circuitry, including the control unit, on one chip. The microprocessor can be divided into three segments for the sake of clarity, as shown in Figure 1.3: Arithmetic/Logic Unit (ALU), Register Array, and Control Unit.

Arithmetic/Logic Unit   This is the area of the microprocessor where various computing functions are performed on data. The ALU unit performs such arithmetic operations as addition and subtraction, and such logic operations as AND, OR, and exclusive OR. Results are stored either in registers or in memory.

Register Array   This area of the microprocessor consists of various registers. These registers are primarily used to store data temporarily during the execution of a program. Some of the registers are accessible to the user through instructions.

Control Unit   The control unit provides the necessary timing and control signals to all the operations in the microcomputer. It controls the flow of data between the microprocessor and memory and peripherals.

Now the question is: what is the relationship among the programmer's instruction (binary pattern of 0s and 1s), the ALU, and the control unit? This can be explained with the example of a Full Adder circuit. A Full Adder circuit can be designed with registers, logic gates, and a clock. The clock initiates the adding operation. Similarly, the bit pattern of an instruction initiates a sequence of clock signals, activates the appropriate logic circuits in the ALU, and performs the task. This is called microprogramming, which is done in the design stage of the microprocessor. The bit patterns required to initiate these microprogram operations are given to the programmer in the form of the instruction set of the microprocessor. The programmer selects appropriate bit patterns from the set for a given task and enters them sequentially in memory through an input device. When the CPU reads these bit patterns one at a time, it initiates appropriate microprograms through the control unit, and performs the task specified in the instructions.

At present, various microprocessors are available from different manufacturers. Examples of widely used 8-bit microprocessors include the Intel 8080/8085, Zilog Z80, and Motorola 6800 and 6809. Earlier microcomputers such as the Radio Shack TRS-80, the Televideo 803, and the Kaypro 4 were designed around the Z80 microprocessor. The recent versions of IBM personal computers, Personal System/2, are designed around 16-bit and 32-bit microprocessors; the model 60 is based on the Intel 80286 (16-bit), the model 80 is based on the Intel 80386 (32-bit), and the models 90 and 95 are based on the 80486 (32-bit) microprocessor. Single-board microcomputers such as the Intel SDK-85, the Motorola MEK-6800-D2, the E&L Instrument Fox Microcomputer Trainer, and the CAMI Research Micro-Trainer are commonly used in college laboratories; the SDK-85 is based on the 8085 microprocessor, the MEK-6800-D2 on the 6800 microprocessor, and the Fox Trainer and the Micro-Trainer on the Z80 microprocessor.

INPUT

The input section transfers data and instructions in binary from the outside world to the microprocessor. It includes such devices as a keyboard, a teletype, and an analog-to-digital converter. Typically, a microcomputer used in college laboratories includes either a hexadecimal keyboard or an ASCII keyboard as an input device. The hexadecimal (Hex) keyboard has 16 data keys (0 to 9 and A to F) and some additional function keys to perform such operations as storing data and executing programs. The ASCII keyboard (explained in Section 1.3) is similar to a typewriter keyboard, and it is used to enter programs in an English-like language. Although the ASCII keyboard is found in most microcomputers, single-board microcomputers generally have Hex keyboards, and microprocessor-based products such as a microwave oven have decimal keyboards.

OUTPUT

The output section transfers data from the microprocessor to such output devices as light emitting diodes (LEDs), a cathode-ray tube (CRT), a printer, a magnetic tape, or another computer. Typically, single-board computers and microprocessor-based products (such as a dishwasher) include LEDs, seven-segment LEDs, and alphanumeric LED displays as output devices.

MEMORY

Memory stores such binary information as instructions and data, and provides that information to the microprocessor whenever necessary. To execute programs, the microprocessor reads instructions and data from memory and performs the computing operations in its ALU section. Results are either transferred to the output section for display or stored in memory for later use. The memory block shown in Figure 1.3 has two sections: **Read-Only Memory** (ROM) and **Read/Write Memory** (R/WM), popularly known as **Random-Access Memory** (RAM).

The ROM is used to store programs that do not need alterations. The monitor program of a single-board microcomputer is generally stored in the ROM. This program interprets the information entered through a keyboard and provides equivalent binary digits to the microprocessor. Programs stored in the ROM can only be read; they cannot be altered.

The Read/Write Memory (R/WM) is also known as user memory. It is used to store user programs and data. In single-board microcomputers, the monitor program monitors the Hex keys and stores those instructions and data in the R/W memory. The information stored in this memory can be easily read and altered.

SYSTEM BUS

The system bus is a communication path between the microprocessor and peripherals; it is nothing but a group of wires to carry bits. In fact, there are several buses in the system that will be discussed in the next chapter. All peripherals (and memory) share the same bus; however, the microprocessor communicates with only one peripheral at a time. The timing is provided by the control unit of the microprocessor.

1.1.3 How Does the Microprocessor Work?

Assume that a program and data are already entered in the R/W memory. (How to write and execute a program will be explained later.) The program includes binary instructions to add given data and to display the answer at the seven-segment LEDs. When the microprocessor is given a command to execute the program, it reads and executes one instruction at a time and finally sends the result to the seven-segment LEDs for display.

This process of program execution can best be described by comparing it to the process of assembling a radio kit. The instructions for assembling the radio are printed in a sequence on a sheet of paper. One reads the first instruction, then picks up the necessary components of the radio and performs the task. The sequence of the process is *read, interpret,* and *perform*. The microprocessor works the same way. The instructions are stored sequentially in the memory. The microprocessor fetches the first instruction from its memory sheet, decodes it, and executes that instruction. The sequence of *fetch, decode,* and *execute* is continued until the microprocessor comes across an instruction to *stop*. During the entire process, the microprocessor uses the system bus to fetch the binary instructions and data from the memory. It uses registers from the register section to store data temporarily, and it performs the computing function in the ALU section. Finally, it sends out the result in binary, using the same bus lines, to the seven-segment LEDs.

1.1.4 Summary of Important Concepts

The functions of various components of a microprocessor-based system can be summarized as follows:

1. The microprocessor
   □ communicates with all peripherals (memory and I/Os) using the system bus.
   □ controls timing of information flow.
   □ performs the computing tasks specified in a program.
2. The memory
   □ stores binary instructions and data, called programs.
   □ provides the instructions and data to the microprocessor on request.
   □ stores results and data for the microprocessor.
3. The input device
   □ enters data and instructions under the control of a program such as a monitor program.
4. The output device
   □ accepts data from the microprocessor as specified in a program.
5. The bus
   □ carries bits between the microprocessor and memory and I/Os.

1.2 FROM LARGE COMPUTERS TO SINGLE-CHIP MICROCONTROLLERS

In the last thirty years, advances in semiconductor technology have had an unprecedented impact on computers. Thirty years ago, computers were accessible only to big corporations, universities, and government agencies. Now, "computer" has become a common word. The range of computers now available extends from such sophisticated, multimillion-dollar machines as the Cray computers to the less-than-$1000 personal computer. All the computers now available on the market include the same basic components shown in Figure 1.3. Nevertheless, it is obvious that these computers are not all the same.

Different types of computers are designed to serve different purposes. Some are suitable for scientific calculations, while others are used simply for turning appliances on and off. Thus, it is necessary to have an overview of the entire spectrum of computer applications as a context for understanding the topics and applications discussed in this text. Until twenty years ago, computers were broadly classified in three categories: mainframe, mini-, and microcomputers. Since then, technology has changed considerably, and the distinctions between these categories have been blurred. Initially, the microcomputer was recognized as a computer with a microprocessor as its CPU. Now practically all computers have various types of microprocessors performing different functions within the large CPU. For the sake of convenience, computers are classified here as large computers, medium-size computers, and microcomputers.

1.2.1 Large Computers

These are large, general-purpose computers designed to perform such data processing tasks as complex scientific and engineering calculations and handling records for large corporations or government agencies. The price is generally beyond $1 million and can range from $10 to $20 million. Typical examples of these computers are the IBM ES9000 series, Unisys A series, and Cray computers; they are generally known as mainframe computers. These are high-speed computers, and their word lengths range from 32 to 64 bits. They are capable of addressing megabytes of memory and handling all types of peripherals.

1.2.2 Medium-Size Computers

In the late 1960s, these computers were designed to meet the instructional needs of small colleges, the manufacturing problems of small factories, and the data processing tasks of medium-size businesses, such as payroll and accounting. They were called **minicomputers**. The price range was anywhere from $25,000 to $100,000. Typical examples include such computers as Digital Equipment Corporation (DEC) PDP 11/45 and Data General Nova.

These computers were slower than the large computers, and their word length generally ranged from 12 to 32 bits. They were capable of addressing 64K to 256K bytes of memory. Some of the larger minicomputers were known as **midicomputers.** However, these classifications are no longer valid. For example, Digital Equipment's VAX series is a 32-bit machine with megabytes of memory addressing capacity. The price ranges from $25,000 to $450,000. The high-end models of the VAX 9000 systems are classified as mainframe computers.

1.2.3 Microcomputers

The 4-bit and 8-bit microprocessors became available in the early 1970s, and initial applications were primarily in the areas of machine control and instrumentation. As the price of the microprocessors and memory began to decline, the applications mushroomed in almost all areas, including video games, word processing, and small business applications. Early arrivals in the microcomputer market, such as Cromemco, North Star Horizon, Radio Shack TRS-80, and Apple, were designed around 8-bit microprocessors. Since then, 16-bit and 32-bit microprocessors such as Intel 8086/88, 80286, 80386, 80486; Motorola 68000; and Zilog Z8000 have been introduced, and recent microcomputers have been designed around these microprocessors. Present-day microcomputers can be classified into three groups: business (or personal), single-board, and single-chip microcomputers.

BUSINESS MICROCOMPUTERS

These microcomputers are being used for a variety of purposes, such as payroll, business accounts, word processing, legal and medical recordkeeping, personal finance, and instruction. They are also known as personal computers. Typically, the price ranges from $1,000 to $5,000 for a single-user system, and it can go higher for a multi-user system. Examples include the IBM personal computer (PC, XT, AT, and personal system 2 series), AT&T 6300 series, Apple and Macintosh, Zenith, and Compaq computers. Figure 1.4 shows an example.

FIGURE 1.4
Microcomputer with Disk Storage: IBM Personal System/2, Model 90XP 486 series

SOURCE: Photograph courtesy of IBM Corporation.

At the low end of the microcomputer spectrum, a typical configuration includes a 16-bit microprocessor, 512K (or higher) bytes of system memory, a cathode ray tube (CRT) terminal, a dot matrix printer, dual disk drive for 5¼- and 3½-inch floppy disks, and a 40 to 80 megabyte (MB) hard disk. The **floppy disk** is a magnetic medium similar to a cassette tape except that it is round like a record. Information recorded on these disks can be accessed randomly using disk drives. Conversely, information stored on a cassette tape is accessed serially. In order to read information at the end of the tape, the user must run the entire tape through the machine. The **hard disk** is similar to the floppy disk except that the magnetic material is coated on a rigid aluminum base that is enclosed in a sealed container and permanently installed in a microcomputer. The hard disk and the floppy disk are used to store programs semipermanently, i.e., the binary information does not disappear when the power is turned off. However, the microprocessor does not have direct access to this information; it must copy this information (programs) into system memory. The hard disk has a large storage capacity; therefore, large and frequently used programs such as compilers, interpreters, system programs, and application programs are stored on this disk. The floppy disk is generally used for user programs. At the high end of the microcomputer spectrum, the basic configuration remains essentially similar. It may include a high-speed, 16- or 32-bit microprocessor, a hard disk with 80 to 120 MB of storage, two disks, a high-resolution CRT terminal, and a laser printer.

SINGLE-BOARD MICROCOMPUTERS

These microcomputers are used primarily in college laboratories and industries for instructional purposes or for evaluating the performance of a given microprocessor. They can also be part of some larger systems. Typically, these microcomputers include an 8-bit microprocessor, from 256 to 2K bytes of user memory, a

Hex keyboard, and seven-segment LEDs for display. The system monitor programs of these computers are generally small; they are stored in less than 2K bytes of ROM. The prices of these single-board computers range from $100 to $800, with the average price being about $300.

Examples of these computers include such systems as Intel SDK-85, Motorola Evaluation Kit, E&L Instrument Fox Microtrainer, and CAMI Research Micro-Trainer (Figure 1.5). These are generally used to write and execute assembly language programs and to perform interfacing experiments.

SINGLE-CHIP MICROCOMPUTERS (MICROCONTROLLERS)

These microcomputers are designed on a single chip, which typically includes a microprocessor, 64 bytes of R/W memory, from 1K to 2K bytes of ROM, and several signal lines to connect I/Os. These are complete microcomputers on a chip; they are also known as **microcontrollers.** They are used primarily for functions such as controlling appliances and traffic lights. Typical examples of these microcomputers include the Zilog Z8, Intel MCS 51 and 96 series, and Motorola 68HC11.

The entire spectrum of computer applications is shown in Figure 1.6, and various applications and categories of the microcomputer are listed in Table 1.1.

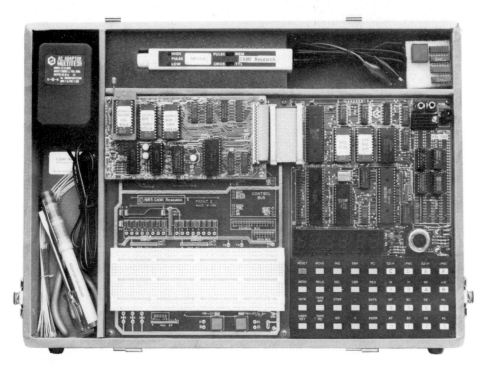

FIGURE 1.5

Single-Board Microcomputer: Micro-Trainer

SOURCE: Photograph courtesy of CAMI Research, Inc.

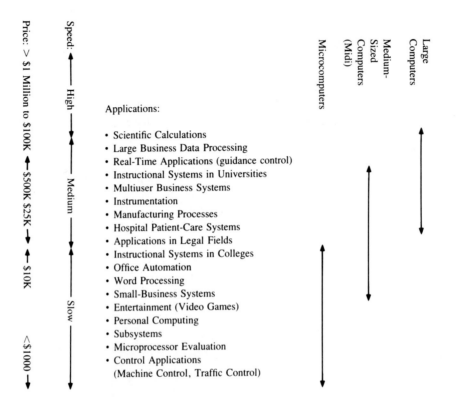

FIGURE 1.6
Applications: From Large Computers to Single-Chip Microcomputers

1.3   MICROPROCESSOR INSTRUCTION SET AND COMPUTER LANGUAGES

Microprocessors recognize and operate in binary numbers. However, each micro-processor has its own binary words, instructions, meanings, and language. The words are formed by combining a number of bits for a given machine. The **word** (or word length), as defined earlier, is the number of bits the microprocessor rec-ognizes and processes at a time. The word length ranges from 4 bits for small, microprocessor-based computers, to 32 bits for such large computers as the IBM ES 9000 series. Another term commonly used to express word length is byte. The **byte** is defined as a group of eight bits. For example, a 16-bit microprocessor has a word length equal to two bytes. The term "nibble," which stands for a group of four bits, is also found in popular computer magazines and books. (A byte has two nibbles.)

TABLE 1.1
Microcomputer Applications

Characteristics	Types		
	Microcomputer (Personal Computer)	Single-Board Microcomputer	Single-Chip Microcomputer
Price range	$1,000–$5,000	$100–$800	<$50
System memory size (ROM & R/WM)	512K—1.2M	256 bytes–2K	64–128 bytes
I/O	ASCII keyboard, CRT	Hex keyboard (rarely ASCII) LEDs and seven-segment LEDs	Keyboard, switches, alpha-numeric LEDs[*]
Languages used	Various types of high-level languages, assembly	Assembly	Assembly and C
Applications	Small business applications, word processing, instructional applications	Evaluation of microprocessors, assembly language instruction; as a subsystem	Industrial control and embedded systems
Storage memory	Floppy and hard disks	No storage memory	No storage memory

*These I/O devices will vary according to the type of microprocessor-based products.

The **instruction** is defined as a complete task (such as Add) the microprocessor can perform; it can be made up of one or more words. Each machine has its own set of instructions based on the design of its CPU or its microprocessor. To be intelligible to the microprocessor, instructions must be written in binary language, also known as **machine language.** However, it is difficult for human beings to write programs in sets of 0s and 1s. Therefore, microprocessor manufacturers have devised English-like words to represent the binary instructions of a machine, and programmers can write programs using these words. These are called **assembly language** programs. Because an assembly language is specific to a given machine, programs written in assembly language are not transferable from one machine to another. To circumvent this limitation, such general-purpose languages as BASIC, FORTRAN, PASCAL, and C have been devised so that a program written in these languages can be machine-independent. These languages are called **high-level languages** (HLL). This section deals with various aspects of these three types of languages: machine, assembly, and high-level. The machine and assembly languages are discussed in the context of the Z80 microprocessor.

1.3.1 Machine Language

The number of bits in a word for a given machine is fixed, and words are formed through various combinations of these bits. For example, a machine with a word length of eight bits can have 256 (2^8) combinations of eight bits—thus a language of 256 words. However, not all of these words need to be used in the machine. The microprocessor design engineer selects combinations of bit patterns and gives a specific meaning to each combination by using electronic logic circuits; this is called an **instruction.** The set of instructions designed into the machine makes up what is called the machine language, a binary language composed of 0s and 1s. Its words, its instructions, and their meanings are specific to each computer. In this book, we are concerned with the language of the Z80 microprocessor from Zilog Corporation, a widely used microprocessor in industrial applications. The primary focus here is on the microprocessor, because it is the microprocessor that determines the machine language and the operations of a microcomputer.

1.3.2   Z80 Machine Language

The Z80 is a microprocessor with 8-bit word length. Its instruction set (or language) is upward compatible with that of the 8080; the Z80 has 158 instruction types that include the entire 8080 set of 72 instruction types. An instruction, as discussed earlier, is a binary pattern entered through an input device to command the microprocessor to perform a specific function. For example:

0011   1100   is an instruction that increments the number in the register called the accumulator by one.

1000   0000   is an instruction that adds the number in the register called B to the number in the accumulator, and keeps the sum in the accumulator.

The Z80 microprocessor has a variety of such bit patterns resulting in its 158 instruction types for performing different operations, called the **instruction set.** The Z80 microprocessor also accepts data in 8-bit words as input from input devices, processes data according to the instructions written by the user, and sends out data in 8-bit words to output devices. This binary language with a predetermined instruction set is called the Z80 machine language.

However, it is tedious and conducive to error for human beings to recognize and write instructions in binary language. Therefore, for convenience, these instructions are written in hexadecimal (or octal) code and entered into a single-board microcomputer by using Hex keys.

For example, the binary instruction 0011 1100 (mentioned previously) is equivalent to 3C in hexadecimal. This instruction can be entered into a single-board microcomputer system with Hex keyboard by pressing two keys: 3 and C. The monitor program of the system translates these keys into their equivalent binary pattern.

1.3.3   Z80 Assembly Language

Even though the instructions can be written in hexadecimal code, it is still not easy to understand such a program. Therefore, each manufacturer of microprocessors has devised a symbolic code for each instruction, called a **mnemonic.** (The word *mnemonic* is based on the Greek word related to *memory aid*.) The mnemonic for a particular instruction consists of letters that suggest the operation to be performed by that instruction.

For example, the binary code 0011 1100 ($3C_{16}$ or $3C_H$* in hexadecimal) of the Z80 microprocessor is represented by the mnemonic INC A:

INC A   INC stands for increment, and A represents the accumulator. This symbol suggests the operation of incrementing the accumulator content by one.

Similarly, the binary code 1000 0000 (80_{16} or 80_H*) is represented as follows:

ADD A, B   ADD stands for addition, and A and B represent the contents in the accumulator and register B, respectively. This symbol suggests the addition of the contents in register B and the accumulator.

Even though these symbols do not specify the complete operations, they suggest the significant portions. The complete description of each instruction must be supplied by the manufacturer. The complete set of Z80 mnemonics is called the Z80 instruction set, and a program written in these mnemonics is called an assembly language program. Again, the assembly language is specific to each microprocessor. For example, the Motorola 6809 microprocessor has an entirely different set of binary codes and mnemonics from that of the Z80. An assembly language program written for one microprocessor is not transferable to a computer with another microprocessor unless the two microprocessors are compatible in their machine codes.

The machine language and the assembly language are microprocessor-specific, and both are considered low-level languages. The machine language is in binary, and the assembly language is in English-like words; however, the microprocessor understands only the binary. How, then, are the assembly language mnemonics entered into a microprocessor system and translated into binary code? In a microcomputer, the mnemonics are entered as ASCII code (explained in the next section) using the keyboard as an input device, and the translation is performed by a program called an **assembler.** In a single-board microcomputer, the user translates mnemonics into Hex digits by looking up the code manually in the instruction set and enters them into the system through the Hex keyboard. This is called **hand assembly.**

1.3.4 Alphanumeric Codes

A computer is a binary machine; in order to communicate with the computer in alphabetic letters and decimal numbers, translation codes are necessary. The commonly used code is known as ASCII—American Standard Code for Information Interchange. It is a 7-bit code with 128 (2^7) combinations, and each com-

---

*Hexadecimal numbers are shown with the subscript H in the text.

bination from 00_H to $7F_H$ is assigned to either a letter, a decimal number, a symbol, or a machine command (see Appendix C). For example, hexadecimal 30_H to 39_H represent 0 to 9, decimal digits, 41_H to $5A_H$ represent capital letters A through Z, 20_H to $2F_H$ represent various symbols, and the initial codes 00_H to $1F_H$ represent such machine commands as carriage return and line feed. Devices that use ASCII characters include ASCII terminals, teletype machines (TTY), and printers. When the key 9 is pressed on an ASCII terminal, the computer receives 39_H in binary, and the system program translates ASCII characters into appropriate binary or BCD numbers.

Another code, called EBCDIC (Extended Binary Coded Decimal Interchange Code) is widely used in IBM computers (except in IBM Personal Computers or microcomputers). This is an 8-bit code representing 256 combinations; however, several combinations are not used.

1.3.5 Writing and Executing an Assembly Language Program

As explained earlier, a program is a set of logically related instructions written in a specific sequence to accomplish a task. To write and execute an assembly language program manually on a single-board computer, with a Hex keyboard for input and LEDs (or seven-segment LEDs) for output, the following steps are necessary:

1. Write the instructions in mnemonics obtained from the instruction set supplied by the manufacturer.
2. Find the hexadecimal machine code for each instruction by searching through the set of instructions.
3. Enter (load) the program in the user memory in a sequential order by using the Hex keyboard as the input device.
4. Execute the program by pressing the *Execute* key. The answer will be displayed by the LEDs.

When the user program is entered by the keys, each entry is interpreted and converted into its binary equivalent by the monitor program, and the machine code is stored as eight bits in each memory location in a sequence. When the *Execute* command is given, the microprocessor fetches each instruction, decodes it, and executes it in a sequence until the end of the program.

The manual assembly procedure is commonly used in single-board microcomputers and is suited for small programs. However, the steps of looking up the machine codes and entering the program, which are tedious and subject to errors, can be avoided by using an assembler on a microcomputer system.

The assembler is a program that translates the mnemonics entered by the ASCII keyboard into the corresponding binary machine codes of the microprocessor. Each microprocessor has its own assembler because the mnemonics and machine codes are specific to the microprocessor being used, and each assembler has certain rules that must be learned by the programmer. Assemblers are discussed in detail in Chapter 7.

1.3.6 High-Level Languages

Programming languages that are intended to be machine-independent are called high-level languages. The list includes such languages as C, FORTRAN, BASIC, PASCAL, and COBOL. These languages have certain sets of rules and draw on symbols and conventions from English. Instructions written in these languages are known as statements rather than mnemonics. A program written in BASIC for a microcomputer with the Z80 microprocessor can generally run on another microcomputer with a different microprocessor.

Now the question is: How do words in English get converted into the binary languages of different microprocessors? The answer lies with another program called either a **compiler** or an **interpreter.** These programs accept English-like statements as their input, called the *source code*. The compiler or interpreter then translates the source code into the machine language compatible with the micro-processor being used in the system. This translation into the machine language is called the *object code* (Figure 1.7). Each microprocessor needs its own compiler or interpreter for each high-level language. The primary difference between a compiler and an interpreter is in the process of generating machine code. The compiler reads the entire program first and then generates the object code, while the interpreter reads one instruction at a time, produces its object code, and ex-ecutes the instruction before reading the next instruction. Compiled programs are executed much faster than interpreted programs. M-Basic is a common example of an interpreter for the BASIC language. Compilers are generally used in such languages as C, FORTRAN, and PASCAL.

Compilers and interpreters require large memory space because each in-struction in English requires several machine codes to translate that instruction into binary. On the other hand, there is a one-to-one correspondence between the assembly language mnemonics and the machine code. Thus, assembly language programs are compact and require less memory space; they are more efficient than the high-level language programs. The primary advantage of high-level lan-guages is in troubleshooting programs, also known as debugging. It is much easier to find errors in a program written in a high-level language than to find them in a program written in assembly language.

In certain applications such as traffic control and appliance control, where programs are small and compact, assembly language is suitable. Similarly, in such real-time applications as converting a high-frequency waveform into digital data, program efficiency is critical. In real-time applications, events and time should closely match with each other without significant delay. Therefore, assembly lan-guage is highly desirable in these applications. On the other hand, for applications

FIGURE 1.7

Block Diagram: Translation of High-Level Language Program into Machine Code

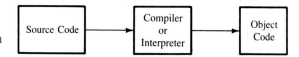

in which programs are large and memory is not a limitation, high-level languages may be desirable. The advantage of time saved in debugging a large program may outweigh the disadvantages of large memory requirements and inefficiency.

SUMMARY

The various concepts and terms discussed in this chapter are summarized below:

Computer Structure
- **Digital Computer**—a programmable machine that processes binary data. It includes four components: CPU (ALU plus control unit), memory, input, and output.
- **CPU**—the Central Processing Unit. The group of circuits that processes data and provides control signals and timing. It includes the arithmetic/logic unit, registers, instruction decoder, and the control unit.
- **ALU**—the group of circuits that performs arithmetic and logic operations. The ALU is a part of the CPU.
- **Control Unit**—The group of circuits that provides timing and signals to all operations in the computer and controls data flow.
- **Memory**—a medium that stores binary information (instructions and data).
- **Input**—a device that transfers information from the outside world to the computer.
- **Output**—a device that transfers information from the computer to the outside world.

Scale of Integration
- **SSI**—Small-Scale Integration. The process of designing a few circuits on a single chip. The term refers to the technology used to fabricate discrete logic gates on a chip.
- **MSI**—Medium-Scale Integration. The process of designing more than 100 gates on a single chip.
- **LSI**—Large-Scale Integration. The process of designing more than 1,000 gates on a single chip. Similarly, the terms VLSI (Very-Large-Scale Integration) and SLSI (Super-Large-Scale Integration) are used to indicate the scale of integration.

Microprocessor-Based Systems
- **Microprocessor**—a semiconductor device (integrated circuit) that is manufactured by using the large-scale integration technique. It includes the ALU, register arrays, and control circuits on a single chip.
- **Microcomputer**—a computer that uses a microprocessor as its CPU. It includes four components: microprocessor, memory, input, and output.

- **Bus**—a group of lines used to transfer bits between the microprocessor and other components of the computer system.
- **ROM**—Read-Only Memory. A memory that stores binary information permanently. The information can be read from this memory but cannot be altered.
- **R/WM**—Read/Write Memory. A memory that stores binary information during the operation of the computer. This memory is used as a writing pad to write user programs and data. The information stored in this memory can be easily read and altered.

Computer Languages

- **Bit**—A binary digit, 0 or 1.
- **Byte**—a group of eight bits.
- **Nibble**—a group of four bits.
- **Word**—a group of bits the computer recognizes and processes as a whole.
- **Instruction**—a command in binary that is recognized and executed by the computer in order to accomplish a task. Some instructions are designed with one word, and some require multiple words.
- **Mnemonic**—a combination of letters to suggest the operation of an instruction.
- **Program**—a set of instructions written in a specific sequence for the computer to accomplish a given task.
- **Machine Language**—the binary medium of communication with a computer through a designed set of instructions specific to each computer.
- **Assembly Language**—a medium of communication with a computer in which programs are written in mnemonics. An assembly language is specific to a given computer.
- **Low-Level Language**—a medium of communication that is machine-dependent, or specific to a given computer. The machine and the assembly languages of a computer are considered low-level languages. Programs written in these languages are not transferable to different types of machines.
- **High-Level Language**—a medium of communication independent of a given computer. Programs are written in English-like words, and they can be executed on a machine using a translator (a compiler or an interpreter).
- **Compiler**—a program that translates English-like words of a high-level language into the machine language of a computer. A compiler reads a given program, called a source code, in its entirety, and then translates the program into the machine language, which is called an object code.
- **Interpreter**—a program that translates the English-like statements of a high-level language into the machine language of a computer. An interpreter translates one statement at a time from a source code to an object code.
- **Assembler**—a computer program that translates an assembly language program from mnemonics to the binary machine code of a computer.
- **Hand Assembly**—a procedure of looking up the machine code manually from the instruction set of a microprocessor and entering those codes into the computer through a keyboard.

☐ **Monitor Program**—a program that interprets the input from a keyboard and converts the input into its binary equivalent.

LOOKING AHEAD

This chapter has given a brief introduction to computer organization and computer languages, with emphasis on the Z80 microprocessor and its assembly language. The chapter has given an overview of the entire spectrum of computers, including their salient features and applications. The primary focus of this book is on the architectural details of the Z80 microprocessor and its industrial applications, and on assembly language programming in the context of these applications. In the microcomputer field, there is hardly any separation between hardware and software, especially in applications where assembly language is necessary. In designing a microprocessor-based product, hardware and software tasks are carried out concurrently because a decision in one area affects the planning of the other area. There are various functions that can be performed through either hardware or software, and a designer needs to consider both approaches. This book focuses on trade-off between the two approaches as a design philosophy.

ASSIGNMENTS

1. List the components of a microprocessor-based system or a computer.
2. Explain the functions of each component of a computer.
3. What is a microprocessor? What is the difference between a microprocessor and a CPU?
4. Explain the difference between a microprocessor and a microcomputer.
5. Explain the following terms: SSI, MSI, and LSI.
6. Define: bit, byte, word, and instruction.
7. How many bytes make a word of 32 bits?
8. Explain the difference between the machine language and the assembly language of the Z80 microprocessor.
9. What is an assembler?
10. What are low- and high-level languages?
11. Explain the difference between a compiler and an interpreter.
12. What are the advantages of an assembly language in comparison with high-level languages?

Microprocessor-Based System: MPU, Memory, and I/O

A microprocessor-based system consists primarily of three components—the microprocessor unit (MPU), memory, and I/O (input/output). The MPU is the central player; it communicates with memory and I/O devices, processes data, and controls timing of all its operations. In this chapter, we will examine what the MPU does and what its requirements are. We then design a model for a generalized MPU that expands on the bus concept discussed in the previous chapter and shows signals necessary for the MPU to communicate with other devices. The model also describes the requirements for processing data and shows registers and logic circuits the MPU needs.

Memory and I/Os are integral parts of a microprocessor-based system. We will discuss memory in terms of its basic elements—latches and registers—and specify the requirements for a memory chip to store information and communicate with the MPU. Based on those requirements, we then develop the concepts of memory addressing and memory maps. We also discuss how the MPU addresses and communicates with I/Os.

OBJECTIVES

□ List the four program-initiated operations performed by the MPU.

□ Define the functions of the address bus, data bus, and control signals.

□ List the externally initiated operations the MPU should respond to.

□ Draw the model of a generalized MPU showing the necessary signals.

□ List the types of registers the MPU needs to process data internally.

□ Explain the internal organization of memory and the requirements of a memory chip to store information and communicate with the MPU.

□ Explain the functions of the control signals: Chip Select ($\overline{CS}$), Read ($\overline{RD}$), and Write ($\overline{WR}$).

□ Explain how memory addresses are assigned to a memory chip and recognize the address range of a given chip in a microprocessor-based system.

□ List the two techniques of addressing I/O devices.

□ Draw a block diagram of a microprocessor-based system showing the MPU, memory, I/Os, and buses.

2.1   GENERALIZED MICROPROCESSOR UNIT (MPU)

The Microprocessor Unit (MPU) is a programmable logic device with a designed set of instructions. In this section, we will examine the functions and requirements of the MPU and derive a generalized model. From the previous chapter, we can recall what the MPU does. It reads or fetches each instruction, one at a time, from memory and performs data manipulation specified by the instruction; it also reads data from input devices, and writes (or sends) data to output devices.

When the MPU is executing a program, it communicates frequently with memory and I/O devices; the process consists of fetch, decode, and execute operations. However, the question is: Can it respond to unexpected events? For example, while printing a long program, can it stop printing temporarily and read any critical data that may arrive at the input? Can it be "interrupted"? Can it wait until a peripheral is ready? For example, when memory response is too slow, can the MPU wait until memory is ready? The answer to all these questions must be affirmative.

In addition to processing data according to the instructions written in memory, the MPU needs to respond to various situations described above. External devices should be able to interrupt and request the attention of the MPU. This communication process and related operations between the MPU and the external devices (memory, I/Os) can be classified into two main categories:

□ Program-initiated operations
□ Peripheral (or externally) initiated operations.

To perform these operations, the MPU requires a group of logic circuits, a set of signals to transfer information, control signals for timing, and clock circuitry; these constitute the architecture. Early microprocessors did not have the necessary circuitry on one chip; the complete units were made up of more than one chip. Therefore, we define here the term Microprocessor Unit (MPU) as a group of devices that can perform operations similar to those of the Central Processing Unit (CPU). For example, the 8080A MPU requires three chips to make it a functional unit. However, since later microprocessors include most of the necessary circuitry on a single chip, the terms MPU and microprocessor are often used synonymously.

2.1.1 Program-Initiated Operations and Buses

To communicate with memory and I/Os, the MPU performs four operations:

1. Memory Read: Reads instructions or data from memory.
2. Memory Write: Writes instructions or data into memory.
3. I/O Read: Accepts data from input devices.
4. I/O Write: Sends data to output devices.

Now the question is: how does the MPU identify a memory register or an I/O device? It does so the same way we identify a house; we give a number. Because it understands only the binary numbers, the MPU identifies each memory register or I/O by a binary number called an address. The next question is: how does the MPU inform the peripherals when it is ready to read or write data? It does so by sending out appropriate timing signals called control signals before it transfers data.

The steps in performing these MPU operations can be summarized as follows (not necessarily in the order listed in every operation):

1. Identify the memory location or the peripheral with its address.
2. Provide timing or synchronization signal.
3. Transfer binary data.

Therefore, the MPU requires three sets of communication lines called buses: the first group of lines, called the address bus, to identify the memory location; the second group, called the data bus, to transfer data; and the third group, called the control lines, for timing signals. In the previous chapter (Figure 1.3), all these different signal lines were grouped together and shown as the system bus. Now we shall describe them individually.

ADDRESS BUS

As mentioned earlier, the MPU identifies each peripheral or memory location with a binary address. Now the question is: how large is this address? The answer depends upon the internal design of the microprocessor and available pins on a chip; it can be eight, 16, 20, or more bits. If the address size is 4 bits, the microprocessor can identify 16 (2^4) different memory locations. The addressing is simply a numbering scheme to identify memory registers. For example, a two-digit decimal numbering scheme can identify only 100 items, from 00 to 99. On the other hand, a four-digit numbering scheme can identify 10,000 items, from 0000

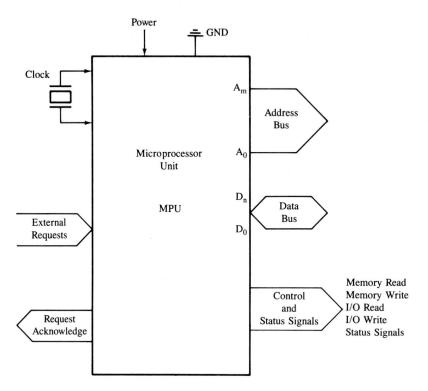

FIGURE 2.1
Generalized Microprocessor Unit (MPU)

to 9999. Thus, the number of bits (address lines) used for addressing by the MPU clearly determines the number of memory registers it can identify.

Figure 2.1 shows one group of lines as the address bus for our generalized MPU. The arrow suggests that these lines are unidirectional—the signals flow from the MPU to peripherals because only the MPU sends out an address. The address lines are generally identified as A_0 to A_m, where m indicates the most significant address bit. Typically, earlier microprocessors such as the 8085, the Z80, and the 6800 have 16 address lines which are capable of addressing 65,536 (2^{16}) memory locations, commonly known as 64K memory. However, recent microprocessors such as the 8086 have 20 address lines, and the 68000 has 23 address lines.

DATA BUS

The second group of lines shown in Figure 2.1 is the data bus. These lines are used to transfer data and are bidirectional—data can flow either direction. These lines are identified as D_0 to D_n, where n signifies the most significant bit (MSB) of the data bus. Again, the size of the data bus determines how large a binary number can be transferred and processed at a time and thus influences the microprocessor architecture considerably. The 8085, the Z80, and the 6800 have eight data lines and thus are called 8-bit microprocessors. On the other hand, the 8086, the 80286, the Z8000, and the 68000 have 16 data lines and are called 16-bit microprocessors.

CONTROL SIGNALS (MPU INITIATED)

These are individual signal lines generated by the MPU to indicate its operations. The MPU generates a specific signal for each of its four operations—Memory Read, Memory Write, I/O Read, and I/O Write. These are timing signals that are used to enable, or activate, peripherals. For example, to fetch (or read) an instruction from a memory location, the MPU sends a timing pulse called Memory Read to enable the memory chip.

2.1.2 Externally Initiated Operations

There are various occasions when ongoing MPU operations need to be interrupted. For the MPU we are designing, we can classify these types of external interruptions or delays into four categories.

☐ Reset: Start again from the beginning. For example, if we are using a microprocessor as a timer, we should be able to reset the timer after each operation or in the middle of an operation and start again.
☐ Interrupt: Stop the ongoing process temporarily; do something now that is more critical, and then go back to the original process. For example, we should be able to stop printing temporarily and read data from a keyboard; then, when the MPU finishes reading that data, it can go back to printing.
☐ Wait: When memory response time is too slow to respond to the speed of the MPU, this signal can be used to delay the MPU operations.
☐ Bus Request: When the MPU operations are too slow compared to the speed of a peripheral, the peripheral can request the use of the buses. For example, when large amounts of data are to be transferred to memory, Direct Memory Access (DMA) controllers can transfer data much faster than can the MPU.

In our generalized MPU model (Figure 2.1), these externally initiated signals are shown as External Requests. To indicate its response to some of these external requests, the MPU needs additional signal lines shown as Request Acknowledge.

2.1.3 Clock Signals and Power

The MPU can be viewed as a complex timer. The timing is very critical in all its operations. The bits of a binary instruction are associated with the microprograms inside the chip; when the MPU executes an instruction, it releases a series of microprograms at precise time intervals. Therefore, the MPU needs circuits that generate clock signals. In addition, it needs electrical power to run all the operations.

Figure 2.1 shows all the signals necessary for our generalized MPU. Presently, because of LSI technology, most of the MPU requirements can be satisfied by single-chip microprocessors with slight variations. For example, the Z80 microprocessor has all the signals of the MPU except clock-generating circuitry, and some of its control signals need to be logically ANDed to generate the specific control signals shown in Figure 2.1. However, the present microprocessors include all the data processing and timing circuitry on one chip; therefore, they can be viewed almost as MPUs. Now we shall examine what is inside the microprocessor to understand how it processes data.

2.1.4 Microprocessor as a Processing Unit

When the microprocessor executes instructions, it does so in a continuous sequence of fetch, decode, and execute operations. After examining these operations in more detail, we can describe the requirements of the internal architecture of our generalized microprocessor.

FETCHING AN INSTRUCTION

To fetch an instruction, the microprocessor places a memory address on the address bus and reads binary information using the data bus. Therefore, it needs a register that can hold memory addresses and increment these addresses after the fetching is completed, a sort of memory pointer.

DECODING AN INSTRUCTION

Once an instruction byte is fetched, it needs to be decoded to answer the following:

☐ Is it a complete instruction? If not, how many more bytes need to be fetched?
☐ What type of operation is required and on what data?

To perform these functions, the microprocessor needs an instruction decoder that can interpret the fetched binary information.

STORING DATA

The microprocessor gets data from memory, I/O, or directly as part of an instruction. Therefore, it needs a set of registers to store data (or addresses) temporarily before it can process the data.

EXECUTING AN INSTRUCTION

The type of data manipulation the microprocessor can perform depends on its internal microprograms, that is, on its instruction set. These operations can be classified as data copy (transfer), arithmetic/logic operations, and decision making. For example, to subtract two numbers, both numbers must be loaded into registers. After the subtraction, it is necessary to indicate whether the result is positive, negative, or zero. This can be indicated by setting or resetting flip-flops called flags. To perform these arithmetic and logic operations, the microprocessor needs a group of logic circuits called Arithmetic/Logic Unit (ALU).

   This description of the requirements of the microprocessor to process data

FIGURE 2.2
MPU Internal Structure

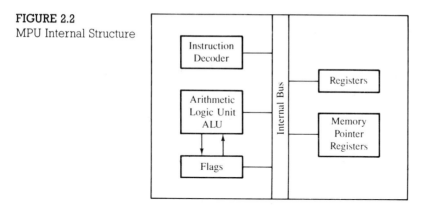

can be summarized in a simplified block diagram shown in Figure 2.2. From this block diagram, we can derive a programming model for a specific microprocessor.

2.1.5 Review of Important Concepts

The description and the requirements of a generalized microprocessor unit can be summarized as follows (see Figure 2.3):

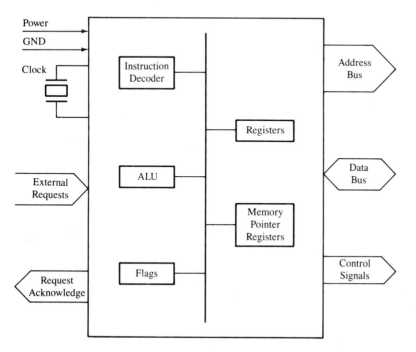

FIGURE 2.3
MPU Architecture

To communicate with memory and I/O devices, the MPU should have the following:

1. Address bus to send the address of a memory register or an I/O.
2. Data bus to transfer data between the MPU and memory and I/O devices.
3. Control signals to identify its operations and provide timing.
4. External Request signal lines to interrupt the MPU operations.
5. Request Acknowledge signals to respond to the requests by peripherals.
6. Clock signals to provide timing and power to operate circuits.

To process data internally, the MPU should include the following:

1. Instruction Decoder to decode the fetched binary information.
2. Registers to store binary data.
3. Registers as memory pointers for addressing memory registers.
4. ALU to perform arithmetic and logic operations.
5. Flags (flip-flops) to indicate data conditions for decision making.

2.2 MEMORY

Memory is an essential component of a microcomputer system; it stores binary instructions and data for the microprocessor. There are various types of memory, and they can be classified in two groups: prime (or main) memory and storage memory. In the last chapter, we saw two examples of prime memory: Read/Write Memory (R/WM) and Read-Only Memory (ROM). Magnetic tapes and disks can be cited as examples of storage memory. First, we will focus on prime memory and then briefly discuss storage memory when we examine various types of memory.

The R/W memory is made up of registers, and each register has a group of flip-flops or field-effect transistors that store bits of information. The user can use this memory to hold programs and store data. On the other hand, the ROM stores information permanently in the form of diodes; the group of diodes can be viewed as a register. In a memory chip, all registers are arranged in a sequence and identified by binary numbers called memory addresses. The MPU uses its address bus to send the address of a memory register and uses data and control buses to read from or write into that register. In the following sections, we examine the basic concepts related to memory—its structure, its addresses, and its requirements for communication with the MPU—and build a model for R/W memory. However, the discussion is equally applicable to ROM except for slight differences in Read/Write control signals.

2.2.1 Flip-Flop or Latch as a Storage Element

What is memory? It is a circuit that can store bits—generally high or low voltage levels representing 1 and 0. A flip-flop or a latch is a basic element of memory.

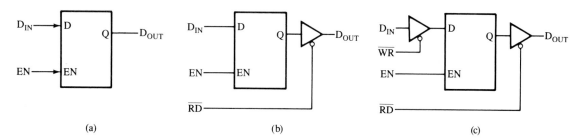

FIGURE 2.4
Latches as Storage Elements

To write or store a bit in the latch, we need an input data bit and an enable signal (Figure 2.4(a)). In this latch, the stored bit is always available on the output line. If a tri-state buffer is connected to the output of the latch (as shown in Figure 2.4(b)), the stored bit can be read only when the buffer is enabled. Similarly, we can also use a tri-state buffer on the input of the latch. Now we can write into the latch (Figure 2.4(c)) by enabling the input buffer and read from it by enabling the output buffer. This latch, which can store one binary bit, is called a memory cell. Figure 2.5(a) shows four such cells or latches grouped together to form a register that has four input lines and four output lines and can store four bits. The size of this register is specified as either 4-bit or 1×4 bit, which indicates one register with four cells or four I/O lines. The number of bits stored in a register is called a memory word. Figures 2.5(b) and (c) show simplified block diagrams of the 4-bit register.

In Figure 2.6(a), four registers with eight cells (or 8-bit memory word) are arranged in a sequence. To write into or read from any one of the registers, a specific register should be identified or enabled. This is a simple decoding function; a 2-to-4 decoder can perform that function. However, two more input lines A_1 and A_0, called address lines, are required to the decoder. These two input lines can carry four different bit combinations (00, 01, 10, 11), and each combination can identify or enable one of the registers named as Register 0 through Register 3.

In Figure 2.6(a), the chip has an 8-bit memory word, and its size can be specified as 32 bits, 4×8 bits, or 4 bytes. If we have a memory chip with a 4-bit memory word, we can combine two such chips in parallel to make an 8-bit memory word as shown in Figure 2.6(b). The address lines and $\overline{RD}/\overline{WR}$ control signals ($^-$ indicates active low) will be connected in parallel, but the memory word will consist of 4 bits from each chip as shown.

Now we can expand the number of registers. If we have eight registers on one chip, we need three address lines and a 3-to-8 decoder. An interesting problem is how to deal with two chips with four registers each. We have a total of eight registers; therefore, we need three address lines. One address line, A_2, is used to select a chip, and the address lines A_1 and A_0 are connected to both chips. Figure

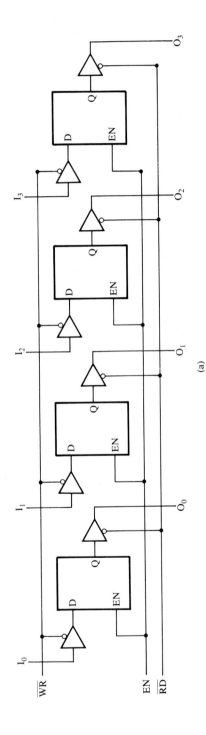

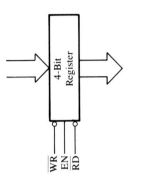

(a)

(b)

(c)

FIGURE 2.5

(a) Four Latches as a 4-Bit Register; (b) and (c) Block Diagrams of a 4-Bit Register

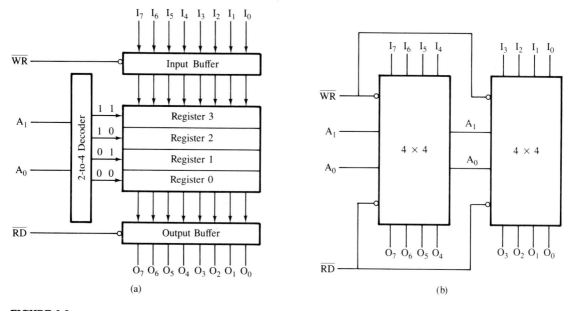

FIGURE 2.6
(a) 4 × 8 Bit Register; (b) Two 4 × 4 Bit Registers

2.7(b) shows that the Chip Select signal $\overline{CS}$ is active low, so that when A_2 is 0 (low), Chip M_1 is selected and when A_2 is 1 (high), Chip M_2 is selected. The addresses on A_1 and A_0 will determine the registers to be selected; thus, by combining the logic on A_2, A_1, and A_0, the memory addresses range from 000 to 111. The concept of the Chip Select signal gives us more flexibility in designing chips and allows us to expand memory size by using multiple chips.

Now let us examine the problem from a different perspective. Assume that we have available four address lines and two memory chips with four registers each as before. Four address lines are capable of identifying sixteen (2^4) registers; however, we need only three address lines to identify eight registers. What should we do with the fourth line? One of the solutions is shown in Figure 2.8. Memory chip M_1 is selected when A_3 and A_2 are both 0; therefore, registers in this chip are identified with the addresses ranging from 0000 to 0011 (0 to 3). Similarly, the addresses of memory chip M_2 range from 1000 to 1011 (8 to B); this chip is selected only when A_3 is 1 and A_2 is 0. In this example, we need three lines to identify eight registers, two for registers and one for Chip Select. However, we used also the fourth line for Chip Select. This is called complete or absolute decoding. Another option is to leave the fourth line as "don't care"; we will further explore this concept later.

After reviewing the above explanation, we can summarize the requirements of a memory chip as follows:

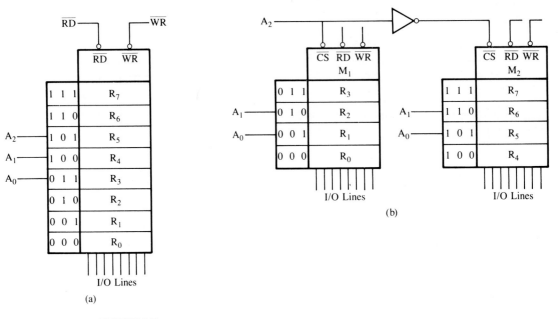

(a)

FIGURE 2.7
(a) Memory Chip with Eight Registers; (b) Two Memory Chips with Four Registers Each

1. A memory chip requires address lines to identify a memory register, a Chip Select $\overline{CS}$ signal to enable the chip, and control signals to read from and write into memory registers.
2. The number of address lines required is determined by the number of registers in a chip (2^n = Number of registers where n is the number of address lines).
3. If additional address lines are available in a system, they are used to enable the Chip Select $\overline{CS}$ signal. The memory address of a register is determined by

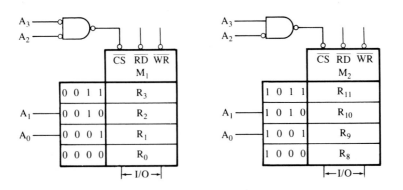

FIGURE 2.8
Addressing Eight Registers with Four Address Lines

the logic levels (0/1) of all the address lines (including the address lines used for $\overline{CS}$).

4. The control signal Read ($\overline{RD}$) enables the output buffer, and data from the selected register are made available on the output lines. Similarly, the control signal Write ($\overline{WR}$) enables the input buffer, and data on the input lines are written into memory cells.

A model of a typical memory chip representing the requirements just stated is shown in Figure 2.9. Figure 2.9(a) represents the R/W memory and Figure 2.9(b) represents the Read-Only Memory; the only difference between the two as far as addressing is concerned is that ROM does not need a $\overline{WR}$ signal. Internally, the memory cells are arranged in a matrix format (in rows and columns), because as the size increases the internal decoding scheme we discussed becomes impractical. For example, a memory chip with 1024 registers would require a 10-to-1024 decoder. If the cells are arranged in six rows and four columns, however, the internal decoding circuitry can be designed with two decoders, one for selecting a row and the other for selecting a column. The internal row and column arrangement does not affect our external interfacing logic.

2.2.2 Memory Map

Typically, in an 8-bit microprocessor system, 16 address lines are available for memory. This means it is a numbering system of 16 binary bits and is capable of identifying 2^{16} (65,536) memory registers, each register with a 16-bit address. The entire memory addresses can range from 0000 to FFFF in Hex. A memory map is like a pictorial representation in which memory devices are located in the entire range of addresses. Memory addresses provide the locations of various memory devices in the system, and the interfacing logic defines the range of memory addresses for each memory device.

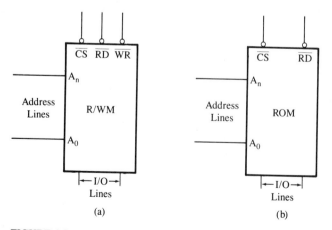

(a)   (b)

FIGURE 2.9

(a) R/W Memory Model; (b) ROM Model

Now let us assume that we have a memory chip with 256 registers that needs only eight address lines (2^8 = 256). How can we assign 16-bit addresses to 256 registers? This can be accomplished by using the remaining eight lines for the Chip Select through appropriate logic gates as illustrated in the next example.

Example 2.1

Illustrate the address range of the memory chip with 256 bytes of memory, shown in Figure 2.10(a), and explain how the address range can be changed by modifying the hardware of the Chip Select $\overline{CS}$ line in Figure 2.10(b).

Solution

Figure 2.10(a) shows a memory chip with 256 registers with 8 I/O lines; the memory size of the chip is expressed as 256 × 8. It has eight address lines A_7–A_0, one Chip Select $\overline{CS}$ signal (active low), and two control signals Read ($\overline{RD}$) and Write ($\overline{WR}$). The eight address lines (A_7–A_0) of the microprocessor are required to identify 256 memory registers. The remaining eight lines (A_{15}–A_8) are connected to the Chip Select ($\overline{CS}$) line through inverters and the NAND gate. The memory chip is enabled or selected when $\overline{CS}$ goes low. Therefore, to select the chip, the address lines A_{15}–A_8 should be at logic 0, which will cause the output of the NAND gate to go low. No other logic levels on the lines A_{15}–A_8 can select the chip. Once the chip is selected (enabled), the remaining address lines A_7–A_0 can assume any combination from 00_H to FF_H and identify any of the 256 memory registers through its decoder. Therefore, the memory addresses of the chip in Figure 2.10(a) will range from 0000_H to $00FF_H$ as shown below.

$$A_{15}\ A_{14}\ A_{13}\ A_{12}\ A_{11}\ A_{10}\ A_9\ A_8 \qquad A_7\ A_6\ A_5\ A_4\ A_3\ A_2\ A_1\ A_0$$
$$0\ \ \ 0\ \ \ 0\ \ \ 0\ \ \ 0\ \ \ 0\ \ \ 0\ \ \ 0 \qquad 0\ \ \ 0\ \ \ 0\ \ \ 0\ \ \ 0\ \ \ 0\ \ \ 0\ \ \ 0 \quad = 0000_H$$
$$\downarrow \qquad\qquad\qquad\qquad \downarrow$$
$$1\ \ \ 1\ \ \ 1\ \ \ 1\ \ \ 1\ \ \ 1\ \ \ 1\ \ \ 1 \quad = 00FF_H$$

Chip Enable or Chip Select   Register Select

The address of the first memory register is 0000_H, and the address of the last register is $00FF_H$. If we numbered these registers in decimal with a four-digit system, the address of the first register will be 0000_{10}, and the last register will be 0255_{10}.

The chip select addresses are determined by the hardware (the inverters and NAND gate); therefore, the memory map of the chip can be changed by modifying the hardware. For example, if the inverter on line A_{15} is removed as shown in Figure 2.10(b), the address required on A_{15}–A_8 to enable the chip will be as follows:

$$A_{15} \qquad A_{14} \qquad A_{13} \qquad A_{12} \qquad A_{11} \qquad A_{10} \qquad A_9 \qquad A_8$$
$$1 \qquad\ 0 \qquad\ 0 \qquad\ 0 \qquad\ 0 \qquad\ 0 \qquad\ 0 \qquad\ 0 \quad = 80_H$$

The memory map for Figure 2.10(b) will be 8000_H to $80FF_H$.

The memory chips in Figures 2.10(a) and (b) are the same chips. However, by changing the hardware of the Chip Select logic, the location of the memory in

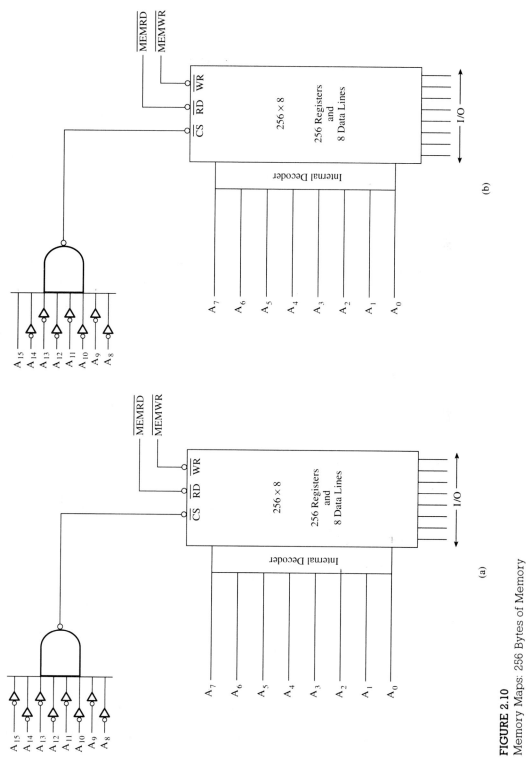

FIGURE 2.10
Memory Maps: 256 Bytes of Memory

the map can be changed, and memory can be assigned addresses in various locations over the entire range of 0000 to $FFFF_H$.

Example 2.2	In Figure 2.10(a), how many 256×4 memory chips would be required to replace the 256×8 memory chip? Redraw Figure 2.10(a) using 256×4 memory chips.
Solution	The memory chip with the size of 256×4 has 256 registers, and each register has four data or I/O lines. Therefore, we would need two 256×4 memory chips to replace the 256×8 memory chip as shown in Figure 2.11. The address lines A_7 to A_0 and $\overline{CS}$ line will be the same for both chips; however, data lines D_7 to D_4 will be connected to the first chip, and the lines D_3 to D_0 will be connected to the second chip.

In a memory system, a 16-bit address can be conceptually organized into two groups of Hex numbers. With two Hex digits, 256 registers can be numbered from 00_H to FF_H as shown in Example 2.1. This is defined as a page with 256 lines (registers) to read from or write on. Similarly, high-order Hex digits in an address can be used to number the pages from 00_H to FF_H; thus, the total range of 64K can be conceptually divided into 256 pages with each page having 256 lines. For example, the memory address $020F_H$ represents line (register) 15 on page 2, and the address $07FF_H$ represents register 255 on page 7. A memory chip with 1K (1,024) byte can be viewed as a chip with four pages. This is just a convenient way of thinking about memory addresses.

Another way of viewing a memory address is in terms of high-order and low-

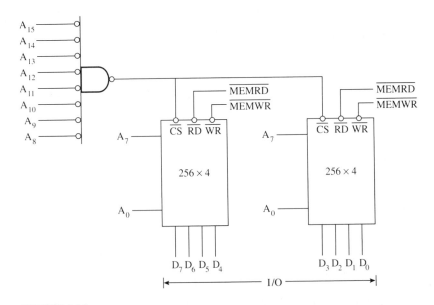

FIGURE 2.11
Memory Circuit Using 256×4 Memory Chips

order addresses. The lines used for chip select are called high-order address lines, and the lines connected to memory address lines are called low-order address lines. Let us use an example of a four-digit (decimal) numbering system in a high-rise apartment building. Generally, the first two digits (high-order) represent a floor and the last two digits (low-order) represent an apartment number. To locate apartment 1241, we go first to the twelfth floor (similar to Chip Select in memory addressing), and then we look for the apartment 41 (similar to selecting a register). Now let us use the example of an apartment complex. Let us assume the complex is divided into sections 1 to 9, and each section has up to 999 apartments. In this situation, the number 2451 would represent Section 2 and apartment number 451; the digit 2 is a high-order address, and 451 is a low-order address. This is similar to memory addresses of 1K memory. The 1K memory chip will require 10 address lines, and the remaining six lines of the address bus will be used for the $\overline{CS}$. Thus, the group of six address lines will be high order, and the remaining ten address lines will be low order. The memory addresses will be determined by combining the logic levels of these address lines. If the number of address lines in a microprocessor is larger than 16, we will use a five-digit Hex numbering scheme.

If the address range of a memory chip is from 4000_H to $43FF_H$, calculate the number of memory registers in the chip.

Example
2.3

The number of registers in Hex: $43FF_H - 4000_H = 3FF_H$
The decimal equivalent of $3FF_H = 1023$
Therefore, the total number of registers in the chip = 1024 (1K). To include the first address, we need to add one to the calculated value.

Solution

2.2.3 How the MPU Writes into and Reads from Memory

To store (write) a byte into a memory location (Figure 2.12), the MPU

1. Places the 16-bit address on the address bus of the memory location where a byte is to be stored. The interfacing logic of the memory chip decodes the address and selects the memory register to be written into.
2. Places the byte on the data bus.
3. Sends the control signal Memory Write to enable the input buffers of the memory and then stores the byte.

To read from memory the steps are similar to that of writing into memory, except the order of steps 2 and 3.

1. The MPU places the 16-bit address on the address bus of the memory location from where a byte is to be read. The interfacing logic of the memory chip decodes the address and selects the appropriate memory register.
2. The MPU sends the control signal Memory Read to enable the output buffer of the memory chip.
3. The memory chip places the data byte on the data bus, and the MPU reads the data byte.

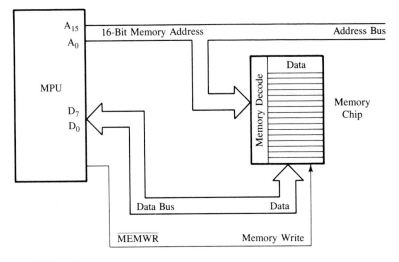

FIGURE 2.12
Memory Write Operation

2.2.4 Memory Classification

Memory can be classified into two groups: prime (or main) memory and storage memory. The R/WM and ROM discussed in the last section are examples of prime memory; this is the memory the microcomputer uses in executing and storing programs. This memory should be able to respond fast enough to keep up with the execution speed of the microprocessor. Therefore, it should be random-access memory, meaning that the microprocessor should be able to access information from any register with the same speed (independent of its place in the chip).

Storage memory includes examples such as magnetic disks and tapes (see Figure 2.13). This memory is used to store programs and results after the completion of program execution. Information stored in these memories is nonvolatile, meaning information remains intact even if the system is turned off. Generally, these memory devices are not a part of any system; they are made part of the system only when stored programs need to be accessed. The microprocessor cannot execute or directly process programs stored in these devices; programs must be copied into the prime memory first. Therefore, the size of the prime memory (e.g., 64K or 128K) determines how large a program the system can process. The size of the storage memory is unlimited; when one disk or tape is full, another can be used.

Figure 2.13 shows two subdivisions of storage memory: secondary storage and backup storage. The secondary storage is similar to what you put on your shelf in your study, and the backup is similar to what you store in your attic. Storage memory includes such devices as disks, magnetic tapes, magnetic bubble memory, and charged-coupled devices (CCD). The primary features of all these

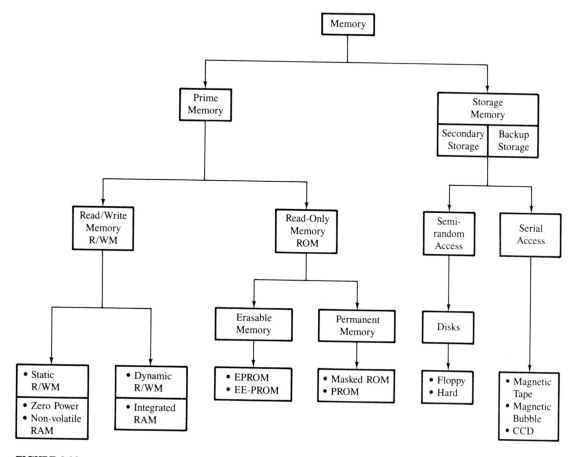

FIGURE 2.13
Memory Classification

devices are high capacity, low cost, and slow access. A disk is similar to a record; the access to the stored information in the disk is semi-random. The remaining devices shown in Figure 2.13 are serial: if information is stored in the middle of the tape, it can be accessed only after running half the tape. We will discuss some of these memory storage devices again in Chapter 7. In this chapter, we will focus on various types of prime memory.

Figure 2.13 shows that the prime memory is divided into two main groups: Read/Write Memory (R/WM) and Read-Only Memory (ROM), and each group includes several different types of memory.

R/WM (READ/WRITE MEMORY)

As the name suggests, the microprocessor can write into or read from this memory, and it is popularly known as Random-Access Memory (RAM). It is used primarily for information that is likely to be altered, such as writing programs or receiving data. This memory is volatile, meaning that when the power is turned off, all its contents are destroyed.

Two types of R/W memories—static and dynamic—are available. Static memory is made of flip-flops, and it stores the bit as a voltage. Dynamic memory is made of MOS transistor gates, and it stores the bit as a charge. The advantages of the dynamic memory are that it has higher density, lower power consumption, and is cheaper than the static memory. The disadvantage is that the charge (bit information) leaks; therefore, stored information needs to be read and written again every few milliseconds. This is called refreshing the memory, and it requires extra circuitry, which adds to the cost of the system. It is generally economical to use dynamic memory when the system memory size is larger than 16K; for smaller systems, the static memory is appropriate.

ROM (READ-ONLY MEMORY)

The ROM is a nonvolatile memory; it retains stored information even if the power is turned off. This memory is used for programs and data that need not be altered because, as the name suggests, the information can be read only so that once a bit pattern is stored, it is permanent or at least semipermanent. The permanent group includes two types of memory: masked ROM and PROM, and the semipermanent group also includes two types of memory: EPROM and EE-PROM as shown in Figure 2.13.

MASKED ROM

In this ROM, a bit pattern is permanently recorded by the masking and metallization process, which memory manufacturers are generally equipped to do. It is an expensive and specialized process, but economical for large production quantities.

PROM (PROGRAMMABLE READ-ONLY MEMORY)

This memory has nichrome or polysilicon wires arranged in a matrix; these wires can be functionally viewed as diodes or fuses. This memory can be programmed by the user with a special PROM programmer that selectively burns the fuses according to the bit pattern to be stored. The process is known as "burning the PROM," and the information stored is permanent.

EPROM (ERASABLE PROGRAMMABLE READ-ONLY MEMORY)

This memory stores a bit by charging the floating gate of a field-effect transistor (FET). Information is stored by using an EPROM programmer, which applies high voltages to charge the gate. All the information can be erased by exposing the chip to ultraviolet light through its quartz window, and the chip can be reprogrammed. Because the chip can be reused many times, this memory is ideally suited for product development, experimental projects, and college laboratories.

EE-PROM (ELECTRICALLY ERASABLE PROM)

This memory is functionally similar to EPROM, except that information can be altered by using electrical signals at the register level rather than erasing all the information. This has an advantage in field and remote control applications. In microprocessor systems, software update is a common occurrence. If EE-PROMs are used in the systems, they can be updated from a central computer by using a remote link via telephone lines. Similarly, in a process control in which timing information has to be changed, it can be done by sending electrical signals from a central place. This memory also includes a chip-erase mode whereby the entire chip can be erased in 10 ms as opposed to 15 to 20 minutes for an EPROM.

RECENT ADVANCES IN MEMORY TECHNOLOGY

Memory technology has advanced considerably in recent years. In addition to static and dynamic R/W memory, there are now more options available in memory devices. Recent examples include Zero Power RAM from MOSTEK, Non-Volatile RAM from Intel, and Integrated RAM from several manufacturers.

The Zero Power RAM is a complementary metal-oxide semiconductor (CMOS) Read/Write memory with battery backup built internally. It includes lithium cells and voltage-sensing circuitry. When the external power supply voltage falls below +3 V, the power switching circuitry connects the lithium battery; thus, this memory provides the advantages of both R/W and Read-Only Memory.

The Non-Volatile RAM is a high speed static R/W Memory array backed up, bit for bit, by an EE-PROM array for nonvolatile storage. When the power is about to go off, the contents of R/W memory are quickly stored in the EE-PROM by activating a STORE signal on the memory chip, and the stored data can be read into the R/W memory segment when the power is turned on again. This memory chip combines the flexibility of static R/W memory with the nonvolatility of EE-PROM.

The Integrated RAM (iRAM) is a dynamic memory with the refreshed circuitry built on the chip. For the user, it is similar to the static R/W memory. The user can derive the advantages of the dynamic memory without having to build the external refreshing circuitry. At present, this memory is economical for a system with medium-sized memory (between 8K and 64K).

INPUT AND OUTPUT (I/O) DEVICES 2.3

Input/Output devices are the means through which the MPU communicates with "the outside world." The MPU accepts binary data as input from devices such as keyboards and analog-to-digital (A/D) converters and sends data to output devices such as LEDs or printers. There are two different methods by which an MPU can identify I/O devices: one uses an 8-bit address and the other a 16-bit address. These methods are described briefly in the following sections.

2.3.1 I/Os with 8-Bit Addresses (Peripheral-Mapped I/O)

In this type of I/O, the MPU uses eight address lines to identify an input or an output device; this is also known as peripheral-mapped I/O. The eight address lines can have 256 (2^8 combinations) addresses; thus, the MPU can identify 256 input devices and 256 output devices with addresses ranging from 00_H to FF_H. The input and output devices are differentiated by the control signals I/O Read for input devices and I/O Write for output devices. The entire range of I/O addresses from 00_H to FF_H is also known as an I/O map, and individual addresses are also referred to as I/O device addresses or I/O port numbers.

If we use LEDs as output or switches as input, we need to resolve two issues: how to assign addresses and how to connect these I/O devices to the data bus. In a bus architecture, these devices cannot be connected directly to the data bus or the address bus; all connections must be made through tri-state interfacing devices so they will be enabled and connected to the buses only when the MPU chooses to communicate with them. In the case of memory, we did not have to be concerned with these problems because of the internal address decoding, Read/Write buffers, and availability of $\overline{CS}$ and control signals of the memory chip. In the case of I/O devices, we need to use external interfacing devices.

The steps in communicating with an I/O device are similar to those in communicating with memory and can be summarized as follows:

1. The MPU places an 8-bit address on the address bus, which is decoded by the external decode logic (explained in Chapter 5).
2. The MPU sends a control signal (I/O Read or I/O Write) to enable the I/O device.
3. Data are transferred on the data bus.

2.3.2 I/Os with 16-bit Addresses (Memory-Mapped I/O)

In this type of I/O, the MPU uses 16 address lines to identify an I/O device; an I/O is connected as if it is a memory register. In memory-mapped I/O, the MPU uses the same control signals (Memory Read or Memory Write) and instructions as those of memory and follows the same steps as when it is accessing a memory register. In some microprocessors, such as the Motorola 6800, all I/Os have 16-bit addresses so that I/Os and memory share the same memory map (64K).

The peripheral- and memory-mapped I/O techniques will be discussed in detail in the context of interfacing I/O devices (see Chapter 5).

2.4 EXAMPLE OF A MICROPROCESSOR-BASED SYSTEM

In the last three sections, we discussed a generalized MPU model, prime memory and its organization model, and I/Os. The discussion can be summarized in the block diagram of a microprocessor-based system as shown in Figure 2.14. It includes a generalized MPU, two types of prime memory, and two I/O devices.

All address lines are used to address memory, and only the low-order address bus is used to identify I/O devices, indicating that they are connected as peripheral-mapped I/O (the details of Chip Select decoding are omitted here). The data bus is bidirectional and common to all devices. The four control signals generated by the MPU are connected to different peripherals, as shown in Figure 2.14.

HOW DOES THE SYSTEM WORK?

Let us assume that a simple program with three instructions is already written and stored in binary in R/W memory. Those instructions are

1. Read on/off switches at input port No. 20_H. (H stands for hexadecimal.)
2. Turn on the devices corresponding to on switches at the output port 80_H.
3. Stop.

To execute these instructions, the MPU performs the following operations:

1. Places the memory address of instruction 1 on the address bus and fetches the instruction using the control signal Memory Read ($\overline{\text{MEMRD}}$). (The MPU may have to fetch instruction codes more than once if the instruction has more than one byte.) It decodes the instruction.
   □ Places the address 20_H of the input port on the address bus, reads data (logic levels 0/1 of the switches) using the control signal I/O Read ($\overline{\text{IORD}}$), and stores the data in one of the registers.
2. Fetches the next instruction by placing the memory address of that instruction on the address bus and the control signal $\overline{\text{MEMRD}}$. Then, it decodes the instruction.
   □ It places the port address 80_H and transfers the data using the control signal I/O Write ($\overline{\text{IOWR}}$) and turns on the devices corresponding to on switches.

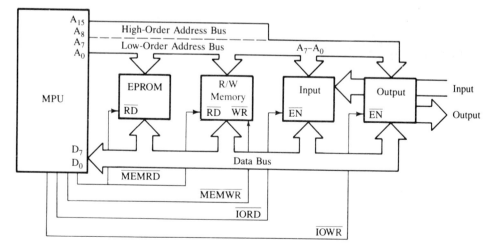

FIGURE 2.14
Example of a Microprocessor-Based System

3. Again fetches the last instruction from memory as before, decodes it, and stops.

This is a simplified description of how the system works; it excludes the details about multibyte instructions, machine cycles, and timing.

SUMMARY

In this chapter, we examined the requirements of the Microprocessor Unit (MPU) to communicate with memory and I/O devices and to process binary data. Based on those requirements, we designed a generalized model of the MPU. We discussed memory in terms of its storage elements, namely, latches and registers and techniques of assigning addresses. The steps required for the MPU to communicate with memory and I/Os were briefly described. The important concepts are summarized as follows.

□ The MPU performs four primary operations: Memory Read, Memory Write, I/O Read, and I/O Write.
□ To communicate with memory and I/Os, the MPU needs three types of buses: the unidirectional address bus to send memory and I/O addresses, the bidirectional data bus to transfer data, and control signals to enable the devices.
□ The MPU should have signal lines to accept and to acknowledge external requests. These requests are Reset (go back to beginning), interrupt (stop the ongoing process and attend to something urgent), wait to synchronize with slow memory, and allow the use of buses to an external device because the MPU response time is slower than that of the external device.
□ To process data, the MPU should include registers to store data, memory pointers to hold memory addresses, ALU to perform arithmetic and logic operations, and flags to indicate data conditions.
□ Memory is a group of registers, arranged in a sequence, to store bits. The number of cells (latches) in a register determines the size of the memory word in a chip.
□ A memory chip requires address lines to identify a memory register, Chip Select signal to select the chip, and control signals to read from and write into memory registers.
□ The range of memory addresses assigned to a memory chip is done through the Chip Select logic.
□ An I/O device can be identified either with an 8-bit address called the peripheral-mapped I/O or with a 16-bit address called the memory-mapped I/O.
□ To communicate with memory or I/O, the MPU places the address of the device on the address bus, sends the appropriate control signal, and places (or receives) data on the data bus.

LOOKING AHEAD

In this chapter, we examined the microprocessor as a programmable logic device and developed a generalized model. Similarly, we discussed memory as a storage element and constructed a memory model. We examined briefly the role of I/Os as channels of communication with "the outside world." These three elements were interconnected through a bus architecture to form a model of a microprocessor-based system. Then we discussed how the MPU communicates with memory and I/Os.

In the next three chapters, we will explore each component and its communication process separately with details and specific examples. In Chapter 3, we will examine the Z80 microprocessor in the context of our generalized model of a programmable logic device. Chapter 4 discusses memory and its interfacing, and Chapter 5 is devoted to interfacing I/O devices.

ASSIGNMENTS

1. List the four operations commonly performed by the MPU.
2. What is a bus?
3. What is the function of the address bus?
4. How many memory locations can be addressed by the MPU with thirteen address lines?
5. How many address lines are necessary to address two megabytes (2048K) of memory?
6. What is the function of the interrupt signal and when is it used?
7. When is the bus request signal used?
8. Specify the number of registers and memory cells in a 128×4 memory chip.
9. How many bits are stored by a 256×4 memory chip? Can this chip be specified as 128-byte memory?
10. If the memory size is 1024×4 bits, how many chips are required to make 1K-byte of memory?
11. If the memory chip size is 1024×1 bits, how many chips are necessary to make 4K (4,096) bytes of memory?
12. What is the function of the $\overline{\text{WR}}$ signal on the memory chip?
13. How many address lines are necessary for the memory chip with 2048×8 size?
14. How many address lines are necessary for the memory chip with 2048×4 size?
15. The memory address range of a 4K (4,096)-byte memory chip begins at the

location 8000_H. Specify the entire memory address range and the number of pages in the chip.

16. The memory address of the last location of an 8K-byte memory chip is $FFFF_H$. Find the starting address.

17. Identify the memory address range in Figure 2.15. List the high-order and low-order address lines. How many pages of memory does the chip include?

18. In Figure 2.15, identify the address range if the inverter of the address line A15 is eliminated and A15 is connected directly to the NAND gate.

19. Figure 2.16 shows an MPU with the address bus containing 12 address lines and the data bus with four data lines; it is interfaced with the 1024×4 memory chip. Find the memory address range.

20. Specify the size of the memory word shown in Figure 2.16.

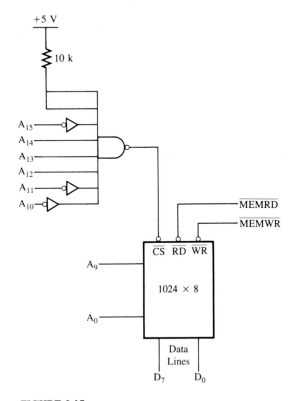

FIGURE 2.15
Identification of Memory Addresses for Assignments 17–18

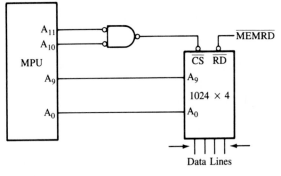

FIGURE 2.16
Identification of Memory Addresses for Assignments 19–20

Z80
Microprocessor
Architecture

The Z80 is one of the most versatile and widely used 8-bit microprocessors, and many microprocessor-based systems are designed around the Z80. The Z80 chip includes most of the logic circuitry for performing computing tasks and necessary bus signals. This chapter discusses the Z80 architecture in terms of the generalized MPU discussed in the previous chapter.

This chapter describes the Z80 hardware model; it shows logic pinout of the chip and classifies the signals in various groups according to their functions. Similarly, the chapter includes a brief description of programming registers and flags. The hardware model lists the operations the Z80 frequently performs and describes how the Z80 communicates with memory and I/Os by using various buses. These operations are illustrated in terms of machine cycles and logic levels of the buses in relation to the system clock.

Finally, the chapter includes the discussion of similar 8-bit microprocessors in terms of the generalized model developed in the last chapter and compares them with the Z80.

OBJECTIVES

☐ List the functional groups of the Z80 signals.
☐ Define the address bus, the data bus, and the control signals, and explain their functions.
☐ List the types of external signals and explain their purposes.
☐ Identify the Z80 programming registers and flags.
☐ List three categories of the Z80's operations.
☐ Explain the terms instruction cycle, machine cycle, and T-state.

☐ List the steps the Z80 performs to execute the Opcode Fetch, the Memory Read, and the Memory Write cycles, and explain their functions.
☐ Show the bus contents and the appropriate control signals in reference to the system clock when these machine cycles are executed.
☐ Describe the 8085, the NSC800, and the 6800 microprocessors in terms of the generalized MPU and compare them with the Z80.

3.1   Z80 HARDWARE AND PROGRAMMING MODELS

The Z80 hardware model described in this section represents the microprocessor unit (MPU) as defined in Chapter 2. The Z80 microprocessor almost qualifies as an MPU, except that an external oscillator circuit is required to provide the operating frequency and appropriate control signals need to be generated to communicate with memory and I/O. In the following sections, we describe the Z80 microprocessor in relation to the model we developed in the previous chapter. Then we examine the timing involved in reading an instruction from memory and generate the necessary control signals by using appropriate logic gates.

3.1.1   Z80 Hardware Model

The Z80 is a general-purpose 8-bit microprocessor with 16 address lines and requires a single +5 V power supply. It is housed in a 40-pin dual-in-line (DIP) package. The different versions of Z80 microprocessors such as Z80, Z80A, Z80B, and Z80H are rated to operate at various frequencies ranging from 2.5 MHz to 8 MHz. Even though the Z80 instruction set is upward compatible with the Intel 8080 set, neither of these microprocessors are pin compatible.

Figure 3.1 shows the pin configuration of the Z80 microprocessor and its hardware model with logic signals. All the signals can be classified into six groups: (1) address bus, (2) data bus, (3) control signals, (4) external requests, (5) request acknowledge and special signals, and (6) power and frequency signals. This Z80 hardware model matches the hardware model of the generalized MPU described in Chapter 2. The specific details of these signals follow.

ADDRESS BUS

The Z80 has 16 tri-state signal lines, A_{15}–A_0, known as the address bus. These lines are unidirectional and capable of addressing 64K (2^{16}) memory. The address bus is used to send (or place) the addresses of memory registers and I/O devices.

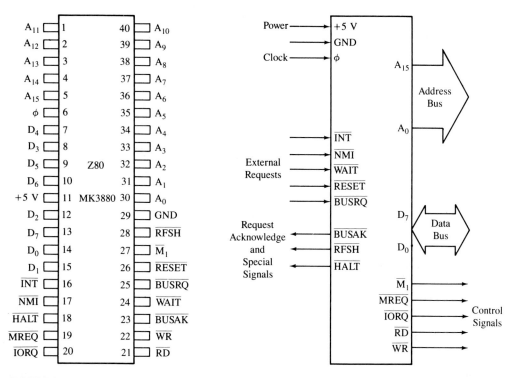

FIGURE 3.1

Z80 Microprocessor Pinout and Logic Signals

SOURCE: Courtesy of Mostek Corporation

DATA BUS

The data bus consists of eight tri-state bidirectional lines D_7–D_0 and is used for data transfer. On these lines, data can flow in either direction—from the microprocessor to memory and I/Os or vice versa.

CONTROL SIGNALS

This group consists of five individual output lines: three can be classified as status signals indicating the nature of the operation being performed, and two as control signals to read from and write into memory or I/Os.

□ $\overline{M_1}$—Machine Cycle One: This is an active low signal indicating that an opcode is being fetched from memory. This signal is also used in an interrupt operation to generate an interrupt acknowledge signal, which will be explained in Chapter 12.

□ $\overline{MREQ}$—Memory Request: This is an active low tri-state line. This signal indicates that the address bus holds a valid address for a memory read or write operation.

☐ IORQ—I/O Request: This is an active low tri-state line. This signal indicates that the low-order address bus (A_7–A_0) holds a valid address for an I/O read or write operation. This signal is also generated for an interrupt operation.

☐ RD—Read: This is an active low tri-state line. This signal indicates that the microprocessor is ready to read data from memory or an I/O device. This signal should be used in conjunction with MREQ for the Memory Read (MEMRD) operation and with IORQ for the I/O Read (IORD) operation.

☐ WR—Write: This is an active low tri-state line. This signal indicates that the microprocessor has already placed a data byte on the data bus and is ready to write into memory or an I/O device. This signal should be used in conjunction with MREQ for the Memory Write (MEMWR) operation and with IORQ for the I/O Write (IOWR) operation.

EXTERNAL REQUESTS

This group includes five different input signals to the microprocessor from external sources. These signals are used to interrupt an ongoing process and to request the microprocessor to do something else.

☐ RESET—Reset: This is an active low signal used to reset the microprocessor. When RESET is activated, the program counter (PC), the interrupt register (I), and the memory refresh register (R) are all cleared to 0. During the reset time, the address bus and the data bus are in high impedance state, and all control signals become inactive. This signal also disables interrupt and refresh. The RESET signal can be initiated by an external key or switch and must be active at least for three clock periods to complete the reset operation.

☐ INT—Interrupt Request: This is an active low signal, initiated by an I/O device to interrupt the microprocessor operation. When the microprocessor accepts the interrupt request, it acknowledges by activating the IORQ signal during the M_1 cycle. The INT signal is maskable, meaning it can be disabled through a software instruction. The interrupt process will be fully discussed in Chapter 12.

☐ NMI—Nonmaskable Interrupt: This is a nonmaskable interrupt; it cannot be disabled. It is activated by a negative edge-triggered signal from an external source. This signal is used primarily for implementing emergency procedures. There is no signal or pin to acknowledge this signal; it is accepted provided the Bus Request signal is inactive. (See Chapter 12 for details.)

☐ BUSRQ—Bus Request: This is an active low signal initiated by external I/O devices such as the DMA (Direct Memory Access) controller. An I/O device can send a low signal to BUSRQ to request the use of the address bus, the data bus, and the control signals. The external device can use the buses, and when its operations are complete, it returns the control to the microprocessor. This signal is used primarily for the direct memory access technique to be discussed in Chapter 16.

☐ WAIT—Wait: This is an active low signal and can be used by memory or I/O devices to add clock cycles to extend the Z80 operations. This signal is used when the response time of memory or I/O devices is slower than that of the

Z80. When this signal goes low, it indicates to the microprocessor that the addressed memory or I/O device is not yet ready for data transfer. As long as this signal is low, the Z80 keeps adding cycles to its operation. The signal will be discussed in Chapter 16 to illustrate how to interface slow memory chips using wait states.

REQUEST ACKNOWLEDGE AND SPECIAL SIGNALS

Among the five external requests described above, only two of the requests need acknowledgment: Bus Request and Interrupt. The interrupt is acknowledged by the $\overline{\text{IORQ}}$ signal in conjunction with the M_1 signal. The Bus Request is acknowledged by a $\overline{\text{BUSAK}}$ (Bus Acknowledge). In addition, the Z80 has two special signals: $\overline{\text{HALT}}$ and $\overline{\text{RFSH}}$.

□ $\overline{\text{BUSAK}}$—Bus Acknowledge: This is an active low output signal initiated by the Z80 in response to the Bus Request signal. This signal indicates to the requesting device that the address bus, the data bus, and the control signals ($\overline{\text{RD}}$, $\overline{\text{WR}}$, $\overline{\text{MREQ}}$, and $\overline{\text{IORQ}}$) have entered into the high impedance state and can be used by the requesting device.
□ $\overline{\text{HALT}}$—Halt: This is an active low output signal used to indicate that the MPU has executed the HALT instruction.
□ $\overline{\text{RFSH}}$—Refresh: This is an active low signal indicating that the address bus A_6–A_0 (low-order seven bits) holds a refresh address of dynamic memory; it should be used in conjunction with $\overline{\text{MREQ}}$ to refresh memory contents.

POWER AND FREQUENCY SIGNALS

This group includes three signals as follows:

□ ϕ — Clock: This pin is used to connect a single phase frequency source. The Z80 does not include a clock circuit on its chip; the circuit must be built separately.
□ +5 V and GND — These pins are for a power supply and ground reference; the Z80 requires one +5 V power source.

3.1.2 Z80 Programming Model

In the last chapter, we developed a model to represent the internal structure of the MPU to process data, shown in Figure 2.3. Now, we will describe a similar model of the Z80 microprocessor as shown in Figure 3.2. The model includes an accumulator and a flag register, general-purpose register arrays, registers as memory pointers, and special-purpose registers. These registers and their functions are briefly described in the following sections; Chapter 6 provides greater detail.

GENERAL-PURPOSE REGISTERS

The Z80 microprocessor has six programmable general-purpose registers named B, C, D, E, H, and L, as shown in Figure 3.2. These are 8-bit registers used for storing data during the program execution. They can be combined as register pairs—BC, DE, HL—to perform 16-bit operations or to hold memory addresses. The programmer can use these registers to load or copy data.

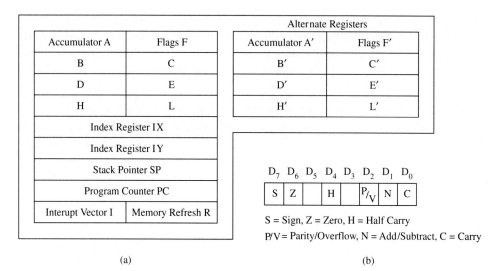

(a)   (b)

FIGURE 3.2
(a) The Z80 Programming Model; (b) Expanded Flag Register with Bit Positions
SOURCE: Courtesy of Mostek Corporation

ACCUMULATOR

The accumulator is an 8-bit register that is part of the arithmetic logic unit (ALU) and is also identified as register A. This register is used to store 8-bit data and to perform arithmetic and logic operations. The result of an operation performed in the ALU is stored in the accumulator.

FLAG REGISTER

The ALU includes six flip-flops that are set or reset according to data conditions after an ALU operation, and the status of these flip-flops, also known as flags, is stored in the 8-bit flag register. For example, after an addition in which the result generates a carry, the carry flip-flop will be set and bit D_0 in the flag register will show logic 1. The bit position of each flag is shown in Figure 3.2(b); bits D_5 and D_3 are unused.

Among the six flags, the H (Half-Carry) and N (Add or Subtract) flags are used internally by the microprocessor for BCD (Binary Coded Decimal) operations. Each of the remaining four flags—S (Sign), Z (Zero), P/V (Parity or Overflow), and C (Carry)—has two Jump or Call instructions associated with it: one when the flag is set and the other when the flag is reset. The details of these flags and their critical importance in programming and decision making are discussed in Chapter 6.

ALTERNATE REGISTER SET

In addition to the general-purpose registers, the accumulator, and the flag register, the Z80 includes a similar set of alternate registers designated as B′, C′, D′, E′,

H', L', the accumulator A', and the flag register F'. These registers are not directly available to the programmer; however, the exchange instructions can exchange information of register pairs with the respective alternate register pairs.

16-BIT REGISTERS AS MEMORY POINTERS

The Z80 microprocessor includes four 16-bit registers, and these registers are used to hold memory addresses; thus, they are classified here as memory pointers. The primary function of memory is to store instructions and data, and the microprocessor needs to access memory registers to read these instructions and data. To access a byte in a memory location, the microprocessor identifies the memory location by using the addresses in these memory pointers. The Z80 has two such specific 16-bit memory pointers, IX and IY, called index registers.

Stack Pointer (SP)   This is also a 16-bit register that is used to point to the memory location called the stack. The stack is a defined area of memory locations in R/W memory, and the beginning of the stack is defined by loading a 16-bit address in the stack pointer. We will discuss the concept of the stack memory in detail when we introduce the topic of subroutines in Chapter 10.

Program Counter (PC)   This register functions as a 16-bit counter. The microprocessor uses this register to sequence the execution of instructions. The function of the program counter is to point to the memory address from which the next byte is to be fetched. When the microprocessor places an address on the address bus to fetch the byte from memory, it then increments the program counter by one to point to the next memory location.

Special-Purpose Registers   The Z80 microprocessor includes two special-purpose registers that are generally absent in other 8-bit microprocessors. These registers are shown in Figure 3.2 as the Interrupt Vector Register (I) and the Memory Refresh Register (R). The functions of these registers will be described in later chapters.

MACHINE CYCLES AND BUS TIMINGS 3.2

The Z80 microprocessor is designed to execute 158 different instruction types. Each instruction has two parts: **operation code** (known as **opcode**) and **operand.** The opcode is a command such as Add, and the operand is an object to be operated on, such as a byte or the contents of a register. Some instructions are 1-byte instructions, and some are multibyte instructions. To execute an instruction, the Z80 needs to perform various operations such as Memory Read/Write and I/O Read/Write. However, there is no direct relationship between the number of bytes of an instruction and the number of operations the Z80 has to perform. For example, the instruction to send the contents of the accumulator to the output port 10_H is a 2-byte instruction: OUT (10H), A.

□ Byte 1: OUT → This is the opcode to output data.
□ Byte 2: (10H*), A → This is the operand to specify that the byte should be sent from the accumulator to port 10_H.

But the Z80 has to perform three operations: (1) read Byte 1 from memory, (2) read Byte 2 from memory, (3) send data to port 10_H.

In the previous section, numerous Z80 signals and their functions were described. Now we need to examine these signals in conjunction with execution of individual instructions and their operations. This task may appear overwhelming at the beginning; fortunately, all instructions are divided into a few basic operations called machine cycles, and these machine cycles are divided into precise *system clock periods*.

The microprocessor external communication functions can be divided into three basic categories:

1. Memory Read and Write.
2. I/O Read and Write.
3. Request Acknowledge.

These functions are further divided into various operations (machine cycles) as shown in Table 3.1. Each instruction consists of one or more of these machine cycles, and each machine cycle is divided into T-states.

To understand various operations, we need to define three terms: instruction cycle, machine cycle, and T-state.

Instruction cycle is defined as the time required to complete the execution of an instruction. The Z80 instruction cycle consists of one to six machine cycles or one to six operations.

Machine cycle is defined as the time required to complete one operation of accessing memory, accessing I/O, or acknowledging an external request. This cycle may consist of three to six T-states.

T-state is defined as one subdivision of the operation performed in one clock period. These subdivisions are internal states synchronized with the system clock, and each T-state is precisely equal to one clock period. The terms T-state and clock period are often used synonymously.

In this chapter, we focus on the first three operations listed in Table 3.1— Opcode Fetch, Memory Read, and Memory Write—and examine the signals on various buses in relation to the system clock. In the next chapter, we will use these timing diagrams to interface memory with the Z80 microprocessor. Similarly, we will discuss timings of other machine cycles in later chapters in the context of their applications. For example, I/O Read/Write machine cycles will be discussed in Chapter 5 and Interrupt Acknowledge will be discussed in Chapter 12.

---

*A hexadecimal number in an instruction is shown as a number followed by the letter H.

TABLE 3.1
The Z80 Machine Cycles and Control Signals

Machine Cycle	$\overline{M_1}$	$\overline{MREQ}$	$\overline{IORQ}$	$\overline{RD}$	$\overline{WR}$
Opcode Fetch ($\overline{M_1}$)	0	0	1	0	1
Memory Read	1	0	1	0	1
Memory Write	1	0	1	1	0
I/O Read	1	1	0	0	1
I/O Write	1	1	0	1	0
Interrupt Acknowledge	0	1	0	1	1
Non-maskable Interrupt	0	0	1	0	1
Bus Acknowledge ($\overline{BUSAK}$ = 0)	1	Z	Z	Z	Z

NOTE: Logic 0 = Active, Logic 1 = Inactive, Z = High Impedance

3.2.1 Opcode Fetch Machine Cycle ($\overline{M_1}$)

The first operation in any instruction is opcode fetch. The microprocessor needs to get (fetch) this machine code from the memory register where it is stored before the microprocessor can begin to execute the instruction. The opcode fetch operation and its timing signals are illustrated in Example 3.1.

The accumulator of the Z80 microprocessor holds the data byte $9F_H$, and the code for instruction LD B, A (opcode) 0 1 0 0 0 1 1 1 (47_H) is stored in memory location 2002_H. This is a 1-byte instruction, and when this opcode is executed, the contents of the accumulator will be copied into register B. List the sequence of events that takes place to execute this machine code and illustrate the signals on various buses in relation to the system clock.

Example
3.1

A = 9F H

We assume here that the Z80 has already completed the execution of the code in memory location 2001_H and the program counter holds the address 2002_H. Before the Z80 can execute the opcode, it needs to fetch the code from the memory location. To fetch the opcode, the Z80 performs the following steps:

Solution

1. The Z80 places the contents of the program counter (2002_H) on the address bus, and increments the program counter to the next address, 2003_H. The program counter always points to the next byte to be executed.
2. The address is decoded by the external decoding circuit, and the register 2002_H is identified.
3. The Z80 sends the control signals ($\overline{MREQ}$ and $\overline{RD}$) to enable the memory output buffer.
4. The contents of the memory register (opcode 47_H) are placed on the data bus and brought into the instruction decoder of the microprocessor.
5. The Z80 decodes the opcode and executes the instruction, meaning it copies the contents of the accumulator into register B.

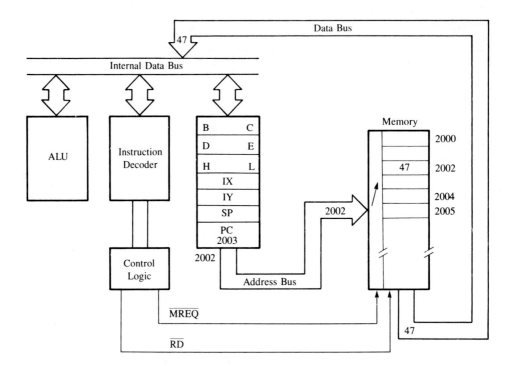

FIGURE 3.3
Z80 Memory Read Operation

Figure 3.3 shows how the Z80 fetches the opcode using the address and the data buses and the control signal. Figure 3.4 shows the timing of the Opcode Fetch machine cycle in relation to the system's clock. The address bus in Figure 3.4 is shown as two parallel lines. This is a commonly used practice to represent logic levels of groups of lines; some lines are high and others are low, and the crossover of the lines indicates that a new address is being placed on the address bus. The high impedance state is shown by a straight line as in the data bus (D_7–D_0). The timing details of these signals are given below.

1. Figure 3.4 shows that the Opcode Fetch cycle is completed in four clock periods or T-states. This machine cycle is also identified as the M_1 cycle.
2. At the beginning of the first clock period T_1, the control signal $\overline{M_1}$ goes low and the contents of the program counter (2002_H) are placed on the address bus.
3. After the falling edge of T_1, the Z80 asserts two control signals—$\overline{MREQ}$ and $\overline{RD}$, both active low. The $\overline{MREQ}$ indicates that it is a memory-related operation, and $\overline{RD}$ suggests that it is a Read operation. Both signals are necessary to read from memory.
4. The internal decoder of the memory and the Chip Select circuit (not shown in Figure 3.4) decode the address and identify register 2002_H. The control signals

FIGURE 3.4

Z80 Opcode Fetch (M₁) and Bus Timings

SOURCE: Courtesy of Zilog Inc. (adapted).

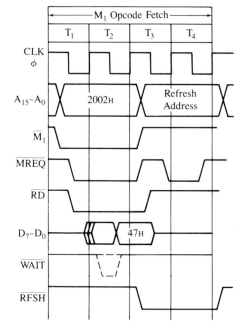

$\overline{\text{MREQ}}$ and $\overline{\text{RD}}$ are used to enable the memory output buffer. The data bus, which was in high impedance state, is activated as an input bus (to the microprocessor) shortly after the leading edge of T_2. After the falling edge of T_2, memory places its register contents (47_H) on the data bus.

5. At the leading edge of T_3, the data on the data bus are read, and the control signals become inactive.

6. During T_3 and T_4, the instruction decoder in the microprocessor decodes and executes the opcode. These are internal operations and cannot be observed on the data bus.

The following two steps are irrelevant to the present problem; however, they are included here as part of the M_1 cycle.

7. During T_3 and T_4, when the Z80 is performing internal operations, the low-order address bus is used to supply a 7-bit address for refreshing dynamic memory. If the system includes dynamic memory, this operation simplifies its interfacing hardware. This aspect of the M_1 cycle will be discussed again when we illustrate interfacing of dynamic memory (Chapter 16).

8. Figure 3.4 shows the signal called $\overline{\text{WAIT}}$. The Z80 samples the Wait line during T_2, and if it is forced low by an external device (such as memory or I/O), the Z80 adds Wait states (clock cycles) to extend the machine cycle and continues to add clock cycles until the Wait signal goes high again. This technique is used

to interface memories with slow response time and will be discussed again in Chapter 16.

3.2.2 Memory Read Machine Cycle

The second machine cycle we want to illustrate is Memory Read. As explained in the next example, this cycle is quite similar to the Opcode Fetch cycle.

Example 3.2

Two machine codes—0 0 1 1 1 1 1 0 ($3E_H$) and 1 0 0 1 1 1 1 1 ($9F_H$)—are stored in memory locations 2000_H and 2001_H, respectively, as shown below. The first machine code ($3E_H$) represents the opcode to load a data byte into the accumulator, and the second code ($9F_H$) represents the data byte to be loaded into the accumulator. Illustrate the bus timings as these machine codes are executed, and calculate the time required to execute the Opcode Fetch and the Memory Read cycles and the entire instruction cycle if the clock frequency is 4 MHz.

Address	Machine Code		Instruction	Comment
2000_H	0 0 1 1 1 1 1 0	→ 3E	LD A, 9FH	;Load 9FH in the accumulator
2001_H	1 0 0 1 1 1 1 1	→ 9F		

Solution

This instruction consists of two bytes; the first is the opcode, and the second is the data byte. The Z80 must first read these bytes from memory and thus requires at least two machine cycles. The first machine cycle is Opcode Fetch, and the second machine cycle is Memory Read, as shown in Figure 3.5. These cycles are described in the following list.

1. The first machine cycle (Opcode Fetch) is identical in bus timings with the machine cycle illustrated in Example 3.1, except for the bus contents. The address bus contains 2000_H, and the data bus contains the opcode $3E_H$. When the Z80 decodes the opcode during the T_3 state, it realizes that a second byte must be read.
2. After the completion of the Opcode Fetch cycle, the Z80 places the address 2001_H on the address bus and increments the program counter to the next address, 2002_H. To differentiate the second cycle from the Opcode Fetch cycle, the M_1 signal remains inactive (high).
3. After the falling edge of T_1 of the Memory Read cycle, the control signals $\overline{MREQ}$ and $\overline{RD}$ are asserted. These signals, along with the memory address, are used to identify the register 2001_H and enable the memory chip.
4. After the leading edge of T_3, the Z80 activates the data bus as an input bus; memory places the data byte $9F_H$ on the data bus, and the Z80 reads and stores the byte in the accumulator during T_3.
5. After the falling edge of T_3, both control signals become inactive (high), and at the end of T_3, the next machine cycle begins.

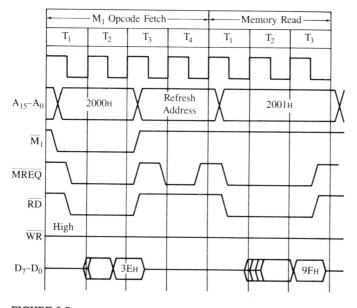

FIGURE 3.5

Memory Read Machine Cycle and Its Timings

SOURCE: Courtesy of Zilog Inc. (adapted).

The execution times of the Memory Read machine cycle and the instruction cycle are calculated as follows:

Clock Frequency f = 4 MHz

T-state = Clock Period (1/f) = 0.25 μs

Execution Time for Opcode Fetch: (4 T) $\times$ 0.25 = 1.0 μs

Execution Time for Memory Read: (3 T) $\times$ 0.25 = 0.75 μs

Execution Time for Instruction: (7 T) $\times$ 0.25 = 1.75 μs.

3.2.3 Memory Write Cycle

Now we want to illustrate the third machine cycle: Memory Write. This machine cycle writes or stores data in a specified memory register as shown in the following example.

Example 3.3

The HL register holds the address 2350_H, and the accumulator has the data byte $9F_H$. The instruction code 0 1 1 1 0 1 1 1 (77_H) is stored in memory location 2003_H. When this code is executed, it stores the contents of the accumulator in the memory location indicated by the address in the HL register. Illustrate the bus contents and timings as this instruction is being executed.

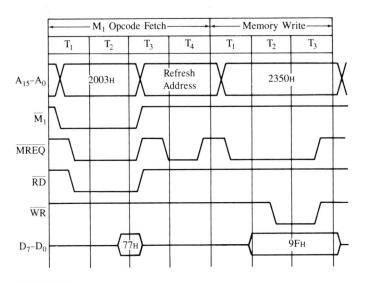

FIGURE 3.6
Memory Write Machine Cycle and Its Timings
SOURCE: Courtesy of Zilog Inc. (adapted)

Instruction: LD (HL), A   ;Copy contents of the accumulator
into memory location, the address
of which is stored in HL register.

Solution

This is a one-byte instruction with two machine cycles: Opcode Fetch and Memory Write. In the first machine cycle, the Z80 fetches the code (77_H), and in the second machine cycle, it copies the byte $9F_H$ from the accumulator into the memory location 2350_H. The timings of these machine cycles are shown in Figure 3.6 and explained below.

1. In the Opcode Fetch machine cycle, the Z80 places the address 2003_H on the address bus and gets the code 77_H by using the control signals $\overline{MREQ}$ and $\overline{RD}$ as in the previous examples. The program counter is also incremented to the next address, 2004_H.
2. During the T_3 and T_4 states, the Z80 decodes the machine code 77_H and prepares for the memory write operation.
3. At the beginning of the next machine cycle (Memory Write), it places the contents (2350_H) of the HL register on the address bus. At the falling edge of T_1, $\overline{MREQ}$ goes low and the data byte $9F_H$ from the accumulator is placed on the data bus.
4. After allowing one T-state (after $\overline{MREQ}$) to stabilize the address, the Z80 asserts the control signal Write ($\overline{WR}$), which is used to write the data byte at the address shown on the address bus.

5. After the falling edge of T_3, both control signals become inactive, and one-half T-state later, the data bus goes into high impedance state.

3.2.4 Review of Important Concepts

1. In each instruction cycle, the first operation is always Opcode Fetch, and it is indicated by the active low $\overline{M_1}$ signal. This cycle can be four to six T-states in duration.
2. The Memory Read cycle is in many ways similar to the Opcode Fetch cycle. Both use the same control signals ($\overline{MREQ}$ and $\overline{RD}$) and read contents from memory. However, the Opcode Fetch reads opcodes and the Memory Read reads 8-bit data or addresses; the two machine cycles are differentiated by the $\overline{M_1}$ signal.
3. The control signals, $\overline{MREQ}$ and $\overline{RD}$, are both necessary to read from memory.
4. In the Memory Write cycle, the Z80 writes (stores) data in memory using the control signals $\overline{MREQ}$ and $\overline{WR}$.
5. In the Memory Read cycle, the Z80 asserts the $\overline{MREQ}$ and $\overline{RD}$ signals to enable memory, and then the addressed memory places the data on the data bus; on the other hand, in the Memory Write cycle, the Z80 asserts the $\overline{MREQ}$, places the data byte on the data bus, and then asserts the $\overline{WR}$ signal to write into the addressed memory.
6. Generally, the Memory Read and Write cycles consist of three T-states; however, they can take four T-states in some instructions. The Memory Read and Write cycles will not be asserted simultaneously; the microprocessor cannot read and write at the same time.

3.2.5 Generating Control Signals

After examining the concepts summarized at the end of the previous section, we may need to generate additional control signals.

1. To read from memory, the $\overline{MREQ}$ and the $\overline{RD}$ signals are necessary, and to read from an input device, the $\overline{IORQ}$ and the $\overline{RD}$ are necessary; all these signals are active low. As a design practice, the $\overline{MREQ}$ is generally combined with a decoded address (discussed in Chapter 4), and $\overline{RD}$ is connected directly to the memory chip. However, control signals $\overline{RD}$ and $\overline{WR}$ can also be combined with $\overline{MREQ}$ and $\overline{IORQ}$ to generate additional signals. We can generate active low Memory Read ($\overline{MEMRD}$) signal either by ANDing these signals in a negative NAND gate as shown in Figure 3.7(a) or by using a 2-to-4 decoder as shown in Figure 3.7(b). The decoder is enabled by the $\overline{MREQ}$ and has $\overline{RD}$ and $\overline{WR}$ signals as input. Both inputs cannot be active at the same time; when one is low, the other will remain high. When $\overline{RD}$ is active low, the input is 0 1, and the output O_1 goes active as $\overline{MEMRD}$.
2. To write into memory, the $\overline{MREQ}$ and the $\overline{WR}$ signals are necessary, and to write a data byte to an output device, the $\overline{IORQ}$ and $\overline{WR}$ signals are necessary;

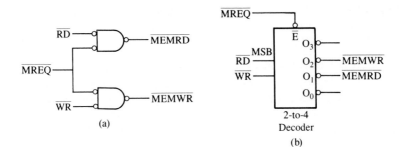

FIGURE 3.7
Generating Memory Control Signals

all these signals are active low. We can generate active low Memory Write ($\overline{\text{MEMWR}}$) signal by ANDing $\overline{\text{MREQ}}$ and $\overline{\text{WR}}$ signals in a negative NAND gate as shown in Figure 3.7(a) or by using the decoder as shown in Figure 3.7(b). Similarly, $\overline{\text{IORD}}$ (I/O Read) and $\overline{\text{IOWR}}$ (I/O Write) signals can be generated; this is discussed in Chapter 5.

3.3   SOME PUZZLING QUESTIONS AND THEIR ANSWERS

After reading the previous sections, the reader may have many unanswered questions. One of the primary reasons for this predicament is that the microprocessor is a programmable and complex device. It interacts with external devices such as memory and I/Os, and some questions cannot be answered until we discuss these other devices. Similarly, some questions will remain unanswered until we start using instructions and writing programs. However, there are some questions that we should answer immediately.

1. *How does the Z80 microprocessor know where to begin after the power is turned on?*

Most microcomputer systems have built-in power-on *reset circuits*, meaning that when the power is turned on, the microprocessor is reset and its program counter is cleared to the address 0000_H. The address 0000_H is placed on the address bus, and the instruction stored at that location determines what happens next.

2. *How does the Z80 know what operation to perform first (Memory Read/Write or I/O Read/Write)?*

The first operation is always an Opcode Fetch.

3. *How does the microprocessor differentiate between an opcode and a data byte?*

When the first opcode is fetched and decoded in the instruction register, the microprocessor recognizes the number of bytes that must be read from memory for the complete instruction. The instructions can range from 1 to 4 bytes in length. Figure 3.5, for example, contains a 2-byte instruction (3E and Data), and the second byte is always considered Data. If that second byte is omitted by mistake, the Z80 will interpret whatever is in that memory location as Data. The byte after the Data will be treated as the next instruction. The microprocessor is a sequential machine; it goes from one memory location to the next unless instructed to do otherwise.

4. *What is the use of the $\overline{M_1}$ signal? It looks as if it will not be connected to any device.*

This signal serves two purposes: (1) it differentiates the Opcode Fetch cycle from other operations, and (2) it can be used to generate the Interrupt Acknowledge signal.

5. *If flags are individual flip-flops, can they be observed on an oscilloscope?*

No, they cannot be observed on an oscilloscope; these flip-flops are internal and not connected to any of the external pins. However, they can be examined by storing them on the *stack memory* (see Chapter 10).

6. *Is the number of T-states required for a given machine cycle constant?*

No. But most Opcode Fetch machine cycles require four T-states, and Memory Read/Write and I/O Read/Write machine cycles, generally, take three or four T-states. However, there are some exceptions.

7. *How does one recognize the machine cycles in a given instruction?*

The number of machine cycles and the T-states required for those machine cycles are listed in the instruction set. There is a repetitive pattern, and one can use the following guidelines.

□ The number of machine cycles in an instruction indicates how many times the microprocessor must access memory or I/O.
□ The first machine cycle in an instruction is always Opcode Fetch.
□ The microprocessor must read all the bytes (codes) from memory before it can execute an instruction.

For example, a 3-byte instruction requires at least three machine cycles. The unconditional Jump instruction is a 3-byte instruction with 10 (4, 3, 3) T-states; it consists of one opcode and a 16-bit address of the jump location. Therefore, by examining the number of T-states, we can easily classify the machine cycles of the Jump instruction as one Opcode Fetch and two Memory Read.

Another example is ADD A, 32H (add a byte 32_H to the contents of the accumulator). This is a 2-byte instruction with 7 (4, 3) T-states. By examining the number of bytes and the number of T-states, we can conclude that it must have two machine cycles—the first is Opcode Fetch, and the second is Memory Read. The addition is performed inside the processor, and it does not need any additional information from memory or I/O.

8. *How does one recognize machine cycles in an instruction when the number of bytes is not the same as the number of machine cycles?*

One has to examine the number of bytes, T-states, and the operation being performed. For example, the instruction **LD (2050H), A** has three bytes and 13 (4, 3, 3, 3) T-states; it copies the contents of the accumulator into the memory location 2050_H. The processor must read the entire instruction first; therefore, the first must be Opcode Fetch, followed by two Memory Read cycles. This accounts for ten T-states. In the remaining three states, the processor must write (copy) the contents of the accumulator into the memory location 2050_H; therefore, it must be the Memory Write cycle.

3.4   ARCHITECTURE OF SIMILAR 8-BIT MICROPROCESSORS

The primary reasons to discuss other 8-bit microprocessors are to examine how the MPU model developed in the last chapter matches with various microprocessors and to confirm that the underlying basic concepts remain similar even though specific details may vary from one chip to another. At present, many 8-bit general-purpose microprocessors are available in the market. We will focus on three: the Intel 8085, the National Semiconductor NSC 800, and the Motorola 6800. These microprocessors are selected to illustrate various strategies used in designing the microprocessor. The recent trend in 8-bit microprocessors can be illustrated by so-called 8-bit super chips, such as the Hitachi HD64180, discussed in Chapter 18.

3.4.1   Intel 8085
The Intel 8085 and its predecessor the 8080 are widely used 8-bit microprocessors. The 8080 MPU is composed of three chips—the 8080 microprocessor, the clock generator, and the system driver—and it needs three power supplies (+5 V, −5 V, +12 V). The 8085 is an upgraded version of the 8080; it operates with one +5 V power supply, and one chip replaces the 8080's three chips. The 8085 is upward

software compatible with the 8080; it has only two more instructions than the 8080. The programming models of both microprocessors are identical; however, the 8085 hardware model differs significantly not only from the 8080 but also from other 8-bit microprocessors. The 8085 has a multiplexed bus (8 lines), which is used as both the 8-bit data bus and the low-order address bus. This feature allows Intel to provide additional interrupt lines.

8085 HARDWARE MODEL

Figure 3.8 represents the hardware model with the logic pinout of the 8085. The six categories of the signals are address bus, data bus, control (and status) signals, external requests, request acknowledge, and power and frequency signals. In addition, the 8085 has two signals for serial I/O.

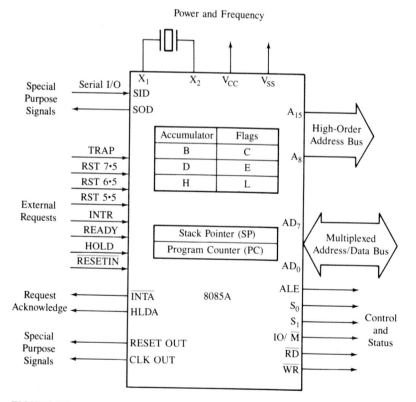

FIGURE 3.8

The Intel 8085 Microprocessor Model

SOURCE: Courtesy of Intel Corporation

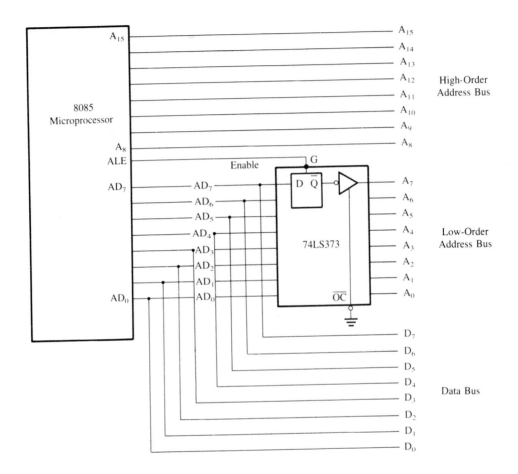

FIGURE 3.9
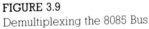
Demultiplexing the 8085 Bus

The 8085 has a 16-bit address bus; however, its low-order address bus is multiplexed with the data bus. These eight lines are time-shared by two functions; in the earlier part of a machine cycle, they are used for a low-order address, and in the later part for data. To interface this chip with memory (without any special features), these lines need to be demultiplexed (separated). The 8085 has a signal called ALE (Address Latch Enable), which can be used to demultiplex the bus, as shown in Figure 3.9. The ALE is asserted at the beginning of each machine cycle, when the bus has an address. Figure 3.9 shows that the ALE is used to latch the address, thus creating a separate low-order bus A_7–A_0. The Z80 does not need this signal because it has separate lines for the data and the address buses.

The 8085 has two status signals S_0 and S_1 to identify various machine cycles, and an IO/$\overline{M}$ signal to differentiate between an I/O operation and a memory operation. In contrast, the Z80 identifies the Opcode Fetch cycle by asserting $\overline{M_1}$ and has two separate signals ($\overline{MREQ}$ and $\overline{IORQ}$) to identify memory and I/O operations. In the 8085, the control signals Memory Read/Write and I/O Read/Write are generated by ANDing IO/$\overline{M}$ and control signals $\overline{RD}$ and $\overline{WR}$.

Figure 3.8 shows that the 8085 provides five interrupt lines as external requests, out of which the TRAP is equivalent to the Z80 nonmaskable interrupt. The Z80 provides various additional interrupt modes through software.

8085 SOFTWARE MODEL

Figure 3.8 also shows the software model of the 8085. It includes one accumulator, a flag register, a general-purpose register array, and two 16-bit registers as memory pointers (program counter and stack pointer). This model matches very well with the requirements of the microprocessor as a processing unit (Figure 2.2). The Z80 includes all the 8085 registers in addition to an alternate set of registers, index registers, and special-purpose registers.

3.4.2 National Semiconductor NSC800

The NSC800 is an 8-bit microprocessor manufactured by National Semiconductor. It is a low-power CMOS device that combines features of the 8085 and the Z80. Because its power consumption is 5 percent of that of n-channel MOSFET (NMOS) devices, it is ideally suited for low-power or battery-operated applications.

The NSC800 has a bus structure similar to that of the 8085: a multiplexed bus with the status signals S_0, S_1, and IO/$\overline{M}$. It has a powerful interrupt scheme that combines the 8085 signals and the Z80 interrupt modes. Its software model, instruction set, and mnemonics are identical with those of the Z80.

In summary, the NSC800 combines the software capability of the Z80 with the bus structure of the 8085; its hardware and software models match with the generalized model we developed in the previous chapter.

3.4.3 Motorola MC6800

The MC6800 was developed at about the same time as the Intel 8080. The hardware model of this processor is similar to any other processor we have discussed, but it has a different internal architecture.

Figure 3.10 represents the 6800's architecture. It has 16 address lines, 8 data lines, and fewer control (and status) signals than the Z80. The fewer control signals result from the lack of peripheral-mapped I/O; all I/Os are interfaced as memory-mapped I/Os. Therefore, the control signals in this processor need not differentiate between memory and I/O operations.

The other significant difference is in its internal architecture; it has two accumulators, one flag register shown as the Condition Code Register, but no general-purpose registers. This processor uses external memory for storing interim

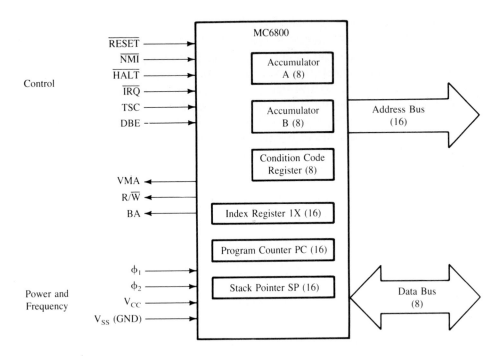

FIGURE 3.10
The Motorola 6800 Microprocessor Model
SOURCE: Courtesy of Motorola, Inc.

calculations and data bytes; it makes extensive use of memory referencing in its operations. The 6800 has simple timing and control signals; the clock period is the same as the machine cycle.

The 6809 is the latest improved version of the 6800 family; however, its machine code is not compatible with that of the 6800. Its internal architecture is similar to that of the 6800, except it has an additional stack pointer, an additional index register, and a register to be used for referencing memory. The basic design philosophy is the same as that of the 6800, but it has eliminated some limitations of the 6800.

3.4.4 Review of 8-bit Microprocessors

In the last section, we examined the architectures of three microprocessors and occasionally compared them with the Z80. Now we can easily conclude that the architectures of various 8-bit microprocessors have similar patterns and can be represented by the hardware and the software models developed in the last chapter. We can classify these processors into two categories: one group, including the Z80, the 8085, NSC800, is register-oriented; the group including the 6800 and the 6809 is memory-reference-oriented.

SUMMARY

- The Z80 signals can be classified into six groups: address bus, data bus, control signals, external requests, request acknowledge, and power and frequency signals (see section 3.1 for definitions of these signals).
- The Z80 address bus has 16 unidirectional address lines; they are capable of addressing 64K memory.
- The Z80 data bus has eight bidirectional data lines, and they are used for data transfer.
- The Z80 microprocessor has six general-purpose 8-bit registers (B, C, D, E, H, and L) as a primary set. In addition, it includes the alternate set of these registers that can be used to exchange information with the primary set. The registers B and C, D and E, and H and L can be combined to perform some 16-bit operations.
- The ALU section of the Z80 includes accumulator A and the flag register to indicate six different data conditions. It also includes the alternate accumulator A′ and the flag register F′, which can be used to exchange information with A and F, respectively.
- Four flags—Sign, Zero, Carry, and Parity/Overflow—can be used for decision making and tested in conjunction with Jump, Call, and Return instructions. Two flags—Half Carry and Add/Subtract—are used internally for BCD operations and are unavailable for the programmer.
- The Z80 has four 16-bit registers—IX, IY, SP, and PC—used as memory pointers. Two index registers IX and IY are used to point to any memory location. The stack pointer (SP) is used to specify memory locations in a defined R/W memory segment called the stack. The program counter (PC) is used to sequence the program execution; it points to the next memory address from where the machine code is to be fetched.
- The Z80 is designed to execute 158 instruction types, and each instruction can be divided into a few basic operations called machine cycles.
- The frequently used machine cycles are Opcode Fetch, Memory Read and Write, and I/O Read and Write.
- The Opcode Fetch and Memory Read are operationally similar; the Z80 reads from memory in both machine cycles. However, the Z80 reads opcode during the Opcode Fetch cycle, and it reads 8-bit data during the Memory Read cycle. In the Memory Write cycle, the Z80 writes data into memory.
- The memory operations are differentiated from I/O operations by two control signals: MREQ and IORQ. The signal MREQ is combined with RD and WR signals to generate MEMRD and MEMWR control signals.
- The Z80 performs three basic steps in any of these machine cycles: It places an address on the address bus, sends appropriate control signals, and transfers data via the data bus.
- The 8-bit microprocessors can generally be classified into two categories: One group is register-oriented, and the other is memory-reference-oriented.

ASSIGNMENTS

1. The MOS Technology 6501 microprocessor chip has 13 address lines. Specify the memory registers it is capable of addressing.
2. If the Intel 8086 microprocessor has 20 address lines, what is its capacity of memory addressing?
3. Explain the functions of the accumulator.
4. List the Z80 programmable registers.
5. What is a flag?
6. What is the function of the program counter?
7. If the Z80 is executing the code fetched from the memory location 1845_H, what is the memory address in the program counter?
8. If the clock frequency is 4 MHz, how much time is required to execute an instruction of 21 T-states?
9. The instruction LD IX, (2050_H) loads 2050_H into the index register. Specify the number of bytes, machine cycles, and T-states of this instruction by checking the instruction set. Calculate the time required to execute the instruction if the system clock frequency is 6 MHz.
10. List the sequence of events that occurs when the Z80 reads from memory.
11. In the Opcode Fetch cycle, what are the control signals required to enable the memory buffer?
12. When is the data byte placed on the data bus in the Memory Write cycle?
13. The memory location 2065_H holds the opcode $F9_H$. If the Z80 begins the Opcode Fetch cycle by placing the address 2065_H on the address bus, specify the contents of the data bus after the falling edge of the T_2 state.
14. The instruction LD B, (HL) copies the contents of the memory location specified by the 16-bit contents in the HL register. It is a 1-byte instruction with two machine cycles. Identify the second machine cycle and its control signals.
15. In Figure 3.7(b), exchange $\overline{RD}$ and $\overline{WR}$ signals and identify the output pins and the control signals that can be generated at the output.
16. Figure 3.11 shows a 3-to-8 decoder with $\overline{MREQ}$, $\overline{RD}$, and $\overline{WR}$ as input signals. Identify the control signals that can be generated at the outputs of the decoder.

FIGURE 3.11

Generating Control Signals Using a 3-to-8 Decoder: Assignment 18

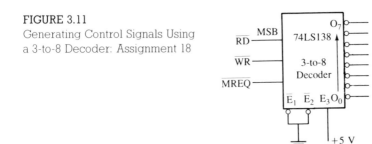

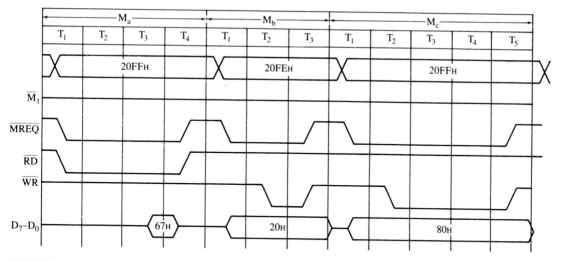

FIGURE 3.12
Machine Cycles for Assignments 19–23

17. Figure 3.12 shows the timings of three machine cycles. Identify the types of operations.

18. Do the three machine cycles in Figure 3.12 represent a complete instruction? Explain.

19. Examine the machine cycle M_b in Figure 3.12 and specify the memory being accessed and its contents.

20. Does the byte on the data bus in the machine cycle M_a in Figure 3.12 represent an opcode?

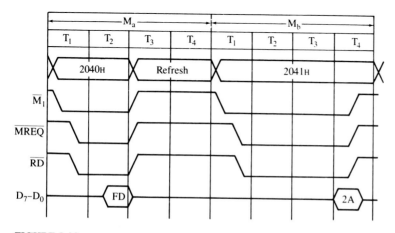

FIGURE 3.13
Machine Cycles for Assignment 22

21. Explain what is being done in machine cycle M_c (Figure 3.12).

22. Identify the machine cycles M_a and M_b in Figure 3.13.

23. Identify the machine cycles in the following instructions:

SUB B	: 1 Byte/1 Machine Cycle/4 T-states
	: Subtract the contents of register B from the accumulator
AND 47H	: 2 B/2 MC/(4, 3) T-states
	: Logically AND 47H with the contents of the accumulator
LD A, (2050H)	: 3 B/4 MC/13 (4, 3, 3, 3) T-states
	: copy the contents of the memory location 2050H into the accumulator
PUSH BC	: 1 B/3 MC/10 (4, 3, 3) T-states
	: copy the contents of BC register into two stack memory locations

Memory Interfacing

Memory is an integral part of a microprocessor-based system, and in this chapter our focus will be on how to interface a memory chip with the microprocessor. We will examine memory structure and requirements to read from it and write into it. We then compare those requirements with those of the Z80 Memory Read and Write machine cycles. From that comparison, we will derive the basic steps necessary to interface memory.

This chapter illustrates two examples of interfacing memory chips, one EPROM and the other static R/W memory. The discussion includes analyses of the following: **decoding circuits, memory maps,** the concepts of **foldback memory** and **absolute decoding.** Finally, an example of memory design is illustrated to synthesize the interfacing concepts.

OBJECTIVES

□ List the requirements to read from memory.
□ List the steps initiated by the Z80 to read from and write into memory.
□ List the steps required to interface a memory chip with the Z80.
□ Analyze given EPROM and static R/W memory interfacing circuits and specify their memory address ranges.
□ Explain the terms absolute decoding and foldback memory.
□ Design a circuit to interface EPROM and R/W memory with the Z80 for given memory addresses.

4.1   INTERFACING MEMORY

While executing a program, the microprocessor needs to access memory frequently to read instruction codes and data stored in memory, and the *interfacing circuit* enables that access. Memory has certain signal requirements for writing into and reading from its registers. Similarly, the microprocessor initiates a set of signals when it wants to communicate with memory. The interfacing process involves designing a circuit that will match the memory requirements with the microprocessor signals. In the following section, we examine memory structure and its requirements and also the Z80 Memory Read and Write machine cycles. Then we derive the basic steps necessary to interface memory with the Z80.

4.1.1 Memory Structure and Its Requirements

Read/Write Memory (R/WM) is a group of registers to store binary information. Figure 4.1 shows a typical R/W memory chip; it has 1024 registers, each of which can store eight bits indicated by eight I/O lines. The chip has ten address lines A_9–A_0, one Chip Select $\overline{CS}$, and two control lines: Read ($\overline{RD}$) to enable the output buffer and Write ($\overline{WR}$) to enable the input buffer. Figure 4.1 also shows the internal decoder to decode the address lines. We may recall from Chapter 2 that to read from or write into one of the memory registers certain requirements have to be met. They are as follows:

1. An address should be placed on the address lines. The low-order address lines are decoded by the internal decoder of the memory chip, and the addressed register is identified.
2. The high-order address should be decoded to generate a Chip Select signal, and the memory chip is selected by asserting the Chip Select $\overline{CS}$ low.
3. To read from the addressed register, the $\overline{RD}$ should be asserted low to enable the output buffer, and then the data byte from the register will be placed on the I/O lines.
4. To write into the addressed register, the $\overline{WR}$ should be asserted low to enable the input buffer, and then data bits from the data lines are stored into the register.

FIGURE 4.1
Logic Diagram: A Typical 1K
Memory Chip

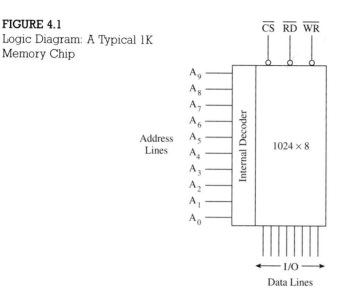

To interface this memory with the Z80 microprocessor, we need to examine the signals the microprocessor asserts when it attempts to communicate with memory.

4.1.2 How Does the Z80 Read from or Write into Memory?

In Chapter 3, we showed the timing diagrams and the Z80 bus contents when an opcode or a data byte is fetched from memory. To read from memory, the Z80 performs the following steps, as shown in Figure 4.2(a):

1. Places a 16-bit address on its address bus (shown as high- and low-order addresses).
2. Asserts the $\overline{\text{MREQ}}$ to indicate that the address bus holds a valid address.
3. Asserts the $\overline{\text{RD}}$ signal low to indicate that it wants to read.

To write into memory, the Z80 performs the following steps, as shown in Figure 4.3:

1. Places a 16-bit address on the address bus.
2. Asserts $\overline{\text{MREQ}}$ and places data on the data bus.
3. Asserts $\overline{\text{WR}}$ signal.

To understand and design an interface circuit, we need to match the memory requirements with the Z80 read/write operations.

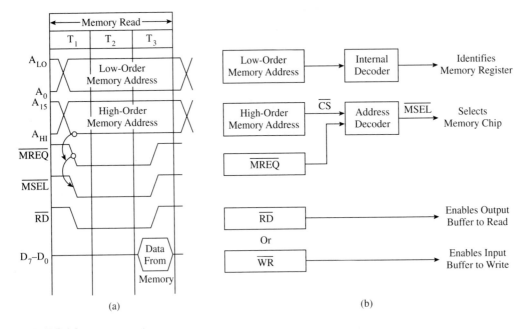

FIGURE 4.2
(a) Memory Read Timing Diagram; (b) Block Diagram: Address Decoding and Memory
Read/Write Operations

SOURCE: (a) Courtesy of Zilog, Inc. (adapted)

4.1.3 Basic Concepts in Memory Interfacing

The primary function of memory interfacing is to allow the microprocessor to read
from and write into a given register of a memory chip. To perform these operations, the microprocessor should

1. Be able to select the chip.
2. Identify the register.
3. Enable the appropriate buffer.

   Let us examine the timing diagram of the Memory Read operation—Figure
4.2(a)—in order to understand how the Z80 can read from memory. In Figure
4.2(a), the address bus is divided into two segments, low order A_0–A_{LO} and high
order A_{HI}–A_{15}, to explain the decoding concepts; the number of address lines represented by the A_{LO} and A_{HI} varies according to the size of the memory chip.

1. The Z80 places a 16-bit address on the address bus, and with this address only
   one register should be selected. For the memory chip in Figure 4.1, only ten
   address lines are required to identify 1,024 registers. Therefore, we can connect
   the low-order address lines A_9–A_0 (A_{LO} = A_9) of the Z80 address bus to the

FIGURE 4.3
Writing into Memory Register

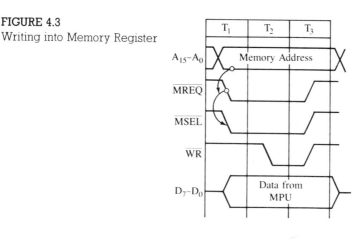

memory chip. The internal decoder of the memory chip will identify and select the register, as shown in Figure 4.2(b).

2. The remaining Z80 address lines A_{15}–A_{10} (A_{HI} = A_{10}) should be decoded to generate a Chip-Select ($\overline{CS}$) signal unique to that combination of address logic.

3. The Z80 provides two signals: $\overline{MREQ}$ and $\overline{RD}$. The $\overline{MREQ}$ can be combined with the decoded address pulse ($\overline{CS}$) to generate a Memory Select ($\overline{MSEL}$) to select the memory chip.

4. The microprocessor asserts the control signal $\overline{RD}$, enables the output buffer of memory, and reads the data byte. Figure 4.2(a) also shows that memory must place the data byte on the data bus at the beginning of T_3.

To write into a register, the microprocessor performs similar steps. Figure 4.3 shows the Memory Write cycle. In the Write operation, the Z80 places the address and data, and asserts the $\overline{MREQ}$ signal. After allowing sufficient time for data to become stable, it asserts the Write ($\overline{WR}$) signal. The $\overline{WR}$ signal enables the input buffer of the memory chip and stores the byte in the selected register.

An alternative to generating the $\overline{MSEL}$ signal (Step 3 in Memory Read) to select the memory chip is to generate the control signals $\overline{MEMRD}$ and $\overline{MEMWR}$ by combining the $\overline{MREQ}$, $\overline{RD}$, and $\overline{WR}$ as shown in Figure 4.4(a). The $\overline{MEMRD}$ can be used to enable the output buffer to read from memory; the $\overline{MEMWR}$ can be used to enable the input buffer to write into memory, and the decoded address pulse ($\overline{CS}$) can be used to select the chip as shown in Figure 4.4(b).

To interface memory with the microprocessor, we can summarize the above steps as follows:

1. Connect the required address lines of the address bus to the address lines of the memory chip.

2. Decode the remaining address lines of the address bus to generate the Chip Select signal, as discussed in the next section (4.1.4).

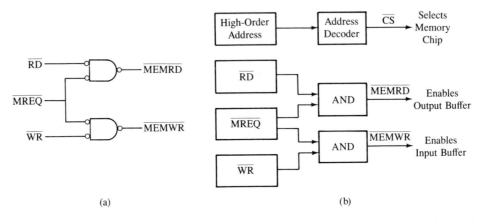

FIGURE 4.4
(a) Generating Control Signals; (b) Block Diagram: Alternative Approach to Memory Read/Write Operations

3. Generate the signal Memory Select ($\overline{\text{MSEL}}$) by combining the decoded address pulse $\overline{\text{CS}}$ and the $\overline{\text{MREQ}}$, and use the $\overline{\text{MSEL}}$ to select the memory chip.
4. Connect the Z80 $\overline{\text{RD}}$ and $\overline{\text{WR}}$ control signals to the $\overline{\text{RD}}$ and $\overline{\text{WR}}$ memory signals to enable memory buffers.
5. An alternative procedure is to generate control signals $\overline{\text{MEMRD}}$ and $\overline{\text{MEMWR}}$ by combining $\overline{\text{RD}}$ and $\overline{\text{WR}}$ signals with the $\overline{\text{MREQ}}$ and to use them to enable appropriate buffers. The decoded address pulse ($\overline{\text{CS}}$) is used to select the memory chip.

4.1.4 Address Decoding

The process of **address decoding** should result in identifying a register with a given address; we should be able to generate a unique pulse for that address. For example, in Figure 4.5(a), the output of the NAND gate goes low (active) only when the address on the address lines is $F7_H$; no other address can cause the output of the gate to go low. This process is called decoding the address. We can also use a decoder for address decoding, as discussed below, or a PROM (Programmable Read-Only-Memory), as discussed in Chapter 16.

Figure 4.5(b) shows a 3-to-8 decoder and a 4-input NAND gate. The decoder has three enable lines: one active high and two active low. The enable line E_1 is connected to address line A_3, and E_2 is connected to address lines A_4–A_7 through the NAND gate. Address lines A_2, A_1, and A_0 are inputs to the decoder, and the enable line E_3 is tied high and is not being used here for decoding.

In this decoder circuit, three input lines can have eight different logic combinations from 000 to 111; each input combination can be identified by the corresponding output line if enable lines are active. For example, if the input is 0 0 0, O_0 goes low (others remain high), and if the input is 1 1 0, O_6 goes low. To

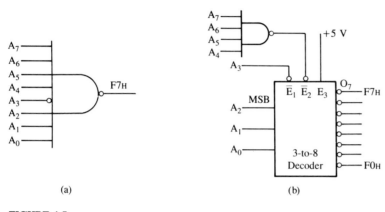

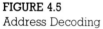

(a)   (b)

FIGURE 4.5
Address Decoding

activate the enable line $\overline{E_1}$, A_3 should be low, and to activate $\overline{E_2}$, address lines A_7–A_4 should be high, causing the output of the NAND gate to go low. If the input to the decoder is 1 1 1, the output line O_7 of the decoder will go low, thus decoding the address $F7_H$.

$$
\begin{array}{ccccc@{\qquad}ccc}
A_7 & A_6 & A_5 & A_4 & A_3 & A_2 & A_1 & A_0 \\
1 & 1 & 1 & 1 & 0 & 1 & 1 & 1
\end{array} = F7_H
$$

Enable   Input

This 3-to-8 decoder can identify or decode eight addresses from $F0_H$ to $F7_H$ as shown in Figure 4.5(b). We will use this address decoding scheme for interfacing memory chips in the following illustrations (Sections 4.2 and 4.3).

ILLUSTRATIVE EXAMPLE 1: INTERFACING 2764 EPROM   4.2

In this section, we will illustrate memory interfacing with the Z80 microprocessor by using an actual chip: the 2764 EPROM (Erasable Programmable Read-Only-Memory). This is a memory chip commonly used in industry to develop microprocessor-based products. In this illustration, we will assume that the chip has been already programmed—that is, the binary patterns representing Z80 instructions are stored in it—and we will only read from it. We focus only on the interfacing concepts, interfacing logic circuit, and memory addresses.

4.2.1 2764 EPROM

This is an 8K (8192 × 8) memory chip with eight data lines and is housed in a 28-pin package; Figure 4.6 shows the logic pinout and the pin configuration. It has thirteen address lines, A_{12}–A_0, to identify 8192 registers, one chip select signal shown as Chip Enable ($\overline{CE}$), and one Output Enable ($\overline{OE}$) signal to enable the

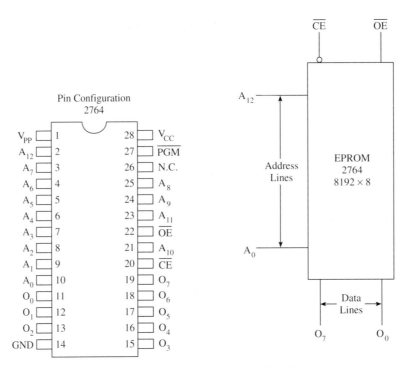

Pin Configuration
2764

V_{PP}	1	28	V_{CC}
A_{12}	2	27	$\overline{PGM}$
A_7	3	26	N.C.
A_6	4	25	A_8
A_5	5	24	A_9
A_4	6	23	A_{11}
A_3	7	22	$\overline{OE}$
A_2	8	21	A_{10}
A_1	9	20	$\overline{CE}$
A_0	10	19	O_7
O_0	11	18	O_6
O_1	12	17	O_5
O_2	13	16	O_4
GND	14	15	O_3

Mode Selection

Pin Names

A_0–A_{12}	Addresses
$\overline{CE}$	Chip Enable
$\overline{OE}$	Output Enable
O_0–O_7	Outputs
$\overline{PGM}$	Program
N.C.	No connect

PINS — MODE	$\overline{CE}$ (20)	$\overline{OE}$ (22)	$\overline{PGM}$ (27)	A_9 (24)	V_{PP} (1)	V_{CC} (28)	Outputs (11–13, 15–19)
Read	V_{IL}	V_{IL}	V_{IH}	X	V_{CC}	V_{CC}	D_{OUT}
Output Disable	V_{IL}	V_{IH}	V_{IH}	X	V_{CC}	V_{CC}	High Z
Standby	V_{IH}	X	X	X	V_{CC}	V_{CC}	High Z
Program	V_{IL}	V_{IH}	V_{IL}	X	V_{PP}	V_{CC}	D_{IN}
Verify	V_{IL}	V_{IL}	V_{IH}	X	V_{PP}	V_{CC}	D_{OUT}
Program Inhibit	V_{IH}	X	X	X	V_{PP}	V_{CC}	High Z

1. X can be V_{IH} or V_{IL}

2. $V_H = 12.0V \pm 0.5V$

FIGURE 4.6

2764 EPROM: Pin Configuration and Logic Symbol

SOURCE: Courtesy of Intel Corporation.

output buffer. It operates from a single $+5$ V power supply in the Read mode and requires $+21$ V pulse V_{pp} to program it. The pinout of this memory chip is compatible with 27128 (16K $\times$ 8) and 27256 (32K $\times$ 8) EPROMs; thus, the memory size can be expanded to 16K or 32K by merely replacing the chip. The chip has a quartz window, and the information stored in this memory can be erased by exposing the window to ultraviolet light for 15 to 20 minutes. The erasing process sets all the bits to logic 1. To avoid accidental erasures from direct sunlight or fluorescent lights, the window should be covered with an opaque label. Once it is erased, the chip can be used again to store a new program. The programming is done by using a circuit called an EPROM programmer that can selectively store logic 0 in bit positions in memory registers by providing a 21 V pulse to V_{pp}.

4.2.2 Interfacing Circuit

Figure 4.7 shows a complete schematic of interfacing the 2764 with the Z80 microprocessor. We will describe this circuit in terms of the four steps required for interfacing, as listed in the previous section.

Step 1: Connect the necessary address lines to the memory chip.

Figure 4.7 shows that the address lines A_{12}–A_0 are connected to the memory chip to identify 8192 registers.

Step 2 Decode the remaining address lines and combine the $\overline{\text{MREQ}}$ with the
&   decoded pulse to generate the Memory Select ($\overline{\text{MSEL}}$) pulse.
Step 3:

In this schematic, two steps—the decoding of the address and generating the Memory Select ($\overline{\text{MSEL}}$)—are combined by using the 74LS138 3-to-8 decoder. The decoder has three inputs, three enable lines, and eight output lines. Two enable lines are active low, and one is active high. Once the decoder is enabled, only one output line, corresponding to the input combination, goes active (low).

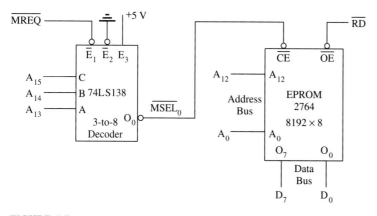

FIGURE 4.7
Schematic of Interfacing 2764 EPROM

In Figure 4.7, the output O_0 of the decoder is shown as Memory Select ($\overline{\text{MSEL}_0}$), which is connected to the Chip Enable ($\overline{\text{CE}}$) of the memory, and O_0 goes active low when the address lines A_{15}–A_{13} and the $\overline{\text{MREQ}}$ are all at logic 0. The control signal $\overline{\text{MREQ}}$ is used to enable the decoder (active low); the address lines A_{15}, A_{14}, and A_{13} are used as input to the decoder; the enable line E_3 is connected to $+5$ V; and E_2 is grounded. No other logic level on these address lines can assert the $\overline{\text{MSEL}_0}$ signal.

Step 4: Connect the Z80 control signal to enable an appropriate buffer.

Figure 4.7 shows that the Z80 Read ($\overline{\text{RD}}$) is connected to the $\overline{\text{RD}}$ signal of the memory chip. When the $\overline{\text{RD}}$ signal is asserted, the output buffer is enabled and the data byte from the selected register is placed on the data bus.

4.2.3 Memory Map

We can obtain the address range of this memory chip by analyzing the possible logic levels on the 16 address lines. The logic levels on the address lines A_{15}–A_{13} have to be 0 to assert the Chip Enable, and the address lines A_{12}–A_0 can assume any combinations from all 0s to all 1s. Therefore, the memory map (the address range) of this chip is from 0000H to 1FFFH as shown below.

$$
\begin{array}{ccc|ccccccccccccc}
A_{15} & A_{14} & A_{13} & A_{12} & A_{11} & A_{10} & A_9 & A_8 & A_7 & A_6 & A_5 & A_4 & A_3 & A_2 & A_1 & A_0 \\
0 & 0 & 0 & 0 & 0 & 0 & 0 & 0 & 0 & 0 & 0 & 0 & 0 & 0 & 0 & 0 = 0000_H \\
\overline{\text{MSEL}_0} & & & \downarrow & & & & & & & & & & & & \downarrow \\
0 & 0 & 0 & 1 & 1 & 1 & 1 & 1 & 1 & 1 & 1 & 1 & 1 & 1 & 1 & 1 = 1\text{FFF}_H
\end{array}
$$

We can verify the memory map in terms of our analogy of page and line numbers. The chip has 8192 bytes of memory that can be viewed as 32 pages with 256 lines each. Let us examine the high-order Hex digits of the map; they range from 00 to 1F indicating 32 pages—0000 to 00FF, 0100 to 01FF, for example.

4.3   ILLUSTRATIVE EXAMPLE 2: INTERFACING STATIC R/W MEMORY

In this example, we will use the MOSTEK MK4802 memory chip to demonstrate both Read and Write operations. To simplify the discussion, we will use the same decoding circuit as in Figure 4.7, except the $\overline{\text{MSEL}_4}$ signal is used as the Chip Enable. This chip has 2K of memory; therefore, two address lines (A_{12} and A_{11}) have to be left as "don't care" to use the previous circuit. Because of the "don't care" address line, the memory registers will have multiple addresses, and the memory chip will occupy more memory space than necessary (explained later).

4.3.1 MOSTEK MK4802 Static R/W Memory

This is a 2K static R/W memory chip, organized as 2048 × 8 format. It has eleven address lines (A_{10}–A_0), eight data lines, and three control signals: $\overline{\text{CE}}$, $\overline{\text{OE}}$, and

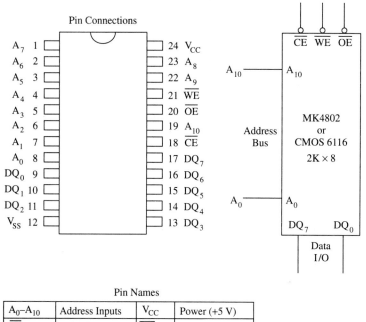

Pin Connections

		Pin Names		
A_0–A_{10}	Address Inputs	V_{CC}	Power (+5 V)	
$\overline{CE}$	Chip Enable	$\overline{WE}$	Write Enable	
V_{SS}	Ground	$\overline{OE}$	Output Enable	
DQ_0–DQ_7	Data In/Data Out			

FIGURE 4.8
MK4802 or CMOS 6116 Static R/W Memory Pin Configuration and Logic Symbol
SOURCE: Courtesy of Mostek Corporation

$\overline{WE}$. We are already familiar with the first two control signals, and the third signal, $\overline{WE}$ (Write Enable), is active low and used to enable the input buffer of the memory. The logic pinout and the pin configuration are shown in Figure 4.8.

4.3.2 Interfacing Circuit

Figure 4.9 shows the interfacing circuit using the MK4802 memory chip. The decoding circuit is the same as in Figure 4.7. We will analyze this circuit in terms of the same three steps outlined previously.

Step 1: The Z80 address lines A_{10}–A_0 are connected to pins A_{10}–A_0 of the memory chip to address 2048 registers. The address lines A_{12} and A_{11} can be used by using a different decoder, but we have left these lines as "don't care" to observe its effects on the memory map. Furthermore, this is a commonly used industrial practice for small microprocessor-based systems.

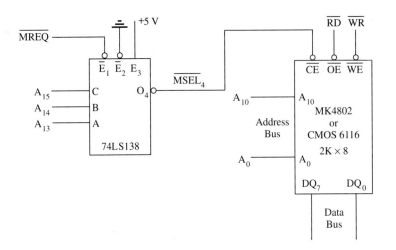

FIGURE 4.9
Schematic of Interfacing Static R/W Memory MK4802

Step 2   The Memory Select $\overline{MSEL_4}$ line, the output O_4 of the decoder, is used as
&   the Chip Enable ($\overline{CE}$). The $\overline{CE}$ is asserted only when the address on A_{15}–
Step 3: A_{13} is 1 0 0.
Step 4: In case of an R/W memory, we need two control signals: Read ($\overline{RD}$) and
             Write ($\overline{WR}$), both active low. The $\overline{RD}$ is connected to $\overline{OE}$, as in the pre-
             vious illustration, to enable the output buffer. The $\overline{WR}$ is connected to
             $\overline{WE}$ (Write Enable) of the memory chip, and when $\overline{WR}$ is asserted low,
             the input buffer of the memory chip is enabled, allowing data to be writ-
             ten into a memory register.

4.3.3 Memory Map

Assuming the "don't care" address lines A_{12} and A_{11} are at logic 0, the first memory address range is from 4000_H to $47FF_H$ as shown below:

A_{15} A_{14} A_{13} A_{12} A_{11} A_{10} A_9 A_8 A_7 A_6 A_5 A_4 A_3 A_2 A_1 A_0

| 1 | 0 | 0 | X | X | 0 | 0 | 0 | 0 | 0 | 0 | 0 | 0 | 0 | 0 | 0 | = 8000_H |

$\overline{MSEL_4}$

| 1 | 0 | 0 | X | X | 1 | 1 | 1 | 1 | 1 | 1 | 1 | 1 | 1 | 1 | 1 | = $87FF_H$ |

Now, to examine the other addresses of this memory chip, we need to consider the remaining combinations of the address lines A_{12} and A_{11}. These two lines
can have four combinations (00, 01, 10, 11). The first combination is already used,
and the remaining three combinations will give us the following address ranges.

A_{15} A_{14} A_{13}	A_{12} A_{11} A_{10} A_9 A_8 A_7 A_6 A_5 A_4 A_3 A_2 A_1 A_0	
1 0 0	0 1 0 0 0 0 0 0 0 0 0 0 0	$= 8800_H$
	0 1 1 1 1 1 1 1 1 1 1 1 1	$= 8FFF_H$
1 0 0	1 0 0 0 0 0 0 0 0 0 0 0 0	$= 9000_H$
	1 0 1 1 1 1 1 1 1 1 1 1 1	$= 97FF_H$
1 0 0	1 1 0 0 0 0 0 0 0 0 0 0 0	$= 9800_H$
	1 1 1 1 1 1 1 1 1 1 1 1 1	$= 9FFF_H$

The entire memory map appears to be from 8000_H to $9FFF_H$; 8K of memory. Actually, we have only 2K of memory occupying the memory space of 8K. Because of the two "don't care" lines, each register can have four addresses. For example, the addresses 8000_H, 8800_H, 9000_H, and 9800_H will select the same register. By convention, the first set of the address (8000_H–$87FF_H$) is considered as the basic memory address range. The remaining duplicate ranges of the memory addresses (8800_H to $9FFF_H$) are generally known as the foldback memory; this memory space cannot be used by any other memory chip. The foldback memory is the result of the partial decoding practices (having "don't care" lines). This is a common practice in microprocessor-based products where memory size is small. Even if such a practice wastes some memory space of the 64K memory map, it reduces the chip count on a board.

ILLUSTRATIVE EXAMPLE 3: DESIGNING MEMORY   4.4

In this section, we will approach the question of memory interfacing from a design point of view. In the previous examples, we analyzed the given schematics of memory interfacing; now we will design an interfacing circuit for given specifications.

4.4.1 Problem Statement
Given a 2K R/W (2048 × 8) static memory chip and one 3-to-8 decoder, design the memory for the beginning address 2800_H. Use the $\overline{MREQ}$ signal to enable one of the decoder lines, and the $\overline{RD}$ and $\overline{WR}$ control signals can be directly connected to the memory chip.

4.4.2 Problem Analysis
1. The 2K memory requires 11 address lines (A_{10}–A_0), and the remaining five address lines A_{15}–A_{11} can be used to generate the Memory Select signal.

2. The 74LS138 decoder has three input lines and three enable lines: two active low and one active high. Of the five address lines, three lines can be used as input to the decoder, and two address lines and the $\overline{\text{MREQ}}$ can be used to enable the decoder.

3. The Z80 control signals $\overline{\text{RD}}$ and $\overline{\text{WR}}$ should be connected to the Output Enable ($\overline{\text{OE}}$) and Write Enable ($\overline{\text{WE}}$) of the memory chip, respectively.

4. To assign the starting address 2800_H. The address lines should have the following logic levels:

$$
\begin{array}{ccccc ccccccccccc}
A_{15} & A_{14} & A_{13} & A_{12} & A_{11} & A_{10} & A_9 & A_8 & A_7 & A_6 & A_5 & A_4 & A_3 & A_2 & A_1 & A_0 \\
0 & 0 & 1 & 0 & 1 & 0 & 0 & 0 & 0 & 0 & 0 & 0 & 0 & 0 & 0 & 0 & = 2800_H
\end{array}
$$

$\underbrace{\phantom{A_{15}\ A_{14}\ A_{13}\ A_{12}\ A_{11}}}_{\overline{\text{MSEL}}_1}$

These logic level requirements dictate that A_{13} and A_{11} should be 1, and that A_{15}, A_{14}, and A_{12} should be 0. We can connect A_{13} to the active high enable line (E_3), and A_{15} and $\overline{\text{MREQ}}$ to the active low enable lines ($\overline{E}_1$ and $\overline{E}_2$) of the decoder, respectively, and by connecting the output O_1 of the decoder to $\overline{\text{CE}}$, we can ensure that the memory chip is selected when A_{14}, A_{12}, and A_{11} are at logic 0 0 1, respectively.

4.4.3 Circuit Analysis

Figure 4.10 shows the schematic of the interfacing circuit based on the problem analysis.

1. The output line O_1 of the decoder is connected to the Chip Enable ($\overline{\text{CE}}$) of the memory chip. The decoder is enabled when $A_{15} = 0$, $A_{13} = 1$, and $\overline{\text{MREQ}}$ is asserted low. The output line O_1 of the decoder is asserted only when input

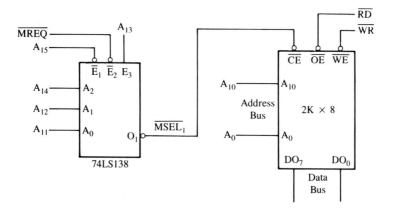

FIGURE 4.10
Schematic of 2K Memory Design

lines are at logic 0 0 1. The logic levels on these address lines will assign the starting address as 2800_H.

2. In this design example, the $\overline{MREQ}$ is used to enable the decoder. The output of the decoder goes low only when the $\overline{MREQ}$ is asserted; thus, the chip is enabled when the $\overline{MREQ}$ is low. The output and the input buffers of the memory chip are enabled directly by the control signals $\overline{RD}$ and $\overline{WR}$.

TESTING AND TROUBLESHOOTING INTERFACING CIRCUITS 4.5

In the last section, we discussed how to design or interface memory for a given address. The next step is to test and verify that we can store a byte at a memory location within the address range of the memory chip and read the byte. At this point, we need to make an assumption that we have a working microcomputer system, and the memory design is an expansion of the existing system. If we are designing a system, we may need to use an in-circuit emulator to test the memory; this is discussed in Chapter 17.

To test the memory, we can simply access an address such as 2800_H through the system keyboard, store a byte, and check the address location again to verify the byte. If there is any fault in the interfacing circuit, the system is likely to show an error message, or a different byte from the one we stored will be displayed. Now we need to troubleshoot the interfacing circuit. The question is: Where do we begin? The obvious step is to check the wiring and the pin connections. After this preliminary check, most traditional methods used in checking analog circuits (such as an amplifier) are ineffective because the logic levels on the buses are dynamic; they constantly change depending upon the operation being performed at a given instant by the microprocessor. In troubleshooting analog circuits, a commonly used technique is signal injection, whereby a known signal is injected at the input, and the output signal is verified against the expected outcome. To use this concept, we need to generate a constant and identifiable signal and check various points in relation to that signal. We can generate such a signal by asking the processor to execute a continuous loop, called a **diagnostic routine,** as shown.

```
START:  LD A, F7H        ;Load F7H into the accumulator
        LD (2800H), A    ;Store accumulator contents in
                         ; location 2800H
        JP START         ;Jump back to beginning and repeat
```

This routine has three instructions. The first instruction loads $F7_H$ into the accumulator (the byte $F7_H$ is selected arbitrarily), and the second instruction stores the byte in the memory location 2800_H. The third instruction is a Jump instruction that takes the program control at the beginning, and these three instructions are repeated continuously. Now we need to examine the machine cycles of these instructions to find an identifiable signal that is repeated at a certain interval. We can analyze the loop in the machine cycles as follows (it will be helpful to have read Chapter 6 to understand the diagnostic routine):

| Instruction | Bytes | T-states | Machine Cycles | | | |
			M_1	M_2	M_3	M_4
LD A, F7H	2	7 (4, 3)	Opcode Fetch	Memory Read		
LD (2800H), A	3	13 (4, 3, 3, 3)	Opcode Fetch	Memory Read	Memory Read	Memory Write
JP START	3	10 (4, 3, 3)	Opcode Fetch	Memory Read	Memory Read	

This loop has 30 T-states and nine operations. To execute the loop once, the microprocessor asserts the $\overline{RD}$ signal eight times (the Opcode Fetch is also a Read operation) and the $\overline{WR}$ signal once. Assuming the system clock frequency is 2 MHz, the loop is executed in 15 μs, and the $\overline{WR}$ signal, repeated every 15 μs, can be observed on a scope. If we sync the scope on the $\overline{WR}$ pulse from the Z80,

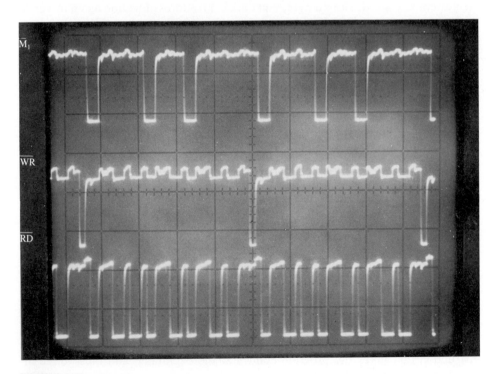

FIGURE 4.11
Timing Signals of Diagnostic Routine
SOURCE: Photograph by Gregg Texido

we can check $\overline{M_1}$, the output of the decoder $\overline{MSEL_1}$ and memory signals $\overline{CE}$, $\overline{WR}$, and $\overline{RD}$; three of these signals are in Figure 4.11.

When the Z80 asserts the $\overline{WR}$ signal, the high-order address A_{15}–A_{11} must be 0 0 1 0 1, and $\overline{MSEL_1}$ must be asserted low. If $\overline{MSEL_1}$ is high, it indicates that the address lines A_{15}–A_{11} or $\overline{MREQ}$ are improperly connected or the decoder chip is faulty.

If $\overline{MSEL_1}$ is low, it confirms that the decoding circuit is functioning properly. Now if we check the entire address bus and the data bus in relation to the $\overline{WR}$ signal, one line at a time, we must read the address 2800_H and the data $F7_H$. If we check the $\overline{RD}$ signal, it must be high when the $\overline{WR}$ is asserted, and we will observe eight $\overline{RD}$ signals between every two $\overline{WR}$ signals, as shown in Figure 4.11.

SOME QUESTIONS AND ANSWERS   4.6

In the above discussion of memory interfacing, we focused on certain aspects of the communication process between the Z80 and memory. However, in order to avoid distraction from basic concepts, we did not address several important issues. Now we will attempt to answer those questions briefly or provide references for them.

1. *How do you determine whether a memory chip is too slow for a given Z80 system?*

The response time of a memory chip is defined in terms of *Access Time*. This is the time delay between when the microprocessor places a memory address on the address bus and when memory places a data byte on the data bus. Typically, Access Time is 50–450 ns for static R/W memory. Similarly, the microprocessor has a timing specification: the time delay after the Z80 places an address on the address bus to when it begins to read data on the data bus. The memory access time must be less than this microprocessor time delay. This will be discussed when we consider advanced topics in memory interfacing.

2. *How do you interface a memory chip with slow response time?*

If the memory response time is slower than the microprocessor read time, the Memory Read cycle can be extended by using the WAIT signal. During the T_2 state of the Memory Read cycle, the Z80 samples the WAIT signal, and if it is low, the Z80 adds Wait states until the signal goes high again. Typically, one Wait state (one clock cycle) provides sufficient time for memory to place data on the data bus. Extra circuitry is necessary for adding Wait states; this is discussed in Chapter 16.

3. *Why did you omit an illustrative example of dynamic memory?*

The dynamic memory stores information as a capacitive charge; therefore, information needs to be refreshed every few milliseconds. In the latter part of the

Opcode Fetch cycle, the Z80 uses the low-order bus for refresh addresses. To interface the dynamic memory, additional refresh circuits that can use the refresh addresses from the Opcode Fetch cycle are necessary. This will also be discussed in Chapter 16.

SUMMARY

□ To read from memory, the address of the register to be read from should be placed on the address lines, and the Chip Enable $\overline{CE}$ and $\overline{RD}$ signals must be asserted low to enable the output buffer.
□ To write into memory, the address of the register to be written into should be placed on the address lines; a data byte should be placed on the data lines, and the Chip Enable $\overline{CE}$ and $\overline{WR}$ signals must be asserted low to enable the input buffer.
□ The Z80 identifies memory operations by initiating the $\overline{MREQ}$ signal. This signal is combined with the decoded address pulse ($\overline{CS}$) to generate Memory Select (MSEL), which is connected to the Chip Enable ($\overline{CE}$) signal of the memory chip. Another alternative is to use the decoded address pulse $\overline{CS}$ to enable the memory chip and generate Memory Read ($\overline{MEMRD}$) and Memory Write ($\overline{MEMWR}$) signals by combining $\overline{MREQ}$, $\overline{RD}$, and $\overline{WR}$ signals.
□ To interface a memory chip with the Z80, the necessary low-order address lines of the Z80 address bus are connected to the address lines of the memory chip. The high-order address lines and the $\overline{MREQ}$ are used to generate the MSEL signal, which enables the chip. The $\overline{RD}$ signal is used to enable the output buffer, and the $\overline{WR}$ signal is used to write into memory by enabling the input buffer.
□ In the absolute decoding technique, all the address lines not used by a memory chip to identify a memory register must be decoded; thus, the Chip Select can be asserted by only one address. In the partial decoding technique, some address lines can be left as "don't care." This technique saves on hardware, but generates multiple addresses, which result in foldback memory space.
□ To troubleshoot an interfacing circuit, a constant and identifiable signal must be generated by writing a continuous loop.

ASSIGNMENTS

1. If a memory chip is organized in a 4096×1 format, specify the number of registers in the chip and the number of bits stored by each register.
2. If $16K \times 1$ memory chips are used in a memory design, how many chips are required to design 64K-byte memory?

3. Specify the number of chips necessary to design 8K-byte memory with 1024×4 memory chips.

4. In Figure 4.7, generate the equivalent $MSEL_0$ signal by using a 4-input $\overline{NAND}$ gate (and inverters) to decode the address lines $A_{15}-A_{13}$ and the $\overline{MREQ}$.

5. Generate the signal equivalent to the $\overline{MSEL_0}$ signal in Figure 4.7 using the 74LS139, which has two 2-to-4 decoders in the package.

6. In Figure 4.7, if we connect the output line O_5 (instead of O_0) of the decoder to the $\overline{CE}$ signal, what will be the memory address range of the circuit?

7. In Figure 4.7, if we use all the output lines (O_7-O_0) of the decoder to select 8 memory chips of the same size as the 2764, what is the total range of the memory map?

8. If the first address of the $8K \times 8$ memory chip is 4000_H, what is the address of the last register?

9. In Figure 4.9, replace the address line A_{15} with A_{11} and find the range of the foldback memory.

10. In Figure 4.9, replace the address lines A_{15} and A_{14} by A_{12} and A_{11}. Find the range of foldback memory.

11. By examining the range of the foldback memory in Figure 4.9, specify the relationship between the range of foldback memory and the number of "don't care" lines.

12. In Figure 4.12, the control signals $\overline{RD}$, $\overline{MREQ}$, and $\overline{WR}$ are used as inputs to the 3-to-8 decoder, and the decoder is enabled. Specify the output lines that can be used as $\overline{MEMRD}$ and $\overline{MEMWR}$ control signals.

13. In Figure 4.12, explain why the output line O_0 cannot be asserted low.

14. In Figure 4.13, specify the memory maps of ROM1, ROM2, and R/WM1.

15. Is there a foldback memory for any one of the chips in Figure 4.13?

16. Sketch the memory map in Figure 4.13.

17. Given a 1K (1024×8) EPROM memory chip and one 3-to-8 decoder, design an interfacing circuit to assign the beginning address at 0400_H. Use the 74LS32 OR gate to generate the control signal $\overline{MEMRD}$.

18. You are given the 74LS139 (two 2-to-4 decoders) and 8K static R/W memory. Use one decoder to assign the starting memory address at 8000_H and

FIGURE 4.12

Generating Control Signals Using the 3-to-8 Decoder

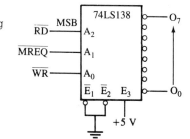

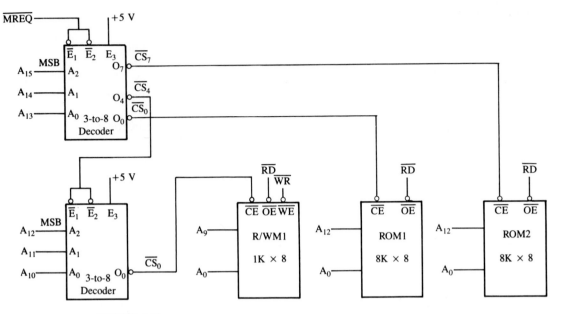

FIGURE 4.13
Schematic for Assignments 14–16

use the other decoder to generate the $\overline{\text{MEMRD}}$ and $\overline{\text{MEMWR}}$ control signals.

The following questions refer to section 4.5 and Figure 4.10.

19. If the diagnostic routine is executed on a system with the clock frequency 4 MHz, specify the time interval between two $\overline{\text{WR}}$ pulses.

20. In the diagnostic routine, how many times is the $\overline{\text{MREQ}}$ signal asserted in one loop?

21. Specify the logic levels of the address lines A_{15} and A_{13} and the data lines D_7 and D_3 when the $\overline{\text{WR}}$ signal is asserted during the diagnostic routine.

22. How many times is the $\overline{M_1}$ signal asserted during the execution of the diagnostic routine?

23. How many times is $\overline{\text{MSEL}_1}$ asserted in one loop.

Interfacing I/O Devices

The I/O (Input/Output) is the third component of a microprocessor-based system. I/O devices, such as keyboards and displays, are the ears and eyes of the MPUs; they are the communication channels to the "outside world." Data can enter or exit in groups of eight bits using the entire data bus; this is called the **parallel I/O mode.** The other mode is the **serial I/O,** whereby one bit is transferred using one data line; typical examples include peripherals such as CRT terminals or cassette tapes. In this chapter, we focus on interfacing I/O devices in the parallel mode; the serial mode will be discussed in Chapter 15.

In the parallel I/O mode, devices can be interfaced using two techniques: peripheral-mapped I/O and memory-mapped I/O. In peripheral-mapped I/O, a device is identified with an 8-bit address and enabled by I/O-related control signals. In memory-mapped I/O, a device is identified with a 16-bit address and enabled by memory-related control signals. The process of data transfer in both is identical. Each device is assigned a binary address through its interfacing circuit. When the Z80 is programmed to transfer data, it places the appropriate address on the address bus, sends the

control signals, enables the interfacing device, and transfers data. The interfacing device is like a gate for data bits, which is opened by the MPU whenever it intends to transfer data.

To grasp the essence of interfacing techniques, we first examine the machine cycles of I/O instructions to determine the timings for I/O data arriving on the data bus, and then latch (or catch) that information. We derive the basic concepts of peripheral-mapped and memory-mapped I/O from the machine cycles. The peripheral-mapped I/O concepts are illustrated with two examples: interfacing LEDs as an output device and switches as an input device. The memory-mapped I/O technique is illustrated with an example of appliance control. The chapter also includes additional interfacing examples that occur frequently in microprocessor-based products.

OBJECTIVES

- □ Illustrate the Z80 bus contents and control signals when OUT and IN instructions are executed.
- □ Explain the necessity of Wait states in I/O machine cycles.
- □ Recognize the device (port) address of a peripheral-mapped I/O by analyzing the associated logic circuit.
- □ Recognize the device (port) address of a memory-mapped I/O by analyzing the associated logic circuit.

- □ Explain the differences between the peripheral-mapped and memory-mapped I/O techniques.
- □ Interface an I/O device to the Z80 microprocessor for a specified device address by using logic gates and such MSI chips as decoders, latches, and buffers.
- □ Explain the concepts in interfacing analog devices such as sensors and motors.

5.1   INTERFACING OUTPUT DEVICES

In peripheral-mapped I/O, a device is identified with an 8-bit address, and I/O-related control signals are used to enable the device. The process of data transfer is in many ways similar to that of reading from or writing into a memory register. The Z80 uses the instruction IN to read (input) data from an input device and uses the instruction OUT to write (send) data to an output device. To understand interfacing of I/O devices, we need to examine the execution and machine cycles of these input/output instructions. In the next section, we will examine the execution of the OUT instruction and discuss the interfacing of output devices, and in Section 5.3, we will examine the IN instruction and discuss the interfacing of input devices.

5.1.1   OUT Instruction

The Z80 microprocessor has several output instructions to send (copy or write) data to an output device. It can send data from the accumulator, internal general-purpose registers, or memory registers to an output device. The Out instructions include the 8-bit address of a device as an operand. Therefore, the address can be any of the 256 8-bit binary combinations from 00_H to FF_H. Thus, an output device can be assigned any 8-bit address between 00_H and FF_H through an appropriate interfacing circuit. The address range from 00_H to FF_H is called the I/O or peripheral map, and an address can be referred to as a device address, port address, or port number. Among the several Out instructions, we will examine the machine cycles and timing of the following instruction.

Opcode	Operand	Description
OUT	(8-bit), A	This is a 2-byte instruction with the hexadecimal opcode D3, and the second byte is the port address of an output device.
		This instruction transfers (copies) data from the accumulator to the output device.

Typically, to display the contents of the accumulator at an output device (such as LEDs) with the address, for example, 07_H, the instruction will be written and stored in memory as follows:

Memory Address	Machine Code	Mnemonics	Memory Contents	
2050	D3	OUT (07H), A ; 2050	1 1 0 1 0 0 1 1	$= D3_H$
2051	07	; 2051	0 0 0 0 0 1 1 1	$= 07_H$

NOTE: The memory locations are chosen here arbitrarily for the illustration.

When the microprocessor reads and executes the machine codes written at memory registers 2050_H and 2051_H, it will transfer (copy) the byte from the accumulator to the LED port with address 07_H and display the byte. Now the question remains: How is the address 07_H assigned to the output port? To answer that question, we need to examine the machine cycles of this instruction, as shown in the next section.

5.1.2   Execution of OUT Instruction and Timing

The OUT instruction has three machine cycles: Opcode Fetch, Memory Read, and I/O Write. The Z80 reads the opcode and the port address from memory in the first two machine cycles and writes into the port in the third cycle. Figure 5.1 shows the timing of the OUT instruction with the port address 07_H.

The first two machine cycles—Opcode Fetch and Memory Read—are similar to the machine cycles shown in Figure 3.5; however, in Figure 5.1, the low-order and high-order address buses are shown separately to illustrate the contents of the low-order bus in the third cycle. In the Opcode Fetch cycle, the Z80 places the address 2050_H on the address bus and fetches the opcode $D3_H$ (1 1 0 1 0 0 1 1) via the data bus. When the Z80 decodes the opcode, it realizes that the instruction consists of two bytes, and that it must read the second byte. In the second machine cycle, the Z80 places the next address, 2051_H, on the address bus and reads the port address 07_H.

In the third machine cycle, M_3 (I/O Write), the following events occur:

1. The Z80 places the port address 07_H on the low-order address bus and the contents of the accumulator on the data bus.

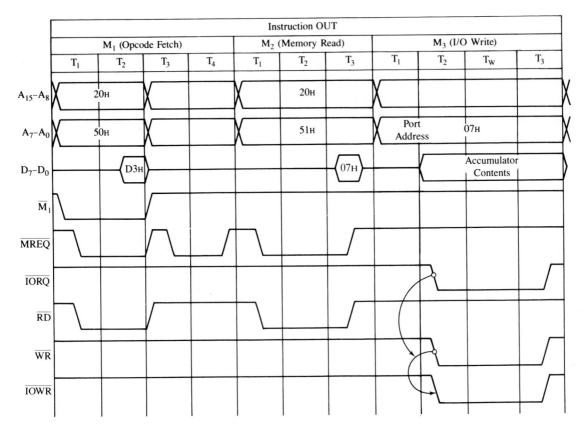

FIGURE 5.1
Z80 Timing for Execution of OUT Instruction

2. During T_2, it asserts the $\overline{\text{IORQ}}$ and $\overline{\text{WR}}$ control signals; the assertion of $\overline{\text{IORQ}}$ indicates that it is an I/O operation.
3. The Z80 automatically inserts a single Wait state T_W after T_2 to allow sufficient response time for an I/O device; this Wait state is added regardless of the WAIT signal status.
4. During T_3, the control signals $\overline{\text{IORQ}}$ and $\overline{\text{WR}}$ become inactive.

   To interface an output device, the information on the buses during the M_3 cycle is critical. From the beginning of T_2 until the end of T_3, we have the port address (07_H) on the low-order address bus and the data byte to be displayed on the data bus. The availability of this information is indicated by the control signals. Now what we must do is to latch (catch) this information using the control signals before it disappears from the buses; we need to open the gate at that precise moment to let the data flow to the "outside world." This is the essence of interfacing.

5.1.3 Basic Concepts in Interfacing Output Devices

The concepts in interfacing output devices are similar to those in interfacing memory. The steps can be listed as follows:

1. Decode the low-order address bus to generate a unique pulse corresponding to the port address on the bus; this is called the I/O address ($\overline{\text{IOADR}}$) pulse.
2. Combine (AND) the I/O address pulse ($\overline{\text{IOADR}}$), $\overline{\text{IORQ}}$, and $\overline{\text{WR}}$ to generate the $\overline{\text{IOSEL}}$ (I/O select) pulse (Figure 5.2(a)). Another approach is to generate the $\overline{\text{IOWR}}$ (I/O Write) by combining $\overline{\text{IORQ}}$ and $\overline{\text{WR}}$, and then combine $\overline{\text{IOWR}}$ with the $\overline{\text{IOADR}}$ (I/O Address) pulse to generate the IOSEL pulse (Figure 5.2(b)). The critical concept here is that the decoded address, $\overline{\text{IORQ}}$, and $\overline{\text{WR}}$ are all necessary to latch the data at the appropriate time; how these signals are combined is often dictated by availability of decoding devices (chips) in the system.
3. Use the IOSEL pulse to enable (activate) the output device.

Let us examine the significance of the I/O select pulse. This pulse is generated by ANDing the decoded address, $\overline{\text{IORQ}}$, and $\overline{\text{WR}}$ signals as shown in Figure 5.2(a); all these signals are active low. The assertion of this pulse indicates two pieces of information: (1) the low-order address bus has the port address (07_H), and (2) the data byte from the accumulator is on the data bus. Thus, this is the

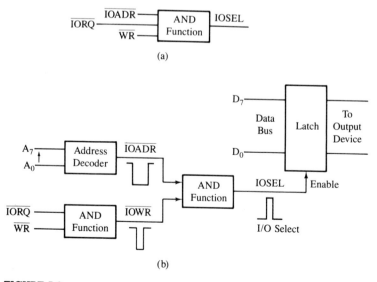

FIGURE 5.2
Block Diagram: Output Interfacing

appropriate time to enable the latch (or open the gate for data). Figure 5.2(b) shows how these control signals are generally ANDed in a typical interfacing circuit to generate the IOSEL pulse and how the I/O select pulse is used to enable the output latch.

5.2   ILLUSTRATIVE EXAMPLE 1: INTERFACING LEDS

In this section, we will analyze an actual interfacing circuit with the port address 07_H to display binary data at an LED port and a single digit at a seven-segment LED. A group of 8 LEDs will be used to indicate binary 1s and 0s and will be connected to the data bus using the 7475 latches. Similarly, an interfacing of a seven-segment LED will be demonstrated using an octal latch 74LS373.

5.2.1 Hardware

Figure 5.3 shows the logic symbols of the 7475 latch. It has four *bistable latches* controlled by the active high enable signals; E_{1-2} enables the first two latches and E_{3-4} enables the remaining two. When E is high, data enter the latch and appear at the Q outputs, and Q outputs correspond to the input data. When E goes from high to low, data will be latched and will remain stable until E goes high again.

When Q output is high, it can supply (source) 400 μA, and when it is low, it can sink 16 mA current. Since most LEDs require a 10–15 mA current to be properly illuminated, they are connected to $\overline{Q}$ output of the latch so that when the input is high, $\overline{Q}$ output is low and the LED is turned on.

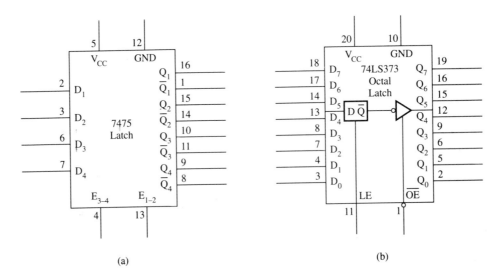

(a)   (b)

FIGURE 5.3
Logic Symbols: (a) 7475 Latch; (b) 74LS373 Octal Latch

Figure 5.3(b) shows the logic symbol of an octal latch 74LS373. This is similar to the 7475 latch, except that the latch is followed by a tri-state buffer. The
latch and the buffer are controlled independently by Latch Enable (LE) and Output Enable (OE). When LE goes high, the data enter the latch, and when LE goes
low, data are latched. The latched data are available on the output lines of the
74LS373 if the buffer is enabled by OE (active low). If OE is high, the output lines
go into high impedance state. The advantage of using the octal latch is that it has
eight latches in a package (vs. four in 7475), and when the buffer is not enabled,
it remains in high impedance state, thus minimizing the loading on the data bus.
In addition, it has two control signals (LE and OE); this can be advantageous in
some interfacing circuits.

5.2.2 Interfacing Circuit

Figure 5.4 shows an interfacing circuit for the LED output port with the address
07_H. We will analyze this circuit in terms of the three steps for interfacing output
devices as outlined in Section 5.1.3.

1. An 8-input NAND gate with five inverters is used to decode the low-order
   address bus A_7–A_0. The output of the NAND gate is asserted when the address
   is 0 0 0 0 0 1 1 1 (07_H); thus, the NAND gate performs the decoding function
   to generate the I/O address (IOADR) pulse.
2. The control signals IORQ and WR are ANDed in a negative AND gate (physically, an OR gate) to generate the control signal IOWR (active low). The
   IOWR is again ANDed (through a NOR gate) with the I/O address pulse to

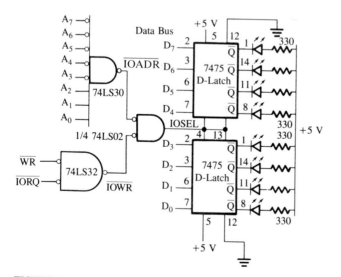

FIGURE 5.4
Schematic: Interfacing LED Output Port

generate the I/O select pulse (active high). The $\overline{\text{IOSEL}}$ pulse is asserted only when the address is 07_H and the control signals $\overline{\text{IORQ}}$ and $\overline{\text{WR}}$ are low.

3. The IOSEL pulse is used to enable the latches 7475. The data bus D_7–D_0 is connected to the D input, and the LED cathodes are connected to the $\overline{Q}$ output of the latch. The LED anodes are connected to the $+5$ V power supply through the current-limiting resistors.

At the beginning of T_2 in the third machine cycle shown in Figure 5.1, the control signals $\overline{\text{IORQ}}$ and $\overline{\text{WR}}$ are asserted, and the I/O select pulse (Figure 5.4) goes high if the address is 07_H. When the I/O select pulse goes high, the data on the data bus enter the latches. During T_3, when the control signals become inactive, the I/O select pulse goes low, and the data are latched. The logic 1s on the data lines turn on the corresponding LEDs because when a data bit is high, the $\overline{Q}$ output is low and the LED is turned on.

INSTRUCTIONS
To display data, for example, 97_H, at this LED port, instructions are as follows:

```
LD A, 97H        ;Load accumulator with the specified byte
OUT (07H), A     ;Display the accumulator contents at port 07H
```

The first instruction (LD) stores the second byte 97_H in the accumulator, and the OUT instruction sends the byte (97_H) from the accumulator to the LED port 07_H. When the I/O select pulse is asserted, the byte 97_H enters the latch and is displayed by the LEDs. When IOSEL goes low (inactive), the byte is latched and continues to be displayed by the LEDs.

5.2.3 Using a Seven-Segment LED as a Display Device
A seven-segment LED consists of seven light-emitting diodes (A through G) and one diode (DP) for the decimal point; these LEDs are physically arranged as shown in Figure 5.5(a). To display a number, the necessary segments are lit by sending an appropriate signal for current flow through diodes. For example, to display 8, all segments should be lit. To display 1, segments B and C must be lit. Seven-segment LEDs are available in two types: common cathode and common anode. They can be represented schematically as in Figures 5.5(b) and (c). The segments, A through G, are usually connected to data lines D_0 through D_6, respectively. If the decimal point is being used, data line D_7 is connected to DP; otherwise it can be left open. Current flow in these diodes must be limited to 20 mA.

Figure 5.6 shows the interfacing of a common-anode seven-segment LED using the latch 74LS373. This circuit assumes the same decoding network as in Figure 5.4, thus assigning the port address 07_H to the latch. The differences between Figures 5.4 and 5.6 are that the binary LEDs in Figure 5.4 are replaced by the seven-segment LED, and the latch 7475 is replaced by the octal latch 74LS373. The binary code required to display a digit is determined by the type of the seven-segment LED (common cathode or common anode) and the connections of the

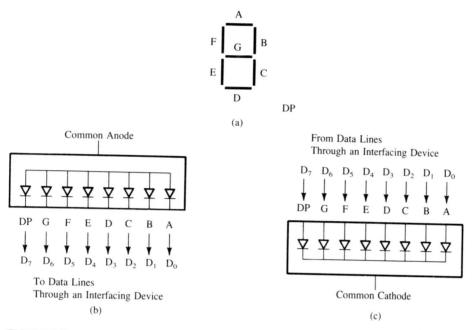

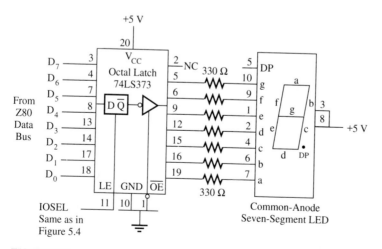

FIGURE 5.5

Seven-Segment LED: (a) LED segments; (b) Common Anode LED; (c) Common Cathode LED

FIGURE 5.6

Interfacing a Seven-Segment LED

data lines. For example, in Figure 5.6, to display digit 1 at the output port, segments B and C should be turned on, and these segments are turned on with logic 0. Therefore, the binary code should be 79_H as follows:

$$\begin{array}{llllllllll}
\text{Data Lines} & D_7 & D_6 & D_5 & D_4 & D_3 & D_2 & D_1 & D_0 \\
\text{Logic} & X & 1 & 1 & 1 & 1 & 0 & 0 & 1 & = 79_H \\
\text{Segments} & NC & G & F & E & D & C & B & A
\end{array}$$

The code for each Hex digit from 0 to F can be determined by examining the connections of the data lines to the segments and the logic requirements.

Instructions   The following instructions are necessary to display digit 1 at the output port:

LD A, 79H   ;Load code for digit 1 in the accumulator
OUT (07H), A   ;Display digit 1 at port 07H
HALT

When the microprocessor executes the OUT instruction, the IOSEL goes active and enables (LE) the latch, and the code 79_H is passed on from the data bus to the latches. The output buffer of the latch is already enabled by grounding $\overline{OE}$; thus, the code displays digit 1 at the seven-segment LED by turning on the segments B and C. The latch can sink 24 mA when the output logic is low; the current limiting resistors 330Ω controls the current flow through the lighted segments. Now the question is, Why not use a common cathode LED? If a common-cathode seven-segment LED is used in this circuit, the output of the latch would have to be high to drive the segments. The latch can supply approximately 2.6 mA when the output is high; this current is insufficient to drive the segments.

5.3   INTERFACING INPUT DEVICES

The interfacing of input devices is almost identical to that of interfacing output devices, but with some differences in bus signals and circuit components. In this discussion, we will assume that you are familiar with the basic concepts of interfacing (Section 5.1.3) and describe only the additional details. First, we examine the execution and timing of the IN instruction and discuss the interfacing of input devices in relation to the timing diagram.

5.3.1   IN Instruction

The Z80 instruction set includes several instructions to read (copy) data from such input devices as switches, keyboards, and A/D data converters. These instructions can read an input device and place the data into the accumulator, Z80 registers, or memory registers. These are two-byte instructions; the first byte is the opcode, and the second byte specifies the port address. Although there are numerous ways of specifying the port address, it is always eight bits long. Thus, the addresses for input devices can range from 00_H to FF_H. Among the several Input instructions available, the machine cycles and timing of the following instruction will be examined.

Opcode	Operand	Description
IN	A, (8-bit)	This is a two-byte instruction with the hexadecimal opcode DB, and the second byte is the port address of an Input device.
		This instruction reads (copies) data from an input device and places the data byte into the accumulator.

To read switch positions, for example, from an input port with the address 84_H, the instructions will be written and stored in memory as follows:

Memory Address	Machine Code	Mnemonics		Memory Contents	
2065	DB	IN A, (84H)	; 2065	1 1 0 1 1 0 1 1	= DB_H
2066	84		; 2066	1 0 0 0 0 1 0 0	= 84_H

NOTE: The memory locations 2065_H and 2066_H are selected arbitrarily for the illustration.

When the microprocessor is asked to execute these instructions, it will first read the machine codes (or bytes) stored at locations 2065_H and 2066_H, then read the switch positions at port 84_H by enabling the interfacing device of the port. The data byte indicating switch positions from the input port will be placed in the accumulator. To design an interfacing circuit with the port address 84_H, we now need to examine the machine cycles and execution timing of the IN instruction.

5.3.2 Execution of IN Instruction and Its Timing

The IN instruction has three machine cycles: Opcode Fetch, Memory Read, and I/O Read. In the first two machine cycles, the Z80 reads the opcode DB and the port address 84_H (see example in previous section). These cycles are identical to the first two machine cycles of the OUT instruction shown in Figure 5.1. In the third machine cycle, the Z80 reads a data byte from the input port as follows (Figure 5.7):

1. The port address 84_H is placed on the low-order address bus at the beginning of the machine cycle M_3 (I/O Read).
2. During T_2, the control signals $\overline{IORQ}$ and $\overline{RD}$ are asserted, and one Wait state is inserted automatically after T_2.
3. During T_3, the Z80 reads the data bus and then causes the control signals ($\overline{IORQ}$ and $\overline{RD}$) to go inactive.

FIGURE 5.7
Z80 Timing for Execution of IN
Instruction

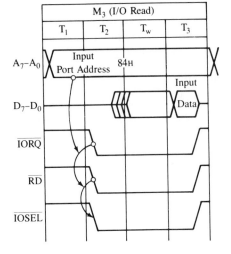

5.3.3 Basic Concepts in Interfacing Input Devices

To interface an input port with the address 84_H, we need to logically AND the information on the address bus with the control signals and enable the input port. The steps are as follows:

1. Decode the low-order bus to generate the I/O address pulse.
2. Combine the I/O address pulse with the control signals $\overline{\text{IORQ}}$ and $\overline{\text{RD}}$ to generate the signal I/O Select ($\overline{\text{IOSEL}}$, Figure 5.8). Another approach is to combine $\overline{\text{IORQ}}$ and $\overline{\text{RD}}$ to generate an $\overline{\text{IORD}}$ signal and then to combine the $\overline{\text{IORD}}$ with the I/O address pulse to generate the I/O select pulse.
3. Enable the input interfacing device using the I/O select pulse.

These steps are identical to those listed for interfacing output devices; the only differences are (1) the control signal is $\overline{\text{RD}}$ instead of $\overline{\text{WR}}$, and (2) data flow from an input port to the accumulator rather than from the accumulator to an output port.

5.4   ILLUSTRATIVE EXAMPLE 2: INTERFACING INPUT SWITCHES

In this section, we will analyze the circuit used for interfacing eight DIP switches as shown in Figure 5.8. The circuit includes the 74LS138 3-to-8 decoder to decode the low-order bus and the tri-state octal buffer (74LS244) to interface the switches to the data bus. The port can be accessed with the address 84_H; however, it also has multiple addresses.

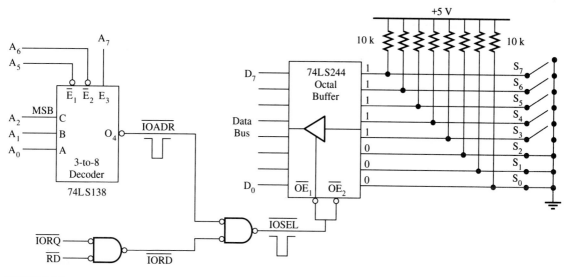

FIGURE 5.8
Interfacing Input Switches

5.4.1 Hardware

Figure 5.8 shows the 74LS244 tri-state octal buffer used as an interfacing device. The device has two groups of four buffers each, and they are controlled by the active low signal $\overline{OE}$. When $\overline{OE}$ is low, the input data appear on the output lines, and when $\overline{OE}$ is high, the output lines assume high impedance state.

5.4.2 Interfacing Circuit

Figure 5.8 shows that the low-order address bus (with the exception of lines A_4 and A_3) is connected to the decoder 74LS138; the address lines A_4 and A_3 are left in the "don't care" state. The output line O_4 of the decoder goes low when the address bus has the following address (we assume the "don't care" lines are at logic 0):

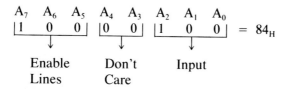

The control signal I/O Read ($\overline{IORD}$) is generated by ANDing the $\overline{IORQ}$ and $\overline{RD}$ in a negative NAND gate, and the I/O select pulse is generated by ANDing the output of the decoder with the control signal $\overline{IORD}$. When the address is 84_H and the control signals $\overline{IORQ}$ and $\overline{RD}$ are asserted, the I/O select pulse enables the tri-state buffer, and the logic levels of the switches are placed on the data bus. The Z80 then reads switch positions during T_3 (Figure 5.7) and places the data byte into the accumulator. When a switch is closed, it has logic 0, and when it is open, it is tied to $+5$ V, representing logic 1. Figure 5.8 shows that the switches S_7–S_3 are open and S_2–S_0 are closed; thus, the input reading will be $F8_H$.

5.4.3 Multiple Port Addresses

In Figure 5.8, the address lines A_4 and A_3 are not used by the decoding circuit; the logic levels on these lines can be either 0 or 1. Therefore, this input port can be accessed by four different addresses, as shown.

A_7	A_6	A_5	A_4	A_3	A_2	A_1	A_0		
1	0	0	0	0	1	0	0	=	84_H
			0	1				=	$8C_H$
			1	0				=	94_H
			1	1				=	$9C_H$

5.4.4 Instructions to Read Input Port

To read data from the input port shown in Figure 5.8, the instruction IN A, (84H) can be used. When this instruction is executed, the Z80 places the address 84_H on the low-order bus, asserts the control signals, and reads the switch positions.

5.5   MEMORY-MAPPED I/O

In memory-mapped I/O, the input and output devices are assigned and identified by 16-bit addresses. To transfer data between the microprocessor and I/O devices, memory-related instructions (such as LD A, (16-bit)) and memory control signals (such as $\overline{\text{MREQ}}$) are used. The microprocessor communicates with an I/O device as if it were one of the memory locations.

5.5.1 Memory-Related Data Transfer Instructions

To understand the memory-mapped I/O technique, we need to examine how a data byte is transferred from the Z80 to a memory location or vice versa. For example, the following instruction will transfer (copy) the contents of the accumulator to the memory location 8000_H. It is assumed here that the instruction is stored in memory locations 2050_H, 51_H, and 52_H.

Memory Address	Machine Code	Mnemonics	Comments
2050	32	LD (8000H), A	;Store contents of accumulator
2051	00		in memory location 8000_H
2052	80		

This is a 3-byte instruction; the first byte is the opcode, and the second and the third bytes specify the memory address. However, the 16-bit address 8000_H is entered in the reverse order; the low-order byte 00 is stored in location 2051, followed by the high-order address 80_H (the reason for the reversed order will be explained in section 5.9). In this example, if an output device instead of a memory register is connected at this address, the accumulator contents will be transferred to the output device. This is called the memory-mapped I/O technique.

Similarly, the instruction LD A, (4000H) will transfer the contents of the memory location 4000_H to the accumulator. To assign this address for a memory-mapped input port, we can interface an input device (for example, a keyboard) instead of memory by using the memory-related control signals ($\overline{MREQ}$ and $\overline{RD}$). When the processor executes the instruction, the accumulator receives data from the input device rather than from a memory register 4000_H.

5.5.2 Execution of Memory-Related Data Transfer Instructions

The execution of memory-related instructions discussed in the previous section is similar to the execution of I/O instructions (Sections 5.1 and 5.3), except that the memory-related instructions have 16-bit addresses.

Figure 5.9 shows the execution of the instruction LD (8000H), A. It has four

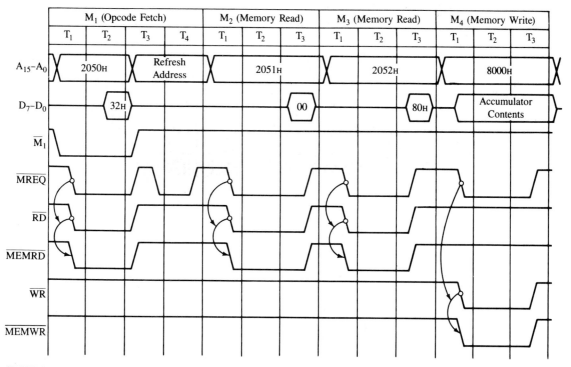

FIGURE 5.9
Z80 Timing for Execution of Instruction LD (8000H), A

machine cycles; in the first three machine cycles, the Z80 reads the three bytes. The fourth machine cycle M_4 (Memory Write) is similar to the machine cycle M_3 of the OUT instruction. In this machine cycle, the Z80 places the 16-bit address 8000_H on the address bus and the accumulator contents on the data bus. This is followed by the assertion of the control signals $\overline{MREQ}$ and $\overline{WR}$. The information available during M_4 can be used to interface a memory-mapped output port with the 16-bit address 8000_H.

In memory-mapped I/O, I/O selection and data transfer require steps similar to those required in peripheral-mapped I/O:

1. Decode the entire address bus $A_{15}-A_0$ (rather than just A_7-A_0).
2. Combine the control signals $\overline{MREQ}$, $\overline{WR}$, and the decoded pulse from Step 1 to generate a pulse similar to the $\overline{MSEL}$ pulse, which will be used to select an I/O rather than memory.
3. Use the I/O select pulse (actually $\overline{MSEL}$) to enable the I/O port.

To interface a memory-mapped input port, the steps are similar to those of the memory-mapped output port. We can use the instruction LD A, (16-bit), which reads data from an input port with the 16-bit address and places it in the accumulator. The instruction has four machine cycles; only the fourth machine cycle differs from M_4 in Figure 5.9. The control signal will be $\overline{RD}$ rather than $\overline{WR}$, and data flow from the input port to the microprocessor.

5.6   ILLUSTRATIVE EXAMPLE 3: APPLIANCE CONTROL USING MEMORY-MAPPED I/O TECHNIQUE

Figure 5.10 shows a schematic of interfacing I/O devices using the memory-mapped I/O technique. The circuit includes one input port with eight DIP switches and one output port to control the appliances. The appliances are turned on and off by the microprocessor according to the corresponding switch positions. For example, the switch S_7 controls the air conditioner and the switch S_0 controls Light 4. All switch inputs are tied high; therefore, when a switch is open (off), it has +5 V, and when a switch is closed (on), it has logic 0. The circuit includes two 3-to-8 decoders and one 8-input NAND gate to decode the address bus and generate the control signals. The eight switches are interfaced using a tri-state buffer 74LS244, and the appliances are interfaced using an octal latch (74LS373) with tri-state output.

5.6.1   Control Signals
In a memory-mapped I/O circuit, the control signals required are $\overline{MREQ}$ (Memory Request) and Read ($\overline{RD}$) or Write ($\overline{WR}$). In this circuit (Figure 5.10), they are used as inputs to a 3-to-8 decoder (labelled #2) to generate additional control signals. The enable lines of the decoder are controlled by the address lines. Assuming the

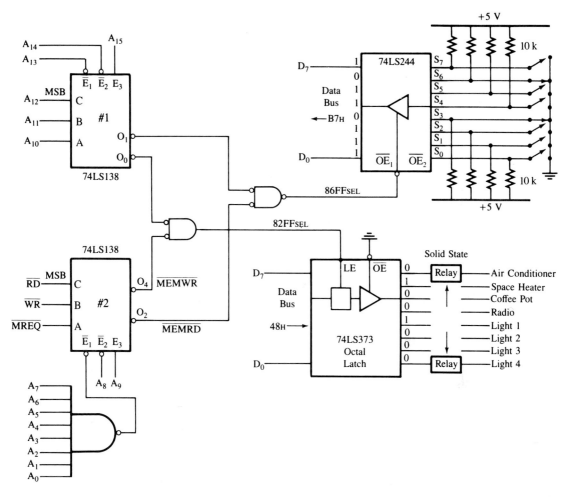

FIGURE 5.10
Interfacing I/O Devices with Memory-Mapped I/O

decoder is enabled by the appropriate address, we need to analyze the input and identify the output lines of the decoder that can be used as control signals.

To assert the Memory Write ($\overline{\text{MEMWR}}$) signal, the input should be $\overline{\text{MREQ}}$ = 0, $\overline{\text{WR}}$ = 0, and $\overline{\text{RD}}$ = 1 ($\overline{\text{RD}}$ and $\overline{\text{WR}}$ cannot be active at the same time). With this input, the output line O_4 goes active and generates the $\overline{\text{MEMWR}}$ signal.

To assert the Memory Read ($\overline{\text{MEMRD}}$) signal, the input should be $\overline{\text{MREQ}}$ = 0, $\overline{\text{WR}}$ = 1, and $\overline{\text{RD}}$ = 0. With this input to the decoder, the output O_2 goes active and generates the $\overline{\text{MEMRD}}$ signal.

5.6.2 Output Port and Its Address

The appliances are connected to the data bus through the latch 74LS373 and solid state relays. If an output bit of the 74LS373 is high, it activates the corresponding relay and turns on the appliance, which remains on as long as the bit stays high. Therefore, to control the appliances, we need to supply the appropriate bit pattern to the latch.

Figure 5.10 shows that the $\overline{OE}$ of the latch is connected to the ground; thus, the latched data will keep the relays on or off according to the bit pattern. The LE is connected to the I/O select pulse, which is asserted when the output O_0 of decoder #1 and the control signal $\overline{MEMWR}$ go low. Therefore, to assert the I/O select pulse, the output port address should be $82FF_H$.

$$\begin{array}{ccc|ccc|cc|cccccccc}
A_{15} & A_{14} & A_{13} & A_{12} & A_{11} & A_{10} & A_9 & A_8 & A_7 & A_6 & A_5 & A_4 & A_3 & A_2 & A_1 & A_0 \\
1 & 0 & 0 & 0 & 0 & 0 & 1 & 0 & 1 & 1 & 1 & 1 & 1 & 1 & 1 & 1
\end{array} = 82FF_H$$

| Enable Lines | Input | Enable | To 8-Input |
| Decoder #1 | to #1 | Lines #2 | NAND Gate |

5.6.3 Input Port and Its Address

The DIP switches are interfaced with the Z80 using the tri-state buffer 74LS244. The switches are tied high and are turned on by grounding as shown in Figure 5.10. The switch positions can be read by enabling the signal $\overline{OE}$ ($\overline{OE}_1$ and $\overline{OE}_2$), which is asserted when both the output O_1 of decoder #1 and the control signal $\overline{MEMRD}$ go low. Therefore, to read the input port, the port address should be $86FF_H$.

$$\begin{array}{ccc|ccc|cc|cccccccc}
A_{15} & A_{14} & A_{13} & A_{12} & A_{11} & A_{10} & A_9 & A_8 & A_7 & A_6 & A_5 & A_4 & A_3 & A_2 & A_1 & A_0 \\
1 & 0 & 0 & 0 & 0 & 1 & 1 & 0 & 1 & 1 & 1 & 1 & 1 & 1 & 1 & 1
\end{array} = 86FF_H$$

| Enable Lines | Input | Enable | To 8-Input |
| Decoder #1 | to #1 | Lines #2 | NAND Gate |

5.6.4 Instructions

To control the appliances according to switch positions, the microprocessor should read the bit pattern at the input port and send that bit pattern to the output port. The following instructions can accomplish this task.

```
READ: LD A, (86FFH)      ;Read the switches
      CPL                ;Complement switch reading, convert "on"
                         ; switch (logic 0) into logic 1 to turn on
                         ; appliances
      LD (82FFH), A      ;Send switch positions to output port and turn
                         ; appliances on or off
      JP READ            ;Go back and read again
```

When this program is executed, the first instruction reads the bit pattern 1 0 1 1 0 1 1 1 ($B7_H$) at the input port $86FF_H$ and places that reading in the accumulator; this bit pattern represents the "on" position of switches S_6 and S_3. The second instruction complements the reading; this instruction is necessary because the "on" position has logic 0, and logic 1 is necessary to turn on solid state relays. The third instruction sends the complemented accumulator contents (0 1 0 0 1 0 0 0 = 48_H) to the output port $82FF_H$. The 74LS373 latches the data byte 0 1 0 0 1 0 0 0 and turns on the space heater and Light 1. The last instruction, JP READ, takes the program back to the beginning and repeats the loop continuously in order to monitor the switches.

ADDITIONAL ILLUSTRATIVE EXAMPLES: INTERFACING SENSORS AND MOTORS 5.7

In previous examples, we illustrated the interfacing of I/O devices that were primarily binary devices (on/off). We now extend the concepts to interface analog devices such as temperature sensors and motors. In interfacing analog devices, the basic procedure remains similar to that of interfacing binary devices; the MPU identifies the device through a binary port address and enables it with an appropriate control signal. However, we need to find a way to detect and to convert the analog signal into the binary format and vice versa. The analog signal is generally handled in two ways: one is to detect the signal when it reaches a predetermined level, and the other is to convert it into binary format proportional to its magnitude. The predetermined level of the analog signal can be detected by using a comparator circuit, and the binary equivalent can be obtained by using an **A/D (Analog-to-Digital) data converter.** In this section, we will focus on interfacing circuits that can detect the predetermined level of analog signals and defer the discussion of interfacing data converters to Chapter 13.

Figure 5.11 shows the interfacing of a temperature sensor. This circuit is designed to detect (through an input port) whether the temperature has risen to 100°C, and at that temperature it turns on the dc motor of a water pump. The dc motor is interfaced with the MPU through an output port.

5.7.1 Hardware: Temperature Sensor LM135 and Comparator LM311

Figure 5.11 shows the LM135 used as a temperature sensor. Its output is connected as one of the inputs to the comparator LM311. The LM135 is an integrated circuit, designed to sense changes in temperature; its output voltage changes 10 mV/°C. It is rated to operate over a temperature range from −55°C to +150°C, and the current range 400 μA to 5 mA. At 25°C, the output of the sensor is typically 2.98 V, and it increases 10mV/°C; therefore, at 100°C, it can reach 3.73 V (2.98 V + 750 mV).

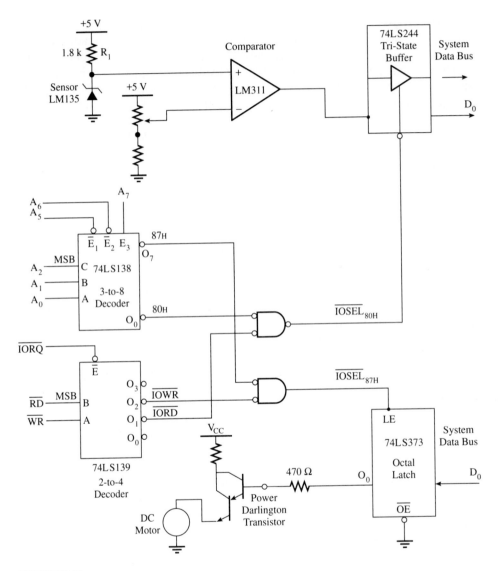

FIGURE 5.11
Interfacing Analog Signals

The LM311 is a voltage comparator that can be operated from a +5 V power supply. The comparator compares two voltages at its input terminals, and if the difference between the two voltages is less than or equal to −10 mV, its output remains at the saturation voltage of about 0.75 V; otherwise, the output is near the power supply voltage.

The output of the sensor is connected to the positive terminal of the comparator, and its negative terminal is set to 3.73 V. At temperatures lower than 100°C the output voltage of the sensor is less than 3.73 V; thus, the comparator output remains at 0.75 V (logic 0). When the temperature reaches 100°C, the output of the sensor is 3.73 V, and the comparator output goes to +4.5 V (logic 1). The output of the comparator is connected to the tri-state buffer 74LS244, which serves as an input port to the MPU.

5.7.2 Interfacing Circuit for the Sensor

Figure 5.11 shows that the 74LS138 (3-to-8) decoder is used for address decoding. This decoding circuit is identical to the circuit shown in Figure 5.8; thus, the outputs of the decoder are asserted for port addresses ranging from 80_H to 87_H ("don't care" lines are assumed to be at logic 0). The control signals $\overline{IORD}$ (I/O Read) and $\overline{IOWR}$ (I/O Write) are generated by using the 74LS139 (2-to-4) decoder; which is enabled by the $\overline{IORQ}$ signal. When the MPU intends to read, it asserts the $\overline{IORQ}$ and $\overline{RD}$ signals. The input of the 2-to-4 decoder becomes 0 1, and the output O_1 goes active low to assert the $\overline{IORD}$ (I/O Read) control signal. The $\overline{IORD}$ is logically ANDed with the decoded address 80_H to generate the $\overline{IOSEL}_{80H}$ (I/O Select) signal, which enables the input buffer 74LS244 to read the output of the comparator. The output voltage of the comparator is connected to the data line D_0 through the buffer, and the MPU can monitor the temperature by monitoring the data line D_0.

5.7.3 Interfacing Circuit for the DC Motor

The dc motor is interfaced with the MPU through the latch 74LS373; the output bit O_0 of the latch can drive the dc motor by turning on the transistor (Darlington pair). The logic level of bit O_0 of the latch is controlled by the data line D_0. The port address of the latch (87_H) is determined by the 3-to-8 decoder; the output line O_7 of the decoder is ANDed with the control signal $\overline{IOWR}$ to generate the $IOSEL_{87H}$, which enables the latch 74LS373. When the temperature reaches 100°C, the MPU sends logic 1 to the latch (port 87_H) to turn on the motor, and when the temperature is less than 100°C, the motor is turned off by the logic 0.

5.7.4 Instructions

START:	IN A, (80H)	;Read the output of the comparator
	AND 00000001B	;Save logic of D_0 and eliminate D_1 through D_7
	OUT (87H), A	;Turn on motor if $D_0 = 1$ or turn off if $D_0 = 0$
	JP START	;Go back and read the output of the comparator

5.7.5 Program and Circuit Description

The first instruction IN A, (80H) enables the buffer 74LS244, reads the entire data bus D_7–D_0, and places the byte in the accumulator. However, we are interested in the logic level of only bit D_0; it has the output of the comparator. Therefore, the next instruction ANDs the contents of the accumulator with the byte 01_H in order to eliminate bits D_1–D_6 and save the logic level of bit D_0. When the temperature exceeds 100°C, the output of the comparator is about $+5$ V, and the MPU reads logic 1 on the data line D_0. When the temperature is lower than 100°C, the comparator output is about 0.7 V, and the MPU reads logic 0 on the data line D_0. The next instruction OUT turns on the transistor if $D_0 = 1$ or turns off the transistor if $D_0 = 0$. When the transistor is on, it supplies the necessary current for the motor to run, and when the transistor is off, the motor is turned off. The last instruction JP takes the program back to the beginning and continuously monitors the changes in the output of the comparator.

5.7.6   Additional Sensors and Output Devices

Figure 5.11 illustrates one example of interfacing a sensor and driving a dc motor. We can extend the same concepts to other sensing and output devices. In Figure 5.11, we used only one data line D_0 to monitor the output of the comparator. We can connect additional sensors such as light detectors, level detectors, and smoke detectors to the remaining data lines, and instructions can monitor all the sensors in a sequence. Similarly, we can connect output devices such as speakers, alarms, and lights by using solid state relays to the remaining output lines of the latch.

5.8   TROUBLESHOOTING I/O INTERFACING CIRCUITS

In the last several sections, we discussed the interfacing of I/O devices and instructions to test them. In Illustrative Example 1 (Figure 5.4), the test program includes two instructions that load the byte 97_H into the accumulator and output the byte to port 07_H. If we execute these instructions and no change is observed at the output port, we must implement the troubleshooting technique similar to that which we used for troubleshooting memory interfacing circuits in the last chapter. After checking the wiring and the pin connections, we can write a diagnostic routine and execute it in a continuous loop to generate a constant and identifiable signal, and then check various points in relation to that signal.

DIAGNOSTIC ROUTINE AND MACHINE CYCLES

We can use the same instructions for the diagnostic routine that we used in Illustrative Example 1; however, to generate a continuous signal, we need to add a Jump instruction, as shown.

Instruction	Bytes	T-states	Machine Cycles		
			M_1	M_2	M_3
START: LD A, 97H	2	7 (4, 3)	Opcode Fetch	Memory Read	
OUT (07H), A	3	11 (4, 3, 4)	Opcode Fetch	Memory Read	I/O Write
JP START	3	10 (4, 3, 3)	Opcode Fetch	Memory Read	Memory Read

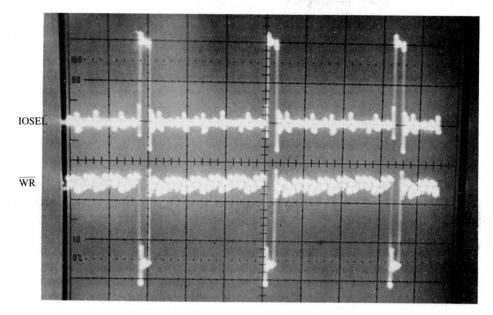

FIGURE 5.12
Timing Signals of Diagnostic Routine

This loop has 28 T-states and eight operations (machine cycles). To execute the loop once, the microprocessor asserts the $\overline{RD}$ signal seven times (the Opcode Fetch is also a Read operation) and the $\overline{WR}$ signal once. Assuming the system clock frequency is 2 MHz, the loop is executed in 14 μs, and the $\overline{WR}$ signal, repeated every 14 μs, can be observed on a scope. If we sync the scope on the $\overline{WR}$ pulse from the Z80, we can check the output of the 8-input NAND gate (IOADR), IOWR, and IOSEL signals; $\overline{WR}$ and IOSEL signals of a working circuit are shown in Figure 5.12.

When the Z80 asserts the $\overline{WR}$ signal, the port address 07H must be on the address bus A_7-A_0, and the output of the NAND gate must be low. Similarly, the IOWR must be low, and the IOSEL must be high. Now if we check the data bus in relation to the $\overline{WR}$ signal, one line at a time, we must read the data byte 97H.

SOME QUESTIONS AND ANSWERS 5.9

During the discussion of interfacing I/O devices, we focused on the basic concepts and avoided some details in order to simplify the presentation. We will now attempt to answer some of those questions.

1. *What are the other I/O instructions in the Z80 instruction set, and how do they differ from the I/O instructions discussed here?*

The Z80 instruction set includes six output instructions, of which we discussed only one. The remaining five instructions perform various types of output functions: for example, output a byte from any of the registers or from a memory location, or output a block of memory. In these instructions, register C is used to specify the port address and register B can be used as a counter.

2. *What are the contents of the high-order bus $(A_{15}-A_8)$ during the M_3 cycle of the IN/OUT instructions?*

The contents of the high-order bus during the M_3 cycle of the I/O instructions, illustrated in Sections 5.1 and 5.3, are generally irrelevant to the interfacing of I/O devices. For the I/O instructions discussed, the contents of the accumulator are placed on the $A_{15}-A_8$ bus. However, in other I/O instructions where the contents of register C are used to specify a port address, the contents of register B are placed on the high-order bus.

3. *Why is one Wait state automatically inserted when an I/O instruction is executed?*

When an I/O instruction is being executed, the control signal $\overline{\text{IORQ}}$ is asserted during T_2 of the M_3 cycle. This does not leave sufficient time for the Z80 to sample the WAIT line. Therefore, a slow-responding I/O device would not be able to decode its address and activate the WAIT line if necessary. Adding one Wait cycle allows the device to activate the WAIT signal for additional Wait states.

4. *In a memory-mapped I/O, what is the reason for not automatically inserting a Wait state?*

In the Memory Read/Write cycles, the $\overline{\text{MREQ}}$ is asserted during T_1; therefore, there is sufficient time to sample the WAIT line during T_2 state.

5. *In a memory-mapped I/O, how does the microprocessor differentiate between I/O and memory, and can an I/O device have the same address as a memory register?*

In the memory-mapped I/O, the microprocessor cannot differentiate between an I/O device and memory; it treats an I/O device as if it is memory. Therefore, an I/O device and memory register cannot have the same address; the entire memory map (64K) of the system has to be shared between memory and I/O.

6. *Why is a 16-bit address (data) stored in memory in the reversed order, i.e., the low-order byte first, followed by the high-order byte?*

In the Z80 microprocessor, the instruction decoder and the associated microprogram are designed to recognize the second byte as the low-order byte in a 3-byte instruction.

SUMMARY

In this chapter, we have examined the machine cycles of the OUT and IN instructions and derived the basic concepts for interfacing peripheral-mapped I/Os. Similarly, we examined the machine cycles of memory-related data transfer instructions and derived the basic concepts for interfacing memory-mapped I/Os. These concepts were illustrated with three examples of interfacing I/O devices and one example of interfacing an analog signal. The interfacing concepts can be summarized as follows.

Peripheral-Mapped I/O

□ The OUT is a 2-byte instruction and copies (transfers or sends) data from the accumulator to the addressed port.
□ When the Z80 executes the OUT instruction, in the third machine cycle it places the output port address on the low-order bus, places data on the data bus, and asserts the control signals $\overline{\text{IORQ}}$ and $\overline{\text{WR}}$.
□ A latch is generally used to interface output devices.
□ The IN instruction is a two-byte instruction and copies (transfers or reads) data from an input port and places the data into the accumulator.
□ When the Z80 executes the IN instruction, in the third machine cycle it places the input port address on the low-order bus, asserts the control signals $\overline{\text{IORQ}}$ and $\overline{\text{RD}}$, and transfers data from the port to the accumulator.
□ A tri-state buffer is generally used to interface input devices.
□ To interface an output or an input device, the low-order address bus needs to be decoded to generate the device address pulse, which must be combined with control signals $\overline{\text{IORQ}}$ and $\overline{\text{RD}}$ (or $\overline{\text{WR}}$) to select the device.

Memory-Mapped I/O

□ Memory-related instructions are used to transfer data.
□ To interface I/O devices, the entire bus must be decoded to generate the device address pulse, which must be combined with the control signals $\overline{\text{MREQ}}$ and $\overline{\text{WR}}$ or $\overline{\text{RD}}$ to generate the I/O select pulse. Data are transferred by using this pulse to enable the I/O device.

ASSIGNMENTS

1. Explain why the number of output ports in peripheral-mapped I/O is restricted to 256 ports.
2. In peripheral-mapped I/O, can an input port and an output port have the same port address?
3. If an output and input port can have the same 8-bit address, how does the Z80 differentiate between the ports?

4. Specify the two control signals required to latch data in an output port.
5. Specify the type of pulse required to latch data in the 7475.
6. Are data latched in the 7475 at the leading edge, during the level, or at the trailing edge of the enable (E) signal?
7. If the control signals $\overline{WR}$ and $\overline{IORQ}$ are asserted at the same time, can data be latched using only the control signal $\overline{WR}$?
8. If the answer to the previous question is yes, what are potential problems with the interfacing circuit?
9. In Figure 5.4, explain why the LED cathodes rather than anodes are connected to the latch.
10. Specify the control signals required to enable an input port.
11. Explain why a latch is used for an output port, but a tri-state buffer can be used for an input port.
12. What are the control signals necessary in memory-mapped I/O?
13. Can the microprocessor differentiate whether it is reading from a memory-mapped input port or from memory?
14. In Figure 5.11, connect the output of the comparator to data line D_7 and also drive the transistor with bit D_7. Make the necessary changes in the instructions.
15. Identify the port address in Figure 5.13.
16. In Figure 5.13, if $\overline{OE}$ is connected directly to the $\overline{WR}$ signal and the output of the decoder is connected to the latch enable (through an inverter), can you display a byte at the output port? Explain your answer.

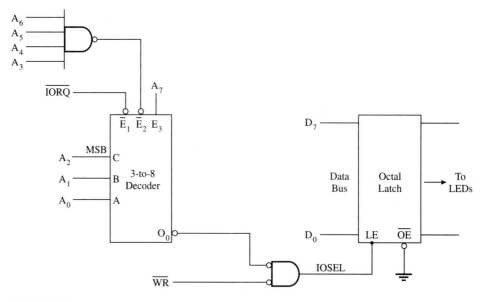

FIGURE 5.13
Schematic for Assignments 15–16

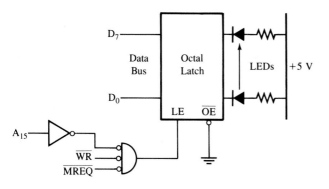

FIGURE 5.14
Schematic for Assignments 17–18

17. In Figure 5.14, determine whether it is the memory-mapped or the peripheral-mapped I/O.
18. In Figure 5.14, what is the port address if all the "don't care" address lines are assumed to be at logic 0?
19. In Figure 5.15, are ports A and B input or output ports?
20. In Figure 5.15, what are the addresses of ports A and B?

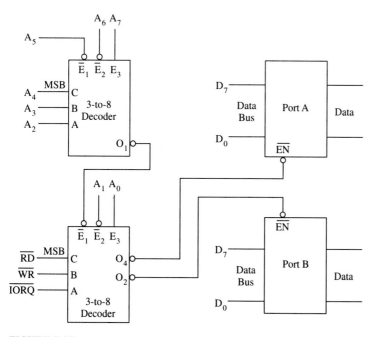

FIGURE 5.15
Schematic for Assignments 19–20

FIGURE 5.16
Schematic for Assignments 21–22

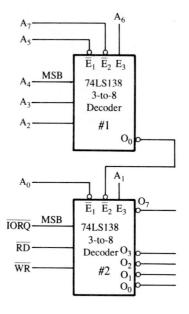

21. In Figure 5.16, identify two output lines of decoder #2 that can be used as control signals and explain their functions. Explain why other output lines cannot be used as control signals.
22. In Figure 5.16, specify the I/O addresses.
23. In Figure 5.17, the decoder 74LS155 and an 8-input NAND gate are used to decode the address bus and generate the control signals. The decoder has two input lines (A_1 and A_0) and four enable lines (pins 1, 2, 14, and 15).

FIGURE 5.17
Schematic for Assignment 23

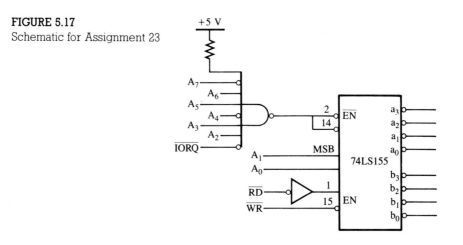

When pins 14 and 15 (active low) are enabled, the four output lines of the "b" group decode the input signal, and when pins 1 (active high) and 2 (active low) are enabled, the four output lines of the "a" group decode the input signals. Identify the addresses that can assert the output lines of the decoder and specify their I/O functions.

24. Sketch the waveforms of the M_1 cycles in the diagnostic routine (section 5.8).

25. Write a similar diagnostic routine to test the circuit in Figure 5.8.

26. Is there a $\overline{WR}$ pulse in your diagnostic routine of **25**? If the answer is no, what is the unique identifiable signal that can be used to sync the scope?

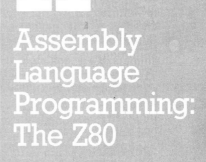

II

Assembly Language Programming: The Z80

Part II of this book is an introduction to Z80 assembly language programming. It explains commonly used instructions, elementary programming techniques and their applications, and the modular approach to software design.

The content is presented in a format similar to one for learning a foreign language. One approach to learning a foreign language is to begin with a few words that can form simple, meaningful, and interactive sentences. After learning a few sentences, one begins writing paragraphs that can convey ideas in a coherent fashion; then, by sequencing a few paragraphs, one can compose a letter. Chapters 6 to 11 are arranged in similar fashion—from simple instructions to applications.

Chapter 6 presents the Z80 programming model and provides an overview of the Z80 instruction set and its capability. Chapter 7 deals with software development systems and Z80 assemblers. Chapters 8 and 9 are concerned primarily with the Z80 instructions that occur most frequently. The instructions are not introduced according to the six groups as classified in Chapter 6; instead, a few instructions that can perform simple tasks are selected from each group. Chapter 8 includes the discussion of instructions from three groups—data copy, arithmetic, and branch—and their various applications. Chapter 9 introduces logic and bit manipulation instructions and their applications. Chapter 10 introduces the concepts of subroutine and stack, which provide flexibility and variety for program design. Chapter 11 synthesizes the programming concepts presented in earlier chapters by illustrating application programs and demonstrates the modular approach to software design.

PREREQUISITES

The reader is expected to know the following topics (refer to Chapters 1 and 2):

☐ Concepts in microprocessor architecture.
☐ Concepts related to memory and I/Os.
☐ Logic operations, and binary and hexadecimal arithmetic.

Introduction to Z80 Assembly Language Programming

An assembly language program is a set of instructions, written in the mnemonics of a given microprocessor, and in a sequence appropriate to a specified task. To write such programs, we should be familiar with the programming model (internal registers) of the microprocessor and its instruction set. This chapter introduces the Z80 programming model and provides such an overview of the Z80 instruction set.

The Z80 instruction set is classified into six categories, and each category is explained with examples. The chapter also discusses the instruction format and various addressing modes. Writing, assembling, and executing a program are illustrated by a simple problem of adding two Hex numbers. The **flowcharting** technique and symbols are discussed in the context of the illustrative program. The chapter concludes with a list of selected Z80 instructions.

OBJECTIVES

□ Draw the Z80 programming model and identify the registers.
□ Explain the functions of the accumulator, general-purpose registers, and alternate registers.
□ Explain the functions of 16-bit registers and special-purpose registers.
□ List the flags and explain the data conditions under which they are set or reset.
□ Explain the terms operation code (opcode) and operand, and illustrate these terms by writing instructions.
□ Classify the instructions in terms of their word size and specify the number of memory registers required to store the instructions in memory.
□ List the six categories of the Z80 instruction set.
□ Define and explain the term **addressing mode.**
□ Write logical steps needed to solve a simple programming problem.
□ Draw a **flowchart** from the logical steps of a given programming problem.
□ Write mnemonics from the flowchart and convert the mnemonics into Hex code for a given programming problem.

6.1   THE Z80 PROGRAMMING MODEL

In Chapter 2, we developed a model to represent the internal structure of the MPU shown in Figure 2.3. We will now describe a similar model of the Z80 microprocessor; however, we will include only those components necessary for the programmer. Figure 6.1 shows such a model, which includes an **accumulator** and a **flag register, general-purpose register arrays,** registers used as **memory pointers,**

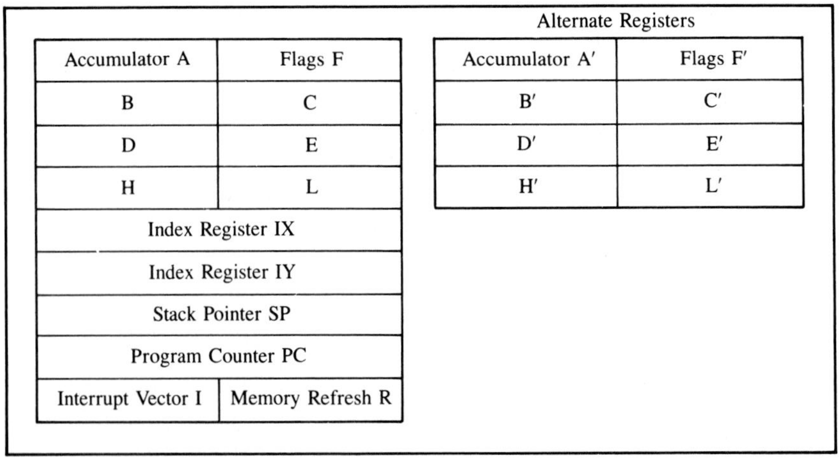

Accumulator A	Flags F
B	C
D	E
H	L
Index Register IX	
Index Register IY	
Stack Pointer SP	
Program Counter PC	
Interrupt Vector I	Memory Refresh R

Alternate Registers	
Accumulator A′	Flags F′
B′	C′
D′	E′
H′	L′

FIGURE 6.1
The Z80 Programming Model
SOURCE: Courtesy of Mostek Corporation

FIGURE 6.2
Flag Register: Bit Identification

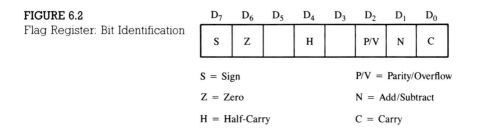

S = Sign   P/V = Parity/Overflow

Z = Zero   N = Add/Subtract

H = Half-Carry   C = Carry

and **special-purpose registers.** These registers and their functions were described briefly in Chapter 3 in the context of the Z80 architecture; now, they are described in detail in the following sections.

6.1.1 Accumulator

The accumulator is an 8-bit register that is part of the Arithmetic/Logic unit (ALU) and is also identified as register A. This register is used to store 8-bit data and to perform arithmetic and logic operations. The result of an operation performed in the ALU is also stored in the accumulator. For example, in an 8-bit addition, the instruction ADD always assumes that one of the numbers is the byte in the accumulator, and the result of the addition is stored in the accumulator by replacing the previous byte.

Figure 6.1 shows an additional accumulator called A' in the alternate register set. A' is not directly accessible to store a byte or perform an ALU operation, but the contents of A' are accessible by using the exchange instruction EX AF,AF'.

6.1.2 Flag Register

The ALU includes six flip-flops that are set or reset according to data conditions after an ALU operation, and the status of each flip-flop, also known as flags, is shown in the flag register F. The status of each of the six flags is stored in the 8-bit flag register so that they can be examined if necessary. The bit position of each flag is shown in Figure 6.2; bits D_5 and D_3 are unused.

Among the six flags, the H (Half-Carry) and N (Add/Subtract) flags are used internally by the microprocessor for **BCD (Binary Coded Decimal)** operations. These two flags cannot be tested by any instruction and are not available to the programmer for decision making. The remaining four flags—S (Sign), Z (Zero), P/V (Parity/Overflow), and C (Carry)*—can be tested in conjunction with Conditional Jump or Call instructions. Each of these four flags has two Jumps or Call instructions associated with it: one when the flag is set and the other when the flag is reset. These flags have critical importance in the decision-making process;

---

*To avoid confusion between C as a register and C as the Carry flag, we will refer to the Carry flag as CY when it does not refer specifically to bit D_0 in the flag register.

all decisions are based on the status of these flags. For example, the instruction JP C, 2050H (Jump on Carry to memory location 2050_H) is implemented to change the sequence of a program when the Carry flag is set.

The details of these flags are described below in the order of frequency of use. They will be discussed again in the context of illustrative programs. At the outset, the descriptions of these flags may appear quite complex. However, when we begin to write programs, we will see that, in general, most flags are ignored except one or two depending upon the operations being performed. For the time being, to understand their function, you should focus on three flags: C (Carry), Z (Zero), and S (Sign).

☐ **C—Carry flag:** If an arithmetic operation generates a carry (in addition) or a borrow (in subtraction), the Carry flag is set; otherwise it is reset.

It is important to remember that when an arithmetic operation does not generate a carry (or borrow), the flag is reset.

The flag is also affected by such other instructions as logic and shift instructions. The details will be discussed when specific instructions are explained.

The Z80 includes instructions SCF—Set Carry Flag—and CCF—Complement Carry Flag—that can set or complement this flag independent of the previous ALU operation.

☐ **Z—Zero flag:** If an 8-bit operation results in zero, the Z flag is set; otherwise it is reset.

In a bit testing operation, if the bit is zero, this flag is set; otherwise it is reset. In comparing two numbers, the Z flag is set when they are equal; otherwise it is reset.

The Z flag is also affected by special input instructions, block I/O instructions, and counting instructions.

☐ **S—Sign flag:** After an ALU operation, if the most significant bit D_7 is 1, the sign flag is set; otherwise it is reset. When the flag is set, you do not necessarily have a negative result. The interpretation of the Sign flag depends upon the number system (unsigned number, signed magnitude, or 2's complement) being used by the programmer. This flag can, of course, be used to indicate negative numbers, but its usage can be confusing. Therefore, it is discussed in detail in the context of the appropriate instructions. This flag is also affected by special input instructions in the Z80 set.

☐ **P/V—Parity/Overflow flag:** This flag is used for two purposes: to check the parity (the number of 1s in a byte) and to check an overflow in dealing with signed numbers.

In the case of a parity check after an operation, if the number of 1s in the result is even (even parity), this flag is set, and if the number of 1s is odd (odd parity), the flag is reset. For example, if the result of ANDing two bytes is 0 0 0 0 0 0 1 1, the parity flag is set to indicate even parity (two 1s). In this example, the magnitude base-ten (3_{10}) is odd; however, the odd or even number has no relationship with the odd or the even parity.

In arithmetic operations of signed numbers where bit D_7 is used to indicate sign, this flag is set to indicate an overflow condition. For example, when bit D_7 is reserved for a sign, the magnitude of a number is represented by the remaining seven bits, the maximum being 0 1 1 1 1 1 1 1 ($+127_{10}$). After an addition, if the sum goes beyond $+127$, bit D_7 changes to 1, a change that would indicate a negative result. In fact, this is an overflow condition and it is indicated by the overflow (V) flag.

This flag is also used for other functions such as block transfer, search, and interrupt.

☐ **H—Half-Carry flag:** In an arithmetic operation, this flag is affected by the carry or borrow between bits D_3 and D_4. In addition, when there is a carry from bit D_3 to D_4, the Half-Carry flag (H) is set; otherwise, it is reset. In a subtraction, when there is a borrow from bit D_4 to D_3, this flag is set; otherwise, it is reset. The flag is used internally for BCD (Binary Coded Decimal) operations, and there are no Jump or Call instructions associated with this flag.

☐ **N—Add/Subtract flag:** This flag is also used internally for BCD operations to distinguish between addition and subtraction. For BCD addition, this flag is 0 and for subtraction it is set to 1.

The **alternate flag register** F' is associated with the alternate accumulator A' as shown in Figure 6.1. The contents of this register can be accessed by using the exchange instruction.

6.1.3 General-Purpose and Alternate Registers

The Z80 microprocessor has six programmable general-purpose registers named B, C, D, E, H, and L, as shown in Figure 6.1. These are 8-bit registers used for storing data during the program execution. They can be combined as register pairs—BC, DE, HL—to perform 16-bit operations or to hold memory addresses.

The programmer can use these registers to *load* or copy data. For example, the instruction LD B, C copies the data from register C into register B. Conceptually, these registers can be viewed as memory locations, except that they are built inside the microprocessor and identified by specific names. Some microprocessors do not have this type of register; instead, they use memory as their registers.

In addition to the general-purpose registers, the Z80 includes a similar set of six **alternate registers** designated as B', C', D', E', H', and L'. They are not directly available to the programmer, except through the exchange instructions; the contents of general-purpose register pairs can be exchanged with the alternate register pairs.

6.1.4 16-Bit Registers as Memory Pointers

The Z80 microprocessor includes four 16-bit registers used to hold memory addresses; they are classified here as memory pointers. The primary function of memory is to store instructions and data, and the microprocessor needs to access memory registers to read these instructions and data. To access a memory register, the microprocessor identifies the register by using the addresses in these memory pointers.

INDEX REGISTERS (IX AND IY)

The Z80 has two 16-bit **index registers** called IX and IY. Each register is used to specify a memory address by the 16-bit address it holds and a displacement count. For example, if the IX register holds 2050_H, a higher memory address such as 2060_H can be specified by adding the displacement count of 10_H. Similarly, a lower memory address such as 2040_H can be specified by adding the negative of 10_H in 2's complement.

In addition to the index registers, the HL pair is frequently used as a memory pointer. Similarly, the BC and DE pairs can be used also as memory pointers in a limited way. However, no displacement byte can be added to the contents of these pairs.

STACK POINTER (SP)

The stack pointer is also a 16-bit register used to point to the memory location called the **stack.** The stack is a defined area of memory locations in R/W memory, and the beginning of the stack is defined by loading a 16-bit address into the stack pointer.

We will discuss the concept of the stack memory in detail when we introduce the topic of subroutines.

PROGRAM COUNTER (PC)

This register functions as a 16-bit counter. The microprocessor uses this register to sequence the execution of instructions. The program counter points to the memory address from which the next byte is to be fetched, and when the microprocessor places an address on the address bus to fetch the byte from memory, it then increments the program counter by one to point to the next memory location.

6.1.5　Special-Purpose Registers

The Z80 microprocessor includes two special-purpose registers, generally absent in other 8-bit microprocessors. These registers are shown in Figure 6.1 as interrupt vector register (I) and the memory refresh register (R).

INTERRUPT VECTOR REGISTER (I)

This is an 8-bit register used in the interrupt process. When an external device interrupts the microprocessor with a request to do something else, the microprocessor should be directed to a 16-bit address in memory where it can find what to do next. The I register is used to store the high-order eight bits of the 16-bit address; the low-order eight bits must be supplied by the interrupting device. We will discuss the details and applications of this register in Chapter 12.

MEMORY REFRESH REGISTER (R)

The memory refresh register (R) is also an 8-bit register that is used as a 7-bit counter to provide an address of memory cells to be refreshed in dynamic memory. As mentioned in Chapter 2, information stored as a capacitive charge in dynamic memory leaks; therefore, bit information should be refreshed, meaning it should be read and stored again every few milliseconds. Applications of the memory refresh register (R) will be discussed in detail with the topic of Interfacing Dynamic Memory.

OVERVIEW: Z80 INSTRUCTION SET 6.2

The instruction set of a microprocessor determines the capability of its operations, the power of its data manipulation, and the ease of programming it. Although it is necessary to have an overall view of the instruction set, our intent here is merely to acquaint you with the overall operations and capability of the Z80 microprocessor. As you progress through the chapters of Part II, you will be exposed to various instructions in more detail along with their applications.

The Z80 microprocessor has 158 instruction types; it includes all the instructions of the Intel 8080 microprocessor and all but two of the 8085. As discussed in Chapter 1, each instruction has two parts: one is the task to be performed (such as Load, Add, and Jump), called the operation code (opcode); and the second identifies the data to be operated on, called the *operand*. First, we will examine various formats of these instructions in terms of number of bytes and then their classification according to their function.

6.2.1 Instruction Format

An instruction is a command to the microprocessor to perform a given task on specified data. The size of Z80 instructions ranges from one to four bytes; thus, the number of memory registers (locations) required to write (or store) them varies. For example, to write a 3-byte instruction into memory requires three memory locations. Most opcodes (operation codes) are specified in one byte; however, some specialized opcodes require two bytes. The operand (or data) can be specified in the following ways: 8-bit data, 16-bit data, registers, register pairs, I/O addresses, and memory addresses. The Z80 instruction set can be classified into four groups according to the length of an instruction: 1-byte to 4-byte instructions. Because the Z80 is an 8-bit microprocessor, the terms "byte" and "word" are used synonymously.

1-BYTE INSTRUCTIONS

In a 1-byte instruction, the opcode and the operand are included in the same byte as shown in the following examples.

Task	Opcode	Operand	Binary Code
Copy the contents of register B into the accumulator A.	LD	A, B	01 111 000 (78H)

In this instruction, the opcode LD is specified by the first two bits (01), and the operand registers A and B are specified by the remaining six bits. (The accumulator A is represented by 111 and register B by 000.) These bits are associated with the internal microoperations of the microprocessor and are not relevant for learning the instruction set.

2-BYTE INSTRUCTIONS

In a 2-byte instruction, the first byte specifies the opcode and the second byte specifies the operand (with exceptions of some Z80 two-opcode instructions).

Task	Opcode	Operand	Binary Code	
Load register B with the hexadecimal number 32. (Opcode for LD B is 06H)	LD	B, 32H*	0000 0110 (06H)	Byte 1
			0011 0010 (32H)	Byte 2

3-BYTE INSTRUCTIONS

In a 3-byte instruction, the first byte specifies the opcode, and the following two bytes specify the 16-bit address or data in a reversed order: low-order byte followed by the high-order byte. For example:

Task	Opcode	Operand	Binary Code	
Load register pair BC with the 16-bit number 2080_H. (Opcode for LD BC is 01H)	LD	BC, 2080H	0000 0001 (01H)	Byte 1
			1000 0000 (80H)	Byte 2
			0010 0000 (20H)	Byte 3

---

*In an instruction, the hexadecimal number is shown as the number followed by capital H, and in the text, the number is shown with the subscript $_H$.

4-BYTE INSTRUCTIONS

The descriptions given above for 2- and 3-byte instructions are valid for the instructions compatible with the 8080 instructions. The Z80 instruction set, however, includes numerous special-purpose instructions that are not compatible with the 8080 instruction set. An 8-bit microprocessor can have a maximum of 256 bit combinations; thus, its instruction set is limited to 256 operation codes. The 8080 has already used 242 combinations for its 72 different instructions, leaving only 14 combinations unused. However, the Z80 microprocessor needs many more combinations to use its additional registers (two index registers, alternate registers, interrupt vector, and refresh). This problem was resolved by designing 2-byte opcodes: unused opcodes combined with instruction opcodes. Z80 4-byte instructions are generally associated with index registers, as shown in the following example.

Task	Opcode	Operand	Binary Code	
Load index register IX with 16-bit address 2000_H.	LD	IX, 2000H	1101 1101 (DDH)	Byte 1
			0010 0001 (21H)	Byte 2
			0000 0000 (00H)	Byte 3
			0010 0000 (20H)	Byte 4

In this instruction, the opcode has two bytes, DD and 21. Now we can discuss various instructions according to their functional classification.

6.2.2 Z80 Instruction Set

The Z80 instruction set can be divided into six major categories as follows:

1. Data Copy (Transfer) or Load Operations
2. Arithmetic Operations
3. Logic Operations
4. Bit Manipulation
5. Branch Operations
6. Machine Control Operations

DATA COPY OR LOAD OPERATIONS

Copying data is one of the major functions the microprocessor needs to perform. The Z80 has numerous instructions that copy data from one location, called **source,** to another location, called **destination,** without modifying the contents of the source. In technical manuals, this function is quite often referred to as data transfer. However, since the term *data transfer* creates the impression that the contents of the source are destroyed, we prefer the term *data copy.* In this text, we have also used the terms Load, Read, and Write to describe data copy operations.

Figure 6.3 shows various categories of data copy operations. The Z80 has several instructions associated with each category, each of which, with its subdivisions, is listed below with examples of instructions.

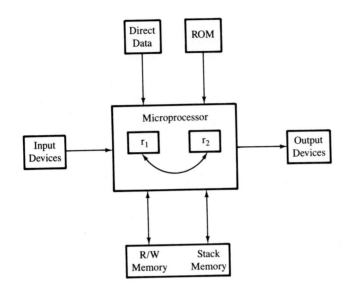

FIGURE 6.3
Types of Data Copy Operations

Data Copy Operations	Examples
1. From one register into another register.	Copy the contents of register B into the accumulator.
	LD, A, B; LD means Load
2. (a) Specific data byte into a register or a memory location.	Load register B with the hexadecimal number 32.
	LD B, 32H
(b) Specific 16-bit data into a register pair.	Load register pair HL with hexadecimal number 2050.
	LD HL, 2050H
3. From a memory location into a register or vice versa.	Copy data from memory location 2080$_H$ into the accumulator.
	LD A, (2080H)*
4. (a) From an input port into the accumulator.	Read data from input port 01$_H$ and copy into the accumulator.
	IN A, (01H)*
(b) From the accumulator into an output port.	Write (send) the contents of the accumulator into port 07$_H$.
	OUT (07H),* A

---

*Parentheses should be read as "contents of," e.g., "contents of memory location 2080H."

Data Copy Operations	Examples
5. From microprocessor registers into stack memory locations and vice versa.	Copy the contents of register pair BC into defined stack memory locations. PUSH BC
6. Exchange contents between registers. (This is a slightly different operation from data copy; this is a data exchange.)	Exchange the contents of general purpose registers (BC, DE, HL) with alternate registers. EXX

General characteristics of these data copy instructions can be listed as follows:

1. In data copy operations, the contents of the source are copied into the destination without affecting the contents of the source (except in Exchange instructions).
2. In an operand, the destination is specified first, followed by the source. For example, in the instruction LD A, B (copy the contents of B into A), the source is register B and the destination is the accumulator. This may appear backward because the flow is generally assumed to be from left to right, the way we read text.
3. The memory and I/O addresses are enclosed in parentheses.
4. In some instructions, operand is implicit (for example, EXX).
5. Data copy instructions do not affect flags.

ARITHMETIC OPERATIONS

The Z80 instruction set includes four types of arithmetic operations: addition, subtraction, increment/decrement, and 1's and 2's complement. In 8-bit arithmetic operations, the accumulator is generally assumed to be one of the operands (with the exception of increment/decrement instructions).

☐ **Addition.** Any 8-bit number, or the contents of a register, or the contents of a memory location can be added to the contents of the accumulator. The result of the addition is stored in the accumulator, and the flags are affected by the result. No two other 8-bit registers can be added directly; for example, the contents of register B cannot be added directly to the contents of register C.

Examples: Add the contents of register B to the contents of the accumulator. → ADD A, B

Add the byte 97_H to the contents of the accumulator. → ADD A, 97H

☐ **Subtraction.** Any 8-bit number, or the contents of a register, or the contents of a memory location can be subtracted from the contents of the accumulator. The subtraction is performed in 2's complement, and the result is stored in the accumulator. The result modifies the flags, and if the result is negative, it is expressed in 2's complement. The following mnemonics indicate that the accumulator is implicitly assumed as one of the operands.

Examples: Subtract the contents of register C from the contents of the accumulator.   → SUB C

Subtract the byte 47_H from the contents of the accumulator.   → SUB 47H

☐ **Increment/Decrement.** The 8-bit contents of a register (including the accumulator) or a memory location can be incremented or decremented by 1. Similarly, the 16-bit contents of a register pair (such as HL) can be incremented or decremented by 1. Unlike Add and Subtract, these operations can be performed in any of the registers. The instructions related to 8-bit contents affect flags (except Carry); on the other hand, instructions related to 16-bit contents do not affect any flags.

Examples: Increment the contents of register B.   → INC B

Decrement the contents of register pair BC.   → DEC BC

☐ **1's and 2's Complement.** The contents of the accumulator can be complemented (1's or 2's complement), and the result is stored in the accumulator. Some flags are affected by the result. These instructions assume that the operand is the accumulator.

Examples: Complement the contents of the accumulator (this is equivalent to 1's complement).   → CPL

Subtract the contents of the accumulator from zero (this is equivalent to 2's complement).   → NEG

Example 6.1

Write instructions in English-like statements to load the two data bytes 53_H and $F5_H$ in registers A and B, respectively, and add the two bytes. Translate these statements into Z80 assembly language. Illustrate the contents of registers affected in the programming model after the execution of each instruction and the status of the Carry and Zero flags.

Solution

	English-like Statements	Assembly Language Statements
	1. Load A with 53_H.	LD A, 53H
	2. Load B with $F5_H$.	LD B, F5H

A [53_H | X] F
B [$F5_H$ | X] C
(a)

A [48_H | C = 1, Z = 0]
B [$F5_H$ | X]
(b)

3. Add registers A and B.   ADD A, B
Result = $53_H + F5_H = 1\ 48_H$
               CY

FIGURE 6.4
Register Contents

This example does not show how to translate these instructions into binary code or how to execute them; this is discussed in the next section. Assuming these instructions are executed by the Z80 microprocessor, Figure 6.4(a) shows the contents of registers A and B after the execution of the first two instructions. The next instruction adds the contents of registers A and B; the sum is 148_H. Figure 6.4(b) shows the accumulator with 48_H and the CY flag set in the flag register. Please note that the flags are not affected by the Load or Copy instructions.

LOGIC OPERATIONS

The instructions related to logic operations can be divided into three groups: logic functions (AND, OR, etc.), bit rotations or shifts, and comparisons (less than, greater than, and equal to) of data bytes.

☐ **Logic Functions.** Any 8-bit number, the contents of a register, or the contents of a memory location can be ANDed, ORed, or Exclusive ORed with the contents of the accumulator. The result is stored in the accumulator, and the flags are affected by the result.

> Examples: Logically AND the contents of register → AND B
> B with the contents of the accumulator.
> Exclusive OR the contents of register   → XOR B
> B with the contents of the accumulator.

☐ **Shift and Rotate.** Each bit in the accumulator, in the registers, or in memory can be shifted either left or right by one position.

> Examples: Rotate the contents of the accumulator   → RRA
> right through Carry flag.
> Rotate left the contents of register B.   → RLC B

☐ **Compare.** Any 8-bit number, the contents of a register, or memory can be compared for equality, greater than, or less than with the contents of the accumulator. The result of the comparison is indicated by appropriate flags.

> Examples: Compare the contents of register B with the   → CP B
> contents of the accumulator.
> Compare the data byte 97_H with the contents   → CP 97H
> of the accumulator.

BIT MANIPULATION

The bit manipulation instructions can be classified into two groups: bit test and bit set/reset.

☐ **Bit Test**—Any one of the eight bits in a register, accumulator, or memory can be verified as 0 or 1, and the Z flag will be modified accordingly.

> Example: Check bit D_7 in register B. → BIT 7, B

☐ **Bit Set/Reset**—Any one of the eight bits in a register, accumulator, or memory can be set or reset.

Examples: Set bit D_5 in the accumulator. → SET 5, A
Reset bit D_2 in register B.   → RES 2, B

BRANCHING OPERATIONS

This group of instructions alters the sequence of program execution either conditionally or unconditionally.

☐ **Jump.** The sequence of program execution can be altered either conditionally or unconditionally. When a conditional Jump instruction is used, the microprocessor checks the specified flag, and if the condition is true, the execution sequence is altered; otherwise, the next instruction is executed. The destination location to which the program should be directed can be specified directly or relative to the contents of the program counter. These instructions are critical to the decision-making process in programming.

Examples: After an operation (such as an addition), → JP C, 2050H
if CY flag is set, jump to location 2050_H.
If Zero flag is not set, jump forward   → JR NZ, 0FH
by 15 locations.

☐ **Call/Return.** These instructions change the sequence of a program by calling a subroutine or returning from a subroutine. The conditional Call and Return instructions check for appropriate flags.

Examples: Go to subroutine located at 2050_H → CALL 2050H
Go to Subroutine located at 2070_H → CALL Z, 2070H
if Z flag is set.

☐ **Restart.** These instructions are used to change the program sequence to one of eight restart locations on memory page 00. The instructions are generally used with interrupts.

Example: Call location 0028_H. → RST 28H

MACHINE CONTROL OPERATIONS

These instructions control microprocessor operations such as Halt and Interrupt.

Examples: Suspend execution of instruction. → HALT
Disable interrupts by resetting the → DI
Interrupt Enable flip-flops.

6.2.3 Review of Important Concepts

Our intent here is to give you an overall view of the instruction set and the capability of the Z80 microprocessor. The Z80 has 158 instruction types with 694 opcodes. These numbers can be overwhelming and intimidating to a beginner. Fortunately, as you begin to use instructions, a logical pattern will begin to emerge. At this point, the important concepts to remember are as follows:

1. Each instruction has two parts: opcode and operand. The opcode specifies the task, and the operand specifies either data or where data are located.
2. Instructions can be classified into four groups according to their word length: one to four bytes.
3. In an instruction, when the data source and the destination are explicitly specified, the destination is shown first and the source second.
4. When an operand is a 16-bit address (or data), it is specified in a reversed order: the low-order byte first, followed by the high-order byte.
5. Instructions are stored in memory in binary format; the microprocessor neither reads nor understands mnemonics or hexadecimal numbers.
6. The number of memory locations required to store an instruction is determined by the word length. For example, a 3-byte instruction would require three memory locations.

HOW TO WRITE, ASSEMBLE, AND EXECUTE A SIMPLE ASSEMBLY LANGUAGE PROGRAM 6.3

An assembly language program is a sequence of instructions written in mnemonics to perform a specific task. These instructions are selected from the instruction set of the microprocessor being used. To write a program, we need to divide a given problem into small steps and translate these steps into the operations the Z80 can perform. For example, the Z80 does not have an instruction that can multiply two binary numbers, but it can add. Therefore, the multiplication problem can be written as a series of additions.

After writing the instructions in mnemonics, you should translate them into binary machine code; this process of translation is called **assembling the code.** Quite often, this process involves intermediate steps, such as translating mnemonics into Hex code and then into binary code. The code assembly can be done manually, as described in this chapter, or using an assembler (a program that translates mnemonics into machine code), as described in the next chapter.

To execute a program, the binary code should be entered and stored in the R/W memory of a microcomputer so that the microprocessor can read and execute the binary instructions written in memory. In a single-board microcomputer the instructions are, generally, entered using a Hex keyboard. This is one of the reasons why we translate mnemonics into Hex code as an intermediate step rather than into binary code directly. When the Hex code is entered, the keyboard program, residing in the microcomputer system, translates the Hex code into binary code. The steps required to write, assemble, and execute a program are illustrated in the next section.

6.3.1   Illustrative Program: Adding Two Hexadecimal Numbers

PROBLEM STATEMENT

Write instructions to load the two hexadecimal numbers 32_H and $A2_H$ into registers B and C, respectively. Add the numbers, and display the sum at the LED output port PORT1.

PROBLEM ANALYSIS

Even though this is a simple problem, it is necessary to divide the problem into small steps in order to examine the process of writing programs. The wording of the problem provides sufficient clues for the necessary steps. They are as follows:

1. Load the numbers into the registers.
2. Add the numbers.
3. Display the sum at the output port PORT1.

FLOWCHART

The steps listed in the problem analysis and the sequence can be represented in a block diagram, called a flowchart. Figure 6.5 shows such a flowchart representing those steps. This is a simple flowchart, and the steps are self-explanatory. We will discuss flowcharting in the next section.

ASSEMBLY LANGUAGE PROGRAM

To write an assembly language program, we need to translate the blocks shown in the flowchart into Z80 operations and then into mnemonics. By examining the blocks in Figure 6.5, we can classify them into three types of Z80 operations: Blocks 1 and 3 are copy operations, Block 2 is an arithmetic operation, and Block

FIGURE 6.5
Flowchart for Adding Two Numbers

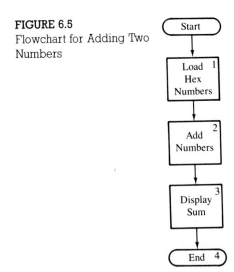

4 is a machine control operation. The translation of each block into mnemonics with comments is shown below.

Block 1:	LD B,32H	;Load register B with 32H.
	LD C,A2H	;Load register C with A2H.
	LD A,C	;Copy contents of C into ; accumulator to perform ; addition. B and C cannot be ; added directly.
Block 2:	ADD A,B	;Add two bytes and save the sum ; in A.
Block 3:	OUT (01H),A	;Display accumulator contents ; at port 01H.
Block 4:	HALT	;End

FROM ASSEMBLY LANGUAGE TO HEX CODE

To convert the mnemonics into Hex code, we need to look up the code in the Z80 instruction set; this is called either manual or hand assembly. The Hex code is as follows:

Mnemonics	Hex Code	
LD B,32H	06 32	2-byte instruction
LD C,A2H	0E A2	2-byte instruction
LD A,C	79	1-byte instruction
ADD A,B	80	1-byte instruction
OUT (01H),A	D3 01	2-byte instruction
HALT	76	1-byte instruction

STORING IN MEMORY AND CONVERTING
FROM HEX CODE TO BINARY CODE

To *store* the program in R/W memory of a single-board microcomputer and display the output, we need to know the memory addresses and the output port address. Let us assume that R/W memory ranges from 2000_H to $20FF_H$, and the system has an LED output port with the address 01_H. To enter the program, the following steps are necessary:

1. Reset the system by pushing the RESET key.
2. Using Hex keys, enter the first memory address at which the program should be stored. Let us assume it is 2000_H.
3. Enter each machine code by pushing Hex keys. For example, to enter the first machine code push 0, 6, and STORE keys. (The STORE key may be labelled

differently in different systems.) When you push the STORE key, the program will store the machine code in memory location 2000_H and upgrade the memory address to 2001_H.

4. Repeat Step 3 until the last machine code 76_H.
5. Reset the system.

Now the question is: How does the Hex code get converted into binary code? The answer lies with the Monitor program stored in the Read-Only Memory (or EPROM) of the microcomputer system. An important function of the Monitor program is to check the keys and convert Hex code into binary code. The entire process of manual assembly is shown in Figure 6.6.

In this illustrative example, the program will be stored in memory as shown:

Mnemonics	Hex Code	Memory Contents	Memory Address	Register Contents After Execution			
LD B,32H	06	0 0 0 0 0 1 1 0	2000	B	32_H	XX	C
	32	0 0 1 1 0 0 1 0	2001				
LD C,A2H	0E	0 0 0 0 1 1 1 0	2002	B	32_H	$A2_H$	C
	A2	1 0 1 0 0 0 1 0	2003				
LD A,C	79	0 1 1 1 1 0 0 1	2004	A / B	$A2_H$ / 32_H	XX / $A2_H$	F / C
ADD A,B	80	1 0 0 0 0 0 0 0	2005	A / B	$D4_H$ / 32_H	FLAGS / $A2_H$	F / C
OUT (01H),A	D3	1 1 0 1 0 0 1 1	2006				
	01	0 0 0 0 0 0 0 1	2007				
HALT	76	0 1 1 1 0 1 1 0	2008				

This program has nine machine codes and will require nine memory locations to store the program. The critical concept to be emphasized here is that the microprocessor can understand and execute only the binary instructions (or data); everything else (mnemonics, Hex code, comments) are for the convenience of those who write and use the assembly language programs.

FIGURE 6.6
Assembling the Code

EXECUTING THE PROGRAM

To execute the program, we need to tell the microprocessor where the program begins by entering the memory address 2000_H. Then, we can push the Execute key (or the key with a similar label) to begin the execution. As soon as the Execute function key is pushed, Z80 loads 2000_H into the program counter, and the program control is transferred from the Monitor program to our program.

The microprocessor begins to read one machine code at a time, and when it fetches the complete instruction, it executes that instruction. For example, it will fetch the machine codes stored in memory locations 2000_H and 2001_H and execute the instruction LD B, 32_H; thus, it loads 32H in register B as shown above in the last column of Register Contents. Next, it loads $A2_H$ into register C and copies $A2_H$ from register C into the accumulator A. It should be emphasized that the contents of register C are not changed in the copying process. When the ADD instruction is executed, the contents of A are changed to $D4_H$, which is the sum of 32_H and $A2_H$. It continues to execute instructions until it fetches the HALT instruction.

6.3.2 Program Documentation or Writing Format

Program documentation is an important aspect of writing programs. The documentation should be able to communicate what the program does and the logic underlying the program, so that it can be debugged and modified if necessary. For our illustrative program, a writing format based on assembler files (discussed in the next chapter) is shown here.

Memory Address	Hex Code	Label	Instruction (Opcode)	(Operand)	Comments
2000	06	START:	LD	B,32H	; Load first byte
2001	32				
2002	0E		LD	C,A2H	; Load second byte to be added
2003	A2				
2004	79		LD	A,C	; Copy one of the bytes into A
2005	80		ADD	A,B	; Add two bytes
2006	D3		OUT	(01H),A	; Display the result
2007	01				
2008	76		HALT		; End

This writing format has five columns: Memory Address, Hex Code, Label, Instruction (Opcode and Operand), and Comments. Each column is described below in the context of a single-board computer.

Memory Addresses These are 16-bit addresses of the system's R/W memory in which the binary code of the user program is stored. In the illustration, we assumed that the R/W memory in our system begins at the address 2000_H, and we chose to store the program starting at the location 2000_H; we could have chosen any other available memory block to store our program.

Hex Codes   These are the hexadecimal codes of the Z80 mnemonics we looked up in the instruction set; they were entered in memory using the Hex keyboard of the single-board microcomputer system. The key monitor program of the system translates these Hex codes and stores the binary equivalents in the proper memory locations.

Labels   They are used to identify a memory location. The program has one label: START. This label is used for documentation; it indicates the beginning of the program. The labels are used to identify memory locations and will be especially useful for Jump instructions when we use assemblers to write programs (discussed in the next chapter).

Instructions   These are the Z80 mnemonics representing the microprocessor operations. Each instruction is divided into two parts: opcode and operand.

Comments   The comments are written as a part of the proper documentation of a program to explain or elaborate the purpose of the instruction used. They thus play a critical role in the user's understanding of the logic behind a program. Because the illustrative program is very simple, the comments shown are either redundant or trivial, but in general comments should not merely describe the meaning of mnemonics.

6.4   FLOWCHARTING

A flowchart is a graphic representation of the logic and sequence of tasks to be performed. A flowchart should assist in clarifying one's thinking process and communicate the programmer's approach and logic in writing the program.

Flowcharting is an art; how much detail it should include requires a subjective decision. At one level, the flowchart includes only the functions to be performed without any reference to a particular microprocessor; at another level, the functions of registers being used are specified in detail. However, it should not duplicate the instructions in the program in a graphic format; this would defeat the whole purpose of drawing the flowchart. It should simply represent a logical approach and sequence of steps in solving the problem.

The six symbols commonly used in flowcharting are shown in Figure 6.7. We have already used three symbols in Figure 6.5. The fourth symbol, shown by the diamond shape, represents the decision-making block. It is used when data conditions need to be checked and the program sequence has to be altered. This symbol is illustrated in Figure 6.8. The fifth symbol, a double-sided rectangle, represents a predetermined process such as a subroutine (discussed in Chapter 10). The last symbol, a circle with an arrow, is used to show continuation of the flowchart to a different column or to a different page.

Symbol	Meaning

Symbol   **Meaning**

Oval: Indicates the beginning
or end of a program.

Arrow: Indicates the direction
of the program execution.

Rectangle: Represents a process or
an operation.

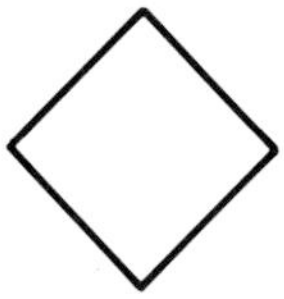

Diamond: Represents a decision-making
block.

Double-sided   Represents a predefined
Rectangle: process such as a subroutine.

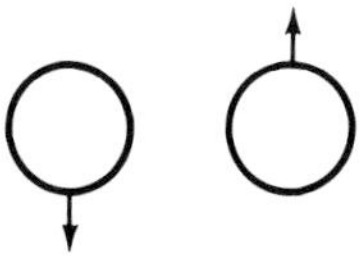

Circle with   Represents continuation
an Arrow: (an entry or exit) to
a different page.

FIGURE 6.7
Flowcharting Symbols

Draw a flowchart to represent the following problem. Load two Hex bytes into Z80 registers, and add the bytes. If the sum is larger than 8 bits, display 01_H as the overload condition at port PORT7; otherwise, display the sum at the output port.

Example
6.2

The problem can be divided into the following steps.

Solution

1. Load bytes into Z80 registers.
2. Add the bytes.
3. Check the sum.
4. If the sum $> FF_H$, display 01_H at the output port.
5. If the sum $< FF_H$, display the sum at the output port.

FIGURE 6.8
Flowchart: Adding Two Hex
Numbers and Checking Carry

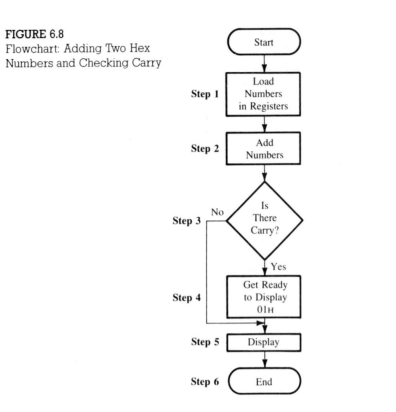

The steps listed in Example 6.2 and the sequence can be represented by the flowchart shown in Figure 6.8. The first two blocks can be easily understood. The third block, shown by the diamond shape, is a decision-making block. In this block the result is checked by examining the CY flag, and the program execution is altered accordingly. If the CY flag is set, the result is larger than FF_H and the program execution goes to the next block. It loads 01_H and displays it at the output port. If the answer to the question in the decision block is "No," the sum is less than FF. The program sequence is then altered; it bypasses Block 4 and displays the sum at the output port.

An interesting question is: Can we interchange the answers "Yes" and "No" at the decision-making block? That is, can the program sequence be changed if CY is set? This is given as a problem at the end of the chapter; you may find that the resulting flowchart will have two end points.

6.5   ADDRESSING MODES

The addressing mode is a way of specifying an operand or pointing to a data location. The Z80 microprocessor has ten addressing modes, as shown in Table

6.1. The first three are explained here as illustrations, and the others will be explained in later chapters.

In Section 6.2.2, we listed various categories of data copy operations. Data can be loaded directly into registers (or memory), or they can be copied from registers and memory, including I/O ports. Here are the addressing modes of these data copy operations.

Addressing Modes	Examples
1. Immediate	In this mode, the byte following the opcode is the operand.

Example: LD A, 32H → Load 32_H into the accumulator
     3E   Opcode
     32   Operand

2. Immediate Extended   In this mode, two bytes following the opcode constitute the operand; the second byte is low-order and the third byte is high-order.

Example: LD HL, 2050H → Load 2050_H into the HL pair.
     21   Opcode
     50   Operand: Low-order
     20   Operand: High-order

3. Register   In this mode, a data byte is copied from one register to another register, and both registers are specified in the instruction.

Example: LD A, B → Copy the contents of register B into A.

At this point, you are unfamiliar with the instruction types; therefore, you should avoid the details of the addressing modes given in Table 6.1. As we begin to use various instructions in following chapters, we will discuss the appropriate addressing modes. As you become more familiar with the instruction set, you will be able to choose an appropriate addressing mode for a given task.

LIST OF SELECTED Z80 INSTRUCTIONS   6.6

The Z80 instruction set includes 158 instructions resulting in 694 machine codes. The following list is a representative sample of each group described in Section 6.2. The purpose of the list is to show you the overall capability of the Z80 and some logical patterns in its instruction. You should not study these instructions in detail; instead, you should search for logical patterns. Once you recognize logical patterns, you will be able to recognize the function of an instruction even if you have not seen it before.

TABLE 6.1

Z80 Addressing Modes	Explanation	Example
1. Immediate :	The byte following the opcode is the operand. This mode is used to load 8-bit data into a register.	
	Load 97_H into register B	LD B, 97H
2. Immediate : Extended	The two bytes following the opcode are the operands. This mode is used to load 16-bit data or address into a register pair.	
	Load 8045_H into register pair BC	LD BC, 8045H
3. Register :	The operand register is included as a part of the opcode. This mode is used to copy data from one Z80 register into another register.	
	Copy data from register A into B	LD B, A
4. Implied :	This refers to operations in which the opcode implies one or more Z80 registers as containing the operands. For example, instructions for logic operations imply that the accumulator is one of the operands and that the result is stored in the accumulator.	
	Logically AND register B with A	AND B
5. Register : Indirect	This mode is used to copy data between the MPU and memory; the 16-bit contents in a register pair are used as a memory pointer.	
	Copy the contents of memory location 2060_H into register B. Register HL contains the address 2060_H.	LD B, (HL)
6. Extended :	The two bytes following the opcode specify the jump location.	
	Jump to location 2080_H.	JP 2080H
7. Relative :	In this mode, the second byte specifies the displacement value in a signed 2's complement for a jump location.	
	Jump forward 20 locations from the address of the next instruction.	JR 14H
8. Indexed :	In this mode, the byte following the opcode specifies a displacement value that is added to one of the index registers to form a memory pointer.	
	The index register IX contains 2060_H; increment the contents of memory location 2070_H.	INC (IX + 10H)

TABLE 6.1
Continued

Z80 Addressing Modes	Explanation	Example
9. Bit :	This mode is used for bit operation (manipulation). In this mode, instruction specifies a bit from a register or a memory location using one of the three addressing modes (register, register indirect, or indexed).	
	Set bit D_7 in register B.	SET 7, B
10. Page Zero :	The instruction set includes eight restart (one-byte call) instructions on memory page zero. In this mode, the memory location can be specified by using the low-order byte, and the high-order byte is assumed to be 00_H.	
	Call restart memory location 0028_H.	RST 28H

Most instructions are compatible with the 8080 instruction set, with a few exceptions. Notations used in the description of the instructions include

r = Z80 8-bit Register rp = Register Pair
r_s = Register Source rx = Index Registers
r_d = Register Destination d = Displacement Byte
m = Memory b = Bit
$( )$ = contents of 16-bit Memory Address
 or 8-bit I/O Address

1. Data Copy (Load) Instructions

Mnemonics	Bytes	Tasks

Data (8 bits and 16 bits) copy or load in registers

LD r_d, r_s	1	Copy data from source register r_s into destination register r_d.
LD r, 8-bit	2	Load 8-bit into a register.
LD rp, 16-bit	3	Load 16-bit into register pair.
LD rx, 16-bit	4	Load 16-bit data into index register.

Data copy between registers and memory

LD A, (16-bit)	3	Load accumulator from memory; the address is specified by 16-bit operand.
LD (16-bit), A	3	Load memory from accumulator; the memory address is specified by 16-bit operand.

Mnemonics	Bytes	Tasks
LD A, (rp)	1	Load accumulator from memory; the memory address is specified by the contents of register pair.
LD (rp), A	1	Load memory from accumulator; the memory address is given by the contents of register pair.
LD r, (HL)	1	Load register from memory; the address is specified by 16-bit contents in HL.
LD (HL), r	1	Load memory from register; the address is specified by 16-bit contents in HL.
LD r, (rx + d)	3	Copy memory contents into register r; the memory address is obtained by adding the contents of index register and the displacement byte d.
LD (rx + d), r	3	Copy register contents into memory address shown by index register and the displacement (rx + d).

2. Arithmetic Instructions*

Mnemonics	Bytes	Tasks
ADD A, r	1	Add register contents to accumulator.
ADD A, 8-bit	2	Add 8-bit data to accumulator.
ADD A, (HL)	1	Add memory contents to accumulator; the memory address is specified by the contents in HL.
SUB r	1	Subtract contents of register from accumulator.
SUB 8-bit	2	Subtract 8-bit data from accumulator.
SUB (HL)	1	Subtract memory contents from accumulator; the memory address is specified by the contents of HL.
INC r	1	Increment the contents of a register.
INC (HL)	1	Increment the contents of memory; the memory address is specified by the contents of HL.
INC rp	1	Increment 16-bit contents in a register pair.
DEC r	1	Decrement the contents of a register.

*Instructions used for 16-bit addition and subtraction are not shown here.

Mnemonics	Bytes	Tasks
DEC (HL)	1	Decrement the contents of memory; the memory address is specified by the contents of HL.
DEC rp	1	Decrement 16-bit contents in a register pair.

3. Logic Instructions*

Mnemonics	Bytes	Tasks
AND r	1	Logically AND the contents of a register with the accumulator.
AND 8-bit	2	Logically AND 8-bit data with accumulator.
AND (HL)	1	Logically AND the contents of memory with accumulator; the memory address is specified by the contents of HL.
CP r	1	Compare the contents of register with accumulator for less than, equal to, or greater than.
CP 8-bit	1	Compare 8-bit data with accumulator for less than, equal to, or greater than.
CP (HL)	1	Compare the contents of memory with accumulator for less than, equal to, or greater than; the memory address is specified by the contents of HL.

4. Bit Rotation

Mnemonics	Bytes	Tasks
RLCA	1	Rotate each bit in the accumulator to the left position.
RLA	1	Rotate each bit in the accumulator including the carry C to the left position.
RRCA	1	Rotate each bit in the accumulator to the right position.
RRA	1	Rotate each bit in the accumulator including the carry C to the right position.

5. Branch Instructions†

Mnemonics	Bytes	Tasks
JP 16-bit	3	Change the program sequence (Jump) to memory location specified by the 16-bit address.

---

*The Z80 instruction set includes similar instructions for logically ORing and Exclusive ORing with mnemonics OR and XOR respectively.

†The Z80 set also includes conditional Call and Return instructions.

Mnemonics	Bytes	Tasks
JP Z, 16-bit	3	Change the program sequence (Jump) to memory location specified by the 16-bit address if the Zero (Z) flag is set.
JP NZ, 16-bit	3	Change the program sequence (Jump) to memory location specified by the 16-bit address if the Zero (Z) flag is reset.
JP C, 16-bit	3	Change the program sequence (Jump) to memory location specified by the 16-bit address if the Carry (C) flag is set.
JP NC, 16-bit	3	Change the program sequence (Jump) to memory location specified by the 16-bit address if the Carry (C) flag is reset.
CALL 16-bit	3	Change the program sequence to the location of the subroutine.
RET	1	Return to the calling program after completing the subroutine sequence.

6. Machine Control Instructions

Mnemonics	Bytes	Tasks
HALT	1	Suspend execution and wait.
NOP	1	Do not perform any operation.

7. Bit Rotation*

Mnemonics	Bytes	Tasks
RLC r	2	Rotate each bit in register r to the left.
RL r	2	Rotate each bit in register r to the left, including Carry flag.
SLA r	2	Shift each bit in register r to the left.

8. Bit Manipulation†

Mnemonics	Bytes	Tasks
BIT b, r	2	Test bit b in register r, affecting the Z flag.
SET b, r	2	Set bit b in register r. ("b" represents bit position 0 to 7)
RES b, r	2	Reset bit b in register r.

9. Z80 Special (Conditional) Repetitive Instructions. The Z80 instruction set includes several instructions that are automatically repeated until a specified reg-

---

*The Z80 set includes similar instructions to shift right as well as to rotate bits in any memory location.

†Similarly, any bit in a memory location can be set or reset.

ister becomes zero. These instructions are quite efficient in dealing with block transfer or counter applications. Some of these instructions are as follows:

CPDR	2	Compare memory contents specified by HL with the accumulator. Increment HL, decrement BC, and repeat until BC = 0. or A = contents of memory specified by HL.
DJNZ d	2	Decrement B, and if B ≠ 0, jump to memory address obtained by adding displacement byte to the program counter.
INDR	2	Read input port indicated by the C register, and store the byte in memory specified by HL register. Decrement B and HL, and continue until B = 0.
OTDR	2	Output the contents of memory specified by HL to port indicated by the C register. Decrement B and HL, and continue until B = 0.

SUMMARY

This chapter introduced the Z80 programming model and provided an overview of the Z80 instruction set and the capability of the Z80 microprocessor. The important concepts and topics discussed in this chapter can be summarized as follows:

□ The Z80 microprocessor has six general-purpose 8-bit registers (B, C, D, E, H, and L) as a primary set. In addition, it includes the alternate set of these registers, all of which can be used to exchange information with the primary set. The registers B and C, D and E, and H and L can be combined to perform some 16-bit operations.

□ The ALU section of the Z80 includes accumulator A and the flag register to indicate six different data conditions. It also includes the alternate accumulator A′ and flag register F′, which can be used to exchange information with A and F, respectively.

□ Four flags—Sign, Zero, Carry, and Parity/Overflow—can be used for decision making and tested in connection with Jump, Call, and Return instructions. Two flags—Half-Carry and Add/Subtract—are used internally for BCD operations and are unavailable for the programmer.

□ The Z80 has four 16-bit registers—IX, IY, SP, and PC—used as memory pointers. Two index registers—IX and IY—can be used to point to any memory location, and an address and the direction (backward or forward) can be specified with a displacement byte. The stack pointer (SP) is used to specify memory locations in a defined R/W memory segment called the stack. The program counter (PC) is used to sequence the program execution; it points to the next memory address from which the machine code is to be fetched.

□ The Z80 includes two 8-bit special-purpose registers: Interrupt Vector (I) and Memory Refresh (R). The I register provides the high-order 8 bits of a 16-bit address to which the program is to be directed after an interrupt. The R register is a 7-bit counter and supplies an address for refreshing memory cells of a dynamic memory.

□ The Z80 microprocessor operations are classified into six major groups: data copy (load), arithmetic, logic, bit manipulation, branch, and machine control.

□ An instruction has two parts: opcode (operation to be performed) and operand (data to be operated on). The operand can be 8- or 16-bit data, an address, register, register pair, or it can be implicit.

□ The method of specifying an operand is called the addressing mode.

□ The instruction set is classified into four groups according to the word size: 1-, 2-, 3-, and 4-byte instructions.

□ To write a simple assembly language program, the problem should be divided into small steps in terms of microprocessor operations, and these steps should be translated into Z80 mnemonics. Then, the Hex code is assembled by looking up the code in the instruction list; this is called either hand or manual assembly.

□ To enter a program into the memory of a single-board microcomputer, Hex keys are used to enter the code, which is converted into binary code by the Key Monitor program of the system and stored in R/W memory. This binary code can then be read and executed by the microprocessor.

ASSIGNMENTS

1. How is the accumulator different from the 8-bit general-purpose registers of the Z80 microprocessor?
2. Explain the function of the alternate registers.
3. What is a flag, and what is its function?
4. If the Z80 adds 87_H and 79_H, specify the contents of the accumulator and the status of the S, Z, and CY flags.
5. If the Z80 is an 8-bit microprocessor, why are the program counter and the stack pointer 16-bit registers?
6. If the Z80 has fetched the machine code located at the memory location $205F_H$, specify the contents of the program counter.
7. The index register IX holds the address 2058_H. Specify the value of the displacement byte needed to make the effective address 2097_H.

8. The index register IY holds the address 2070_H. Specify the value of the displacement byte in 2's complement needed to make the effective address 2050_H.

9. List the six types of operations the Z80 performs.

10. Define opcode and operand, and specify the opcode and the operand in the instruction LD A, B.

11. Explain the instruction LD A, B. Specify the data source and destination.

12. If the instruction LD A, B is stored in memory location 2005_H, what are the contents of the memory register?

13. Explain the instruction SUB H. List the operand implicit in the instruction.

14. Write mnemonics to load $F8_H$ into register C, and show the Hex codes with the memory address starting at 1800_H.

15. Write logical steps to load the following three Hex numbers (2F, 47, and 7A) into Z80 registers B, C, and D, respectively. Add the numbers, and save the sum in register H.

16. Translate the steps in the previous question into Z80 assembly language.

17. Redraw the flowchart in Figure 6.5 by interchanging the answers of the decision block. For example, the program sequence will be altered if the answer is "Yes." (Hint: The flowchart can have two End statements.)

18. Draw a flowchart to represent the following problem. Load two numbers into Z80 registers, and subtract the second number from the first number. If the result generates a borrow, display FF_H at the output port of the system; otherwise, display the second number.

Software Development Systems and Assemblers

A **software development system** is a computer that enables the user to develop programs (**software**) with the assistance of other programs. The development process includes writing, modifying, testing, and debugging of the user programs. In the previous chapter, we discussed how to write a simple assembly language program and translate its mnemonics into Hex code manually. In this chapter, we will develop assembly language programs with the help of four other programs: Editor, Assembler, Linker, and Debugger. These programs enable the user to write programs in mnemonics, translate mnemonics into Hex and binary code, and debug the code. All the activities of the computer—hardware and software—are directed by another program, called the **operating system.**

This chapter describes an IBM PC (Personal Computer)-based software development system, its hardware, and related programs. It also describes its operating systems MS-DOS (Microsoft-Disk Operating System) and illustrates the use of the assembler to write assembly language programs.

OBJECTIVES

□ Describe the components of a software development system.
□ List various types of floppy disks, and explain how information is accessed from the disk.
□ Define the operating system of a microcomputer, and explain its function.
□ Explain the functions of these programs:

Editor, Assembler, Cross-assembler Linker (Loader), and Debugger.
□ List the advantages of the assembler over manual assembly.
□ List the assembler directives, and explain their functions.
□ Write assembly language programs with appropriate directives.

7.1 MICROPROCESSOR-BASED SOFTWARE DEVELOPMENT SYSTEMS

A software development system is simply a computer that enables the user to write, modify, debug, and test programs. In a microprocessor-based development system, a microcomputer is used to develop software for a particular microprocessor. Generally, the microcomputer has a large R/W memory (640K bytes or higher), disk storage, and a video terminal with a typewriter-like keyboard. The keyboard enables the user to write programs in alphanumeric (alphabet and number) characters, which are translated into American Standard Code for Information Interchange (ASCII) binary code; the keyboard (or the terminal) is known as ASCII keyboard (or terminal). The system includes programs that enable the user to develop software in either assembly language or high-level languages. This text will focus on developing programs in the **Z80 assembly language.**

Conceptually, this type of microcomputer is similar to a single-board microcomputer except that it has additional features that can assist in developing large programs. Programs are accessed and stored under a file name (title), and they are written by using such other programs as text editors and translated into binary code by using assemblers. The system (I/Os, files, programs, etc.) is managed by a program called the **operating system.** The various hardware and software features of a typical software development system are described in the next sections.

7.1.1 System Hardware and Storage Memory

Figure 7.1 shows a typical software development system; it includes an ASCII keyboard, a CRT terminal, an MPU board with R/W memory (around 640K) and disk controllers, and two disk drives. The disk controller is an interfacing circuit through which the MPU can access a disk and provide Read/Write control signals. The disk drives have Read/Write elements that are responsible for reading and writing data on the disk. Two types of floppy disks are in use: 5¼-inch and 3½-inch. A 5¼-inch single-density disk can store about 90K bytes of data; the storage capacity can be doubled by using double-density disks, and quadrupled (to 360K) by using both sides of the disks. A high-density 5¼-inch disk can store 1.2M bytes. A 3½-inch double-sided double-density disk stores 740K bytes, and high-

FIGURE 7.1
A Typical Software Development
System: AT&T PC 6300 Plus
SOURCE: Photograph Courtesy of AT&T.

density stores 1.44M bytes. In addition, most systems nowadays have a permanently installed hard disk with memory capacity of 10M to 120M bytes.

FLOPPY DISK

A **floppy disk**—Figure 7.2(a)—is made of a thin magnetic material (iron oxide) that can store logic 0s and 1s in the form of magnetic directions. The surface of the disk is divided into a number of concentric tracks, each track divided into sectors, as shown in Figure 7.2(b). The large hole in the center of the disk is locked by the disk drive when it spins the disk. The small hole shown in Figure 7.2(a) is known as the indexing hole. The disk drive uses this hole as a reference to count the sectors. The oblong cutout, called the head slot, is the reading/recording segment; this is the only segment of the surface that comes in contact with the R/W head. At the edge of the disk, near the head slot, is a notch called the Write Protect notch. If this notch is covered, data cannot be written on the disk; the disk is then "Write Protected." Figure 7.2(c) shows a typical 3½-inch disk.

Each sector and track is assigned a binary address by using a program (FORMAT); this is called formatting a disk. The MPU can access any information on the disk with the sector and the track addresses; however, the access is semi-

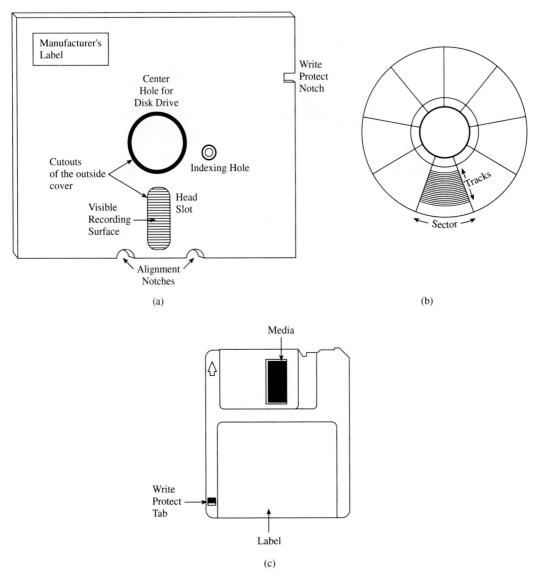

FIGURE 7.2
(a) A Typical 5¼-Inch Floppy Disk and (b) Its Sectors and Tracks; (c) A Typical
3½-Inch Disk.

random. To go from one track to another, the access is random. Once the track is found, the system waits for the index hole and then locates the sector serially by counting the sectors. Once data bytes are located, they are transferred to the system's R/W memory. These data transfer functions between a floppy disk and the system are performed by the **disk controller** and controlled by the **operating system,** also known as the Disk Operating System (DOS), described in Section 7.12.

HARD DISK

Another type of storage memory used with computers is called a **hard disk** or **Winchester disk.** The hard disk is similar to the floppy disk except that the magnetic material is coated on a rigid aluminum base and enclosed in a sealed container. While it is highly precise and reliable, the hard disk requires sophisticated controller circuitry. However, its storage capacity is quite large. Hard disks are available in various sizes; 3½-inch, 5¼-inch, and 14-inch. Storage capacity can range from several megabytes to several gigabytes.

OPERATING SYSTEMS 7.2

The **operating system** of a computer is a group of programs that manages or oversees all the operations of the computer. The computer transfers information constantly among peripherals such as a floppy disk, printer, keyboard, and video monitor. It also stores user programs under file names on a disk. (A **file** is defined as related records stored as a single entity.) The operating system is responsible primarily for managing the files on the disk and the communication between the computer and its peripherals. The functional relationship between the operating system and the computer's various subsystems is shown in Figure 7.3.

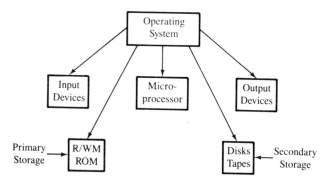

FIGURE 7.3

Operating System and Its Functional Relationship with Various Components of a Computer System

Each computer has its own operating system. Nowadays, the most widely used operating system for IBM PC-compatible microcomputers is MS-DOS. In the 1970s and early 1980s when most microcomputers were designed to use 8-bit microprocessors, the CP/M (Control Program/Monitor) operating system was commonly used. The MS-DOS and CP/M are in many ways similar to each other, except that the MS-DOS is designed to handle 16-bit (or 32-bit) microprocessors and 1M byte memory, and the CP/M was designed for 8-bit microprocessors and 64K byte memory.

7.2.1 MS-DOS Operating System

In 16-bit microcomputers, such as IBM PC, XT, AT, and PS/2, the MS-DOS (Microsoft Disk Operating System) is so widely used that it has become the industry standard. Initially, when it was installed on IBM PC, it was known as PC-DOS; the terms MS-DOS and PC-DOS are interchangeable. The MS-DOS is designed to handle 16-bit data word and large-size one-megabyte system memory and disks with high memory capacity such as 720K and 1.44M. Similarly, it can support a hard disk and includes a hierarchical file directory. The latest version of MS-DOS is geared toward handling communication between multiuser systems.

The MS-DOS operating system is divided into four components: Boot Record, IO.SYS, MSDOS.SYS, and COMMAND.COM. In the PC-DOS, these components are identified as ROM-BIOS, IBMBIO, IBMDOS, and COMMAND.COM, respectively. In a typical 1M (1,024K) system, the memory space is divided into 16 blocks from 0 to F, each being 64K byte memory; the Hex address ranges from 00000 to FFFFFH. Generally, the lowest addresses in 0 block are reserved for system software, the highest block F is used for IO.SYS, and approximately ten blocks (640K) are reserved as the user memory. The remaining blocks are used for such various purposes as video display and BIOS extensions. See Figure 7.4(a).

BOOT RECORD AND ROM-BIOS

The boot record works in conjunction with the set of instructions stored permanently in ROM. The boot record is a program that loads the MS-DOS into the system memory, and ROM includes the program to initialize the hardware. The boot record is stored on track 0 and sector 1 of a formatted disk. When the system is turned on or reset, the program in ROM initializes the hardware parameters and reads the first sector of track 0. Then the boot record loads IO.SYS and MSDOS.SYS into beginning locations of the system memory and passes the control to IO.SYS.

IO.SYS (IBMBIO.COM)

The primary function of this program is to communicate with I/O devices when it receives commands from a user's program; it works in conjunction with a set of instructions in ROM. The program defines peripheral port addresses and enables additions of new peripherals; thus, it is device-dependent and -modified by hard-

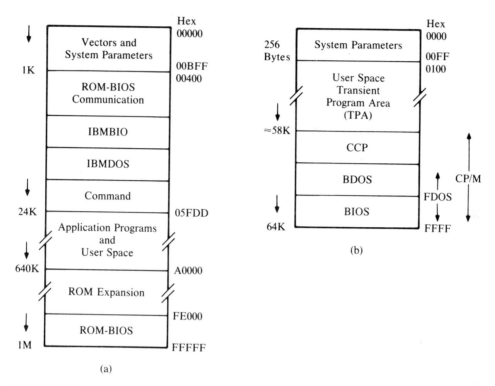

FIGURE 7.4
Memory Maps: (a) MS-DOS with 1M Memory; (b) CP/M with 64K Memory

ware manufacturers. The IO.SYS passes the control to MS-DOS after initializing the peripheral.

MS-DOS (IBMDOS)

This program directs the activities of the disk controller and also contains DOS service routines; these service routines include such programs as DIR (Directory), FORMAT (Formatting Disk), and COPY (Copying files). The program generates the tables in memory that are used by the COMMAND.COM program.

COMMAND.COM

This program reads and interprets the commands from the keyboard and differentiates between the DOS services (such as COPY) and the utility programs (such as DEBUG). This is an interface between the user and the MS-DOS.

Once the COMMAND.COM is executed, the booting process is completed, and the MS-DOS is ready to accept commands from the user. Figure 7.4(a) shows where the MS-DOS resides in the system memory and the memory space available for the user's programs. The user writes programs in a transient portion of the memory, and when the Save command is given, the MS-DOS takes control of the system, determines where to save the program on the disk under a file name, and regains control of the system.

7.2.2 CP/M Operating System

The CP/M operating system is designed to handle 8-bit data words and 64K bytes system memory. It is divided into three components: BIOS (Basic Input/Output System), BDOS (Basic Disk Operating System), and CCP (Console Command Processor).

When CP/M is loaded into a system's R/W memory, it occupies approximately 6K of memory at the highest available locations, as shown in Figure 7.4(b). In addition, the first 256 locations (from 0000 to 00FFH) are reserved for system parameters. The rest of the R/W memory (approximately 58K) is available for the user. Once the operating system is loaded into R/W memory, the user can write, assemble, test, and debug programs by using **utility programs** (described in the next section).

7.2.3 Tools for Developing Assembly Language Programs

In addition to the operating system of a computer, various programs called utility programs are necessary to develop assembly language programs. These programs can be classified in two categories: (1) file-management utilities and (2) program-development utilities. The file-management utilities are programs that enable the user to perform such functions as copying, printing, erasing, and renaming files. In MS-DOS, some programs such as COPY (Copy), DEL (Delete), and DIR (Directory) are part of the internal commands, meaning these programs are loaded into system memory along with the operating system. Other programs, such as PRINT (Print), FORMAT (Formatting Disk), and MODE (to set up printer options) are part of the external commands, meaning these programs are stored on the disk under file names and copied into system memory whenever they are needed. The program development utilities enable the user to write, assemble, and test assembly language programs; they include programs such as Editor, Assembler, Linker (or Loader), Debugger, and cross-assemblers. The descriptions of various programs and the assembly process described below may vary in details depending upon an operating system, its utility programs, and an assembler being used.

EDITOR

The Editor is a program that allows the user to enter, modify, and store a group of instructions or text under a file name. The Editor programs can be classified in two groups: line editors and full-screen editors. Line editors, such as EDLIN (Edit Line) in MS-DOS, work with and manage one line at a time. On the other hand, full-screen editors (also known as word processors), such as PC-Write, Word Star, and Word Perfect, manage the full screen or a paragraph at a time. To write text, the user must call the Editor under the control of the operating system. As soon as the Editor program is transferred from the disk to the system memory, the program control is transferred from the operating system to the Editor program. The Editor has its own commands, and the user can enter and modify text by using those commands. At the completion of writing a program, the exit command of the Editor program will save the program on the disk under the file name and will transfer the program control back to the operating system. This file is known as a source file or a source program. If the source file is intended to be a program in the Z80 assembly language, the user should follow the syntax of the assembly language and the rules of the assembler that are described next.

The Editor program is not concerned with whether one is writing a letter or an assembly language program. The full-screen editors are convenient to write either line- or paragraph-oriented text; they automatically adjust lines as words are typed, and the text can be modified or erased with ease.

ASSEMBLER

The Assembler is a program that translates source code or mnemonics into the binary code, called object code, of the microprocessor and generates a file called the Object file. This function is similar to manual assembly, whereby the user looks up the code for each mnemonic in the listing. In addition to translating mnemonics, the Assembler performs various functions, such as error checking and memory allocations. The Assembler is described in more detail in Section 7.3.

LINKER

The Linker (or Loader) is a program that takes the object file generated by the Assembler program and generates a file in binary code called the COM file or the EXE file. The COM (or EXE) file is the only executable file—i.e., the only file that can be executed by the microcomputer. To execute the program, the COM file is called under the control of the operating system and executed. In different assemblers or cross-assemblers, the COM file may be labelled by other names such as TSK file.

DEBUGGER

The Debugger is a program that allows the user to test and debug the object file. The user can employ this program to perform the following functions:

□ Make changes in the object code.
□ Examine and modify the contents of memory.
□ Set breakpoints, execute a segment of the program, and display register contents after the execution.
□ Trace the execution of the specified segment of the program, and display the register and memory contents after the execution of each instruction.
□ Disassemble a section of the program, i.e., convert the object code into the source code or mnemonics.

MS-DOS AND CROSS-ASSEMBLERS

The MS-DOS is an operating system designed primarily for 16-bit microprocessors. This raises a question: Why are we discussing the operating system meant for 16-bit processors in the context of 8-bit microprocessors such as the Z80? The answer lies with the widespread use of IBM PCs or their compatibles on college campuses. However, the microprocessor used in the IBM PC (Intel 8088 type family) has different mnemonics than that of the Z80; thus, we need a program that can translate the Z80 mnemonics but operate under the 16-bit microprocessor. Such a program is called a cross-assembler. The assembly process using a cross-assembler (described in Section 7.4) is similar to that of an assembler under a Z80 system. After assembling a program, the Hex file (discussed later) can be directly transferred to the R/W memory of a Z80 single-board microcomputer by using a download program. Thus, programs and/or hardware-related laboratory experiments can be easily performed.

7.3   ASSEMBLERS

The assembler (or the cross-assembler), as defined before, is a program that translates assembly language mnemonics or source code into binary executable code. Here, we are using the term **assembler** to include all the utility programs (such as Assembler and Linker) necessary for the assembly process. This translation process requires that the source program be written strictly according to the specified syntax of the assembler. The assembly language source program includes three types of statements:

1. The *program statements* in Z80 mnemonics, which are to be translated into binary code.
2. *Comments,* which are reproduced as a part of the program documentation.
3. *Directives* to the assembler that specify such items as starting memory locations, label definitions, and required memory spaces for data.

The first two types of statements have been used in the program of adding two Hex numbers in the last chapter. The format of these statements as they appear in an assembly language source program is identical to the format used here. The third type—directives—and their functions will be described in Section 7.3.2.

7.3.1   Assembly Language Format

A typical assembly language programming statement is divided into four parts, called **fields:** *label, operation code* (opcode), *operand,* and *comments.* These fields are separated by **delimiters** as shown in Table 7.1.

The **assembler statements** have a free-field format, which means that any number of blanks can be left between fields. Comments are optional but are generally included for good documentation. A label for an instruction is also optional,

TABLE 7.1
Delimiters Used in Assembler
Statements

Delimiter	Placement
Colon	After label (optional in some assemblers)
Space	Between an opcode and an operand
Comma	Between two operands*
Semicolon	Before the beginning of a comment

*Some assemblers may not tolerate space between comma and the operand.

but its use greatly facilitates specifying jump locations. As an example, a typical assembly language statement is written as follows:

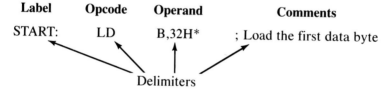

Label	Opcode	Operand	Comments
START:	LD	B,32H*	; Load the first data byte

Delimiters

Delimiters include the colon following START, the space following LD, the comma following B, and the semicolon preceding the comment.

7.3.2 Assembler Directives

The **assembler directives** are the instructions to the assembler concerning the program being assembled; they are also called *pseudo operations* or *pseudo-ops*. These instructions are neither translated into machine code nor assigned any memory locations in the object file. Some of the important assembler directives for the Z80 assembler are listed and described here.

Assembler Directives	Example	Description
1. ORG (Origin)	ORG 0100H	The next block of instructions should be stored in memory locations starting from 0100_H.

---

*Some assemblers do not tolerate a space between the comma and the second operand, 32H.

Assembler Directives	Example	Description
2. END	END	End of assembly. The HALT instruction suggests the end of a program, but that does not necessarily mean the end of assembly.
3. EQU (Equate)	PORT1 EQU 01H	The value of the term PORT1 is equal to 01_H. Generally, this means the PORT1 has the port address 01_H.
	INBUF EQU 1899H	The value of the term INBUF is 1899_H. This may be the memory location used as input buffer.
	OUTBUF EQU INBUF + 4	The equate can be expressed by using the label of another equate. This example defines the OUTBUF memory location in terms of INBUF.
4. DB or DEFB (Define Byte)	DATA: DEFB A2H, 9FH	Initializes an area byte by byte, in some assemblers either symbol (DB or DEFB) can be used. Assembled bytes of data are stored in successive memory locations until all values are stored. This is a convenient way of writing a data string. The label is optional.
5. DW or DEFW (Define Word)	DEFW 2050H	Initializes an area of two bytes at a time. In some assemblers either symbol (DW or DEFW) can be used. This statement reserves two locations for 2050_H.

Assembler Directives	Example	Description
6. DS or DEFS (Define Storage)	OUTBUF: DEFS 4	Reserves a specified number of memory locations. In this example, four memory locations are reserved for OUTBUF.
7. Constant Suffix D, B, Q, H	32H 0A5H 97	Numerical values can be expressed in decimal (D), binary (B), octal (Q), or Hex (H). Hexadecimal digits from A to F must be preceded by 0 as shown by 0A5H, and any number without a suffix is considered decimal.

7.3.3 Advantages of the Assembler

The assembler is a tool for developing programs with the assistance of the computer. Assemblers are absolutely essential for writing industry-standard software; manual assembly is quite time-consuming for programs larger than 50 instructions. The assembler performs many functions in addition to translating mnemonics, and it has several advantages over manual assembly. The salient features of the assembler are as follows:

1. The assembler translates mnemonics into binary code with speed and accuracy, thus eliminating human errors in looking up the codes.
2. The assembler assigns appropriate values to the symbols used in a program. This facilitates specifying jump locations.
3. It is easy to insert or delete instructions in a program; the assembler can quickly reassemble the entire program with new memory locations and modified addresses for jump locations. This avoids rewriting the program manually.
4. The assembler checks syntax errors, such as wrong labels and expressions, and provides error messages. However, it cannot check logic errors in a program.
5. The assembler can reserve memory locations for data or results.
6. The assembler can provide files for documentation.
7. A Debugger program can be used in conjunction with the assembler to test and debug an assembly language program.

CAUTION

A correctly assembled program with zero errors does not mean it is a working program. The assembler cannot check the logic of the program; it checks only the syntax of the program.

7.4   WRITING PROGRAMS USING A CROSS-ASSEMBLER

This section describes a commercially available Z80 cross-assembler and the process of assembling a program. The description in the following sections is equally applicable to both assemblers and cross-assemblers; therefore, the term *assembler* should be interpreted as the representation of both. The assembly process is illustrated with a simple example from the last chapter.

7.4.1   Z80 Cross-Assembler

The Z80 cross-assembler from 2500AD Software, Inc.* is one among several of such commercially available products. It includes two programs: X80 and LINK. In this assembler, translating mnemonics into binary code is a two-step process. The X80 translates the source file into modules of the Z80 code and generates two files: one is called the list (LST) file, and the other is called the object (OBJ) file. (This assembly process and the file names may vary slightly from assembler to assembler.) In addition to translating mnemonics, the assembler performs various functions, such as error checking and memory allocations.

The list (LST) file includes the source file plus the memory addresses and the Hex code of each instruction. This file is primarily used for documentation and may look like the hand-assembled file shown in the last chapter under program documentation or writing format.

The object file is an intermediate file that is used by the Link program to generate an executable binary COM (or TSK) file. The object file is necessary to combine different modules (or programs) and relocate the modules from one block of memory to another block of memory. In addition, the object file is used to generate the Hex file that can be used to transfer the program from the IBM PC to a Z80 single-board computer. This transfer of files among different systems is called downloading and uploading of files. This program assembly process is described in more detail in section 7.4.2 with an illustrative program. In addition, some editors also generate a back (BAK) file. When the user calls the source file for reediting, the editor copies the source file as the BAK file before the user begins to reedit, in case the user elects to retrieve the original file.

The complete assembly process on a software system such as the IBM PC can be summarized in the following steps:

1. Call up an editor program such as PC-Write or Wordstar, and write an assembly language program (statements) using an editor. Save the program. This is called the source program.
2. Call an assembler such as X80, use the source program as the input to the X80, and generate the object (OBJ) file and the list (LST) file.
3. If the assembler finds errors in the program, go back to Step 1 and correct the errors in the source program. Then repeat Step 2.

---

*Address: 17200 E. Ohio Dr., Aurora, CO 80017.

4. If the file needs to be transferred directly to a single-board computer, call the Link program (LINK2) to generate the HEX file. This file is used to download the program from the IBM PC to the single-board computer if the download facility is available in the system. Otherwise, the Hex code can be loaded manually using the Hex keyboard into R/W memory of the single-board computer.

5. A binary executable file called COM or TSK file can be generated from the object file by using another Link program (LINK1). Generally, this step is unnecessary because the Z80 binary code cannot be executed by a system such as IBM PC.

Upon completion of the assembly process, the user can have the following files:

☐ **Source file.** This is the file written by the user using an editor. Generally, a file name can be eight characters long with an extension of three characters. The file name and the extension are separated by a period. For example, the file name can be DELAY1.ASM; the extension ASM suggests that it is an assembly language file.

☐ **OBJ file.** This is a binary file generated by the assembler (X80) without any specific reference to the user memory. This file is used to generate an executable binary file called TSK (or COM) file and relocate the entire program for storage to specified memory locations.

☐ **LST file.** This is the list file generated by the assembler program (X80) for documentation purposes. It contains memory locations, Hex code, mnemonics, and comments. This file looks like a manually assembled program, as shown in Section 6.3.2.

☐ **HEX file.** This is generated by the Linker (LINK2) program and contains program code in hexadecimal notations. This file can be used for debugging the program and transferring files from one system to another system.

☐ **TSK file.** This is the executable file generated by the Linker (LINK1) program, and it contains binary code; this is the only file that can be understood and executed by the microprocessor.

☐ **BAK file.** When the source file is called for reediting, the previous file is saved as the BAK file.

7.4.2 Illustrative Program: Addition of Two Hexadecimal Numbers

To illustrate how to write a source program, the example is taken from the last chapter, where it was assembled manually. The source program is written using an editor under the file name PROGRAM1.ASM and assembled using the assembler X80 described earlier. The problem statement is repeated here for convenience; refer to section 6.3.1 for analysis.

PROBLEM STATEMENT

Write instructions to load the two hexadecimal numbers 32_H and $A2_H$ into registers B and C, respectively. Add the numbers, and display the sum at the LED output port PORT1.

SOURCE PROGRAM

;This program adds two Hex bytes and displays the sum.

```
        ORG    1800H         ; BEGIN ASSEMBLY AT 1800H
PORT1   EQU    01H           ; OUTPUT PORT ADDRESS
START:  LD     B,32H         ; LOAD FIRST BYTE
        LD     C,0A2H*       ; LOAD SECOND BYTE TO BE ADDED
        LD     A,C           ; COPY ONE OF THE BYTES INTO A
        ADD    A,B           ; ADD TWO BYTES
        OUT    (PORT1),A     ; DISPLAY THE RESULT
        HALT                 ; END
        END
```

This program illustrates the following assembler directives:

□ ORG

The object code will be stored starting at the location 1800_H.

□ EQU

The program defines one equate: PORT1. In this program it would have been easier to write the port address directly with the instructions. However, equates are essential in development projects where hardware and software design are done concurrently, and they are also useful in long programs because they make it easy to change or redefine port addresses.

□ Label

The program illustrates one label: START. This label represents the memory location 1800_H. In this illustration, the label is not particularly useful; generally, labels are used to specify Jump and Call addresses. In writing assembly language programs, it is convenient to identify a Jump or Call address by a label because absolute addresses are not known in the beginning. Also, if any changes (deletions and additions) are made in the source program, the assembler will reassign all label addresses when it is reassembled. In manual assembly, the entire program must be rewritten with new addresses if any changes are to be made.

□ End

The end of assembly.

TWO-PASS ASSEMBLER

To assemble the program, the assembler scans through the program twice; this is known as a **two-pass assembler.** In the first pass, the first memory location is determined from the ORG statement, and the counter known as the location counter is initialized. Then the assembler scans each instruction and records locations in the address column of the first byte of each instruction; the location

---

*Any Hex number that begins with A through F must be preceded by zero.

counter keeps track of the bytes in the program. The assembler also generates a symbol table during the first pass. When it comes across a label, it records the label and its location. In the second pass, each instruction is examined, and mnemonics and labels are replaced by their machine codes.

ASSEMBLED LIST FILE

A list (LST) file generated from the source program (PROGRAM1.ASM) by the X80 assembler is shown here.

```
           2500 A.D. Z80 CROSS ASSEMBLER - VERSION 3.01C

      INPUT   FILENAME  :  PROGRAM1.ASM
      OUTPUT  FILENAME  :  PROGRAM1.OBJ

  1   ; THIS PROGRAM ADDS TWO HEX BYTES AND DISPLAYS THE SUM.
  2
  3
  4   1800                        ORG 1800H      ; BEGIN ASSEMBLY AT 1800H
  5
  6          01 00     PORT1   EQU 01H       ; OUTPUT PORT ADDRESS
  7
  8   1800   06 32     START:  LD B ,32H     ; LOAD FIRST BYTE
  9   1802
 10   1802   0E A2             LD C ,0A2H    ; LOAD SECOND BYTE TO BE
                                             ; ADDED
 11   1804
 12   1804   79                LD A ,C       ; COPY ONE OF THE BYTES
                                             ; INTO A
 13   1805
 14   1805   80                ADD A ,B      ; ADD TWO BYTES
 15
 16   1806   D3 01             OUT (PORT1) ,A ; DISPLAY THE RESULT
 17   1808
 18   1808   76                HALT          ; END
 19
 20   1809                     END

                   SYMBOLIC REFERENCE TABLE

PORT1 = 0001  START 1800
         LINES ASSEMBLED: 20   ASSEMBLY ERRORS: 0
```

The LST file has five columns: memory addresses, Hex codes, labels, mnemonics, and comments. It lists the memory addresses of the first byte of each instruction with its Hex codes on the same line. For example, the listing shows that the first memory address is 1800 and the first two Hex codes are 06 32; the next address is 1802. Therefore, it is understood that the memory address 1801 and holds the Hex byte 32. In addition to the program listing, the LST file includes the list of symbols, equates, and error messages.

Error Messages   In addition to translating the mnemonics into object code, the assembler also gives error messages. These messages are of two types: *terminal error messages* and *source program error messages*. In the first case, the assembler is not able to complete the assembly. In the second case, the assembler lists the errors, but it is able to complete the assembly.

GENERATING COM (TSK) AND HEX FILES

This assembler has two Linker programs: LINK1 and LINK2; these programs use the OBJ file generated by the X80 program. The LINK1 generates the executable binary (TSK) file, and the LINK2 creates the HEX file that can be used to transfer the file from the IBM PC system to a single-board computer.

Precautions in Writing Programs   Assembler programs are available from various software companies, and for the most part, they follow a similar format. However, we suggest the following precautions in writing assembly language programs.

1. Some assemblers impose a rigid format in which the source code must be written. For example, X80 must have a label starting in column 1. Similarly, it generates an error code if there is a space between operands. For example, in the first instruction (LD B,32H), if there is a space between B and the comma, or between the comma and 32H, the X80 will generate an error message.
2. The letter following a number specifies the type of a number. A hexadecimal number is followed by the letter "H," an octal by letter "O," a binary by letter "B." A number without a letter is interpreted as a decimal number.
3. Any Hex number that begins with A through F must be preceded by zero; otherwise, the assembler interprets the number as a label and gives an error message because it cannot find the label.
4. Some assemblers require a colon after a label.
5. When a 16-bit address is used in a mnemonic (such as Jump to 1850H), the X80 prints the address as 1850; however, it is stored in the reverse order in memory. Some assemblers print the address as 50 18.

USING AN INTEGRATED EDITOR-ASSEMBLER PROGRAM

An integrated editor-assembler software development package is available from CAMI Research* to assemble Z80 programs. One of the drawbacks of the assembly process described earlier is the need to go back and forth between the editor and the assembler until all the errors are corrected. This integrated software pack-

---

*CAMI Research, Inc., 75 Westmoreland Ave., Arlington, MA 02174.

age is menu driven, and the programs (editor, assembler, and linker) are integrated in one package. The program can identify errors and enable the user to edit them.

SUMMARY

A software development system and an assembler are essential tools for writing, assembling, testing, and debugging large assembly language programs.

A disk-based microcomputer, its operating system, and assembler programs can serve as a development system. All the operations of the computer are managed and directed by the operating system of the computer. The Assembler and other utility programs assist the user in developing software. The Editor allows the user to enter text, and the Assembler translates mnemonics into machine code and provides error messages. The Debugger assists in debugging the program. The cross-assembler is an assembler program that operates under one type of MPU and can translate mnemonics of another MPU.

The program thus assembled is in many ways similar to that of the hand assembly program except that the program written for the assembler includes assembler directives, which are instructions concerning how to assemble the program. The assembler has many advantages over manual assembly; without the assembler, it would be extremely difficult to develop industry-standard software.

ASSIGNMENTS

Check the appropriate answer in **1–10.**

1. The process of accessing information on a floppy disk is
   a. random.
   b. serial.
   c. semirandom.
2. The operating system of a computer is defined as
   a. hardware that operates the floppy disk.
   b. a program that manages files on the disk.
   c. a group of programs that manages and directs hardware and software in the system.
3. The Editor is
   a. an assembly language program that reads and writes information on the disk.
   b. a high-level language program that allows the user to edit programs.

     c. a program that allows the user to write, modify, and store text in the computer system.

4. The Assembler is

     a. a compiler that translates statements from high-level language into assembly language.

     b. a program that translates mnemonics into binary code.

     c. an operating system that manages all the programs in the system.

5. A file is

     a. a group of related records stored as a single entity.

     b. a program that transfers information between the system and the floppy disk.

     c. a program that stores data.

6. The COM (TSK) file

     a. consists of Hex digits and is used for communication.

     b. is the only file that can be interpreted and executed by the microprocessor.

     c. consists of Z80 mnemonics.

7. The Hex file generated by the Assembler is used primarily

     a. to reduce the memory requirement for storing files.

     b. to transfer a file from one system to another.

     c. to transfer a file between a floppy disk and the system's R/W memory.

8. The assembler directive DB (or DEFB)

     a. reserves a specified number of memory locations.

     b. stores data bytes written after the directive in successive memory locations.

     c. defines bytes as decimal, Hex, or Octal.

9. A disk controller is

     a. a program that manages the files on the disk.

     b. a circuit that interfaces the disk with the microcomputer system.

     c. a mechanism that controls the spinning of the disk.

10. The MS-DOS is

     a. an operating system that is designed primarily to handle the communication between the 16-bit microprocessor and its peripherals.

     b. a master disk that stores all system programs.

     c. an application program that handles communication between various systems.

11. Assemble the following program with the starting address 1820_H, and print the LST file. The address of the output port OUTPRT is 07_H.

START:	LD B,32H	;Load B with first data byte
	LD C,0A2H	;Load C with second data byte
	LD A,C	;Copy (C) into A for addition

```
            ADD A,B                 ;Add two bytes

            JP NC, DSPLAY           ;If sum < FFH, display sum at PORT7

            LD A,01H                ;If sum > FFH, load 01 to display
                                    ; as overload

DSPLAY:     OUT (OUTPRT),A          ;Display result at PORT7

            HALT

            END
```

Introduction to Z80 Instructions and Programming Techniques

When a microcomputer is asked to execute a program stored in its memory, it reads one instruction at a time and performs the task specified by the instruction. Each instruction in the program is a command, in binary, to the microprocessor to perform an operation. In Chapter 6, we examined briefly the Z80 instruction set and its capability. In this chapter, we will introduce a few selected instructions and illustrate them with examples. These instructions are selected from three groups: data copy, arithmetic, and branch operations.

A computer is at its best, relative to human capability, when it is asked to repeat such simple tasks as adding or copying. The programming techniques—such as **looping, indexing,** and **counting**—necessary to perform such tasks are introduced and illustrated with two programs. This chapter also includes a brief discussion of debugging programs.

Finally, a group of special Z80 instructions that perform multiple tasks are introduced with illustrative examples.

OBJECTIVES

□ Explain the functions of data copy instructions and how the contents of the source register and the destination registers are affected.

□ List four types of data copy operations and explain the term *addressing mode*.

□ Explain how a memory address is specified to copy data from and to a memory register.

□ Explain how data are transferred from and to I/O devices.

□ Explain the functions of arithmetic instructions (ADD, SUB, INC, DEC) and how flags are affected by these instructions.

□ Write a set of commands using data copy and arithmetic instructions to perform a given task.

□ Explain the functions of unconditional and conditional jump instructions and how they are used for decision making.

□ Draw a flowchart of a conditional loop to illustrate the indexing and counting techniques.

□ List the seven blocks of a generalized flowchart illustrating data acquisitions and data processing.

□ Write a program to copy data from one block of memory to another block including the case of overlapping blocks.

□ Write a program to perform arithmetic operations on given data stored in memory.

□ List the types of errors that frequently occur in writing assembly language programs and in hand assembling the code. Recognize the errors in a given program.

□ List Z80 special instructions and explain how they provide more flexibility and improve efficiency in writing Z80 programs.

□ Modify the previously written programs using the Z80 special instructions.

8.1 DATA COPY (LOAD) OPERATIONS

In this section, we focus on three types of **data copy operations:** data copy related to microprocessor registers, memory, and I/Os. Instructions frequently used are illustrated below, and the Z80 block transfer instruction will be discussed later in the chapter. In addition, one machine control instruction—HALT—is introduced; this instruction is necessary to indicate the end of a program.

8.1.1 Data Copy (Load) Among Registers

In this group, we have three types of instructions: data copy from one register to another, loading 8-bit data into a register, and loading 16-bit data into a register pair.[*]

Opcode	Operand	Bytes	Addressing Modes	Description
LD	r_d, r_s[†]	1	Register	Copy data from source register r_s to destina-

---

[*]Appendix A includes complete descriptions of these instructions in alphabetical order with illustrative examples.

[†]r_d, r_s, and r can be any one of the registers such as A, B, C, D, E, H, or L (including I and R) but not the alternate registers.

Opcode	Operand	Bytes	Addressing Modes	Description
	Example:	LD B,C		tion register r_d. In this mode, operand is a part of the opcode.
LD	$r^\dagger$, 8-bit	2	Immediate	Load 8-bit data of the second byte into the
	Example:	LD B,32H		specified register. In this mode, the second byte is the operand.
LD	rp, 16-bit	3	Immediate Extended	Load 16 bits into the specified register
	Example	LD HL,1850H		pair. In this mode, two bytes following the opcode are the operands.
LD	rx, 16-bit	4	Immediate Extended	Load 16 bits into the specified index
	Example	LD IX,2050H		register.
HALT		1		This is a machine control instruction. The processor stops executing and enters into Wait state.

General Characteristics

1. Copy (Load) instructions do not affect flags.
2. The operands of copy instructions specify a destination register first, followed by a source register; they are separated by a comma.
3. The data byte is copied without modifying the contents of a source register.
4. A 16-bit operand is stored in two consecutive memory locations in the reversed order: the low-order byte first, followed by the high-order byte.
5. The instructions related to the index registers IX and IY have two-byte opcodes.
6. Data cannot be loaded directly into the flag register, program counter (PC), and alternate registers; the immediate addressing mode is not available for these registers.

Write instructions to load 97_H into the accumulator, 2050_H into HL registers, and 2075_H into the index register IX. Copy the contents of the accumulator into register C and the contents of register H into register B. Write the HALT instruction at the end of the sequence. Enter the machine codes of these instructions in R/W memory starting from 2000_H, and show the contents of each register after the execution.

Example 8.1

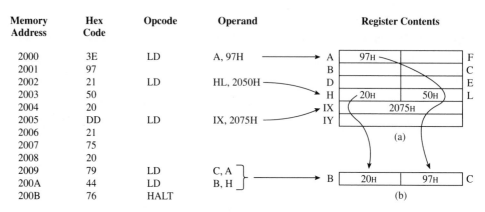

Memory Address	Hex Code	Opcode	Operand
2000	3E	LD	A, 97H
2001	97		
2002	21	LD	HL, 2050H
2003	50		
2004	20		
2005	DD	LD	IX, 2075H
2006	21		
2007	75		
2008	20		
2009	79	LD	C, A
200A	44	LD	B, H
200B	76	HALT	

FIGURE 8.1
Instructions and Register Contents

Solution

Description

1. The first instruction LD A, 97_H is a 2-byte instruction; the opcode $3E_H$ and the operand 97_H are stored in the first two memory locations. This instruction loads 97_H into the accumulator (Figure 8.1(a)).
2. The second instruction is a 3-byte instruction that loads 16-bit data (2050_H) into the HL registers (Figure 8.1(a)). The low-order byte (50_H) is stored first in memory location 2003_H, followed by the high-order byte (20_H).
3. The third instruction (IX, 2075H) is a 4-byte instruction; it has a 2-byte opcode (DD and 21). This instruction loads 16-bit data (2075_H) into the index register IX.
4. The remaining two instructions are 1-byte instructions; they copy data from one register to another as shown in Figure 8.1(b). It is important to note that the copy operations do not destroy the contents of the source registers. Figure 8.1 shows that registers A and H retain their contents after the copy operations.
5. The last instruction (HALT) is a machine control instruction; it forces the machine into the Wait state.

8.1.2   Data Copy Between Z80 Registers and Memory

To copy data from and into memory, the 16-bit address of a selected memory register must be specified, and this memory address can be specified by using indirect, direct, or other addressing modes. In the indirect addressing mode, the address of a memory location is loaded into the HL register, and the register (HL) with the parentheses is used as a memory pointer to copy data. Registers BC and DE can also be used in this manner, with some restrictions. In the direct addressing mode, the 16-bit address of a memory location is used as the operand of the copy instruction. Methods using index registers are discussed after the discussion of 2's complement arithmetic because the index registers include a displacement byte, which is expressed as a signed 2's complement number. In Z80 mnemonics, the memory address is enclosed in parentheses, as shown in the following list.

Opcode	Operand	Bytes	Addressing Modes	Description
LD	r, (HL)	1	Register Indirect	Copy contents of memory into register r. The memory address is specified indirectly by the number in the HL register; therefore, this is called register indirect addressing.
	Example: LD B, (HL)			
LD	(HL), r	1	Register Indirect	Copy contents of register r into memory, the address of which is in HL.
	Example: LD (HL), C			
LD	(HL), 8-bit	2	Register Indirect & Immediate	Copy 8-bit data into memory. This mode is a combination of indirect and immediate addressing.
	Example: LD (HL), 97H			

Note: In these three instructions, the memory address is specified by the contents of register HL, and register r can be any one of the general-purpose registers.

Opcode	Operand	Bytes	Addressing Modes	Description
LD	A, (rp)	1	Register Indirect	Copy contents of memory into accumulator.
LD	(rp), A	1	Register Indirect	Copy contents of accumulator into memory.
	Example: LD (BC), A			

Note: In the preceding two instructions, the memory address is shown by the contents of a register pair (BC or DE). However, these instructions can copy data from and into the accumulator only.

Opcode	Operand	Bytes	Addressing Modes	Description
LD	A, (16-bit)	3	Extended	Copy contents of memory into accumulator.
LD	(16-bit), A	3	Extended	Copy contents of accumulator into memory.
	Example: LD (2050H), A			

Note: In these instructions, the memory address is the 16-bit operand, and these instructions can copy data from and into the accumulator only.

General Characteristics

1. No flags are affected by these data copy operations.
2. Memory-related data copy operations can be recognized by the parentheses around the operand.
3. Register HL is a versatile memory pointer; a data byte can be copied from any

memory location to any general-purpose register and vice versa. In addition, HL can be used to load a byte directly into memory.

4. A 16-bit direct address and other register pairs (BC and DE) can be used as memory pointers to copy data from a memory location into the accumulator and vice versa. However, these memory pointers cannot be used to copy data between general-purpose registers and memory.

Example 8.2

The memory location 2050_H contains the data byte 37_H. Write instructions to copy the byte from the memory location into register B. Illustrate three different ways of transferring the byte from memory to the microprocessor, and list the associated machine codes.

Solution

1. The first method of copying a byte from memory into the microprocessor is by using the HL register as a memory pointer; this is an illustration of indirect addressing. First, we need to load the memory address into the HL register and then use the contents of HL as a memory pointer (Figure 8.2(a)).
2. The second method of copying a byte from memory into the microprocessor is by using BC or DE as a memory pointer; this is also the indirect addressing (Figure 8.2(b)). However, these registers (BC and DE) can be used as pointers to copy into A only. Therefore, one more instruction is necessary to copy from A into B.
3. The third technique is to use the direct extended addressing (Figure 8.2(c)) that copies a data byte from memory into A and then into B.

Example 8.3

The memory location 2040_H contains the data byte $F2_H$. Copy the data byte $F2_H$ from the memory location 2040_H into 2070_H using memory pointers. Then, clear the memory location 2040_H. Enter the machine codes of these instructions in memory locations starting from 2000_H. Describe how data copy operations are performed.

Solution

Memory Address	Hex Code	Opcode	Operand	Comments
2000	21	LD	HL, 2040H	; Set up HL as memory pointer
2001	40			for 2040H
2002	20			
2003	01	LD	BC, 2070H	; Set up BC as memory pointer
2004	70			for 2070H
2005	20			
2006	7E	LD	A, (HL)	; Copy data (F2H) into
				accumulator
2007	02	LD	(BC), A	; Copy data into memory (2070H)
2008	36	LD	(HL), 00	; Clear location 2040H
2009	00			
200A	76	HALT		

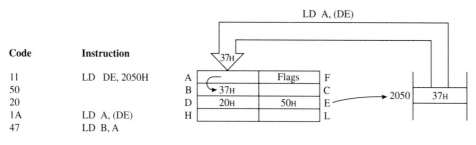

Code	Instruction
21	LD HL, 2050H
50	
20	
46	LD B, (HL)

FIGURE 8.2
(a) Indirect Addressing Using HL

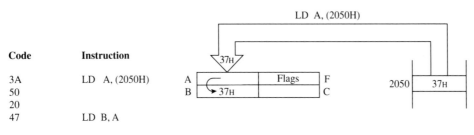

Code	Instruction
11	LD DE, 2050H
50	
20	
1A	LD A, (DE)
47	LD B, A

FIGURE 8.2
(b) Indirect Addressing Using BC

Code	Instruction
3A	LD A, (2050H)
50	
20	
47	LD B, A

FIGURE 8.2
(c) Extended Addressing

Description

1. The first two instructions load registers HL and BC with the numbers 2040_H and 2070_H, respectively. These are not memory-related data copy instructions because the operands lack parentheses.

2. The next two instructions copy the data byte ($F2_H$) stored in memory location 2040_H into the accumulator and from the accumulator into location 2070_H (see Figure 8.3).

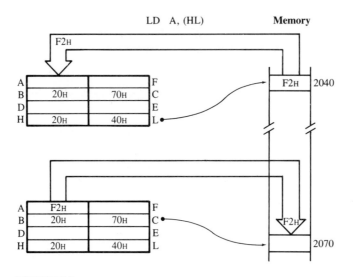

FIGURE 8.3
Data Copy between Microprocessor and Memory

3. The next instruction LD (HL), 00 is a 2-byte instruction; it clears the memory location 2040_H by loading 00 into the memory location pointed to by the HL register.

8.1.3   Data Copy Between Accumulator and I/Os

In the Z80 instruction set, input and output devices are identified by 8-bit addresses. The set includes several instructions that can read data from an input device (also known as input port) and write data into an output device (or output port). Two of these I/O instructions are described here:

Opcode	Operand	Bytes	Description
IN	A, (8-bit)	2	Read data from an input port into the accumulator.
OUT	(8-bit), A	2	Write data to an output port from the accumulator.

General Characteristics

1. These I/O instructions do not affect flags. (Some Z80 I/O instructions do affect flags; they are discussed later.)
2. The I/O instructions have 8-bit operands; thus, the Z80 is capable of addressing 256 input and 256 output ports with addresses from 00 to FF_H.
3. The 8-bit I/O addresses are enclosed in parentheses similar to those of memory addresses.

Read the switches connected to the input port 01_H (Figure 8.4). Display the reading at the LED output port 07_H and store it in memory location 2060_H.

Example
8.4

Instructions are as follows:

Solution

Opcode	Operand	Comments
IN	A, (01H)	; READ INPUT SWITCHES
OUT	(07H), A	; DISPLAY SWITCH READING AT OUTPUT PORT
LD	(2060H), A	; STORE SWITCH READING IN MEMORY
HALT		

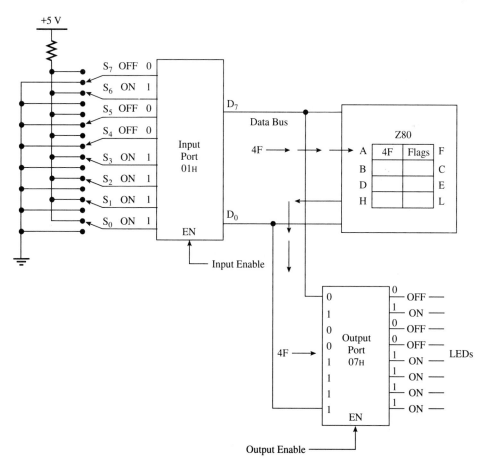

FIGURE 8.4
Reading Data at Input Port and Sending Data to Output Port

Description

1. Figure 8.4 shows that the switch positions of the input port 01_H provide the reading 0 1 0 0 1 1 1 1 ($4F_H$). The first instruction reads the switch positions and places the reading in the accumulator.
2. The OUT instruction sends the accumulator contents to the output port 07_H and displays the corresponding LEDs (Figure 8.4).
3. The last instruction stores the accumulator contents in memory location 2060_H.

8.2 ARITHMETIC OPERATIONS

The Z80 microprocessor performs various **arithmetic operations** such as *addition, subtraction, increment/decrement,* and *1's and 2's complement.* Most of these operations are concerned with 8-bit operands. The instruction set also includes some 16-bit operations that will be discussed in later chapters. (See Appendix A for a complete alphabetical listing of the Z80 instruction set and how flags are affected by the instructions.)

8.2.1 Addition and Subtraction

The addition and subtraction operations are performed in relation to contents of the accumulator. We focus here on three types of operands: register contents, 8-bit data, and memory contents.

Opcode	Operand	Bytes	Description
ADD	A, r	1	Add contents of register r to the contents of the accumulator, and store the result in the accumulator.
ADD	A, 8-bit	2	Add 8-bit data directly to the accumulator.
ADD	A, (HL)	1	Add memory contents to the accumulator.
SUB	r	1	Subtract contents of register r from the accumulator.
SUB	8-bit	2	Subtract 8-bit data from the accumulator.
SUB	(HL)	1	Subtract memory contents from the accumulator.

General Characteristics

These arithmetic instructions:

1. Assume that the accumulator is one of the operands.
2. Modify all the flags according to the result of the operation.
3. Place the result in the accumulator.
4. Do not affect the contents of the operand register or memory.

8.2.2 Increment/Decrement Instructions

The following instructions are special types of arithmetic instructions; they increment or decrement the contents of the operand by one. These instructions are generally used in counting and indexing.

Opcode	Operand	Bytes	Description
INC	r	1	Increment the contents of register r.
INC	(HL)	1	Increment the contents of memory.
INC	rp	1	Increment the contents of register pair rp (Register pairs are BC, DE, HL, and SP).
DEC	r	1	Decrement the contents of register r.
DEC	(HL)	1	Decrement the contents of memory.
DEC	rp	1	Decrement the contents of register pair rp.

General Characteristics

1. In these instructions, the operand can be any of the 8-bit registers r, memory, or register pairs rp. The result is stored back into the same operand register.
2. The instructions dealing with 8-bit registers affect all the flags except the Carry (CY) flag.
3. The instructions dealing with register pairs do not affect any flags. This is important to remember when a register pair is used as a 16-bit counter.

8.2.3 1's and 2's Complement Instructions

The Z80 instruction set includes the following instructions that perform complement operations with the contents of the accumulator. The addressing mode is implied; the accumulator is implied as the operand.

Opcode	Operand	Bytes	Description
CPL		1	Invert each bit of the accumulator. This can also be classified as the NOT function. No flags (except H and N) are affected.
NEG		2	Subtract the contents of the accumulator from 00; this is equivalent to 2's complement of the number in the accumulator. This instruction affects all the flags.

Load two unsigned numbers $F2_H$ and 68_H in registers B and C, respectively, and store $A2_H$ in memory location 2065_H, using the HL register as a memory pointer. Subtract 68_H from $F2_H$, complement the result, and add $A2_H$ from memory. Store the final answer in memory location 2066_H. Show register contents and the status of S (Sign), Z (Zero), and CY (Carry) flags as each instruction is being executed.

Example
8.5

Solution	Instructions		Register Contents					Flags		
	Mnemonics		*A*	*B*	*C*	*H*	*L*	*S*	*Z*	*CY*
	1. LD BC, F268H		X	F2	68	X	X	Not affected		
	2. LD HL, 2065H		X			20	65			
	3. LD (HL), A2H $\boxed{\text{A2}}$ 2065		X							
	4. LD A, B		F2							
	5. SUB C → (F2 − 68)		8A					1	0	0
	6. CPL → (Invert 8A)		75					NA	NA	NA
	7. ADD A, (HL) (75 + A2)		17					0	0	1
	8. INC HL					20	66	0	0	NA
	9. LD (HL), A $\boxed{\text{17}}$ 2066							NA	NA	NA
	HALT Result		**17**	**F2**	**68**	**20**	**66**	**0**	**0**	**1**

Description

1. The first instruction loads register BC with the given bytes. This could be achieved by using two separate load instructions for each register, but loading a register pair is slightly more efficient.

2. The second instruction sets up HL as a memory pointer for location 2065_H, and the third instruction loads $A2_H$ into the memory location indicated by HL.

3. To subtract C from B, it is necessary to copy the contents of B into the accumulator (Instruction 4).

4. Instructions 1 through 4 are all data copy instructions; they do not affect flags. All the flags will remain in their initial conditions before the program is executed.

5. Instruction 5 performs the subtraction in 2's complement and places $8A_H$ in the accumulator as shown below. The subtraction method using 2's complement involves three steps: (1) Find 2's complement of the subtrahend, (2) Add the 2's complement to the minuend, and (3) Complement CY. (Refer to Appendix B if you are unfamiliar with the technique.)

Register C = 68_H → 0110 1000 Subtrahend

2's Com. of 68_H → 1001 1000⎫ 2's Complement of Subtrahend
Accumulator = $F2_H$ → + 1111 0010⎭ Minuend

1 1000 1010 Sum
Complement CY → 0 1000 1010 →$8A_H$ Final Result
Flags: S = 1, Z = 0, and CY = 0

The result of this subtraction sets the Sign flag and resets the Zero and Carry flags. However, the result is not a negative number. After an arithmetic operation, if bit $D_7 = 1$, the Sign flag is set. In this subtraction, the Sign flag should be ignored because data bytes are not signed numbers (see further discussion in Section 8.2.4).

6. The instruction CPL inverts the contents of the accumulator $8A_H$; the result is 75_H. This instruction does not affect any flags, so the flags set by the previous instruction are preserved.

$$1\ 0\ 0\ 0\ 1\ 0\ 1\ 0\ (8A_H) \rightarrow 0\ 1\ 1\ 1\quad 0\ 1\ 0\ 1\ (75_H)$$

7. Instruction 7 adds $A2_H$ from the memory location pointed to by HL to the accumulator contents (75_H). The result is 117_H. The instruction places 17_H into the accumulator, sets the CY flag, and resets the S and Z flags.

$$
\begin{array}{r}
\text{Accumulator} = 75_H \rightarrow \quad 0\ 1\ 1\ 1\quad 0\ 1\ 0\ 1 \\
\text{Memory } (2065_H) = A2_H \rightarrow + \quad 1\ 0\ 1\ 0\quad 0\ 0\ 1\ 0 \\
\hline
\text{CY} \rightarrow 1\quad 0\ 0\ 0\ 1\quad 0\ 1\ 1\ 1 \rightarrow 117_H \\
\text{Flags: } S = 0,\ Z = 0,\ CY = 1
\end{array}
$$

8. Instruction 8 increments HL to point to the next location 2066_H, and the next instruction stores the result in the memory location 2066_H.

9. The HALT is a machine control instruction; it does not affect any registers or the flags. The final result is shown in the box.

8.2.4 Flags and Decision Making

As described in Chapter 6, the Z80 architecture includes six flags, which are flip-flops that are set or reset after the execution of arithmetic and logic operations, with some exceptions. Four of the flags (S, Z, P/V, and CY) can be used by the programmer for decision making in conjunction with Jump and Call instructions; the remaining two (H, N) are used internally by the microprocessor for BCD arithmetic. The thorough understanding of flags is critical to writing assembly language programs.

In many ways the flags are like signs on an interstate highway that help drivers in decision making. A driver sees one or more signs at a time, but continues along the highway ignoring the signs until the appropriate sign is found, and then he or she changes direction or takes an exit. Flags function similarly as signs of data conditions. After an operation, one or more flags are set (or reset) and can be used to change the direction of program sequence by using Jump instructions (discussed in the next section). The following illustrations from Example 8.5 may clarify some of the critical issues.

1. In Example 8.5, Instruction 5 sets the Sign flag and resets the other flags. However, the Sign flag can be ignored because the numbers loaded into registers are unsigned numbers. The Sign flag is relevant when the programmer is dealing with signed numbers.

2. Instruction 7 sets the Carry flag and resets the other flags. If the programmer is adding numbers and is interested in finding the total, the Carry flag must be used to test for a sum larger than an 8-bit number.
3. Another important observation that can be made after the execution of Instruction 7 is that the flags set by Instruction 5 are altered by Instruction 7. Thus, if the programmer is interested in making a decision based on the Sign flag, it should be made before that flag is altered by another operation.

8.2.5 Signed Numbers and Flags

The microprocessor is incapable of understanding a + or − sign unless the sign is represented in the form of binary digits. Therefore, in 8-bit microprocessors, bit D_7 is reserved for the sign by the user when signed numbers are used in arithmetic operations. For a positive number, bit D_7 is 0, and for a negative number, D_7 is set to 1; the remaining seven bits represent the magnitude of a number. If a number is negative, it is represented in 2's complement. In an 8-bit microprocessor, the largest positive number is 0111 1111 ($7F_H = +127_{10}$), and the largest negative number is 1000 0000 ($80_H = -128_{10}$).

The Z80 microprocessor has two flags to indicate the status of the arithmetic results in signed numbers: Sign and Overflow. After an arithmetic (or logical) operation, if bit $D_7 = 1$, the Sign flag is set, and if $D_7 = 0$, the Sign flag is reset. However, this flag can be misleading when the result of an addition exceeds the magnitude $7F_H$ or that of the subtraction exceeds 80_H. These conditions are known as overflow and are indicated by the P/V flag.

The P/V flag is a dual-purpose flag; in logical operations it indicates a parity, and in arithmetic operations it indicates an overflow. In arithmetic operations, if the sum of two positive numbers exceeds 7F, bit D_7 becomes 1, indicating a negative number. However, the Z80 sets the P/V flag to indicate the error in the result. The critical point to remember is that the Z80 does not know whether the numbers are signed, unsigned, or just individual digits. The interpretation of the flags is the responsibility of the user.

Example 8.6

Add two signed numbers: $+29_H$ and $+76_H$. Indicate the status of the flags S, P/V, and CY if the operation is performed by the Z80 microprocessor. Explain how the flags are affected if the numbers are unsigned.

Solution

$$
\begin{array}{rl}
+29_H = & 0010\ \ 1001 \\
+ & \\
+76_H = & 0111\ \ 0110 \\
\hline
+9F_H = & 1001\ \ 1111
\end{array}
$$

CY = 0 because the sum does not exceed FF_H,
 S = 1 because $D_7 = 1$, and
P/V = 1 because the sum exceeds $7F_H$.

In this addition of two positive numbers, the sign flag erroneously indicates that the sum is negative; however, the overflow flag (P/V) suggests that the result has an overflow from bit D_6 and that the result is therefore inaccurate. The user must check the P/V flag and correct the sum.

If these numbers were unsigned numbers, the interpretation of the result would therefore be different; the user should ignore the S and P/V flags and check for the CY flag. In this example, the sum is $9F_H$ with no carry.

Another common misunderstanding is that bit D_0 in the result $9F_H$ is 1; therefore, bit D_0 in the flag register must be 1, thus setting the CY flag. There is no relationship between bit D_0 of a result and bit D_0 of the flag register.

BRANCH OPERATIONS 8.3

The **branch instructions** and their associated flags are the key to the power of a computer or its microprocessor. These instructions can change the sequence of execution based on certain data conditions indicated by the flags; thus, they are decision-making instructions.

The branch instructions are classified into three categories, as listed in Chapter 6: (1) *Jump instructions*, (2) *Call and Return instructions*, and (3) *Restart instructions*. In this chapter, we concentrate on Jump instructions.

8.3.1 Jump Instructions

The Jump instructions can be divided into two groups: *absolute jump* and *relative jump*. In case of absolute jump, the operand specifies the 16-bit address to which the program sequence should be transferred; these are 3-byte instructions. The relative jump instructions are 2-byte instructions and contain an operand that specifies 8-bit displacement, forward or backward (in 2's complement), in relation to the address of the Jump instruction; these instructions are discussed in the next section.

The absolute jump instructions can be further classified into two groups: *unconditional* and *conditional jump*. The conditional jump instructions are implemented based on the status of four flags: S (Sign), Z (Zero), CY (Carry), and P/V (Parity/Overflow). Two instructions are associated with each flag: one for when the flag is set and the other for when it is reset. The list of Jump instructions follows:

Opcode	Operand	Bytes	Description
JP	16-bit	3	Jump unconditional to memory location specified by the 16-bit operand.
JP	C, 16-bit	3	Jump on carry to 16-bit address (CY = 1).
JP	NC, 16-bit	3	Jump on no carry to 16-bit address (CY = 0).

Opcode	Operand	Bytes	Description
JP	Z, 16-bit	3	Jump on zero to 16-bit address ($Z = 1$).
JP	NZ, 16-bit	3	Jump on no zero to 16-bit address ($Z = 0$).
JP	M, 16-bit	3	Jump on minus to 16-bit address ($S = 1$).
JP	P, 16-bit	3	Jump on positive to 16-bit address ($S = 0$).
JP	PE, 16-bit	3	Jump on parity even to 16-bit address ($P/V = 1$).
JP	PO, 16-bit	3	Jump on parity odd to 16-bit address ($P/V = 0$).

General Characteristics

1. The Jump (JP) instructions are 3-byte instructions. The second byte specifies the low-order address, and the third byte specifies the high-order address.
2. A conditional jump instruction checks for the appropriate flag. If the condition is true, the program sequence is changed to the memory location specified by the operand; otherwise, the execution continues to the next instruction.
3. The Jump instructions do not affect any flags.

Example 8.7

Write instructions to load two Hex bytes BYTE1 and BYTE2 into registers B and C, respectively, and add the bytes. If the sum is larger than 8 bits, display 00H as the overload condition at output port PORT1, and clear the memory location OUTBUF; otherwise, store the sum in memory location OUTBUF. Draw a flowchart, and assemble the program starting at location 2000_H. The data bytes and the labels are defined as follows:

$$BYTE1 = 9A_H, BYTE2 = A7_H, PORT1 = 01_H, \text{ and } OUTBUF = 2050_H$$

Solution

This problem is similar to Example 6.2 with some variations in display and data storage. A flowchart is shown in Figure 8.5. Each block in the flowchart is then translated into mnemonics, and by looking up the instruction set, each mnemonic is converted into Hex code. The program should be assembled starting at location 2000_H. The last column in Figure 8.5 shows the corresponding memory addresses for each Hex code.

Program Description

1. In this program, data bytes and memory locations are shown with labels; this is called symbolic representation. These symbols are defined generally in the beginning of a program. This is a common practice in writing assembly language programs, especially when using an assembler.
2. The first four instructions (mnemonics for blocks 1 and 2) are similar to those we used previously and need no additional explanation.
3. Block 3 is concerned with decision making, and it is important to understand how this block is translated into Hex code. If the ADD instruction generates a carry, the program follows the straight-line path; if it does not generate a carry,

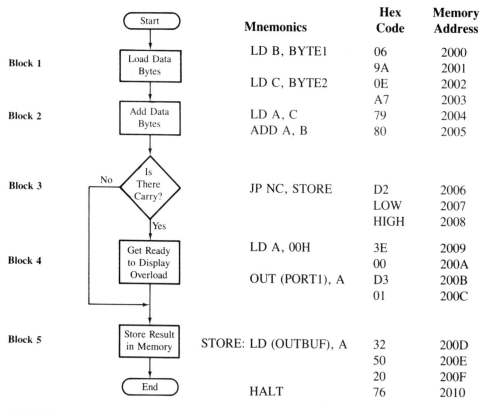

Mnemonics	Hex Code	Memory Address
LD B, BYTE1	06	2000
	9A	2001
LD C, BYTE2	0E	2002
	A7	2003
LD A, C	79	2004
ADD A, B	80	2005
JP NC, STORE	D2	2006
	LOW	2007
	HIGH	2008
LD A, 00H	3E	2009
	00	200A
OUT (PORT1), A	D3	200B
	01	200C
STORE: LD (OUTBUF), A	32	200D
	50	200E
	20	200F
HALT	76	2010

FIGURE 8.5
Flowchart for Example 8.7

the program is branched. Initially, when we write the branch instruction (JP NC, STORE) for the decision-making block, we do not know the address of the jump location. Therefore, we just label the address as STORE and leave the two memory locations (2007_H and 2008_H) for the address to be filled in later.

4. Now we can assemble the straight-line segment of the flowchart (blocks 4 and 5). The instructions shown in these blocks are self-explanatory. The critical point to remember in entering memory addresses is that the 16-bit number is entered in the reversed order—low-order byte first, followed by the high-order byte.

5. After completing the translation of blocks 4 and 5, we can specify the address of the Jump location STORE (200DH) and fill in the blanks for LOW and HIGH bytes; $0D_H$ is entered in location 2007_H, and 20_H is entered in location 2008_H.

Example 8.8

Write instructions to read incoming data from input port INPORT, count the number of readings, and add the readings. When the sum exceeds FF_H, stop reading the port, store the number of readings added in memory location OUTBUF, and display 01 at the output port OUTLED to indicate the overload.

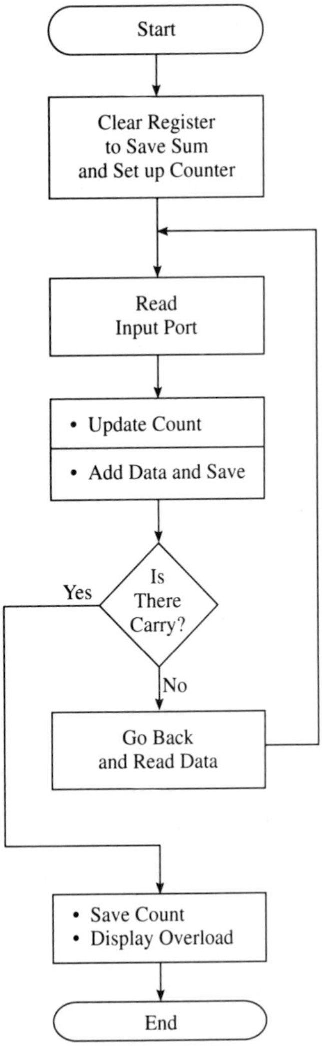

Flowchart		Mnemonics	Comments
Start			
Clear Register to Save Sum and Set up Counter		LD BC, 0000H	;Clear B to save the sum and C to ; count the number of readings
Read Input Port	READ:	IN A, (INPORT)	;Read data

• Update Count
• Add Data and Save
		INC C
		ADD A, B
		LD B, A
			;Add count
			;Add new data to previous sum
			;Save the sum

Is There Carry? (Yes)		JP C, OVRLOD	;Check for overload
(No) Go Back and Read Data		JP READ	;Go back to read next data

• Save Count
• Display Overload
	OVRLOD:	LD HL, OUTBUF
		LD (OUTBUF), C
		LD A, 01H
		OUT (OUTLED), A
		HALT
			;Set up HL as memory pointer
			;Save the count in memory
			;Load 01 as overload indicator
			;Display overload indicator
			;End of program

End			

FIGURE 8.6
Flowchart for Example 8.8

Program Description

1. This program uses two labels—READ AND OVRLOD—to specify jump memory locations. Similarly, I/O ports are shown with labels: INPORT and OUTLED. To assemble this program, these labels must be replaced by appropriate addresses.
2. Register B is used to save the sum, and register C is used to count the number of readings added.
3. Initially, registers B and C are cleared. If they are not cleared in the first operation the sum and the count will have the residual contents of registers B and C.
4. The IN instruction reads the input port, and register C counts the number of data bytes read. The two following instructions add the data bytes and save the result in register B.
5. If the addition does not generate a carry, the READ loop is repeated. When the addition generates a carry, the microprocessor sets the CY flag to indicate an overload. The program jumps to location OVRLOD, whereby the count is saved in memory location OUTBUF, and the overload is indicated by displaying 01_H at the output port.

8.3.2 Relative Jump Instructions

The Z80 instruction set includes two types of relative Jump instructions: *unconditional* and *conditional*. The new address to which the program sequence is redirected is specified by an 8-bit offset (displacement) value relative to the Jump instruction. The displacement can be positive (**forward jump**), specified by the seven bits D_6-D_0 (the MSB $D_7 = 0$), or negative (**backward jump**) specified in 2's complement. The total offset values range from -126 to $+129$ bytes (explained in Example 8.9). The list of relative Jump instructions is (d = displacement):

Mnemonics	Bytes	Description
JR d	2	;Jump relative unconditionally
JR Z, d	2	;Jump relative if Z = 1
JR NZ, d	2	;Jump relative if Z = 0
JR C, d	2	;Jump relative if CY = 1
JR NC, d	2	;Jump relative if CY = 0

Note: There are no relative Jump instructions based on Sign and Parity flags.

General Characteristics

1. These are 2-byte instructions; therefore, they are more efficient than 3-byte absolute jump instructions in terms of memory space and, in some situations, execution time.
2. Relative jumps are limited to 256 memory locations.
3. No flags are affected by these instructions.

Example 8.9

The unconditional relative Jump instruction is stored in memory locations 2100 and 2101_H, as shown below. Find the memory address of the forward jump location if the displacement byte is $7F_H$, and find the memory address for the backward jump if the displacement byte is $9C_H$.

```
2100    18              JR d  ; JUMP RELATIVE
                              ; TO GIVEN OFFSET
2101    OFFSET d
2102    NEXT OPCODE
```

Solution

1. When the jump instruction is executed, the program counter (PC) contains the address 2102 (PC always points to the next machine code to be fetched). By adding the displacement byte to the program counter, the address of the jump location becomes 2181_H ($2102_H + 7F_H$).

   For an 8-bit displacement byte, $7F_H$ is the largest offset value for a forward jump. Therefore, relative to the memory location of the first code of the Jump instruction, the maximum displacement is $7F_H$ plus two memory locations of the instruction. The decimal equivalent of 81_H (7F + 2) is 129; thus, the positive range extends to 129 memory locations.

2. If the displacement byte is $9C_H$, it is in 2's complement because $D_7 = 1$. The memory address for the backward jump location from 2102_H (contents of the program counter) can be calculated two ways: (a) by adding the negative displacement $9C_H$ or (b) by subtracting the positive displacement 64_H, which is the 2's complement of $9C_H$.

	(a)	**(b)**
Program Counter:	2 1 0 2	2 1 0 2
Displacement Byte:	+ 9 C	− 6 4 2's Complement of $9C_H$
In 2's Complement:	9 E	2 0 9 E
Complement CY and:	1 9 E	
Subtract from 21_H:	2 0 9 E	

The memory address of the Jump location is $209E_H$. In the first calculation, after adding a negative number, the sum is $9E_H$ without a carry. Therefore, in 2's complement addition, the ninth bit must be set to 1, indicating a borrow that is subtracted from 21_H. If you are unfamiliar with 2's complement arithmetic, review section B.2 in Appendix B. In the second calculation, 64_H is a positive number obtained by taking 2's complement of the negative number, and it is subtracted from 2102_H.

Z80 INSTRUCTIONS RELATED TO INDEX REGISTERS 8.4

The Z80 microprocessor includes two 16-bit index registers IX and IY, and they are used primarily as memory pointers. In the previous sections, we discussed instructions concerning data copy, arithmetic, and branch operations. The Z80 can perform these operations with the contents of memory registers using the index registers.

The following group shows data copy, arithmetic, and unconditional jump instructions related to the IX registers; there is an identical set for the IY register.

Opcode	Operand	Bytes	Description
LD	IX, 16-bit	4	Load 16-bit data into IX register (this instruction was discussed in Section 8.1.1)
LD	(IX + d), 8-bit	4	Load 8-bit into memory location IX + d*
LD	r, (IX + d)	3	Copy from memory IX + d into register r
LD	(IX + d), r	3	Copy from register r into memory IX + d
ADD	A, (IX + d)	3	Add contents of memory IX + d to A
SUB	(IX + d)	3	Subtract contents of memory IX + d from A
INC	IX	2	Increment 16-bit contents of IX
INC	(IX + d)	3	Increment contents of memory IX + d
DEC	IX	2	Decrement 16-bit contents of IX
DEC	(IX + d)	3	Decrement contents of memory IX + d

General Characteristics

1. Index registers IX and IY are used as memory pointers. The memory address is calculated by adding the displacement byte (also known as offset) to the contents of the index register. The displacement byte is an 8-bit number; it can be either positive or negative. The magnitude of a positive offset is specified by the seven bits D_6-D_0, and the positive sign is indicated by bit D_7 being 0.

---

*d is an offset value added to the contents of the index register to obtain in the memory location (see Example 8.10).

For a negative offset, the displacement byte is expressed in 2's complement (illustrated in Example 8.10). The total offset ranges from $+127$ to -128 memory locations.

2. When the operand is memory, it is specified by enclosing the memory address in the parentheses (as in any other memory-related instructions), and when the operand is the index register, it is written without parentheses.

3. The instructions listed above follow the same pattern as discussed in the previous sections.

4. These instructions have 2-byte opcodes; therefore, the number of bytes in index-related instructions ranges from two to four bytes.

Example 8.10

Set up index registers IX and IY as memory pointers to locations 2050_H and 2185_H, respectively. Load data bytes 32_H into location 2090_H and 97_H into 2120_H using the index registers. Add the bytes, and save the sum in the accumulator.

Solution

Mnemonics	Descriptions
LD IX, 2050H	;Point IX to location 2050H
LD IY, 2185H	;Point IY to location 2185H
LD (IX + 40H), 32H	;Load byte into location (2050H + 40H) = 2090H
LD (IY + 9BH), 97H	;Load byte into location 2120H Offset is (2185H − 2120H) 65H locations backward. 2's complement of 65H = 9BH.
LD A, (IX + 40H)	;Copy first byte (32H) into A
ADD A, (IY + 9BH)	;Add second byte
HALT	

The memory addresses are calculated by adding the offset to the low-order byte of the index register.

$$IX + 40 = 20 \quad \begin{array}{r} 50 \\ +40 \\ \hline 90_H \to 2090_H \end{array} \qquad IY + 9B = \quad 21 \quad \begin{array}{r} 85 \\ +9B \\ \hline 1\ 20 \end{array}$$

$$\begin{array}{lrr} \text{Complement CY} \to & & 0\ 20 \\ \text{Result} \to & 21 & 20_H \end{array}$$

Because the second operation is a 2's complement addition, the carry is complemented.

8.5 PROGRAMMING TECHNIQUES: LOOPING, COUNTING, AND INDEXING

The examples illustrated in the previous sections are simple and can be solved manually. However, a computer is at its best, surpassing human capability, when it has to repeat such tasks as adding a large set of numbers or copying bytes from one block of memory locations to another. It is fast and accurate.

To perform a given repetitive task, commonly used techniques are looping, counting, and indexing. To add data bytes stored in memory, for example, the following steps are necessary.

1. Define the task to be repeated: **Looping.**
   A loop is set up by using either a conditional Jump or an unconditional Jump as illustrated in Examples 8.7 and 8.8.
2. Specify how many times the task is to be repeated: **Counting.**
   The counter is set by loading a count (number of times the task is to be repeated) into a register or a register pair, and the counting is done by decrementing the count every time the loop is repeated. The counter can also be set up to count from 0 to the final count using increment instructions.
3. Specify the location of the data: **Indexing.**
   The starting location of the data can be specified by loading the memory address into a register pair and using the register pair as a memory pointer or index.
4. Indicate the end of the repetitive task: **Setting Flags.**
   The end of repetition is indicated by the flag of the conditional Jump instruction. When the condition is true, the loop is repeated; when the condition is false, the loop execution is terminated, and the execution goes to the next instruction in memory.

These steps are further clarified in Example 8.11.

Draw a general flowchart to add ten bytes of data stored in memory starting at a given location, and display the sum. Explain the blocks in the flowchart.

Example 8.11

To draw a flowchart, the problem must be divided into steps as follows:

Solution

1. Set up a counter to count the number of bytes.
   Set up a memory pointer (index) to locate where data bytes are stored.
   Clear a register if necessary (either to store partial results or count the number of carries).
2. Transfer data from memory to the microprocessor.
3. Perform addition, checking for carry.
4. Save the partial result.
5. Update the counter and the memory pointer for the next operation.
6. Check the flag to indicate the completion of the task. If the condition is true, repeat the task; otherwise go to the next instruction.
7. Display or store the result.

These steps and their sequence can be represented in the form of a flowchart as shown in Figure 8.7.

Blocks

1. Initialization

This is a planning stage where all initial conditions and requirements are defined. In our example, this block should set up a counter, memory index (pointer), carry register, and temporary storage register.

2. Data Acquisition

Data are generally stored in memory or read from an input port. This step is concerned with bringing data into the microprocessor.

3. Data Processing

This step involves data manipulation, such as arithmetic or logical operations. In the example, we add a data byte, check for a carry, and update the carry register if necessary.

4. Temporary Storage

This step involves storing of partial results so that the previous result will not be destroyed by the next data processing operation.

5. Getting Ready for Next Operation

Before we can check whether the task is completed, we need to update the initial conditions; the index and the counter should be incremented or decremented.

6. Decision Making

In this step, the flag is checked. If the condition is true, the loop is repeated; otherwise, the program goes to the next block to display the result.

7. Output

In this Block, the result is either sent to an output port or stored in memory.

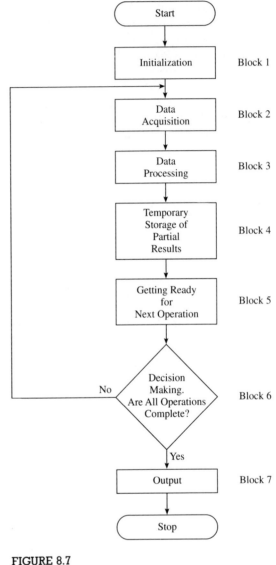

FIGURE 8.7
Generalized Programming Flowchart

LOOKING AHEAD

In the previous sections, we introduced three groups of instructions: data copy, arithmetic, and branching. These instructions were illustrated with examples. In the last section, we discussed the programming techniques with the generalized flowchart (Figure 8.7). Now we will illustrate two programs using the instructions and the programming techniques that were introduced and discussed. We will attempt to analyze the programming problems in terms of the blocks shown in Figure 8.7 and modify these blocks if necessary.

ILLUSTRATIVE PROGRAM 1: BLOCK TRANSFER OF DATA BYTES 8.6

In practical applications, data transfer from one memory block to another is a common occurrence. This illustrative program demonstrates how to copy data bytes from one block of memory to another using the instructions discussed previously.

8.6.1 Problem Statement
Ten bytes of data are stored in a block of memory; the first location is labeled SOURCE (1850_H). Transfer all data bytes to a new block starting with the location labeled OUTBUF (Output Buffer = 1870_H). When the data transfer is complete, display 01 at the output port PORT0.

8.6.2 Problem Analysis
Ten bytes are already stored in the memory block from 1850_H to 1859_H (Figure 8.8). These bytes must be copied into the memory block from 1870_H to 1879_H; these are called nonoverlapping memory blocks. This problem is similar to Example 8.3 repeated ten times. Therefore, we must copy one byte from 1850_H into

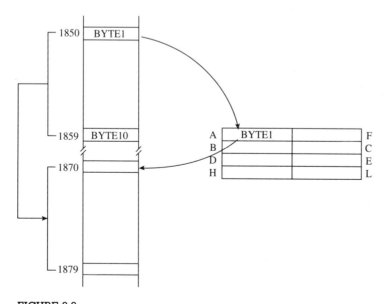

FIGURE 8.8
Data Copy from Memory to Memory in Nonoverlapping Blocks

the Z80 microprocessor and then copy the byte into 1870_H as shown in Figure 8.8. This process should be repeated ten times for the remaining bytes.

We can analyze this problem in terms of the generalized flowchart (Figure 8.7).

1. *Initialization:* In this problem, we need one counter to count ten bytes and two memory pointers: one for SOURCE memory and the other for OUTBUF memory.
2. *Data Acquisition:* In this problem, when a data byte is transferred from memory to the microprocessor, it is immediately transferred to a new memory location. There is no data processing; thus, we can eliminate blocks 3 and 4.

The flowchart is shown in Figure 8.9; blocks 5, 6, and 7 are identical to the blocks shown in Figure 8.7.

8.6.3 Program and Flowchart

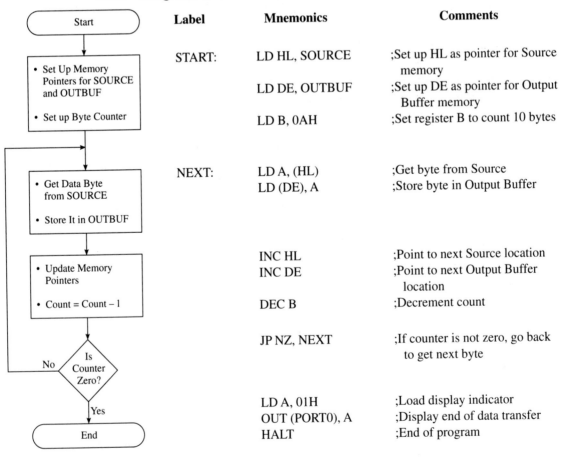

Label	Mnemonics	Comments
START:	LD HL, SOURCE	;Set up HL as pointer for Source memory
	LD DE, OUTBUF	;Set up DE as pointer for Output Buffer memory
	LD B, 0AH	;Set register B to count 10 bytes
NEXT:	LD A, (HL)	;Get byte from Source
	LD (DE), A	;Store byte in Output Buffer
	INC HL	;Point to next Source location
	INC DE	;Point to next Output Buffer location
	DEC B	;Decrement count
	JP NZ, NEXT	;If counter is not zero, go back to get next byte
	LD A, 01H	;Load display indicator
	OUT (PORT0), A	;Display end of data transfer
	HALT	;End of program

FIGURE 8.9
Flowchart: Block Transfer of Data Bytes

8.6.4 Program Description and Execution

In this program, several labels are used to specify memory locations and I/O ports; this is a common industrial practice. When an assembler is used to write programs, labeling provides convenience and flexibility. In manual assembly, labels make it easy to read a program. In this problem, we need to specify or define absolute values of the labels SOURCE, OUTBUF, and PORT0, as well as the label START, the location where the program begins.

The flowchart in Figure 8.9 is similar to the generalized flowchart of Figure 8.7. In the first block, registers HL and DE are used as memory pointers and register B as a counter to count ten bytes. In the next block, a byte is transferred from SOURCE memory to the accumulator using HL as the memory pointer, and the same byte is stored in OUTBUF memory using DE as the memory pointer.

The statements shown in the next block update the memory pointers and the counter. These statements may appear strange as algebraic equations; in fact, they are not algebraic statements but value assignments. The statement Count = Count − 1 means the new value is obtained by decrementing the previous value at the completion of one loop. It is important to remember that updating should be done before the decision making because once the Jump instruction finds that the Zero flag is not set, the program execution will go back to location NEXT. When the counter B is decremented to 0, the DEC B instruction sets the Zero flag. The program execution falls out of the loop and displays 01 at PORT0; this is shown as End in the flowchart.

An example of the assembled program using an assembler is shown below. The assembler used is ZAD from CAMI Research, and the starting memory address is 1800H. In the following program, note that (1) instruction codes are shown on one line, (2) the memory addresses are skipped accordingly, and (3) the 16-bit numbers are entered in the reverse order, i.e., low order first, followed by high order. If you are assembling this program manually, you should ignore label definitions and assembler directives such as ORG.

ASSEMBLY OF DATACOPY.ASM

```
              0001   ;THIS PROGRAM COPIES DATA FROM ONE MEMORY BLOCK
              0002   ; TO ANOTHER
              0003   ;HL AND DE REGISTERS ARE USED AS MEMORY
              0004   ; POINTERS.
              0005   ;COMPLETION OF DATA TRANSFER IS INDICATED BY
              0006   ; DISPLAYING 01.
              0007   ;
1850=         0008   SOURCE   EQU    1850H    ;STARTING MEMORY
              0009                            ; BLOCK
1870=         0010   OUTBUF   EQU    1870H    ;DESTINATION WHERE
              0011                            ; DATA TO BE COPIED
0001=         0012   OUTPRT   EQU    01H      ;OUTPUT PORT ADDRESS
```

```
1800=           0013                    ORG    1800H      ;BEGIN ASSEMBLY HERE
                0014    ;
                0015    ;
1800  215018    0016    START:  LD HL, SOURCE   ;SET UP HL AS POINTER
                0017                             ; FOR DATA SOURCE
1803  117018    0018            LD DE, OUTBUF    ;SET UP DE AS POINTER
                0019                             ; FOR DESTINATION
1806  060A      0020            LD B, 10         ;SET UP B AS A COUNTER
                0021                             ; FOR 10 BYTES
1808  7E        0022    NEXT:   LD A, (HL)       ;GET BYTE FROM SOURCE
1809  12        0023            LD (DE), A       ;STORE BYTE IN OUTPUT
                0024                             ; BUFFER
180A  23        0025            INC HL           ;POINT TO NEXT BYTE TO
                0026                             ; BE COPIED
180B  13        0027            INC DE           ;POINT TO NEXT STORAGE
                0028                             ; LOCATION
180C  05        0029            DEC B            ;DECREMENT COUNTER
180D  C20818    0030            JP NZ, NEXT      ;IF ALL BYTES ARE NOT
                0031                             ; YET COPIED,
                0032                             ; GET NEXT BYTE
1810  3E01      0033            LD A, 01         ;LOAD DISPLAY BYTE
1812  D301      0034            OUT (OUTPRT), A  ;DATA COPY COMPLETE
1814  76        0035            HALT             ;END OF PROGRAM
                SYMBOL TABLE
NEXT     1808           OUTBUF  1870   OUTPRT  0001   SOURCE     1850
START    1800

THERE WERE 0 ASSEMBLY ERRORS.
```

8.7 ILLUSTRATIVE PROGRAM 2: ADDITION WITH CARRY

The following program adds the number of bytes stored in memory and counts the number of carries generated. The maximum sum can be up to 16-bit.

8.7.1 Problem Statement

Add the following ten data bytes stored in memory with the starting address INBUF (Input Buffer). Store the sum in two memory locations; the low-order byte of the sum should be stored in OUTBUF and the high-order byte in OUTBUF + 1.

Data (H): A2, 37, 4F, 97, 22, 6B, 75, 8E, 9A, C7.

8.7.2 Problem Analysis

This problem is similar to Example 8.11 and can be very easily analyzed in terms of the blocks shown in the generalized flowchart in Figure 8.7.

1. In the initialization block, we need to set up a counter to count ten bytes, a memory pointer for INBUF, and registers to save the partial sum and carries. We use the accumulator for addition. The memory pointer for OUTBUF is not necessary until the data processing is completed; thus, the memory pointer used for INBUF can also be used for OUTBUF.
2. In this problem, the data processing block needs to be expanded because of the carries. Whenever a carry is generated after an addition, the carry register will be incremented; thus, the high-order byte of the sum will be saved in the carry register, and the low-order byte will be in the accumulator.

8.7.3 Program Description and Execution

The comments written in the program (see Figure 8.10) explain the function of each instruction, and the blocks drawn around the instructions show the sequence of execution. However, Figure 8.10 should not be used or viewed as an illustration of a flowchart.

In the initialization block, the accumulator and register C are cleared for use in arithmetic operations; otherwise, residual data would cause erroneous results. However, register D need not be specifically cleared because the first load instruction replaces its residual data.

This program has two types of loops; one loop repeats the addition-related instructions if the counter is not zero, and the second loop skips the carry counter if there is no carry. The instruction ADC (Add with Carry) is inappropriate for this problem; this instruction is used for 16-bit addition (see Appendix A).

In the output block, the HL register is used again as a memory pointer for the output buffer memory. After all bytes have been added, the low-order byte of the result, which is in the accumulator, is stored in the memory location OUTBUF, and the high-order byte (carries) in register C is stored in the next memory location OUTBUF + 1.

8.7.4 Program Assembly (Assembly of ADDITION.ASM)

This section shows an illustration of the listing file of the program assembled using an assembler. This listing illustrates how to store data using the Define Byte (DEFB) pseudo-op.

```
0001    ;THIS PROGRAM ADDS TEN BYTES STORED IN MEMORY
0002    LOCATIONS
0003    ; STARTING AT INBUF AND STORES THE SUM IN MEM-
0004    ORY LOCATION
0005    ; OUTBUF AND OUTBUF + 1,
0006    ; ---------------------------------------------------
```

```
1850 =              0007    OUTBUF    EQU      1850H         ;ADDRESS TO STORE THE
                    0008                                    ; SUM
000A =              0009    COUNT     EQU      10            ;COUNT FOR TEN BYTES
1800                0010              ORG      1800H         ;BEGIN ASSEMBLY HERE
                    0011    ; --------------------------------------------------
1800  3E00          0012    START:    LD       A,00H         ;CLEAR A FOR ADDITION
1802  4F            0013              LD       C,A           ;CLEAR C TO SAVE
                    0014                                    ; CARRIES
1803  212018        0015              LD       HL,INBUF      ;SET UP HL AS A POINTER
                    0016                                    ; FOR DATA
1806  060A          0017              LD       B,COUNT       ;SET UP B AS A COUNTER
1808  56            0018    NXTBYT:   LD       D,(HL)        ;GET DATA BYTE
1809  82            0019              ADD      A,D           ;ADD DATA BYTE
180A  D20E18        0020              JP       NC,SKIPCY     ;IF NO CARRY, SKIP
                    0021                                    ; CARRY REGISTER
180D  0C            0022              INC      C             ;SAVE CARRY BIT
180E  23            0023    SKIPCY:   INC      HL            ;POINT TO NEXT BYTE
180F  05            0024              DEC      B             ;DECREMENT COUNTER
1810  C20818        0025              JP       NZ,NXTBYT     ;IF ALL BYTES ARE NOT
                    0026                                    ; ADDED, GO BACK TO
                    0027                                    ; GET NEXT BYTE
1813  215018        0028              LD       HL,OUTBUF     ;SET UP HL TO STORE
                    0029                                    ; THE SUM
1816  77            0030              LD       (HL),A        ;STORE LOW-ORDER BYTE
                    0031                                    ; OF THE SUM
1817  23            0032              INC      HL            ;POINT TO MEMORY
                    0033                                    ; OUTBUF + 1
1818  71            0034              LD       (HL),C        ;STORE HIGH-ORDER BYTE
                    0035                                    ; OF THE SUM
1819  76            0036              HALT                   ;END OF PROGRAM
                    0037    ; --------------------------------------------------
                    0038    ;DATA BYTES ARE STORED IN MEMORY STARTING AT
                    0039    ; LOCATION 1820H
1820 =              0040              ORG      1820H
1820  A2374F97      0041    INBUF:    DEFB     0A2H,37H,4FH,97H
1824  226B758E      0042              DEFB     22H,6BH,75H,8EH
1828 9AC7           0043              DEFB     9AH,0C7H
                    0044              END                    ;END OF THE ASSEMBLY
COUNT       000A    INBUF     1820      NXTBYT     1808      OUTBUF      1850
SKIPCY      180E    START     1800
```

THERE WERE 0 ASSEMBLY ERRORS.

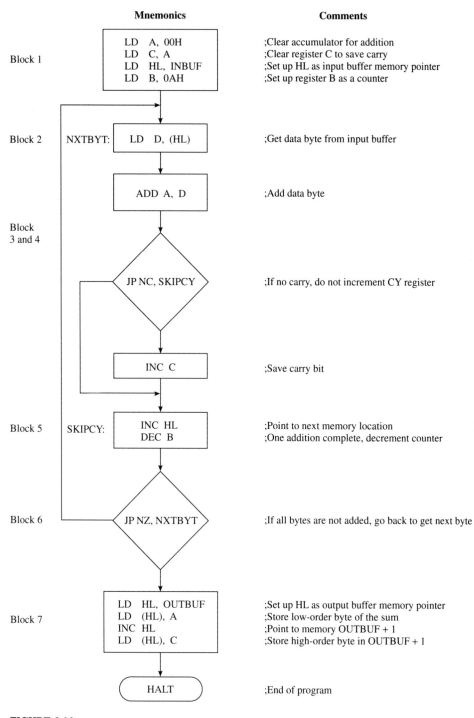

	Mnemonics	**Comments**

Block 1	LD A, 00H
	LD C, A
	LD HL, INBUF
	LD B, 0AH
		;Clear accumulator for addition
		;Clear register C to save carry
		;Set up HL as input buffer memory pointer
		;Set up register B as a counter

Block 2	NXTBYT: LD D, (HL)	;Get data byte from input buffer
	ADD A, D	;Add data byte
Block 3 and 4	JP NC, SKIPCY	;If no carry, do not increment CY register
	INC C	;Save carry bit
Block 5	SKIPCY: INC HL DEC B	;Point to next memory location ;One addition complete, decrement counter
Block 6	JP NZ, NXTBYT	;If all bytes are not added, go back to get next byte

Block 7	LD HL, OUTBUF
	LD (HL), A
	INC HL
	LD (HL), C
		;Set up HL as output buffer memory pointer
		;Store low-order byte of the sum
		;Point to memory OUTBUF + 1
		;Store high-order byte in OUTBUF + 1

	HALT	;End of program

FIGURE 8.10

Program to Add Ten Bytes

8.8   DEBUGGING A PROGRAM

Debugging a program is similar to troubleshooting hardware, but it is much more difficult and cumbersome. When a program fails to work, very few clues alert you to what exactly went wrong. Therefore, it is essential to search carefully for the errors in the program logic, machine code, and execution.

The debugging procedure can be divided into two parts: **static debugging** and **dynamic debugging.** Static debugging is similar to visual inspection of a circuit board; it is the paper-and-pencil check of a flowchart and machine code. Dynamic debugging involves observing outputs, register contents, and flags following the execution of either instruction (the single-step technique) or a group of instructions (the breakpoint technique).

8.8.1   Static Debugging of Machine Code

Translating the assembly language into the machine code is similar to building a circuit from a schematic in that the machine code will have errors just as would the circuit board. If an assembler is used to translate the code, most of the errors involved in hand assembly can be eliminated. The following errors are common in manual assembly:

1. Selecting a wrong code.
2. Forgetting the second byte or third byte of an instruction.
3. Specifying the wrong jump location.
4. Not reversing the order of high and low bytes in a Jump instruction.
5. Writing memory addresses in decimal, thus specifying wrong jump locations.

The debugging problems given in the Assignments section at the end of the chapter will illustrate some of these errors.

8.8.2   Dynamic Debugging

Dynamic debugging is concerned with observations of data after executing an instruction or a set of instructions. These observations may include verifying output displays, checking flags, examining register contents, and tracing execution flow. The process is similar to that of the signal-injection technique in troubleshooting analog circuits, which involves injecting a signal into a hardware system (such as an amplifier) and checking signals at various points against the expected outputs. Similarly, in debugging programs, we execute a few instructions and check register contents or outputs against the expected results. The commonly used techniques and tools are (1) **Single Step,** (2) **Register Examine,** and (3) **Breakpoint.**

SINGLE STEP

The single step technique allows us to execute one instruction at a time and to observe the results following each instruction. As we advance through each in-

struction, we will be able to observe memory addresses and codes as they are executed. With the single step technique, we can spot
□ Incorrect addresses.
□ Incorrect jump locations for loops.
□ Incorrect data or missing codes.

This technique is generally used in conjunction with the Register Examine facility (described below), and it is very useful for short programs (50–100 machine codes). For larger programs, the technique is cumbersome and time consuming.

REGISTER EXAMINE

The Register Examine facility allows us to examine the contents of the microprocessor registers and the flags. We can examine registers after the execution of each instruction or after the execution of a group of instructions and compare the contents with the expected outcomes.

BREAKPOINT

The breakpoint technique allows us to check the program in segments. We can set a breakpoint at the end of a program segment or multiple breakpoints at various memory locations. When the microprocessor is asked to execute the program, it executes the codes until it comes across the first breakpoint, where it returns the control to the breakpoint subroutine in the system. At this point, we can examine the registers for expected results. If the segment of the program is found satisfactory, the program can be executed up to the next breakpoint. With the breakpoint technique, we can isolate the segments of the programs with errors and debug those segments with the single step technique. The breakpoint technique is generally used to check out timing loops, I/O sections, and interrupts.

COMMON SOURCES OF ERRORS

In addition to the errors mentioned in Section 8.8.1, other common errors in the types of programs discussed in this chapter are:
□ Failure to clear the accumulator when it is used to add data.
□ Failure to clear registers when they are used to store partial results or carries.
□ Failure to update an index or a counter.
□ Failure to set a flag before using a conditional Jump instruction or use of an inappropriate flag.
□ Inadvertently changing a flag before using a Jump instruction.

Z80 SPECIAL INSTRUCTIONS 8.9

The Z80 instruction set includes some instructions that perform more than one task. These instructions improve programming efficiency considerably. Some of these instructions are:

Mnemonics	Description
DJNZ d	Decrement B and Jump Relative on no zero (Z = 0)
	The instruction decrements register B, and if B ≠ 0, it jumps to the memory address specified by the offset value d.
LDI	Load and Increment
	The instruction copies a data byte from the memory location shown by HL into the memory location indicated by DE. Registers HL and DE are incremented, and BC is decremented.
LDIR	Load, Increment, and Repeat
	This is similar to the instruction LDI, except that it is repeated until BC = 0.
LDD	Load and Decrement
	The instruction copies a data byte from the memory location shown by HL into the memory location pointed to by DE. Registers HL, DE, and BC are decremented.
LDDR	Load, Decrement, and Repeat
	This instruction is similar to LDD, except that it is repeated until BC = 0.

Example 8.12

Modify the illustrative program Addition with Carry (Section 8.7) using the instruction DJNZ and the offset value.

Solution

The following mnemonics are repeated from a segment of the program in Figure 8.10; we assume that the segment is stored in memory locations starting from 1808_H.

Location	Label	Mnemonics	Comments
1808	NXTBYT:	LD D, (HL)	;Get data byte from input buffer
1809		ADD A, D	;Add data byte
180A		JP NC, SKIPCY	;If no carry, do not save CY
180D		INC C	;Save carry bit
180E	SKIPCY:	INC HL	;Point to next memory location
180F		DJNZ F7H	;Decrement counter B, and if B ≠ 0, jump to location 1008 to get the next byte

Program Description and Calculation of the Offset Value In this program, the instruction DJNZ replaces two instructions—DEC B and JP NZ, NXTBYT—from the program in Figure 8.10. The instruction DJNZ assumes that register B is used as a counter. When the Z80 executes the 2-byte instruction DJNZ, the program counter holds the address 1811_H. This is a backward jump; therefore, the offset value must be in 2's complement. The offset value for the jump location NXTBYT (1808_H) is obtained as follows:

$$
\begin{array}{lccc}
\text{Program Counter:} & 1\ 8 & & 1\ 1 \\
& & - & \\
\text{Jump Location:} & 1\ 8 & & 0\ 8 \\
\hline
& & & 0\ 9_H \quad (0\ 0\ 0\ 0\ 1\ 0\ 0\ 1) \\
\text{2's Complement of } 09_H & & & F\ 7_H \quad (1\ 1\ 1\ 1\ 0\ 1\ 1\ 1) \\
\text{for backward jump:} & & &
\end{array}
$$

ILLUSTRATIVE PROGRAM 3: BLOCK TRANSFER OF DATA BYTES USING Z80 SPECIAL INSTRUCTIONS 8.10

This program transfers data from one memory block to another using the Z80 instruction LDIR.

8.10.1   Problem Statement

Modify the illustrative program (Section 8.6.3) using the instruction LDIR with the problem statement as follows: Transfer 1024 (1K) bytes from the memory block SOURCE (0000H) to the memory block OUTBUF (1900H), and indicate the end of data transfer by displaying 01 at PORT0.

8.10.2   Problem Analysis

To use the instruction LDIR, the HL register should be used to point to memory SOURCE and the DE register to the destination OUTBUF, and the register BC should be used as the counter with the 16-bit count ($03FF_H = 1024$ bytes).

8.10.3   Program

Label	Mnemonics	Comments
START:	LD HL, SOURCE	;Set up HL as pointer for SOURCE memory
	LD DE, OUTBUF	;Set up DE as pointer for OUTBUF memory
	LD BC, 03FFH	;Specify the number of bytes in BC
	LDIR	;Transfer data byte from SOURCE to OUT-; BUF and repeat until BC = 0
	LD A, 01H	;Load display indicator
	OUT (PORT0), A	;Display end of data transfer
	HALT	;End of program

8.10.4   Program Description

In this program, the instruction LDIR is the workhorse; it replaces several instructions from the illustrative program in Section 8.6.3. The instruction performs three operations: (1) copies a data byte from the memory location shown by the

HL register into the memory location indicated by the DE register, (2) updates memory pointers (HL and DE) and the counter (BC), and (3) makes the decision to repeat or terminate the loop based on the count in the BC register. When all 1024 (1K) bytes are copied into new locations, the counter BC becomes zero, and the program goes on to display 01 at PORT0.

SUMMARY

In this chapter, we illustrated a group of instructions from the Z80 set frequently used in writing programs. Instructions were selected from three groups: data copy, arithmetic, and branch. These instructions range from 1 byte to 4 bytes long. General characteristics of these instructions are as follows:

1. The data copy and load instructions copy the contents of the source into the destination without affecting the source contents. They do not affect the flags.
2. The arithmetic instructions (with some exceptions) assume one of the operands is the accumulator, and the result of an operation is usually stored in the accumulator. Most of these instructions affect the flags.
3. The conditional Jump instructions are decision-making instructions and are executed according to the status of the flags. Not all instructions affect the flags; in particular, the data copy instructions and 16-bit increment/decrement instructions do not affect the flags.
4. The Z80 microprocessor includes two index registers (IX and IY), which are used primarily as memory pointers. The instructions related to index registers have 2-byte opcodes and perform data copy and arithmetic operations with the contents of memory registers.

Programming techniques such as looping, counting, and indexing were discussed and a generalized flowchart was illustrated. Two illustrative programs were discussed in the context of this generalized flowchart.

Finally, some Z80 special instructions were introduced. These instructions perform multiple tasks; thus, they improve programming efficiency.

ASSIGNMENTS

Note: In the following assignments, substitute high-order memory address XX with the high-order address and PORT with the output port address of your single-board microcomputer system. Use your own data if data are not given, and specify memory addresses for labels such as INBUF and OUTBUF.

Section 8.1

1. Write mnemonics to load 39_H into register B and 92_H into register D. Save the contents of B in register L, and display the contents of D at PORT1.
2. Write instructions to load 47_H into register B and $F2_H$ into register C using one instruction. Store the contents of C in memory location $XX80_H$ and display the contents of B at PORT1. Assemble the Hex code and store the code in memory.
3. Write instructions to load $A2_H$ into register D and $XX80_H$ into register HL. Copy the contents of D into memory location $XX80_H$.
4. Write instructions to load $A7_H$ into register D and $XX55_H$ into register BC. Copy the contents of D using BC as a memory pointer.
5. Write instructions to load 98H in memory location XX40H and F9H in location XX70H. Exchange the contents of these memory locations. Assemble and execute the code.
6. Specify the register contents and the flag statuses after execution of the following instructions. Show only the changes in register contents, and when flags are not affected, write NA.

Registers						**Flags**	
A	B	C	H	L	Z	CY	
34	7F	FF	01	00	0	1 (Initial Conditions)	

```
LD A, 00H
LD BC, 8058H
LD B, A
LD HL, 2040H
LD L, C
LD (HL), A
HALT
```

7. Write instructions to read the input port 80_H and output the reading to the port 05_H (see Figure 8.11). What appliances will be turned on with this output?
8. Write comments to explain the functions of the following instructions:

```
LD HL, 2065H
LD (HL), 00H
HALT
```

Section 8.2

9. What are the contents of the accumulator after the execution of the instruction SUB A? Specify the status of the Z and CY flags.
10. Write the instructions to load FF_H into the accumulator and increment A. Specify the status of the S, Z, and CY flags after the execution of the increment instruction.

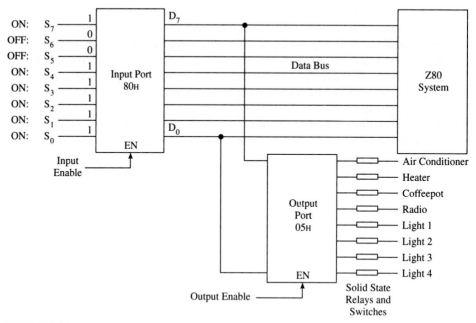

FIGURE 8.11
Appliance Control

11. In the previous assignment (**#10**), replace the increment instruction with the instruction ADD A, 01H and explain how the flags S, Z, and CY are affected after the addition.

12. Specify the register contents and the flag status after the execution of the following instructions. What is being displayed at OUTPRT?

	Register Contents			Flags		
	A	B	C	S	Z	CY
	FF	77	89	1	0	1 (Initial Conditions)

```
SUB A
LD B,A
ADD A,A9H
LD C,57H
ADD A,C
DEC A
OUT (OUTPRT), A
HALT
```

13. Write instructions to load $40FF_H$ into register HL and increment HL. Specify the contents of register HL.
14. Register HL contains $20FF_H$. What are the contents of register HL if the byte 01_H is added (not incremented) to register L? What are the statuses of the S, Z, and CY flags after the addition?
15. Write instructions to perform the operations listed in **14**, and assemble the code showing memory addresses.
16. Show the contents of the registers and the memory locations that are affected after the execution of the following instructions. Explain the difference between the two INC instructions shown below.

```
LD HL, 209FH
LD (HL), FFH
INC (HL)
INC HL
HALT
```

17. Find the results of the following operations and explain the difference between the two results.

```
SUB A            SUB A
LD HL,971FH      LD HL,971FH
LD BC,8F9CH      LD BC,8F9CH
ADD A,L          ADD A,L
ADD A,C          ADD A,C
ADD A,B          SUB H
SUB H            ADD A,B
HALT             HALT
```

Section 8.3

18. Load $48A2_H$ into register BC. Subtract the contents of C from B. If the answer is in 2's complement, display 01_H at PORT; otherwise, display the result. Assemble the code and execute the program.
19. Execute the program in **18** by loading $F247_H$ in register BC.
20. Three data bytes are stored in memory locations XX50, XX51, and $XX52_H$. Write instructions to subtract the bytes stored in memory locations XX50 and XX51 from the byte stored in location $XX52_H$. If the answer is in 2's complement, display FF_H at PORT; otherwise, display the answer. Execute the instructions with the following set of data in Hex.

    Set 1: XX50 = 32, XX51 = 78, XX52 = F9
    Set 2: XX50 = 67, XX51 = 98, XX52 = F9

21. The Relative Jump instruction JR NZ, 68H is stored in memory locations $XXA7_H$ and $XXA8_H$. Calculate the jump location.

22. If the opcode of the Relative Jump instruction JR NC, 8FH is located at memory location $XX50_H$, calculate the jump location.
23. Assemble the code in Illustrative Program 1 (Section 8.6.3) and replace the instruction JP NZ, NEXT with the appropriate Relative Jump instruction and offset.
24. In Illustrative Program 2 (Figure 8.10), assemble the code and replace the Jump instructions JP NC, SKIPCY; and JP NZ, NXTBYT with the appropriate Relative Jump instructions and their offsets.

Section 8.4

25. Rewrite the instructions in Figures 8.2 (a), (b), and (c) using the index registers IX and IY as memory pointers.
26. Write instructions to load $XX70_H$ into the IY index register. Using the register IY as a memory pointer with appropriate offsets, store the bytes $A2_H$ and 32_H in memory locations $XX4F_H$ and $XX9F_H$, respectively.
27. Calculate the value of the memory pointer if register IX contains 2000_H with the displacement byte 80_H.
28. Calculate the values of two memory pointers if register IY contains $20FF_H$ and it is combined with the displacement bytes $7F_H$ and $8F_H$.
29. Assuming the index register IX contains 2050_H, explain the difference between the instructions INC IX and INC (IX + 0).
30. Rewrite Illustrative Program 1 (Section 8.6), Block Transfer of Data Bytes, using the index registers as memory pointers.

Section 8.5

31. Draw a flowchart to add the numbers stored in memory location INBUF (Input Buffer). When the result generates a carry, subtract the last byte and display the sum.
32. Modify the above program to count and display the number of bytes added (excluding the last one).
33. You are given a long grocery list and asked to buy the items from number 20 to 47. Any item that costs more than $10.00 should be excluded. Add up the total cost and show the total expenses. Draw a flowchart for performing these tasks.
34. Modify the above flowchart to include a ceiling of $100 on total expenses.
35. Draw a flowchart to add the string of numbers stored in memory locations BUFFER. The end of the string is indicated by the number 00. Display the sum.

Section 8.6

36. The following block of data is stored in memory locations INBUF. Transfer the data to the locations OUTBUF in the reverse order.

    Data (H) 47, 97, F2, 9C, A2, 98

37. Ten bytes are stored in memory locations starting from INBUF. To insert an additional five bytes at the beginning locations, it is necessary to shift the first ten bytes by five locations. Write a program to shift the data string by five memory locations.

38. Ten 16-bit readings are stored in memory locations SOURCE; the low-order byte is stored first, followed by the high-order byte. Write a program to copy the low-order bytes only to a new location BUFFER in a sequence.

39. Given the initial conditions in **38,** ignore the high-order readings and pack the low-order readings in consecutive memory locations SOURCE.

Section 8.7

40. Draw a flowchart to modify Illustrative Program 2 (Section 8.7) to include the instruction Jump on Carry instead of Jump on No Carry (JP NC, SKIPCY). You may have to use an additional Jump instruction, and the flowchart may have to be altered significantly.

41. Modify Illustrative Program 2 (Section 8.7) using the DE register as a memory pointer instead of HL.

42. Modify Illustrative Program 2 (Section 8.7) using the DE register as a memory pointer and a memory location as a counter (instead of register B).

43. Write a program to add the following string of data bytes until a carry is generated. When the Carry flag is set, subtract the last byte added and display the sum at OUTPRT.

   Data (H) 89, 32, 2B, 7A, B5, 68, 2F, . . .

44. Modify the program in **43** to count the number of bytes added (excluding the byte that generates the carry) and display the count at the second port.

45. Ten 16-bit readings are stored in memory locations SOURCE; the low-order byte first, followed by the high-order byte. Write a program to add the low-order bytes. Display the sum at two different ports and store the sum in two memory locations OUTBUF and OUTBUF + 1.

46. Two sets of data, ten bytes each, are stored in memory locations INBUF1 and INBUF2. Subtract each data byte stored at INBUF2 from the corresponding data byte at INBUF1. Add the remainders, and if the sum of the remainders generates a carry, display FFH at PORT; otherwise, display the sum at PORT.

Section 8.8

47. Find the errors in the following instructions.

   a. The following instructions add two Hex bytes (06 and 52) and display the sum at PORT7.

```
XX00   06   LD B, 06H      ;Load data bytes
XX01   06
XX02   0E   LD C,52H
```

XX03	52		
XX04	80	ADD A,B	;Add data bytes
XX05	81	ADD A,C	
XX06	D3	OUT (07H),A	;Display the sum
XX07	76	HALT	

b. The following instructions add five bytes stored in memory locations starting from $XX50_H$. The sum will be less than FF_H.

XX00	9F	SUB A	;Clear A
XX01	21	LD HL,XX50H	;Set up HL as memory pointer
XX02	XX		
XX03	50		
XX04	78	LD B,05H	;Set up B as a counter
XX05	05		
XX06	86	ADD A,(HL)	;Add byte
XX07	23	INC HL	;Point to next byte
XX08	05	DEC B	;Reduce count
XX09	D2	JP NZ,XX04H	;If B ≠ 0, get next byte
XX10	04		
XX11	XX		
XX12	76	HALT	;End of program

c. The following program transfers 100_H bytes of data starting at the memory location 2100_H to a new location starting at 2800_H.

```
        LD HL, 2100H      ;Set up HL as index for source
        LD BC, 2800H      ;Set up BC as index for new memory
        LD DE, 0100H      ;Set up DE as counter
NEXT.   LD A, (HL)        ;Get byte
        LD (BC),A         ;Transfer byte to new memory
        INC HL            ;Update indexes and counter
        INC BC
        DEC DE
        JP NZ, NEXT       ;If transfer is not complete, go back and get
                            next byte
        HALT              ;End of data transfer
```

Section 8.9

48. A data set with 512 bytes is stored in memory locations with the starting address INBUF1 ($XX00_H$). Shift the entire data set by 256 locations with the starting address INBUF2 on the next page (XX + 1.00). Use the instruction LDDR.

49. Rewrite Illustrative Program 2 (Section 8.7) using the instructions DJNZ and JR NC.

50. Rewrite Illustrative Program 1 (Section 8.6) using the index registers IX and IY as memory pointers and the instruction DJNZ.

51. Rewrite Illustrative Program 1 (Section 8.6) to copy 512 bytes by using the IX and IY registers as memory pointers. Define the SOURCE and OUTBUF memory locations accordingly, and use BC register as a counter. (Hint: The decrement instructions for a register pair (such as DEC BC) do not affect any flags. Set the zero flag by ORing the contents of registers B and C.)

Logic and Bit Manipulation Instructions

The microprocessor is a programmable logic device; it can perform all the logic functions of hardware gates, such as AND, OR, and Ex-OR (exclusive-OR). It can compare two bytes and indicate the comparison (less than, equal to, or greater than) by setting appropriate flags. In addition, it can rotate and shift bytes, and manipulate individual bits.

In this chapter, Z80 instructions related to logic and compare operations and bit manipulation are introduced. These instructions are illustrated with examples, and their applications are shown in two illustrative programs, one of which demonstrates how to design time delays using software instructions. This chapter also includes a section on debugging, which lists errors that commonly occur in writing these types of programs and suggests debugging techniques using a counter program.

Finally, this chapter introduces Z80 special instructions related to the compare operations. These special instructions perform multiple tasks such as comparing two bytes, up-

dating registers that are used as memory pointers and a counter, and making a decision to change the program sequence. For example, one of the Compare instructions can search for a specific byte in a given memory block.

OBJECTIVES

□ Explain how logic instructions (AND, OR, and XOR) perform their operations and how flags are affected by these instructions.

□ Write a set of instructions to illustrate logic operations and explain how these instructions are used in masking, setting, and resetting bits.

□ Explain how the Compare instructions perform a comparison and modify flags to indicate the comparison of two bytes.

□ Explain the Rotate instructions and their effects on the contents of the accumulator and the CY flag.

□ Write a set of instructions (programs) to illustrate the use of Compare and Rotate instructions.

□ Explain how a specific bit in a register or memory can be checked and set or reset by using bit manipulation instructions.

□ Write a program to set/reset specific bits at a given interval.

□ Explain the Z80 special instructions related to search and compare operations.

□ Write a set of instructions to illustrate these Z80 special instructions and explain their advantages.

9.1   LOGIC AND COMPARE OPERATIONS

The microprocessor is basically a programmable logic chip. It can perform all the logic functions of the hard-wired logic through its instruction set. However, the logic operations are slightly different from the hard-wired logic. The AND gate shown in Figure 9.1(a) has two inputs and one output. On the other hand, in an 8-bit microprocessor, the AND instruction simulates eight 2-input AND gates. Figure 9.1(b) shows ANDing the contents of register B with the contents of the accumulator. Register B contains 77_H and the accumulator has 81_H. After ANDing, the result (01_H) is stored back into the accumulator. The other logic functions are performed similarly. In the following sections, we discuss instructions related to AND, OR, and XOR logic functions; the instruction related to the NOT function was discussed as 1's complement in the last chapter.

9.1.1 Logic AND, OR, and XOR Instructions

Logic instructions are examples of implied addressing; the implied operand is the 8-bit word of the accumulator. The other operand can be an 8-bit data word or the contents of a register or memory. When the second operand is a memory location, the memory address can be specified either by the 16-bit number in the HL register or the 16-bit number in an index register with an offset byte. (See Appendix A for complete descriptions with examples of these instructions.)

Opcode	Operand	Bytes	Description
AND	r	1	AND contents of a register with the accumulator
AND	8-bit	2	AND 8-bit data with the accumulator

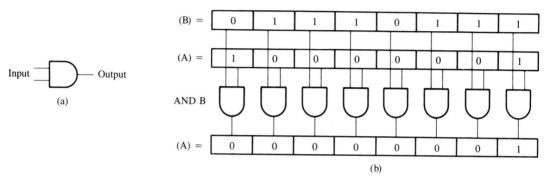

FIGURE 9.1
(a) AND Gate, and (b) a Simulated AND Instruction

AND	(HL)	1 }	AND contents of memory with the accumulator
AND	(IX + d)*	3 }	
OR	r	1	OR contents of a register with the accumulator
OR	8-bit	2	OR 8-bit data with the accumulator
OR	(HL)	1 }	OR contents of memory with the accumulator
OR	(IX + d)*	3 }	
XOR	r	1	Exclusive OR contents of a register with the accumulator
XOR	8-bit	2	Exclusive OR 8-bit data with the accumulator
XOR	(HL)	1 }	Exclusive OR contents of memory with the accumulator
XOR	(IX + d)*	3 }	

General Characteristics

These logic instructions

1. Implicitly assume that the accumulator is one of the operands.
2. Reset (clear) Carry (CY) flag and modify S, Z, and P/V flags according to the data conditions of the result.
3. Place the result in the accumulator.
4. Do not affect the contents of the operand register or memory.

Figure 9.2 shows an input port (PORT1) with three switches connected to data lines D_0, D_1, and D_2; when a switch is on, it provides logic 1 to the respective data line. Write instructions to read the port, mask bits D_3–D_7, and save the reading of the three switches in memory location INBUF.

Example 9.1

---

*The similar instructions related to the index register IY are not shown here.

FIGURE 9.2
Reading Switches from an Input
Port

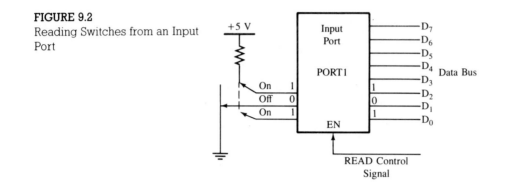

Solution

```
IN A, (PORT1)        ;Read the switch positions
AND 07H              ;Mask data bits D₃–D₇
LD (INBUF), A        ;Store the reading in memory INBUF
HALT
```

The first instruction reads the switch positions at PORT1. Even if only three switches are connected, the reading will be 8-bit data; bits D_3–D_7 will be random. Therefore, bits D_3–D_7 should be masked or eliminated without affecting the switch positions. This is accomplished by ANDing the input reading with an appropriate masking byte (07_H). The masking byte is obtained by placing 0s in bit positions that are to be masked and by placing 1's in bit positions where switches are connected. The masking is performed as follows, and the switch positions (1 0 1) are stored in memory INBUF.

		D_7	D_6	D_5	D_4	D_3	D_2	D_1	D_0
Input Reading in Accumulator:		X	X	X	X	X	1	0	1
	AND								
Masking Byte (07_H):		0	0	0	0	0	1	1	1
Result in Accumulator:		0	0	0	0	0	1	0	1
Flag Status:		S = 0, Z = 0, CY = 0

Example 9.2

A microcomputer with two input ports ($F1_H$ and $F2_H$) and one output port ($F3_H$) is designed to monitor various processes (conveyor belts) on the floor of a manufacturing plant (Figure 9.3). The input ports have seven switches, and the conveyor belts can be started only if corresponding switches of both ports are turned on (logic 1). (The data line D_7 of the output port is connected to an emergency signal and not a part of this example.)

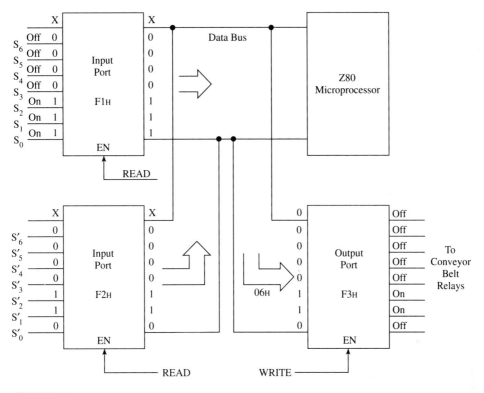

FIGURE 9.3
Microprocessor-Controlled Conveyor Belts

Write instructions to:

1. Turn on and off the seven conveyor belts according to ON/OFF positions of switches S_6–S_0 at port $F1_H$ and switches S_6'–S_0' at port $F2_H$.
2. Monitor the switches continuously.

Solution

			Refer to Figure 9.3	
START:	IN A,(F1H)	;Read switches at F1H	X 0 0 0 0 1 1 1	(A)
		AND		
	AND A,7FH	;Mask bit D_7	0 1 1 1 1 1 1 1	
	LD B,A	;Save reading from F1H	0 0 0 0 0 1 1 1	(A) → (B)

IN A,(F2H)	;Read switches at F2H	X 0 0 0 0 1 1 0	(A)
AND B	;Check ON switches	0 0 0 0 0 1 1 1	(B)
	from both ports	0 0 0 0 0 1 1 0	(A)
OUT (F3H), A	;Turn on/off appropriate	0 0 0 0 0 1 1 0	(A)
	conveyor belts		
JP START	;Go back and read		
	switches again		

Description The three switches S_0, S_1, and S_3 at port F1H are turned on as shown in Figure 9.3. Initially, these switch positions are read, bit D7 is masked, and the reading is saved in register B. At port F2H, the switches S_1 and S_2 are on; this means only two conveyor belts should be running. This is checked by ANDing the two readings from the input ports, and the result (0 0 0 0 0 1 1 0) is sent to the output port to turn on the belts connected to bits D_1 and D_2.

9.1.2 Compare Instructions

The Compare instructions test a byte for less than, equal to, or greater than the contents of the accumulator, and the comparison is indicated by the flags without affecting the operands. The instructions can test the contents of a register, memory, or 8-bit data against the contents of the accumulator. The instructions are as follows:

Opcode	Operand	Bytes	Description
CP	r	1	Compare the contents of a register with the accumulator
CP	8-bit	2	Compare 8-bit data with the accumulator
CP	(HL)	1 ⎫	Compare the contents of memory with the
CP	(IX + d)	3 ⎭	accumulator

General Description These instructions compare the operand (data byte, register contents, or memory contents) with the contents of the accumulator by subtracting the operand from the accumulator. However, no contents are modified; the comparison is indicated by setting the flags.

1. If (A) < operand, the Carry flag is set and the Zero flag is reset.
2. If (A) = operand, the Zero flag is set and the Carry flag is reset.
3. If (A) > operand, the Carry and Zero flags are reset.
4. Other flags are also affected according to the result of the subtraction.
5. When the operand is memory, the address is specified by the contents of the HL register or index registers with an offset byte.

Example 9.3 Write instructions to compare the byte in memory location 1850_H with 80_H. If the byte is equal to 80_H, jump to location CHECK, and if it is higher than 80_H, jump to OVRLOD to indicate the circuit overload.

```
LD    HL, 1850H    ;Set up HL as memory pointer
LD    A, 80H       ;Load comparison byte
CP    (HL)         ;Compare memory byte with 80H
JR    Z, CHECK     ;If memory byte = 80H, begin CHECK procedures
JR    C, OVRLOD    ;Indicate overload
```

A Relative Jump instruction can be used with a label; the assembler will automatically calculate the offset value. However, in manual assembly, the magnitude of the offset must be calculated by the user.

ROTATE (SHIFT) OPERATIONS AND BIT MANIPULATION 9.2

The rotate instructions shift each bit either to the right or to the left. These instructions are used primarily for mathematical operations and serial I/O, where one bit is transmitted over a single line. The Z80 has a set of rotate instructions that can rotate bits not only in the accumulator but in any register and memory location.

Another group of instructions that makes the Z80 one of the most attractive microprocessors in control applications is bit manipulation. The Z80 can test, set, or reset any bit in an 8-bit register or memory. In other microprocessors, the user must write a set of instructions to test a bit in a register or memory.

In this section, we first introduce the Rotate instructions dealing with the accumulator bits and then discuss the Rotate instructions dealing with registers and memory. Finally, we examine the bit manipulation instructions.

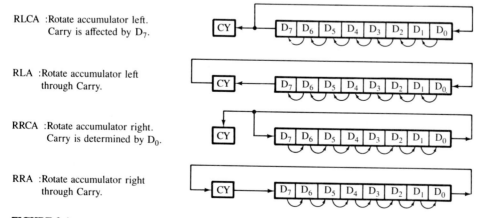

RLCA :Rotate accumulator left. Carry is affected by D_7.

RLA :Rotate accumulator left through Carry.

RRCA :Rotate accumulator right. Carry is determined by D_0.

RRA :Rotate accumulator right through Carry.

FIGURE 9.4
Rotate Instructions

9.2.1 Rotate Instructions (Accumulator)

The following Rotate instructions deal with the bits in the accumulator. The rotate operations can be classified into two groups: Rotate Left and Rotate Right. Each group can be further classified into (1) 8-bit rotation and (2) 9-bit rotation through Carry. In an 8-bit rotation, each bit of the accumulator is shifted to the adjacent position. In this operation, the Carry flag is affected by the rotation, but it is not a part of the rotation. On the other hand, in a 9-bit rotation, the CY flag is one of the bits in the rotation. These instructions are shown in Figure 9.4.

Example
9.4

The accumulator contains 81_H with the Carry flag reset. Illustrate the contents of the accumulator and the status of the Carry flag after the execution of each rotate instruction.

Solution

Figure 9.5 shows how the byte 81_H in the accumulator is changed after various rotate instructions. The first two instructions rotate bits to the left; however, RLCA is an 8-bit rotation and RLA is a 9-bit rotation. In instruction RLCA, bit D_7 is rotated into bit D_0; yet, in instruction RLA, CY is rotated into bit D_0. Both instructions modify the CY flag according to bit D_7. Similarly, RRCA is an 8-bit and RRA a 9-bit rotate right instruction.

Example
9.5

The memory location 1850_H contains a 4-bit number. Write instructions to multiply the number by ten and store the result in the same memory location.

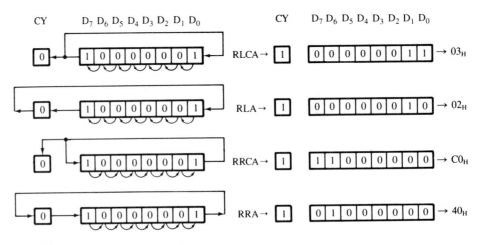

FIGURE 9.5
Rotate Instructions and Accumulator Contents

```
LD HL, 1850H      ;Set up memory pointer
LD A, (HL)        ;Get the number
RLCA              ;Multiply by 2
LD B, A           ;Save result to use it later
RLCA              ;Multiply by 4
RLCA              ;Multiply by 8
ADD A, B          ;To multiply by 10, add multiply-by-2
LD (HL), A        ;Save result in memory
HALT
```

Rotating bits to the left by one position is equivalent to multiplying the number by two, and rotating to the right is equivalent to dividing by two. For example, if the number is 01_H, the instruction Rotate Left makes it 02_H. This technique is valid until bit D_7 does not rotate 1 into bit D_0. For example, rotating the number 80_H left makes it 01_H. However, 80_H can be divided by two by rotating it right.

In the above instructions, the number is multiplied by eight by rotating the accumulator contents three times. Adding the result of multiply-by-two to the result of multiply-by-eight is equivalent to multiply-by-ten.

9.2.2 Rotate and Shift Instructions (Registers and Memory)

The Z80 instruction set has several rotate instructions; these instructions can rotate bits in a register or memory. In addition, the Z80 has shift instructions that shift bits in a given direction. In the following instructions, r represents any register (A, B, C, D, E, H, or L), and m stands for a memory location in R/W memory. In these instructions, a memory location can be specified by HL or an index register. The instructions are as follows:

Opcode	Operand	Description
RLC	r or m	Rotate bits left in a register or memory.
RL	r or m	Rotate bits left through Carry in a register or memory.
RRC	r or m	Rotate bits right in a register or memory.
RR	r or m	Rotate bits right through Carry in a register or memory.
SLA	r or m	Shift bits left through CY in a register or memory and insert 0 in bit position D_0.
SRL	r or m	Shift bits right through CY in a register or memory and insert 0 in bit position D_7.

The set also includes the instructions SRA, RLD, and RRD. (See Appendix A for their complete description.)

General Characteristics

1. In these instructions, the memory address can be specified either by using the HL register or an index register with an offset.
2. Flags S, Z, and P/V are modified according to data conditions. The CY flag is determined by D_7 in left rotation (or shift) and by D_0 in right rotation (or shift).
3. The Shift instructions (SLA and SRA) differ from the rotate instructions in their operations. In Shift instructions, bits are shifted into the next position and 0s are inserted from the other direction. (See Appendix A for a complete description of these instructions.)

Example 9.6

In a Key Monitor program, register B is used to store binary codes of data keys of the Hex keyboard. When a key is pressed, the accumulator receives the 4-bit binary code, and it is stored as the low-order four bits in register B. When a new key is pressed, the previous 4-bit code in register B is shifted to the left and the new key code is stored as the low-order four bits. Write instructions to store a new key code in register B.

Solution

```
SLA B        ;Shift low-order key code to left
SLA B        ;and clear bit positions D₃–D₀ in B
SLA B
SLA B
OR B         ;Store new key code as low-order bits
LD B, A
```

9.2.3 Bit Manipulation

The bit manipulation group has three types of instructions: Bit Test, Bit Set, and Bit Reset. These instructions can test, set, or reset a bit in a register or memory. The instructions are as follows:

Opcode	Operand	Description
BIT	b, r, or m	Test bit b in register or memory. If bit is 0, set Z flag, and if it is 1, reset Z flag.
SET	b, r, or m	Set bit b in register or memory.
RES	b, r, or m	Reset bit b in register or memory.

General Characteristics

1. The operand "b" represents any bit from D_7 to D_0; it is specified as a number between 0 and 7.
2. The memory address can be specified by using either the HL register or an index register.
3. The Set/Reset instructions do not affect any flags.

Example
9.7

Write instructions to read a byte from PORT1, reset bit D_7, and store the reading in memory INBUF.

```
IN A, (PORT1)      ;Read PORT1
RES 7, A           ;Eliminate the parity bit
LD (INBUF), A      ;Store reading in memory
```

To cite a practical use for these instructions, bit D_7 is used to indicate the parity in ASCII characters; therefore, to process these characters, bit D_7 must be eliminated (this will be discussed in Chapter 15).

ILLUSTRATIVE PROGRAM 1: SEARCHING FOR A MAXIMUM NUMBER 9.3

This program searches for a maximum number in a given set of data bytes stored in memory. It compares two numbers at a time, saves the higher number, and continues the process until the end of the data set.

9.3.1 Problem Statement

A set of ten readings is stored in memory locations starting from INBUF. Write a program to find the highest reading in the set, and store that reading in memory OUTBUF.

9.3.2 Problem Analysis

1. Initialization: In this problem, we need one counter to count ten readings and a memory pointer for the INBUF memory. In addition, we need one register and the accumulator for comparison.
2. Data Processing: This block involves comparing two numbers and saving the larger one for the next comparison. This process is continued until the counter is zero.

9.3.3 Program

```
START:    XOR A             ;Begin with minimum reading (00)
          LD B, 0AH         ;Set up register B as a counter
          LD HL, INBUF      ;Set up HL as memory pointer for INBUF
NEXT:     CP (HL)           ;Compare memory reading with accumulator
          JP NC, SKIP       ;If reading is lower, do not save
          LD A, (HL)        ;Save reading
SKIP:     INC HL            ;Point to next memory location
          DEC B             ;One comparison complete, decrement
                              count
          JP NZ, NEXT       ;Get next reading if counter ≠ 0
```

```
LD HL, OUTBUF        ;Set up HL as memory pointer for
                     ; OUTBUF
LD (HL), A           ;Save the highest reading
HALT                 ;End of program
```

9.3.4 Program Description

In this program, the new concept is a comparison of two numbers; otherwise, the remaining program is similar to the programs in the previous chapter.

This program begins by clearing the accumulator and then compares the reading in memory INBUF with the accumulator. If the data byte in the accumulator (A) is larger than the data byte in memory (HL), the CY flag is reset, and the program does not save the byte. If the data byte in memory is larger than (A), the CY flag is set, and the byte is saved for the next comparison. This process is continued until all the readings are compared.

9.4 ILLUSTRATIVE PROGRAM 2: GENERATING DELAYS AND WAVEFORMS

The microprocessor can be used to produce time delays and generate various types of waveforms using time delays and appropriate hardware. This program generates a square wave for a given frequency by turning on/off a bit of an output port at the specified time interval.

9.4.1 Problem Statement

Write a program to generate a square wave with a period of 500 μs if the system frequency is 2 MHz. Use bit D_0 of the output PORT1 to display the waveform. Illustrate how time delays can be increased into several milliseconds or seconds.

9.4.2 Problem Analysis

This problem is somewhat different from the previous data transfer or arithmetic programs. It involves generating a time delay of 250 μs (half the period) and turning bit D_0 on or off by outputting 0 and 1 alternately every 250 μs. Figure 9.6 shows the flowchart.

The initialization block is simple. It includes the loading of bit pattern into the accumulator; it does not even require a counter or a memory pointer. The bit manipulation block is similar to the data processing block; it gets ready appropriate bits for an output, and the output block turns bit D_0 on or off. The time delay block provides appropriate delay for the output pulse. Various ways to generate and calculate time delays are discussed in the next section.

TIME DELAYS

A time delay is generated by keeping the microprocessor busy in a loop executing instructions. This can be accomplished by loading a general-purpose register with an appropriate count and setting up a loop to decrement the count until it reaches

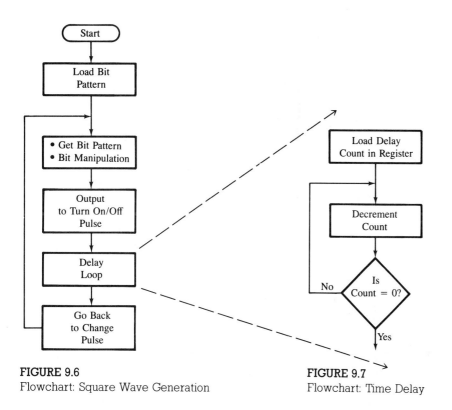

FIGURE 9.6
Flowchart: Square Wave Generation

FIGURE 9.7
Flowchart: Time Delay

zero. The delay is determined by the time required by the microprocessor to execute the loop; thus, the delay depends upon the clock period of the system, the number of instructions in the loop, and the number of times the loop is repeated. A typical set of instructions representing the time delay is shown here, and Figure 9.7 shows the flowchart for these instructions.

Mnemonics	T-states	Comments
LD B, 64H	7	;Delay Count
LOOP:DEC B	4	;Delay Loop
JP NZ, LOOP	10	

To calculate the time delay in this loop, we need to find how much time the microprocessor takes to execute the instructions in the loop once and multiply that time by the number of times the loop is repeated. The execution time for each instruction is given by the T-states; one T-state is equivalent to one clock period of the system. For example, the instruction DEC B has four T-states; it means that the Z80 executes the instruction in four clock periods. The loop includes two instructions with 14 T-states, and the loop is repeated 100 (64H = 100) times; the first instruction LD B, 64H is not part of the loop. Therefore, the loop delay T_L:

$$T_L = (T_C \times L_T \times N_{10})$$

where T_L = Time delay in the loop

T_C = System clock period (f = 2 MHz; T_C = 1/f = 0.5 μs)

L_T = T-states in the loop (14)

N_{10} = Count in decimal (64H = 100)

$T_L = (0.5 \times 10^{-6} \times 14 \times 100)$

= 700 μs

To calculate the total delay, we need to include the execution time outside the loop. In this example, one instruction (LD B, 64H) is outside the loop. It has seven T-states and will require 3.5 μs.

Total Delay $T_D = T_o + T_L$

where T_o = Delay outside the loop

T_L = Loop delay

T_D = 700 μs + 3.5 μs

= 703.5 μs

In most applications, the delay outside the loop is insigificant and can be ignored.

We calculated the time delay for a given count in the example above. However, in many situations—as in this illustrative program—we know the delay required, and we need to calculate a count for the delay loop. For example, let us calculate a count for 400 μs delay for the above loop (ignoring any outside instructions).

If the loop delay: $T_L = (T_C \times L_T \times N_{10})$

Count: $N_{10} = \dfrac{T_L}{T_C \times L_T}$

$= \dfrac{400 \times 10^{-6}}{(0.5 \times 10^{-6} \times 14)} = 57.14 \approx 57$

Now to calculate the delay of 250 μs for the illustrative program, we need to write the program first. In addition, the delay outside the loop will be significant, as shown in the next section; therefore, it cannot be ignored.

9.4.3 Program

	Mnemonics	T-states	Comments
1.	START: LD C, 01010101B		;Load bit pattern
2.	ROTATE: LD A, C	(4)	;Place bit pattern in A

3.		RLCA	(4)	;Change bit pattern for next output
4.		LD C, A	(4)	;Save bit pattern
5.		AND 01H	(7)	,Mask bits D_7–D_1
6.		OUT (PORT1),A	(11)	;Change pulse voltage
7.		LD B, COUNT	(7)	;Load register B with a delay count
8.	DELAY:	DEC B	(4)	;Set up delay loop
9.		JP NZ, DELAY	(10)	
10.		JP ROTATE	(10)	;Go back to change pulse voltage

9.4.4 Program Description

The bit pattern is selected for this program in such a way that when it is rotated, it provides logic 0 and 1 alternately at bit D_0. The bit pattern is masked by ANDing with the byte 01 to eliminate bits D_7–D_1. Bit D_0 is turned on and off at the interval of 250 μs to generate a square wave with the period of 500 μs. In this program, we are concerned with the delay between two consecutive outputs and not just the delay in the loop. The loop count for the total delay of 250 μs is calculated as follows:

1. The DELAY loop consists of two instructions (**8** and **9**) with a total of 14 T-states; however, the number of times the loop is repeated (COUNT) needs to be calculated.

$$\text{Delay in the loop } T_L = (0.5 \times 10^{-6} \times 14 \times \text{Count})$$
$$= 7 \times 10^{-6} \times \text{Count}$$

2. In this problem, we are concerned with not just the delay in the loop, but how long the pulse stays on. After the execution of the OUT instruction (**6**), all the delay caused by the instructions in addition to the delay loop should be accounted for until the OUT instruction is executed again. This is labeled as ROTATE loop in the program. The instructions that are executed once in the ROTATE loop are **2** through **7** and **10**. Therefore,

$$\text{T-states outside the DELAY loop} = 47.$$
$$\text{Delay outside the loop } T_O = (0.5 \times 10^{-6} \times 47) = 23.5 \text{ μs}$$

3. Total delay $T_D = T_o + T_L$

$$250 \text{ μs} = 23.5 + 7 \times 10^{-6} \times \text{Count}$$
$$\text{Count} = (250 - 23.5)/7 \approx 32$$

In this program, the delay outside the loop is quite significant, ten percent of the total delay. The loop will be repeated 32 (20_H) times.

9.4.5 Increasing Time Delay Using the Loop-within-a-Loop Technique

To increase the time delay in a loop, the count must be increased. This can be accomplished by using either a register pair or the loop-within-a-loop technique. Use of a register pair is included in assignment **38**; a program for the loop-within-a-loop technique is shown below.

1.		LD C, 1EH		1.		LD C, 1EH
2.	LOOP:	LD B, 64H	7T	2.	LOOP:	LD B, 64H	7T

3. LOOP1:	DEC B	4T
4.	JP NZ,LOOP1	10T

$T_{L1} = 700 \; \mu s$

5.		DEC C	4T	5.		DEC C	4T
6.		JP NZ,LOOP	10T	6.		JP NZ,LOOP	10T

Delay Calculations Assuming the clock frequency is 2 MHz, the delay in LOOP1 = 700 μs, as calculated earlier. The instructions on the right are the same as on the left, except that the delay in LOOP1 is replaced by $T_{L1} = 700 \; \mu$s. Now we can calculate the delay T_L in the main LOOP as if it is one loop. This LOOP with 21 T-states (T-states of instructions 2, 5, and 6) + T_{L1} is executed 30 times because of the count ($1E_H = 30_{10}$) in register C. Therefore, total loop delay:

$$T_L = 30 \, (T_{L1} + 21 \text{ T-states} \times 0.5 \; \mu s)$$
$$= 30 \, (700 \; \mu s + 10.5 \; \mu s) = 21.31 \text{ ms}$$

To achieve higher accuracy, the instruction outside LOOP (LD C) can also be included, but generally it is insignificant. This delay can be increased considerably by using register pairs. Similarly, the time delay within a loop can be increased by adding instructions (such as NOP) that will not affect the program except to increase the delay.

9.5   DEBUGGING PROGRAMS

The debugging techniques discussed in the previous chapter can be used to check errors in programs similar to those discussed in this chapter. Common sources of errors in these types of programs are as follows:

1. Failure to update a memory pointer or a counter.
2. Failure to set a flag before using a conditional Jump instruction. This is especially true with 16-bit increment/decrement instructions.
3. Failure to save partial results.
4. Specifying Jump instruction on a wrong flag. This error occurs frequently with the Compare instructions.

5. Use of wrong Rotate instruction or improper combination of Rotate instructions.
6. Errors in counting T-states in a delay loop. Typically, the first instruction—to load a delay register—is mistakenly included in the loop.
7. Errors in recognizing how many times a loop is repeated.
8. Failure to convert a delay count from a decimal number into its hexadecimal equivalent or vice versa.
9. Conversion error from decimal to hexadecimal number or vice versa.
10. Specifying the wrong jump location, thus possibly setting up an infinite loop.

Z80 SPECIAL INSTRUCTIONS 9.6

In this section, we introduce additional Z80 special instructions. The Z80 has Compare instructions that are capable of searching for a given byte in memory; some instructions can search through 64K bytes of memory.

Instructions

CPI   Compare and Increment

This instruction compares the contents of the memory location specified by register HL with the contents of the accumulator. Register HL is incremented and register BC is decremented.

CPIR   Compare, Increment, and Repeat

This instruction is similar to the previous instruction CPI, except that the instruction is repeated until BC = 0 or the contents of memory are equal to the contents of the accumulator.

CPD   Compare and Decrement

This instruction compares the contents of the memory location specified by register HL with the contents of the accumulator. Registers HL and BC are decremented.

CPDR   Compare, Decrement, and Repeat

This instruction is similar to the previous instruction CPD, except that the instruction is repeated until BC = 0 or the contents of memory are equal to the contents of the accumulator.

General Characteristics

1. These are 2-byte instructions.
2. The Zero (Z) flag is set when a match is found, meaning the memory byte is the same as the accumulator byte.
3. The Sign (S) flag is set if the memory byte is larger than the accumulator byte.
4. The Parity/Overflow (P/V) flag is reset when BC = 0.
5. The Carry flag is not affected.

Example 9.8	The input buffer memory (INBUF) contains 256 bytes of data. Search for the byte (character) 24H in the input buffer. If it is found, jump to location START; otherwise, jump to location ERROR.

Solution

```
LD HL, INBUF      ;Set up HL as memory pointer
LD BC, 0100H      ;Set up BC as a counter
LD A, 24H         ;Load the byte to be searched
CPIR              ;Search for 24H in the input buffer
JR Z, START       ;Character found, start the process
JR ERROR          ;Display error message
```

The instruction CPIR will be repeated until it finds the character 24_H. When it finds the character, the Z flag is set, the loop is terminated, and the program jumps to location START. If there is no match, the instruction is repeated until BC = 0, and the P/V flag is reset. This flag can be used for decision making if necessary. (The P/V flag is not used in this example.)

SUMMARY

In this chapter, instructions related to logic (AND, OR, XOR) operations, compare operations, bit rotation, and bit manipulation were introduced. The chapter is concluded with the illustrations of Z80 special instructions related to compare operations. General characteristics of these instructions are as follows:

1. Logic operations can be performed with the contents of the accumulator and the contents of a register, memory, or 8-bit data. The AND, OR, and XOR instructions reset the CY flag and modify other flags according to the result of an operation.
2. A byte can be compared with the contents of the accumulator; the byte can be direct 8-bit or from a register or memory. The Compare instructions perform the comparison by subtracting the byte from the accumulator, and the comparison is indicated by setting appropriate flags without affecting the contents. When (A) < the byte, the CY flag is set; when (A) = the byte, the Z flag is set, and when (A) > the byte, the CY and Z flags are reset. All other flags are affected according to the result of the subtraction.
3. The rotate instructions can rotate bits in the accumulator, register, or memory either left or right by one position. Bit rotations can be performed either for eight bits or for nine bits including the CY flag. In either rotation, the status of the CY flag is determined by D_7 in the left rotation and by D_0 in the right rotation.

4. The shift instructions can shift each bit in the accumulator, register, or memory either left or right by one position. When bits are shifted to the left, bit D_7 is placed into the CY flag and 0 is inserted into bit D_0. When bits are shifted to the right, bit D_0 is placed into the CY flag and 0 is inserted into bit D_7.

5. Bit manipulation instructions can test, set, or reset any bit in a register or memory.

Two applications programs—searching for a maximum number in a data set and generating a square wave—were illustrated. The square wave program also illustrated how to design time delays. Errors that commonly occur in writing these programs were listed.

Finally, the Z80 special instructions related to block compare operations were illustrated. These Compare instructions can be used for searching a byte in memory.

ASSIGNMENTS

Section 9.1

1. Write instructions to load 80_H and $7F_H$ into registers B and C, respectively. Logically AND the bytes and save the answer in memory INBUF. Specify the status of the S, Z, and CY flags after ANDing the bytes.

2. If the bytes in **1** are ORed instead of ANDed, specify the contents of the accumulator and the flag statuses (S, Z, CY).

3. Specify the contents of the accumulator and the flag statuses (S, Z, CY) after executing the instruction XOR A.

4. Write instructions to read PORT1. If the reading is 00_H, set the Z flag and jump back to read the port again. Specify a 1-byte logic instruction that can set the Z flag without affecting the input reading.

5. Write instructions to read the input port (INPORT) and mask bit D_7.

6. Load bit pattern 97_H into register D and mask high-order bits D_7–D_4.

7. In **6**, mask high-order bits D_7–D_4 by using the XOR instruction with an appropriate byte.

8. Write instructions to load BYTE1 and BYTE2 into registers D and E, respectively. Check bit D_0 in both bytes, and if either one is at logic 1, turn on the indicator connected to bit D_0 at the output port OUT1.

9. Eight lights are connected to output port OUT1. These can be turned on from the corresponding switches from either of the input ports INPUT1 or INPUT2. Write instructions to read INPUT1 and INPUT2. If all the switches are off in both ports, continue to read the input ports. When a switch (or switches) is on in either port, turn on the corresponding light(s) at OUT1.

10. Write instructions to load 37_H into the accumulator and $6F_H$ into register B. Compare the two bytes, and specify the statuses of the S, Z, and CY flags.

11. When BYTE2 in register B is compared with BYTE1 in the accumulator, the CY flag is reset. Explain the significance of the CY flag status.

12. The following instructions read the switches S_7–S_0 from port INPUT1 and S_7'–S_0' from port INPUT2. When a switch is ON, it provides logic 1 to the corresponding data line (for example, S_7 to D_7). The readings are processed and used for decision making. Read the instructions, and answer the questions following. You may refer to Figure 9.3 as a reference even if this problem is different from Example 9.2.

```
START:   LD HL, 2065H
         LD (HL), 80H
READ:    IN A, (INPUT1)
         LD B, A
         IN A, (INPUT 2)
         AND B
         JP Z, READ
         LD B, A
         AND 80H
         CP (HL)
         JP Z, URGENT
         OUT (OUT1), A
         Continue—
```

a. What is the output at OUT1 when switches S_0, S_1, S_3', and S_7' are turned ON? Explain your answer.

b. Does the program jump to location URGENT when switches S_7, S_7', and S_0 are ON, or does it go back to READ?

c. Specify the output if switches S_7, S_6, S_5, S_1, and S_0 from INPUT1 and S_5', S_4', S_1', and S_0' from INPUT2 are ON.

Section 9.2

13. The accumulator contains the byte 77_H. What is the byte in the accumulator and the CY flag status after the execution of the instruction RRCA?

14. The accumulator contains the data byte $C1_H$, and the CY flag is 0. Specify the contents of the accumulator and the status of the CY flag if the instruction RLCA is executed twice.

15. In **14**, specify the contents of the accumulator and the status of the CY flag if the instruction RLA is used instead of the instruction RLCA.

16. What is in the accumulator and the CY flag after the execution of the following instructions?

```
LD A, F3H
OR A
RLA
RRCA
```

17. Register B holds the byte $3F_H$, representing the values of two Hex keys, 3 and F. The accumulator holds 02_H, representing a new key. Specify the contents of register B after the execution of the following instructions and explain the function of the instruction OR A.

```
                LD L, A          ;Save new key in register L
                LD C, 04H        ;Set up C as a counter
                LD A, B          ;Get previous two keys
SHIFT:          OR A             ;The next four instructions shift low-order
                RLA              ; four bits of register B (now in A) into high-
                DEC C            ; order positions D₇–D₄ and clear D₃–D₀
                JP NZ, SHIFT
                OR L             ;Place bits of new key into D₃–D₀
                LD B, A          ;Save key bits in B
```

18. Write instructions using the masking technique and four RLCA instructions to perform the same shift function as in **17**.
19. Write instructions to shift high-order bits D_7–D_4 of the byte in the accumulator into low-order position D_3–D_0, and multiply the bits by eight.
20. In **19**, mask the low-order bits D_3–D_0 and shift the remaining bits to the right by one position. Is the result the same as in **19**?
21. Mask the high-order bits D_7–D_4 of the accumulator, and add the remaining bits D_3–D_0 four times using the instruction ADD A, A. Explain the result.
22. Can you achieve the same result as in **21** by using the shift instruction?
23. Write instructions to reset the bit D_7 in the accumulator and check whether the number is odd. If it is odd, jump to the memory location REJECT routine; otherwise, continue.
24. Write instructions to check bits D_7 and D_0 in the accumulator, and if both bits are high, jump to the URGNCY location.

Section 9.3

25. Rewrite Illustrative Program 1 (Section 9.3) to find the minimum number in a given data set.

    Data (H) 32, F8, 6A, 47, 1F, AF, 97, 20, 2F, C2

26. A set of ten readings is stored in memory DATA. Write a program to check whether the byte 30_H exists in the set. If it does, stop checking, and display its memory location; otherwise, output FFH.

    Data (H) 48, 8F, C7, 68, 9F, 9C, 30, 33, B8, D9

27. A set of ten readings, representing the power consumption in watts of each house in the area, is stored in memory INBUF. The limit on consumption

per house is set at 200_{10} watts. Check each reading, and count all the readings that exceed the limit and display the number.

Data (H) A9, B3, 98, C8, C7, F5, C8, 89, D2, E7

28. A set of eight current readings is stored in memory INBUF. The readings are expected to be positive ($<128_{10}$). Write a program to check each reading, reject the negative readings, and add the positive readings. Display the answer at the output port, or store it in the output buffer memory OUTBUF.

    Data (H) 74, 6F, A1, 7F, 76, 87, 5B, 8C

29. In **28**, modify the program to add the positive readings until the sum exceeds FFH. If the addition generates a carry, stop the addition, and display 01H at the output port; otherwise, display the sum.

    Data (H) 27, A1, 2A, 1F, 38, 81, 19, 9A
    Data (H) 87, 22, 5F, 3A, 47, 52, 35, 81

30. A data string is stored in memory INBUF, and the end of the data string is indicated by the data byte 00_H. Copy the data string into new memory OUTBUF.

    Data (H) 67, 89, 7F, F5, C8, 9A, 4B, 00, F8, F8

31. Write a program to check 1K byte of R/W memory in your system starting from XX00 to X3FF$_H$. Determine whether each memory cell can store logic 0 and logic 1. (Hint: Check each memory register by loading the byte 55H and reading the byte back to compare with the original byte. Repeat the same steps with the byte AAH.) If any of the memory location is found to be faulty, display 01H at PORT1; otherwise, display FFH as an indicator of a successful memory check.

32. Write a program to check the size of the user memory, and display the last memory address available to the user. (Hint: Check each register by loading and checking a byte as in **31** until you get an error.)

33. In a single-board microcomputer, when an INS (Insert) key is pressed at a given address, the program shifts the entire memory contents by one location and clears that memory location. Write a program to simulate this key. Assume that the memory address where the INS key is pressed is available in the HL register, and use the last available user memory location from your system. (16-bit subtraction instructions are introduced in Chapter 11; therefore, to find the differences between the memory address and the last user memory location, use the 8-bit subtraction: subtract the low-order addresses first, and then subtract the high-order addresses.

Section 9.4

34. Calculate the period of the square wave in Illustrative Program 2 if the COUNT in the delay loop is changed to 44_H.

35. Write a program to generate a square wave with the period of 750 μs. Use bit D_7 to output the square wave.

36. Write a program to generate a rectangular wave with a 300 μs on-period and 500 μs off-period.

37. Calculate the delay in LOOP1, and then calculate the total delay in LOOP including LOOP1 (f = 4 MHz).

	Instructions	T-states
START:	LD B, 64H	7
LOOP:	LD D, FAH	7
LOOP1:	NOP	4
	NOP	4
	DEC D	4
	JP NZ, LOOP1	10
	DEC B	4
	JP NZ, LOOP	10

38. In **37,** replace the instructions (LD D, FAH) with (LD DE, 03FFH), and (DEC D) with (DEC DE). However, the instruction (DEC DE) does not set any flags. Add instructions before the instruction (JP NZ, LOOP1) to set the zero flag when register DE becomes zero.

Section 9.5

39. The following program checks eight numbers stored in memory INBUF, rejects the negative numbers, and adds the positive numbers. If the sum generates a carry, it displays 01_H for an overload condition; otherwise, it displays the sum. However, it appears that the program works only for certain data sets. Debug the program, and execute it for the given three data sets. After debugging the program, when it works for Set 2, make sure that it also works for Set 3.

Set 1 (H) 77, 8F, 68, 32, 47, 92, 89, 6C   Expected Output: 01_H
Set 2 (H) 32, 10, 2A, 8A, A2, B5, 22, 15   Expected Output: $A3_H$
Set 3 (H) 87, 2C, 19, 22, CF, F2, 41, D3   Expected Output: $A8_H$

PROGRAM

```
START:   LD HL, INBUF      ;Set up HL as memory pointer
         LD C, 08H         ;Set up register C as a counter
         LD B, 00H         ;Clear B to save partial results
NEXT:    LD A, (HL)        ;Get the byte
         RLA               ;Place D7 in CY
         JP C, REJECT      ;If D7 = 1, reject number
         RRCA              ;If number is positive, restore it
         ADD A, B          ;Add the previous sum
         JP C, OVRLOD      ;If sum > FFH, it is overload
         LD B, A           ;Save the sum
```

REJECT:	INC HL	;Point to the next number
	DEC C	;Update counter
	JP NZ, NEXT	;If all numbers are not checked, go back and get the next number
	OUT (PORT1), A	;Display the sum
	HALT	;End
OVRLOD:	LD A, 01H	;Load overload indicator
	OUT (PORT1), A	;Display overload signal
	HALT	;End

Section 9.6

40. Write a program to transfer a block of data from memory INBUF to new memory locations OUTBUF. The end of the data string is indicated by 00_H. The suggested Z80 special instructions to be used are LDI (Load and Increment) and JR (Jump Relative).

41. The following ten data bytes are stored in memory locations starting at XX50H. Write a program using the instruction CPIR to search for the first byte 30H and store its address at XX70 and XX71 (or display the address at output ports).

Data: 32H, 6FH, 7AH, 30H, 42H, 30H,
      F2H, 30H, 30H, A5H.

42. Rewrite the program in **41** to count the number of times the byte 30H is repeated in the data strings.

Stacks and Subroutines

The **stack** is a group of memory locations in a system's R/W memory that is used to store register contents and memory addresses temporarily during the execution of a program. The starting location of the stack is defined by loading a 16-bit address into the stack pointer, and space is reserved, usually at the high end of the memory map. This method of information storage resembles the process of stacking books, one above another, so that information is always retrieved from the top of the stack; hence, the particular group of memory locations is called the stack. In this chapter, the processes of information storage into the stack and retrieval from the stack and associated instructions are introduced. An illustrative program demonstrates how to use these instructions to examine and manipulate the flags.

The latter part of the chapter deals with the subroutine technique. A **subroutine** is a group of instructions that performs a subtask (for example, time delay) that is required repeatedly in a program. The subroutine is written as a separate unit, apart from the main program, and can be called whenever it is necessary. When a main program calls a subroutine, the program execution is transferred to the subroutine, and after the completion of the subroutine, the program execution returns to the main program. The microprocessor uses the stack to store the return address of the subroutine.

The subroutine and the stack offer a great deal of flexibility in writing programs. The subroutine technique eliminates the need to repeat the instructions for a subtask; thus, memory is used efficiently and programs can be written concisely. The use of a stack can provide a practically unlimited number of microprocessor registers. When a subroutine is written, the contents of the registers being used by the calling program can be stored on the stack, and the registers can be reused in the subroutine to perform the subtask. At the end of the routine, the register contents of the calling program can be retrieved. The illustrative program, Traffic Signal Controller, demonstrates the use of the subroutine technique.

In the industrial environment, a large software project is generally divided into subtasks called modules. These modules can be developed and tested independently as subroutines by different programmers. This **modular approach to software design** provides flexibility and ease in writing programs. The modular approach is demonstrated by designing a BCD counter and its seven-segment display, and techniques are suggested for debugging modular programs.

OBJECTIVES

☐ Define the stack and initialize it at a given memory location using the stack pointer (register).

☐ Explain how information is stored and retrieved from the stack using the instructions PUSH and POP and the stack pointer (register).

☐ Demonstrate how the contents of the flag register can be examined and how a given flag can be set or reset.

☐ Define the subroutine and explain its uses.

☐ Explain the sequence of program execution when a subroutine is called and executed.

☐ Explain how information is exchanged between the program counter and the stack, and identify the contents of the stack pointer (register) when the CALL and RET (Return) instructions are executed.

☐ Write a subroutine for a given task.

☐ List and explain conditional Call and Return instructions.

☐ Explain multiple call, nested, and multiple ending subroutines.

☐ Explain the modular programming technique and demonstrate the technique by writing a program.

10.1 STACK

The stack is a group of memory locations in R/W memory, defined by loading a memory address into the *stack pointer (register)*.* The stack is used to store binary information temporarily during the execution of a program. Theoretically, the size of the stack is unlimited, restricted only by the available R/W memory in a microcomputer system.

In Z80 systems, the beginning of the stack is defined in the program by using the instruction LD SP, 16-bit (Load Stack Pointer), which loads the 16-bit address into the stack pointer (register). The contents of register pairs (BC, HL, for example, but not just a single register) can be stored in two consecutive stack memory locations by using the instruction PUSH and can be retrieved from the stack into register pairs by using the instruction POP. The microprocessor keeps track

---

*Initially, we are using the term *stack pointer (register)* to emphasize the difference between the stack as memory and the stack pointer as a 16-bit register.

of the next available stack memory location by incrementing or decrementing the address in the stack pointer (register). The address in the stack pointer (register) always points to the top of the stack and indicates that the next memory location (SP − 1) is available to store information.

Once the stack pointer is loaded with a 16-bit address—for example, 1899_H— the storing of information begins at the next location SP − 1 (1898_H) in the decreasing order. The contents of a register pair are stored at SP − 1 and SP − 2 (1898_H and 1897_H), and the address in the stack pointer is decremented by two from 1899_H to 1897_H. The storing of information can continue in the reversed numerical order (decreasing memory addresses). Therefore, as a general practice, the stack is initialized at the highest possible memory location to prevent the user program from being destroyed by the stack information. The process of information retrieval from the stack is opposite to the storing process; it begins at the location indicated by the stack pointer whenever a POP instruction is executed, and the stack pointer is incremented twice. This process will be further clarified in Example 10.1.

The stack is shared by the programmer and the microprocessor to store information. The programmer can store and retrieve the contents of register pairs by using PUSH and POP instructions. Similarly, the microprocessor can automatically store and retrieve the contents of the program counter when a subroutine is called (discussed later in the chapter).

10.1.1 Stack Instructions

The instructions used to store information on and retrieve information from the stack are:

Opcode	Operand	Description
LD	SP, 16-bit	Load 16-bit address into the stack pointer register. This is a load instruction, similar to other 16-bit load instructions discussed previously.
PUSH PUSH	rp rx	This is a 1- or 2-byte instruction and copies the contents of the specified register pair or index register onto the stack as described below. Instructions for four register pairs and index registers are listed here.
PUSH PUSH PUSH	AF BC DE	The instruction first decrements the stack pointer (register) and copies the high-order byte of the register pair or the index register on the stack location SP − 1.
PUSH PUSH PUSH	HL IX IY	Then it again decrements the stack pointer and copies the low-order byte of the register pair or the index register onto the stack location SP − 2.

POP	rp	This is a 1- or 2-byte instruction and copies the con-
POP	rx	tents of the top two locations of the stack into the
		specified register pair or the index register.
POP	AF	First, the instruction copies the contents of the stack
POP	BC	indicated by SP into the low-order register (for ex-
POP	DE	ample, register C of the BC pair) or as a low-order
POP	HL	byte into the index register and then increments the
POP	IX	stack pointer to SP + 1.
POP	IY	It copies the contents of the SP + 1 location into the
		high-order register (for example, register B of the
		BC pair) or as a high-order byte into the index regis-
		ter and increments the stack pointer to SP + 2.

The Z80 instruction set includes six PUSH and six POP instructions associated with six register pairs (AF, BC, DE, HL, IX, and IY). These instructions belong to the data copy group; thus, flags are affected, but the stack pointer is adjusted according to the instructions.

Example 10.1

The R/W Memory of the system ranges from 2000_H to $23FF_H$. A program is stored in memory locations starting from 2000_H, and the stack is initialized at the location 2400_H.

1. Explain why the stack is initialized at 2400_H when, in fact, the R/W memory extends up to $23FF_H$.
2. Explain the data transfer between the registers and the stack when PUSH and POP instructions are executed.
3. Change the sequence of POP instructions to exchange the contents of BC and HL when the contents are retrieved from the stack.

PROGRAM

```
2000    LD SP, 2400H
2003    LD HL, 22A2H
2006    LD BC, 2110H
2009    LD A, (HL)
200A    PUSH BC
200B    PUSH HL
200C    PUSH AF
200D    POP AF
200E    POP HL
200F    POP BC
2010    HALT
```

Solution

1. Because the stack pointer is initialized at 2400_H, the first available stack memory location for storage is $23FF_H$; the location 2400_H will never be used to store information with a PUSH instruction. This is an efficient way of using R/W memory.

FIGURE 10.1
Register Contents

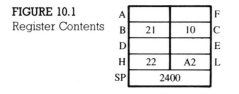

2. The first three instructions load the contents as shown in Figure 10.1. The instruction at location 200A$_H$ (PUSH BC) decrements the stack pointer to SP − 1 and stores the contents of B (21$_H$) in location 23FF$_H$. It then decrements the stack pointer to SP − 2 (23FE$_H$) and stores the contents of C (10$_H$) in the location 23FE$_H$. Figure 10.2 shows the stack contents after the execution of three PUSH instructions; the stack pointer is at location 23FA$_H$.

3. Figure 10.3 shows how the contents are retrieved to their respective registers by POP instructions in the Last-In-First-Out (LIFO) sequence. By examining the sequence of PUSH and POP instructions, you may notice that the contents are placed on the stack in BC, HL, and AF sequence and retrieved in reversed

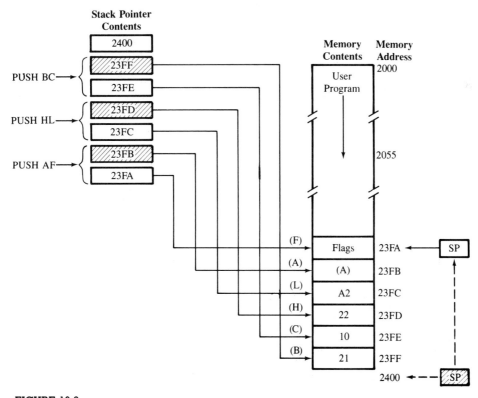

FIGURE 10.2
Contents of Stack Pointer and Stack After Execution of PUSH Instructions

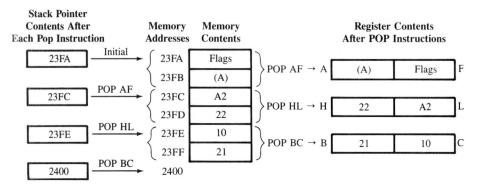

FIGURE 10.3
Register Contents After Execution of POP Instructions

order: AF, HL, and BC. This retrieval sequence is necessary to retrieve the original register contents.

The last two bytes placed on the stack by the instruction PUSH AF are on the top of the stack, and the stack pointer points to the top location ($23FA_H$). The instruction POP AF places the contents of the top location into the flag register, increments the stack pointer to $23FB_H$, places the contents of $23FB_H$ into the accumulator, and again increments the stack pointer to $23FC_H$. The process is repeated for the next two POP instructions, and the stack pointer returns to its original address, 2400_H.

4. To exchange the contents of BC and HL registers during the retrieval of information from the stack is a simple task that can be accomplished by exchanging the positions of POP BC with POP HL in the program. The critical aspect to remember about the POP instructions is that they copy the top of the stack into the specified register pair irrespective of how the bytes were stored on the stack.

10.1.2 Review of Important Concepts

The following points can be summarized from the above example:

1. Memory locations in R/W Memory can be employed as temporary storage during the execution of a program by loading a 16-bit address (initializing) into the stack pointer (register). The contents of register pairs can be stored beginning from the next location (SP − 1).
2. The stack space grows upward in the numerically decreasing order of memory addresses.
3. The stack can be initialized anywhere in the user memory map. However, as a general practice, the stack is initialized at the highest user memory location so that it will be less likely to interfere with a program.
4. The PUSH instructions are used to store contents of register pairs on the stack, and the POP instructions are used to retrieve the information from the stack.

The address in the stack pointer (register) always points to the top of the stack, and the address is decremented or incremented as information is stored or retrieved, respectively.

5. The storage and retrieval of data bytes on the stack should follow the LIFO (Last-In-First-Out) sequence.

6. Information in the stack locations is not destroyed until new information is stored in those locations.

10.1.3 Additional Instructions: Exchange

The Z80 includes an alternate set of registers, and these registers can be used to store the contents of general-purpose registers, the accumulator, and the flags. The contents can be saved by using Exchange instructions. The alternate registers serve a function similar to that of the stack. The following list also includes exchange instructions that exchange contents between an index register or the HL register and the stack.

Instruction	Description
EXX	Exchange the contents of general-purpose registers (BC, DE, HL) with the contents of their corresponding alternate registers.
EX AF, AF′	Exchange contents of the accumulator and the flag register with the contents of the corresponding alternate registers.
EX (SP), IX EX (SP), IY EX (SP), HL	Exchange the contents of an index register or HL register with the contents of the two top locations of the stack.
EX DE, HL	Exchange the contents of the DE register with the contents of the HL register.

General Characteristics

1. These are 1-byte instructions (except instructions EX (SP), IX and EX (SP), IY) and are similar to copy instructions, except that the copying is performed both ways—from the source to destination and vice versa.

2. These instructions do not affect the flags.

3. The Exchange instructions related to the alternate registers can be used (instead of PUSH and POP instructions) for temporary storage of register contents into alternate registers.

ILLUSTRATIVE PROGRAM 1: EXAMINING AND MANIPULATING FLAGS   10.2

The following program demonstrates that the flags can be examined and manipulated if necessary. The program clears all the flags and shows that the increment instruction does not set the CY flag but does affect the other flags.

10.2.1   Problem Statement

Write a program to perform the following functions:

1. Clear the accumulator and all the flags.
2. Load FF_H into the accumulator, increment the contents of the accumulator, and display how the S, Z, and CY flags are affected by the increment instruction.

10.2.2   Problem Analysis

The problem is concerned with clearing the flags and examining the flags after the increment instructions. There are no instructions in the set that can change the contents of the flag register directly. However, the flags can be examined and modified by storing the flags on the stack and retrieving them in any one of the general-purpose registers.

10.2.3   Program

```
START:  LD SP, STACK       ;Initialize the stack
        LD DE, 0000H       ;Load register DE with 00 to clear
                           ; A and F registers
        PUSH DE            ;Place (DE) on stack
        POP AF             ;Clear accumulator and flags
        LD A, FFH          ;Load the given byte in A
        INC A              ;Increase (A) beyond FFH
        PUSH AF            ;Place flags on stack
        POP DE             ;Retrieve flags in register E
        LD A, E            ;Copy flags into A
        AND 11000001B      ;Mask all flags except S, Z, and CY
        OUT (PORT1), A     ;Display flags
        HALT               ;End of program
```

10.2.4   Program Description

After initializing the stack, register DE is cleared and the contents of DE placed on the stack. Assuming the stack is initialized at 2099_H, the instruction PUSH DE clears the locations 2098_H and 2097_H, and the stack pointer points to 2097_H. The next instruction POP AF copies the top of the stack into the flag register and clears the accumulator and the flags. (In this problem, we are not particularly interested in the contents of registers D and A.)

After loading the byte FF_H into the accumulator and incrementing it, the flags are placed on the stack and retrieved in register E. The masking instruction saves the status of S, Z, and CY flags and eliminates the others. The increment instruction increases the accumulator contents to 00; however, it does not affect the CY flag. Therefore, the output will be 40_H, indicating Z flag set and S and CY reset as shown:

		S	Z	H		P/V	N	CY	
Flags		0	1	0	0	0	1	0	0
	AND								
Masking Byte		1	1	0	0	0	0	0	1	(CI_H)
		0	1	0	0	0	0	0	0	(40_H)

SUBROUTINE 10.3

A **subroutine** is a group of instructions written separately from the main program to perform a function that can be used repeatedly in the main program. For example, if a time delay is required between three successive events, a time delay subroutine can be written once instead of three times. The subroutine is written separately from the main program, and is called by the main program when needed. The subroutine technique enables an efficient use of memory.

A subroutine is implemented with two associated instructions: Call (call a subroutine) and Return (return from the subroutine). The Call instruction is written in the main program (except in the nested subroutines) to call a subroutine, and the Return instruction is written in the subroutine to return to the main program.

When a subroutine is called, the contents of the program counter, which is the address of the instruction following the Call instruction, are stored on the stack, and the program execution is transferred to the subroutine address. When the Return instruction is executed at the end of the subroutine, the memory address stored in the stack is retrieved and the sequence of execution is resumed in the main program. The procedure is demonstrated in Example 10.2. In addition, Restart (RST) instructions, which are equivalent to 1-byte Call instructions, are described later.

10.3.1 Subroutine Instructions

The Z80 microprocessor has two groups of instructions to implement the subroutine technique: unconditional and conditional.

Opcode	Operand	Description
CALL	16-bit	Call subroutine unconditionally located at the memory address specified by 16-bit operand. This instruction places the address of the next instruction on the stack and transfers the program execution to the subroutine address.

RET   Return unconditionally from the subroutine.
                             This instruction locates the return address on the top
                                 of the stack and transfers the program execution
                                 back to the calling program.

Conditional Call and Return

CALL	Z, 16-bit	Call subroutine if Z flag is set (Z = 1)
CALL	NZ, 16-bit	Call subroutine if Z flag is reset (Z = 0)
CALL	C, 16-bit	Call subroutine if CY flag is set (C = 1)
CALL	NC, 16-bit	Call subroutine if CY flag is reset (C = 0)
CALL	M, 16-bit	Call (On Minus) if S flag is set (S = 1)
CALL	P, 16-bit	Call (On Plus) if S flag is reset (S = 0)
CALL	PE, 16-bit	Call (On Parity Even) if P/V flag is set (P/V = 1)
CALL	PO, 16-bit	Call (On Parity Odd) if P/V flag is reset (P/V = 0)

RET	Z	Return if Z flag is set (Z = 1)
RET	NZ	Return if Z flag is reset (Z = 0)
RET	C	Return if CY flag is set (C = 1)
RET	NC	Return if CY flag is reset (C = 0)
RET	M	Return (On Minus) if S flag is set (S = 1)
RET	P	Return (On Plus) if S flag is reset (S = 0)
RET	PE	Return (On Parity Even) if P/V flag is set (P/V = 1)
RET	PO	Return (On Parity Odd) if P/V flag is reset (P/V = 0)

General Characteristics

1. The Call instructions are 3-byte instructions; the second byte specifies the low-order byte, and the third byte specifies the high-order byte of the subroutine address.
2. The Return instructions are 1-byte instructions.
3. A Call instruction must be used in conjunction with a Return instruction (conditional or unconditional) in the subroutine.

Example 10.2

In the following example, the main program begins at 1800_H and ends at 1830_H, and the stack pointer is initialized at location 1895_H. The program has a Call instruction at location 1825_H, and the subroutine is located at 1850_H apart from the main program. The subroutine ends at location 1865_H with a Return instruction. Explain the flow of program execution and contents of the stack.

Solution

The program initializes the stack pointer at 1895_H and continues execution until the Call instruction is stored in locations 1825_H, 26_H, and 27_H (Figure 10.4). However, the program in Figure 10.4 does not list the instructions until the Call instruction because they are irrelevant to this example. When the Z80 completes the fetching of the 3-byte CALL instruction, the program counter holds 1828_H, always one address ahead of the execution. When the instruction is decoded, the Z80 recognizes that it is a Call instruction. It places the contents of the program

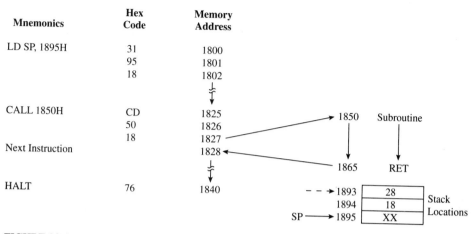

Mnemonics	Hex Code	Memory Address		
LD SP, 1895H	31	1800		
	95	1801		
	18	1802		
CALL 1850H	CD	1825	1850	Subroutine
	50	1826		
	18	1827		
Next Instruction		1828		
			1865	RET
HALT	76	1840		

FIGURE 10.4
Program Flow and Stack Contents in Call Execution

counter (1828_H) on the stack, 18_H in location 1894_H, and 28_H in location 1893_H, and transfers the program execution to location 1850_H as shown in Figure 10.4. At the end of the subroutine, when the Z80 decodes the Return instruction, it retrieves the address (1828_H) from the top of the stack and returns the execution back to the main program at 1828_H. The instruction Return can be functionally interpreted as Jump to memory location, the address of which is stored on the top of the stack; however, the Jump instruction would not increment the address in the stack pointer.

10.3.2 Restart (RST) Instructions

These are 1-byte Call instructions that transfer the program execution to a specific location on the page 00H as listed below. These are executed the same way as that of Call instructions. When an RST instruction is executed, the Z80 first stores the address of the next instruction on the top of the stack and then transfers the program to the Restart (Call) location specified by the operand. After completion of the subroutine at the Restart location, the RET instruction (in the subroutine) returns the program execution to the address on the top of the stack.

Opcode	Operand	Description
RST	00 to 38H	Go to (Call) memory location on page 0; the low-order address is specified by the operand. This is called Modified Page Zero addressing mode. No flags are affected.
RST 00H		Call location 0000_H
RST 08H		Call location 0008_H
RST 10H		Call location 0010_H

Opcode	Operand	Description
RST	18H	Call location 0018_H
RST	20H	Call location 0020_H
RST	28H	Call location 0028_H
RST	30H	Call location 0030_H
RST	38H	Call location 0038_H

Example 10.3

Specify the contents of the stack and the stack pointer after the execution of the instruction RST 30H shown below. Where will the program execution be transferred?

Instructions:

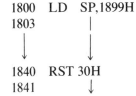

```
1800   LD   SP,1899H
1803        |
            |         |
            ↓         ↓
1840   RST 30H
1841        ↓
```

Solution

The stack pointer is initialized at 1899H. The RST 30H is a one-byte call instruction to location 0030_H. When the RST instruction is executed, the Z80 places the contents of the program counter 1841_H (which is the address of the instruction following the RST instruction) on the stack, the stack pointer is decremented to 1897_H, and the program execution is transferred to location 0030_H. The contents of the stack and the stack pointer after the execution of RST instruction are as follows:

Stack

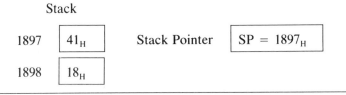

| 1897 | 41_H | Stack Pointer | SP = 1897_H |

| 1898 | 18_H |

10.4   ILLUSTRATIVE PROGRAM 2: TRAFFIC SIGNAL CONTROLLER

This program controls the traffic signal lights by turning them on or off at a specified interval. The subroutine technique is used to write the delay routine, and a register pair is used as a delay register. The significance of using the register pair is that the increment/decrement instructions do not affect any flags. Thus, a procedure needs to be built in to set the zero flag when the delay count in the register pair reaches zero.

10.4.1 Problem Statement

Write a program to provide the specified on/off time to three traffic lights (Green, Yellow, and Red) and two pedestrian signs (WALK and DON'T WALK). The signal lights and signs are turned on and off by the data bits of an output port as shown.

Lights	Bit	Time
1. Green	D_0	15 seconds
2. Yellow	D_2	5 seconds
3. Red	D_4	20 seconds
4. WALK	D_6	15 seconds
5. DON'T WALK	D_7	25 seconds

The traffic and pedestrian flow are in the same direction; the pedestrian should cross the road only when the Green light is on.

10.4.2 Problem Analysis

The problem is primarily concerned with providing various time delays for a complete sequence of 40 seconds. The lights and signs can be turned on by providing logic 1s and turned off by providing logic 0s to appropriate data bits of the output port. The on/off times for the traffic signals and pedestrian signs are as follows:

Time Sequence in Seconds	DON'T WALK D_7	WALK D_6	D_5	Red D_4	D_3	Yellow D_2	D_1	Green D_0	Hex Code
0									
(15) ↓ 15	0	1	0	0	0	0	0	1	= 41H
(5) ↓ 20	1	0	0	0	0	1	0	0	= 84H
(20) ↓ 40	1	0	0	1	0	0	0	0	= 90H

The output needs three different codes at three different intervals as shown above. Three different delays (15, 5, and 20 seconds) can be conveniently obtained by writing a half-second delay subroutine and specifying the delay instructions as necessary. This is known as **parameter passing** (discussed in Section 10.5).

10.4.3 Program

```
          LD SP, STACK        ;Initialize stack pointer
START:    LD A, 01000001B     ;Load bit pattern for Green
                              ; light and WALK sign
```

```
          OUT (PORT1), A        ;Turn on Green light and WALK
                                ; sign
          LD B, 30              ;Set up B to count 15 seconds
                                ;Pass this information to
                                ; DELAY routine
          CALL DELAY            ;Wait for 15 seconds
          LD A, 10000100B       ;Load bit pattern for Yellow
                                ; light and DON'T WALK sign
          OUT (PORT1), A        ;Turn on Yellow and DON'T WALK
                                ; and turn off Green and WALK
          LD B, 10              ;Set up B to count 5 seconds
          CALL DELAY            ;Wait for 5 seconds
          LD A, 10010000B       ;Load bit pattern for Red and
                                ; DON'T WALK
          OUT (PORT1), A        ;Turn on Red, keep DON'T WALK
                                ; on, and turn
                                ; off Yellow light
          LD B, 40              ;Set up B to count 20 seconds
          CALL DELAY            ;Wait for 20 seconds
          JP START              ;Go back to repeat the
                                ; sequence
DELAY:    ;This is 0.5 second delay routine and provides delay
          ; according to the count in register B
          ;Input: Appropriate delay count is specified in B; it is twice the
                  number of desired seconds
          ;Output: None
          ;Registers Modified: B
          PUSH  DE              ;Save contents of DE and AF
          PUSH  AF
WAIT:     LD    DE, COUNT       ;Load DE for 0.5 second delay
LOOP:     DEC   DE
          LD    A, D            ;Place (D) in A for flag checking
          OR    E               ;Set Z flag if (D) and (E) are both zero
          JP    NZ, LOOP        ;Repeat if COUNT ≠ 0
          DEC   B               ;End of 0.5 second delay,
                                ; decrement B
          JR    NZ, WAIT        ;Is it sufficient delay? If not, go back
                                ; to WAIT
          POP   AF              ;Retrieve contents of saved registers
          POP   DE
          RET                   ;Go back to main program
```

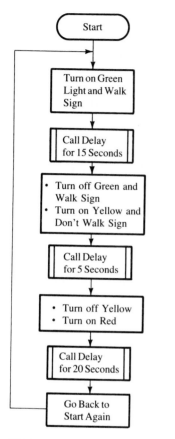

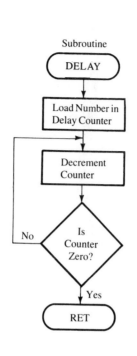

FIGURE 10.5
Flowchart for Traffic Signal Controller

10.4.4 Program Description

Figure 10.5 shows the flowchart of this program; it includes the symbol of the predetermined process used for the delay subroutine. As shown in the flowchart (Figure 10.5), the program turns on the specified lights and calls the delay routine. The main program begins with loading the stack pointer; the initialization of the stack is essential to use Call instructions. The program loads the appropriate bit pattern into the accumulator, sends it to the output port, specifies the total delay in register B, and calls the delay routine. Register B is loaded with a delay count*

---

*In this program, the delay counts are shown in decimal, and the bit patterns are shown in binary; these numbers must be converted into Hex numbers for manual assembly. This is a standard industrial practice if you are using an assembler.

in the main program, but the information in B is used in the subroutine. This is called parameter passing.

The DELAY subroutine is similar to delays discussed in the previous chapter. However, this routine has four additional features:

1. At the beginning of the subroutine, the registers being used (A, D, and E) for the delay loop are saved on the stack and retrieved before the end of the routine.
2. The subroutine ends with the Return instruction.
3. The delay loop uses register pair DE; however, the decrement instruction for register pairs does not affect any flags. When COUNT is decremented to 0, the Z flag needs to be set. To set the flag, the contents of register D are placed in A and logically ORed with the contents of E. The OR instruction sets the Z flag when both bytes, in D and E, are equal to 0; otherwise, the loop is repeated.
4. The WAIT loop includes a conditional relative Jump instruction, which requires 12 T-states if the specified condition is met; otherwise, it takes seven T-states. In this example, when the Z flag is not set, the Jump instruction takes 12 T-states and the loop is repeated. When register B goes to zero, the Z flag is set and the Jump instruction takes seven T-states and the program proceeds to the next instruction. In general, the difference in execution time of these two conditions is insignificant.

The main program calls the subroutine three times as shown in Figure 10.6; this is known as a **multiple call subroutine.**

10.5 SUBROUTINE DOCUMENTATION AND PARAMETER PASSING

In a large program, subroutines are scattered all over the memory map and are called from many locations. Information may be passed between a calling program and a subroutine, a procedure called **parameter passing.** Typically, software design and implementation are performed by a team. Since subroutines and calls may be written by different team members, it is important to document a subroutine clearly so that the team members will know the consequences of using a subroutine. The documentation should include at least

1. Functions of a subroutine
2. Input/Output parameters
3. Registers modified—often called "destroyed"
4. List of other subroutines called by this subroutine.

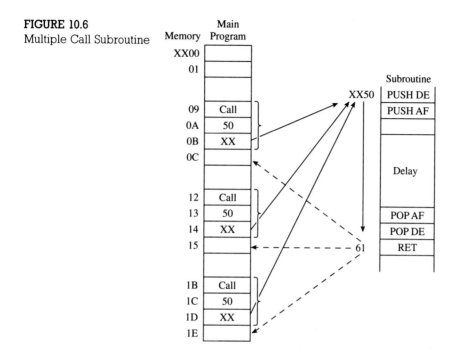

FIGURE 10.6

Multiple Call Subroutine

The DELAY subroutine in Traffic Signal Controller shows one example of subroutine documentation.

FUNCTIONS OF THE SUBROUTINE

This is a brief summary of the purpose of the subroutine and the functions it performs. The user should be able to understand whether it is an appropriate subroutine without going through its instructions.

INPUT/OUTPUT PARAMETERS

The parameters (information) passed on to a subroutine are listed as inputs, and the parameters returned to the calling program are listed as outputs. For example, in the DELAY subroutine, the count in register B determines the number of times the WAIT loop is repeated. This parameter is supplied by the main program and used by the subroutine. Therefore, the count in register B becomes an input to the subroutine. However, this subroutine passes no information back to the main program, so there is no output.

When many parameters must be passed, R/W Memory locations are frequently used to store them, and memory pointers (HL or index registers) are used to point to those locations. The stack can also be used to store and pass parameters.

REGISTERS MODIFIED OR DESTROYED

Registers used in a subroutine may have been used by the calling program. There-fore, it is necessary to save the register contents of the calling program on the stack at the beginning of the subroutine and to retrieve the contents before re-turning to the calling program.

In the DELAY routine, the contents of DE and AF registers are saved on the stack at the beginning of the routine because these registers are used in the delay loop. Their contents are restored at the end of the routine using the LIFO method.

LIST OF SUBROUTINES CALLED

If a subroutine is calling other subroutines, the user should be provided with that information. This enables the user to check which parameters need to be passed to various subroutines and which registers are modified in the process.

10.6   ADVANCED SUBROUTINE CONCEPTS

Types of subroutines generally used are:

1. Multiple Call
2. Nested
3. Multiple Ending

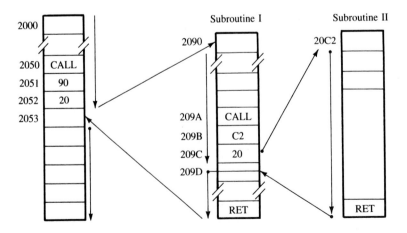

FIGURE 10.7
Nested Subroutines

MULTIPLE CALL SUBROUTINE

This is a subroutine called from many locations in the main program. For example, the DELAY routine in Section 10.4.3 is a **multiple call subroutine.** These types of routines are easy to trace and need minimal stack space.

NESTED SUBROUTINE

A subroutine called by another subroutine is said to be **nested.** The extent of nesting is limited only by the number of available stack locations. When a subroutine calls another subroutine, all return addresses are stored on the stack.

Nested subroutines are shown in Figure 10.7. The main program calls Subroutine I from location 2050_H. The address of the next instruction, 2053_H, is placed on the stack, and the program is transferred to Subroutine I at 2090_H. Subroutine I calls Subroutine II from location $209A_H$. The address $209D_H$ is placed onto the stack, and the program is transferred to Subroutine II. Figure 10.7 shows how the sequence of execution returns to the main program.

MULTIPLE ENDING SUBROUTINE

A subroutine that can be terminated at more than one place is called a **multiple ending subroutine,** as shown in Figure 10.8. The subroutine has two conditional returns (RET Z—Return On Zero—and RET C—Return on Carry) and one unconditional return (RET). If the Z flag is set, the subroutine returns from location

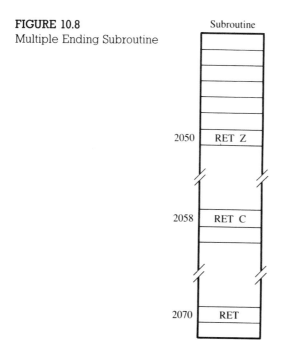

FIGURE 10.8
Multiple Ending Subroutine

2050_H, and if the CY flag is set, it returns from location 2058_H. If neither flag is set, the subroutine returns from location 2070_H.

10.7 SOFTWARE DESIGN FOR BCD COUNTER AND ITS SEVEN-SEGMENT LED DISPLAY

This program is concerned with designing a BCD (Binary Coded Decimal) counter that counts in BCD and displays BCD digits at seven-segment LED output ports. This program demonstrates

1. How to adjust a binary number to a decimal number using the instruction DAA.
2. Table look-up technique to get seven-segment codes.
3. Nested and multiple ending subroutines.

10.7.1 Problem Statement

Design a BCD counter to count from 0 to 60_{BCD} to simulate a 60-second timer, and display each two-digit BCD count at two seven-segment LED ports (PORT0, PORT1); the time interval between each count should be 1 second. The display should go up to 59, and when the count reaches 60, the counter should be reset to 00. The output ports have common-cathode seven-segment LEDs, and the appropriate codes to display digits from 0 to 9 are stored in memory locations labelled as CODE.

10.7.2 Problem Analysis

This software design can be divided into three segments: (1) counting in BCD, (2) getting seven-segment LED code, and (3) creating a 1-second delay. (See Section 11.5 for additional explanation of BCD numbers.)

COUNTING IN BCD

The designing of a binary (or Hex) counter using software instructions is a simple process; it involves clearing a register and incrementing the count at a given interval until the final count is reached. However, to count in BCD some adjustment is necessary; this is done by using the instruction DAA. The concepts underlying the DAA instruction are explained in Appendix A.

The microprocessor is a binary machine; it does not recognize BCD numbers. In BCD, any number from A through F is invalid. When the count goes from digit 9 to A, the DAA instruction can adjust the count to 10. The microprocessor interprets this number as equivalent to 10 in Hex; however, we view the low-order four bits as 0 and the high-order four bits as 1, stored side by side in an 8-bit register. This is called **packed BCD**. To display 10_{BCD}, the low-order and high-order bits need to be separated (called **unpacking**) and displayed by two seven-segment LEDs.

INSTRUCTION
DAA: Decimal Adjust Accumulator

1. This is a 1-byte instruction. After an arithmetic operation, this instruction adjusts an 8-bit number in the accumulator to form two packed BCD numbers by using the process described above.
2. It uses the H and C flags to perform the adjustment.
3. In arithmetic addition, if there is a carry from bit D_3 to bit D_4, the Half-Carry flag (H) is set. Similarly, in subtraction, if there is a borrow from bit D_4, the H flag is set. The DAA instruction uses the H and CY flags internally to adjust the result to BCD digits. The CY flag is used in 16-bit addition; this is discussed in the next chapter.

It must be emphasized that the instruction DAA

☐ Adjusts the result of a BCD addition or subtraction.
☐ Does not convert a binary number into BCD numbers.

GETTING SEVEN-SEGMENT LED CODES
When a BCD number is to be displayed by a seven-segment LED, it should be converted into its seven-segment code. The code is determined by hardware considerations such as common cathode versus common anode LED. For example, to display 0 in the common anode LED, six elements are turned on by supplying logic 0 and the center element is turned off by supplying logic 1. (See section 5.2 for hardware details of seven-segment LEDs and related codes.)

The code has no direct relationship to binary numbers. The codes of BCD digits (0–9) are stored sequentially in memory and obtained using the **table look-up technique.** To use the technique, the BCD number must be unpacked. For example, the BCD number 28 must be converted into binary equivalents of 02_{BCD} and 08_{BCD}. Then, the conversion program locates the code of a digit based on its magnitude and copies the code into the accumulator (or register) to send to the seven-segment LED port.

ONE-SECOND DELAY
A 1-second delay can be generated by using a register pair, similar to the DELAY subroutine in Traffic Signal Controller (section 10.4). However, there is no need to pass a parameter to repeat the delay loop from the main program; it can be written into the routine itself.

10.7.3 Program
This program consists of a main program and five subroutines: UNPACK, DSPLAY, LOOKUP, DELAY, and UPDATE. To illustrate use of an assembler, this program begins at memory location 1800H and defines the stack location at 1900H.

```
STACK      EQU 1900H            ;Stack location
BUFF1      EQU 1901H            ;Storage for unpacked BCD1
BUFF2      EQU 1902H            ;Storage for unpacked BCD2
           ORG 1800H            ;Begin assembly at this
                                ; location
MAIN:      LD SP, STACK         ;Initialize the stack
           LD B, 00H            ;Load initial BCD count
NEXT:      CALL UNPACK          ;Unpack BCD number and store
                                ; digits in output buffer
           CALL DSPLAY          ;Get codes and display at
                                ; ports
           CALL DELAY           ;Wait for one second
           CALL UPDATE          ;Go to next count and adjust
                                ; for BCD
           JP    NEXT           ;Continue
UNPACK:    ;This subroutine unpacks the BCD number from
           ; the accumulator and stores two unpacked BCD
           ; digits in memory output buffers BUFF1 and
           ; BUFF2.
           ;Input: Packed BCD number in register B
           ;Output: BCD_1 in BUFF1 and BCD_2 in BUFF2
           ;Registers modified: Accumulator and HL
           LD HL, BUFF1         ;Set up HL as memory pointer
                                ; for BUFF1
           LD A, B              ;Get BCD number
           AND 0FH              ;Keep low-order 4 bits (BCD_1)
           LD (HL), A           ;Store BCD_1 in BUFF1
           INC HL               ;Point to BUFF2
           LD A, B              ;Shift BCD_2 to D_3–D_0 and insert
                                ; 0 from left
           SRL A
           SRL A
           SRL A
           SRL A
           LD (HL), A           ;Store BCD_2 in BUFF2
           RET
DSPLAY:    ;This subroutine gets BCD digits from the
           ; output buffer, calls the LOOKUP routine,
           ; and displays digits at the output ports with
           ; appropriate codes.
           ;Input: Memory pointer to BUFF2 in HL registers
           ;Output: None
           ;Registers modified: HL registers
           ;Calls LOOKUP subroutine
           LD A,(HL)            ;Get BCD_2 from BUFF2
```

```
                CALL LOOKUP          ;Get seven-segment code
                OUT (PORT2), A       ;Display BCD₂ at PORT2
                DEC HL               ;Move memory pointer to BUFF1
                LD A,(HL)            ;Get BCD₁ from BUFF1
                CALL LOOKUP          ;Get seven-segment code
                OUT (PORT1),A        ;Display BCD₁ at PORT1
                RET                  ;Go back to main program
LOOKUP:         ;This subroutine takes an unpacked BCD digit,
                ; updates the memory pointer, and gets the
                ; seven-segment code of the digit from
                ; memory.
                ;Input: Unpacked BCD digit in the accumulator
                ;Output: Seven-segment code in the accumulator
                ;Registers modified: Accumulator
                PUSH HL              :Save (HL) on the stack
                LD    HL, CODE       ;Set up HL as memory pointer to
                                     ; LED code
                ADD  A, L            ;Add memory pointer to digit
                                     ; to be displayed
                LD    L, A           ;Update memory pointer to
                                     ; locate LED code
                LD    A, (HL)        ;Get LED code
                POP  HL              ;Retrieve from the stack
                RET                  ;Return to the calling program
CODE:           DEFB 40H, 79H, 24H   ;Common-anode LED codes for 0 to 2
                DEFB 30H, 19H, 12H   ;Codes for 3 to 5
                DEFB 02H, 78H, 00H   ;Codes for 6 to 8
                DEFB 18H             ;Code for 9
UPDATE:         ;This subroutine updates the BCD count and
                ; adjusts for BCD number. When the BCD count
                ; reaches 60, it resets the counter.
                ;Input: Count in register B
                ;Output: Updated and BCD adjusted count in B
                ;Registers modified: Accumulator and register B
                LD A, B              ;Get the last count
                ADD A, 01H           ;Update the count
                DAA                  ;Adjust for BCD
                LD B, A              ;Save the count
                CP 60H               ;Is count 60?
                RET NZ               ;If not, go back to main
                                     ; program
                LD B, 00H            ;Reset the counter
                RET
```

```
DELAY:      ;This is a 1-second delay routine
            ;Input/Output: None
            ;Registers Modified: None
            PUSH DE              ;Save contents of DE, AF, BC
            PUSH AF
            PUSH BC
            LD   B, 10           ;Load B to repeat loop ten
                                 ; times
WAIT:       LD   DE, COUNT       ;Load DE for 100-ms delay
LOOP:       DEC  DE
            LD   A, D            ;Place (D) in A for flag
                                 ; checking
            OR   E               ;Set Z flag if (D) and (E) are
                                 ; both zero
            JP   NZ, LOOP        ;Repeat if COUNT ≠ 0
            DEC  B               ;End of 100-ms delay,
                                 ; decrement B
            JP   NZ, WAIT        ;Is it 1-second delay? If not,
                                 ; go back to WAIT
            POP  BC              ;Retrieve contents of saved
                                 ; registers
            POP  AF
            POP  DE
            RET                  ;Go back to the calling
                                 ; program
```

10.7.4 Program Description

In this program, the problem is divided into various small tasks, each of which is assigned to a subroutine. The main program initializes the stack and the counter and calls subroutines in a sequence.

The first subroutine unpacks the BCD number and stores the unpacked digits in the output buffer BUFF1 and BUFF2. The unpacking is performed by separating the two digits and shifting the high-order digit into low-order bit positions D_3–D_0. For example, if the BCD number is 27, the digit 07 will be stored in BUFF1 and 02 will be stored in BUFF2, both in binary format.

The next subroutine DSPLAY is an example of the nested routines. It gets the BCD digits from the output buffer and calls the LOOKUP subroutine. In the LOOKUP routine, the seven-segment codes are stored sequentially from 0 to 9, and the HL register points to the first code. The DSPLAY subroutine supplies a digit in the accumulator that is added to register L, and the sum is saved in L. In effect, the memory pointer is moved to the location where the code of the digit is stored. For example, if the memory pointer is initially at the starting code location

1850_H and the digit is 02, the pointer is shifted after addition to 1852_H, where the code for the digit 2 is stored. Then the code is moved to the accumulator and passed back to the subroutine DSPLAY, which displays the code at the output port PORT2. The same process is repeated for BCD_1. However, this technique will work properly only if the code is stored on the same memory page (see Assignment 15).

The UPDATE subroutine is an example of a multiple-ending subroutine. This subroutine adds one to the previous count and adjusts for BCD using the instruction DAA. It compares the count with 60 and uses the conditional Return instruction to check for the Z flag. If Z is reset, the subroutine returns to the main program, and if it is set, it clears the register B to start the counter again.

MODULAR PROGRAMMING AND DEBUGGING 10.8

The program discussed in the last section is an example of industry-standard software even though it is a small program. The problem is divided into small tasks, and a subroutine is written for each task. The main program consists primarily of calling these subroutines. This is known as the **modular approach.**

The modular approach has several advantages. The approach provides flexibility in writing and modifying programs, especially in a team project. It is also easy to debug individual modules; each module can be tested separately for the expected outputs because each module has a specific task to perform. For example, the UNPACK subroutine is expected to accept a packed BCD number, unpack it, and store the digits in the output buffer. This can be written and tested separately from any other modules. Similar tests can be performed for the other modules. In addition, when all the modules are combined, the entire program can be debugged by setting breakpoints at the end of each module.

DEBUGGING MODULAR PROGRAMS

At the outset, it appears that if each module is tested individually, the whole program should work perfectly when they are combined, and the programmer can live happily ever after. But this seldom happens. As soon as the modules are combined, the interaction between the modules can cause quite a few trouble spots. Following is a list of common errors.

1. Mismatch between PUSH and POP instructions, the number of PUSH instructions being different from the number of POP instructions.
2. Improper sequence of PUSH and POP instructions (not following the LIFO sequence).
3. Destroying the contents in other modules.
4. Passing on wrong parameters or failure to pass parameters.
5. Failure to initialize the stack.
6. Failure to end a subroutine with a Return instruction.
7. Using a wrong flag for a conditional Call and Return instruction.

To illustrate a debugging procedure for the BCD Counter program (section 10.7), we can set up a breakpoint at the end of the subroutine UNPACK and examine registers and two memory locations BUFF1 and BUFF2. We are starting with digit 00, and after unpacking the digit, we should have both locations cleared. The second breakpoint can be set up at the end of the DSPLAY subroutine, and 00 should be displayed at PORT1 and PORT2. If we do not observe what we expect, we can check the output of the subroutine LOOKUP and continue to check each module until the entire program is debugged. This is somewhat similar to trouble-shooting an amplifier; we inject a signal at the input and check the expected output. In this program, an output of one subroutine becomes an input of the next subroutine, and we can check each module by setting breakpoints and examining registers for expected outputs. When we do not observe what we expect, the single-step technique can be used to troubleshoot within the module.

SUMMARY

- □ The stack is a group of memory locations in the system's R/W memory that is defined by loading an address into the stack pointer register.
- □ The programmer uses the stack to store and retrieve the contents of register pairs temporarily during the execution of a program, and the microprocessor uses the stack to store and retrieve the return address when a subroutine is called.
- □ The contents of register pairs are stored on the stack by using PUSH instructions and retrieved by using POP instructions. The stack pointer tracks the storing and retrieving process by adjusting its address.
- □ When a PUSH instruction is executed, the stack pointer register is decremented once, and the high-order byte is stored; then, the stack pointer is decremented again, and the low-order byte is stored.
- □ When a POP instruction is executed, the byte at the top of the stack is retrieved in the low-order register, and the stack pointer is incremented; the next byte is retrieved in the high-order register, and the stack pointer is incremented again.
- □ The Exchange instructions (EXX and EX AF, AF') are used to exchange contents between general-purpose registers and alternate registers; these instructions can be used (instead of PUSH and POP instructions) for temporary storage of register contents into alternate registers.
- □ A subroutine is a group of instructions that performs a subtask of repeated occurrence; it is written separately from the main program.
- □ The program is transferred to a subroutine by using a Call instruction (conditional or unconditional) and returned to the calling program by using a Return

(conditional or unconditional) instruction. A Call instruction should always be used in conjunction with a Return instruction.

□ When a Call instruction is executed, the return address is stored on the stack before the program execution is transferred to the subroutine.

□ When a Return instruction is executed, the program is transferred to the address stored at the top two locations of the stack.

□ The DAA instruction adjusts a binary number in the accumulator to its BCD digits by using the Half-Carry (H) and the Carry (CY) flags. When a group of 4 bits (high or low) exceeds the magnitude 9_{10}, the instruction adds 6 and adjusts digits to their BCD values.

□ In a seven-segment LED display, the codes required to display digits are unrelated to the binary values and dependent on hardware configuration. Therefore, the table look-up technique is used to display these digits.

□ Modular programming is a software design process whereby the programming problem is divided into subtasks (or modules) with definite functions to perform, and each module is written and tested separately as a subroutine. This approach provides flexibility in writing and ease in debugging the program.

ASSIGNMENTS

1. Specify the contents of the BC registers and the stack pointer after the execution of the following instructions.

```
            LD SP, 18F5H
            LD HL, 2055H
            PUSH HL
            POP BC
            HALT
```

2. Specify the address in the stack pointer and the contents of memory locations 1890_H–1899_H after the execution of the following instructions.

```
            LD SP, 189AH
            XOR A
            LD H, A
            LD L, A
            LD B, 05H
LOOP:       PUSH HL
            DEC B
            JP NZ, LOOP
            HALT
```

3. Read the following program and answer the questions.

No.	Instructions
1.	LD SP, 84F9H
2.	LD HL, 8138H
3.	LD BC, 0001H
4.	LD DE, 235AH
5.	LD A, D
6.	OR A
7.	PUSH HL
8.	PUSH AF
9.	PUSH BC
	↓
20.	POP AF

a. What is stored in the stack pointer after the execution of instruction 1?

b. What are the contents of locations $84F8_H$ and $84F7_H$ after the execution of instruction 7 (PUSH HL)?

c. Specify the bytes in the accumulator and the flag register after the execution of the instruction OR A.

d. What is the address in the stack pointer when instruction 9 is executed and what are the contents of the two top locations of the stack?

e. Specify the status of the S, Z, and C flags after the execution of instruction 20 (POP AF).

4. If the stack pointer is initialized at $20C8_H$ and the Call instruction located at 2052_H calls the subroutine at 2075_H, specify the contents of the stack locations $20C7_H$ and $20C6_H$ and the contents of the stack pointer after the execution of the Call instruction.

5. The following program has a delay subroutine located at 1860_H. Read the program and answer the questions following.

Memory Addresses	Instructions	Comments
1800	LD SP, 1900H	;Main Program
1803	LD HL, 1850H	
1806	LD BC, 000AH	
1809	CALL 1860H	
180C	OUT (PORT1), A	
	↓	
1860	PUSH HL	;Delay Subroutine
1861	PUSH BC	
1862	LD HL, A2FFH	
	↓	
1872	POP BC	

1873	POP HL
1874	RET

a. When the Call instruction located at 1809_H is executed, specify the contents of the stack location $18FE_H$ and the address in the stack pointer.

b. List the stack locations and their contents after the execution of the instructions PUSH HL and PUSH BC in the subroutine.

c. List the address in the stack pointer and the contents of the BC registers after the execution of the instruction POP BC.

d. Where does the program return after the execution of the instruction RET at the end of the subroutine?

e. Specify the contents of the stack pointer after the execution of the RET instruction.

6. The following program is a continuous Hex counter with an appropriate delay between two counts. Read the program and answer the questions.

Memory Addresses	Instructions	Comments
2000	LD SP, 20FAH	;Main program
2003	LD HL, 2065H	
2006	LD BC, 0010H	
2009	LD A, 00H	
200B	OUT (PORT1), A	
200D	CALL 2065H	
2010	INC A	
2011	JP 200BH	
	↓	
2065	PUSH HL	;Delay Subroutine
2066	PUSH BC	
2067	LD HL, 10FFH	
206A	DEC HL	
	↓	
2070	POP BC	
2071	RET	

a. List the stack locations and their contents after the instruction PUSH BC is executed.

b. Where does the program return after the execution of the RET instruction and what are the contents of the stack pointer?

c. What is being displayed at PORT1? Explain your answer.

7. Write a program to add the two Hex numbers 8A and 93. Store the sum at location OUTBUF and the flag status at location OUTBUF − 1. Initialize the stack at an appropriate memory address.

8. Write a program to initialize the stack pointer at memory location STACK,

add two Hex numbers (97 and A1), and store the flag status in location
STACK $-$ 2 and the accumulator contents in location STACK $-$ 1.

9. Write a program to meet the following specifications.

   □ Initialize the stack pointer at $XX99_H$.
   □ Clear the memory locations starting from $XX90_H$ to $XX9F_H$.
   □ Load register pairs BC, DE, and HL with data $024F_H$, 4835_H, and 2050_H, respectively.
   □ Store the contents of the registers BC, DE, and HL on the stack.
   □ Execute the program and verify the memory locations from $XX90_H$ to $XX9F_H$.

   Note: For XX substitute high-order memory address (page number) of your system.

10. Write a program to clear the initial flags, load the data $FFFF_H$ into register BC, and increment the register pair BC. Display the flag status at an output port or store it on the stack. Explain your results.

11. Write a 20-ms time delay subroutine using register pair BC. Clear the Z flag without affecting any other flags in the flag register and return to the main program.

12. Write a delay subroutine for 750 ms. Use the subroutine to simulate a flashing yellow light with 750 ms on and off.

13. Given a binary LED output port with eight LEDs, turn on one LED at a time for 750 ms; the output should appear as a rotating light display. Use the delay subroutine from **12**.

14. Write a delay subroutine to generate the tone of "high C" with frequency ≈ 4185 Hz. This delay subroutine should include a constant (parameter) in a register that should enable a calling program to increase the delay and generate tones of various frequencies. (Refer to section 10.4.3, parameter passed on to the DELAY routine in register B.)

15. Modify the subroutine LOOKUP to include the situation when the code is stored in a sequence but crosses the memory page boundary (for example, when the seven-segment code is stored from $18FA_H$ to 1903_H).

16. Modify the BCD Counter program (section 10.7) to make it a 10-minute timer, and display the minutes at the LED ports.

Application Programs and Software Design

In the last three chapters, most of the Z80 instructions were introduced and illustrated with examples and application programs, such as block transfer, time delays, bit manipulations, and some arithmetic operations. The subroutine technique, discussed in Chapter 10, provides us with the most powerful features of programming: modularity and flexibility.

In this chapter we first introduce the Z80 instructions dealing primarily with 16-bit operations (copy, exchange, and arithmetic) and illustrate them using the subroutine technique. The illustrations will include examples such as multiprecision addition, multiplication, division, and code conversions.

In computer applications, various number systems and codes are used to input data or to display results. The ASCII (American Standard Code for Information Interchange) terminal is a standard Input/Output device in disk-based microcomputer systems. The code conversion subroutines demonstrated in this chapter are

commonly used to exchange alphanumeric (letters and numbers) information between the microprocessor and peripherals such as terminals and printers.

OBJECTIVES
□ Explain and illustrate the instructions used to copy or exchange 16-bit data between registers and memory locations.
□ Explain and illustrate the instructions that perform addition or subtraction with carry.
□ Write subroutines to perform arithmetic op-
erations such as multiplying, dividing, and adding numbers larger than 8 bits.
□ Write subroutines to perform code conversions for BCD, binary, and ASCII characters.
□ Write a program to illustrate the modular approach in software design.

11.1   16-BIT OPERATIONS

Most of the instructions discussed in the last several chapters deal primarily with 8-bit data. However, there are instances when we need to manipulate data larger than 8 bits, especially in arithmetic manipulations and stack operations. Even though the Z80 is an 8-bit microprocessor, its architecture allows specific combinations of 8-bit registers to form 16-bit registers. There are several instructions in the set to manipulate data larger than 8 bits. These instructions will be introduced in this section and illustrated with examples.

11.1.1   16-Bit Data Copy and Data Exchange Group

Opcode	Operand	Bytes	Description
LD	HL, (16-bit)	3	Load HL register from the contents of memory specified by the 16-bit operand and the next memory location.
LD	(16-bit), HL	3	Load the contents of HL register into memory location specified by the 16-bit operand and the next memory location.
LD	SP, HL	1	Load the contents of HL register into the stack pointer register.
JP	(HL)	1	Load the contents of HL register into the program counter. This instruction is equivalent to LD PC, HL.
EX	DE, HL	1	Exchange the contents of DE and HL.
EX	(SP), HL	1	Exchange the contents of HL register and the contents of the top two locations of the stack.

General Characteristics
1. The first four instructions copy 16-bit data between the HL register pair and memory, the stack pointer, and the program counter.
2. The Exchange instructions exchange (copy both ways) 16-bit data.
3. These instructions do not affect the flags.

Example
11.1

The memory locations 2050_H and 2051_H contain $3F_H$ and 42_H, respectively, and the register pair DE contains $856F_H$. Write instructions to exchange the contents of DE with the contents of the memory locations.

Memory Contents   Solution

Before Instructions: D | 85 | 6F | E   2050 | 3F |

                                                  2051 | 42 |

LD HL, (2050H)   ;   H | 42 | 3F | L   2050 | 3F |

                                                  2051 | 42 |

EX DE, HL   ;   D | 42 | 3F | E

                   ;   H | 85 | 6F | L

LD (2050H), HL   ;   2050 | 6F |

                                                  2051 | 85 |

11.1.2 Arithmetic Instructions: Addition with Carry

ADC	A, r	These instructions add the contents of the operand, and
ADC	A, 8-bit	the carry, and the accumulator, and the result is placed
ADC	A, (HL)	in the accumulator.
ADC	A, (rx*+d)	Generally, these instructions are used to add numbers larger than 8 bits, as shown in Example 11.2.

*rx represents index registers IX and IY.

Example
11.2

Registers BC contain 2793_H, and registers DE contain 3182_H. Add these two 16-bit numbers, and place the sum in memory locations 2050_H and 2051_H.

Solution

Before Instructions: B | 27 | 93 | C

                         D | 31 | 82 | E

Instructions to add 16 bits:

LD A, C   A | 93 | X | F $93_H \rightarrow$ (A)

ADD A, E   A | 15 | C = 1 | F $+ 82_H \rightarrow$ (E)

                                               ——————
                                               $1\ 15_H$

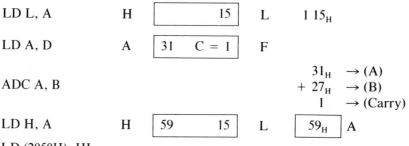

LD (2050H), HL

The 16-bit addition is performed in two stages: add low-order bytes ($93_H + 82_H$), and then add high-order bytes ($27_H + 31_H$). These two stages are necessary because the addition is performed with the contents of the accumulator, which can hold only eight bits. If the addition of the low-order eight bits generates a carry, it should be added to the ninth bit position of the 16-bit numbers.

In this example, the addition of 93_H and 82_H generates the sum 15_H and a carry. The sum (15_H) is stored in register L, and the carry is added as a ninth bit to the high-order bytes 27_H and 31_H by the instruction ADC A, B. The result 59_H is saved in register H. Finally, the sum of the two 16-bit numbers (contents of HL) is stored in memory locations 2050_H and 2051_H.

11.1.3   Arithmetic Instructions: Subtraction with Carry

SBC	A, r	These instructions subtract the contents of the operand
SBC	A, 8-bit	and the borrow from the contents of the accumulator,
SBC	A, (HL)	and the result is placed in the accumulator.
SBC	A, (rx + d)	

Example 11.3

Registers BC contain 8538_H and registers DE contain $62A5_H$. Subtract the contents of DE from the contents of BC, and place the result in BC.

Solution

                    LD A, C   85   38
                    SUB E
                    LD C, A   − 62   − A5

                    LD A, B   − 1 ←   93

                    SBC A, D   22   93
                    LD B, A

This is a 16-bit subtraction performed in two stages similar to that of 16-bit addition in the previous example. The low-order byte $A5_H$ is first subtracted from 38_H. The result (93_H) is saved in register C, and the borrow generated by this operation is subtracted as a ninth bit from the high-order byte 85_H ($85_H - 62_H - 1$ Borrow $= 22_H$). Finally, the result is saved in register B.

11.1.4 Arithmetic Instructions: 16-Bit Addition

ADD HL, rp   Add register pair to register HL

ADD HL, BC	This instruction adds the contents of the operand (register
ADD HL, DE	pair or stack pointer) to the contents of the HL register,
ADD HL, HL	and the result is placed in the HL register.
ADD HL, SP	The Carry flag is altered to reflect the result of the 16-bit addition. No other flags are affected.
	These instructions use HL as a 16-bit accumulator.

The register HL contains a 16-bit number (4 Hex digits). Write instructions to shift all the digits by four positions to the left and clear bits D_3–D_0. For example, if the register contains 1231_H, it should have 2310_H after the instructions are executed.

Example 11.4

The solution to this problem lies in the fact that a binary number added to itself shifts the number to the left by one position. To shift the number by four positions, we need to add the number four times. This is equivalent to shifting Hex digits to the left by one position. This is illustrated below in the comment section, beginning with the number 1231_H in HL register.

Solution

ADD HL, HL	; 1231 + 1231 = $\boxed{2462_H}$	HL
ADD HL, HL	; 2462 + 2462 = $\boxed{48C4_H}$	HL
ADD HL, HL	; 48C4 + 48C4 = $\boxed{9188_H}$	HL
ADD HL, HL	; 9188 + 9188 = $\boxed{2310_H}$	HL

    A practical example of this problem is entering a 16-bit address in a single-board microcomputer using the Hex keyboard. When a new key is pressed, the display drops off the most significant Hex digit, shifts the three remaining digits to the left, and places the new key as the least significant digit.

11.1.5 Miscellaneous Instructions

These instructions are used in a bit manipulation, usually in conjunction with rotate instructions. (See Appendix A for illustrative examples.)

CCF: Complement the carry flag
        If C = 1, the CY flag is reset, and
        if C = 0, the CY flag is set.
SCF: Set the Carry Flag. C is set to logic 1.

11.2 ILLUSTRATIVE PROGRAM: MULTIPRECISION ADDITION

Even though the Z80 has an 8-bit accumulator, it can be used to add multibyte numbers. The instruction set includes several instructions specifying arithmetic operations with carry (for example, add with carry or subtract with carry). Descriptions of these instructions convey an impression that these instructions can be used to add (or subtract) 8-bit numbers when the addition generates carries. In fact, when a carry is generated, it is added to bit D_0 of the accumulator in the next operation. Therefore, these instructions are used primarily in multibyte addition and subtraction as illustrated in this program, which adds two 32-bit numbers and stores the result in memory locations of the first number.

11.2.1 Problem Statement

Two 32-bit numbers, each occupying four memory locations starting with the low-order byte, are stored in locations BUF1 and BUF2. Write a subroutine to add the numbers and store the result in BUF1. Pass the following parameters from the main program to the subroutine: the addresses of BUF1 and BUF2 and the number of bytes in a number.

11.2.2 Problem Analysis

To add multibyte numbers, two issues need to be resolved: (1) how to add a carry generated by the addition of low-order bytes to the next order bytes, and (2) how to save multibyte results. The first issue can be resolved by using the instruction ADC (Add with Carry), and multibyte results can be stored in memory by assigning appropriate memory locations.

In this problem, we need to set up one counter to count the number of bytes to be added and two memory pointers to point to BUF1 and BUF2.

11.2.3 Program

```
MAIN:   LD HL, BUF1          ;Initialize memory pointers
        LD DE, BUF 2
        LD B, 04H            ;Set up register B as a counter to
                             ; specify the size of number to be added
        CALL ADBYTE          ;Call subroutine to add multibyte
                             ; numbers
        HALT
ADBYTE: ;This subroutine adds any two multibyte numbers
        ; and saves the
        ; result in memory by replacing the first number.
        ;Input: Addresses of numbers to be added in HL and
        ;         DE registers
        ;       : The size of the number in bytes in
        ;         register B
        ;Output: None, the result is stored in memory
```

```
            ;Modifies registers: B, DE, and HL
  START: XOR A              ;Clear carry
  NEXT:  LD A, (DE)         ;Get byte from BUF2
         ADC A, (HL)        ;Add byte from BUF1
         LD (HL), A         ;Save partial result
         INC HL             ;Update memory pointers
         INC DE
         DEC B              ;Update counter for next addition
         JR NZ, NEXT        ;If counter ≠ 0, get next-order
                            ; byte

         RET
```

11.2.4 Program Description

The main program initializes the memory pointers DE and HL, sets up register B to count four bytes (32 bits), and calls the subroutine ADBYTE. The subroutine begins by clearing the CY flag; if a carry has been generated by the calling program in the previous operation, it must be cleared. The program adds the low-order bytes from BUF1 and BUF2 by using the memory pointers and the instruction ADC and saves the partial result in the first memory location of BUF1. In the following instructions, the pointers are upgraded to point to the next bytes, and the counter is decremented. The loop is repeated until all four bytes are added, and the complete result, starting from the low-order byte, is stored in four memory locations of BUF1.

This subroutine can be used to add numbers of any size specified by the calling program in register B; however, it does not account for a carry generated by the last addition. For example, in this program, if the sum is larger than 32 bits, the result will have an error. To subtract multibyte numbers, this subroutine can be used by replacing the instruction ADC with SBC.

BINARY MULTIPLICATION   11.3

Multiplication can be viewed as repeated addition. For example, the product of 20 and 5 (20 × 5) can be obtained by adding 20 five times. To write a program, we can set up a counter for five and add 20 until the counter is zero. It is, however, a rather inefficient technique for a large multiplier. A more efficient technique can be devised by following the model of manual multiplication of decimal numbers.

$$
\begin{array}{r}
1\,2\,5 \\
\times 1\,0\,1 \\
\hline
\end{array}
$$

Step 1: $(125 \times 1) =$ 1 2 5
Step 2: Shift left and add (125×0) +   0 0 0
Step 3: Shift left and add (125×1) +1 2 5
                                                    _____
                                                    1 2 6 2 5

In this example, the multiplier multiplies each digit of the multiplicand, starting from the right, and adds the product by shifting to the left. When the multiplier digit is 1, we add multiplicand (125), and when the multiplier digit is 0, we add 0 (or nothing). The same process can be applied in binary multiplication. The binary multiplier has only two digits, 0 and 1. Therefore, we can set up the algorithm to check each digit of the multiplier; if the digit is 1, we will add the multiplicand, and if it is 0, we will skip the addition.

11.3.1 Problem Statement
A multiplicand is stored in memory location BUF1, and a multiplier is stored in location BUF1 + 1. Write a main program to

1. Transfer the two numbers from memory locations to the H and L registers.
2. Store the product in the output buffer OUTBUF.

Write a subroutine to

1. Multiply two unsigned numbers placed in registers H and L.
2. Return the result into the HL pair.

11.3.2 Problem Analysis
The problem is concerned with multiplying two unsigned 8-bit numbers. Since the result will be larger than 8 bits, it will require a 16-bit register for storage. To implement the algorithm discussed above, we need to set up a counter to check eight bits of the multiplier. When the multiplier bit is 1, the multiplicand can be added to itself by using the instruction (ADD HL, HL) for 16-bit addition.

11.3.3 Program

```
MAIN:       LD SP, STACK         ;Initialize the stack
                                 ; pointer
            LD HL, (BUF1)        ;Place multiplicand in L and
                                 ; multiplier in H
            EX DE, HL            ;Place multiplicand in E and
                                 ; multiplier in D
            CALL MLTPLY          ;Multiply two numbers
            LD (OUTBUF), HL      ;Store the product in the
                                 ; output buffer
            HALT
MLTPLY:     ;This subroutine multiplies two 8-bit unsigned
            ; numbers.
            ;Input: Multiplicand in register E and
            ; multiplier in register D
            ;Output: Result in HL register
            ;Modifies registers: A, B, D, E, H, and L
```

```
                  LD A, D              ;Transfer multiplier to
                                       ; accumulator
                  LD D, 0              ;Clear D to save partial
                                       ; result
                  LD HL, 0             ;Clear HL
                  LD B, 08H            ;Set up register B to count
                                       ; eight rotations
NXTBIT:           RRA                  ;Check if multiplier bit is 1
                  JR NC, NOADD         ;If not, skip adding
                                       ; multiplicand
                  ADD HL, DE           ;If multiplier is 1, add
                                       ; multiplicand to HL
                                       ; and place partial result
                                       ; in HL
NOADD:            EX DE, HL            ;Place multiplicand in HL
                  ADD HL, HL           ; and shift left
                  EX DE, HL            ;Retrieve shifted
                                       ; multiplicand
                  DEC B                ;One operation is complete,
                                       ; decrement counter
                  JR NZ, NXTBIT        ;Go back to next bit if not
                                       ; done
                  RET
```

11.3.4 Program Description

1. The objective of the main program is to demonstrate uses of 16-bit data copy and exchange instructions. The main program transfers the two bytes—multiplier and multiplicand—from memory locations to the HL registers and places them in the DE registers by using the exchange instruction. It calls the MLTPLY routine and places the result in the output buffer.

2. The multiplier routine follows the format—add and shift to the left—illustrated earlier. The routine places the multiplier into the accumulator and rotates it eight times until the counter (B) becomes zero. Register D is cleared to use it for 16-bit addition (ADD HL, DE).

3. After each rotation, when a multiplier bit is 1, the instruction ADD HL, DE performs the addition, and ADD HL, HL performs the shifting of bits to the left. When a bit is 0, the subroutine skips the instruction ADD HL, DE and just performs the shifting.

BINARY DIVISION 11.4

The division of two numbers can be performed by subtracting the divisor repeatedly from the dividend (the number to be divided) until the remainder becomes smaller than the divisor; the number of times the subtraction is repeated then becomes the quotient. For example, to divide 19 by 5, we can subtract 5 three times from 19 until the remainder is 4, and the quotient is equal to 3. Conceptually, this procedure is simple, but it can be time-consuming. An efficient algorithm that imitates the manual division of two decimal numbers can be devised. For example, to divide 203 by 5, we perform the following steps.

	Divisor	Dividend	Quotient
Step 1: Take the most significant digit (MSD) from the dividend and divide it by the divisor. If the divisor > MSD, place the quotient as 0; otherwise find the remainder.	5	203 2 R = 2	0
Step 2: Take the next digit from the dividend and combine it with the remainder of Step 1 and divide the new number by the divisor. Find quotient and remainder.	5	2 0 −2 0 R = 0 0	0 4
Step 3: Take the last digit from the dividend and combine it with the remainder of Step 2. Divide it by the divisor. If the divisor > the partial dividend, the quotient is 0. Find the remainder.	5 5	0 0 3 R = 3	0 4 0 4 0

In this example, the quotient is 40 and the remainder is 3. From this illustration, two critical points need to be emphasized: (1) when the divisor is larger than the partial dividend, the quotient is 0, and (2) the quotients of successive steps are not added but combined with the previous result in appropriate columns.

In Step 2, integer 20 is divided by 5 to obtain the quotient 4, and then the remainder is obtained by subtracting the product of 5 and 4 from 20. This algorithm appears to be complicated; however, in binary numbers, it can be performed simply by subtraction because the quotient can only be either 1 or 0. Similarly, the remainder is obtained by subtracting the divisor from the dividend; the product of the divisor and the quotient is the same as the divisor when the quotient is 1.

11.4.1 Problem Statement

Write necessary subroutines to divide two unsigned 8-bit numbers. The calling program places the dividend in register E and the divisor in register D. The subroutine should place the quotient in register L and the remainder in register C.

11.4.2 Problem Analysis

To implement the algorithm suggested in the above example, the following steps are necessary.

1. In Step 1, the MSD is separated from the dividend and divided by the divisor. In case of the binary number, the MSB can be isolated by rotating bit D_7 into the Carry flag and from the Carry flag into bit D_0 of the accumulator (or of any other register). Now, the MSB can be divided by subtracting the divisor; in binary numbers, the quotient can be either 0 or 1. If the Carry flag is set after the subtraction, the divisor is larger than the MSB; thus, the quotient is 0 and the MSB should be retained as a remainder. If the divisor can be subtracted from the MSB, the quotient is 1 and the remainder should be passed on to the next operation.

2. In the next operation, bit D_6 of the dividend is combined with the remainder by rotating the bits, and the above process is repeated until the dividend is rotated left eight times.

11.4.3 Program

```
DIVIDE:      ;This subroutine divides two 8-bit integers.
             ;Input: Dividend in register D and divisor in
             ; register E
             ;Output: Quotient in register L and remainder
             ; in register C
             ;Registers modified: B, C, and L
             ;Calls two subroutines: DIV8 and RESULT
             LD B, 08H        ;Set up register B to count eight
                              ; rotations
             LD L, 0          ;Clear L to save quotient
             LD C, L          ;Clear C to save partial
                              ; remainder
NXTBIT:      CALL DIV8        ;Call routine to divide two
                              ; numbers
             CALL RESULT      ;Call routine to save results
             DEC B            ;Decrement bit-count
             JR NZ NXTBIT     ;If all bits are not checked, get
                              ; next bit
             RET
DIV8:        ;This subroutine gets one bit at a time from the
             ; dividend to form a partial dividend and subtracts the divisor
             ; from it and passes the status of CY flag and the remainder to
             ; the subroutine RESULT
             ;Input : Dividend in register D and divisor in
             ; register E
             ;           : Partial remainder in register C
```

```
                          ;Output: Remainder in accumulator and CY flag
                          ; status
                          ;Registers modified: A, C, D
        LD A, D           ;Get dividend
        RLCA              ;Shift bit into CY
        LD D, A           ;Save remaining dividend
        LD A, C           ;Place partial remainder in A
        RLA               ;Combine CY bit with remainder
                          ; to form partial dividend
        CP E              ;Check if divisor > partial
                          ; dividend
        RET C             ;Return if CY = 1, divisor >
                          ; partial dividend
        SUB E             ;Subtract divisor from partial
                          ; dividend
        RET
RESULT:                   ;This subroutine saves the remainder and
                          ; adjusts the quotient according to the
                          ; result of the previous routine.
                          ;Input: Remainder in the accumulator and CY
                          ; status
                          ;Output: Quotient in register L and remainder
                          ; in register C
        LD C, A           ;Save partial remainder
        CCF               ;Set CY to 1 or 0 as a quotient
        LD A, L           ;Get previous quotient
        RLA               ;Add quotient from CY flag
        LD L, A           ;Save partial quotient
        RET
```

11.4.4 Program Description

The subroutine DIVIDE initializes register B to count 8-bit rotation; for a 16-bit division, the counter would be set up to count 16. Register L is cleared to save the quotient and register C to save the partial dividend. This routine calls the subroutines DIV8 and RESULT eight times until the counter = 0.

The primary function of the subroutine DIV8 is to take bit D_7 from the dividend (register D) and place the bit as D_0 into register C using the accumulator. This is similar to the procedure shown in the example—taking one digit from the dividend and combining it with the remainder from the previous step. The dividend from register D is copied into A and D_7 is shifted into the CY flag. Then the accumulator contents are replaced by the partial remainder from register C, and the CY flag is shifted into the accumulator to form the partial dividend. The divisor (register E) is compared with the new partial dividend. If the divisor is larger than the dividend, the CY flag is set and the program returns; otherwise, the divisor is subtracted from the partial dividend before returning.

In the subroutine RESULT, the remainder is saved in register C, and the CY flag is complemented. When the divisor is larger than the partial dividend, the CY flag is set, but the quotient is zero. On the other hand, when the divisor can be subtracted from the partial dividend, the Carry is reset, but the quotient is 1. Thus, the CY flag needs to be complemented before placing it as D_0 into register L.

ILLUSTRATIVE PROGRAM: BCD TO BINARY CONVERSION 11.5

In most microprocessor-based products, data are entered and recorded in decimal numbers. For example, in an instrumentation laboratory, readings such as voltage and current are maintained in decimal numbers, and data entry may be done through a decimal keyboard. The system monitor program of the instrument converts each key into an equivalent 4-bit binary number, and stores two BCD numbers in an 8-bit register or a memory location as a packed BCD. Even if data are entered in decimal digits, it is inefficient to process data in BCD numbers because, in each 4-bit combination, the digits A through F are unused. Therefore, BCD numbers are generally converted into binary numbers for data processing.

The conversion of a BCD number into its binary equivalent employs the principle of *positional weighting* in a given number.

For example, $72_{10} = 7 \times 10 + 2$.

The digit 7 represents 70, based on its second position from the right. Therefore, to convert 72_{BCD} into its binary equivalent requires multiplying the second digit by 10, and adding the first digit.

Converting a two-digit BCD number into its binary equivalent requires the following steps:

1. Separate an 8-bit packed BCD number into two 4-bit unpacked BCD digits: BCD_1 and BCD_2.
2. Convert each digit into its binary value according to its position.
3. Add both binary numbers to obtain the binary equivalent of the BCD number.

Convert 72_{BCD} into its binary equivalent.

$72_{10} = 0111\ 0010_{BCD}$

Step 1: $0111\ 0010 \rightarrow 0000\ 0010$ Unpacked BCD_1
$\rightarrow 0000\ 0111$ Unpacked BCD_2
Step 2: Multiply BCD_2 by 10 (7 × 10)
Step 3: Add BCD_1 to the answer in Step 2.

Example 11.5

Solution

The multiplication of BCD_2 by 10 can be performed by various methods. One method is multiplication with repeated addition: add 7 ten times. The technique is illustrated in the next program.

11.5.1 Problem Statement

A two-digit BCD number between 0 and 99 is stored in an R/W memory location called the Input Buffer (INBUF). Write a program that utilizes an unpacking subroutine (UNPACK) and a conversion subroutine (BCDBIN) to convert the BCD number into its equivalent binary number. Store the result in a memory location defined as the Output Buffer (OUTBUF).

11.5.2 Program

```
START:      LD SP, STACK       ;Initialize stack pointer
            LD HL, INBUF       ;Point HL index to the Input
                               ; Buffer memory location
                               ; where BCD number is stored
            LD BC, OUTBUF      ;Point BC index to the Output
                               ; Buffer memory where
                               ; binary number will be
                               ; stored
            LD A, (HL)         ;Get BCD number
            LD HL, BUFF1       ;Set up HL as memory pointer for
                               ; BUFF1
            CALL UNPACK        ;Call routine to unpack BCD
                               ; number
            CALL BCDBIN        ;Call BCD to binary conversion
                               ; routine
            LD (BC), A         ;Store binary number in the
                               ; Output Buffer
            HALT               ;End of program

UNPACK:     ;This subroutine unpacks the BCD number from the
            ; accumulator and stores two unpacked BCD
            ; digits in output buffer memory BUFF1 and
            ; BUFF1 + 1
            ;Input: Packed BCD number in the accumulator, and
            ; storage address for unpacked BCD in HL
            ;Output: None, but stores unpacked BCD in BUFF1
            ; and BUFF1 + 1
            ;Registers modified: Accumulator and HL

            PUSH BC
            LD B, A            ;Save BCD number temporarily
```

```
            AND 0FH              ;Keep low-order 4 bits BCD1
            LD (HL), A           ;Store BCD₁ in BUFF1
            INC HL               ;Point to BUFF1 + 1
            SRL B                ;Shift BCD₂ to right to get it
                                 ; into bits D₃–D₀
            SRL B
            SRL B
            SRL B
            LD (HL), B           ;Store BCD₂ in BUFF1 + 1
            POP BC
            RET
```

BCDBIN: ;This subroutine converts an unpacked BCD number
            ; into its binary equivalent.
            ;Input: Two unpacked BCD numbers in BUFF1 and BUFF1 + 1,
            ; low-order BCD₁ in BUFF1 and BCD₂ in BUFF1 + 1
            ;Output: A binary number in the accumulator.
            ;Registers modified: A, E, H, and L

```
            LD HL, (BUFF1)       ;Get BCD₁ in L and BCD₂ in
                                 ; H registers
            XOR A                ;Clear accumulator
            LD E, 10             ;Set register E as multiplier of ten
SUM:        ADD A, H             ;Add BCD₂ ten times
            DEC E                ;Reduce count by one
            JR NZ SUM            ;Is multiplication complete? If
                                 ; not repeat
            ADD A, L             ;Add BCD₁
            RET
```

11.5.3 Program Description

1. In modular programming, the main program is concerned primarily with initializations and passing parameters on to subroutines. In this illustration, the main program initializes the stack pointer and two memory indexes. It brings the BCD number into the accumulator, initializes location BUFF1, and passes these parameters to the subroutine. It calls two subroutines: UNPACK and BCDBIN.

2. After the return from the subroutines, the main program stores the binary equivalent in the Output Buffer memory.

3. The conversion from BCD to binary involves multiplying BCD₂ by its positional weighting factor (10) and adding BCD₁ as explained in the example.

The illustrated multiplication routine is easy to understand; however, it is rather long and inefficient. Another method is to multiply BCD_2 by shifting, as illustrated in Assignment **19** at the end of this chapter. We could have used also the MLTPLY (section 11.3.3) subroutine with a few modifications.

11.6 ILLUSTRATIVE PROGRAM: BINARY TO BCD CONVERSION

In most microprocessor-based products, numbers are displayed in decimal. However, since data processing inside the microprocessor is performed in binary, it is necessary to convert the binary results into their equivalent BCD numbers just before the display.

The conversion of binary to BCD is performed by dividing the number by the powers of ten; the division can be performed either by the subtraction method or the algorithm shown in the subroutine DIVIDE (Section 11.4.3).

For example, assume the binary number is

$$1111 \quad 1111_2 \, (FF_H) = 255_{10}.$$

To represent this number in BCD requires 12 bits or three BCD digits, labelled here as BCD_3 (MSB), BCD_2, and BCD_1 (LSB).

$$
\begin{array}{ccc}
0\ \ 0\ \ 1\ \ 0 & 0\ \ 1\ \ 0\ \ 1 & 0\ \ 1\ \ 0\ \ 1 \\
BDC_3 & BCD_2 & BCD_1
\end{array}
$$

The conversion can be performed as follows:

	Example	Quotient
Step 1: If the number is less than 100, go to Step 2; otherwise, subtract 100 repeatedly until the remainder is less than 100. The quotient is the most significant BCD digit BCD_3.	255 $-100 = 155$ $-100 = \ \ 55$ $BCD_3 = 2$	1 1
Step 2: If the number is less than 10, go to Step 3; otherwise subtract 10 repeatedly until the remainder is less than 10. The quotient is BCD_2.	55 $-10 = 45$ $-10 = 35$ $-10 = 25$ $-10 = 15$ $-10 = 05$ $BCD_2 = 5$	1 1 1 1 1
Step 3: The remainder from Step 2 is BCD_1.	$BCD_1 = 5$	

These steps can be converted into a program as illustrated below.

11.6.1 Problem Statement

An 8-bit binary number is stored in memory location BINBYT. Convert the number into BCD, and store each BCD as unpacked BCD digits in an output buffer.

11.6.2 Problem Analysis

The problem can be divided into three tasks.

1. The first task is to get the byte from memory. This can be part of the main program.
2. After getting the byte, it has to be divided by 100 and 10. These divisors need to be supplied.
3. Convert the binary number into BCD numbers and store them in the output buffer.

11.6.3 Program

This program converts an 8-bit binary number into a BCD number, so it requires 12 bits to represent three BCD digits. The result is stored as three unpacked BCD digits in three output buffer memory locations.

```
START:      LD SP, STACK        ;Initialize stack pointer
            LD HL, BINBYT       ;Point HL index to where binary
                                ; number is stored.
            LD A, (HL)          ;Transfer byte
            CALL BINBCD         ;Call conversion subroutine
            HALT
BINBCD:     ;This subroutine supplies the powers of ten in
            ; register B
            ; and calls the BCD conversion routine.
            ;Input: Binary number in the accumulator.
            ;Output: Powers of ten and stores BCD₁ in the
            first output buffer.
            ;Calls BCD routine and modifies register B.
            LD HL, OUTBUF       ;Point HL index to output-
                                  buffer memory
            LD B, 100           ;Load 100 into register B (in
                                ; hand assembly 100 should
                                ; be converted to 64H)
            CALL BCD            ;Call conversion
            LD B, 10            ;Load 10 into register B
            CALL BCD
            LD (HL), A          ;Store BCD₁
            RET
```

```
BCD:            ;This subroutine converts a binary number into
                ; BCD and stores BCD₂ and BCD₃ in the output
                ; buffer.
                ;Input: Binary number in accumulator and powers
                ; of ten in B.
                ;Output: None, but stores BCD₂ and BCD₃ in output
                ; buffer.
                ;Modifies accumulator content.
                LD (HL), 0FFH ;Load buffer with (zero minus one)
STORE:          INC (HL)        ;Clear buffer and increment for
                                ; each subtraction
                SUB B           ;Subtract power of ten from
                                ; binary number
                JR NC, STORE ;Is number larger than power of
                                ; ten?
                                ; If yes, go back and add 1 to
                                ; buffer
                ADD A, B        ;If no, add power of ten to get
                                ; back remainder
                INC HL          ;Go to next buffer location
                RET
```

11.6.4 Program Description

This program illustrates the concepts of the nested subroutine and multiple call subroutine. The main program calls the subroutine BINBCD; in turn, the BINBCD calls the BCD subroutine twice.

1. The main program transfers the byte to be converted to the accumulator and calls the BINBCD subroutine.
2. The subroutine BINBCD supplies the powers of ten by loading register B and the address of the first output buffer memory location, and calls the conversion routine BCD.
3. In the BCD conversion routine, the output buffer memory is used as a register whose contents are incremented in each subtraction loop. This step can also be achieved by using a register in the microprocessor. The BCD routine is called twice, once after loading register B with 100, and again after loading register B with 10.
4. During the first Call of BCD, the subroutine clears the output buffer, stores BCD₃, and points the HL registers to the next output buffer location. The instruction ADD A, B is necessary to restore the remainder because one extra subtraction is performed to check the borrow.
5. During the second Call of BCD, the subroutine again clears the output buffer, stores BCD₂, and points to the next buffer location. BCD₁ is already in the

accumulator after the ADD instruction, which is stored in the third output buffer by the instruction LD (HL), A in the BINBCD subroutine.

ILLUSTRATIVE PROGRAM: ASCII TO BINARY CODE CONVERSION 11.7

A computer is a binary machine; it understands and communicates in binary language. However, human beings communicate using alphanumeric symbols (letters and numbers). Therefore, we need to translate between alphanumeric symbols and the binary language; ASCII (American Standard Code for Information Interchange) is a commonly used code for such a translation. It is a seven-bit code with 128 (2^7) combinations. In the 8-bit word format, the ASCII code ranges from 00_H to $7F_H$, bit D_7 being 0. Each combination is assigned to a letter, a decimal number, or a machine command (see Appendix C). For example, hexadecimals 30_H to 39_H represent numerals 0 to 9, and 41_H to $5A_H$ represent capital letters from A to Z.

The ASCII keyboard is a standard input device for most microcomputers. When an ASCII character is entered, the microprocessor receives the binary equivalent of the ASCII Hex number. For example, when the ASCII key for digit 9 is pressed, the microprocessor receives the code 0 0 1 1 1 0 0 1 (39_H), which must be converted to the binary equivalent of 09 (0 0 0 0 1 0 0 1) for arithmetic operations. Similarly, to display digit 9 at the video terminal, the microprocessor must send out the ASCII code 39_H. In some systems, bit D_7 of the ASCII code is used for the parity check. The parity check conveys the information whether the number of 1s in a transmitted ASCII byte is odd or even (see Chapter 15 for details). For example, in a system with the odd parity check, ASCII 9 will be transmitted with D_7 as 1 to keep the number of 1s odd in the byte; ASCII 9 will be $B9_H$. At this point, we do not need to know the details of parity check except that bit D_7 should be masked to translate from ASCII to binary code.

11.7.1 Problem Statement

Write a subroutine to convert an ASCII Hex digit (0 to F) into its binary equivalent. A calling program places the ASCII Hex digit including the parity bit into the accumulator.

11.7.2 Problem Analysis

The ASCII codes for digits 0 to 9 range from 30_H to 39_H, and for digits A to F, they range from 41_H to 46_H; there is a break in the range. Therefore, to set up a conversion routine, we need to check two ranges. If the digit is between 0 and 9, it can be obtained by subtracting 30_H from the ASCII code. If it is between A to F, we need to subtract an additional 07_H from the remainder because there are seven ASCII codes between the code of 9 (39_H) and code of A (41_H).

11.7.3 Program

```
ASCBIN:     ;This subroutine takes an ASCII Hex digit,
            ; strips the parity bit, and
            ; converts it into its binary equivalent. In
            ; the comment section, the routine
            ; is explained assuming ASCII F (46H) as an
            ; illustration.
            ;Input: ASCII Hex digit (with parity bit) in the
            ; accumulator
            ;Output: Binary equivalent in the accumulator
            ;Modifies the contents of the accumulator
            ;                                          Example
            ;                                    A|0100  0110|   46H
            ;                                     |0111  1111|   7FH
AND 7FH     ;Mask parity bit                    _____
SUB 30H     ;Subtract 0 bias from the digit           4 6H
                                                     − 3 0H
                                                    _____
CP 10       ;Is the digit between 0 and 9?            1 6H
RET C       ;If yes, conversion done
SUB 7       ;If not, subtract 7 to find digit         1 6H
            ; between A and F                         0 7 H
                                                    _____
RET                                                   0 F H
```

11.7.4 Program Description

This is an illustration of the multiple ending subroutine. If the digit is between 0 and 9, its comparison with 10 results in a return on the Carry flag. Otherwise, the subroutine returns after subtracting an additional 7. However, this routine does not check whether the ASCII character is beyond the range of Hex digits.

11.8 ILLUSTRATIVE PROGRAM: BINARY TO ASCII CODE CONVERSION

The binary to ASCII code conversion is necessary to display text or numbers at an ASCII terminal (or print at a printer). For example, to display digit 9 at the terminal, the microprocessor should send out 39_H. The following subroutine illustrates binary to ASCII conversion.

11.8.1 Problem Statement

Write a subroutine to convert a byte in the accumulator into two ASCII characters and store them in output buffer OUTBUF and OUTBUF + 1.

11.8.2 Problem Analysis

A byte in the accumulator is equivalent to 2 Hex digits. Therefore, the byte should be unpacked. The conversion process is opposite the previous subroutine ASCBIN. If the digit is between 0 to 9, it is converted by adding 30_H, and if the digit is between A to F, an additional 07_H must be added to the digit.

11.8.3 Program

```
BINASC:      ;This subroutine converts the byte in the
             ; accumulator into two ASCII
             ; characters and saves them in memory OUTBUF
             ; and OUTBUF + 1
             ;Input: Byte in the accumulator and the memory
             ; pointer for OUTBUF
             ; in BC
             ;Output: None; two ASCII characters are stored
             ; in OUTBUF
             ;Registers modified: A, B, C, H, and L
             ;Calls two subroutines: UNPACK and ASCII
             CALL UNPACK       ;Unpack the byte from the
                               ; accumulator and
                               ; place nibbles as low-order
                               ; 4-bit in BUFF1 and
                               ; BUFF1 + 1
             LD HL, (BUFF1)    ;Place unpacked nibbles into
                               ; HL register
             LD A, L           ;Place digit from BUFF1 into A
                               ; for conversion
             CALL ASCII        ;Convert into ASCII character
             LD (BC), A        ;Store first ASCII in OUTBUF
             INC BC            ;Memory pointer to OUTBUF + 1
             LD A, H           ;Place digit from BUFF1 + 1
                               ; into A for
                               ; conversion
             CALL ASCII        ;Convert second digit into
                               ; ASCII character
             LD (BC), A        ;Place second ASCII into
                               ; OUTBUF + 1
             HALT              ;End
UNPACK:      ;This subroutine is written in Section 11.5.3.

ASCII:       ;This subroutine converts low-order 4-bit into
             ; ASCII Hex code
```

```
        ;Input : Binary digit from 0 to F as low-order 4-
        ; bit in the accumulator
        ;Output: ASCII Hex code in the accumulator
        ;Modifies accumulator contents
        CP 10              ;Is digit less than 10?
        JR C, BASE         ;If yes, go to add ASCII base
                           ; of 30H
        ADD A, 07H         ;Add 7H to get code for digits
                           ; between A and F
BASE:   ADD A, 30H         ;Add ASCII base 30H
        RET
```

11.9   SOFTWARE DESIGN

In previous sections of this chapter, we illustrated various subroutines related to 16-bit arithmetic operations and code conversions. These subroutines are written as independent modules dealing with a simple task. We can now combine these independent modules to design a simple project. The following project can be viewed as part of a communication process between the microcomputer and its terminal. The project is concerned with how to process ASCII characters after they have been received, how to form binary numbers for arithmetic operations, and how to convert any arithmetic results into ASCII characters for display.

11.9.1 Project Statement

Four ASCII characters are stored sequentially in the input buffer INBUF. The first two characters represent an 8-bit multiplicand and the remaining two represent an 8-bit multiplier. Each number is stored low-order digit first, followed by the high-order digit. Convert the ASCII characters into binary digits, multiply the numbers, and store the result in the output buffer OUTBUF as ASCII characters.

11.9.2 Project Analysis

This is a simple software design project, and it can be divided into various segments. To clarify the analysis, the steps are illustrated with the example of the following four ASCII characters: 32_H, 41_H, 46_H, and 35_H (Figure 11.1).

1. First, we need to convert ASCII characters into their binary equivalents. Four ASCII characters will have four binary digits; thus, they can be placed as unpacked binary digits (02, 0A, 0F, and 05) back into INBUF. (See Appendix C for the ASCII table to obtain the Hex equivalents for ASCII characters.)
2. The first two represent a multiplicand ($A2_H$), and the remaining two represent a multiplier ($5F_H$). These four digits need to be packed as two binary numbers (Figure 11.1(b)).

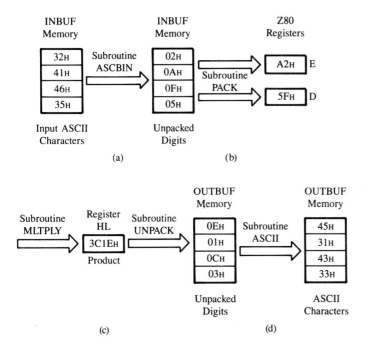

FIGURE 11.1
Memory and Register Contents After Execution of Subroutines

3. When these two 8-bit numbers are multiplied, the result can be as large as a 16-bit number (or four Hex digits). In our example, the result is $3C1E_H$.

4. To convert the result into ASCII characters, all four digits should be converted into unpacked digits as 0E, 01, 0C, and 03 (Figure 11.1(c)).

5. Now the unpacked digits can be converted into ASCII characters as 45_H, 31_H, 43_H, and 33_H and stored sequentially in the output buffer OUTBUF (Figure 11.1(d)).

11.9.3 Program

```
START:   LD SP, STACK          ;Initialize the stack
         LD HL, INBUF          ;Set up HL as memory pointer
                               ; to ASCII characters
         LD B, 04H             ;Set up register B to count
                               ; ASCII characters
CHAR:    LD A, (HL)            ;Get ASCII character
         CALL ASCBIN           ;Convert into binary
         LD (HL), A            ;Place unpacked binary digit
                               ; into INBUF
```

```
              INC HL               ;Next buffer memory location
              DEC B                ;One conversion complete
              JR NZ, CHAR          ;If all characters are not
                                   ; yet converted, get next one
              LD HL, INBUF         ;Set up HL as memory pointer
                                   ; for unpacked
                                   ; digits
              CALL PACK            ;Pack digits of the
                                   ; multiplicand
              LD E, A              ;Place the multiplicand in
                                   ; register E
              CALL PACK            ;Pack digits for the
                                   ; multiplier
              LD D, A              ;Place the multiplier in
                                   ; register D
              CALL MLTPLY          ;Multiply two numbers and
                                   ; place result in HL
              EX DE, HL            ;Save the result in DE
              LD HL, OUTBUF        ;Set up HL as memory pointer
                                   ; for OUTBUF
              LD A, E              ;Get low-order byte of the
                                   ; result
              CALL UNPACK          ;Unpack the low-order byte
                                   ; and store in
                                   ; OUTBUF
              LD HL, OUTBUF + 2    ;Update memory pointer
              LD A, D              ;Get high-order byte of the
                                   ; result
              CALL UNPACK          ;Unpack high-order byte and
                                   ; store in OUTBUF
              LD HL, OUTBUF        ;Set up HL as memory pointer
                                   ; for OUTBUF
              LD B, 04H            ;Set up register B to count
                                   ; four digits
DIGIT:        LD A, (HL)           ;Get binary digit
              CALL ASCII           ;Convert binary digit into
                                   ; ASCII character
              LD (HL), A           ;Save ASCII character in
                                   ; OUTBUF
              INC HL               ;Next buffer memory location
              DEC B                ;One conversion complete
              JR NZ, DIGIT         ;If all digits are not yet
                                   ; converted, get next digit
```

```
                HALT
PACK:           ;This subroutine takes two unpacked digits from
                ; memory and packs
                ; them into an 8-bit number in the accumulator.
                ;Input: Memory address in HL
                ;Output: Packed number in the accumulator
                ;Modifies registers: A, B, H, and L


        LD B, (HL)              ;Get low-order unpacked
                                ; digit
        INC HL                  ;Point to the next digit
        LD A, (HL)              ;Get high-order unpacked
                                ; digit
        SLA A                   ;Place digit into bit
                                ; positions D7–D4
        SLA A                   ; and clear D3–D0.
        SLA A
        SLA A
        OR B                    ;Pack both digits
        INC HL                  ;Point to the next memory
                                ; location
        RET
```

11.9.4 Program Description and Debugging

This program is made up of several subroutines written previously, and the comments explain the functions of each subroutine. This is a demonstration of how a problem can be divided into small modules and how these modules can be written as subroutines and combined into a program.

The program begins by initializing a memory pointer for ASCII characters stored in INBUF and the counter to get these characters into the microprocessor. The program segment starting with the label CHAR gets these characters and converts them into unpacked digits using the subroutine ASCBIN. Figure 11.1(a) shows the process with the four specific ASCII characters as examples. The subroutine PACK converts them into binary numbers—a multiplicand and a multiplier—and stores them in registers E and D, respectively. The next subroutine MLTPLY multiplies these numbers and places the product $3C1E_H$ into register HL (Figure 11.1(c)). The product is again unpacked and stored as four unpacked digits in memory OUTBUF. Finally, these digits are converted into ASCII characters by the subroutine ASCII (Figure 11.1(d)). We could have used the subroutine BINASC, with some modifications, instead of the last two subroutines.

The subroutines used in this project are taken from the previous programs, except PACK, which is included at the end of the program. In troubleshooting this program, you have to be careful in checking the parameters that are passed from one module to another. However, this type of program is easy to debug. The programmer can set up breakpoints at the end of a module and check register contents and parameters being passed. For example, a breakpoint can be set up just before the subroutine PACK is called, and the contents of memory INBUF can be verified. If unexpected results are found, you can examine the initialization instructions or the subroutine ASCBIN. On the other hand, if the expected results are found, you can proceed to check the output after the subroutine PACK. The keys to troubleshooting software are modularity and knowledge of the expected outputs at critical junctures.

SUMMARY

This chapter illustrated subroutines dealing with arithmetic operations such as multiprecision addition, multiplication, and division, and code conversions for BCD and ASCII. The programs were written as independent modules, and the design of a simple software project was illustrated using these modules. The project demonstrated how to break down a given problem into small manageable modules, and how these modules can be written as subroutines and combined in a program to accomplish a given task.

However, single-board microcomputer systems are unsuitable for writing, coding, and debugging programs larger than fifty instructions. To write a large program, it is necessary to have access to an assembler and a disk-based system, as discussed in Chapter 7.

ASSIGNMENTS

Section 11.1
1. Register BC contains the 16-bit number $72F2_H$. Add $F5_H$ to the number, and save the result in BC.
2. Two 16-bit numbers ($82F7_H$ and $24A2_H$) are stored in memory locations $XX50_H$ to $XX53_H$, low-order byte first followed by the high-order byte. For example, the location $XX50_H$ holds $F7_H$, and $XX51_H$ holds 82_H. Add the numbers. If the sum is larger than 16-bit, call the ERROR routine; otherwise, store the sum in memory locations $XX60_H$ and $XX61_H$.
3. Register BC contains $A7F2_H$, and register DE contains $5F18_H$. Add the numbers. If the sum is larger than 16-bit, call the OVRLOD routine; otherwise, save the result in register BC.

4. Register BC contains $87A9_H$. Subtract the byte $F8_H$, and save the result in register BC.

5. Register BC holds $F538_H$, and register DE holds $A279_H$. Subtract the contents of DE from the contents of BC, and save the result in BC.

6. Register D holds the number $C4_H$. Shift the entire number to the left by four positions and clear bits D_3–D_0 (the result should be 40_H).

7. Write instructions to get the address from the stack pointer, and save it on the stack.

8. Assuming the HL register holds 1888_H, write a 1-byte instruction to transfer the program execution to 1888_H.

Section 11.2

9. Two 24-bit numbers, each occupying three memory locations, are stored in addresses starting with 1850_H and 1860_H. The numbers are stored with high-order byte first; locations 1850_H and 1860_H hold the high-order byte of each number. Write a subroutine to add the numbers and store the result in memory locations starting with the low-order byte at 1870_H. The calling program should pass the memory addresses to the subroutine.

10. A string of 16-bit numbers is stored in memory locations starting at BUF1; the numbers are stored with low-order byte first. Write a subroutine to add the string and save the result in the output buffer OUTBUF; the result is limited to 24 bits. The calling program should supply the memory addresses and the length of the string.

11. Modify the program in **10** to increase the limit of the result to 32 bits.

12. In **10,** save the contents of the stack pointer from the main program, point the stack pointer to the location BUF1, and transfer the readings to registers by using the POP instruction. Add the readings as in **10**; however, the original contents of the stack pointer should be retrieved after the addition is completed.

13. Assume that the monitor program stores a memory address in the DE registers. When a Hex key is pressed to enter a new memory address, the keyboard subroutine places the 4-bit binary code of the key pressed into the accumulator. Write a subroutine to shift out the most significant 4 bits of the old address and to insert the new code from the accumulator as the least significant 4 bits in register E.
Hint: See Example 11.4 to shift the four low-order bits in a 16-bit register.

Sections 11.3 and 11.4

14. Rewrite the MLTPLY subroutine to multiply two 16-bit unsigned numbers; the multiplier is given in register DE and the multiplicand in register HL.

15. Rewrite the MLTPLY subroutine using the technique of successive addition for two 8-bit unsigned numbers.

16. Write a subroutine to divide two unsigned 8-bit numbers using the technique of successive subtraction. The calling program passes the dividend in register D and the divisor in register E.

17. Write a subroutine to divide two unsigned 16-bit numbers using the technique shown in section 11.4. The calling program passes the dividend in register HL and the divisor in register DE.

Section 11.5

18. Modify the Illustrative Program: BCD to Binary Conversion as follows. The number of BCD digits to be converted is specified by the main program in register D and passed on as a parameter to the subroutine.

19. Rewrite the multiplication section of the BCDBIN routine using the RLCA (Rotate Left) instruction.
    Hints: Rotating left once is equivalent to multiplying by two. To multiply a digit by ten, rotate left three times and add the result of the first rotation (times 10 = times 8 + times 2).

20. An 8-bit packed BCD is in the accumulator. Save BCD_1 in one of the registers and delete BCD_1 from the accumulator, leaving BCD_2 in high-order positions D_7–D_4. Clear the CY flag, and shift BCD_2 to the right by one position. Explain that rotating BCD_2 to the right once from the high-order position is equivalent to multiplying it by eight from the low-order position.

Section 11.6

21. Assume the STACK is defined as $XXB8_H$ in the illustrative program. Specify the stack addresses and their (symbolic) contents when the BCD subroutine is called the second time.

22. Rewrite the main program to supply the powers of ten in registers B and C and to store converted BCD numbers in the output buffer. Modify the subroutine BCD to accommodate the changes in the main program, and eliminate the subroutine BINBCD.

23. Rewrite the program to convert a given number of binary data bytes into their BCD equivalent, and store them as unpacked BCDs in the output buffer. The number of data bytes is specified in register D in the main program. The converted numbers should be stored in groups of three consecutive memory locations. If the number is not large enough to occupy all three locations, zeros should be loaded into those locations.

24. A set of ten BCD readings is stored in the input buffer. Convert the numbers into binary, and add the numbers. Store the sum in the output buffer; the sum can be larger than FF_H.

Sections 11.7, 11.8, and 11.9

25. Rewrite the subroutine PACK using an appropriate Rotate instruction.

26. A set of ASCII Hex digits is stored in the input buffer. Write a program to convert these numbers into binary. Add these numbers in binary, and store the result in the output buffer.

27. Extend the program in **26** to convert the result from binary to ASCII Hex code.

III

Interfacing
Peripherals,
Programmable
I/O Devices,
Applications,
and Design

Part III of this book is concerned with the interfacing of peripherals using programmable I/O devices and design processes of microcomputer-based systems. The primary objectives of Part III are

1. To examine the concepts and processes of various data transfers between the microprocessor and peripherals.
2. To illustrate applications of programmable I/O interface devices.
3. To synthesize the concepts of microprocessor architecture, software, and interfacing by designing simple microprocessor-based systems.

The primary function of the microprocessor (MPU) is to accept data from such input devices as keyboards and A/D converters, read instructions from memory, process data according to the instructions, and send the results to such output devices as LEDs, printers, and video monitors. These input and output devices are called either **peripherals** or **I/Os**; memory can

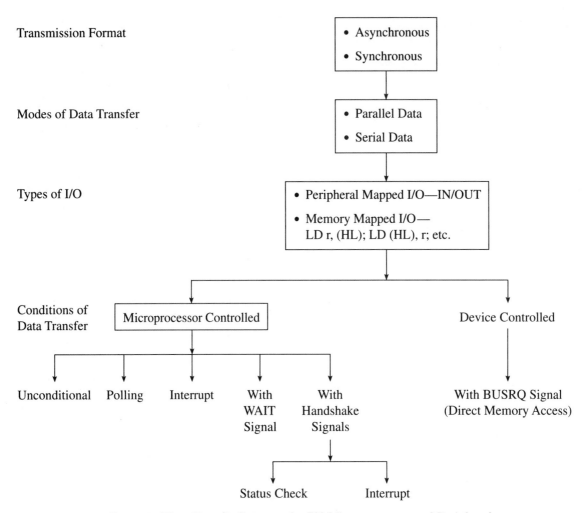

Process of Data Transfer Between the Z80 Microprocessor and Peripherals

be viewed as a special type of I/O. The designing of logic circuits (hardware) and the writing of instructions (software) to enable the microprocessor to communicate with these peripherals is called **interfacing,** and the logic circuits are called **I/O ports** or **interfacing devices.**

The microprocessor (MPU) communicates with the peripherals in either the **asynchronous** or **synchronous** format. Similarly, it can transfer data in one of two modes: **parallel I/O** or **serial I/O.** The Z80 identifies peripherals either as **memory-mapped I/O** or **peripheral-mapped I/O** based on their interfacing logic circuits (see Chapter 5). Data transfer between the microprocessor and peripherals can take place under various conditions, as shown in the chart. The modes, techniques, instructions, and conditions of data transfer are briefly described in the following paragraphs.

FORMATS OF DATA TRANSFER: SYNCHRONOUS AND ASYNCHRONOUS

Synchronous means at the same time; transmitter and receiver are synchronized with the same clock. *Asynchronous* means at irregular intervals. The synchronous format is used in high-speed data transmission, and the asynchronous format is used for low-speed data transmission. Our focus here is primarily on asynchronous data transfer.

MODES OF DATA TRANSFER: PARALLEL AND SERIAL

The microprocessor receives (or transmits) binary data in either of two modes: parallel or serial. In the parallel mode, the entire word (8-bit, 16-bit, or 32-bit) is transferred at the same time. In the Z80, an 8-bit word is transferred simultaneously over the eight data lines as illustrated in Chapter 5. The peripherals commonly used for parallel data transfer are keyboards, seven-segment LEDs, printers, data converters, and memory.

In the serial mode, data are transferred one bit at a time over a single line between the microprocessor and a peripheral. For data transmission from the microprocessor to a peripheral, a word is converted into a stream of eight bits; this is called parallel-to-serial conversion. For reception, a stream of eight bits is converted into a parallel word; this is called serial-to-parallel conversion. The serial I/O mode is commonly used with such peripherals as a teletype (TTY), CRT terminals, modems (digital communication over telephone lines), and cassette tapes.

TYPES OF I/O: PERIPHERAL AND MEMORY-MAPPED

In Z80-based systems, I/O devices can be classified into two categories: peripheral-mapped I/Os or memory-mapped I/Os. In peripheral-mapped I/O, a peripheral is identified with an 8-bit address, and I/O related control signals are used for data transfer. In memory-mapped I/O, a peripheral is connected as if it were a memory location, and it is identified with a 16-bit address. Data transfer is implemented by using memory-related control signals.

CONDITIONS OF DATA TRANSFER

The process of data transfer between the microprocessor and peripherals is controlled either by the microprocessor or by the peripherals. Data transfer is generally implemented under the microprocessor control when the peripheral response is slow relative to that of the microprocessor.

MICROPROCESSOR-CONTROLLED DATA TRANSFER

Most peripherals respond slowly in comparison to the speed of the microprocessor. Therefore, it is necessary to set up conditions for data transfer so that data will not be lost during the transfer. Microprocessor-controlled data transfer can take place under four different conditions: (1) unconditional, (2) status check (also known as polling), (3) interrupt, and (4) with WAIT signal. In many situations, the status check and the interrupt are implemented by using specific signals called *handshake* signals. These conditions of data transfer are described briefly.

Unconditional Data Transfer   In this form of data transfer, the microprocessor assumes that a peripheral is always available. For example, to display data at an LED port, the microprocessor simply enables the port, transfers data, and goes on to execute the next instruction.

Data Transfer with Status Check (Polling)   In this form of data transfer, the microprocessor is kept in a loop to check the status of a peripheral; this is also called polling. When the status condition is satisfied, data transfer is implemented. For example, to read data from an input keyboard in a single-board microcomputer, the microprocessor can keep polling the port until a key is pressed.

Data Transfer with Interrupt   In this form of data transfer, when a peripheral is ready to transfer data, it sends an interrupt signal to the microprocessor. The microprocessor stops the execution of the program, accepts the data from the peripheral, and then returns to the program. The advantage of the interrupt technique is that the processor is free to perform other tasks rather than waiting in a status check or polling loop.

Data Transfer with WAIT Signal   When peripheral response time is slower than the execution time of the microprocessor, the WAIT signal can be used to add T-states, thus extending the execution time. This technique provides sufficient time for the peripheral to complete the data transfer and is commonly used in a system with slow memory chips.

As mentioned above, in many systems, **Handshake Signals** are exchanged between the microprocessor and a peripheral prior to actual data transfer. The function of handshake signals is to ensure the readiness of the peripheral and to synchronize the timing of the data transfer. For example, when an A/D converter is used as an input device, the microprocessor needs to wait because of the slow conversion time of the converter. At the end of the conversion, the A/D converter sends the Data Ready (DR), also known as End of Conversion, signal to the microprocessor. Upon receiving the DR signal, the microprocessor reads the data and acknowledges by sending a signal to the converter that the data have been read. During the conversion period, the microprocessor keeps checking the DR signal; this technique is called the status check with handshake signals and is functionally similar to the polling method.

Rather than using the handshake signals for the status check, the signals can be used to implement data transfer with interrupt. In the above example of the A/D converter, the DR signal can be used to interrupt the microprocessor.

Handshake signals prevent the microprocessor from reading the same data more than once from a slow device and from writing new data before the device has accepted the previous data.

PERIPHERAL-CONTROLLED DATA TRANSFER

The last category of data transfer is peripheral-controlled I/O. This type of data transfer is employed when the peripheral is much faster than the microprocessor. For example, in the case of Direct Memory Access (DMA), the DMA controller sends a BUSRQ (Bus Request) signal to the microprocessor; the microprocessor acknowledges the request and releases its data bus, address bus, and control signals to the DMA controller; and data are transferred at high speed without the intervention of the microprocessor.

CHAPTER TOPICS

Chapter 12 is concerned with the Z80 interrupt I/O process, whereby an external peripheral can interrupt the processor and indicate its readiness for data communication. The chapter discusses various modes of the Z80 interrupt and illustrates them with applications.

Chapter 13 deals with the programmable interface devices: the Z80 PIO and the Intel 8255A. These devices can be set up to perform various I/O tasks by instructions written in their control registers; they are thus called programmable devices. The chapter explains the basic concepts underlying the devices and illustrates various operational modes of these devices with examples.

Chapter 14 describes two programmable timers: the Z80 CTC and the Intel 8254. While time delays and counters were designed using software instructions in earlier chapters, this chapter illustrates the hardware approach.

Chapter 15 focuses on serial data communication, whereby data bits are transferred one bit at a time over one line. First, the chapter discusses the basic concepts in serial I/O and the software approach to serial data transfer. Then it illustrates how the concepts can be implemented using programmable serial interface devices such as the Z80 SIO and the Intel 8251A.

Chapter 16 is concerned with advanced topics in memory interfacing and concepts in the direct memory access (DMA). The topics include the need for Wait states, interfacing of dynamic memory, and data transfer using DMA techniques.

Chapter 17 discusses the design processes in a microprocessor-based product. The primary objective of this chapter is to synthesize the various concepts, both hardware and software, discussed in all the previous chapters.

Chapter 18 reviews various 8-bit, 16-bit, and 32-bit microprocessors and single-chip controllers and suggests trends in microprocessor technology.

PREREQUISITES

☐ Basic concepts of microprocessor architecture, memory, and I/Os (Part I).
☐ Familiarity with the Z80 instruction set and programming techniques (Part II).

Interrupts

In the introduction to Part III, we classified the processes of data transfer between the microprocessor and peripherals into four categories: unconditional, polling, interrupt, and using Wait states. In this chapter, we focus on the interrupt process. The interrupt I/O is a process of data transfer whereby an external device or a peripheral can inform the processor that it is ready for communication and requests attention. The process is initiated by an external device, and is asynchronous, meaning that it can be initiated at any time without reference to the system clock. However, the response to an interrupt request is directed or controlled by the microprocessor.

The interrupt requests are classified in two categories: **maskable interrupt** and **nonmaskable interrupt.** A maskable interrupt request can be ignored or delayed by the microprocessor if it is performing some critical task; however, it has to respond to a nonmaskable request immediately. The maskable interrupt is somewhat like a telephone that can be kept off the hook if one is not interested in receiving any calls. The nonmaskable interrupt is like a smoke detector requiring immediate attention if set off.

The interrupt process allows the microprocessor to respond to these external requests for its attention or service on a demand basis and leaves the microprocessor free to perform other tasks. On the other hand, in the program-controlled (or polled) I/O, the microprocessor remains in a loop, continuously checking the I/O device and doing nothing else, until the device is ready for data transfer.

This chapter describes the basic concepts in the interrupt process and provides an overview of the Z80 nonmaskable interrupt and three modes of the maskable interrupt: Modes 0, 1, and 2. The interrupts are illustrated with examples and industrial applications, such as the interfacing of an A/D data converter. Finally, it includes discussion of how multiple interrupts are implemented with one interrupt line and how priorities are determined.

OBJECTIVES

□ Explain an interrupt process and the difference between a nonmaskable and a maskable interrupt.
□ List the modes of the maskable interrupt and differences among them.

□ Explain the instructions EI, DI, and RST, and their functions in the Z80 interrupt process.
□ List the eight steps to initiate and implement an interrupt in Z80.
□ Design and implement an interrupt with a given RST instruction in Mode 0.
□ Design and implement an interrupt in Mode 2 for a given memory address as a restart location.
□ Interface an external device such as an A/D converter with the interrupt I/O.
□ Explain how to connect multiple-interrupting peripherals with the INT interrupt line and how to determine their priorities using logic circuits.

12.1 BASIC CONCEPTS IN INTERRUPT I/O

The interrupt I/O is a communication process through which the MPU can be interrupted by using one of the external request signals. In Chapter 3, we discussed briefly five such request signals (pins): Reset, Interrupt ($\overline{\text{INT}}$), Nonmaskable Interrupt ($\overline{\text{NMI}}$), Wait ($\overline{\text{WAIT}}$), and Bus Request ($\overline{\text{BUSRQ}}$) in the context of the Z80 architecture. They are shown in Figure 12.1(a). In this chapter, we focus primarily on two external request signals, $\overline{\text{INT}}$ and $\overline{\text{NMI}}$ (Figure 12.1(b)), and their functions in the I/O communication process.

The interrupt signal can be compared with a telephone in an office; a person in the office can continue to work until interrupted by a phone ring. After an-

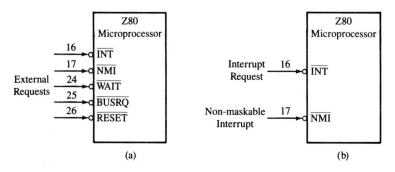

FIGURE 12.1
(a) Z80 External Request Signals; (b) Z80 Interrupt Pins

swering the phone, the person can go back to work. In a microcomputer system, an external device can interrupt the microprocessor by using the interrupt signal. For example, let us assume the microcomputer is executing a program and occasionally needs to read data from a data converter whenever a new reading is available. The data converter can be interfaced with the microprocessor using the interrupt line, so that it can interrupt the processor whenever a new data byte is available. The processor can then read the data byte and go back to executing the program. The interrupt process allows the microprocessor to execute the program and also attend to various peripherals on a demand basis. Otherwise, in our example, the processor would be kept busy just waiting for data and occasionally reading data from the data converter input port.

What happens in the office of busy or high-powered executives when the phone rings? Generally, the secretary or the administrative assistant answers the phone, then transfers the call to the person you asked for; you may even have to go through one more secretary. When the Z80 microprocessor is interrupted, the program execution is transferred to specific locations in memory to get further instructions for what to do next; this group of instructions is called a service routine. In our example, the service routine may consist of reading a data byte. The Z80 microprocessor has various processes for transferring the program execution to these specific locations in memory similar to the various office protocols for answering telephones. These processes are called interrupt modes and are described in the next section.

12.1.1 Overview of Z80 Interrupts

The Z80 interrupts are divided into two groups: nonmaskable interrupt ($\overline{NMI}$, pin 17) and maskable interrupt ($\overline{INT}$, pin 16). The maskable interrupt is the interrupt that can be masked, meaning it can be disabled or enabled. On the other hand, the nonmaskable interrupt cannot be disabled. The maskable interrupt has three different modes (Modes 0, 1, and 2), as shown in Figure 12.2, and they are explained in the following sections. (The nonmaskable interrupt is discussed later.)

MASKABLE INTERRUPT

The Z80 maskable interrupt is controlled by the Interrupt Enable flip-flops (IFF1 and IFF2), which are internal to the processor. These flip-flops are set to logic 1 by using the software instruction EI to enable the interrupt process. The maskable interrupt can be disabled by using the instruction DI; this instruction resets the flip-flops IFF1 and IFF2.

Instruction: EI—Enable Interrupt

☐ This is a 1-byte instruction.
☐ The instruction sets the Interrupt Enable flip-flops IFF1 and IFF2 and enables the interrupt process.
☐ The interrupt process is disabled by the instruction DI, an interrupt acknowledgment by the Z80, or system Reset. The instruction EI must be used to enable the interrupt.

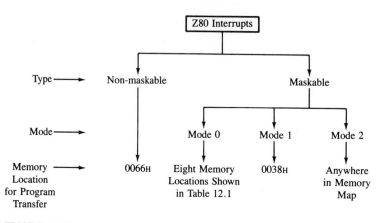

FIGURE 12.2
Z80 Interrupt Modes

Instruction: DI—Disable Interrupt

☐ This is a 1-byte instruction.
☐ The instruction resets the Interrupt Enable flip-flops and disables the maskable interrupt.
☐ This instruction should be included in a program segment where an interrupt from an outside source cannot be tolerated.

The Z80 microprocessor can be interrupted from whatever it is doing if

☐ the flip-flops IFF1 and IFF2 are set (through software).
☐ the input to the interrupt signal $\overline{\text{INT}}$ (pin 16) is caused to go low by a signal from an external device or a peripheral until the microprocessor has time to sample the $\overline{\text{INT}}$. The $\overline{\text{INT}}$ signal is level sensitive, meaning it is not accepted (or stored) immediately on transition from high to low (see the details in Mode 0).

What happens after the Z80 is interrupted is dependent on the mode it has been programmed for by the programmer. The Z80 instruction set has three instructions to set the interrupt mode: IM 0 (Mode 0), IM 1 (Mode 1), and IM 2 (Mode 2).

Mode 0: The program execution can be transferred to one of the eight memory locations from 0000_H to 0038_H shown in Table 12.1 by using additional hardware. (Refer to Section 10.3.2 for explanation of the RST instructions.)

Mode 1: The program execution is directly transferred to memory location 0038_H without any additional hardware.

Mode 2: The program execution can be transferred to any memory location by using external hardware and the address in the interrupt vector register I.

interrupts

TABLE 12.1
Restart Instructions*

Mnemonics				Binary Code					Hex Code	Call Location (Hex)	
	D_7	D_6	D_5	D_4	D_3	D_2	D_1	D_0			
RST 00H	1	1	0	0	0	1	1	1	C7	0000	_ready_
RST 08H	1	1	0	0	1	1	1	1	CF	0008	"
RST 10H	1	1	0	1	0	1	1	1	D7	0010	"
RST 18H	1	1	0	1	1	1	1	1	DF	0018	FFE9 FF
RST 20H	1	1	1	0	0	1	1	1	E7	0020	1806 10
RST 28H	1	1	1	0	1	1	1	1	EF	0028	0038 C5
RST 30H	1	1	1	1	0	1	1	1	F7	0030	1806 10
RST 38H	1	1	1	1	1	1	1	1	FF	0038	1806 10

*Refer to section 10.9 for explanation.

The next step is dependent on what is written at these memory locations; this is similar to what happens to your phone call when the secretary transfers it to the appropriate person. In the following sections, we discuss the hardware and software details of how to transfer the program execution to these memory locations and how to get back to the program execution prior to the interrupt. Remember that the person you called has to get back to work after the phone call.

NONMASKABLE INTERRUPT

This interrupt is not controlled through the Interrupt Enable flip-flops. The instruction DI therefore has no effect on this interrupt, and the instruction EI is not necessary to enable it. This interrupt can be compared to the smoke detector in an office, rather than a telephone. When the smoke detector sets off the alarm, it has to be responded to immediately.

The $\overline{NMI}$ (pin 17) is an active low, edge-sensitive interrupt. When the $\overline{NMI}$ goes low, the Z80 completes the execution of the current instruction and transfers the execution to memory location 0066_H without any external hardware. The details of this interrupt process are discussed later in the chapter.

12.1.2 Interrupt Process in Mode 0

The interrupt in Mode 0 is compatible to the interrupt (INT) in the 8080 and (INTR) in the 8085 microprocessors. We selected Mode 0 to describe the interrupt process because it includes all the basic concepts in the interrupt I/O; other modes can be described as special cases of Mode 0.

One way to describe the Z80 interrupt process is with the analogy of the telephone in an office, this time with a blinking light instead of a ring. Assume that the office has one telephone serving eight engineers, and it is monitored by the secretary. The secretary is generally busy typing, and when the phone begins to blink, he or she stops typing to answer the phone. In order for the secretary to receive and respond to a telephone call, typically, the following activities take place:

1. The telephone system is enabled, meaning that the receiver is on the hook.
2. The secretary glances at the light at certain intervals to check whether someone is calling.
3. When the light begins to blink, the secretary completes the sentence being typed, answers the phone, and waits for a response. Once the phone is picked up, the line is busy, and no more calls can be received on that line until the receiver is placed back on the hook.
4. The caller specifies the message; for our example, assume the caller is the manager of the group and wants to cancel the scheduled meeting with one of the engineers, Ms. Peterson. The secretary performs the following steps:
5. makes a pencil mark at the beginning of the next sentence on the typing draft as a reminder to start typing at that point later on.
6. places the receiver back on the hook.
7. informs Ms. Peterson about the cancellation of the meeting.
8. goes back to the pencil mark on the typing draft and starts typing again.

In some instances, steps **6** and **7** are interchanged, depending on the urgency of the request. If the request is critical and the secretary does not want to be interrupted again while attending to the request, step **7** will be performed first.

The Z80 interrupt process can be described in terms of these eight steps.

Step 1: The interrupt process should be enabled by writing the instruction EI, and the interrupt Mode 0 should be specified by the instruction IM 0 in the main program. This is similar to keeping the phone receiver on the hook.

Step 2: When the microprocessor is executing a program, it checks the INT line in the last T-state of each instruction.

Step 3: If the interrupt flip-flop is enabled and the INT signal goes active (low) and remains active until the end of the instruction being executed, the microprocessor samples the INT signal, completes the instruction, disables the interrupt flip-flop, and sends a signal called INTA—Interrupt Acknowledge (active low). The processor cannot accept any further interrupt requests until the interrupt flip-flops are enabled again.

Step 4: The signal INTA is used to insert an instruction, preferably a restart (RST) instruction, through additional hardware, as shown in Figure 12.3 (discussed in the next section).

Step 5: If the instruction is one of the RST instructions, the microprocessor saves the memory address of the next instruction on the stack and transfers the program to the memory location of the RST instruction. This is similar to the secretary's making a mark on the draft before walking to the engineer to relay the message.

FIGURE 12.3
A Circuit to Implement the Instruction RST 30H

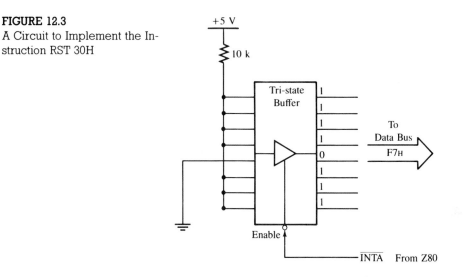

Step 6: Assuming that the task to be performed is written as a subroutine at the specified location, the processor performs the task. This subroutine is known as a service routine.

Step 7: The service routine should include the instruction EI to enable the interrupt again. This is similar to putting the receiver back on the hook.

Step 8: At the end of the subroutine, the RET instruction retrieves the memory address where the program was interrupted and continues the execution. This is similar to finding the mark made on the typing draft after the secretary was interrupted by the phone call and continuing to type.

12.1.3 Restart Instructions and Mode 0

As mentioned in the previous discussion (Steps 4 and 5), the program execution can be transferred, after an interrupt, to a Restart (RST) location through additional hardware. As discussed in section 10.3, the Z80 has eight Restart instructions. These are 1-byte Call instructions that transfer the program execution to a specific location on the page 00_H as listed in Table 12.1. We can use these RST instructions in conjunction with the interrupt Mode 0.

When an interrupt is acknowledged, the program execution is halted, and the processor waits for a further instruction. We can insert one of the RST instructions in the microprocessor using external hardware and the signal $\overline{INTA}$, and begin the program execution again by redirecting the processor to one of the Restart memory locations. Figure 12.3 shows such a circuit. The input to the tri-state buffer is $F7_H$, which is the code for the RST 30H instruction (see Table 12.1). When this buffer is enabled by the $\overline{INTA}$, the instruction RST 30H will be placed on the data bus and brought into the microprocessor. When it is executed, the program will be transferred to the memory location 0030_H. Generation of INTA and its timing are discussed in the next section.

12.1.4 Interrupt Request/Acknowledge Machine Cycles

Figure 12.4(a) shows the timing of the Z80 Interrupt Request and Acknowledge. The interrupt signal ($\overline{INT}$) is sampled by the Z80 with the rising edge of the last clock at the end of every instruction. If the Interrupt Enable flip-flop is already enabled by the EI instruction and the $\overline{INT}$ is low, the Z80 acknowledges the interrupt by generating the $\overline{IORQ}$ signal during the M_1 (Opcode Fetch) cycle. Normally, the $\overline{MREQ}$ control signal goes low during the M_1 cycle to read an opcode from memory. Thus, the interrupt is recognized when M_1 and $\overline{IORQ}$ are active (Figure 12.4(a)). By logically ANDing these two signals in a negative NAND gate (De Morgan's equivalent of an OR gate), we can generate the Interrupt Acknowledge (INTA) control signal. The INTA signal can be used to place an 8-bit instruction (such as RST) onto the data bus. Figure 12.4(a) shows that the Z80 adds two wait states during the Interrupt Acknowledge cycle; these wait states allow sufficient time to determine priorities in multiple interrupts (this will be discussed later). Once the Z80 recognizes that the instruction received is an RST (Call) instruction, it issues two more machine cycles M_2 and M_3 to store the program counter on the stack. During M_1, the program counter holds the memory address of the next instruction, which should be stored on the stack so that the processor can return to the program where it was interrupted after the service routine. During M_2 (Figure 12.4(b)), the address of the stack pointer minus one ($SP - 1$) location is placed onto the address bus, and the high-order address of the program counter is stored on the stack. During M_3, the low-order address of the program counter is stored in the next location ($SP - 2$) of the stack. Figure 12.4(b) shows that the machine cycles M_2 and M_3 are Memory Write cycles.

In the next instruction cycle, the program is transferred to location 0030_H, assuming we use the circuit shown in Figure 12.3 to insert the RST instruction. However, there is a space of eight memory locations between any two RST instructions; RST 38H, the next restart instruction, begins at 0038_H. If the service routine requires more than eight locations, the routine is written somewhere in memory, and the jump instruction is written at 0030_H to specify the address of the service routine. All these steps are illustrated in the next section.

12.2 ILLUSTRATION: AN IMPLEMENTATION OF THE Z80 INTERRUPT IN MODE 0

The following example is concerned primarily with demonstrating the basic concepts in the interrupt I/O, rather than illustrating an industrial application. Hardware circuitry is kept to a minimum so that it can be easily built and tested in a laboratory. Similarly, programs are chosen for the ease of the implementation of the interrupt.

In this example, the Z80 MPU is kept busy counting in binary, and when it is interrupted, it flashes FF_H at one of the output ports. The program is illustrated

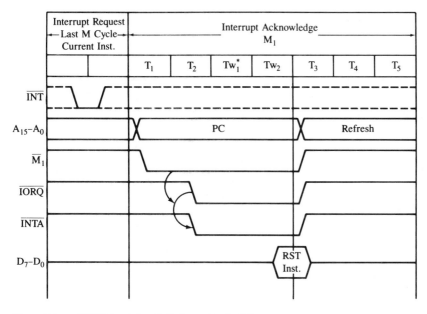

*T_{w_1} and T_{w_2} are Wait States, Automatically Inserted by the Z80

(a)

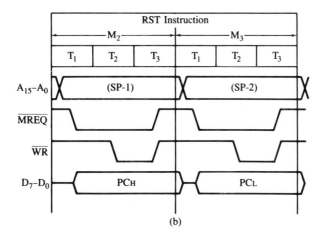

(b)

FIGURE 12.4

(a) Interrupt Request/Acknowledge and RST Fetch Machine Cycles; (b) RST Instruction: M_2, M_3 Machine Cycles

SOURCE: Courtesy of Zilog, Inc.

with specific memory locations starting at 1800_H to explain the details of the interrupt process.

12.2.1 Problem Statement

The main program counts continuously in binary with a one-second delay between each count and displays the count at PORT1. A service routine is written at 1870_H to flash FF_H five times when the program is interrupted, with some appropriate delay between each flash.

1. Design a circuit to insert the instruction RST 30H when the MPU is interrupted by a push-button key.
2. Explain the interrupt process.

PROGRAM

```
            0001    ;THE FOLLOWING PROGRAM IS A CONTINUOUS COUNTER
            0002    ; USED TO DEMONSTRATE MODE 0 INTERRUPT. WHEN
            0003    ; IT IS INTERRUPTED, RST 30H IS SUPPLIED
            0004    ; EXTERNALLY. IT CALLS DELAY SUBROUTINE FROM
                    ; SECTION 10.7. THIS ROUTINE IS NOT ASSEMBLED
                    ; HERE.
            0005
00C1 =      0006    PORT1   EQU     0C1H            ;OUTPUT PORT
                                                    ; ADDRESS
1899 =      0007    STACK   EQU     1899H           ;STACK
                                                    ; INITIALIZATION
1800 =      0008            ORG     1800H           ;ASSEMBLE
                                                    ; PROGRAM AT
                                                    ; 1800H
            0009    ;_____
1800 319918 0010    START:  LD      SP,STACK        ;INITIALIZE
                                                    ; STACK POINTER
1803 ED46   0011            IM      0               ;SET UP INTERRUPT
                                                    ; IN MODE 0
1805 FB     0012            EI                      ;ENABLE
                                                    ; INTERRUPT
                                                    ; FLIP-FLOPS
1806 3E00   0013            LD      A,00            ;START COUNTER
1808 D3C1   0014    NXTCNT: OUT     (PORT1),A       ;DISPLAY COUNT
180A CD8418 0015            CALL    DELAY           ;WAIT ONE SECOND
180D 3C     0016            INC     A               ;NEXT COUNT
180E C30818 0017            JP      NXTCNT          ;CONTINUE
            0018    ;_____
0030 =      0019            ORG     0030H           ;WE ARE ASSUMING
                                                    ; THAT THE SYSTEM
            0020                                    ; DESIGNER HAS
```

```
                                                   ; WRITTEN THE
                                                   ; JUMP
                    0021                           ; INSTRUCTION TO
                                                   ; TRANSFER
                                                   ; PROGRAM
0030 C37018         0022           JP      1870H   ; TO 1870H
                    0023   ;_____
1870 =              0024           ORG     1870H   ;LOCATION OF THE
                                                   ; SERVICE ROUTINE
1870 =              0025   FLASH:           ;SERVICE ROUTINE TO DISPLAY FFH FIVE
                                            ; TIMES.
1870 C5             0026           PUSH    BC       ;SAVE REGISTERS
1871 F5             0027           PUSH    AF
1872 060A           0028           LD      B,10     ;LOAD COUNT FOR
                                                    ; FIVE FLASHES
                    0029                            ; AND FIVE BLANKS
1874 3E00           0030           LD      A,00     ;BYTE TO BLANK
                                                    ; DISPLAY
1876 D3C1           0031   DSPLAY:  OUT    (PORT1),A ;OUTPUT 00 AND
                                                     ; FFH
                                                     ; ALTERNATELY
1878 CD8418         0032           CALL    DELAY
187B 2F             0033           CPL              ;COMPLEMENT
                                                    ; DISPLAY BYTE
187C 05             0034           DEC     B        ;NEXT COUNT
187D C27618         0035           JP      NZ,DSPLAY
1880 F1             0036           POP     AF       ;RESTORE
1881 C1             0037           POP     BC       ; REGISTERS
1882 FB             0038           EI               ;ENABLE INTERRUPT
                                                    ; PROCESS
1883 C9             0039           RET              ;RETURN TO
                                                    ; CALLING PROGRAM
                    0040
1884 =              0041   DELAY:          ;USE DELAY SUBROUTINE ILLUSTRATED IN
                                           ; SECTION 10.7
                    0042           END              ;END OF PROGRAM
                                                    ; ASSEMBLY
```

12.2.2 Circuit Design

The circuit is concerned with designing the instruction RST 30H. The machine code for the instruction is $F7_H$. We can design such an instruction by using the 74LS244, a tri-state buffer, as shown in Figure 12.5. All the input lines are tied

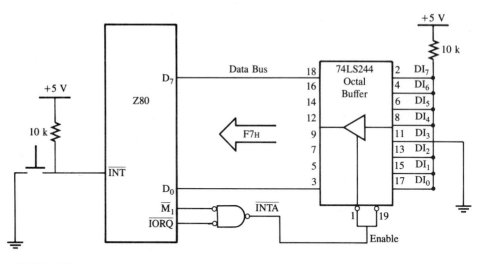

FIGURE 12.5
Schematic to Implement Mode 0 Interrupt

high to represent logic 1 except line DI_3, which is grounded to insert logic 0. The output lines of the buffer are connected to the data bus of the Z80 MPU. When the Enable signal of the buffer goes active (low), the input of the buffer, 1 1 1 1 0 1 1 1 ($F7_H$), is placed onto the data bus.

The Interrupt Acknowledge ($\overline{INTA}$) signal from the Z80 is generated by ANDing $\overline{M_1}$ and $\overline{IORQ}$ in a negative NAND gate, and it is connected to the Enable line of the buffer. The $\overline{INT}$ line of the Z80 is pulled high through a 10 k resistor, and an interrupt is asserted by grounding the $\overline{INT}$ through the push button key as shown in Figure 12.5.

12.2.3 Interrupt Operation

1. The main program initializes the stack pointer at 1899_H and enables the interrupts. The program will count continuously from 00_H to FF_H with a delay of one second between each count.
2. When the key is pushed to interrupt the processor, the $\overline{INT}$ line goes low.
3. Assuming the key is pushed when the processor is executing the instruction OUT at memory location 1808H, the following sequence of events occurs. The Z80

   □ Samples the $\overline{INT}$ line in the last T-state of the OUT instruction
   □ Senses that the $\overline{INT}$ is low, and the interrupt is enabled
   □ Completes the execution of the instruction OUT
   □ Disables the interrupt, and sends out two signals: $\overline{M_1}$ and $\overline{IORQ}$.

4. The $\overline{\text{INTA}}$ (Interrupt Acknowledge) signal goes active at the output of the negative NAND gate.

5. The $\overline{\text{INTA}}$ enables the buffer, and the code $F7_H$ is placed onto the data bus.

6. The Z80 recognizes the instruction as one of the RST instructions. It saves the address $180A_H$ of the next instruction (CALL DELAY) on the stack at locations 1898_H and 1897_H.

7. The program is transferred to memory location 0030_H. The locations 0030, 0031, and 0032_H should have the following Jump instruction to transfer the program to the service routine: JP 1870H.

   (Let us assume that this Jump instruction is already written at 0030_H by the system designer. Otherwise, you do not have access to write at 0030_H. Generally, in a system, ROM (or EPROM) is mapped into the initial memory locations. See the next section.)

8. The program jumps to the service routine at 1870_H.

9. The service routine saves the registers being used in the subroutine and loads the count ten into register B to output five flashes and also five blanks.

10. The service routine enables the interrupt before returning to the main program.

11. When the service routine executes the RET instruction, the microprocessor retrieves the memory address $180A_H$ from the top of the stack and continues the binary counting in the main program.

12.2.4 Testing Interrupts on a Single-Board Microcomputer System

Step 7 in the preceding description assumes that you are designing the system and have access to locations in EPROM or ROM on page 00_H. In reality, you have no direct access to restart locations if the system has already been designed. Then how do you transfer the program control from a restart location to the service routine?

In single-board microcomputers, some restart locations are usually reserved for users, and the system designer provides a Jump instruction at a restart location to jump somewhere in R/W memory. By writing one more Jump instruction at this location in R/W memory, we can transfer the program to location 1870_H.

12.2.5 Issues in Implementing Interrupts

In the above illustration, we deliberately avoided some of the complex issues in the interrupt I/O to maintain clarity in the discussion. These issues are discussed here.

1. *Is there a minimum pulse width required for the $\overline{\text{INT}}$ signal?*

The interrupt in Mode 0 is level sensitive, meaning the pulse has to be active until the Z80 has time to sample it. The Z80 samples the $\overline{\text{INT}}$ signal on the rising edge of the last clock cycle of every instruction, and the longest instruction in the Z80 set is 23 T-states. In the worst case, if the $\overline{\text{INT}}$ goes active in the last cycle of an instruction, it may have to stay on for 23 clock periods.

2. *How long can the $\overline{INT}$ pulse stay low?*

The $\overline{INT}$ pulse can remain low until the interrupt flip-flops are set by the EI instruction in the service routine. If it remains low after the execution of the EI instruction, the processor will be interrupted again, as if it were a new interrupt.

3. *How can we keep the pulse long enough to interrupt the processor but not so long that it can be misinterpreted as a new interrupt?*

One of the solutions to this dilemma is to latch the $\overline{INT}$ pulse in a flip-flop and clear the flip-flop before enabling the interrupt again. This can be accomplished by interfacing the flip-flop as shown in Figure 12.6. The interrupt source is connected to the clock input of an edge-triggered flip-flop, and the output Q is connected to the $\overline{INT}$ pin of the processor. The $\overline{INT}$ signal will stay active low until the processor acknowledges the interrupt request by asserting M_1 and $\overline{IORQ}$, and these signals are used to reset the flip-flop as shown in Figure 12.6.

4. *Can the microprocessor be interrupted again before the completion of the first interrupt service routine?*

The answer to this question is determined by the programmer. After the first interrupt, the interrupt process is automatically disabled. In our illustration, the service routine enables the interrupt at the end of the service routine; in this case, the microprocessor cannot be interrupted before the completion of this routine. If the instruction EI were written at the beginning of the routine, the microprocessor could be interrupted again during the service routine.

5. *Is there any problem in connecting the key to interrupt the processor as shown in Figure 12.5?*

Yes. When a mechanical push-button key is pressed or released, the metal contacts of the key momentarily bounce before giving a steady-state reading, as

FIGURE 12.6
Latching and Clearing Interrupt
Request

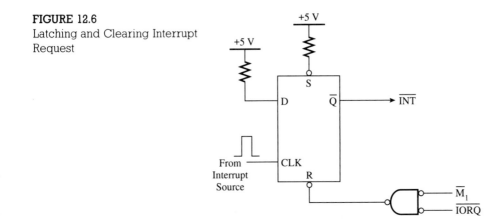

shown in Figure 12.7(a). The bounce can last for more than 20 ms, and if the interrupt service routine clears the flip-flop before the bounce is settled, the key bounce will be interpreted as a new interrupt.

The key bounce can be eliminated from the $\overline{INT}$ signal by connecting the key through a pair of NAND gates, as shown in Figure 12.7(b). Initially, the output of gate G_1 is logic 1 and that of gate G_2 is logic 0. When the key is pushed, and when it loses its contact with terminal A, the input A_1 to the gate G_1 goes high, but the input A_2 is still low. Thus, the output does not change. When the key makes the contact with terminal B, the input B_1 to gate G_2 goes low and the output of G_2 changes from logic 0 to logic 1. This changes the input A_2 from logic 0 to logic 1. Thus, the output of G_1 changes to logic 0.

The key bounce is eliminated because when the key bounces, meaning it bounces from no-contact to contact with the same terminal, the output will not change. In our illustration, the problems of the key bounce and the duration of the $\overline{INT}$ pulse are avoided by keeping the service routine unusually long.

6. *What is the reason to have two flip-flops IFF1 and IFF2 to enable the interrupt?*

In Mode 0, it does not make any difference. In the nonmaskable interrupt, the status of IFF1 is copied into IFF2 when the Z80 is interrupted, and the status is copied back into IFF1 at the end of the service routine (see section 12.5).

7. *What are the differences among RET (Return), RETI (Return from Interrupt), and RETN (Return from Nonmaskable Interrupt) instructions?*

The RET instruction is used to return from a subroutine. This instruction copies the return address from the stack in the program counter and returns to

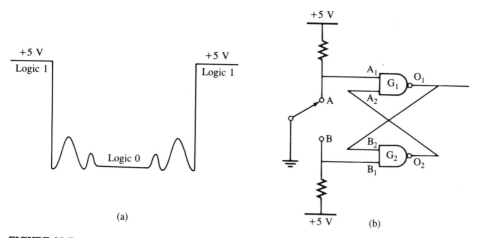

FIGURE 12.7
(a) Key Bounce; (b) Key Debounce Using Two NAND Gates

the calling program. The RETI instruction performs the function similar to that of RET, but it is specially designed to be recognized by Z80 peripherals (such as Z80 PIO) and used to reset the Z80 daisy-chain interrupt logic (see section 13.3.5). The RETN instruction is used in service routines associated with the nonmaskable interrupt. This instruction copies the contents of IFF2 into IFF1 to restore the status of the interrupt flag before the NMI is asserted.

8. *When does EI in the service routine (memory location 1882_H) become effective?*

The EI instruction becomes effective immediately after the execution of the next instruction. In the service routine, the processor will not be prematurely interrupted until after the execution of the RET instruction.

9. *If the Interrupt Enable flip-flops are set and the $\overline{INT}$ is low long enough, will an interrupt request always be acknowledged?*

The interrupt request will not be acknowledged if the $\overline{BUSRQ}$ (Bus Request) is active or if the Z80 is servicing a higher priority request (see section 12.6).

12.3 ILLUSTRATION: INTERFACING A/D CONVERTER IN INTERRUPT MODE 1

The interrupt Mode 1 is a special case of the interrupt Mode 0; all the basic concepts of the interrupt I/O discussed in the previous section are applicable in this mode. However, the implementation is simple because most of the external circuitry required for Mode 0 is already built into the Z80. After reviewing the interrupt I/O in Mode 1, we will illustrate the interrupt Mode 1 by interfacing the ADC0801, an A/D converter manufactured by National Semiconductor. This A/D converter is specially designed to be compatible with the microprocessor control signals. Refer to Appendix E for basic concepts in data converters and specifications of ADC0801.

12.3.1 Interrupt Process in Mode 1

The initial requirements of Mode 1 to interrupt the Z80 processor are similar to those of Mode 0:

□ The Interrupt Enable flip-flops should be set by the instruction EI.
□ The mode should be specified.
□ The $\overline{INT}$ signal should go low and stay low until the Z80 can sample it.

After the Z80 acknowledges the interrupt, it

□ Resets the Interrupt Enable flip-flops, thus disabling further interrupts
□ Places the address of the next instruction (the contents of the program counter) on the stack

□ Transfers the program execution to location 0038_H (without any external hardware).

The primary difference between Mode 0 and Mode 1 is that in Mode 1, the external hardware to insert the RST instruction is not necessary; it is already built into the processor, and it is activated by setting the Mode. The other difference is that the program can be transferred to only one location, unlike the eight RST instructions in Mode 0; Mode 1 uses the memory location of RST 38H.

12.3.2 Interfacing an A/D Converter

To interface an A/D converter with the microprocessor, the following conditions need to be satisfied. The Z80 should

□ Provide a START pulse to initialize the conversion process by writing to the device as an output port.
□ Wait until the end of the conversion.
□ Read the binary equivalent when the DATA READY signal goes active.

We need to interpret these conditions in terms of circuitry and control signals. The microprocessor can communicate with any external device through a port address and its Read and Write control signals. To meet the above requirements we need to build

□ One output port to send a START pulse
□ One input port with a latch so that the Z80 can read the binary data
□ A circuit to sense the end of the conversion

Fortunately, manufacturers have begun to include latches, buffers, and control logic on the same chip with data converters so that data converters can be easily interfaced with the microprocessor. For our illustration, we selected the National Semiconductor ADC0801 because it has all the necessary interfacing circuitry built in.

ADC0801

This is an 8-bit A/D converter (Figure 12.8(a)) available as an integrated circuit on a chip. The analog signal is connected to $V_{in(+)}$, and the binary output is available on eight data lines, DB_7–DB_0. The maximum input signal can be +5 V or it can be connected as a differential input by using the pin $V_{in(-)}$. The signal V_{ref} is used to limit the maximum input voltage; if it is not connected externally, it is set for +5 V internally. The internal clock is determined by the RC network connected to pins 19 and 4.

To interface the A/D converter with the microprocessor requires three signals: $\overline{CS}$, $\overline{WR}$, and $\overline{RD}$. To start the conversion, the chip should be selected and $\overline{WR}$ asserted low. When $\overline{WR}$ goes low, the chip is reset, and when it goes high, the conversion begins. At the end of the conversion, it initiates the signal $\overline{INTR}$; this can be used to interrupt the microprocessor. When the microprocessor reads

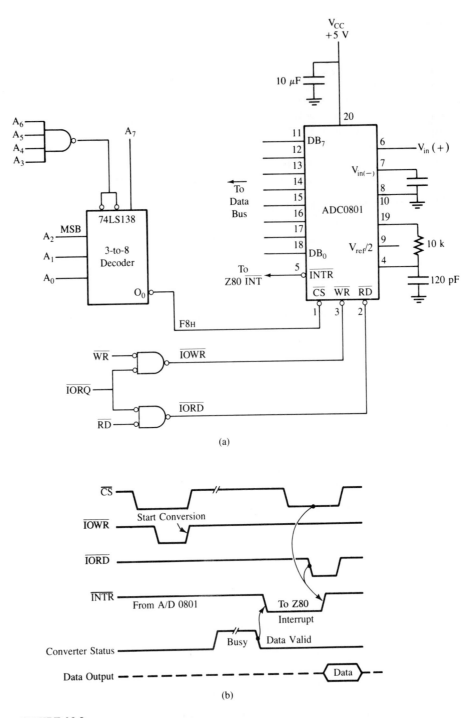

FIGURE 12.8

(a) Interfacing A/D Data Converter ADC0801; (b) Timing Diagram for Reading Data from A/D Converter

SOURCE: **(b) Reprinted with permission of National Semiconductor Corporation.**

the output, the $\overline{INTR}$ is reset (see the timing waveforms in Figure 12.8(b)). The ADC0801 is ideally suited for interfacing as an interrupt I/O not only because it generates the $\overline{INTR}$ pulse, but also because it is turned off after the data byte is read. This eliminates our concern about the $\overline{INT}$ pulse width for the Z80 microprocessor.

12.3.3 Interfacing Circuit

To interface the ADC0801, three signals are necessary: $\overline{WR}$, $\overline{RD}$, and $\overline{CS}$. Figure 12.8(a) shows such a circuit. The output line O_0 of the 3-to-8 decoder is connected to the $\overline{CS}$ signal of the converter. The converter is selected when the address on the address lines from A_7–A_0 is $F8_H$; thus, the converter is assigned the port address $F8_H$. To start the conversion, the Z80 should write to port $F8_H$; however, we are interested not in writing anything, but in asserting the $\overline{WR}$ signal. At the end of the conversion, the converter asserts the $\overline{INTR}$, which is connected to the $\overline{INT}$ signal of the Z80.

Assuming the Z80 interrupt is enabled and is set for Mode 1, the program will be transferred to memory location 0038_H. If the system is being designed, the service routine to read data can be written at 0038_H. Otherwise, a Jump instruction should have already been written here to give access to the service routine in the system's R/W memory. When the service routine reads the data byte, the $\overline{RD}$ signal will remove the interrupt.

12.3.4 Program

The following program is set up to collect a number of readings from the data converter, and the readings are stored in memory labelled as BUFFER. The number of readings to be recorded is defined by the term BYTE. To verify this illustration in a laboratory, the terms STACK, BUFFER, and BYTE need to be defined. The program has three segments: main program to initialize the parameters, the restart segment, and the service routine to record data.

MAIN PROGRAM

```
START:    LD SP, STACK      ;Initialize stack pointer
          IM 1              ;Set up interrupt Mode 1
          LD HL, BUFFER     ;Set up HL as memory pointer
          LD B, BYTE        ;Set up counter to count the number of
                            ; readings
          EI                ;Enable interrupt flip-flops
          OUT (F8H), A      ;Start conversion
WAIT:     NOP
          JP NZ, WAIT       ;If all data readings are not yet recorded,
                            ; wait
          HALT
0038      JP ADC            ;This is Mode 1 Restart location; go to data
                            ; Converter service routine
```

SERVICE ROUTINE

ADC: ;This service routine reads data from the A/D converter, saves data in
        ; memory, and starts conversion for the next reading.
        ;Input: Address of memory pointer in HL and the number of readings
        ; to be recorded in register B.
        ;Modifies registers A, B, and HL

IN A, (F8H)	;Read data byte from the converter
EI	;Enable the interrupt
LD (HL), A	;Save data in memory
INC HL	;Next memory location
DEC B	;One reading is recorded, decrement counter
OUT (F8H), A	;Start conversion for the next reading
RET	

PROGRAM DESCRIPTION

The main program initializes the stack pointer, the memory pointer, and the counter. It enables the interrupt, starts the conversion by writing to port $F8_H$, and waits in the loop. In a real industrial application, the main program would have continued to monitor other activities.

When the conversion is complete, the data converter causes $\overline{INTR}$ to go low, which interrupts the processor. Because the interrupt is set up in Mode 1, the Z80 disables the interrupt, stores the contents of the program counter on the stack, and transfers the program to 0038_H automatically. The Jump instruction at 0038_H transfers the program to the service routine.

The service routine first reads the output of the data converter, and the Read signal removes the interrupt from the INT pin. This logic is built inside the ADC0801; in the previous illustration, we needed to use a flip-flop to turn off the interrupt (see Figure 12.6). The routine enables the interrupt so that the subsequent interrupts can be accepted, then upgrades the memory pointer, decrements the counter, and initiates the conversion for the next reading. The final instruction in the service routine (RET) is critical; when the RET instruction is executed, the Z80 gets the address from the top of the stack and returns to the main program. The main program has the instruction Jump on No Zero; the Zero flag is set in the service routine when the register B goes to zero.

12.4   INTERRUPT MODE 2

In Mode 0 and Mode 1, once the interrupt request is acknowledged, the program is transferred to specific locations on memory page 00. This is quite a limitation because these locations are, generally, reserved for ROM (or EPROM) and can be used for only eight interrupts. On the other hand, in Mode 2, the program control can be transferred to any memory location in the memory map. This is one of the powerful features of the Z80 microprocessor.

The process of interrupt request and acknowledge in Mode 2 is similar to that of Mode 0. However, the response to the interrupt request is quite different.

12.4.1 Interrupt Process in Mode 2

Assuming that the interrupt is enabled and set up to operate in Mode 2 by the instructions EI and IM 2, and that the $\overline{\text{INT}}$ signal goes low, the Z80 acknowledges the interrupt by asserting two signals $\overline{M_1}$ and $\overline{\text{IORQ}}$. The $\overline{\text{INTA}}$ signal, generated by ANDing $\overline{M_1}$ with $\overline{\text{IORQ}}$, is used to place a byte onto the data bus. The Z80 disables the interrupt and stores the contents of the program counter onto the stack. This is similar to Mode 0.

However, in Mode 2, the Z80 interprets the eight bits from external hardware as the low-order byte of a 16-bit memory address rather than an instruction as in Mode 0. The Z80 takes the eight bits from the interrupt register (I) as the high-order byte and combines it with the external byte to form a 16-bit vector address or a pointer. The program is then transferred to the memory location identified by the 16-bit address. Let us assume it is $18F8_H$. Then the contents of the two memory locations $18F8_H$ and $18F9_H$ are interpreted as the 16-bit memory address of the service routine; the byte in $18F8_H$ is the low-order byte, and the byte in $18F9_H$ is the high-order byte. This process is demonstrated in the next example.

---

1. Write initialization instructions to set up the Z80 interrupt in Mode 2 and the interrupt vector with 18_H as the high-order byte.
2. Design a circuit to place the byte $F8_H$ onto the data bus using the $\overline{\text{INTA}}$ signal.
3. Specify the contents of the vectored memory locations if the service routine is located at $19A7_H$.

Example 12.1

1. Initialization Instructions

Solution

```
MODE2:  LD SP, STACK    ;Initialize stack pointer
        LD A, 18H        ;Load high-order byte of interrupt vector
        LD I, A          ;Load register I with high-order byte
        IM 2             ;Set up Z80 interrupt in Mode 2
        EI               ;Enable interrupt flip-flops
```

2. Circuit for the Byte $F8_H$

   Figure 12.9 shows the circuit to place the byte $F8_H$ onto the data bus. The input lines DI_0–DI_2 of the tri-state buffer are grounded and the remaining lines are tied high. When the buffer is enabled by the interrupt acknowledge ($\overline{\text{INTA}}$) signal, the byte $F8_H$ is placed onto the data bus.
3. Memory Vector and Service Routine Addresses

   When the Z80 acknowledges an interrupt request, it forms the memory vector by combining the contents of the interrupt register I (18_H) and the data byte

FIGURE 12.9
Schematic to Place the Byte $F8_H$
onto the Data Bus

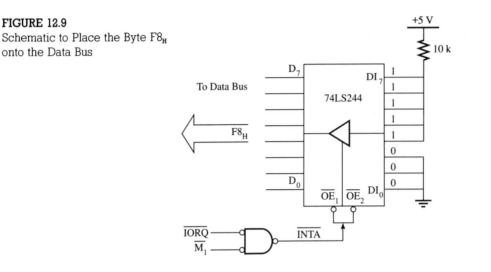

($F8_H$); thus, the address of the vector becomes $18F8_H$. To transfer the program control to the service routine located at $18A7_H$, the low-order byte $A7_H$ must be stored at location $18F8_H$ and the high-order byte 19_H at location $18F9_H$.

$$18F8 \rightarrow A7_H$$
$$18F9 \rightarrow 19_H$$

At this point, it is necessary to clarify the potential confusion in implementing Mode 2 interrupt. The 16-bit address formed by combining the byte in interrupt register I and the byte placed on the data bus is the vector address (or the memory pointer) and not the address of the service routine. The address of the service routine is located at memory locations identified by the vector address. Thus, on one page of memory (256 bytes), a table of 128 vectors pointing to service routines can be stored. Another puzzling question is how to design multiple interrupts using only one $\overline{\text{INT}}$ signal; this question is discussed in section 12.6.

12.5   NONMASKABLE INTERRUPT

The Z80 has a separate input (pin 17) for the **nonmaskable interrupt.** As mentioned before, this interrupt cannot be disabled and has the highest priority among the interrupts. When the Z80 acknowledges the $\overline{\text{NMI}}$, it transfers the program to memory location 0066_H. The $\overline{\text{NMI}}$ is used, generally, for emergency situations such as power failure or activities with high priority, such as a system clock.

12.5.1 Nonmaskable Interrupt Process

The nonmaskable interrupt differs from the maskable interrupts in the following ways.

□ It cannot be disabled by the DI instruction and need not be enabled by the EI instruction; it is independent of the EI and DI instructions.

□ It is edge sensitive, meaning it does not have to be active until the Z80 samples it.

□ It has a higher priority than the maskable interrupts, meaning it will always be acknowledged at the end of the current instruction being executed if $\overline{\text{BUSRQ}}$ (Bus Request) is inactive.

The steps in the nommaskable interrupt are as follows.

1. When the $\overline{\text{NMI}}$ is caused to go low by an external device, the interrupt request is latched internally on the falling edge of the $\overline{\text{NMI}}$.
2. When the Z80 samples the $\overline{\text{NMI}}$ (as well as $\overline{\text{INT}}$) in the last T-state of the instruction being executed, it accepts the $\overline{\text{NMI}}$ request after completing the current instruction if $\overline{\text{BUSRQ}}$ is inactive.
3. Once the $\overline{\text{NMI}}$ is accepted, the Z80 stores the contents of the program counter on the stack.
4. The Z80 copies the status of the interrupt enable flip-flop IFF1, determined by the previously executed instructions EI (or DI), into IFF2 and resets IFF1 to prevent any interruptions from maskable interrupts.
5. The program is transferred to location 0066_{H} without any external hardware; this is similar to Mode 1 in the maskable interrupt.

If the service routine is terminated by the special instruction RETN (Return from Nonmaskable Interrupt), the Z80

6. Copies IFF2 into IFF1 to restore the status of the maskable interrupt
7. Copies the contents of the top two locations of the stack into the program counter, and the program returns to the instruction where it was interrupted.

MULTIPLE INTERRUPTS AND PRIORITIES 12.6

The Z80 microprocessor has one $\overline{\text{INT}}$ pin for the maskable interrupt. However, Mode 0 suggests that at least eight different peripherals can be connected, and their requests can be transferred to eight restart locations. Mode 2 suggests almost unlimited possibilities to vector interrupt requests anywhere in memory. This raises two questions:

1. How do we connect more than one interrupting device to one interrupt line?
2. What happens if multiple interrupting devices request service simultaneously?

The method of connecting multiple devices to the $\overline{INT}$ line of the Z80 is determined by the process of identifying an interrupting device. After the acknowledgment of an interrupt, the interrupting device can be identified either by the **polling method** (software technique) or by the **interrupt vector method** (hardware technique). In the polling method, the microprocessor queries each device using software instructions, identifies the device, and transfers the program to the appropriate service routine. On the other hand, in the interrupt vector method, the device identifies itself by supplying either an instruction or an address.

The next question is: What happens when devices request the service at the same time? In the polling technique, software determines the priority among the requesting devices and serves those devices in the sequence specified in the program. In the interrupt vector technique, priority is determined by the hardware. We will illustrate these techniques in the next two sections.

12.6.1 Polling Technique

Figure 12.10 shows an example in which two A/D converters are interfaced with the Z80 in interrupt Mode 1. The $\overline{INTR}$ lines from the ADC0801 are logically ORed, and the output of the gate is connected to the $\overline{INT}$ line of the Z80; either one or both converters can interrupt the processor. Figure 12.10 does not include any circuitry to turn off the $\overline{INT}$ because the $\overline{INTR}$ line of the ADC0801 goes inactive when the microprocessor reads the output.

To identify the interrupting data converters, an additional input port with the tri-state inverter (74LS366) is designed, and the $\overline{INTR}$ lines of both converters are connected to the data bus lines (D_1 and D_0) through the 74LS366. The following subroutine identifies the interrupting devices and determines the priority between the two converters if they request the service simultaneously.

SERVICE ROUTINE

MODE1:   ;This is an interrupt service routine, written at location 0038_H to
             ;respond to Mode 1 interrupt requests. It determines the priority
             ;between the two data converters and identifies them. In this
             ;routine Device 1 has higher priority than Device 2. After
             ;identifying the interrupting converter(s), it reads and stores data
             ;received from the converter(s), and initiates the next conversion.

PUSH AF	;Save register contents
IN A, (STATUS)	;Read tri-state inverter port
AND 00000011B	;Mask data lines D_7–D_2
RRA	;Place D_0 in CY flag
CALL C, DVICE1	;If $D_0 = 1$, go to DVICE1 to read data
RRA	;Place D_1 in CY flag
CALL C, DVICE2	;If $D_1 = 1$, go to DVICE2 to read data
POP AF	;Retrieve register contents
EI	;Enable interrupt
RET	

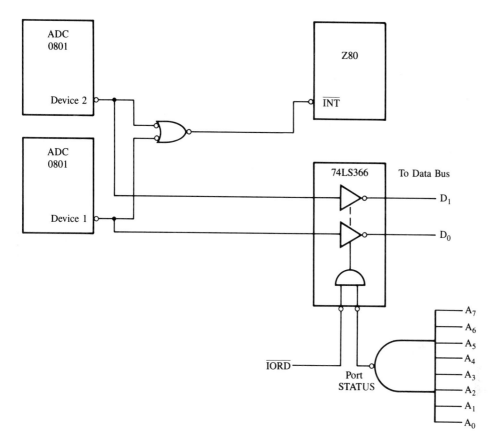

FIGURE 12.10
Multiple Interrupts with Polling Technique

```
DVICE1:    PUSH AF           ;Save interrupt status
           IN A, (ADC1)      ;Read data from Device 1 and turn off
                             ; INT
           LD (HL), A        ;Save data in memory
           OUT (ADC1), A     ;Start next conversion
           POP AF            ;Retrieve register contents
           RET
DVICE2:    PUSH AF           ;Save interrupt status
           IN A, (ADC2)      ;Read data from Device 2 and turn off
                             ; INT
           LD (DE), A        ;Save data in memory
           OUT (ADC2), A     ;Start next conversion
           POP AF            ;Retrieve register contents
           RET
```

PROGRAM DESCRIPTION

This service routine assumes that the main program sets up the interrupt mode and initializes memory pointers (HL and DE) to store data. Data converters are assigned port addresses ADC1 and ADC2 for both input and output, and the tri-state buffer is assigned the address STATUS as an input port.

To identify the interrupting device, the service routine reads the tri-state buffer and saves bits D_1 and D_0. The routine checks first whether D_0 is at logic 1 (the 74LS366 inverts the interrupt request) by rotating D_0 into the CY flag because Device 1 has higher priority than Device 2. If D_0 is high, the routine calls DVICE1 to read data. To check whether Device 2 has also requested the service, the input reading from the STATUS port is rotated again to the right to place D_1 into the CY flag. If the CY is 1, the routine calls DVICE2; otherwise, it returns control to the main program.

Figure 12.10 shows only two interrupting devices; however, the polling technique and the circuit shown can be extended to include many devices. In place of the negative OR gate in Figure 12.10, interrupt requests from many devices can be tied together using open collector logic devices. The disadvantage of the polling technique is the delayed response in servicing requests.

12.6.2   Interrupt Vector Technique

The schematic shown in Figure 12.11 implements multiple interrupting devices using the 8-to-3 priority encoder 74LS148. The encoder has eight input lines and three output lines; the output ranges from 000 to 111, thus encoding the eight inputs. However, the output is inverted. For example, when the input I_7 is active, the output is 000, and when the input I_0 is active, the output is 111. In addition to encoding the input, the encoder also determines the priorities among interrupting devices; the higher input signal has higher priority. For example, if I_6 and I_4 are active at the same time, the encoder ignores I_4 and places the code of I_6 on the output lines. The encoder provides appropriate combinations on its output lines A_0, A_1, and A_2, which are connected to data lines D_1, D_2, and D_3; other data lines are tied high. The data line D_0 must be kept at zero because the Z80 expects the vector address to be even in Mode 2.

When an interrupting device requests service, one of the input lines goes low, which makes the line $\overline{\text{GS}}$ low and interrupts the microprocessor. When the interrupt is acknowledged and the signal $\overline{\text{INTA}}$ enables the buffer 74LS366, the code corresponding to the input is placed on lines D_3, D_2, and D_1, and D_0 is kept at logic 0 by connecting one of the input signals as shown in Figure 12.11. For example, if the interrupting device on line I_0 goes low, the output of the encoder will be 111. This code is inverted by the buffer 74LS366 and placed on data lines D_3, D_2, and D_1. Other data lines are high and $D_0 = 0$; thus, the byte 1111 0000 ($F0_H$) is placed on the data lines. Assuming that the Z80 is set up for interrupt Mode 2, and the interrupt register I is loaded with the byte 20_H, the Z80 forms a vector address $20F0_H$ for the interrupting device connected to I_0. The program is transferred to location $20F0_H$ to get the 16-bit address of the service routine stored

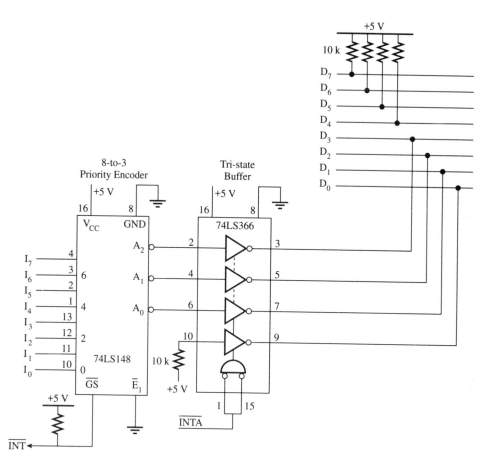

FIGURE 12.11
Implementing Multiple Interrupts

in memory locations $20F0_H$ and $20F1_H$. If the input I_2 goes low, the byte 1111 0100 is placed on the data bus, and the program is transferred to location $20F4_H$. The Z80 expects the interrupt vector to be an even memory address and uses two consecutive memory locations to obtain the address of a service routine.

If there are simultaneous requests, the priorities are determined by the encoder; it responds to a higher level input, ignoring a lower level input. One of the drawbacks of this scheme is that the interrupting device connected to the input I_6 always has the highest priority.

The interrupt scheme, similar to that illustrated in Figure 12.11, can also be implemented by using devices such as the Parallel Input/Output (PIO) controller, to be discussed in the next chapter. A programmable interrupt controller, such as the AMD AM9519A can also be used in implementing interrupts. This is quite a versatile device; it can accept interrupts from eight different devices, hold the requests, resolve priorities, and process them according to their priorities. It is also programmable, meaning its various operating modes can be determined by writing instructions into its internal register.

SUMMARY

- The interrupt is an asynchronous process of communication with the microprocessor and is initiated by an external peripheral.
- The Z80 has two active low interrupt signals: maskable interrupt and nonmaskable interrupt ($\overline{\text{NMI}}$). The maskable interrupt is level sensitive, and the nonmaskable is edge sensitive.
- The maskable interrupt can be enabled or disabled through the program control instructions EI and DI, and it has three operating modes: Modes 0, 1, and 2. The nonmaskable interrupt cannot be disabled.
- The maskable interrupt is disabled after (1) the execution of the DI instruction, (2) the acknowledgment of an interrupt request, and (3) the system reset.

TABLE 12.2
Summary of Z80 Interrupt Process

Interrupts	Conditions to Accept Interrupt Requests	Software Instruction	External Hardware	Restart Locations
Nonmaskable Interrupt (NMI) ☐ Edge Sensitive ☐ Pin 17 (NMI)	$\overline{\text{BUSRQ}}$ Inactive $\overline{\text{NMI}}$ Active Low	No Effect of EI or DI	Not Required	0066_H
Maskable Interrupt ☐ Level Sensitive ☐ Pin 16 ($\overline{\text{INT}}$)	$\overline{\text{BUSRQ}}$ Inactive $\overline{\text{NMI}}$ Inactive $\overline{\text{INT}}$ Active Low	Must Be Enabled by EI and Can Be Disabled		
Mode 0			RST Instruction	Eight locations: See Table 12.1
Mode 1			Not Required	0038_H
Mode 2		Uses I Register for High-Order Byte	Low-Order Byte	Even Address Memory Location

□ The Z80 instruction set includes eight RST instructions (refer to Chapter 10), which are equivalent to 1-byte calls to specific locations on memory page 00_H. These can be used as software instructions to transfer the program control to their vectored locations on memory page 00_H or can be inserted through external hardware in interrupt Mode 0.

□ When the Z80 accepts a request in maskable interrupt I/O, it acknowledges the request by issuing a special $\overline{M_1}$ cycle. During M_1, the I/O Request ($\overline{IORQ}$) signal goes active. The signals ($\overline{M_1}$ and $\overline{IORQ}$) are logically ANDed to generate the Interrupt Acknowledge (INTA) signal, which can be used to insert a hardware instruction or a byte.

□ The general steps in the interrupt process are as follows. The Z80

1. Disables the interrupt
2. Stores the contents of the program counter on the stack
3. Transfers the program to the memory location specified either by the external hardware or by the mode operation
4. Services the interrupt request
5. Fetches one of the return instructions, gets the address from the top of the stack, and returns to the program where the program was interrupted.

The operational details are summarized in Table 12.2.

ASSIGNMENTS

1. Answer the following questions.
   a. What are the differences between the nonmaskable and the maskable interrupt?
   b. When does the Z80 check the $\overline{INT}$ and $\overline{NMI}$ signals?
   c. How is the Interrupt Acknowledge cycle differentiated from the Opcode Fetch and the I/O Read machine cycles?
   d. How is the INTA (Interrupt Acknowledge) signal generated?
   e. Specify the three conditions that are necessary to acknowledge the $\overline{INT}$.
   f. Assuming the system's clock frequency is 2 MHz, and if the $\overline{INT}$ goes low in the first T-state of the OUT instruction (11 T-states), specify the period for which the $\overline{INT}$ has to remain active to be acknowledged.
   g. In a system with the clock frequency of 1 MHz, the Z80 begins to execute an instruction with ten T-states. If at the beginning of the instruction, the $\overline{NMI}$ goes active for 0.5 μs, will the NMI be accepted, and if the answer is yes, when will it be accepted?
   h. The instruction CALL 2085H is written at memory locations 2017–18–19_H. If it is interrupted during its execution, what is the address that is stored on the stack?

FIGURE 12.12
RST Instruction for Assignment 2

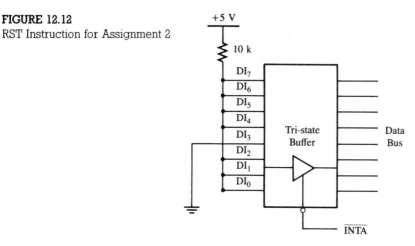

i. The execution of the unconditional Call instruction requires 17 T-states. In a system with 2 MHz clock frequency, if the $\overline{\text{INT}}$ (set up in Mode 1) goes active at the beginning of the Call instruction and stays on for 8.5 μs, and if the $\overline{\text{NMI}}$ goes active 2 μs later than the $\overline{\text{INT}}$ and stays on for 1 μs, where will the program be transferred?

j. Does the system Reset disable the maskable interrupt?

k. If the Z80 is initialized in the interrupt Mode 1, what is the status of the interrupt flip-flop IFF2 when the Z80 acknowledges the $\overline{\text{NMI}}$?

l. If the instruction RST 20H is written in a program at location 2051_H, where will the program be transferred and what will be stored on the stack when the instruction is executed?

2. Identify the RST instruction shown in Figure 12.12 and answer the following questions.

a. Specify the Restart memory location when the microprocessor is interrupted.

b. If the instruction in the monitor program at 0030 is CALL $20BF_H$ and the service routine is written at $20BF_H$, what instruction is necessary at location 0033_H?

3. The main program is stored beginning at 0100_H. The main program has called the subroutine at 0150_H, and when the microprocessor is executing the instruction at location 0151_H (LD), it is interrupted. Read the program and then answer the questions that follow.

```
START:    0100      LD SP, 0400H
          0103      IM 1
          0104      EI
           ↓         ↓
          0120      CALL 0150H
           ↓         ↓
```

SUB:	0150	PUSH BC
	0151	LD BC, 10FFH
	0154	LD C, A
	↓	↓
	015E	POP BC
	015F	RET

   a. Specify the contents of the stack location $03FF_H$.

   b. Specify the stack locations where the contents of registers BC are stored.

   c. When the program is interrupted, what is the memory address stored on the stack?

4. In **3**, if the program is changed as follows and the circuit in Figure 12.9 is used to supply the byte, specify the location to which the program will be transferred when it is interrupted and the location of the service routine.

START:	0100	LD SP, 2400H
	0103	IM 2
	0104	LD A, 01H
	0106	LD I, A
	0107	LD HL, 01F8H
	010A	LD (HL), 80H
	010C	INC HL
	010D	LD (HL), 23H
	010F	EI
	0110	↓

5. In Figure 12.11, if the input I_4 goes active, specify the location to which the program will be transferred.

6. In Figure 12.11, if the inputs I_4 and I_6 go active simultaneously, specify the location to which the program will be transferred.

7. In Figure 12.11, connect the output lines A_2, A_1, and A_0 of the encoder (through the buffer 74LS366) to the data bus D_5, D_4, and D_3 and tie D_7, D_6, D_2, and D_1 data lines high. If the Z80 is set up in the interrupt Mode 0, and if the input I_4 goes active, where will the program be transferred?

8. Redraw and combine Figures 12.8 and 12.9 without any additional components to meet the following specifications.

   a. Port address of ADC0801 = 78_H

   b. Low-order interrupt vector = 80_H

9. In reference to Figures 12.8 and 12.9, write and assemble a program to set up interrupt Mode 2, and record and store ten readings in the buffer location starting at 1900_H. The service routine should be located at 1850_H.

Programmable
Interface Devices

A **programmable interface device** is designed to perform various input/output functions, and these functions can be programmed into the device by writing an instruction (or instructions) in its internal register, called the control register. Functions can also be changed by writing a new instruction in the control register. These devices are flexible, versatile, and economical; they are widely used in microprocessor-based products.

In Chapter 5, we used simple integrated circuits, such as latches and tri-state buffers, for I/O functions. However, they are limited in their capabilities; each device can perform only one function, and they are hardwired. In this chapter, we first discuss the basic concepts in programmable devices and then examine the Z80 **Parallel Input Output (PIO) device** in the context of these concepts. The PIO is an I/O device specially designed to function with the Z80, and it is commonly used in Z80-based systems. The PIO has two I/O ports, and it can be programmed in various modes ranging from bit mode to bidirectional data transfer mode. These

modes are illustrated with several interfacing applications, such as keyboard and seven-segment display, and bidirectional data transfer between two microcomputers. Finally, another widely used peripheral device, the Intel 8255, is described and compared with the Z80 PIO.

OBJECTIVES

□ List elements and characteristics of a typical programmable device.

□ Explain the functions of handshake signals.

□ List the elements of the Z80 PIO (Parallel Input Output) and explain its various operating modes.

□ Write initialization instructions to set up the PIO in a given mode.

□ Design an interfacing circuit to set up the PIO

in a handshake mode, and write instructions to transfer data using the interrupt I/O.

□ List the elements of the Intel 8255 Programmable Peripheral Interface and its various operating modes.

□ Write initialization instructions to set up the 8255 in a given mode.

□ Compare the features of the Z80 PIO and the 8255.

13.1   BASIC CONCEPTS IN PROGRAMMABLE DEVICES

In Chapter 5, we discussed the interfacing of simple input (switches) and output (LEDs) devices. In the illustrations, we assumed that the I/O devices were always ready for data transfer. In fact, that assumption may not be valid in many data transfer situations. The MPU needs to check whether a peripheral is ready before it reads from or writes into a device because the execution speed of the microprocessor is much faster than the response of a peripheral such as a printer. For example, when the MPU sends data bytes (characters) to a printer, the microprocessor can execute the instructions to transfer a byte in microseconds, but the printer can take 10–25 ms to print a character. After transferring a character to the printer, the MPU should wait until the printer is ready for the next character; otherwise data will be lost. To prevent the loss of data or the MPU's reading the same data more than once, signals are exchanged between the MPU and a peripheral prior to actual data transfer; these signals are called **handshake signals.** To provide such signals in the illustrations of Chapter 5, we need to build additional logic circuitry.

In Chapter 12, we interfaced an A/D converter using the interrupt I/O; however, the interrupt signal was generated by the internal logic of the data converter. Many peripherals may not have that capability; such signals may have to be provided by the interfacing circuitry. In some applications, data flow is bidirectional (such as data transfer between two computers). In such a situation, the interfacing device should be capable of handling **bidirectional data flow.** Based on the above discussion and the illustrations of Chapters 5 and 12, we can summarize the requirements for a programmable interfacing device as follows. The device should include the following:

1. Input and output registers (a group of latches to hold data).
2. Tri-state buffers.
3. Capability for bidirectional data flow.
4. Handshake and interrupt signals.

FIGURE 13.1
Logic Symbol of 74LS245 Bidirectional Buffer

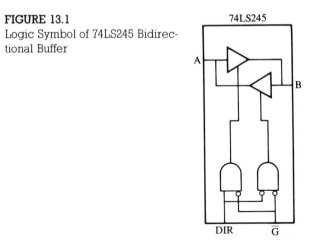

74LS245

A

B

DIR $\overline{G}$

5. Control logic.
6. Chip Select logic.
7. Interrupt control logic.

To understand the programmability of such a device, we illustrate a simple example of building a programmable device using a transceiver (bidirectional buffer) in the next section.

13.1.1 Making the 74LS245 Transceiver Programmable

The 74LS245 is a bidirectional tri-state octal buffer, and the direction of the data flow is determined by the signal DIR. Figure 13.1 shows the logic diagram of the 74LS245; it shows one buffer (rather than eight) in each direction. The buffer is enabled when G is active low; however, the direction of the data flow is determined by the DIR signal. When the DIR is high, data flow from A to B, and when it is low, data flow from B to A. In fact, this is a hardwired programmable device; the direction of the data flow is programmed through DIR. However, we are interested in a device that can be programmed by writing an instruction through the MPU. This can be accomplished by adding a register called the control register, as shown in Figure 13.2, and by connecting the DIR signal to bit D_0 of the control register. When $D_0 = 1$, data flow from A to B as output, and when $D_0 = 0$, data flow in the opposite direction as input.

Now the question is, How would the MPU write into the control register? It does so the same way it would with any other I/O port, through a port address. Figure 13.2 shows that the address lines A_7-A_1 are used to select the chip through a NAND gate and A_0 is used to differentiate between the control register and the transceiver. When A_0 is high, the control register is enabled, and when A_0 is low, the transceiver is enabled. Thus, the MPU could access the control register through the port address FF_H, and the transceiver through FE_H. To set up the

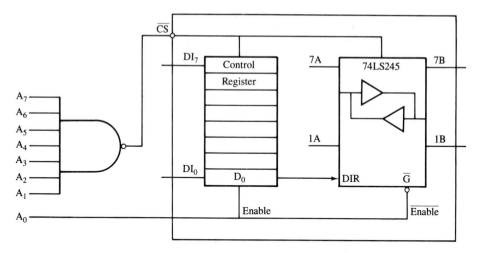

FIGURE 13.2
Making 74LS245 Programmable

transceiver as an output device, the control word would be 01_H, and to set it up as an input device, the control word would be 00_H.

Example 13.1

Write instructions to initialize the hypothetical chip (Figure 13.2) as an output buffer and send a byte.

Solution

Instructions

LD A, 01H	;Set $D_0 = 1$, D_1 through D_7 are "don't care" lines
OUT (FFH), A	;Write in the control register
LD A, BYTE1	;Load data byte
OUT (FEH), A	;Send data out

In the previous section, we used the 74LS245 as a tri-state buffer. However, in microprocessor applications, we often need registers that can be used as I/O ports. We can build a latch with a buffer, and by controlling the enable signal of the latch, we can program it to function as an input port or an output port. Similarly, we can build an interrupt logic and control it through a flip-flop that, in turn, can be enabled or disabled by a bit in the control register. Thus, we can build a programmable device to meet the requirements specified in the previous section, and by writing an appropriate word (byte) in the control register, we can specify its functions.

Z80 PARALLEL INPUT/OUTPUT DEVICE (PIO) 13.2

The **Z80 PIO** is a programmable I/O interfacing device, specially designed for the Z80. It has two 8-bit I/O ports, A and B, and its signals are divided into six groups as shown in Figure 13.3; they are described in the next section. Ports A and B can be used in three different modes: byte output (Mode 0), byte input (Mode 1), and bit input/output (Mode 3) as shown in Figure 13.4. In addition, Port A can be configured in the bidirectional mode (Mode 2).

☐ **Modes 0 and 1.** Mode 0 is for output and Mode 1 is for input. In these modes, Ports A and B can be used in two ways: simple I/O without handshake signals or interrupt I/O with handshake signals. Each port has two handshake signals: **Strobe** and **Ready.**

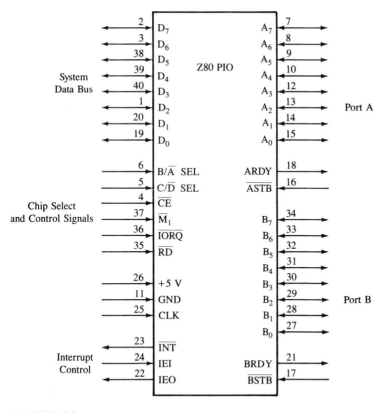

FIGURE 13.3
Z80 PIO Logic Pinout
SOURCE: Courtesy of Zilog, Inc.

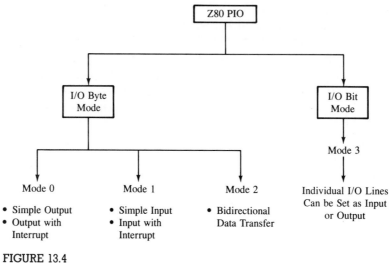

FIGURE 13.4
Z80 PIO Modes

□ **Mode 2.** This mode specifies the bidirectional data flow. Only Port A can be configured in this mode, and it uses all four handshake signals.

□ **Mode 3.** This is a bit mode whereby each bit of Port A and Port B can be configured as input or output. The handshake signals cannot be used in this mode.

13.2.1 Z80 PIO Signals

As shown in Figure 13.3, the PIO signals are grouped in six categories.

1. Data bus—D_7–D_0: This is an 8-bit bidirectional, tri-state data bus, used to transfer information between the Z80 MPU and the PIO.
2. I/O lines—A_7–A_0: These are bidirectional tri-state I/O lines of Port A, used to transfer information between the PIO and a peripheral. These lines can source 250 μA in logic 1 state and sink 2 mA in logic 0 state.
   B_7–B_0: These are Port B I/O lines similar to those of Port A. These lines can supply 1.5 mA at 1.5 V to drive Darlington transistors.
3. Handshake signals: The PIO has four handshake signals, two for each port. However, all of them are used for Port A when it is configured in the bidirectional mode.

   □ $\overline{\text{ASTB}}$—This is an active low Port A input signal from a peripheral to the PIO. When Port A is configured as an output port, this signal indicates the acknowledgment of the byte received by the peripheral. When Port A is configured as an input port, this signal indicates that a byte has been placed in Port A by a peripheral.

☐ ARDY—This is an active high Port A output signal from the PIO to a peripheral. In the output mode, the signal indicates that a byte has been placed in the Port A register and is ready for data transfer. In the input mode, it indicates that the Port A register is empty and ready to accept the next byte from the peripheral.

☐ BSTB and BRDY—These are handshake signals for Port B similar to those of Port A. However, these are used by Port A when Port A is configured in the bidirectional mode.

4. Power and clock: The PIO operates with a single power supply with +5 V and uses a single phase system clock as an input for internal operations.

5. Interrupt control logic: The PIO has three signals to handle the interrupt I/O.

☐ $\overline{\text{INT}}$—Interrupt: This is an active low open collector output signal from the PIO; it is used to interrupt the Z80 MPU.

☐ IEI—Interrupt Enable In: This is an active high input signal used to form a priority interrupt daisy chain when multiple peripherals are connected in the interrupt I/O (see section 13.3.5 for the discussion of daisy chain priority interrupts). The high on this pin indicates that no other peripherals with higher priority are being serviced.

☐ IEO—Interrupt Enable Out: This is an active high output signal used in daisy chain priority interrupts. This signal goes high when IEI is high and the Z80 is not servicing an interrupt from this PIO. This signal blocks lower priority devices from interrupting when a higher priority device is being serviced.

6. Control signals: The PIO has six control signals. The first three signals ($\overline{\text{CE}}$, B/$\overline{\text{A}}$, and C/$\overline{\text{D}}$) determine the port addresses of the I/O registers A and B and their control registers. The remaining three signals define the type of the operation (Read or Write) being performed.

☐ $\overline{\text{CE}}$—Chip Enable: This is an active low signal and is connected to a decoded address bus of the Z80.

☐ B/$\overline{\text{A}}$—Port B or A Select: When this signal is high, Port B is selected, and when it is low, Port A is selected. This signal is generally connected to address line A_0 of the MPU.

☐ C/$\overline{\text{D}}$—Control or Data Select. When this signal is high, the control register is selected to write a command, and when it is low, the I/O (Port A or Port B) register is selected to transfer data between the MPU and the PIO. This signal is generally connected to address line A_1 of the MPU. The port selection is summarized in Table 13.1.

☐ $\overline{\text{M}}_1$, $\overline{\text{RD}}$, and $\overline{\text{IORQ}}$—All these signals are connected to the corresponding control signals of the Z80. The $\overline{\text{M}}_1$ signal synchronizes the internal operation and the interrupt logic of the PIO and performs various functions in conjunction with the other two control signals as described below.

TABLE 13.1
Z80 PIO Port Selection

$\overline{CE}$	$C/\overline{D}$	$B/\overline{A}$	Selected Port
0	0	0	Data Port A
0	0	1	Data Port B
0	1	0	Control Register A
0	1	1	Control Register B
1	X	X	PIO Not Selected

a. Read: When the $\overline{RD}$ and $\overline{IORQ}$ signals are active low, the MPU reads from the selected register.
b. Write: When the $\overline{IORQ}$ is active, but the $\overline{RD}$ is inactive, the MPU writes into the selected register. There is no specific control signal to write into register; it is a default condition.
c. Interrupt Acknowledge: When $\overline{M_1}$ and $\overline{IORQ}$ are active, the MPU acknowledges the interrupt from the PIO.
d. Reset: When $\overline{M_1}$ is active and both $\overline{RD}$ and $\overline{IORQ}$ are inactive, the PIO is reset.

Example 13.2

Figure 13.5 shows a circuit interfacing the PIO with the Z80 microprocessor. Identify the port addresses of Ports A and B and control registers.

Solution

In Figure 13.5, the output line O_0 of the 74LS138 decoder is connected to the Chip Enable of the PIO. To assert the output line O_0 of the decoder, the address line A_7 should be at logic 1 and the remaining lines at logic 0. By combining these address lines with address lines A_1 and A_0, the port addresses are as follows (refer to Table 13.1).

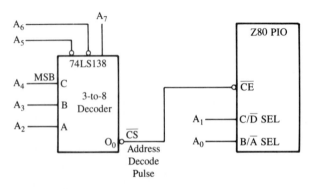

FIGURE 13.5
Interfacing PIO

FIGURE 13.6
Z80 PIO Mode Word

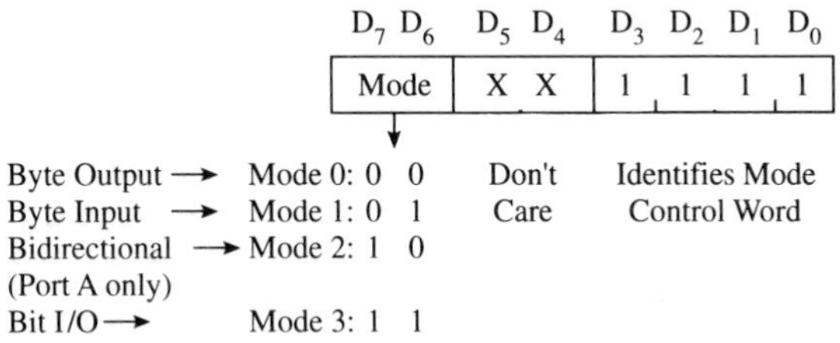

$$D_7\ D_6\quad D_5\ D_4\quad D_3\ D_2\ D_1\ D_0$$

| Mode | X X | 1 1 1 1 |

Byte Output → Mode 0: 0 0   Don't   Identifies Mode
Byte Input → Mode 1: 0 1   Care   Control Word
Bidirectional → Mode 2: 1 0
(Port A only)
Bit I/O → Mode 3: 1 1

A_7	A_6	A_5	A_4	A_3	A_2	A_1	A_0		
						$C/\overline{D}$	$B/\overline{A}$		
1	0	0	0	0	0	0	0	$= 80_H$	Data Port A
						0	1	$= 81_H$	Data Port B
						1	0	$= 82_H$	Control Register A
						1	1	$= 83_H$	Control Register B

13.2.2 Control Word

Figure 13.4 shows that the PIO can operate in four different modes. To set up an operating mode, the appropriate control word must be written in the control register of the port being used. The control word is determined by the internal logic (as discussed in section 13.1), and it is specified by the manufacturer. The control word for the PIO to specify the modes is shown in Figure 13.6, and how to initialize a port is illustrated in Example 13.3.

In Figure 13.7, eight DIP switches are connected to Port A and seven LEDs and one speaker are connected to Port B (the buffer is necessary to supply sufficient current to the LEDs). Write instructions to initialize Port A as an input port and Port B as an output port. Read Port A, and if switch S_7 is on (logic 0), output an emergency signal to the speaker; otherwise, turn on corresponding LEDs at Port B. Assume that the decoding logic is the same as in Figure 13.5, and the program should continue to monitor the switches.

Example 13.3

To initialize Port A as an input port, $D_7 = 0$ and $D_6 = 1$, and to initialize Port B as an output port, D_7 and D_6 should be both 0. Thus, the control words are

Solution

Port A as Input Port: 0 1 0 0 1 1 1 1 = $4F_H$

Mode 1

Port B as Output Port: 0 0 0 0 1 1 1 1 = $0F_H$

Mode 0

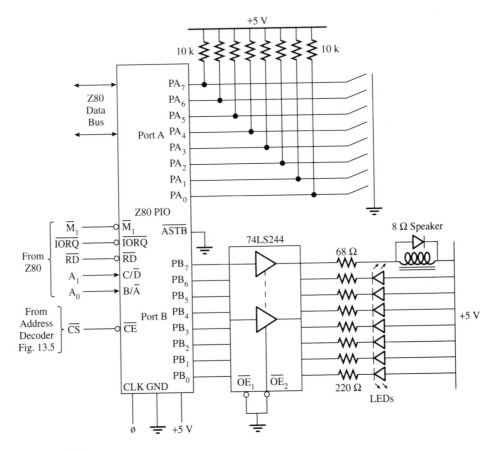

FIGURE 13.7
Interfacing PIO in Mode 0 for Simple I/O

Instructions

```
                  ;The following port addresses refer to Figure 13.5
PORTA    EQU 80H          ;Port A address
PORTB    EQU 81H          ;Port B address
CNTRLA   EQU 82H          ;Control Register A
CNTRLB   EQU 83H          ;Control Register B
         LD A, 01001111B  ;Control word 4FH for Port A
         OUT (CNTRLA), A  ;Write in control register A
         LD A, 00001111B  ;Control word 0FH for Port B
         OUT (CNTRLB), A  ;Write in control register B
READ:    IN A, (PORTA)    ;Read DIP switches
         BIT 7,A          ;Check Switch S7
         JR NZ, LED       ;If it is off, turn on LEDs
```

```
SPEKER:  LD A,0FFH              ;If S₇ is on,
         OUT (PORTB),A          ;turn on speaker and turn off LEDs
         CALL DELAY             ;Wait
         LD A,7FH               ;Load 0 for D₇
         OUT (PORTB),A          ;Turn off speaker
         CALL DELAY             ;Wait
         JR SPEKER              ;Repeat speaker output
LED:     OUT (PORTB),A          ;Turn on LEDs
         JR READ                ;Continue to check DIP switches
```

Description Initially, all ports are defined by writing equates; these port addresses are from Figure 13.5. Then, Ports A and B are initialized by writing control words in their respective control registers. The IN instruction reads DIP switches, and the BIT instruction checks bit D_7 for logic 0, which indicates the on position of S_7. Then, the program outputs FFH to Port B. Bit D_7 of the byte FFH turns on the speaker and turns off all LEDs. By calling delay and subsequently turning on/off bit D_7, an emergency tone is generated at the speaker. If switch S_7 is off, the program jumps to location LED and turns on the corresponding LEDs for the switches that are on; the speaker does not generate a tone for constant output. The switches that are turned on provide logic 0 reading in the accumulator, and logic 0 turns on LEDs because LED anodes are connected to +5 V. For example, if switches S_0, S_1, and S_2 are on, the IN instruction will read 1 1 1 1 1 0 0 0 (F8H), and if this reading is sent out to Port B, it will turn on LEDs connected to B_0, B_1, and B_2 lines of Port B.

In Example 13.3, switches and LEDs are connected as simple I/O devices, similar to illustrations in Chapter 5. The only difference in writing instructions is the initialization instructions. The next section shows how to interface peripherals using the handshake signals and the interrupt I/O.

MODES 0, 1, AND 2 WITH HANDSHAKE SIGNALS AND INTERRUPT I/O   13.3

As described earlier, the PIO has two handshake signals, Strobe and Ready ($\overline{STB}$ and RDY), associated with each port and one interrupt ($\overline{INT}$) signal. The handshake signals are used to indicate the readiness of the peripheral. The interpretation of the handshake signals is somewhat dependent on the mode being used; therefore, they will be explained separately.

The interrupt signal is used to request service from the MPU. To generate an $\overline{INT}$ signal, the interrupt flip-flop of the port being used must be enabled; each port has its interrupt enable flip-flop. (These flip-flops should not be confused with the Z80 interrupt flip-flops, IFF1 and IFF2.)

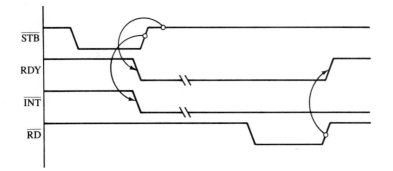

FIGURE 13.8
PIO Input Mode 1: Timing Waveforms
SOURCE: Courtesy of Zilog, Inc.

13.3.1   Input Mode 1 and Handshake Signals

Figure 13.8 shows the sequence of events and timing when the selected port is configured as an input port and a byte is transferred from the peripheral to the PIO and then to the MPU.

1. The peripheral causes the $\overline{\text{STB}}$ (Strobe) to go low and informs the PIO that a data byte has been placed in the input register.
2. The rising edge of the $\overline{\text{STB}}$ activates the interrupt ($\overline{\text{INT}}$), and the other handshake signal RDY (Ready) goes inactive, indicating that the input register is full.
3. Let us assume that the Z80 and the PIO interrupt flip-flops are enabled, and that the Z80 MPU is set up in the interrupt Mode 2. When the Z80 acknowledges the interrupt request, a preprogrammed 8-bit vector is placed onto the data bus (see section 13.3.3 for interrupt vector definition). This vector is combined with the byte in the interrupt register, IR, of the Z80 to form a 16-bit address, and the program is transferred to this memory address to get the address of the service routine. These interrupt activities are not shown in the timing diagram.
4. When the service routine reads the byte from the port, the RDY goes active on the rising edge of the $\overline{\text{RD}}$ signal, indicating that the PIO is ready for the next byte.

13.3.2   Output Mode 0 and Handshake Signals

Figure 13.9 shows the sequence of events and the timing when the port is configured as an output port and a data byte is transferred from the MPU to the PIO and then to the peripheral.

1. When the Z80 executes the OUT instruction, it places the byte in the PIO register and activates the RDY signal, indicating to the peripheral that a byte is available in the register.

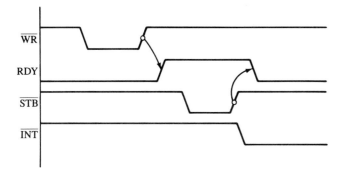

FIGURE 13.9
PIO Output Mode 0: Timing Waveforms
SOURCE: Courtesy of Zilog, Inc.

2. The RDY signal stays high until the peripheral sends the $\overline{\text{STB}}$ signal. The rising edge of the $\overline{\text{STB}}$ activates the interrupt, indicating to the MPU that the byte has been received by the peripheral, and that it is ready for the next byte.
3. When the $\overline{\text{INT}}$ is acknowledged, the program is transferred to the service routine as described in step **3** of Mode 1.

In Figure 13.9, the $\overline{\text{WR}}$ signal needs clarification because the PIO does not have a $\overline{\text{WR}}$ pin. This signal is generated internally by the PIO when CE, C/D, and $\overline{\text{IORQ}}$ are active, but $\overline{\text{RD}}$ is inactive.

13.3.3 Interrupt Enable Word and Interrupt Vector

To set up the PIO ports in the interrupt I/O, the interrupt flip-flop of the port being used must be enabled by writing an instruction in the control register. In addition, the low-order byte must be programmed to form the interrupt vector to locate the address of the service routine. The definitions of the interrupt enable word and the interrupt vector are shown in Figure 13.10. To set up the PIO ports in the interrupt I/O, we need to write three instructions (control words) in the control register of the port being used: mode word, interrupt enable word, and interrupt vector. This is illustrated in the next example.

Assuming the same Chip Select logic as in Figure 13.5, write instructions to set up the Z80 MPU and the PIO for the interrupt I/O. Initialize Port A as an input port and Port B as an output port. The addresses of the service routines for Port A and Port B are stored in locations 1896_H and 1898_H, respectively.

Example 13.4

Initialization Instructions
;Setting up Port A as input port with interrupt I/O

Solution

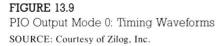

```
START:    LD A, 4FH          ;Control word for Mode 1
          OUT (CNTRLA), A    ;Initialize Port A as input port
```

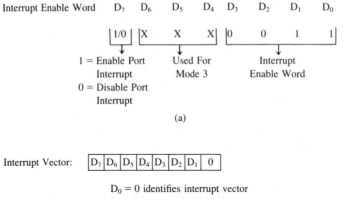

Interrupt Enable Word D_7 D_6 D_5 D_4 D_3 D_2 D_1 D_0

| 1/0 | X   X   X | 0   0   1   1 |

1 = Enable Port   Used For   Interrupt
    Interrupt   Mode 3   Enable Word
0 = Disable Port
    Interrupt

(a)

Interrupt Vector: D_7 D_6 D_5 D_4 D_3 D_2 D_1 0

$D_0 = 0$ identifies interrupt vector
$D_7 - D_1 =$ user defined bits
$D_7 - D_0$ specify the low-order byte of the interrupt vector

(b)

FIGURE 13.10
Definitions of: (a) Interrupt Enable Word; (b) Interrupt Vector

```
LD A, 83H              ;Interrupt enable control word
OUT (CNTRLA), A        ;Enable Port A Interrupt flip-flop
LD A, 96H              ;Low-order byte of the interrupt vector
                       ; for Port A

OUT (CNTRLA), A        ;Specify interrupt vector for Port A


;Setting up Port B as output port with interrupt I/O
LD A, 0FH              ;Control word for Mode 0
OUT (CNTRLB), A        ;Initialize Port B as output port
LD A, 83H              ;Interrupt enable control word
OUT (CNTRLB), A        ;Enable Port B interrupt flip-flop
LD A, 98H              ;Low-order byte of the interrupt vector
                       ; for Port B

OUT (CNTRLB), A        ;Specify interrupt vector for Port B


;Setting up Z80 MPU in interrupt Mode 2
LD SP, STACK           ;Initialize stack pointer
LD A, 18H              ;High-order address for interrupt vector
LD I, A                ;Initialize Z80 interrupt register
IM 2                   ;Set up Z80 in interrupt Mode 2
EI                     ;Enable Z80 interrupt
```

Description   The above instructions are divided into three groups: initialization of Port A, Port B, and Z80. To initialize Port A and Port B for the interrupt I/O and in Mode 0 and 1, three control words are necessary: Mode Word, Interrupt Enable, and Interrupt Vector. These words can be executed in any sequence; however, we have used a certain sequence to clarify the concepts. Now the question is: How does the PIO differentiate these words, especially when they are written in the same control register? These words are differentiated by identifying certain bit patterns. For example, a mode word is recognized when D_3–D_0 are all 1s, and an interrupt vector is recognized when bit $D_0 = 0$.

The instructions in the third group set up the Z80 MPU in the interrupt Mode 2, and specify the high-order byte (18_H) of the interrupt vector in register I. By keeping the instruction EI at the end, the initialization of the PIO will not be disturbed even if an interrupt were to occur in the system.

When the Z80 acknowledges an interrupt from Port A, the byte (18_H) in register I is combined with the low-order byte 96_H, specified as the interrupt vector for Port A, to form the 16-bit memory addresses 1896_H. The program is then transferred to location 1896_H. The byte stored in memory location 1896_H provides the low-order address and the byte in location 97_H the high-order address of the service routine for Port A. For Port B interrupt, the program is transferred to location 1898_H in a similar manner.

13.3.4 Mode 2: Bidirectional Data Transfer

Port A of the PIO can be set up as a bidirectional input and output port. This is called Mode 2, which is the combination of Mode 0 and Mode 1. In Mode 2, Port A uses all four handshake lines; thus, Port B cannot be used as an I/O port with an interrupt-generating capability. Port B must be set in Mode 3 without its logic checking capability (Mode 3 is discussed in Section 13.4). In bidirectional data transfer (Mode 2), when Port A functions as the output port, the handshake signals of Port A (ASTB and ARDY) are used, and when it functions as an input port, the handshake signals for Port B (BSTB and BRDY) are used. Similarly, the interrupt vector for the output is programmed in the control register of Port A, and the interrupt vector for the input is programmed in the control register of Port B. In this mode, the process of data transfer is as follows:

1. *Output Mode.* When the Z80 writes a byte in Port A, ARDY goes high. When the peripheral asserts ASTB and reads the byte, an interrupt is generated (if enabled) to signal the Z80 that the next byte can be sent. This is identical to Mode 0 except that a data byte is allowed onto the data bus of Port A when ASTB is active.
2. *Input Mode.* When the peripheral places a data byte on the data lines and asserts the BSTB signal, an interrupt (if enabled) is generated to indicate that the byte is placed in Port A. When the Z80 reads the byte, the BRDY goes active to indicate to the peripheral that the Z80 is ready for the next byte.

The timing and additional details of Mode 2 are further explained in section 13.6.

13.3.5   Interrupt Priority

When multiple peripherals are interfaced with the interrupt I/O, it is essential to have a priority scheme built into the system. The PIO can be used to set the *daisy chain priority* scheme, whereby the first PIO connected to Z80 has the highest priority. Figure 13.11 shows four PIOs connected in the daisy chain format; PIO-1 has the highest priority and PIO-4 has the lowest priority. The design of the daisy chain priority scheme is based on two PIO signals IEI and IEO and the Z80 instruction RETI.

- □ IEI—Interrupt Enable In: This is an active high input signal to the PIO. When this signal is high, it indicates that no other PIOs of higher priority are being serviced by the Z80. When it is low, it indicates that a higher priority PIO is being serviced and no interrupt can be generated from this PIO.
- □ IEO—Interrupt Enable Out: This is an active high output signal. This remains high if IEI is high and remains low if IEI is low. When IEI is high and IEO is low, it indicates that either the PIO is being serviced or an interrupt is pending from this PIO.
- □ RETI—Return from Interrupt: This is a 2-byte (ED 4D) instruction, and the PIO logic can recognize it. When the PIO reads this instruction, it sets IEO high, thus indicating the end of the service routine and allowing lower priority PIOs to interrupt the processor.

To further explain the daisy chain interrupt operation, let us assume that all IEI and IEO signals in Figure 13.11 are high. When PIO-2 generates an interrupt and it is accepted, the IEO_2 goes low, thus causing IEI_3 to go low. The signal ripples through PIO-3 and PIO-4 and disables these devices. Let us assume that when PIO-2 is being serviced, it is interrupted by PIO-1, causing IEI_2 to go low. At the end of the service routine, PIO-1 reads the instruction RETI and sets the IEI_2 high; thus, the service routine of PIO-2 can continue.

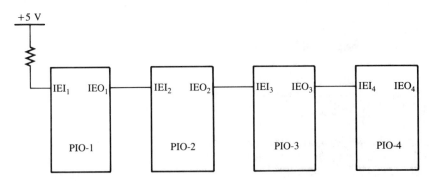

FIGURE 13.11
Daisy Chain Interrupt Priority

This daisy chain using the PIO has two drawbacks: (1) it is limited to four PIOs (it can be extended to include more PIOs by using additional logic), and (2) the priority is fixed.

MODE 3: BIT MODE 13.4

Mode 3 is a bit mode whereby each bit of Port A and Port B can be individually assigned input or output function. The features of this mode are as follows:

1. Each individual line of the port can be assigned either input or output function by writing a control word in the control register of the port.
2. The handshake signals are not used; Ready is kept low, and Strobe is disabled.
3. Bits are read or written into by use of the normal Read and Write functions of the I/O ports.
4. Individual bits can be masked by writing a mask word in the control register.
5. An interrupt can be generated if a predefined logical combination occurs in the input lines. The logical combination (AND/OR) can be defined by writing an interrupt control word in the control register, and the logic level can be active low or active high. For example, we can specify that bits D_0–D_7 be inputs and two bits, D_7 and D_6, be active low with AND function. With this specification, when the PIO reads both bits D_7 and D_6 low, an interrupt signal is generated. In OR logic function, when one of the input lines (D_7 or D_6) is active, the interrupt is activated.

To set up the PIO in Mode 3 with the interrupt capability, four different words should be written in the control register of the port being used.

1. Mode control word for Mode 3.
2. I/O register control word to assign input or output function to individual bits.
3. Interrupt control word to define the logic conditions to generate the interrupt.
4. Mask control word to specify a mask word.

The Mode control word is already defined in Figure 13.7, and the remaining three words are defined in Figure 13.12. The use of these words is illustrated in Example 13.5.

Port A of the Z80 PIO is set up in Mode 3 to drive traffic light signals and monitor any conflict between Red and Green lights; these lights should never be on at the same time. Bits A_4 to A_0 are set as output lines to drive traffic signal lights and Walk/Don't-Walk signs as shown in Figure 13.13. Bits A_7 and A_6 are used as inputs to monitor Red (bit A_4) and Green (bit A_2) lights to prevent both being on at the same time. When both bits A_4 and A_2 are turned on (logic 1) by some error, an interrupt is generated to flash a yellow light and turn off the remaining lights.

Example
13.5

FIGURE 13.12
Word Definitions for Mode 3

D_7	D_6	D_5	D_4	D_3	D_2	D_1	D_0

0 = Output
1 = Input

(a) I/O Register Control Word

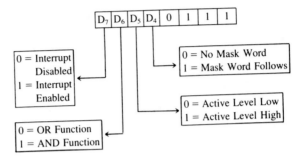

D_7	D_6	D_5	D_4	0	1	1	1

0 = No Mask Word
1 = Mask Word Follows

0 = Interrupt Disabled
1 = Interrupt Enabled

0 = Active Level Low
1 = Active Level High

0 = OR Function
1 = AND Function

(b) Interrupt Control Word

D_7	D_6	D_5	D_4	D_3	D_2	D_1	D_0

Bit is monitored if it is set to 0 for input readings.

(c) Mask Control Word

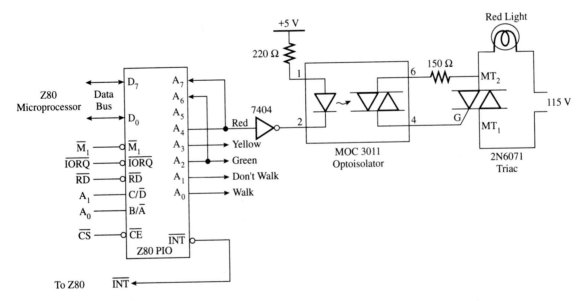

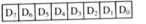

FIGURE 13.13
Interfacing PIO in Mode 3 with Traffic Signal Lights (Figure shows a driver circuit only for red light; driver circuits for the remaining lights are not shown.)

Write instructions to initialize the PIO and monitor the process. Port addresses are the same as previously defined in Example 13.2.

To initialize the PIO as specified in the problem statement, we need to define the four words as follows:

Solution

Mode Word (refer to Figure 13.6)

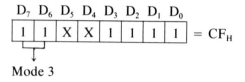

$$D_7 \ D_6 \ D_5 \ D_4 \ D_3 \ D_2 \ D_1 \ D_0$$

| 1 | 1 | X | X | 1 | 1 | 1 | 1 | = CF$_H$

Mode 3

I/O Register Word (refer to Figure 13.12(a))

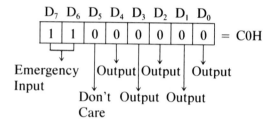

$$D_7 \ D_6 \ D_5 \ D_4 \ D_3 \ D_2 \ D_1 \ D_0$$

| 1 | 1 | 0 | 0 | 0 | 0 | 0 | 0 | = C0H

Emergency   Output Output   Output
Input
       Don't   Output Output
       Care

Interrupt Control Word (refer to Figure 13.12(b))

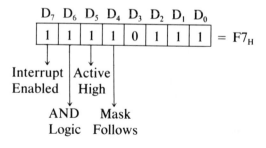

$$D_7 \ D_6 \ D_5 \ D_4 \ D_3 \ D_2 \ D_1 \ D_0$$

| 1 | 1 | 1 | 1 | 0 | 1 | 1 | 1 | = F7$_H$

Interrupt   Active
Enabled   High

       AND   Mask
       Logic   Follows

Mask Control Word (refer to Figure 13.12(c))

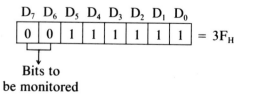

$$D_7 \ D_6 \ D_5 \ D_4 \ D_3 \ D_2 \ D_1 \ D_0$$

| 0 | 0 | 1 | 1 | 1 | 1 | 1 | 1 | = 3F$_H$

Bits to
be monitored

Instructions

```
;Initialization of Port A in Mode 3
START:      LD A, 0CFH          ;Mode control word
            OUT (CTRLA), A      ;Write in control register A
            LD A, 0C0H          ;Control word to set up I/O functions
            OUT (CTRLA), A
            LD A, 18H           ;High-order address of interrupt vector
            LD I, A             ;Initialize interrupt register I in Z80
            LD A, 72H           ;Low-order address of interrupt vector
            OUT (CTRLA), A
            LD A, 0F7H          ;Enable interrupt with AND logic
            OUT (CTRLA), A
            LD A, 3FH           ;Mask to check D7 and D6
            OUT (CTRLA), A
            LD SP, STACK        ;Initialize stack pointer
READ:       CALL TRAFIC         ;Refer to program in section 10.4
                                ;Must be modified to match light positions
                                ;Port A should be read after every bit
                                ; pattern
```

Program Description The control words are already explained, and they are written in the control register of port A. The interrupt vector is specified as 1872_H. The interrupt control word 1 1 1 1 0 1 1 1 ($F7_H$) sets up the PIO to check for active high AND logic. This is followed by the masking word 0 0 1 1 1 1 1 1 ($3F_H$); this word specifies that bits D_7 and D_6 should be monitored for active high AND logic. This masking word specifies that if bits D_7 and D_6 are both logic 1, the PIO will generate an interrupt. Then the program will be transferred to location 1872_H to find the address of the service routine.

The subroutine TRAFIC is not shown here. It will be similar to the traffic signal controller program in section 10.4. However, it should be modified to: (1) convert a program into a subroutine, (2) include different bit positions of the lights, and (3) read Port A whenever a new bit pattern is outputted to change a light. Reading of Port A for a new light pattern is necessary to monitor Red and Green lights; if bits A4 and A2 are at logic 1 simultaneously, the PIO will generate an interrupt, and the service routine can take an appropriate action.

Hardware Figure 13.13 shows that the traffic light signal (Red) connected to bit A_4 is driven by the optically isolated triac driver (MOC 3011); similar connections to bits A_0–A_3 are assumed but not shown in the figure. When A_4 is at logic 1, the output of the inverter is at logic 0, which turns on the LED of the optoisolator. This LED must have at least 10 mA of current to turn on the triac driver. However, the PIO bit is unable to sink such a current; therefore, the optoisolator is driven by the inverter. The triac driver of the optoisolator switches the power triac 2N6071 and turns on the Red light. For low-power applications (less than

500 mW), the power triac can be eliminated, and AC load driven by power line (115 V) can be connected directly to pin 6 of the optoisolator. The primary purpose of the optoisolator is to isolate digital signals from high voltage signals; therefore, the digital ground and the AC ground should never be connected together.

ILLUSTRATION: INTERFACING KEYBOARD AND SEVEN-SEGMENT DISPLAY 13.5

This illustration is concerned with interfacing a push-button keyboard and a seven-segment LED display using the PIO. The PIO is connected as a peripheral I/O as in Example 13.2, with the same port addresses. The emphasis in this illustration is not particularly on the features of PIO but on how to integrate hardware and software. When a key is pressed, the binary reading of the key has almost no relationship to what we intend to represent. Similarly, to display a number at a seven-segment LED, the binary value of the number needs to be converted into the seven-segment code, which is primarily decided by the hardware consideration. This illustration demonstrates how the microprocessor monitors the changes in hardware reading, and how we can convert the reading into the appropriate binary format using the Z80 instructions.

13.5.1 Problem Statement

A push-button keyboard is connected to Port A and a seven-segment LED is connected to Port B of the PIO, as shown in Figure 13.14. Port A should be configured in the input Mode 1 and Port B in the output Mode 0; this is a simple I/O configuration without the use of handshake signals or the interrupt.

Write a program to monitor the keyboard to sense a key pressed and display the number of the key at the seven-segment LED. For example, when the key K_7 is pressed, the digit 7 should be displayed at Port B.

13.5.2 Problem Analysis

In this problem, the address decoding circuit and the port addresses are the same as in Example 13.2, and the initialization instructions for the PIO are the same as in Example 13.3; therefore, these aspects of the problem will not be discussed here.

The keyboard circuit shown in Figure 13.14 is similar to that in Figure 5.6 except that the DIP switches are replaced by push-button keys and the buffer is replaced by the PIO. When a push-button key is pressed, it bounces (makes and breaks contact) a few times before it makes a firm contact. To prevent the multiple readings of the same key, it is necessary to debounce the key. We have already discussed the hardware solution to this problem in Chapter 12. The software solution to this problem is to wait for 10–20 ms until the key is settled and then check the key again. The display circuit in Figure 13.14 uses a common anode seven-segment LED, connected to Port B of the PIO. To display a digit, it is

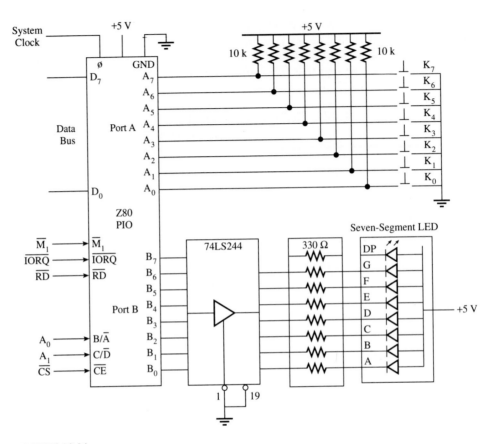

FIGURE 13.14
Interfacing a Keyboard and a Seven-Segment LED

necessary to turn on the appropriate segments of the LED. The appropriate binary code can be obtained by using the table look-up technique, described in section 13.5.4. The programming of this problem can be divided into the following categories:

1. Check whether a key is pressed.
2. Debounce the key.
3. Identify and encode the key in appropriate binary format.
4. Obtain the seven-segment code and display it.

The instructions for these steps can be written in separate modules, as shown in the next section.

13.5.3 Keyboard

The keys K_7–K_0 are tied high through 10 k resistors, and when a key is pressed, the corresponding line is grounded. When all keys are open and if the Z80 reads

Port A, the reading on the data bus will be FF_H. When any key is pressed, the reading will be less than FF_H. For example, if K_7 is pressed, the output of Port A will be 0111 1111 ($7F_H$). This reading should be encoded into the binary equivalent of the digit 7 (0 1 1 1) by using software routines. The following subroutines—KYCHK and KYCODE—accomplish the tasks of checking a key pressed and encoding the key in appropriate binary format.

;KYCHK: This subroutine first checks whether all keys are open.
           ;Then, it checks for a key closure, debounces the key, and
           ; places the reading in the accumulator. See Figure 13.15 for
           ; flowchart.

FIGURE 13.15
Flowchart: Key Check Subroutine

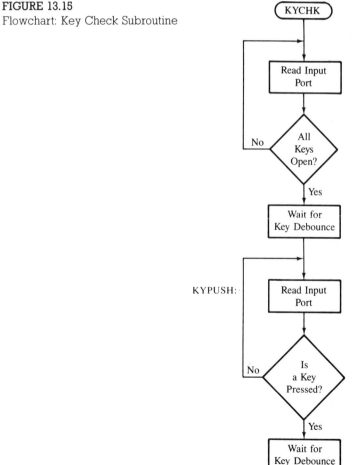

```
KYCHK:  IN A, (PORTA)        ;Read keyboard
        CP 0FFH              ;Are all keys open?
        JP NZ, KYCHK         ;If not, wait in loop
        CALL DBONCE          ;If yes, wait 20 ms
KYPUSH: IN A, (PORT A)       ;Read keyboard
        CP 0FFH              ;Is key pressed?
        JP Z, KYPUSH         ;If not, wait in loop
        CALL DBONCE          ;If yes, wait 20 ms
        CPL                  ;Set 1 for key closure
        OR A                 ;Set 0 flag for an error
        JP Z, KYPUSH         ;It is error, check again
        RET
```

Description This subroutine is based on hardware; when all keys are open the keyboard reading is FF_H, and when a key is pressed, the reading is less than FF_H. The routine begins with the loop to check whether all keys are open, and it stays in the loop until all keys are open. This prevents a reading of the same key repeatedly if someone were to hold the key for a long time. When it finds that a key has been released, it waits for 20 ms for a key debounce.

The loop starting at KYPUSH checks whether a key is pressed. When a key is pressed, the reading is less than FF_H; thus, the compare instruction does not set the Z flag and the program goes to the next instruction for a key debounce. The CPL instruction complements the accumulator reading; thus, the reading of the key pressed is set to 1, and other bits are set to 0. The next two instructions check for an error. If it is momentary contact (false alarm), all bits are 0s. The OR instruction sets the Z flag, and the Jump instruction takes the program back to checking keys.

```
KYCODE:      ;This routine converts (encodes) the binary hardware reading
             ; of the key
             ; pressed into appropriate binary format according to the
             ; number of the key.
             LD C, 08H        ;Set code counter
NEXT:        DEC C            ;Adjust key code
             RLCA             ;Place MSB in CY
             JP NC, NEXT      ;If bit = 0, go back to check next bit
             LD A, C          ;Place key code into the accumulator
             RET
```

Description Conceptually, this is an important routine; it establishes the relationship between the hardware and the number of the key. For example, if key K_7 is pressed, the reading from the routine KYCHK in the accumulator will be 1 0 0 0 0 0 0 0 (the reading is already complemented). The KYCODE routine sets register C for the count of eight and immediately decrements the count to seven. The instruction RLCA places bit D_7 into the CY flag, and the next instruction checks for the CY flag. If it is set, the key K_7 must be pressed, and the key code (digit 7) is in register C. If CY = 0, the program loops back to check the next bit (D_6). The loop is repeated until 1 is found in CY, and at every iteration of the loop, the key code in register C is adjusted for the next key. If more than one key is pressed, this routine ignores the low-order key. Finally, the subroutine places the key code into the accumulator and returns.

```
DBONCE:        ;This is a 20 ms delay routine.
               ;The delay COUNT should be calculated based on system
               ; frequency.
               ;This does not destroy any register contents.
               ;Input and Output = None
               PUSH BC              ;Save register contents
               LD B, COUNT1         ;Count for DJNZ
REPEAT:        LD C, COUNT2         ;Load delay count
  LOOP:        NOP                  ;Add delay
               DEC C                ;Repeat until C = 0
               JR NZ, LOOP
               DJNZ REPEAT          ;Loop until B = 0
               POP BC               ;Restore register contents
               RET
```

Description This is a simple delay routine similar to the delay routines discussed in Chapter 9. The inner loop is repeated until C = 0. The NOP instruction is included in the loop to increase the delay. The DJNZ instruction decrements the number in B and repeats the loop until B = 0. In this routine, delay counts in registers B and C should be calculated based on the clock frequency of the system and the T-states in the loop (see Chapter 9 for details).

13.5.4 Seven-Segment Display

Figure 13.14 shows that a common anode seven-segment LED is connected to Port B through the driver 74LS244. The driver is necessary to increase the current capacity of Port B; each LED segment requires 15–20 mA of current.

The driver 74LS244 (Figure 13.14) is an octal noninverting driver with tri-state output and the current sinking capacity of 24 mA. It has two active low enable lines, and the driver is permanently enabled by grounding these lines. In this circuit, the driver functions simply as a current amplifier; whatever logic is at Port B will be at the output of the driver.

To display the number of the key pressed, a routine is necessary that will send an appropriate code to Port B. The routine KYCODE supplies the binary number of the key pressed; however, there is no relationship between the binary value of a digit and its seven-segment code. Therefore, the table look-up technique (section 10.7) will have to be used to find the code for the digit supplied by KYCODE; this is shown in the next routine, DSPLAY.

```
DSPLAY:     ;This routine takes the binary number and converts it into its
            ; common anode seven-segment LED code. The codes are
            ; stored in memory sequentially starting from the
            ; address CACODE.
            ;Input: Binary number in accumulator
            ;Output: None
            ;Modifies contents of HL and A
            LD HL, CACODE      ;Load starting address of code table in
                                  HL
            ADD A, L           ;Add digit to low-order address in L
            LD L, A            ;Place code address in L
            LD A, (HL)         ;Get code from memory
            OUT (PORTB), A     ;Send code to Port B
            RET

CACODE:     ;Common anode seven-segment codes are stored sequentially in
               memory
            DEFB 40H, 79H, 24H,     ;Codes for digits from 0 to 5
              30H, 19H, 12H
            DEFB 02H, 78H           ;Codes for digits 6 and 7
```

Description In this routine the HL register is used as a memory pointer to code location. The digit to be displayed is in the accumulator, supplied by the routine KYCODE, and the seven-segment code is stored sequentially in memory starting from location CACODE. The basic concept in this routine is to modify the memory pointer by adding the value of the digit to the base address and get the code location. For example, let us assume that the starting address of CACODE is 1850_H and the digit 7 is in the accumulator. The code for digit 0 is in location 1850_H; consequently, the code for digit 7 is in location 1857_H. Therefore, to display digit 7, the routine adds the contents of the accumulator (7) to the low-order byte 50_H in register L, resulting in the sum 57_H. Thus, the memory pointer in HL is modified to 1857_H, and the code for digit 7 is obtained by using this memory pointer.

13.5.5 Program

To monitor the keyboard and display the key pressed, we need to initialize the PIO ports and combine the software modules discussed previously.

```
KYBORD:     ;This program first initializes the PIO ports: Port A in Mode 1 and
            ;    Port B in Mode 0 and then calls the subroutine modules
            ;    discussed previously to monitor the keyboard.
            PORT A      EQU 80H      ;Port A address
            PORT B      EQU 81H      ;Port B address
            CNTRLA      EQU 82H      ;Control register A
            CNTRLB      EQU 83H      ;Control register B
```

```
              WORDA     EQU 4FH      ;Mode 1 control word
              WORDB     EQU 0FH      ;Mode 0 control word
              STACK     EQU 18A7H    ;Beginning stack address
              LD SP, STACK
        PIO:  LD A, WORDA
              OUT (CNTRLA), A
              LD A, WORDB           ;Set up Port A in Mode 1
              OUT (CNTRLB), A       ;Set up Port B in Mode 0
     NEXTKY:  CALL KYCHK            ;Check if a key is pressed
              CALL KYCODE           ;Encode the key
              CALL DSPLAY           ;Display key pressed
              JP NEXTKY             ;Check the next key pressed
```

Description   This is the main program, which involves the initialization of the PIO and the stack pointer. The port addresses defined here are from Example 13.3 (Figure 13.7), and the address of STACK (stack pointer initialization) is shown as an illustration; it has no specific significance. Because the problem is divided into small modules, the main program consists primarily of calling these modules.

13.5.6   Comments and Alternative Approaches

The interfacing of the push-button keyboard and seven-segment display is a simplified illustration of industrial applications. The illustration is deliberately kept simple to emphasize the conceptual framework between hardware and software. However, as an application, it has several limitations.

1. This method of connecting the keyboard limits the number of keys in proportion to the number of I/O ports; only eight keys can be connected to an 8-bit port. Generally, keys are connected in a matrix format (section 13.5.7). For example, in the matrix format, 16 keys can be connected to one 8-bit port or 64 keys can be connected to two 8-bit ports.
2. This method of connecting a seven-segment LED needs excessive hardware: one port and a driver per seven-segment LED. Furthermore, it consumes large current (100–150 mA per display). To minimize hardware and power consumption, the technique of multiplexing is generally used (section 13.5.8).

In this illustration, the primary emphasis is on software. For example, in the keyboard, the debouncing and encoding is performed by using instructions. However, interfacing chips that can sense a key closure, debounce the key, and encode the key are currently available commercially. These chips can also generate an interrupt signal when a key is pressed. Similarly, in the seven-segment display, the table look-up can be replaced by a decoder/driver. However, the hardware approach increases unit price. On the other hand, the software approach involves considerable labor (programming and debugging) cost. The choice is generally determined by the production volume and the total unit price.

13.5.7 Matrix Keyboard

In a matrix keyboard, keys are arranged in a matrix form, as shown in Figure 13.16. It has 20 keys, arranged in four rows and five columns. When a key is pressed, it shorts one row and one column; otherwise, the row and column have no contact. This keyboard requires nine data lines instead of the 20 required if the keys are connected as in Figure 13.14.

The interfacing of a matrix keyboard requires two I/O ports: one output port and one input port. Rows are connected to the output port, and the columns are connected to the input port. To sense a key closure, we can use either the software approach or the hardware approach.

A software technique called matrix scan is used to sense a key closure. In this technique, rows are grounded by sending 0s to all the rows through the output

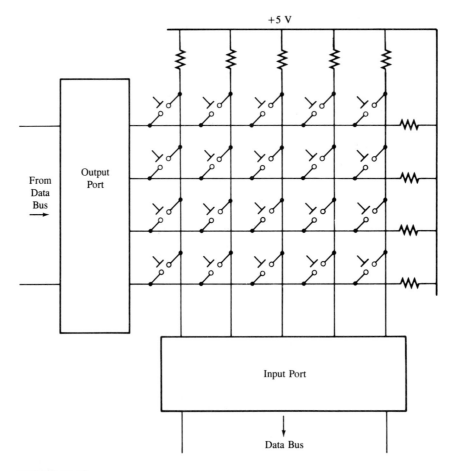

FIGURE 13.16
Interfacing a Matrix Keyboard

port, and a key closure is checked by reading the data on columns through the input port. If no key is pressed, all bits of the input reading are high, and if a key is pressed, one of the bits will be 0. Then the program grounds one row at a time, locates the key pressed, and encodes the key. The basic concepts in interfacing a matrix keyboard are similar to those discussed in the above illustration, except that the software is somewhat complex. An illustration of interfacing a matrix keyboard is discussed in Chapter 17.

The hardware approach is to use a commercially available chip, such as National Semiconductor MM54/74C923; this is a key encoder for a 20-key matrix. When a key is pressed, the internal circuit of the encoder senses a key closure, debounces and encodes the key, and generates an interrupt to inform the MPU that a key has been pressed. For example, when the "A" key is pressed, the output of the key encoder will be 0 1 0 1 0. The task for software is to read the code. (Refer to section 17.5.4 for additional details.)

13.5.8 Multiplexing and Scanned Display

The display technique in the above illustration is quite limited. It needs one I/O port and a driver for one seven-segment LED; this technique can be quite costly for multiple-digit display. The number of hardware chips needed for multiple-digit display can be minimized by using the technique called multiplexing, whereby the data lines are time-shared by various seven-segment LEDs.

Figure 13.17 shows a block diagram for a multiplexed display. The diagram has two output ports: one port P_A to drive LED segments, and a second port P_B

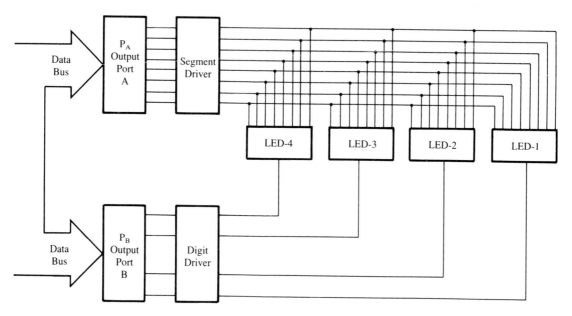

FIGURE 13.17
Block Diagram of Multiplexed Output Display

to turn on the corresponding cathodes. The output lines of port P_A are connected to seven segments of each LED, and the output lines of port P_B are connected to the cathodes of each LED. To display a digit, the code is sent to the segments through port P_A, and an LED is turned on by sending a bit to the appropriate cathode through port P_B. To display a four-digit number, each seven-segment LED is turned on and off sequentially. For example, to display 2001, the code for digit 1 is sent first and LED-1 is turned on. Next, the code for digit 0 is placed on the segment data lines; simultaneously, LED-1 is turned off and LED-2 turned on. The cycle is repeated fast enough that the display appears stable. This multiplexing technique reduces the power consumption and the number of chips.

Two ports shown in Figure 13.17 are incapable of driving eight seven-segment LEDs. In a common cathode seven-segment LED, all segments are driven by the output lines, which should supply at least 10–15 mA of current to each segment. The cathode should sink seven or eight times that current. The I/O ports of the PIO are limited in current capacity; therefore, additional transistors or ICs, called segment and digit drivers, are required, as shown in Figure 13.17. An illustration of multiplexed scanned display is shown in Chapter 17. Another approach is to replace software with hardware, as shown in Figure 13.18. It has two types of displays: HP 5082/7340 and seven-segment LEDs with a Hex decoder/driver. The HP 5082/7340 display has an internal decoder/driver; thus, two digits per port

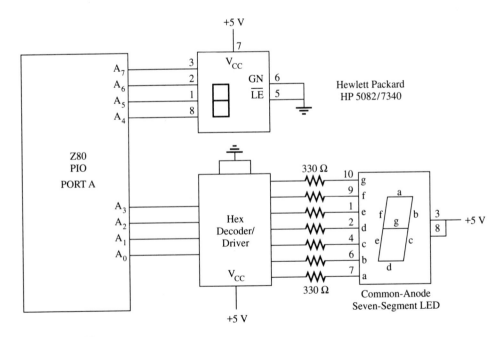

FIGURE 13.18
Hardware Alternatives to Multiplexed Display

can be displayed. The seven-segment LED has a separate decoder/driver; however, both displays are functionally similar. In this approach, the task of the software instructions is reduced simply to outputting the byte to be displayed to the port. For example, to display 87_H, the Z80 needs only to output 87_H to that port. Replacing software with hardware can increase the unit price of a display and the power consumption.

ILLUSTRATION: BIDIRECTIONAL DATA TRANSFER BETWEEN TWO MICROCOMPUTERS USING PIO IN MODE 2   13.6

The bidirectional data transfer is a common occurrence in the computer world. Typical examples include data transfer between two microcomputers or between a floppy disk and a microcomputer. The bidirectional communication between two microcomputers can be accomplished using the PIO in Mode 2.

13.6.1   Problem Statement
Design an interfacing circuit to set up bidirectional data communication between two Z80 microcomputers: Micro-1 and Micro-2. Use the PIO in Mode 2 as the interfacing device with Micro-1, and the interrupt technique for data transfer. Set up Micro-2 using a tri-state buffer as the interfacing device and implement data transfer under program control (status check). Write necessary software to transfer a block of data from Micro-1 to Micro-2.

13.6.2   Problem Analysis
Figure 13.19 shows a block diagram to set up the bidirectional communication between two microcomputers. The block diagram shows two bidirectional data

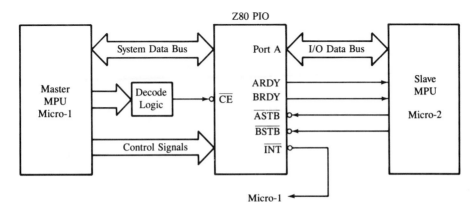

FIGURE 13.19
Block Diagram: Bidirectional Communication Between Two Microcomputers Using PIO

buses—system data bus and I/O data bus—interconnected through the PIO, which serves as the interfacing device of Micro-1. Port A of the PIO is used for bidirectional data transfer. Micro-1 uses the handshake signals of Port A ($\overline{\text{ASTB}}$ and ARDY) for output control, and the handshake signals of Port B ($\overline{\text{BSTB}}$ and BRDY) for input control. The communication process is the combination of Mode 0 and Mode 1.

Both microcomputers require I/O ports to read and write data and to check the status of handshake signals. Therefore, it is necessary to analyze carefully these I/O functions between the MPUs. Data transfer for Micro-2 is to be accomplished under program control with the status check and through the interrupt process for Micro-1. The steps in the data transfer operations between the two MPUs and the timing are as follows.

Data Output from Micro-1 to Micro-2

1. The Micro-1 writes data into Port A and causes the signal ARDY to go high, indicating to Micro-2 that a byte is available to be read (Figure 13.20). This is an output function for Micro-1.
2. The Micro-2 continues to check ARDY, and when it goes high, it asserts the $\overline{\text{ASTB}}$ signal low. This places the data byte onto the data bus (Figure 13.20). For Micro-2, checking ARDY is an input function.
3. Once the data byte is on the bus, it can be latched or read by Micro-2 on the rising edge of the $\overline{\text{ASTB}}$ signal. Therefore, the asserting of $\overline{\text{ASTB}}$ low and

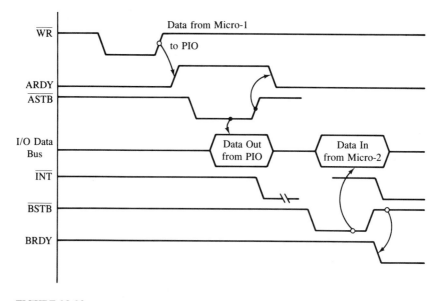

FIGURE 13.20
Timing Waveforms for Bidirectional Data Transfer

reading the byte can be performed by a Read operation of Micro-2. Thus, asserting the $\overline{\text{ASTB}}$ is an input operation of Micro-2.
4. When the byte is read by the Micro-2, ARDY goes low and the $\overline{\text{INT}}$ is generated to indicate to Micro-1 that the next byte can be sent.

Data Input to Micro-1 from Micro-2

1. Micro-2 places a data byte onto the I/O data bus as it asserts the $\overline{\text{BSTB}}$ signal. This is an output function for Micro-2.
2. On the rising edge of the $\overline{\text{BSTB}}$, the $\overline{\text{INT}}$ is generated to inform Micro-1 that a byte is available in Port A to be read. Similarly, when $\overline{\text{BSTB}}$ goes high, it causes BRDY to go low, indicating to Micro-2 to wait until a byte is read, so Micro-2 continues to read BRDY. This is an input function for Micro-2.
3. When an interrupt is generated, Micro-1 reads the byte, and the $\overline{\text{RD}}$ signal causes the BRDY to go high, indicating to Micro-2 that the next byte can be sent.

This analysis leads to certain hardware requirements, which are discussed in the next section.

13.6.3 Hardware Description

To clarify the hardware requirements, we can summarize the bidirectional data transfer operations as follows.

1. To send a byte from Micro-1 and to receive it in Micro-2:

   □ Micro-1 writes a byte into Port A of the PIO whenever an interrupt is generated.
   □ Micro-2 reads ARDY until it goes high, and then reads the byte by asserting the $\overline{\text{ASTB}}$.

2. To receive a data byte by Micro-1:

   □ Micro-1 performs an input operation whenever an interrupt is generated.
   □ Micro-2 performs two operations: one input operation to monitor BRDY and one output operation to write a data byte and assert the $\overline{\text{BSTB}}$.

Thus, for Micro-1, Port A of the PIO needs to be set up in the bidirectional mode, and the Z80 in the interrupt Mode 2. Micro-2 needs one input port to monitor ARDY and BRDY, another input port to read a byte and assert $\overline{\text{ASTB}}$, and one output port to send a byte and assert $\overline{\text{BSTB}}$.

Figure 13.21 shows the complete schematic of the necessary ports and their decoding logic. The decoding logic for Port A of the PIO is the same as in Example 13.2; thus, port addresses range from 80_H to 83_H. All the handshake signals are being used for bidirectional data transfer by Port A; the $\overline{\text{INT}}$ signal of the PIO is connected to the $\overline{\text{INT}}$ signal of the Z80 MPU of Micro-1, and Port B is not being used in this illustration.

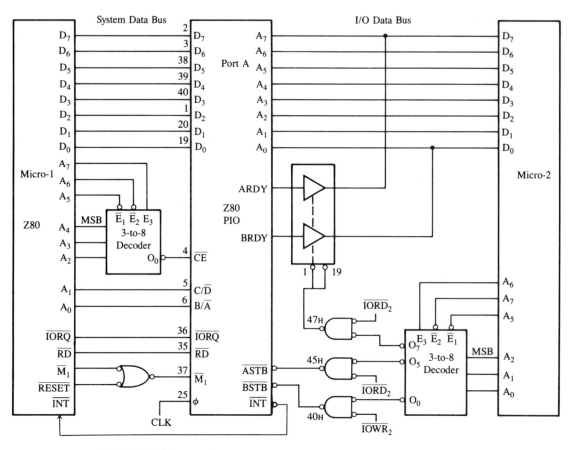

FIGURE 13.21
Interfacing Schematic for Bidirectional Data Transfer Between Two Microcomputers

The two handshake signals—ARDY and BRDY—are tied, respectively, to bits D_7 and D_0 of the I/O data bus through a tri-state buffer so that they can be monitored by Micro-2; this port is labeled as input port STATUS. The signal $\overline{ASTB}$ is asserted by reading PORTIN, and the signal $\overline{BSTB}$ is asserted by writing in PRTOUT. The decode logic for these ports is generated by using the 74LS138 (3-to-8) decoder. Assuming the "don't care" address lines (A_4 and A_3) are at logic 0, the port addresses are as follows:

	A_7	A_6	A_5	A_4	A_3	A_2	A_1	A_0		
Status Port:	0	1	0	X	X	1	1	1	$= 47_H \rightarrow$	STATUS
Input Port:						1	0	1	$= 45_H \rightarrow$	PORTIN
Output Port:						0	0	0	$= 40_H \rightarrow$	PRTOUT

Two output lines of the decoder are combined with the $\overline{\text{IORD}}$ control signal of Micro-2 to generate two input device select pulses (45_H and 47_H). Port 47_H is used to read status on the data lines D_7 and D_0, and Port 45_H is used to assert the $\overline{\text{ASTB}}$ signal. The decoder line with the address 40_H is combined with the $\overline{\text{IOWR}}$ signal of Micro-2 to generate the $\overline{\text{BSTB}}$ signal.

13.6.4 Program

This illustration requires two programs: one for Micro-1 to send a block of data bytes and another for Micro-2 to receive those data bytes. These programs will be similar, but will vary in details because Micro-1 uses the PIO with the interrupt I/O while Micro-2 transfers data under program control. Data transfer from Micro-2 to Micro-1 is not included in the problem statement; it is left as an assignment.

Micro-1 Program
;This program initializes Z80 in interrupt Mode 2 and the PIO in the
; bidirectional data transfer Mode 2 and sends out a block of data bytes to
   Micro-2.
;The interrupt vector for Port A is 2090H and for Port B is 2092H.

```
MICRO1:   LD A, 10001111B      ;Control word (8FH) for Mode 2
          OUT (CNTRLA), A      ;Set up Port A for bidirectional data
                                  transfer
          LD A, 10000011B      ;Interrupt enable word (83H)—Figure
                                  13.10(a)
          OUT (CNTRLA), A      ;Enable interrupt for Port A
          OUT (CNTRLB), A      ;Enable interrupt for Port B
          LD A, 90H            ;Interrupt vector for Port A
          OUT (CNTRLA), A      ;Write interrupt vector to Port A
          LD A, 92H            ;Interrupt vector for Port B
          OUT (CNTRLB), A      ;Write interrupt vector to Port B
          LD SP, STACK1        ;Initialize stack for Z80 of Micro-1
          IM 2                 ;Set up Z80 in interrupt Mode 2
          LD HL, DATA          ;Set up HL as memory pointer where
                               ; data bytes are located
          LD B, BYTES          ;Load number for bytes to be
                                  transferred
          CALL SEND            ;Send first to get things started
LOOP:     JP LOOP              ;Wait for an interrupt
SEND:     ;This is a service routine for Port A to send data to Micro-2.
          ;The routine outputs one byte at a time to PIO Port A until all
          ; bytes are transmitted.
          LD A, (HL)           ;Get byte from memory
          OUT (PORTA), A       ;Send byte to Port A of PIO
```

```
        INC HL              ;Next byte location
        DEC B               ;Decrement byte counter
        EI                  ;Enable Z80 interrupt
        RET NZ              ;Return if byte counter ≠ 0
        JP END              ;Jump to end message subroutine
```

Micro-2 Program (See Figure 13.22)
;This program receives the block of data from Micro-1 under program control.
;It checks the status of ARDY. When ARDY is high, it reads PORTIN.

```
  RECIVE:   LD SP, STACK2       ;Initialize stack pointer for Micro-2
            LD HL, STORE        ;Point index to first memory location
                                 where data bytes should be stored
```

FIGURE 13.22

Flowchart: Program to Receive
Data Bytes by Micro-2

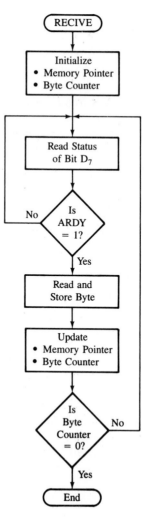

```
          LD B, BYTES          ;Specify number of bytes to be received
          IN A, (PORTIN)       ;This is dummy read to generate
                                 interrupt for PIO
ARDY:     IN A, (STATUS)       ;Check ARDY
          RLA                  ;Place bit D₇ into Carry
          JP NC, ARDY          ;If ARDY is low, wait in loop
          IN A, (PORTIN)       ;Read data
          LD (HL), A           ;Store data byte
          INC HL               ;Next memory location
          DJNZ NZ, ARDY        ;Go back to read next byte if all bytes
                               ; are not yet received

          HALT
```

PROGRAM DESCRIPTION

1. To transfer a block of data from Micro-1 to Micro-2, both programs need to be executed at the same time.
2. The program for Micro-1 waits in a loop after the initialization; ordinarily, in real application, the program would continue to perform other tasks until an interrupt is generated.
3. The program RECIVE for Micro-2 performs a dummy read operation to start the data transfer and continues to check ARDY. When Micro-2 reads PORTIN the first time, the $\overline{ASTB}$ signal goes low and an interrupt is generated for Micro-1.
4. In Micro-1, because of the interrupt the program is transferred to the service routine. It writes a byte in the PIO, causing ARDY to go high; decrements the byte counter; and if the counter is not zero, returns to the main program to wait in the loop.
5. When ARDY goes high, bit D_7 goes high because the $\overline{ARDY}$ is tied to data line D_7. The program RECIVE reads the byte; this causes $\overline{ASTB}$ to go low, and an interrupt is generated for the next byte.
6. Every time a byte is transferred by Micro-1 and received by Micro-2, the respective counters (registers B) are decremented, and the data transfer continues until the counters go to 0. In Micro-1, when the byte counter is 0, the program control jumps to an End message routine. It is expected that the message routine will include the instructions EI and RET.
7. The programs given can transfer a block of data from Micro-1 to Micro-2, but not vice versa. To transfer a block of data from Micro-2 to Micro-1, additional routines are necessary (see Assignment 24). The service routine for Micro-1 will involve reading PORTA whenever an interrupt is generated. For Micro-2, an additional set of instructions is necessary. These instructions will monitor the BRDY signal. When the BRDY goes high, it means $\overline{PORTA}$ is ready to receive a byte. Then Micro-2 can write a byte causing $\overline{BSTB}$ to go low; an interrupt will be generated and Micro-1 can read the byte.

13.7 THE 8255A PROGRAMMABLE PERIPHERAL INTERFACE

The Intel 8255A is another widely used, programmable, parallel I/O device, similar to the Z80 PIO. It is the revised version of Intel's 8255 and is commonly referred to as the 8255 rather than the 8255A. It can be programmed to transfer data under various conditions—from simple I/O to interrupt I/O. It is flexible, versatile, and economical, but somewhat complex. It is a general purpose I/O device and can be used with almost any microprocessor. Because of its wide use in industry it is discussed here briefly. (See Gaonkar, *Microprocessor Architecture,* 1988, for a full description.)

The 8255A has 24 I/O pins, and they can be grouped into two 8-bit parallel ports, A and B, and an 8-bit port C. The eight bits of Port C can be used as individual bits or grouped into two 4-bit ports: C_U and C_L (Figure 13.23(a)). Ports A and B of the 8255A are similar to Ports A and B of the Z80 PIO, and Port C is similar to the bit mode of the PIO. The functions of these ports are defined by writing a control word in the control register.

Figure 13.23(b) shows all the functions of the 8255A. They are classified according to two modes: the Bit Set/Reset (BSR) mode and the I/O mode (byte mode). The **BSR mode** is used to set or reset the bits in Port C. The I/O mode is further divided into three modes: Mode 0, Mode 1, and Mode 2. In Mode 0, all ports function as simple I/O ports. Mode 1 is a **handshake mode,** whereby Ports

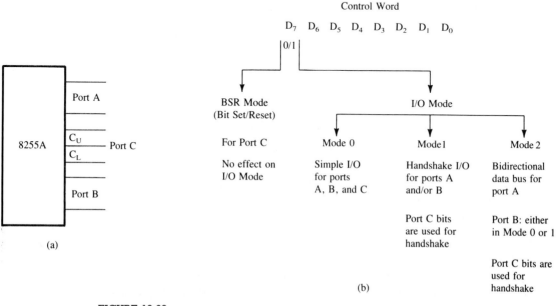

FIGURE 13.23
(a) 8255A I/O Ports and (b) Their Modes

A and/or B use bits from Port C as handshake signals. In the handshake mode, two types of I/O data transfer can be implemented: status check under program control and interrupt. In Mode 2, Port A can be set up for bidirectional data transfer using handshake signals from Port C, and Port B can be set up in either Mode 0 or Mode 1. The definitions of Mode 0 and Mode 1 in the 8255A are quite different from those in the PIO and should not be confused.

13.7.1 Block Diagram of the 8255A

The block diagram in Figure 13.24(a) shows two 8-bit ports (A and B), two 4-bit ports (C_U and C_L), the data bus buffer, and control logic. Figure 13.24(b) shows a simplified but expanded version of the internal structure, which includes a control register. This block diagram includes all the elements of a programmable device; Port C performs functions similar to those of the status register.

CONTROL LOGIC

The control section has six lines. Their functions and connections are as follows:

☐ $\overline{RD}$—Read: This control signal enables the Read operation. When the signal is low, the MPU reads data from a selected I/O port of the 8255A.
☐ $\overline{WR}$—Write: This control signal enables the Write operation. When the signal goes low, the MPU writes into a selected I/O port or the control register.
☐ RESET—Reset: This is an active high signal and clears all the registers of the 8255A.
☐ $\overline{CS}$, A_0, and A_1—Chip Select Signals: These signals are used for selecting the device. $\overline{CS}$ is connected to a decoded address, and A_0 and A_1 are generally connected to the system address lines A_0 and A_1, respectively.

The $\overline{CS}$ signal is the master Chip Select, and A_0 and A_1 specify one of the I/O ports or the control register as shown.

$\overline{CS}$	A_1	A_0	Selected
0	0	0	Port A
0	0	1	Port B
0	1	0	Port C
0	1	1	Control Register
1	X	X	8255 is not selected.

As an example, the port addresses in Figure 13.25 are determined by the $\overline{CS}$, A_0, and A_1 lines. The $\overline{CS}$ line goes low when $A_7 = 1$ and A_6 through A_2 are at logic 0. Combining these signals with A_0 and A_1 yields port addresses ranging from 80_H to 83_H, as shown in Figure 13.25(b).

CONTROL WORD

The 8255A has one control register, and the contents of this register, called the control word, specify an I/O function for each port. This register can be assessed to write a control word when A_0 and A_1 are at logic 1, as mentioned previously. The register is not accessible for a Read operation.

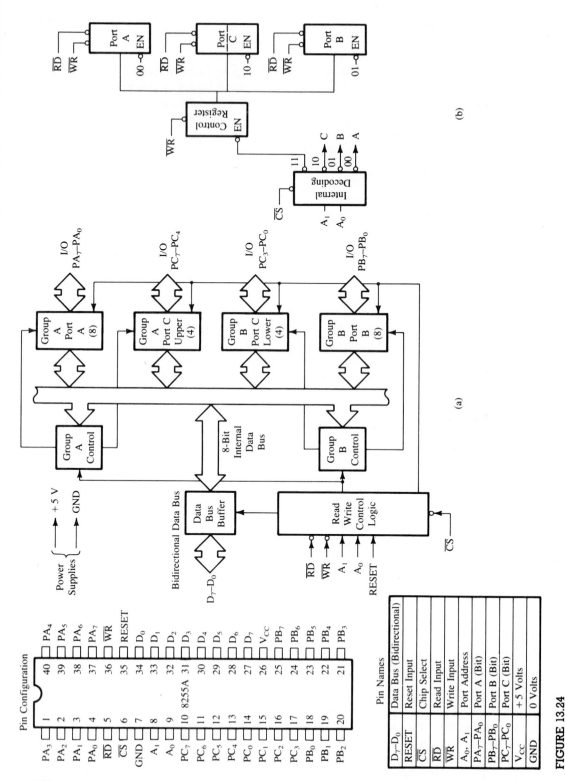

FIGURE 13.24

(a) 8255A Block Diagram; (b) Expanded Version of the Control Logic and I/O Ports

SOURCE: (a) Reprinted by permission of Intel Corporation, copyright 1979.

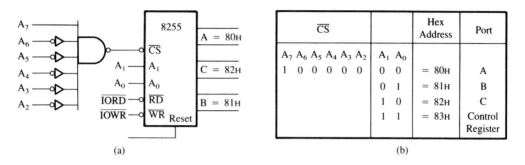

FIGURE 13.25
(a) 8255A Chip Select Logic and (b) I/O Port Addresses

Bit D_7 of the control register specifies either the I/O function or the Bit Set/Reset function, as shown in Figure 13.23(b). If bit $D_7 = 1$, bits D_0–D_6 determine I/O functions in various modes, as shown in Figure 13.26. If bit $D_7 = 0$, Port C operates in the Bit Set/Reset (BSR) mode. The BSR control word does not affect the functions of Ports A and B; the BSR mode will be described later.

To communicate with peripherals through the 8255A, the following three steps are necessary:

1. Determine the addresses of Ports A, B, and C and of the control register according to the Chip Select logic and the address lines A_0 and A_1.
2. Write a control word in the control register.
3. Write I/O instructions to communicate with peripherals through Ports A, B, and C.

13.7.2 Mode 0: Simple Input or Output

In this mode, Ports A and B function as two 8-bit I/O ports and Port C as two 4-bit ports. Each port (or half port, in the case of C) can be programmed to function as simply an input or output port. The input/output features in Mode 0 are as follows:

1. Outputs are latched.
2. Inputs are not latched.
3. Ports do not have handshake interrupt capability.

13.7.3 BSR (Bit Set/Reset) Mode

The BSR mode is concerned only with the 8 bits of Port C, which can be set or reset by writing an appropriate control word in the control register. A control word with bit $D_7 = 0$ is recognized as a BSR control word, and it does not alter any previously transmitted control word with bit $D_7 = 1$; thus, the I/O operations of Ports A and B are not affected by a BSR control word. In the BSR mode, individual bits of Port C can be used for applications such as an on/off switch.

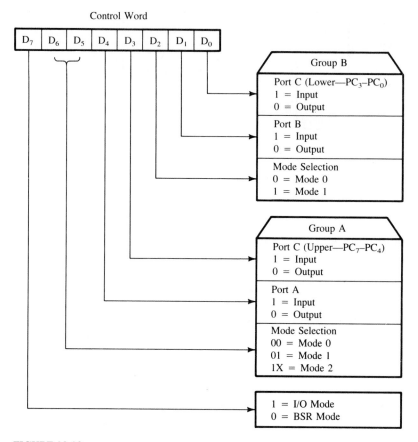

FIGURE 13.26
8255A Control Word Format for I/O Mode
SOURCE: Adapted from Intel Corporation, copyright 1981.

BSR CONTROL WORD

This control word, when written in the control register, sets or resets one bit at a time, as shown in Figure 13.27.

13.7.4 Illustration: Interfacing an A/D Converter Using the 8255A in Mode 0 and BSR Mode

PROBLEM STATEMENT

Design an interfacing circuit to read data from an A/D converter, using the 8255A in the peripheral-mapped I/O.

1. Set up Port A to read data.
2. Set up bit PC_0 to start conversion and bit PC_7 to read the ready status of the converter.

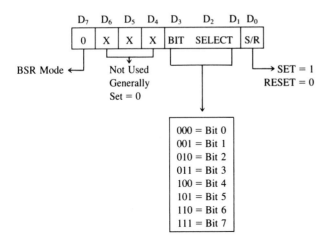

FIGURE 13.27
8255A Control Word Format in the BSR Mode

PROBLEM ANALYSIS

The Chip Select logic in Figure 13.28 is similar to that in the previous examples. The port addresses can be obtained by examining the decoding logic of the $\overline{CS}$ signal and combining that with the A_1 and A_0 signals. The port addresses range from 20_H to 23_H, as shown.

A_7	A_6	A_5	A_4	A_3	A_2	A_1	A_0		
0	0	1	0	0	0	0	0	$= 20_H$	Port A
						0	1	$= 21_H$	Port B
						1	0	$= 22_H$	Port C
						1	1	$= 23_H$	Control Register

MODE 0 CONTROL WORD

The configuration of the ports is specified as follows:

□ Port A as an input port.
□ Port C_L as an output port because bit PC_0 is being used to start conversion.
□ Port C_U as an input port to read the status at PC_7.
□ Port B not being used.

Therefore, the control word necessary to meet the requirements is 98_H as shown.

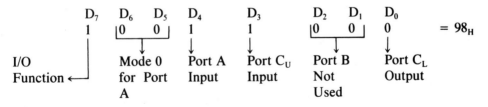

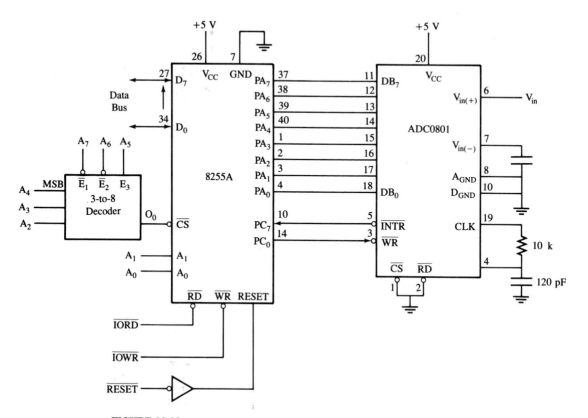

FIGURE 13.28
Schematic: Interfacing the A/D Converter ADC0801 Using the 8255A in Mode 0 and BSR Mode

BSR CONTROL WORD FOR START PULSE

Bit PC_0 is being used as a start pulse. To set and reset PC_0, the BSR control word is as follows (refer to Figure 13.27):

D_7	D_6	D_5	D_4	D_3	D_2	D_1	D_0	
0	0	0	0	0	0	0	1/0	$= 01_H$ to Set
↓					↓		↓	↓
BSR Mode		"Don't Care"			Bit 0		Set/ Reset	$= 00$ to Reset

SUBROUTINE

```
PORTA   EQU 20H      ;Port A address
PORTC   EQU 22H      ;Port C address
CNTRL   EQU 23H      ;Control register address
A/D:    LD C, 23H    ;Set up Z80 C register as pointer to 8255A
                     ; control register
```

```
                LD A, 10011000B        ;Load the Mode 0 control word (98H)
                OUT (C), A             ;Write in the control register to set up A
                                       ; and C_U as inputs
                LD A, 00H              ;Load BSR control word to reset PC_0
                OUT (C), A             ;Send WR pulse
                CALL DELAY             ;Wait for sufficient pulse width
                LD A, 01H              ;Load BSR control word to set PC_0
                OUT (C), A             ;Start conversion
READ:           IN A, (C)              ;Read bit PC_7
                RLA                    ;Place PC_7 in the carry
                JP C, READ             ;Wait in the loop until the end of
                                          conversion
                IN A, (20H)            ;Read A/D converter
                RET
```

PROGRAM DESCRIPTION

The 8255A ports are initialized by placing the control word 98_H into the control register. To provide a start pulse to the converter, logic 0 is sent to bit PC_0 in Port C, and after a sufficient delay, bit PC_0 is set to start the conversion. The end of conversion is checked by verifying the status of line PC_7. When PC_7 goes low, the instruction IN A, (20H) reads and places data into the accumulator.

13.7.5 Mode 1: Input or Output with Handshake

In Mode 1, handshake signals are exchanged between the MPU and peripherals prior to data transfer. The features of this mode are as follows:

1. Two ports—A and B—function as 8-bit I/O ports. They can be configured either as input or output ports.
2. Each port uses three lines from Port C as handshake signals. The remaining two lines of Port C can be used for simple I/O functions.
3. Input and output data are latched.
4. Interrupt logic is supported.

In the 8255A, the specific lines used from Port C for handshake signals vary according to the I/O function of a port. Therefore, input and output functions in Mode 1 are discussed separately.

MODE 1: INPUT CONTROL SIGNALS

Figure 13.29(a) shows the associated control signals used for handshaking when Ports A and B are configured as input ports. Port A uses the upper three signals—PC_3, PC_4, and PC_5—while Port B uses PC_2, PC_1, and PC_0. The functions of these signals are:

□ $\overline{STB}$ (Strobe Input): This signal (active low) is generated by a peripheral device to indicate that it has transmitted a data byte. The 8255A, in response to $\overline{STB}$, generates IBF and INTR, as shown in Figure 13.30.

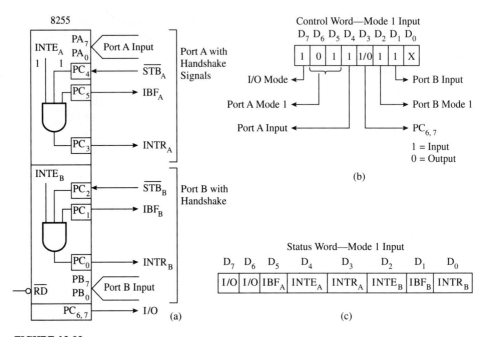

FIGURE 13.29
8255A Mode 1: Input Configuration
SOURCE: Adapted from Intel Corporation, copyright 1981.

□ IBF (Input Buffer Full): This signal is an acknowledgment by the 8255A to indicate that the input latch has received the data byte. This is reset when the MPU reads the data (Figure 13.30).

□ INTR (Interrupt Request): This is an output signal that may be used to interrupt the MPU. This signal is generated if $\overline{STB}$, IBF, and INTE (internal flip-flop) are all at logic 1, and is reset by the falling edge of the $\overline{RD}$ signal (Figure 13.30).

□ INTE (Interrupt Enable): This is an internal flip-flop used to enable or disable the generation of the INTR signal. The two flip-flops $INTE_A$ and $INTE_B$ are set/reset through the BSR mode. The $INTE_A$ is enabled/disabled through PC_4, and $INTE_B$ is enabled/disabled through PC_2.

CONTROL AND STATUS WORDS

Figure 13.29(b) uses control words derived from Figure 13.26 to set up Port A and Port B as input ports in Mode 1. Similarly, Figure 13.29(c) shows the status word, which will be placed into the accumulator if Port C is read.

PROGRAMMING THE 8255A IN MODE 1

The 8255A can be programmed to function using either status check I/O or interrupt I/O. Figure 13.31(a) shows a flowchart for the status check I/O. In this flowchart, the MPU continues to check data status through the IBF line until it goes

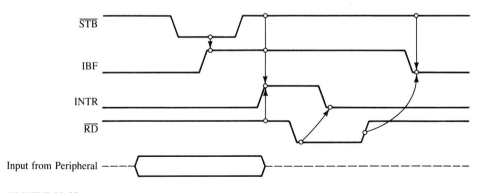

FIGURE 13.30
8255A Mode 0: Timing Waveforms for Strobed Input (with Handshake)
SOURCE: Adapted from Intel Corporation, copyright 1981.

high. This is a simplified flowchart and does not show how to handle data transfer if two ports are being used. The technique is similar to that of Mode 0 combined with the BSR mode. The disadvantage of the status check I/O with handshake is that the MPU is tied up in the loop.

The flowchart in Figure 13.31(b) shows the steps required for the interrupt I/O, assuming that vectored interrupts are available. The confusing step in the interrupt I/O is to set INTE for either Port A or Port B. Figure 13.30(a) shows that the $\overline{\text{STB}}$ signal is connected to pin PC_4 and the $INTE_A$ is also controlled by the pin PC_4. (In Port B, the pin PC_2 is used for the same purposes.) However, the $INTE_A$ is set or reset in the BSR mode and the BSR control word has no effect when Ports A and B are set in Mode 1.

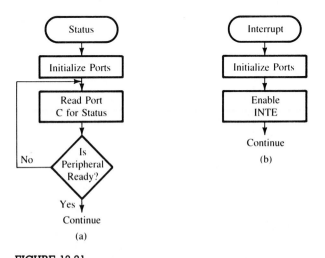

FIGURE 13.31
Flowcharts: (a) Status Check I/O; (b) Interrupt I/O

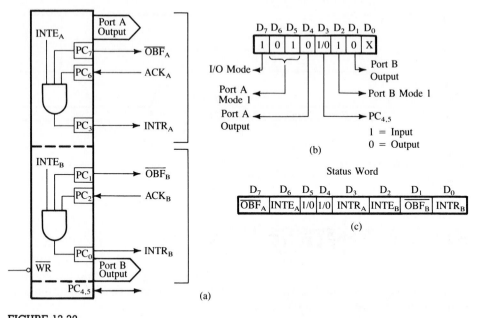

FIGURE 13.32
8255A Mode 1: Output Configuration
SOURCE: Adapted from Intel Corporation, copyright 1981.

In case the INTR line is used to implement the interrupt, it may be necessary to read the status of $INTR_A$ and $INTR_B$ to identify the port requesting an interrupt service and to determine the priority through software, if necessary.

MODE 1: OUTPUT CONTROL SIGNALS

Figure 13.32 shows the control signals when Ports A and B are configured as output ports. These signals are defined as follows:

☐ $\overline{OBF}$ (Output Buffer Full): This is an output signal that goes low when the MPU writes data into the output latch of the 8255A. This signal indicates to an output peripheral that new data are ready to be read (Figure 13.33). It goes high again after the 8255A receives an $\overline{ACK}$ (Acknowledge) from the peripheral.

☐ $\overline{ACK}$ (Acknowledge): This is an input signal to the 8255A from a peripheral, which must output a low when the peripheral receives the data from the 8255A ports (Figure 13.33).

☐ INTR (Interrupt Request): This is an output signal, and it is set by the rising edge of the $\overline{ACK}$ signal. This signal can be used to interrupt the MPU to request the next data byte for output. The INTR is set when $\overline{OBF}$, $\overline{ACK}$ and INTE are all one (Figure 13.33) and reset by the falling edge of $\overline{WR}$.

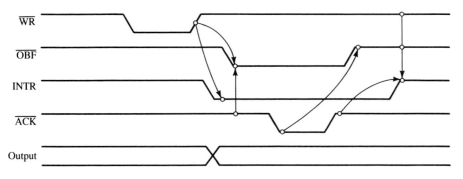

FIGURE 13.33
8255A Mode 1: Timing Waveforms for Strobed Input (with Handshake)
SOURCE: Adapted from Intel Corporation, copyright 1981.

□ INTE (Interrupt Enable): This is an internal flip-flop to a port and needs to be set to generate the INTR signal. The two flip-flops $INTE_A$ and $INTE_B$ are controlled by bits PC_6 and PC_2, respectively, through the BSR mode.
□ PC_4 and PC_5: These lines can be set up as either input or output.

CONTROL AND STATUS WORDS
Figure 13.32(b) shows the control word needed to set up Port A and Port B as output ports in Mode 1. Similarly, Figure 13.32(c) also shows the status word, which will be placed into the accumulator if Port C is read.

13.7.6   Mode 2: Bidirectional Data Transfer
This mode is used primarily in applications such as data transfer between two microcomputers or floppy disk controller interfaces. In this mode, Port A can be configured as the bidirectional port and Port B in either Mode 0 or Mode 1. Port A uses five signals from Port C as control signals for data transfer. The remaining three signals from Port C can be used either as simple I/O or as handshake signals for Port B. Figure 13.34 shows two configurations of Mode 2.

13.7.7   Comparison of the Z80 PIO and the 8255A
The Z80 PIO and the Intel 8255A are two widely used peripheral interface devices, and they are designed to serve similar functions. However, the 8255A is a general-purpose device and can be used with any microprocessor. On the other hand, the PIO is specifically designed to work with the Z80 microprocessor. Therefore, the PIO can offer some special features, such as daisy chain interrupt priority, based on its ability to recognize the instruction RETI. The PIO has some other attractive features, such as its ability to recognize predefined logic conditions in the bit mode. The advantages of the 8255A over the PIO are that the 8255A has three

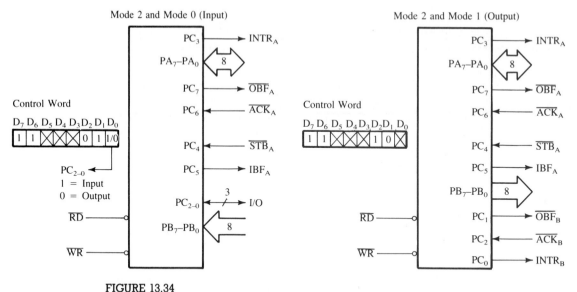

FIGURE 13.34

8255A Mode 2: Bidirectional Input/Output

SOURCE: Adapted from Intel Corporation, copyright 1981.

I/O ports and the status of the handshake signals can be monitored by reading Port C. In the 8255A, data transfer can be set up under the program control or the interrupt control; the PIO is better suited for the interrupt control. The comparison of these two devices is shown in Table 13.2.

TABLE 13.2

Comparison of the Z80 PIO and the 8255A

	PIO	8255A
1. Number of 8-bit Ports	Two: A and B	Three: A, B, and C Port C Consists of Two 4-bit Ports.
2. I/O Lines in Bit Mode	16 Lines	8 Lines in Addition to Ports A and B
3. Handshake and Interrupt Signals	Ports A and B Separate Available Lines	Ports A and B Use Lines of Port C
4. Bidirectional Mode	Port A	Port A
5. Status Check of Handshake Signals	Not Available	Available through Port C
6. Interrupt I/O	Ports A and B	Ports A and B
7. Logic Check and Interrupt	Bit Mode	Not Available
8. Daisy Chain Interrupt Priority	Available	Not Available

ILLUSTRATION: INTERFACING A STEPPER MOTOR 13.8

A stepper motor is a commonly used device in various products such as printers, disk drivers, and X-Y plotters. The stepper motor converts electrical pulses into mechanical rotations in precise degrees. The angle of rotation per pulse is determined by the design of a motor. Typically, stepper motors used in microprocessor-based products (such as printers) have a stepping angle from 1.8° to 7.5°. A stepper motor with 1.8° requires 10 pulses (steps) to rotate the shaft through 18°; thus, 200 steps are required for a complete rotation of 360°. In a printer (set up for 6 lines/inch), when the LF (Line Feed) key is pushed, the stepper motor rotates the paper exactly through one line (⅙ inch) and for a page feed, it rotates through 66 steps. The following illustration shows how to interface a stepper motor using the 8255A, and demonstrates its hardware and programming requirements.

13.8.1 Problem Statement
Figure 13.35 shows a circuit interfacing a stepper motor using the 8255A in Mode 0. Explain how the circuit works. Write instructions to initialize the 8255A and to rotate the motor clockwise through 66 steps. This will be a simulation of a page feed in a printer.

13.8.2 Hardware
The circuit in Figure 13.35 shows a stepper motor with four windings. Each winding is driven by individual bits of the 8255A through an optocoupler and a power transistor driver. The connections of bits PC_0 are shown in Figure 13.35; the similar connections to bits PC_1, PC_2, and PC_3 are omitted from the schematic.

When the processor outputs logic 1 to bit PC_0, it is inverted by the inverter, the input LED of 4N26 is turned on, and that activates the phototransistor. As the phototransistor conducts, it pulls the base of the power transistor below its turned on voltage. Thus, the power transistor is turned off and the winding is deactivated. To activate the winding, logic 0 must be sent to the inverter. The optocoupler isolates the low voltage of digital circuits from the high voltages due to the inductive loads of the stepper windings. The 10-Ω resistor drops enough voltage across the resistor and adjusts the winding voltage to its requirement (6 V), and the diode across the winding suppresses surge voltages of the inductive load.

Now we need to examine the pulse sequence required to turn the motor in steps: either clockwise or counter-clockwise. The motor shown in Figure 13.35 has four coils (or windings) and two sections: upper half and lower half. On each half, two coils are wound in the opposite direction. Therefore, to rotate the motor through one step, one winding from the upper half and one winding from the lower half should be turned on in a sequence. Table 13.3 shows the full-step sequence, and Table 13.4 shows the half-step sequence for both: clockwise and counter-clockwise directions.

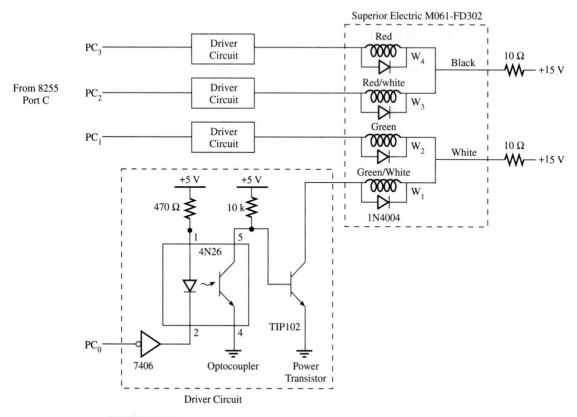

FIGURE 13.35
Interfacing a Stepper Motor

SOURCE: Adapted from *Experiments in 8085 Microprocessor Programming and Interfacing,* David Delker, Merrill, an imprint of Macmillan Publishing Company, 1989.

TABLE 13.3
Full-Step Sequence

Step	Windings			
	W_1	W_2	W_3	W_4
1	On	Off	On	Off
2	On	Off	Off	On
3	Off	On	Off	On
4	Off	On	On	Off

TABLE 13.4
Half-Step Sequence

Step	Windings			
	W_1	W_2	W_3	W_4
1	On	Off	On	Off
2	On	Off	Off	Off
3	On	Off	Off	On
4	Off	Off	Off	On
5	Off	On	Off	On
6	Off	On	Off	Off
7	Off	On	On	Off
8	Off	Off	On	Off

We will use the same decoding circuit as in Figure 13.28. Thus, the addresses of Port C and the control register are 22_H and 23_H, respectively.

13.8.3 Program

This subroutine is expected to simulate a page feed on a printer by outputting 66 pulses to the windings. These windings should be turned on/off in a sequence shown in Table 13.3, and after activating a winding, a 5 ms delay is required to provide enough time for the motor to turn through its step.

```
Main: ;This is a main program that initializes the 8255A and
      ; calls the STEPER routine.
PORTC       EQU   22H              ;Port C address
CNTRL       EQU   23H              ;Control port address
STACK       EQU   1899H            ;Initialize stack

            ORG 1800H              ;Begin assembling at 1800H
            LD C,22H               ;Set up register C for the port address
            LD A, 10000000         ;Lower Port C is set as output by setting
                                      D₀ = 0
            OUT (CNTRL), A         ;Initialize Port C
            LD D, 66               ;Set up D as a counter for 66 pulses
            CALL STEPER            ;Rotate motor through 66 steps
            HALT

STEPER:     ;This is a subroutine that turns the stepper motor through 66
               steps
REPEAT:     LD E,4                 ;Set up counter for four patterns
            LD HL, STEP            ;Point HL to winding bit pattern
NEXT:       LD B,(HL)              ;Get bit pattern
            OUT (C),B              ;Turn on winding
            CALL 5MS               ;Wait until motor turns
            INC HL                 ;Next bit pattern
            DEC D                  ;Next total count
            JR Z,STOP              ;Did motor step through 66 turns? If yes,
                                      stop
            DEC E                  ;Next count of the bit pattern
            JR NZ,NEXT             ;Did we finish four bit patterns?
            JR REPEAT              ;If yes, load and start again
STOP:       RET
STEP        DEFB 0AH, 06H, 05H, 09H
```

In the line "LD A, 10000000", the subscript should read $D_0 = 0$.

PROGRAM DESCRIPTION

The main program initializes the 8255A, sets up register D as a counter to count 66 pulses, and calls the STEPER routine. This subroutine repeatedly outputs the four bit patterns that are stored in memory starting at location STEP. The basic requirement to turn the motor through one step is that a set of two windings on the opposite stator must be turned on. For example, the first bit pattern to turn the motor clockwise is 1 0 1 0, which turns on W_3 and W_1 windings; in this circuit, logic 0 turns on a winding. The second bit pattern 0 1 1 0 turns on W_1 and W_4 windings, followed by W_4 and W_2 and W_2 and W_3.

The subroutine begins by setting the counter E to 4 and initializes the HL pointer to the first bit pattern. The program outputs four bit patterns in a sequence with 5 ms delay after each output. Once the bit pattern counter (register E) becomes 0, the program resets the counter to 4 and starts from the first bit pattern again. This is continued until the count in D becomes 0, and then the subroutine returns to the main program. To turn the motor in the counter-clockwise direction, the subroutine should begin by outputting the last bit pattern and continue in the reverse direction.

SUMMARY

This chapter has been concerned with the basic concepts (such as control register, control logic, and handshake signals) underlying a programmable device. Based on these concepts, the Z80 PIO (Programmable Input/Output) device was discussed in detail with illustrative applications. Finally, another widely used peripheral interfacing device, the Intel 8255A, was discussed and compared with the PIO. The important points can be summarized as follows:

☐ A programmable interface device is designed to perform various I/O functions, and these functions can be specified by writing an appropriate control word (or words) into its control registers.

☐ A programmable I/O device generally includes multiple I/O ports, control register(s), handshake signals, and interrupt capability.

☐ The signals that are exchanged between the MPU and peripherals prior to data transfer are called handshake signals. These signals check whether a peripheral is ready for data transfer and inform the MPU accordingly.

☐ The Z80 PIO is a programmable I/O device with two I/O ports (A and B), and it has four operating modes: Mode 0 (output), Mode 1 (input), Mode 2 (bidirectional), and Mode 3 (bit mode).

☐ Each PIO port has two handshake signals, and each port can be used to transfer data under interrupt control.

☐ In PIO, only Port A can be used for bidirectional data transfer, and all handshake lines are used for this data transfer. Port A handshake lines are used for output control and Port B handshake lines for input control.

☐ Both PIO ports can be set up in the bit mode, whereby each line can be assigned either input or output function. For input lines, AND or OR logic function can be specified in the control register, and an interrupt can be generated when the conditions exist.

- The PIO has two signals—IEI and IEO—which are used to set up daisy chain priority.
- The Intel 8255A is a general purpose programmable interfacing device, and it has three ports. It can also operate in various modes similar to the PIO.

ASSIGNMENTS

1. List the internal components found in a typical programmable device.
2. Explain the functions of handshake signals.
3. List the operating modes of the PIO and their features.
4. If the PIO does not include the Write signal, specify the control signals necessary to perform a Write operation.
5. Write instructions to set up Port A in Mode 0 and Port B in Mode 1.
6. In Figure 13.5, identify the addresses of Port A and Port B and their control registers if the output line O_7 of the decoder is connected to the $\overline{CE}$ signal of the PIO.
7. In Figure 13.5, identify the addresses of Ports A and B and their control registers if the address lines A_0 and A_1 are interchanged.
8. In Figure 13.5, exchange the address lines A_7 and A_5 of the decoder, and identify port addresses.
9. In Figure 13.36, address lines A_6 and A_5 are "don't care." Specify the multiple addresses that can access Ports A and B.
10. Identify the addresses of Ports A and B and their control registers in Figure 13.37, assuming all "don't care" lines at logic 0.
11. Port A of the PIO is initialized in Mode 3 with bits D_7–D_5 as input and D_4–D_0 as output. The PIO generates an interrupt when bits D_7 and D_6 are both at logic 0. Write initialization instructions.

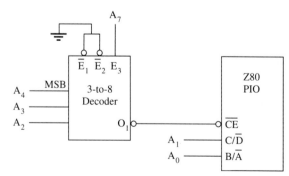

FIGURE 13.36
PIO Interfacing for Assignment 9

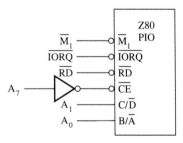

FIGURE 13.37
PIO Interfacing for Assignment 10

12. Explain the functions of the handshake signals $\overline{\text{ASTB}}$ and ARDY if PIO Port A is initialized as an input port.

13. List the control words that need to be written into the control register to set up PIO Port B in Mode 1 for interrupt control I/O.

14. If PIO Port B is initialized as an output port, list the sequence of events that occurs when a data byte is transferred to a peripheral under interrupt I/O.

15. The PIO Ports A and B are initialized as output ports to transfer data under interrupt control. Write instructions for the Z80 MPU to initialize the stack at $18A7_H$ and the interrupt register at 18_H. Assume that the service routine for Port A is at 1872_H and for Port B at 1897_H, and that the interrupt vectors are located at 1848_H and $184A_H$ for Ports A and B, respectively.

16. Write a service routine to output a byte to the peripheral in Assignment 15. Show the memory addresses where the service routine is to be stored.

17. In 15, an interrupt occurs from Port A when the Z80 MPU is executing a 3-byte instruction located at 1822_H–1824_H. List the stack addresses and their contents when the interrupt is acknowledged and the program control is transferred to the service routine.

18. In Figure 13.11, if PIO-3 is being serviced, specify the status of the pins IEI and IEO of PIO-2 and PIO-3.

19. The keyboard routine for Figure 13.14 gives the priority from key K_7 to key K_0 in that sequence. Modify the subroutine to change the priority sequence so that key K_0 has the highest priority.

20. When two keys are pressed simultaneously (Figure 13.14), the subroutine recognizes only the higher priority key. Modify the subroutine to recognize both keys.

21. Redraw Figure 13.14 to replace the PIO with an octal buffer (such as the 74LS240) and an octal latch (such as the 74LS373).

22. Modify Figure 13.16 to show how a 4 × 4 matrix keyboard can be connected to Port A of the PIO. Write initialization instructions to set up Port A in Mode 3 to generate an interrupt whenever a key is pressed.

23. Write initialization instructions to set up Port A in the bidirectional mode and Port B in Mode 3. Assign lines B_7–B_4 as input and B_3–B_0 as output. Can you write the control word to generate an interrupt when the lines B_7 and B_6 are at logic 1? Explain your answer.

24. Write necessary software to transfer 100 bytes of data from Micro-2 to Micro-1 (Figure 13.21).

25. List the operating modes of the 8255A Programmable Peripheral Interface.

26. Specify the bit of a control word for the 8255A that differentiates between the I/O mode and the BSR mode.

27. Write initialization instructions for the 8255A to set up Ports A and B in the handshake mode with the interrupt I/O.

28. Modify the schematic in Figure 13.28 to use Mode 1 with the handshake lines for Port A and bit PC_6 to start the conversion. Rewrite the program to monitor the $\overline{\text{STB}}$ input line and record the data converter readings.

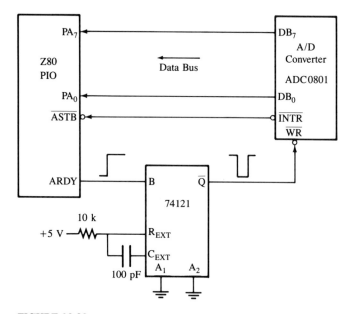

FIGURE 13.38
Interfacing the ADC0801 Using the Z80 PIO in Mode 1 with Handshake

29. Modify the schematic (Figure 13.28) and the subroutine to use the interrupt.

30. Figure 13.38 shows an interfacing of the data converter ADC0801 using Port A of the Z80 PIO; Port A is set up in Mode 1. The handshake signal ARDY is used to start the conversion by connecting it to $\overline{\text{WR}}$ through the one-shot multivibrator 74121, and $\overline{\text{ASTB}}$ is used to detect the end of the conversion by monitoring the line $\overline{\text{INTR}}$ of the converter. To start the conversion, one dummy Read instruction IN A, (PIOA) is executed. Explain the need for the one-shot multivibrator. (Hint: The data converter needs a pulse transition low-to-high to start the conversion.)

31. Write instructions to set up the Z80 PIO Port A in Mode 1 and the Z80 in interrupt Mode 2 with the interrupt vector 1870_H. Initialize the memory pointer at 1850_H to store data and the counter to record ten readings, and start the conversion. Write also an interrupt service routine to read the port, store data in memory (for ten readings), start the conversion again, and enable the interrupt.

32. In Figure 13.39, Port A of the Z80 PIO is initialized in Mode 0, and its handshake signals ARDY and $\overline{\text{ASTB}}$ are tied together. When we execute the instruction OUT (PIOA), A, a pulse equal to one system clock period is generated at the output of ARDY that can be used as a strobe to start a process at a peripheral. Explain the output pulse of ARDY. (Hint: In Mode 0, the

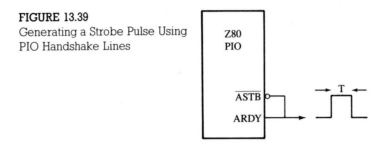

FIGURE 13.39
Generating a Strobe Pulse Using
PIO Handshake Lines

transition low-to-high of the $\overline{\text{STB}}$ signal turns off the RDY signal—see Figure 13.9.)

33. Modify the subroutine STEPER in section 13.8 to rotate the stepper motor in the counter-clockwise direction.

34. Modify the subroutine STEPER in section 13.8 to rotate the stepper motor through half-steps.

Programmable Timers and Counters

A programmable timer/counter device is designed to generate accurate time delays using the system's clock and to count occurrences of external events. It can be used for applications such as a real-time clock, an event counter, and a signal generator.

This chapter is concerned primarily with the Z80 CTC—Counter/Timer Circuit—and its applications. The CTC has four timer/counter channels and can be programmed to function as timers or counters by the user's writing control words into appropriate internal registers. The CTC is also capable of generating interrupt signals at a specified time delay or count. The CTC is widely used as a timer/counter and has become an integral part of Z80-based microprocessor systems. This chapter also includes the description of another widely used timer/counter—the Intel 8254—and its features are compared with those of the CTC.

OBJECTIVES

□ List the elements of the block diagram of the Z80 CTC (Counter/Timer Circuit) and explain functions of each element.

□ List the operating modes of the CTC and explain the differences in these modes.

□ Explain how the CTC operates as a counter and a timer and its interrupt capability.

□ Identify port addresses of each counter channel in a given circuit.

□ Write initialization instructions to set up the CTC in either the counter or the timer mode.

□ Design a circuit to interface the CTC for given port addresses and write instructions to set up the CTC as a timer or a counter.

□ List the elements of the Intel 8254 Programmable Interval Timer and its operating modes.

□ Design a circuit to interface the 8254 for given port addresses and write instructions to set up the device for a given mode.

14.1   Z80 CTC—COUNTER/TIMER CIRCUIT

The **Z80 CTC (Counter/Timer Circuit)** is a 28-pin programmable chip, specially designed to work with the Z80 microprocessor. The block diagram (Figure 14.1) shows that the chip includes four counter/timer channels, control logic, interrupt control, and the system data bus. The CTC requires +5 V power supply and the Z80 system clock (CLK).

The system data bus, D_7–D_0, consists of bidirectional tri-state lines and is connected to the data bus of the Z80 microprocessor. These bus lines transfer all data and commands between the Z80 and the CTC.

The four channels can be independently programmed in either the timer or the counter mode. An 8-bit number ("count" or "time constant") is loaded into the register of a channel and is decremented on every clock pulse. At the end of the count, it generates a pulse at the ZC/TO (Zero Count/Time Out) pin, reloads the count into the register, and begins the next operation. If the CTC is programmed to use the interrupt, it generates an interrupt pulse at the end of the count, and its IEI and IEO signals can be used to set up the daisy chain interrupt priorities. The delay interval between two pulses is similar to that of software delays (discussed in section 9.4) whereby a register is loaded with a count, the count is decremented in a loop until it becomes zero, and the delay is calculated from the count, T-states in the loop, and the clock period.

14.1.1 Interfacing the CTC

The CTC has an 8-bit bidirectional data bus, one output signal per channel (except Channel 3), and seven control signals including the chip enable signal, as shown in Figure 14.1. These signals are connected to the appropriate signals of the Z80 microprocessor.

□ D_0–D_7 (Data Bus): This is a tri-state bidirectional data bus that transfers data and commands between the Z80 and the CTC.

□ CLK (Clock): This is an input from the Z80 system clock.

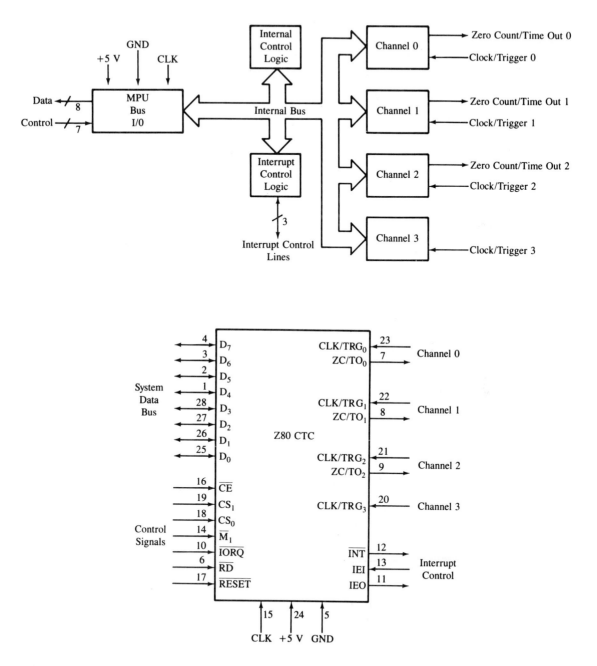

FIGURE 14.1
Z80 CTC: Block Diagram and Logic Pinout
SOURCE: Courtesy of Zilog, Inc.

TABLE 14.1
Control Operations and Signals

Operations	$\overline{\text{IORQ}}$	$\overline{\text{RD}}$	M_1
Read	Low	Low	High
Write	Low	High	High
Interrupt Acknowledge	Low	High	Low

- CLK/TRG (Clock/Trigger): This is an external input signal. In the counter mode, it is used to count external events, and its active level (high or low) is specified in the control word. In the timer mode, an active edge starts the timer.
- ZC/TO (Zero Count/Time-Out): This is an active high output, generated when the down-counter has been decremented to zero. Channel 3 does not have this output signal because of an insufficient number of pins in a 28-pin package. However, Channel 3 can generate an interrupt signal when the counter reaches zero.
- $\overline{\text{IORQ}}$ (I/O Request), $\overline{\text{M}_1}$ (Machine Cycle 1), and $\overline{\text{RD}}$ (Read): These are three active low signals that perform Read/Write/Interrupt Acknowledge operations as described below.
- Read: This operation is performed when $\overline{\text{IORQ}}$ and $\overline{\text{RD}}$ are active low and $\overline{\text{M1}}$ is high. In this operation, the contents of the counter of the selected channel can be read.
- Write: There is no separate signal for the Write operation. When $\overline{\text{RD}}$ is high, the CTC generates the Write signal internally. In this operation, a control word and a count can be written in the selected channel.
- Interrupt Acknowledge: The Z80 acknowledges the interrupt by asserting two control signals ($\overline{\text{IORQ}}$ and $\overline{\text{M1}}$) low, and the highest priority interrupting channel places its interrupt vector on the data bus. (This operation is discussed in detail in sections 14.1.3 and 14.1.4.)
- The control operations and the active level of the associated control signals are summarized in Table 14.1.
- $\overline{\text{RESET}}$ (Reset): This is an active low signal that terminates the counting operation and disables the interrupts; all outputs go inactive, and the data bus D_7–D_0 goes to the high impedance state.
- $\overline{\text{CE}}$ (Chip Enable): This is an active low signal connected to the decoded low-order address bus of the Z80. When this signal is active, the CTC is selected.
- CS_0 and CS_1 (Channel Select): These two lines are generally connected to the address lines A_0 and A_1, respectively, and the logic combination of these lines (as shown in the following list) selects one of the four channels of the CTC to write into or read from. The decoded address of the Chip Enable and the logic levels of CS_0 and CS_1 determine the port address of the selected counter channel.

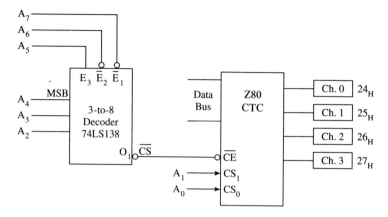

FIGURE 14.2
Interfacing the CTC

$\overline{CE}$	CS_1	CS_0	Selected Channel
0	0	0	Channel 0
0	0	1	Channel 1
0	1	0	Channel 2
0	1	1	Channel 3

Example 14.1 illustrates the use of these signals in interfacing the CTC.

Determine the port addresses of the CTC channels shown in Figure 14.2.

Example 14.1

To select the CTC, the output line O_1 of the decoder should go low. Therefore, the logic levels of the address lines A_7–A_2 should be as shown. Combining the logic levels of A_7–A_2 with those of A_1 and A_0 gives us port addresses of the counter channels ranging from 24_H to 27_H.

Solution

A_7	A_6	A_5	A_4	A_3	A_2	A_1	A_0		
0	0	1	0	0	1	0	0	$= 24_H$	Channel 0
						0	1	$= 25_H$	Channel 1
	↓			↓		1	0	$= 26_H$	Channel 2
	Decoder Enable			Decoder Input		1	1	$= 27_H$	Channel 3
						Channel Select			

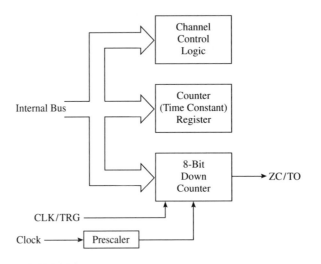

FIGURE 14.3

Internal Architecture of a Channel

SOURCE: Adapted from *Z80 CTC Technical Manual*. Courtesy of Zilog, Inc.

14.1.2   Programming the CTC

The CTC can be programmed to operate in either the timer mode or the counter mode. Each channel consists of *channel control logic, time constant (counter) register,* and the *down-counter,* as shown in Figure 14.3. To program the CTC, a control word should be written into the channel, and it must be followed by an 8-bit count loaded into the counter register. The control word determines such parameters as the operating mode, the active trigger level (falling or rising edge), and the interrupt logic (see Figure 14.4). The count, which can be from 1 to 256 (0 = 256), is loaded into the counter register and decremented according to the specified mode operation. When the count reaches zero, it is automatically reloaded into the register. Figure 14.3 also shows a block called prescaler. This is used only in the timer mode; it divides the system clock frequency by either 16 or 256. The output of the prescaler decrements the down-counter in the timer mode.

The channel control word is shown in Figure 14.4 and is illustrated in Example 14.2.

Example 14.2

Write instructions to program Channel 0 of the CTC (Figure 14.2) in the timer mode to provide a pulse every 20 ms if the system clock is 1 MHz.

Solution

Channel 0 of the CTC in Figure 14.2 has the port address 24_H. To program the channel in the timer mode, we need to send two words to the channel port: a channel control word and a proper count to provide 20 ms delay. Assuming the

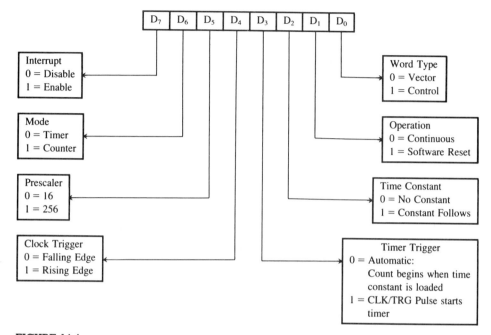

FIGURE 14.4
Channel Control Word

prescaler is 256, the system clock frequency will be divided by 256; in other words, the clock period will be multiplied by 256. Therefore the total delay between two consecutive outputs is

$$T_d = T_{CLK} \times PS \times N_{10}$$
$$\text{where } T_{CLK} = \text{System clock period}$$
$$PS = \text{Prescaler}$$
$$N_{10} = \text{Count in decimal}$$

This formula is similar to that of software loop delay calculations ($T_L = T_C \times L_T \times N_{10}$) in section 9.4; the only differences are that the Prescaler is fixed and the T-states in the loop vary according to the instructions in the loop. The system has a 1 μs clock period; therefore, the number in the counter register will be decremented every 256 μs because the prescaler is 256. The count necessary to obtain a 20 ms delay is

$$20 \text{ ms} = 1 \text{ μs} \times 256 \times N_{10} \text{ (Count)}$$
$$\text{Count } (N_{10}) = \frac{20 \text{ ms}}{256 \text{ μs}} = 78.125 \cong 78 = 4E_H.$$

Assuming the counter will begin at the rising edge of the system clock as soon as the count is loaded into the register, the control word is as follows:

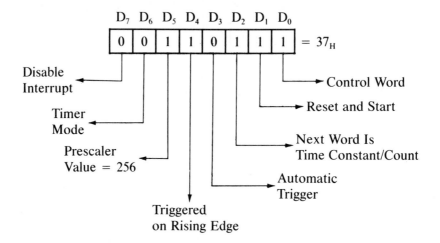

Instructions   The following instructions will set up the CTC in the timer mode with the specified parameters.

```
CNTRL     EQU 37H          ;Defines channel control word
COUNT     EQU 4EH          ;Count
PORT0     EQU 24H          ;Port address of Channel 0
SETUP:    LD A, CNTRL      ;Channel control word
          OUT (PORT0), A   ;Send control word to Channel 0
          LD A, COUNT
          OUT (PORT0), A   ;Load time constant in Channel 0
          HALT
```

Description   The first instruction writes the channel control word in Channel 0 (Port 24_H), and it is followed by the count (COUNT = $4E_H$). As soon as the count is loaded into the channel, the down-counter begins. Because the prescaler divides the system clock by 256, the count is decremented every 256 μs. The countdown continues until the count ($4E_H$) goes to zero, and at the end of the count, a high pulse, approximately 1.5 times the system clock period in width, is generated at the output (ZC/TO = Zero Count/Time Out) of Channel 0. The channel word has specified continuous operation; therefore, the count is automatically loaded again into the channel register and the down-counter continues generating a pulse every 20 ms.

14.1.3   Using the CTC Interrupts

The CTC architecture includes the interrupt control logic shown in the block diagram (Figure 14.1). This logic is used to generate an interrupt request pulse and

D7 D6 D5 D4 D3 D2 D1 D0

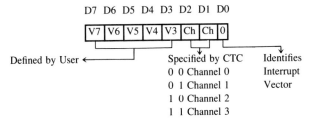

Defined by User ←   Specified by CTC   Identifies
                       0   0   Channel 0   Interrupt
                       0   1   Channel 1   Vector
                       1   0   Channel 2
                       1   1   Channel 3

FIGURE 14.5
Bit Definition of Interrupt Vector

to determine the priorities among the four channels as well as among various CTC devices if the system includes more than one CTC. The CTC has three signals associated with the interrupt: $\overline{INT}$, IEI, and IEO. These signals are functionally similar to those of the Z80 PIO described in the last chapter. The $\overline{INT}$ signal is again described here, and the other two are described in section 14.1.4.

☐ $\overline{INT}$ (Interrupt Request): This is an active low output signal, and if the interrupt is enabled in the channel control word, it goes low when the down-counter reaches zero.

To use the interrupt process, the Z80 should be set in the interrupt Mode 2, and the CTC should be programmed to supply the low-order byte of the interrupt vector. The CTC generates an interrupt request ($\overline{INT}$) when the down-counter of a channel reaches zero. When the Z80 acknowledges the interrupt request, the Interrupt register I of the Z80 supplies the high-order byte and the CTC supplies the low-order byte of the interrupt vector address. The low-order byte of the interrupt vector and the identification of the channel requesting the interrupt are defined as shown in Figure 14.5. Bits D_7–D_3 are defined by the user; bits D_2–D_1 are supplied by the CTC to identify the channel that has reached the count of zero, and bit D_0 must be zero to differentiate the interrupt vector from the control word. To form the interrupt vector, initially, bits D_2 and D_1 can be at any logic level; they are specified by the CTC when a channel requests an interrupt. Once the interrupt vector address of Channel 0 is defined, the remaining vector addresses are automatically defined; they are consecutive addresses with two memory locations for each channel.

Modify the instructions in Example 14.2 to program Channel 0 of the CTC (Figure 14.2) in the timer mode to provide a pulse and generate an interrupt every 20 ms. The address of the interrupt service routine is at memory locations 1850_H and 1851_H.

            Example
            14.3

Solution   To program the CTC, we need to load three words into Channel 0.

1. Channel control word: The word is similar to the word in Example 14.2 except that bit D_7 should be 1 to enable the interrupt. Therefore, the word should be changed from 37_H to $B7_H$.
2. Count: It is the same as in Example 14.2.
3. Interrupt vector for location 1850_H: The high-order byte should be loaded into the interrupt vector register I of the Z80 and the low-order byte into Channel 0.

Instructions

```
CNTRL   EQU B7H              ;Channel control word
COUNT   EQU 4EH              ;Count
PORT0   EQU 24H              ;Channel 0 Port address
SETUP:  DI                   ;Disable interrupt
        IM 2                 ;Set up Z80 in interrupt Mode 2
        LD A, 18H            ;High-order byte of interrupt vector
        LD I, A              ;Load interrupt register with high-order
                               byte
        LD A, CNTRL          ;Channel control word = B7H
        OUT (PORT0), A       ;Initialize Channel 0
        LD A, COUNT          ;Count = 4EH as in Example 14.2
        OUT (PORT0), A       ;Load count into Channel 0
        LD A, 50H            ;Low-order byte of interrupt vector
        OUT (PORT0), A       ;Load interrupt vector in CTC
        EI                   ;Enable Z80 interrupt
        ↓                    ;Continue with program
```

Description   The first instruction DI disables, and the last instruction EI enables, the Z80 interrupt. This is necessary to avoid any false interrupts when the CTC is being initialized. The interrupt vector for Channel 0 is initialized at 1850_H; therefore, the interrupt service routine address for Channel 0 must be stored in locations 1850_H and 1851_H. The interrupt vector addresses for Channels 1 through 3 are automatically defined; they range from 1852_H to 1857_H. The interrupt service routine should be terminated by the instruction RETI (Return from Interrupt). The CTC is designed to recognize the RETI instruction, and when it does so, the interrupt is automatically removed.

14.1.4 Interrupt Priorities

Among the four CTC channels, Channel 0 has the highest priority and Channel 3 has the lowest priority. When multiple CTC devices are used in a system, they can be connected in the daisy chain format; the CTC has two signals (IEI and IEO) to set up the daisy chain priorities among CTC devices.

□ IEI (Interrupt Enable In): This is an active high input signal, used to set up daisy chain interrupt priorities. A high level on this pin indicates that no other interrupting devices of higher priority in the daisy chain are being serviced by the Z80.

□ IEO (Interrupt Enable Out): This is an output signal, used in conjunction with the IEI signal to set up the daisy chain priority in a system. The IEO signal remains high if the IEI is high and the Z80 is not servicing any interrupt from any CTC channel. This signal blocks lower priority devices from interrupting while a higher priority interrupting device is being serviced.

Figure 14.6 shows three CTC devices connected in the daisy chain format. The IEI of Device #1 is tied to +5 V, and its IEO signal is fed to Device #2. In this schematic, Device #1 has the highest priority, and Device #3 has the lowest priority; within each device, the priority goes from Channel 0 to Channel 3.

14.1.5 Counter and Timer Applications

The CTC operations in the counter mode and the timer mode appear to be similar; this apparent similarity can cause confusion in applications. For example, either of the modes can be used to design a clock. Therefore, it is necessary to discuss the differences between these two operations.

The counter mode is used to count external events indicated by the CLK/TRG pulse. When an external circuit causes the CLK/TRG pin to go active, the down-counter in the CTC is decremented. Thus, the down-counter continues to count the events until it reaches zero, and then the output (ZC/TO) pulsed high indicates the end of the count. The down-counter is automatically loaded again, and the next cycle of counting continues.

On the other hand, the timer mode is used to provide time delays and is based on the internal clock (CLK). However, the clock frequency is divided by a number called prescaler (16 or 256), which is specified in the control word. Thus, the down-counter is decremented every 16th or 256th clock pulse. When the

FIGURE 14.6
CTCs Connected in Daisy Chain
Format

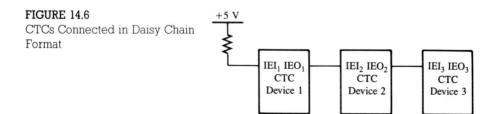

down-counter reaches zero, an output pulse is generated, similar to that in the counter mode, and the counter is loaded again for the next time delay.

The CTC can be used in the timer mode to design a clock to indicate the time of day; the accuracy is determined primarily by the system clock. Similarly, the CTC can be used in the counter mode to count pulses from a 60 Hz power line, and a clock can be designed as illustrated in section 14.3.

14.2 ILLUSTRATION: DESIGNING A BAUD (RATE) GENERATOR USING THE CTC IN THE TIMER MODE

A typical application of the CTC in the timer mode is a programmable **baud (rate) generator** for serial I/O data communication (see Chapter 15). The baud generator is a frequency generator that provides a pulse at a predetermined frequency. In serial I/O, data bits are generally transmitted from 110 bits to 9,600 bits per second. For example, to send data over telephone lines, the transmission rate ranges normally from 300 to 2,400 bits per second. The clock frequency for serial I/O circuitry is generally 16 to 64 times the transmission rate. This illustration is concerned with designing a baud generator using the CTC.

14.2.1 Problem Statement

Design a programmable baud (frequency) generator using the CTC to provide two frequencies: $300 \times 16 (= 4.8 \text{ kHz})$ and $1200 \times 16 (= 19.2 \text{ kHz})$; the system clock is 3.6864 MHz. Identify the port addresses of Channels 1 and 2 and program Channel 1 to generate 4.8 kHz and Channel 2 for 19.2 kHz.

14.2.2 Problem Analysis

The port addresses of the channels can be obtained by analyzing the decoding logic in Figure 14.7. The circuit uses the 74LS139 2-to-4 decoder; it has address lines A_7 and A_6 as inputs, A_5 as the enable line (active low), and lines A_4, A_3, and A_2 as "don't care." The address lines A_1 and A_0 are connected to the CTC, and they determine the channel selection. Assuming the "don't care" lines at logic 0, Channel 1 can be accessed with the port address 91_H and Channel 2 with the port address 92_H, as shown.

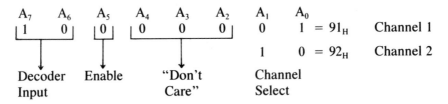

To program the channels for the specified frequencies, we need to initialize the channels in the timer mode and calculate the count; this step is similar to

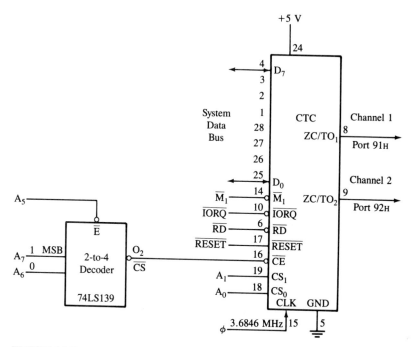

FIGURE 14.7
Schematic: Baud Generator Using CTC in the Timer Mode

Example 14.2. The delay formula in Example 14.2 ($T_d = T_{CLK} \times PS \times N_{10}$) gives a time period between output pulses. The frequency (that is, BAUD) can be calculated by taking the reciprocal as follows:

$$f_{BAUD} = \frac{1}{T_d} = \frac{1}{T_{CLK} \times PS \times N_{10}}$$

$$= \frac{f_S \text{ (System frequency)}}{PS \times N_{10}} \qquad (f_S = 1/T_{CLK})$$

In this example, let us assume the prescaler is 16; for Channel 1, the output or the baud (rate) should be 4.8 kHz as shown below.

$$4.8 \text{ kHz} = \frac{3.6864 \text{ MHz}}{16 \times N_{10}} \qquad N_{10} = 48$$

Similarly, the count for 19.2 kHz = 12.

The channel control word for both channels is 17_H as shown in the following diagram; this is a continuous operation without the interrupt capability.

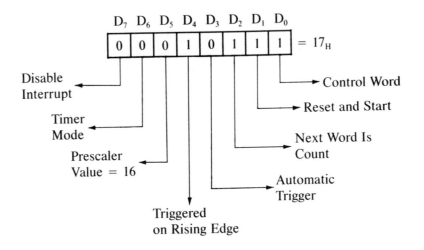

Instructions The following instructions will set up the CTC in the timer mode: Channel 1 for 4.8 kHz output and Channel 2 for 19.2 kHz.

```
CNTRL    EQU   17H        ;Defines channel control word
COUNT1   EQU   30H        ;Count 48 for Channel 1
COUNT2   EQU   0CH        ;Count 12 for Channel 2
CTC1     EQU   91H        ;Port address of Channel 1
CTC2     EQU   92H        ;Port address of Channel 2
SETUP:   LD A, CNTRL      ;Channel control word
         OUT (CTC1), A    ;Send control word to Channel 1
         LD A, COUNT1     ;Count for Channel 1
         OUT (CTC1), A    ;Load count into Channel 1
         LD A, CNTRL      ;Channel control word
         OUT (CTC2), A    ;Send control word to Channel 2
         LD A, COUNT2     ;Count for Channel 2
         OUT (CTC2), A    ;Load count into Channel 2
         HALT
```

Description The first two instructions write the channel control word into Channel 1 (Port 91_H), and it must be followed by the count (COUNT1 = 30_H). This operation is repeated for Channel 2 by the subsequent instructions. When the count is loaded, it resets the channel and begins the countdown at the rising edge of the system clock. When the count reaches zero, a high pulse equal to 1.5 times (0.41 μs) the system clock period is generated at the output (ZC/TO = Zero Count/Time Out) of the channel; thus, Channel 1 provides a 4.8 kHz clock and Channel 2 provides a 19.2 kHz clock.

ILLUSTRATION: USING THE CTC IN THE COUNTER MODE WITH INTERRUPT

14.3

In the counter mode, the CTC counts external events whenever the input signal at the CLK/TRG pin of a channel goes active. The CLK/TRG pin can be activated by either a leading edge or trailing edge pulse input; it is specified by the channel control word. The channel operation is similar to that in the timer mode; an 8-bit count is loaded into the channel register, and the count is decremented whenever the CLK/TRG input goes active. When the count reaches zero, the output ZC/TO goes active for approximately 1.5 times the clock period and the count is reloaded into the register.

This illustration concerns designing a clock by counting a 60 Hz power line, which provides an accurate time base.

14.3.1 Problem Statement

Design a minute timer using a 60 Hz powerline as an external trigger to the CLK/TRG pin of Channel 3 as shown in Figure 14.8. The CTC should interrupt the Z80 MPU every second to update the seconds display, and at the end of 60 minutes

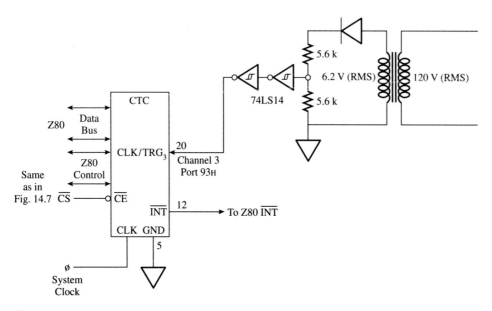

FIGURE 14.8

Schematic: CTC in the Counter Mode (Note: Digital grounds should be separate from the AC ground.)

the clock should be reset and start again. The vector address for Channel 3 = 1856_H.

14.3.2   Problem Analysis

This problem has three parts:

1. Getting an appropriate pulse from the 60 Hz power line.
2. Setting up the CTC in the counter mode with the interrupt capability.
3. Writing subroutines to upgrade the displays of seconds and minutes.

The AC power line provides 120 V (RMS) with 60 Hz frequency. Thus, it can provide a signal with a 16.6 ms period; however, the voltage should be converted into a 5 V pulse to be compatible with TTL logic. Figure 14.8 shows a step-down transformer with a rectifier; the output of the rectifier will be approximately +10 V, and the resistor divider network adjusts the output to +5 V. The inverters are used as a wave-shaping circuit to convert the sine wave into a square wave pulse. The output of the inverters will be a 5 V square wave with a 16.6 ms period, connected to the CLK/TRG pin of the CTC Channel 3. This pulse triggers the CTC channel 60 times per second.

The CTC channel counter should be set up to count these pulses, and at the end of the count, the CTC should generate an interrupt. Thus, the interrupts are generated every second, and the interrupt service subroutine should upgrade the seconds display.

14.3.3   Initializing the CTC in the Counter Mode

To initialize the CTC in the counter mode with interrupt capability, we need to send three words: channel control word and count (time constant) to Channel 3, and interrupt vector to Channel 0.

The channel control word is as follows (assuming "don't care" bits at logic 0):

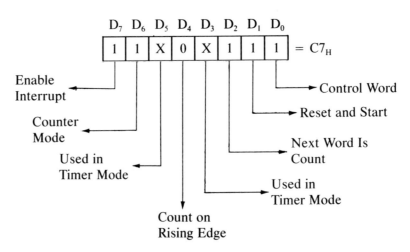

The count $= 3C_H$ to count 60 pulses. The low-order vector address $= 50_H$ for Channel 0; the high-order address is supplied by the interrupt register I (see Figure 14.5).

14.3.4 Program

In this illustration, the program can be divided into three sections: CTC initialization, the main program to display minutes and seconds, and the interrupt service routine to update the timer registers.

CTC Initialization The following instructions are written as a subroutine to set up the CTC Channel 3 in the counter mode with interrupt enable.

```
CNTRL     EQU   C7H         ;Defines channel control word
COUNT3    EQU   3CH         ;Count 60 for 1 second
LOVECT    EQU   50H         ;Low-order address of interrupt vector
CTC3      EQU   93H         ;Port address of Channel 3
CTC0      EQU   90H         ;Port address of Channel 0.
SETCTC:   LD A, CNTRL       ;Channel control word
          OUT (CTC3), A     ;Send control word to Channel 3
          LD A, COUNT 3     ;Count for 60 pulses
          OUT (CTC3), A     ;Load count into Channel 3
          LD A, LOVECT      ;Low-order interrupt vector
          OUT (CTC0), A     ;Load interrupt vector address into Channel 0
          RET
```

Main Program The main program initializes the stack pointer, the interrupt register, and registers for minutes and seconds. It calls the SETCTC subroutine, enables the Z80 interrupt, and stays in the display loop.

```
START:    LD SP, STACK      ;Initialize stack pointer
          IM 2              ;Set up Z80 in interrupt Mode 2
          LD A, 18H         ;Load high-order byte of interrupt vector
          LD I, A           ;Load interrupt register
          CALL SETCTC       ;Initialize CTC
          LD BC, 0000       ;Set B for minutes and C for seconds
          EI                ;Enable Z80 interrupts
DSPLAY:   LD A, B
          OUT (PORT1), A    ;Display minutes
          LD A, C
          OUT (PORT2), A    ;Display seconds
          JP DSPLAY
```

Interrupt Service Routine This routine is concerned primarily with updating the registers for seconds and minutes and decimal adjusting the values in the registers for BCD display. When register C reaches 60 seconds, it clears the register and increments register B. Register B is incremented until it reaches 60 minutes, and then the timer is reset to start again.

```
TIMER:     PUSH AF           ;Save (A) and (F)
           LD A, C           ;Get previous reading
           ADD A, 01H        ;Update seconds
           DAA               ;Decimal adjust seconds
           LD C, A           ;Save BCD value of seconds
           CP 60H            ;Is time = 60 seconds?
           JR NZ, GOEND      ;If not, go to end and return
           LD C, 00          ;If yes, clear seconds
           LD A, B           ;Get previous minutes
           ADD A,01H         ;Update minutes
           DAA               ;Decimal adjust minutes
           LD B, A           ;Save BCD value of minutes
           CP 60H            ;Are minutes = 60?
           JR NZ, GOEND      ;If not, go to end and return
           LD B, 00          ;If yes, clear minutes
GOEND:     POP AF            ;Retrieve (A) and (F)
           EI                ;Enable Z80 interrupt
           RETI
```

PROGRAM DESCRIPTION

The main program initializes the CTC Channel 3 and remains in the DSPLAY loop displaying the contents of registers B and C at output ports. The CTC channel register is loaded with the count 60, and whenever the powerline source triggers the CLK/TRG pin, the CTC register is decremented. When the register reaches zero, the interrupt request (INT) goes active and interrupts the Z80; thus, the Z80 is interrupted every second. Channel 3 does not have a ZC/TO output signal; therefore, the interrupt request INT must be used to indicate that the register has reached zero.

When the Z80 acknowledges the interrupt request, the CTC supplies the low-order address (56_H) of the interrupt vector, and it is combined with the high-order address (18_H) from the Z80 interrupt register. The program execution is transferred to location 1856_H, where the address of the service routine is stored in two consecutive memory locations (1856_H and 1857_H), and then the program is transferred to the service routine TIMER.

The service routine increments the seconds in register C, adjusts the value for BCD, and checks whether the number has reached 60. If it has not, the routine jumps to the end to enable the interrupt and returns to the main program. When the instruction RETI (Return from Interrupt) is executed, it is recognized by the CTC, which clears the INT signal. When register C does eventually reach 60, the routine clears register C and increments the minutes in register B. When register B reaches the count of 60 minutes, register B is cleared, and the timer is reset to start all over.

THE 8254 PROGRAMMABLE INTERVAL TIMER 14.4

The Intel 8254 is another widely used general purpose programmable interval timer/counter, and it is in many ways similar to the Z80 CTC. The 8254 includes three identical 16-bit counters that can operate independently in any one of six modes (described later). It is packaged in a 24-pin DIP and requires a single $+5$ V power supply. For operation as a counter, a 16-bit count is loaded in its register, and on command, it begins to decrement the count until it reaches zero. At the end of the count, it generates a pulse that can be used to interrupt the MPU. The counter can count in either binary or BCD. In addition, a count can be read by the MPU while the counter is decrementing.

The 8254 is an upgraded version of the earlier timer device 8253, and they are pin-compatible. The features of these two devices are almost identical except that

☐ The 8254 can operate with higher clock frequency range (DC to 8 MHz and 10 MHz for 8254-2), and the 8253 can operate with clock frequency from DC to 2 MHz.

☐ The 8254 includes a Status Read-Back Command that can latch the count and the status of the counters.

14.4.1 Block Diagram of the 8254

Figure 14.9 shows the block diagram of the 8254; it includes three 16-bit counters (0, 1, and 2). Each counter has two input signals—clock (CLK) and GATE—and one output signal—OUT. GATE can be used to initiate, enable, or disable counting. The diagram also shows three blocks: data bus buffer, Read/Write control logic, and a control word register.

Data Bus Buffer This is a tri-state 8-bit, bidirectional buffer connected to the data bus of the MPU.

Control Logic This control section has five signals: $\overline{RD}$ (Read), $\overline{WR}$ (Write), $\overline{CS}$ (Chip Select), and the address lines A_0 and A_1. In the peripheral I/O mode, the $\overline{RD}$ and $\overline{WR}$ signals are connected to $\overline{IORD}$ and $\overline{IOWR}$, respectively. In memory-mapped I/O, these are connected to $\overline{MEMRD}$ (Memory Read) and $\overline{MEMWR}$ (Memory Write). Address lines A_0 and A_1 of the MPU are usually connected to lines A_0 and A_1 of the 8254, and $\overline{CS}$ is tied to a decoded address.

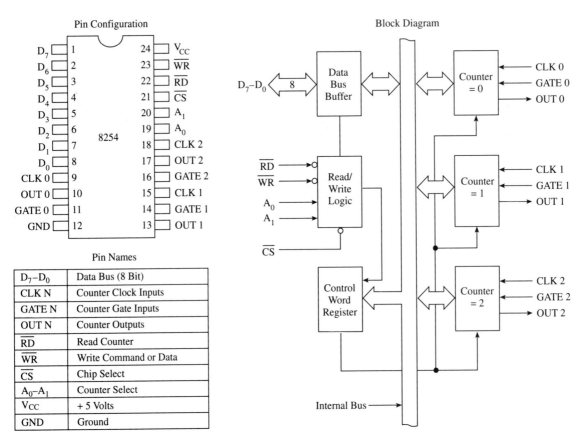

FIGURE 14.9

8254 Block Diagram

SOURCE: Reprinted by permission of Intel Corporation, copyright 1979.

The control word register and counters are selected according to the signals on lines A_0 and A_1, as shown.

A_1	A_0	Selection
0	0	Counter 0
0	1	Counter 1
1	0	Counter 2
1	1	Control Word Register

Control Word Register   This register is accessed when lines A_0 and A_1 are at logic 1. It is used to write a command word that specifies the counter to be used, its mode, and either Read or Write operation. The control word format is shown in Figure 14.10.

| | D₇ | D₆ | D₅ | D₄ | D₃ | D₂ | D₁ | D₀ |

D_7 D_6 D_5 D_4 D_3 D_2 D_1 D_0

| SC1 | SC0 | RW1 | RW0 | M2 | M1 | M0 | BCD |

SC—Select Counter:

SC1 SC0

0	0	Select Counter 0
0	1	Select Counter 1
1	0	Select Counter 2
1	1	Read-Back Command (See Read Operations)

RW—Read/Write:

RW1 RW0

0	0	Counter Latch Command (see Read Operations)
0	1	Read/Write least significant byte only.
1	0	Read/Write most significant byte only.
1	1	Read/Write least significant byte first, then most significant byte.

M—MODE:

M2 M1 M0

0	0	0	Mode 0
0	0	1	Mode 1
X	1	0	Mode 2
X	1	1	Mode 3
1	0	0	Mode 4
1	0	1	Mode 5

BCD:

0	Binary Counter 16-bits
1	Binary Coded Decimal (BCD) Counter (4 Decades)

Note: Don't Care Bits (X) Should Be 0 to Ensure Compatability with Future Intel Products.

FIGURE 14.10
8254 Control Word Format
SOURCE: Intel Corporation, *Component Data Catalog* (Santa Clara, CA.: Author, 1982).

Mode The 8254 can operate in six different modes, as shown in Figure 14.11. The gate of a counter is used either to disable or enable counting, as shown in Figure 14.12.

14.4.2 Programming the 8254

The 8254 can be programmed to provide various types of outputs (Figure 14.11) through Write operations, or to check a count while counting through Read operations. The details of these operations are given below.

Write Operations To initialize a counter, the following steps are necessary.

1. Write a control word into the control register.
2. Load the low-order byte of a count into the counter register.
3. Load the high-order byte of a count into the counter register.

Mode 0: Interupt on Terminal Count

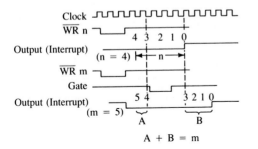

Mode 1: Programmable One-Shot

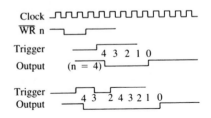

Mode 2: Rate Generator Clock

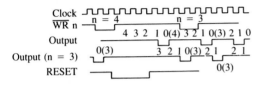

Mode 3: Square Wave Generator

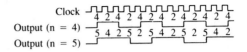

Mode 4: Software Triggered Strobe

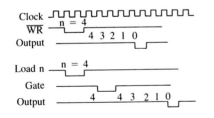

Mode 5: Hardware Triggered Strobe

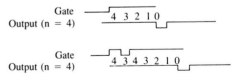

FIGURE 14.11
8254 Operating Modes
SOURCE: Reprinted by permission of Intel Corporation, copyright 1981.

With a clock and an appropriate gate signal to one of the counters, the above instructions should be able to start the counter and provide appropriate output according to the control word.

Read Operations   In some applications, especially in event counters, it is necessary to read the value of the count in progress. This can be done by one of two methods. One method involves reading a count after inhibiting (stopping) the counter to be read. The second method involves reading a count while counting is in progress (reading on the fly).

In the first method, counting is stopped (or inhibited) by controlling the gate input or the clock input of the selected counter, and two I/O Read operations are

Modes / Signal Status	Low or Going Low	Rising	High
0	Disables counting	—	Enables counting
1	—	(1) Initiates counting (2) Resets output after next clock	—
2	(1) Disables counting (2) Sets output immediately high	(1) Reloads counter (2) Initiates counting	Enables counting
3	(1) Disables counting (2) Sets output immediately high	Initiates counting	Enables counting
4	Disables counting	—	Enables counting
5	—	Initiates counting	—

FIGURE 14.12

Gate Settings of a Counter

SOURCE: Reprinted by permission of Intel Corporation, copyright 1981.

performed by the MPU. The first I/O operation reads the low-order byte, and the second reads the high-order byte.

In the second method, an appropriate control word is written into the control register to latch a count in the output latch, and two I/O Read operations are performed by the MPU.

14.4.3 The 8254 as a Square Wave Generator

One of the attractive features of the 8254 is that it has several modes that can be used for various purposes, whereas the CTC is primarily restricted to two modes: counter and timer. The following example illustrates how to set up the 8254 as a square wave generator.

---

1. Identify the port addresses of the control register and the counter 2 in Figure 14.13.

Example 14.4

2. Calculate the count necessary to obtain a 20 kHz square wave if the clock frequency is 2 MHz and the counter is set up in Mode 3.
3. Write instructions to initialize Counter 2 in Mode 3 to obtain a 20 kHz square wave.

1. *Port Addresses*

Solution

The Chip Select is enabled when $A_7 = 1$ (see Figure 14.13), and the control register is selected when A_1 and $A_0 = 1$. Similarly, Counter 2 is selected when

FIGURE 14.13
Schematic: Interfacing the 8254

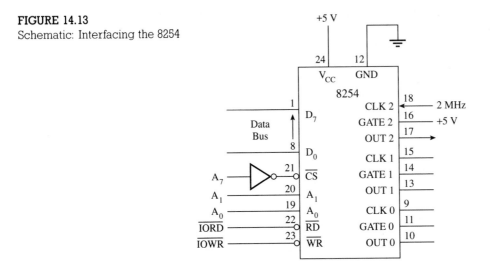

$A_1 = 1$ and $A_0 = 0$. Assuming that the unused address lines A_6 to A_2 are at logic 0, the port addresses will be as follows:

$$\text{Control Register} = 83_H$$
$$\text{Counter 2} = 82_H.$$

2. *Count to Generate 20 kHz in Mode 3*

The clock frequency (CLK 2) is 2 MHz with the period of 0.5 μs. In Mode 3, the output remains high for half the count and low for the remaining half of the count. This is accomplished by decrementing the count by two at every falling edge of the clock. Therefore, with 2 MHz clock frequency, the count will be decremented by two every 0.5 μs. To obtain the square wave with 20 kHz frequency (50 μs period), the output should remain high for 25 μs and low for 25 μs.

$$\frac{\text{Count} \times \text{Clock Period}}{2} = \text{Half Period of Square Wave}$$

$$\text{Count} = 2 \times \frac{25 \ \mu s}{0.5 \ \mu s} = 100$$

3. *Control Word and Instructions to Initialize the Counter*

To initialize the 8254 for Counter 2 in Mode 3, the following control word is necessary.

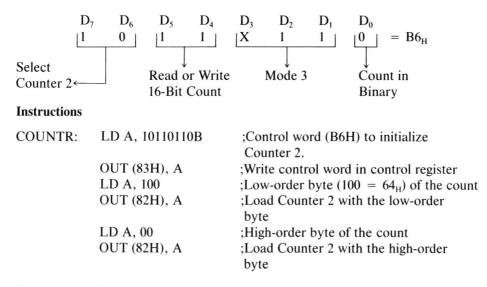

D₇	D₆	D₅	D₄	D₃	D₂	D₁	D₀	

$$\begin{array}{cccccccc} D_7 & D_6 & D_5 & D_4 & D_3 & D_2 & D_1 & D_0 \\ 1 & 0 & 1 & 1 & X & 1 & 1 & 0 \end{array} = B6_H$$

Select
Counter 2 ←   Read or Write   Mode 3   Count in
                 16-Bit Count   Binary

Instructions

COUNTR:	LD A, 10110110B	;Control word (B6H) to initialize Counter 2.
	OUT (83H), A	;Write control word in control register
	LD A, 100	;Low-order byte (100 = 64_H) of the count
	OUT (82H), A	;Load Counter 2 with the low-order byte
	LD A, 00	;High-order byte of the count
	OUT (82H), A	;Load Counter 2 with the high-order byte

Description   The first instruction loads the control word into the control register of the 8254 to set up Counter 2 in Mode 3. The subsequent instructions load the count 0064H (100_{10}) to obtain a 20 kHz square wave. In Figure 14.13, the gate (Gate 2) is tied high; therefore, the counter begins as soon as the count is loaded.

14.4.4   Modes and Status
As mentioned earlier, the 8254 can operate in six different modes; we already illustrated Mode 3 in Section 14.4.3. Now we will describe briefly various modes of the 8254 including Mode 3.

MODE 0: INTERRUPT ON TERMINAL COUNT
In this mode, initially the OUT is low. Once a count is loaded in the register, the counter is decremented every cycle, and when the count reaches zero, the OUT goes high. This can be used as an interrupt. The OUT remains high until a new count or a command word is loaded. Figure 14.11 also shows that the counting (m = 5) is temporarily stopped when the Gate is disabled (G = 0), and continued again when the Gate is at logic 1.

MODE 1: HARDWARE-RETRIGGERABLE ONE-SHOT
In this mode, the OUT is initially high. When the Gate is triggered, the OUT goes low. At the end of the count, the OUT goes high again, thus generating a one-shot pulse (Figure 14.11, Mode 1).

MODE 2: RATE GENERATOR
This mode is used to generate a pulse equal to the clock period at a given interval. When a count is loaded, the OUT stays high until the count reaches 1, and then

the OUT goes low for one clock period. The count is reloaded automatically, and the pulse is generated continuously. The count = 1 is illegal in this mode.

MODE 3: SQUARE-WAVE GENERATOR

In this mode, when a count is loaded, the OUT is high. The count is decremented by two at every clock cycle. When it reaches zero, the OUT goes low, and the count is reloaded again. This is repeated continuously; thus, a continuous square wave with period equal to the period of the count is generated. In other words, the frequency of the square wave is equal to the frequency of the clock divided by the count. If the count (N) is odd, the pulse stays high for $(N + 1)/2$ clock cycles and stays low for $(N - 1)/2$ clock cycles.

MODE 4: SOFTWARE-TRIGGERED STROBE

In this mode, the OUT is initially high; it goes low for one clock period at the end of the count. The count must be reloaded for subsequent outputs.

MODE 5: HARDWARE-TRIGGERED STROBE

This mode is similar to Mode 4, except that it is triggered by the rising pulse at the gate. Initially, the OUT is low. When the Gate pulse is triggered from low to high, the count begins. At the end of the count, the OUT goes low for one clock period.

READ-BACK COMMAND

The Read-Back Command in the 8254 allows the user to read the count and the status of the counter; this command is unavailable in the 8253. The format of the command is shown in Figure 14.14(a).

The command is written in the control register, and the count of the specified counter(s) can be latched if $D_5 = 0$. The latched count is held until it is read or the counter is reprogrammed. Similarly, the counter status can be read if $D_4 = 0$; the format of the status byte is shown in Figure 14.14(b).

14.4.5   Comparison of the Z80 CTC and Intel 8254

The Intel 8254 is a general-purpose programmable timer/counter. It includes three 16-bit counters. Its control logic requires $\overline{RD}/\overline{WR}$ control signals and the decoded address. Each counter can have its own independent clock, and the counter operation can be controlled using the gate input. The 8254 can operate in six different modes to provide various types of outputs, such as a single pulse at the end of the count or a square wave output.

On the other hand, the CTC is specially designed to work with the Z80; it requires $\overline{M_1}$ and $\overline{IORQ}$ control signals in addition to the $\overline{RD}$ signal. The CTC has four independent channels with an 8-bit counter register. The counting is initiated by software instructions; it does not have a gate input signal. It can operate only in two modes: counter and timer. However, the CTC has a very powerful interrupt scheme; it can generate an interrupt request signal at the end of the count and set up the daisy chain priority scheme.

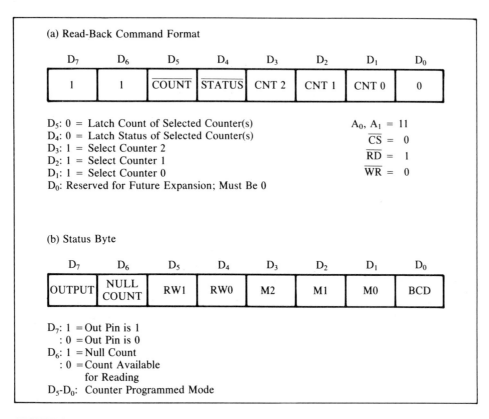

FIGURE 14.14

(a) Read-Back Command Format and (b) Status Byte

SOURCE: Intel Corporation, *Component Data Catalog* (Santa Clara, CA.: Author, 1982).

SUMMARY

Programmable timer/counter circuits are designed to provide accurate time delays and to count external events. These integrated circuits are used in various applications such as time delays, counters, one-shot, and waveform generation. This chapter has been concerned with applications of programmable timer/counter devices, specifically, the Z80 Counter/Timer Circuit (CTC). The CTC was described in detail, and it was illustrated with two applications: baud generator and timer (clock) design using a 60 Hz power line signal. In addition, the Intel 8254 timer was described and compared with the CTC. A summary of the important features of the programmable timer circuits follows.

□ A programmable timer/counter device generally includes multiple timer/counter circuits and can operate in various modes.

□ The control logic of the timer includes a control register and a counter register. The operation mode and the selection of a timer is specified by writing a control word into the control register, and an appropriate count is loaded into the counter register.

□ The Z80 CTC has two modes of operation: the timer mode and the counter mode.

□ In the timer mode, the CTC provides the time delay based on the frequency of the system clock, the prescaler specified in the control word, and the count loaded into the counter register. After the count is loaded, the counter can be initiated either automatically or by an external pulse. Once the operation is initiated, the down-counter is decremented at every clock pulse, and when it reaches zero, an active high pulse is generated at the output. The count is automatically loaded again, and the operation continues.

□ In the counter mode, the CTC counts external events indicated by the input from an external circuit. In this mode, the counter is decremented whenever it receives an active pulse from the external event, and when the counter reaches zero, an active high pulse is generated at the output and the count is automatically reloaded into the counter register.

□ The Z80 CTC is capable of generating an interrupt request pulse. If the interrupt is enabled, the CTC generates an interrupt request pulse when the count reaches zero. The CTC also includes interrupt control logic to set up several CTCs in a daisy chain priority.

□ The Intel 8254 is also a widely used general purpose timer/counter circuit. It has three 16-bit counters that can operate independently in six different modes.

ASSIGNMENTS

1. Explain the operations of the Z80 CTC in the counter mode and the timer mode.
2. What is the function of the prescaler when the CTC is set up in the timer mode?
3. Calculate the time delay for the following parameters: System clock frequency = 4 MHz, prescaler = 256, and the count = 150.
4. Calculate the count to obtain a pulse every 400 μs if the system clock is 4 MHz and the prescaler value is 16.
5. Identify the port addresses of Channel 1 and Channel 2 in Figure 14.2 if address lines A_7 and A_4 are interchanged.
6. Specify the control word for Channel 1 (Figure 14.7) to set up the CTC in the timer mode with the automatic trigger on the falling edge and the interrupt disabled.

7. Write instructions to initialize Channel 2 (Figure 14.7) in the timer mode to provide a pulse approximately every 5 ms.
8. Specify the control word to set up Channel 2 in the counter mode with the interrupt enabled.
9. Write instructions to set up Channel 2 (Figure 14.8) in the counter mode to count 120 events. At the end of 120 events, the CTC should generate an interrupt request. After the interrupt acknowledge, the program should be transferred to the location $189F_H$, where the service routine is located. The interrupt vector address for Channel 0 is specified as 1848_H.
10. Show output connections of Channel 1 and Channel 2 (Figure 14.8) to count 1000 events. Initialize the channels with appropriate time constants.
11. Design a five-minute timer using two channels of the Z80 CTC. Assuming the system clock to be 2 MHz, set up one channel as a timer and another as a counter. Connect the output of the timer to CLK/TRG input of the counter. The counter channel should generate an interrupt request every second, and the service routine should count the seconds until the total time is five minutes.
12. Write initialization instructions to set up Channel 0 as a timer with the pre-scaler equal to 16 and the count equal to 256. If the clock frequency is 4 MHz, calculate the delay obtained at the output of Channel 0.
13. Set up Channel 1 as a counter with the maximum count (256) and trigger the CLK/TRG1 from the output of Channel 0 in Assignment 12. Calculate the delay interval at ZC/TO1.
14. Set up Channels 2 and 3 as counters and generate an interrupt after one hour by using the output of Assignment 13.

Serial I/O and Data Communication

The Z80 microprocessor is a parallel device; it transfers data bits simultaneously over its eight data lines. This is called the **parallel I/O mode,** as discussed in previous chapters. However, in many situations, the parallel I/O mode is either impractical or impossible. For example, parallel data communication over a long distance can become very expensive. Similarly, devices such as a CRT terminal and a cassette tape are not designed for parallel I/O. In these instances, the **serial I/O mode** is used, whereby one bit at a time is transferred over a single line.

In *serial transmission* (from the MPU to a peripheral), an 8-bit parallel word should be converted into a stream of eight serial bits; this is known as **parallel-to-serial conversion.** After the conversion, one bit at a time is transmitted over a single line at a given rate called the **baud** (bits per second). In *serial reception,* on the other hand, the MPU receives a stream of eight bits, and they should be converted into an 8-bit parallel word; this is known as **serial-to-parallel conversion.** In addition to the conversion, information such as the beginning and the end of transmission and error check is necessary in serial communication. This chapter first discusses these basic concepts in serial data communica-

tion and explains how serial communication can be implemented using microprocessor instructions (software). However, in industrial applications, the hardware approach through programmable devices is generally used. This chapter illustrates applications with two such devices: the Intel 8251 and the Z80 SIO (and DART).

OBJECTIVES

□ Explain how data transfer occurs in the serial I/O mode and how it differs from the parallel I/O mode.

□ Explain the terms: synchronous and asynchronous transmission; simplex, and half and full duplex transmission; baud; and parity check.

□ Explain how data bits are transmitted (or received) in the asynchronous format, and calculate the delay required between two successive bits for a given baud.

□ Explain the RS-232C serial I/O standard and compare it with the RS-422 and -423 standards.

□ Explain how serial I/O communication can be implemented in the asynchronous format using software.

□ Explain the block diagram and the functions of each block of the Intel 8251 USART (Programmable Communication Interface).

□ Design an interfacing circuit using the 8251, and write initialization instructions to set up data communication between a microcomputer and a serial peripheral.

□ Explain the block diagram and the functions of each block of the Z80 SIO (Serial Input/Output Controller) and the DART (Dual Asynchronous Receiver and Transmitter).

□ Write initialization instructions to set up the Z80 SIO (or DART) for given specifications to implement the asynchronous communication.

□ Write interrupt service routines to implement communication between the Z80 MPU and a terminal when the Z80 SIO is set up in the interrupt mode.

15.1   BASIC CONCEPTS IN SERIAL I/O

The basic concepts concerning the serial I/O mode can be classified into the following categories.

1. Interfacing requirements
2. Serial I/O format and requirements
3. Error checks in data communication
4. Data communication over long distance
5. Standards in serial I/O
6. Software versus perogrammable hardware approaches

15.1.1   Interfacing Requirements

The interfacing requirements for a serial I/O peripheral are the same as those of a parallel I/O device. The microprocessor identifies the peripheral through a port address and enables it using a Read or Write control signal. The primary difference between the parallel I/O and the serial I/O is in the number of lines used for data transfer: the parallel I/O uses the entire data bus, and the serial I/O uses only one data line. Figure 15.1 shows a typical configuration of serial I/O transmission; the MPU selects the peripheral through Chip Select and uses the control signals READ to receive data and WRITE to transmit data. The serial peripheral can be interfaced either under program control (status check) or interrupt control.

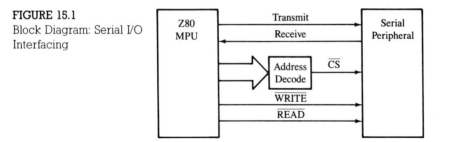

FIGURE 15.1
Block Diagram: Serial I/O
Interfacing

15.1.2 Serial I/O Format and Requirements

The serial transmission format is concerned with such issues as synchronization between a receiver and a transmitter, direction of data flow, and rate or speed of transmission. These topics are briefly described below. Topics concerning errors in transmission and data communication over long distances are discussed in the subsequent sections.

Synchronous Versus Asynchronous Transmission   Serial communication occurs in one of two formats: synchronous or asynchronous. In the synchronous format, a receiver and a transmitter are synchronized with the same clock, and a block of characters is transmitted along with the synchronization (Sync) characters, as shown in Figure 15.2(a). Error check characters called CRC (Cyclic Redundancy Check—discussed later), are also included. This format is generally used for high-speed transmission (more than 20 k bits/second).

The asynchronous format is character-oriented as shown in Figure 15.2(b). The asynchronous transmission, as the name suggests, can occur any time; it is unpredictable in relation to time. Therefore, each character must carry information about when the transmission begins and when it ends; this information is included in each character by adding the Start and the Stop bits (Figure 15.2(b)). When no data are being transmitted, a receiver stays in the high state. Transmission begins with a low Start bit, followed by a character and one or two high Stop bits. This is also known as **framing.** Figure 15.2(b) shows the transmission of 11 bits for an ASCII character in the asynchronous format: one Start bit, eight character bits, and two Stop bits. In serial I/O, logic 1 is known also as Mark and logic 0 as Space. The format shown in Figure 15.2(b) is similar to Morse Code, but dots and dashes are replaced by logic 0s and 1s. The asynchronous format is generally used in low-speed transmission (less than 20 k bits/second).

Simplex and Duplex Transmission   Serial communication can also be classified according to the direction and simultaneity of data flow.

In **simplex transmission,** data are transmitted in only one direction. An example is the transmission from a microcomputer to a printer.

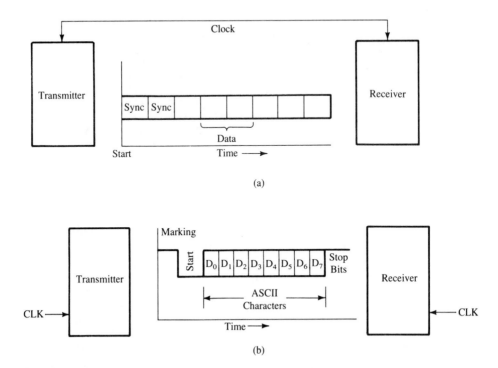

FIGURE 15.2
Transmission Format: (a) Synchronous; (b) Asynchronous

In **duplex transmission,** data flow in both directions. However, if the transmission is one way at a time, it is called *half duplex;* if it is both ways simultaneously, it is called *full duplex.* Generally, transmission between two computers or between a computer and a terminal is full duplex.

Rate of Transmission   In parallel I/O, data bits are transferred when a control signal enables the interfacing device; the transfer takes place in less than three T-states. However, in serial I/O, one bit is sent out at a time; therefore, how long the bit stays on or off is determined by the speed at which the bits are transmitted. Furthermore, the receiver should be set up to receive the bits at the same rate as the transmission; otherwise, the receiver may not be able to differentiate between two consecutive 0s or 1s.

The rate at which the bits are transmitted—bits/second—is called a **baud;** however, technically, it is defined as the number of signal changes/second. Each piece of equipment has its own baud requirement. For example, a teletype (TTY) generally runs on a 110 baud. However, in most terminals and printers, the baud is adjustable, typically ranging from 50 to 9,600 baud. Figure 15.3 shows how the ASCII character I (49_H) will be transmitted with 1,200 baud with the framing in-

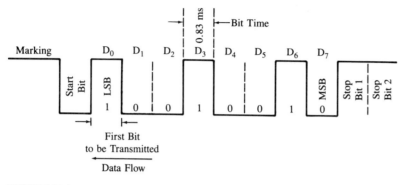

FIGURE 15.3
Serial Bit Format for ASCII Character "I" at 1,200 Baud

formation of one Start and two Stop bits. The transmission begins with active low Start bit, followed by the LSB D_0. The bit time—the delay between any two successive bits—is 0.83 ms; this is determined by the baud as shown in Figure 15.3.

$$1,200 \text{ bits} = 1 \text{ second}$$
$$\text{For 1 bit} = 1/1,200 = 0.83 \text{ ms}$$

Therefore, to transmit one character, a parallel byte (49_H) should be converted into a stream of 11 bits by adding framing bits (one Start and two Stop bits), and each bit must be transmitted at the interval of 0.83 ms. This can be implemented either through software or through programmable hardware chips. To receive a character in the serial mode, the process is reversed: bits are received one at a time and converted into a parallel word.

15.1.3 Error Checks in Data Communication

During transmission, various types of errors can occur. For example, data bits may change because of noise or can be misunderstood by the receiver because of differences in receiver and transmitter clocks. These errors need to be checked; therefore, additional information for error checking is sent during the transmission. The receiver can check the received data against the error check information, and if an error is detected, the receiver can request the retransmission of that data segment. Three methods used in common practice are **parity check, checksum,** and **cyclic redundancy check.**

PARITY CHECK

This is used to check each character by counting the number of 1s in the character, and in the ASCII code transmission, bit D_7 is used to transmit parity check information. The technique is based on the principle that in a given system, each character is transmitted with either an even number or an odd number of 1s.

In an even parity system, when a character has an odd number of 1s, the bit D_7 is set to 1 and an even number of 1s is transmitted. For example, the code for the character I is 49_H (01001001) with three 1s. When the character I is transmitted in an even parity system, the transmitter will set the bit D_7 to 1, making the code $C9_H$ (1100 1001). On the other hand, in an odd parity system, the character I is transmitted by keeping bit D_7 at 0; thus, the code remains 49_H.

In the Z80 system, the parity check is easy to implement and detect because the Z80 has the parity flag, and this flag can be used to check parity information in each character. However, the parity check cannot detect multiple errors in any given character if the number of errors is even.

CHECKSUM

The checksum technique is used when blocks of data are transferred. It involves adding all the bytes in a block without carries. Then, the 2's complement of the sum (negative of the sum) is transmitted as the last byte. The receiver adds all the bytes, including the 2's complement of the sum; thus, the result should be zero if there is no error in the block.

CYCLIC REDUNDANCY CHECK (CRC)

This technique is commonly used when data are transferred from and to a floppy disk and in a synchronous data communication. The technique is based on mathematical relationships of polynomials. A stream of data can be represented as a polynomial that is divided by a constant polynomial called the generator polynomial. The remainder of the division is sent out as a check for errors. The receiver checks the remainder to detect an error in the transmission. The mathematical details are as follows.

1. A stream of data bits can be represented as
   $M(x) = b_n x^0 + b_{n-1} x^1 + \ldots + b_0 x^n$, where
   b_0 = least significant bit
   b_n = most significant bit.
   For example, the polynomial of the Hex number $8A_H$ (1 0 0 0 1 0 1 0) is
   $M(x) = 1x^0 + 0x^1 + 0x^2 + 0x^3 + 1x^4 + 0x^5 + 1x^6 + 0x^7$
   $= 1x^0 + 1x^4 + 1x^6 = x^6 + x^4 + 1$.

2. Let us assume the length of the CRC code is four bits, although normally it is 16 bits. To obtain proper division, the polynomial is first multiplied by the power of the CRC code length (in our example it is x^4) and divided by the agreed-upon generator polynomial $G(x)$. The formula is

$$\frac{M(x) \times x^4}{G(x)} = Q(x) + R(x)$$

where $Q(x)$ is the quotient obtained by Modulo-2 arithmetic (see Appendix B for Modulo-2 arithmetic) and R(x) is the remainder.

3. Assuming $G(x) = x^4 + 1$

$$\frac{M(x) \times x^4}{G(x)} = \frac{x^{10} + x^8 + x^4}{x^4 + 1} = (x^6 + x^4 + x^2) + x^2 \qquad \text{(see Appendix B)}.$$

$$\text{Quotient } Q(x) \quad \text{Remainder } R(x)$$

4. This remainder is added to the modified polynomial
$M(x) \times x^4 + R(x) = x^{10} + x^8 + x^4 + x^2$ and transmitted as

x^{10}		x^8					x^4		x^2		
0	1	0	1	0	0	0	1	0	1	0	0
D_0	D_1	D_2	D_3	D_4	D_5	D_6	D_7	D_8	D_9	D_{10}	D_{11}

$$\text{Data} = 8A_H \qquad\qquad \text{CRC}$$

The transmitted stream of bits includes the original byte $8A_H$ in reverse order, appended by the CRC bits at the end.

5. The receiver divides the transmitted polynomial by $G(x)$, and if the remainder is 0, it indicates no error (divides $x^{10} + x^8 + x^4 + x^2$ by $x^4 + 1$ and checks the answer).

The CRC check is a somewhat complex technique; it is discussed briefly here because the Z80 SIO is capable of generating and checking the CRC code if the SIO is used in the synchronous mode.

15.1.4 Data Communication over Telephone Lines

The serial I/O technique can be used to send data over long distance through telephone lines. However, telephone lines are designed to handle voice; the bandwidth of telephone lines ranges from 300 Hz to 3,300 Hz, while a digital signal, with rise time in nanoseconds, requires a bandwidth of several megahertz. Therefore, data bits are converted into audio tones using modems.

A **modem** (Modulator/Demodulator) is a circuit that translates digital data into audio tone frequencies for transmission over telephone lines and converts audio frequencies into digital data for reception. The modems are designed to transfer data at rates of 300–9,600 bps (bits per second); 1200 and 2400 baud are in common use. Generally, two types of modulation techniques are used: *frequency shift keying* (FSK) for low-speed modems and *phase shift keying* (PSK) for high-speed modems.

Computers can exchange information over telephone lines by using two modems—one on each side (Figure 15.4). A calling computer (or terminal), also known as the originator, contacts a receiving (answering) computer through a telephone number, and a communication link is established after control signals have been exchanged between computers and modems.

A typical process of communication for a 300 bps modem is shown in Figure

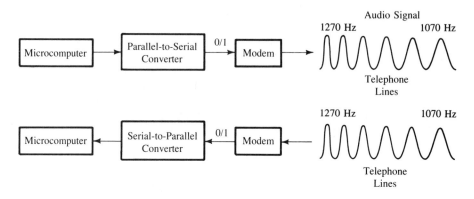

FIGURE 15.4
Communication over Telephone Lines Using Modems

15.4. A parallel word is converted into serial bits; in turn, the originator modem generates two audio frequencies: 1,070 Hz for logic 0 (Space) and 1,270 Hz for logic 1 (Mark). These audio frequencies are transmitted over telephone lines. At the answering end, audio frequencies are converted back into 0s and 1s, and serial bits are converted into a parallel word that can be read by the computer. When the answering computer needs to transmit, it transmits on 2,025 Hz (Space) and 2,225 Hz (Mark).

15.1.5 Standards in Serial I/O

The serial I/O technique is commonly used to interface terminals, printers, and modems. These peripherals and computers are designed and manufactured by various companies. Therefore, a common understanding must exist among various manufacturing and user groups that can ensure compatibility among different equipment. When this understanding is defined and generally accepted in industry (and by users), it is known as a standard. A standard is normally defined by a professional organization, such as the Institute of Electrical and Electronic Engineers (IEEE); however, a widespread practice can occasionally become a de facto standard. A standard may include such items as assignment of pin positions for signals, voltage levels, speed of data transfer, length of cables, and mechanical specifications.

In serial I/O, data can be transmitted either as current or voltage. Typically, 20 mA (or 60 mA) current loops are used in teletype equipment. When a teletype is Marking or at logic 1, current flows; when it is at logic 0 (or Space), the current flow is interrupted. The advantage of the current loop method is that signals are relatively noise-free.

When data are transmitted as voltage, the commonly used standard is known as **RS-232C.** It is defined in reference to Data Terminal Equipment (DTE) and Data Communication Equipment (DCE)—terminal and modem—as shown in Figure 15.5(a); however, its voltage levels are not compatible with TTL logic levels.

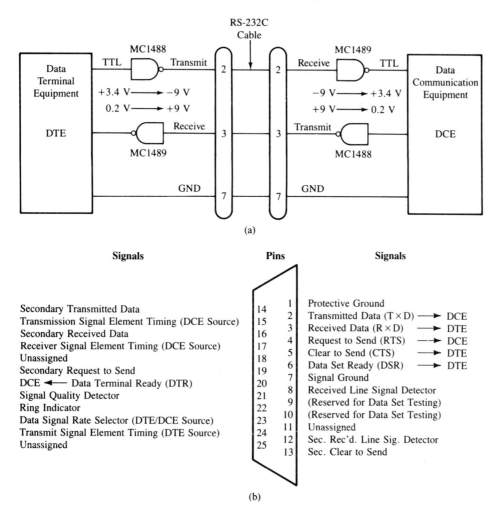

FIGURE 15.5

(a) Minimum Configuration of RS-232C Signals and Voltage Levels; (b) RS-232C Signal Definitions and Pin Assignments

SOURCE: Courtesy of Electronic Industries Association.

The rate of data transmission in RS-232C is restricted to a maximum of 20 kbaud and the distance is limited to 50 ft. For high-speed data transmission, two new standards—RS-422A and RS-423A—have been developed in recent years; however, they are not yet widely used.

To appreciate the difficulties and confusion in this standard, one has to examine its historical background. The RS-232 standard was developed during the initial days of computer timesharing, long before the existence of TTL logic, and its primary focus was to have compatibility between a terminal and a modem. However, the same standard is now being used for communications between computers and peripherals, and the roles of a data terminal and a modem have become ambiguous. Should a computer be considered a terminal or a modem? The answer is that it can be either. Therefore, the lines used for transmission and reception will differ, depending on how the manufacturer designs the equipment.

RS-232C

Figure 15.5(b) shows the RS-232C 25 pins and associated signals. The signals are divided into four groups: **data signals, control signals, timing signals,** and **grounds.** For data lines, the voltage level from $+3$ V to $+15$ V is defined as logic 0, and from -3 V to -15 V is defined as logic 1 (normally, voltage levels are ± 12 V). This is negative true logic. Because of incompatibility with TTL logic, voltage translators, called **line drivers** and **line receivers,** are required to interface TTL logic with the RS-232 signals, as shown in Figure 15.5(a). The line driver, MC1488, converts logic 1 into approximately -9 V and logic 0 into $+9$ V (Figure 15.5(a)). Before the signal is received by the DCE, it is again converted by the line receiver, MC1489, into TTL compatible logic. This raises the question: If the received signal is to be converted back to the TTL levels, what is the reason to convert the transmitted signal to higher voltages in the first place? The primary reason is that the standard was defined before the TTL levels came into existence; before 1960, most equipment was designed to handle higher voltages. The other reason is that this standard provides a higher level of noise margin, from -3 V to $+3$ V.

The minimum interface between a computer and a peripheral requires three lines: pins 2, 3, and 7, as shown in Figure 15.5(a). These lines are defined in relation to the DTE; the terminal transmits on pin 2 and receives on pin 3. On the other hand, the DCE transmits on pin 3 and receives on pin 2. Now the dilemma is: How does a manufacturer define the role of its equipment? For example, the user may connect its microcomputer to a printer configured as a DTE or to a modem configured as a DCE. Therefore, to remain compatible with the defined signals of the RS-232C, the computer must be defined as a DCE for the printer connection and a DTE for the modem. One of the solutions to this dilemma is for the manufacturer to provide two serial ports, one for a modem and the other for a printer. Another solution is to reconfigure the RS-232 cable as shown in Figure 15.6. In Figure 15.6, the microcomputer is defined as a DTE, and it can be connected to the modem, defined as a DCE, without any modification in the RS-232 cable, as shown in Figure 15.6(a). However, when it is connected to the printer, the transmit and the receive lines must be crossed as shown in Figure 15.6(b).

Typically, data transmission with a handshake requires eight lines, listed in Table 15.1. Specific functions of handshake lines differ in different peripherals and, therefore, should be referred to in the manufacturers' manuals.

For high-speed transmission, the standards RS-422A and RS-423A are used. These standards use differential amplifiers to reject noise levels and can transmit data at higher speed with longer cable. The RS-422A allows a maximum speed of

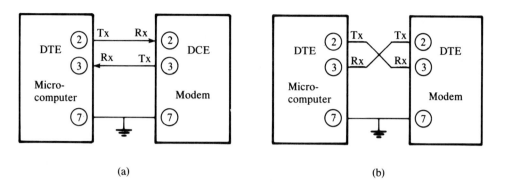

FIGURE 15.6
RS-232C Connections: (a) DTE to DCE and (b) DTE to DTE

10 Mbaud for a 40-ft distance and 100 kbaud for 4000 ft. The RS-423A is limited to 100 kbaud for a 30-ft distance and 10 kbaud for 300 ft. See Table 15.2 for comparison of the three standards: RS-232C, RS-422A, and RS-423A.

15.1.6 Review of Serial I/O Concepts and Approaches to Implementation

Serial data transmission can be implemented through either software or programmable I/O devices. The software and the hardware approaches are conceptually similar. In asynchronous data transmission, the steps can be summarized as follows:

1. Inform the receiver that the transmission is beginning with the Start pulse.
2. Convert a parallel word into a stream of serial bits.

TABLE 15.1
RS-232C Signals Used with Handshake Data Communication

Pin No.	Signals[a]		Functions
2	Transmitted Data	TxD	Output; transmits data from DTE to DCE
3	Received Data	RxD	Input; DTE receives data from DCE
4	Request to Send	RTS	General-purpose output from DTE
5	Clear to Send	CTS	General-purpose input to DTE; can be used as a handshake signal
6	Data Set Ready	DSR	General-purpose input to DTE; can be used to indicate that DCE is ready
7	Signal Ground	GND	Common reference between DTE and DCE
8	Data Carrier Detect	DCD	Generally used by DTE to disable data reception
20	Data Terminal Ready	DTR	Output; generally used to indicate that DTE is ready

[a]Signals are referenced to DTE.

TABLE 15.2
Comparison of Serial I/O Standards

Specifications	RS-232C	RS-422A	RS-423A
Speed	20 kbaud	10 Mbaud at 40 ft	100 kbaud at 30 ft
		100 kbaud at 4000 ft	1 kbaud at 4000 ft
Distance	50 ft	4000 ft	4000 ft
Logic 0	> +3 to +25 V	B> A[a]	+4 to +6 V
Logic 1	< −3 to −25 V	B < A	−4 to −6 V
Receiver Input	± 15 V	±7 V	± 12 V

[a]B and A are differential input to the op amp.

3. Transmit data one bit at a time with appropriate time delay using one data line of an output port. The time delay is determined by the speed of the transmission.
4. Transmit parity check bit.
5. Inform the receiver that transmission is ending by sending Stop bits.

In data reception, the process is reversed. The receiver needs to

1. Recognize the beginning of the transmission.
2. Receive data one bit at a time and convert the bits into a parallel byte.
3. Check for errors and recognize the end of the transmission.

In the software approach, the speed of transmission is set up by using an appropriate delay between the transmission of two consecutive bits, and the entire word is converted into a serial stream by rotating the byte and outputting one bit at a time using one of the data lines of an output port. The software provides the time delay between the two consecutive bits and adds framing bits and the parity bit; this is discussed in section 15.2.

In the hardware approach, the above functions are performed by a programmable device (chip). The device contains a parallel-to-serial register and 1-bit output port for transmission, and a serial-to-parallel register and 1-bit input port for reception. The rate of transmission and reception is determined by the clock. The programmable chip also includes a control register that can be programmed to add framing and error-check information, and to specify the number of bits to be transferred. The microprocessor transfers a parallel byte using the data bus, and the programmable chip performs the remaining functions for serial I/O.

The software approach is suitable for slow-speed asynchronous data communication where timing requirements are not critical. The approach is simple and inexpensive. The hardware approach is suitable for both asynchronous and synchronous formats. The approach is flexible, and chips can be programmed to accommodate changing requirements. In industrial and commercial products, the hardware approach has become almost universal. This chapter includes the detailed discussion and illustrations of two programmable chips: the Intel 8251 and

TABLE 15.3
Summary of Synchronous and Asynchronous Serial Data Communication

Format	Synchronous	Asynchronous
Data Format	Groups of Characters	One Character at a Time
Speed	High (20 k bits/second or Higher)	20 k bits/second or Lower
Framing Information	Sync Characters Are Sent with Each Group	Start and Stop Bits Present with Every Character
Implementation	Hardware	Hardware or Software
Data Direction	Simplex, Half, and Full Duplex	Simplex, Half, and Full Duplex

the Z80 SIO. However, for learning the basic concepts in serial I/O, the software approach is more suitable than the hardware approach; thus, the software approach is described here prior to the discussion of the programmable serial I/O devices. We will limit our discussion to the asynchronous communications mode, which is commonly used in the microcomputer. Synchronous data communication is a specialized technique and will not be discussed here.

The basic concepts concerning serial I/O discussed in the previous sections are summarized in Table 15.3.

SOFTWARE-CONTROLLED ASYNCHRONOUS SERIAL I/O 15.2

In the software-controlled asynchronous serial mode, the program should perform the following tasks.

1. Output a Start bit.
2. Convert the character to be sent into a stream of serial bits with appropriate delay.
3. Add parity information if necessary.
4. Output one or two Stop bits.

Figure 15.7 shows the accumulator with the code for the ASCII character "I," and it is converted into a stream of 11 bits, including one Start bit and two Stop bits. After the Start bit, the character bits are transmitted with bit D_0 first and bit D_7 last; for ASCII characters, bit D_7 can be used to add parity information. The bit time—the delay between two successive bits—is determined by the transmission baud. Figure 15.7 shows the transmission with 1,200 baud; the delay between the two consecutive bits is thus 0.83 ms.

Data reception in the serial mode involves the reverse process: receiving one bit at a time and forming an 8-bit parallel word. The receiving program should continue to read the input port until it receives the Start bit, and then begin to count character bits with appropriate delay.

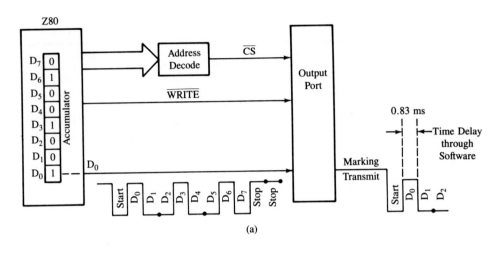

(a)

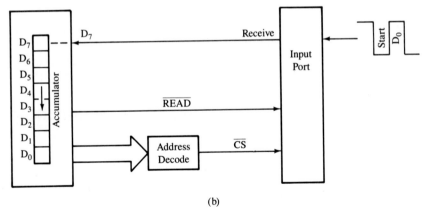

(b)

FIGURE 15.7
(a) Serial Data Transmission and (b) Serial Data Reception Under Software Control

15.2.1 Serial Data Transmission

Figure 15.8(a) shows a flowchart to transmit an ASCII character, and it can be explained in the context of the block diagram shown in Figure 15.7(a). When no character is being transmitted, the transmit line of the output port stays high in the Mark position. The transmission begins with the Start bit, active low. The initialization block of the flowchart includes setting up a counter to count eight character bits; Start and Stop bits are sent out separately. The program waits for bit time—0.833 ms for 1,200 baud—and begins to send one character-bit at a time over the data line D_0 at the interval of 0.83 ms. To get ready for the next bit, the program rotates the bits—for example, D_1 into D_0. It repeats the loop eight times, and finally sends out two Stop bits. Assuming that the character is being sent to

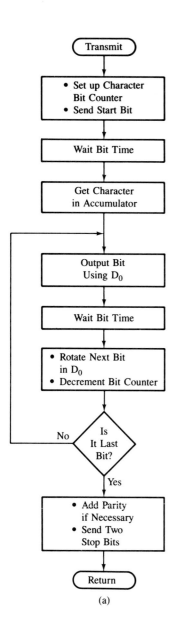

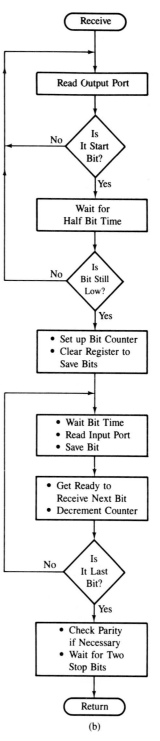

FIGURE 15.8

Flowcharts: (a) Transmission and (b) Reception of an ASCII Character

a printer, the printer waits until it receives all the bits serially, checks the parity if necessary, forms a character, and prints it during the Stop bits. The Stop bits perform two functions: They allow sufficient time for the printer to print the character, and they leave the transmit line in the Mark position at the end of the character.

15.2.2 Serial Data Reception

In serial data reception, the program begins by reading the input port. When no character is being received, the input line stays high. The program stays in the loop and continues to read the port until the Start bit (active low) is received, as shown in the flowchart (Figure 15.8(b)).

When the Start bit is received, the program waits for half the bit time and samples the character bits in the middle of the pulse rather than at the beginning to avoid errors in transition. Then it checks again to confirm that it is really a Start bit and not a false start such as a noise spike. In the next block, it initializes the counter to count eight bits and clears a register to save the partial readings. The program reads the input port at the interval of bit time until it reads all the character bits, checks the parity bit, and ignores the last two bits by just waiting for two bit times. The character reception also begins with the LSB; that is, the microprocessor will receive bit D_0 first. In Figure 15.7(a), the data line D_7 is used for the reception. The line D_7 provides some programming convenience for serial-to-parallel conversion; the word can be formed by shifting bits to the right whenever a bit is read, and eventually the LSB will reach its proper position.

15.3 PROGRAMMABLE COMMUNICATION INTERFACE— INTEL 8251A: HARDWARE APPROACH TO SERIAL I/O

The hardware approach to serial I/O incorporates the same basic principles and requirements necessary for the software approach. The various functions performed separately under software control must be performed by the hardware, designed in an integrated circuit. Such a device should

1. Transfer a parallel word between the microprocessor and the device.
2. Have an input port to receive and an output port to transmit serial data, both with one I/O line each.
3. Perform parallel-to-serial and serial-to-parallel conversion.
4. Provide framing and error-check information.
5. Transmit (or receive) serial data according to the clock connected to the device.

The integrated circuit that meets these requirements is generally called a USART (Universal Synchronous/Asynchronous Receiver/Transmitter). Because of technological advances in IC fabrication, such devices have become quite inexpensive and are commonly used for serial I/O. We will focus on two widely used devices: the Intel 8251A and the Z80 SIO. The 8251A is discussed in this section and the Z80 SIO is described in section 15.5. The discussion of the 8251A is included prior to the discussion of the SIO because the initialization of the 8251A is easier than that of the SIO.

15.3.1 8251A Programmable Communication Interface: Overview

The 8251A is a programmable chip designed for synchronous and asynchronous serial data communication, packaged in a 28-pin DIP. The 8251A is the enhanced version of its predecessor, the 8251, and is compatible with the 8251. Figure 15.9 shows the block diagram of the 8251A. It includes five sections: Read/Write Control Logic, Transmitter, Receiver, Data Bus Buffer, and Modem Control.

The control logic interfaces the chip with the MPU, determines the functions of the chip according to the control word in its register (explained later), and monitors the data flow. The transmitter section converts a parallel word received from the MPU into serial bits and transmits them over the TxD line to a peripheral. The receiver section receives serial bits from a peripheral, converts them into a parallel word, and transfers the word to the MPU. The modem control is used to establish data communication through modems over telephone lines. The 8251A is a complex device, capable of performing various functions. For the sake of clarity, this chapter focuses only on the asynchronous mode of serial I/O and excludes any discussion of the synchronous mode and the modem control. The asynchronous mode is commonly used for data communication between the MPU and such serial peripherals as terminals and floppy disks.

Figure 15.10 shows an expanded version of the 8251A block diagram. The block diagram shows all the elements of a programmable chip; it includes the interfacing signals, the control register, and the status register. The functions of various blocks are described next.

15.3.2 Read/Write Control Logic and Interfacing

This section has six input signals, control logic, and three buffer registers: data register, control register, and status register.

Input Signals

□ $\overline{CS}$—Chip Select: When this signal goes low, the 8251A is selected by the MPU for communication. This is usually connected to a decoded address bus.

□ C/$\overline{D}$—Control/Data: When this signal is high, the control register or the status register is addressed; when it is low, the data buffer is addressed. The control register and the status register are differentiated by $\overline{WR}$ and $\overline{RD}$ signals, respectively.

□ $\overline{WR}$—Write: When this signal goes low, the MPU either writes in the control register or sends output to the data buffer. This is connected to $\overline{IOWR}$ or $\overline{MEMWR}$.

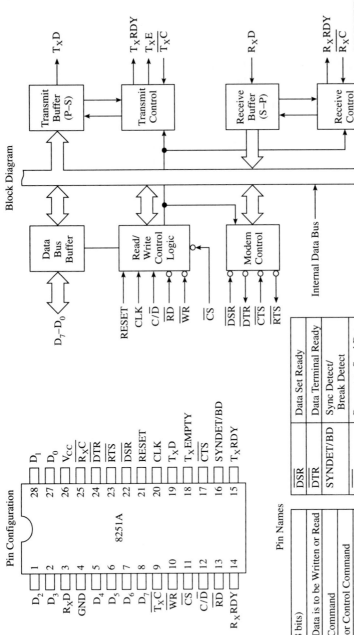

Block Diagram

Pin Configuration

8251A

D_2	1	28	D_1
D_3	2	27	D_0
R_XD	3	26	V_{CC}
GND	4	25	R_XC
D_4	5	24	$\overline{DTR}$
D_5	6	23	$\overline{RTS}$
D_6	7	22	$\overline{DSR}$
D_7	8	21	RESET
$\overline{T_XC}$	9	20	CLK
$\overline{WR}$	10	19	T_XD
$\overline{CS}$	11	18	$\overline{T_XEMPTY}$
$C/\overline{D}$	12	17	$\overline{CTS}$
$\overline{RD}$	13	16	SYNDET/BD
R_XRDY	14	15	T_XRDY

Pin Names

$D_7–D_0$	Data Bus (8 bits)
$C/\overline{D}$	Control or Data is to be Written or Read
$\overline{RD}$	Read Data Command
$\overline{WR}$	Write Data or Control Command
$\overline{CS}$	Chip Enable
CLK	Clock Pulse (TTL)
RESET	Reset
$\overline{T_XC}$	Transmitter Clock
T_XD	Transmitter Data
$\overline{R_XC}$	Receiver Clock
R_XD	Receiver Data
R_XRDY	Receiver Ready
T_XRDY	Transmitter Ready
$\overline{DSR}$	Data Set Ready
$\overline{DTR}$	Data Terminal Ready
SYNDET/BD	Sync Detect/Break Detect
$\overline{RTS}$	Request to Send Data
$\overline{CTS}$	Clear to Send Data
T_XE	Transmitter Empty
V_{CC}	+5 Volt Supply
GND	Ground

FIGURE 15.9

The 8251A: Block Diagram, Pin Configuration, and Description

SOURCE: Adapted from Intel Corporation, copyright 1990.

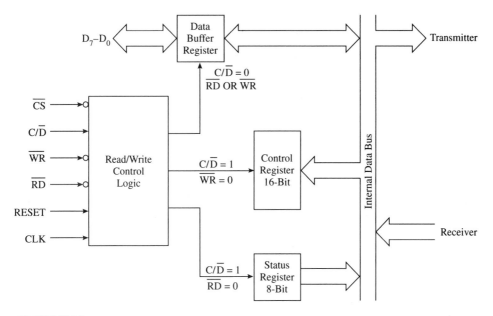

FIGURE 15.10
The 8251A: Expanded Block Diagram of Control Logic and Registers

□ $\overline{\text{RD}}$—Read: When this signal goes low, the MPU either reads a status from the status register or accepts (inputs) data from the data buffer. This is connected to either $\overline{\text{IORD}}$ or $\overline{\text{MEMRD}}$.

□ RESET—Reset: A high on this input resets the 8251A and forces it into the idle mode.

□ CLK—Clock: This is the clock input, usually connected to the system clock; the clock frequency must be between 740 kHz and 3.125 MHz. This clock does not control either the transmission or the reception rate. This clock is necessary to synchronize internal operations of the 8251A.

Control Register   This 16-bit register for a control word consists of two independent bytes; the first byte is called the **mode instruction** (word), and the second byte is called the **command instruction** (word). This register can be accessed as an output port when the C/$\overline{\text{D}}$ pin is high.

Status Register   This input register checks the ready status of a peripheral. This register is addressed as an input port when the C/$\overline{\text{D}}$ pin is high; it has the same port address as the control register.

Data Buffer   This bidirectional register can be addressed as an input and an output port when the C/$\overline{\text{D}}$ pin is low. Table 15.4 summarizes all the interfacing and control signals.

TABLE 15.4
Summary of Control Signals for the 8251A

$\overline{CS}$	$C/\overline{D}$	$\overline{RD}$	$\overline{WR}$	Function
0	1	1	0	MPU Writes Instructions in the Control Register
0	1	0	1	MPU Reads Status from the Status Register
0	0	1	0	MPU Outputs Data to the Data Buffer
0	0	0	1	MPU Accepts Data from the Data Buffer
1	X	X	X	USART Is Not Selected

Example 15.1

Identify port addresses of the control register and the data register in Figure 15.11 and explain the functions of each control register.

Solution

In Figure 15.11, the address line A_0 is connected to the $C/\overline{D}$ pin of the 8251A. When A_0 is high, the MPU communications with the control register, and when it is low, it selects the data register. The 8251A is selected when the output line O_4 of the decoder goes low. Therefore, the control register is accessed with the port address $F9_H$, and the data register is accessed with the port address $F8_H$ as shown.

A_7	A_6	A_5	A_4	A_3	A_2	A_1	A_0			
1	1	1	1	1	0	0	1	$= F9_H$	Control Register
							0	$= F8_H$	Data Register

$\overline{CS}$ $C/\overline{D}$

The control register is an output port and the status register is an input port; they are identified by $\overline{WR}$ and $\overline{RD}$ signals even if their port addresses are the same.

The data register is selected when the $C/\overline{D}$ line goes low. Thus, the port address of the data register is $F8_H$. The register is bidirectional, and the same address is used to receive or transmit data. The input and output functions are identified by $\overline{RD}$ and $\overline{WR}$ signals.

The 8251A does not have an $\overline{IORQ}$ signal; it has $\overline{RD}$ and $\overline{WR}$ signals. However, the Z80 identifies its I/O operation using the $\overline{IORQ}$ signal. Therefore, the control signals $\overline{IORD}$ and $\overline{IOWR}$ are generated by ANDing (physically OR gate) $\overline{RD}$ and $\overline{WR}$ with the $\overline{IORQ}$ signal as shown in Figure 15.11. The RESET signal from the Z80 can reset the 8251A, thus clearing all the previous commands, and the Z80 clock signal is used by the 8251A to perform internal functions.

15.3.3 Transmitter Section

The transmitter accepts parallel data from the MPU and converts them into serial data. It has two registers: a buffer register to hold 8 bits and an output register to

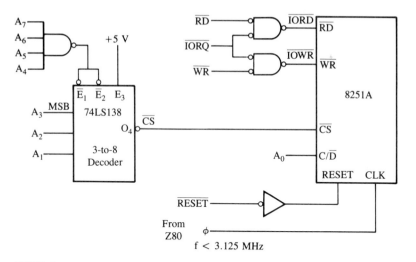

FIGURE 15.11
Interfacing the 8251A

convert 8 bits into a stream of serial bits (Figure 15.12). The MPU writes a byte in the buffer register, and whenever the output register is empty, the contents of the buffer register are transferred to the output register. This section transmits data on the TxD pin with the appropriate framing bits (Start and Stop). Three output signals and one input signal are associated with the transmitter section.

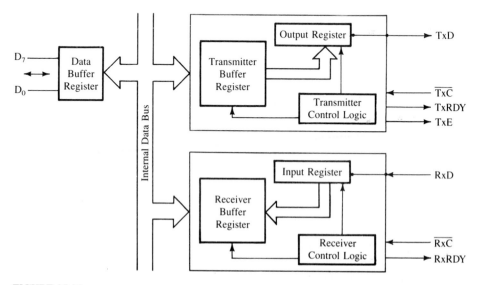

FIGURE 15.12
The 8251A: Expanded Block Diagrams of Transmitter and Receiver Sections

□ TxD—Transmit Data: Serial bits are transmitted on this line.
□ $\overline{\text{TxC}}$—Transmitter Clock: This input signal controls the rate at which bits are transmitted by the USART. The clock frequency must be 1, 16, or 64 times the baud.
□ TxRDY—Transmitter Ready: This is an output signal. When it is high, it indicates that the buffer register is empty and the USART is ready to accept a byte. It can be used either to interrupt the MPU or to indicate the status. This signal is reset when a data byte is loaded into the buffer.
□ TxE—Transmitter Empty: This is an output signal. Logic 1 on this line indicates that the output register is empty. This signal is reset when a byte is transferred from the buffer to the output register.

15.3.4 Receiver Section

The receiver accepts serial data on the RxD line from a peripheral and converts them into parallel data. The section has two registers: the receiver input register and the buffer register (Figure 15.12). When the RxD line goes low, the control logic assumes it is a Start bit, waits for half a bit time, and samples the line again. If the line is still low, the input register accepts the next bits, forms a character, and loads it into the buffer register. Subsequently, the parallel byte is transferred to the MPU when requested. In the asynchronous mode, two input signals and one output signal are necessary, as described below.

□ RxD—Receive Data: Bits are received serially on this line and converted into a parallel byte in the receiver input register.
□ $\overline{\text{RxC}}$—Receiver Clock: This is a clock signal that controls the rate at which bits are received by the USART. In the asynchronous mode the clock must be set to 1, 16, or 64 times the baud.
□ RxRDY (Receiver Ready): This is an output signal. It goes high when the USART has a character in the buffer register and is ready to transfer it to the MPU. This line can be used either to indicate the status or to interrupt the MPU.

15.3.5 Programming the 8251A

To implement serial communication, the MPU must inform the 8251A of all details such as mode, baud, Stop bits, and parity. Therefore, prior to data transfer, a set of control words must be loaded into the 16-bit control register of the 8251A. In addition, the MPU must check the readiness of a peripheral by reading the status register. The control words are divided into two formats: mode word and command word. The mode word specifies the general characteristics of operation (such as baud, parity, number of Stop bits), and the command word enables data transmission and/or reception. The status word, which can be read by the MPU, provides information concerning register status and transmission errors. Figure 15.13 shows the definitions of these words.

To program the 8251A in the asynchronous mode, the following sequence of steps must be followed.

1. Reset the 8251A. This can be done either through a system reset (RESET signal) or software reset of the 8251A (bit D_6 in the command word).
2. Write a mode word in the control register to specify baud, parity, number of stop bits (see Figure 15.13(a) for definition). This word must be followed by a command word (see Step 3).
3. Write a command word in the control register to enable data transfer (see Figure 15.13(b) for definition). The command word can be changed anytime during the operation without resetting the 8251A.
4. To modify the mode word, the 8251A must be reset prior to writing a new mode word. This can be accomplished by setting bit D_6 to logic 1 in the command word.

The 8251A is designed to recognize the first word written to the control register as a mode word. However, the software reset is accomplished by the bit D_6 in the command word. If we were to load a command word with bit $D_6 = 1$, it would be interpreted as the mode word. The solution to this dilemma is to send the first word as a dummy mode word, followed by the command word that resets the 8251A. Therefore, the sequence of programming the 8251 is as follows:

1. Send dummy mode words (00) to the control register. (See Initialization Subroutine in Example 15.2 for an explanation for sending three dummy words in the beginning.)
2. Send command word with bit $D_6 = 1$ to reset the 8251A.
3. Send mode word to specify communication parameters (baud, parity, etc.).
4. Send command word to enable transmission/reception.

After this sequence, any word sent to the control register will be interpreted as a command word until the 8251A is reset. The above sequence is adequate in most situations; however, on rare occasions the 8251A may be set up for synchronous mode by a random word when the system is turned on. In such a case, it would interpret the next two words written in the control register as Sync characters. Therefore, to deal with the worst possible situation at power turned on, three dummy words are sent to the control register, followed by the command word to reset the 8251A.

Figure 15.11 shows a schematic of interfacing the 8251A with the Z80 MPU.

1. Identify the mode and the command words to initialize the 8251A to transmit data with the following requirements:

   □ Asynchronous mode with 9,600 baud.
   □ Character length: seven bits and two Stop bits.
   □ No parity check.

2. Write a subroutine SETUP to initialize the 8251A.

Example
15.2

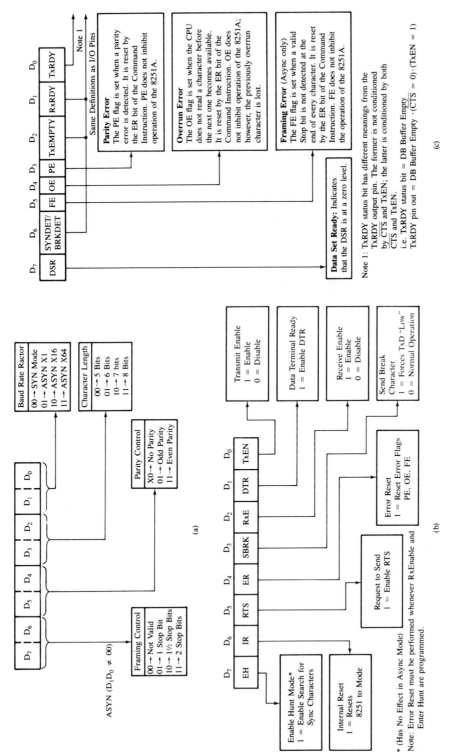

FIGURE 15.13

(a) Mode Word, (b) Command Word, and (c) Status Word Format

SOURCE: (a) and (c) reprinted by permission of Intel Corporation, copyright 1990.

458

1. The mode word to meet the following requirements (refer to Figure 15.13(a)):   Solution

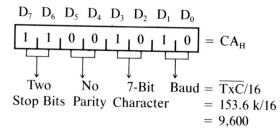

D_7 D_6 D_5 D_4 D_3 D_2 D_1 D_0

| 1 | 1 | 0 | 0 | 1 | 0 | 1 | 0 | = CA_H

Two   No   7-Bit   Baud = $\overline{TxC}/16$
Stop Bits Parity Character   = 153.6 k/16
                                                       = 9,600

Reset command word—Figure 15.13(b):

D_7 D_6 D_5 D_4 D_3 D_2 D_1 D_0

| X | 1 | X | X | X | X | X | X | = 40_H

Reset
8251A

Command word to enable transmitter—Figure 15.13(b):

D_7 D_6 D_5 D_4 D_3 D_2 D_1 D_0

| X | 0 | X | 1 | X | 0 | X | 1 | = 11_H

Do Not Error   Receive   Transmit
Reset   Reset   Disable   Enable

Status Word—Figure 15.13(c):

D_7 D_6 D_5 D_4 D_3 D_2 D_1 D_0

| X | X | X | X | X | X | X | 1 | = 01_H

Transmitter
Ready

2. Initialization Subroutine:

```
CNTRL      EQU F9H          ;8251A control port address
PORT       EQU F8H          ;8251A data port address
RESET      EQU 40H          ;Reset command
MODE       EQU CAH          ;Mode word
```

```
COMAND      EQU 11H            ;Command word to enable transmitter
SETUP:      LD C, CNTRL        ;Load control port address into C
            LD B, 00           ;Load dummy word
            OUT (C), B         ;Send dummy word three times
            OUT (C), B
            OUT (C), B
            LD B, RESET        ;Load reset command
            OUT (C), B         ;Reset 8251A
            LD B, MODE         ;Load mode word = CAH
            OUT (C), B         ;Specify communication parameters
            LD B, COMAND       ;Load command word (11H) to enable
                               ; transmission
            OUT (C), B         ;Enable transmitter
            RET
```

As the power is turned on, the 8251A can come up in either the asynchronous or the synchronous mode. If it is set up in the synchronous mode, it expects the next two words as Sync pulses. Therefore, this initialization routine sends three dummy words at the beginning; the first two will be interpreted as Sync characters and the third as the Mode word, which is followed by the Reset command word. Then the Mode and Command words are sent in a sequence. If the 8251A comes up in the asynchronous mode, it will interpret the first dummy word as the Mode word, followed by Command and Mode words; thus, it will interpret the Reset as a Command and not as a Mode word.

15.4   ILLUSTRATION: INTERFACING AN RS-232 TERMINAL USING THE 8251A IN THE POLLED MODE

CRT terminals are serial I/O devices, generally connected using the RS-232C standard. The terminal has two sections: the ASCII keyboard as an input port and the video screen as an output port. To transmit data using the RS-232C standard, the TTL logic levels should be converted into RS-232C levels by using line drivers; to receive data, line receivers should be used to convert back into TTL logic levels.

15.4.1   Problem Statement

1. Figure 15.14(a) shows a schematic of interfacing a CRT terminal using RS-232C. The port decoding logic is the same as in Figure 15.11 with the control port address $F9_H$ and the data port address $F8_H$. Explain the RS-232C signals and the operations of the line driver (MC 1488) and the line receiver (MC 1489).
2. Write a program to transmit a message from a Z80 single-board microcomputer

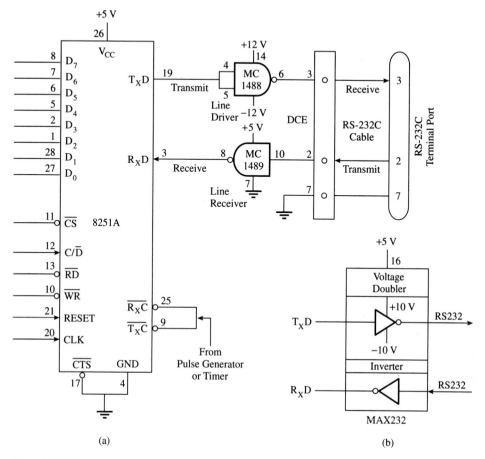

FIGURE 15.14

(a) Schematic: Interfacing a CRT Terminal Using RS-232 with the 8251A in the Polled Mode; (b) MAX 232 Logic Diagram

to a CRT terminal under program control (status check). The requirements are as follows:

- ☐ A message is stored in ASCII characters (without parity) in memory locations starting at $XX70_H$.
- ☐ The message specifies the number of characters (excluding the first byte) to be transmitted in the first byte and concludes with the characters for the carriage return and the line feed.
- ☐ Use subroutine SETUP to initialize the 8251A as in Example 15.2.
- ☐ Explain the necessary modifications in the program to receive data into the Z80 system.

15.4.2 RS-232C Signals

In Figure 15.14(a), the addresses of the control port and the data port are $F9_H$ and $F8_H$, respectively; these addresses are from Figure 15.11. The transmit and receive signals are connected to the terminal using the line driver (MC 1488) and the line receiver (MC 1489), as shown in Figure 15.14(a). Line drivers and receivers are integrated circuits designed to interface TTL logic levels with the RS-232C signal levels. They are used primarily in interfacing data terminal equipment (DTE) with data communication equipment (DCE).

Line Driver: MC 1488 This is a quad line driver that converts TTL input levels to a maximum $+15$ V_{DC} output signal. Typically, it is used with ± 12 V power supply. For logic 0 input (< 0.8 V_{DC}) the output is around $+10$ V, and for logic 1 input ($> +2.4$ V_{DC}) the output is around -10 V; thus, the positive true logic is converted into negative true logic for RS-232C signals. The internal circuit of the MC 1488 functions much like a comparator. For an input lower than the threshold voltage, the output approaches positive power supply voltage, and for an input higher than the threshold voltage, the output approaches negative power supply voltage.

Line Receiver: MC 1489 This is a quad line receiver that converts high voltage signals ($+15$ V) into TTL logic levels. Output voltages usually range from 0.2 V (low) to 4.0 V (high). The internal circuit functions as an on/off transistor. When the transistor base has a negative input voltage, the transistor is turned off and the collector voltage (the output of the MC 1489) is high. When the transistor base has a positive input voltage, the transistor is driven into saturation to 0.2 V.

RS-232 Drivers/Receivers: MAX 232 One of the drawbacks of the line driver MC 1488 is that it requires additional voltages ± 12 V from a power supply. Typically, such voltages are unavailable in systems compatible with the TTL logic. This difficulty can be resolved by using a specialized integrated device, MAX 232 (Figure 15.14(b)). It includes drivers and receivers (two each), and it generates ± 10 V internally by using a voltage doubler and inverter circuits. The MAX 232 can replace the 1488 and 1489 and eliminate the need for ± 12 V power supplies.

15.4.3 Program (See Figure 15.15)

PROGRAM DESCRIPTION

According to the problem statement, the first character of the message specifies the number of characters to be transmitted. Therefore, the instruction LD B, (HL) loads the first character (in this case 08_H) into register B and sets that register as counter. The subroutine SETUP (described earlier in Example 15.2) initializes the 8251A for the given specifications.

The next group of instructions, starting with the label STATUS, continues to read the status port and check bit D_0 until it is 1. Bit D_0 indicates the status of

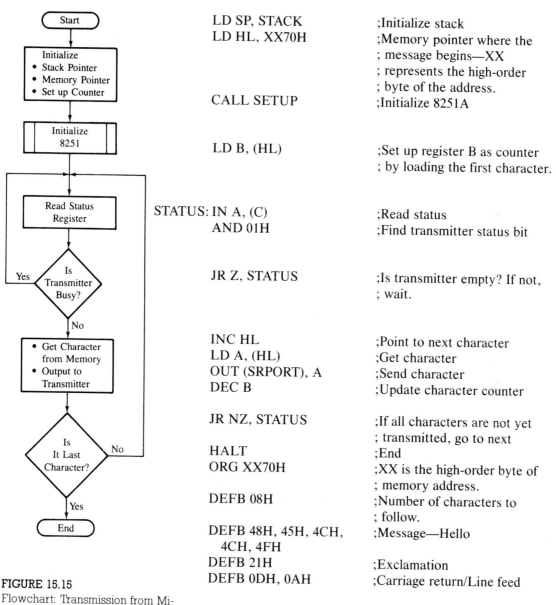

LD SP, STACK	;Initialize stack
LD HL, XX70H	;Memory pointer where the ; message begins—XX ; represents the high-order ; byte of the address.
CALL SETUP	;Initialize 8251A
LD B, (HL)	;Set up register B as counter ; by loading the first character.
STATUS: IN A, (C)	;Read status
AND 01H	;Find transmitter status bit
JR Z, STATUS	;Is transmitter empty? If not, ; wait.
INC HL	;Point to next character
LD A, (HL)	;Get character
OUT (SRPORT), A	;Send character
DEC B	;Update character counter
JR NZ, STATUS	;If all characters are not yet ; transmitted, go to next
HALT	;End
ORG XX70H	;XX is the high-order byte of ; memory address.
DEFB 08H	;Number of characters to ; follow.
DEFB 48H, 45H, 4CH, 4CH, 4FH	;Message—Hello
DEFB 21H	;Exclamation
DEFB 0DH, 0AH	;Carriage return/Line feed

FIGURE 15.15

Flowchart: Transmission from Microcomputer to Terminal

the transmitter; logic 1 indicates that the transmitter buffer is empty and ready for the next character. When bit D_0 goes to logic 1, the program points to the next character, loads it into the accumulator, and sends it to the transmitter. This loop is repeated until the counter B becomes 0, indicating the completion of the message.

15.4.4 Data Reception

To receive data from the terminal, the command word should be modified to enable the receiver section of the 8251A by setting $D_2 = 1$. Thus, to enable only the receiver, the command word is as follows:

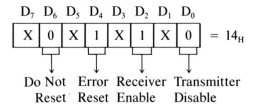

$$D_7 \quad D_6 \quad D_5 \quad D_4 \quad D_3 \quad D_2 \quad D_1 \quad D_0$$

| X | 0 | X | 1 | X | 1 | X | 0 | $= 14_H$ |

Do Not Error Receiver Transmitter
Reset Reset Enable Disable

The program for data reception (Figure 15.16) should begin with reading the status port as in the transmission program and checking bit D_1 for receiver ready, instead of bit D_0 for transmitter ready (Figure 15.13(c)). When a character is placed into the receiver buffer by the terminal, bit D_1 is set to logic 1, and then the program should read the data port for the character.

15.5 SERIAL INPUT/OUTPUT CONTROLLERS: Z80 SIO AND DART

The Z80 **Serial Input/Output Controller (SIO)** is another commonly used programmable device in serial communication. It has two channels (equivalent of two

FIGURE 15.16
Flowchart: Data Reception

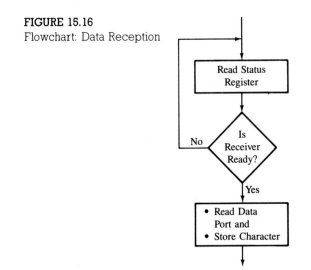

devices), and both channels can be used for asynchronous or synchronous communication. It is functionally similar to the Intel 8251A (section 15.3) but includes two channels and additional features such as CRC error check. It is a versatile device but requires many more programming instructions to set up than does the 8251A. The Z80 **DART (Dual Asynchronous Receiver/Transmitter)** is similar to the SIO, but it is designed to handle only asynchronous serial communication. It also has two channels, and they are identical to the asynchronous sections of the SIO.

In 8-bit microprocessors, serial communication is generally asynchronous; thus, we will focus on applications using the DART or the asynchronous section of the SIO. The SIO can be set up to communicate data in three different ways: program control (status check), interrupt control, and block transfer. In the last section, we illustrated the 8251A under program control; in this section, we focus on interrupt control.

15.5.1 Z80 SIO and DART: Overview

The Z80 SIO is a dual channel interfacing device in a 40-pin package as shown in Figure 15.17(a). The logic pin-out shows seven sections: Channel A and Channel B, modem control for each channel, parallel data bus, control signals for interfacing, and interrupt control.

Channel A and Channel B are two independent channels and can support both asynchronous and synchronous communications. The SIO has a versatile interrupt structure and can be used to set up daisy-chained interrupt priority. The parallel data bus and the control signals are used to interface the device with the Z80, and the modem control signals are used for communication through telephone lines.

The SIO has three versions: **SIO/0, SIO/1,** and **SIO/2.** The internal structure of these versions is identical; however, to provide all the necessary signals for two independent channels, 41 pins are necessary. To accommodate 41 signals in a 40-pin package, one function must be restricted or combined with some other pin. For example, Channel B of the SIO/0 has a common clock for the receiver and the transmitter; thus, the clock frequency for the receiver and the transmitter must be the same.

The DART is designed to support only asynchronous communication; it is functionally and architecturally identical with the asynchronous section of the SIO. Figure 15.17(c) shows the pin-out of the DART. It is pin compatible with the Z80 SIO/0 except for two pins, which can be used for general-purpose inputs or ignored.

Figure 15.18 shows the expanded block diagram of the DART (or the asynchronous section of the SIO) with Channel A only. The Read/Write control section and the data bus are used for interfacing the device with the MPU. The device includes several control and status registers shown as the Control/Status block. The parameters of communications, such as number of bits per character, parity, and transmission rate in relation to the clock have to be specified or programmed. Prior to implementing communication, these control registers must be programmed.

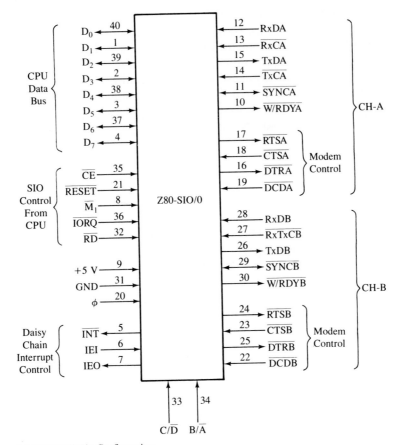

(a) Z80-SIO/0 Pin Configuration

FIGURE 15.17
Z80 SIO/0 and DART Logic and Pin Configurations
SOURCE: Courtesy of Zilog, Inc.

To transmit a byte, the MPU accesses the device through a port address and sends a parallel byte. The control and status circuitry of Channel A frames the byte by adding a Start bit, Stop bits, and a parity bit; places it into the register to transmit data; and then transmits one bit at a time by using the shift register. The baud is determined by the transmitter clock and multiplying factor specified in the control register. To receive data, the process is reversed. In addition, the data go through error logic to check errors. The following sections describe various signals and illustrate the serial communication process.

15.5.2   Read/Write Control Logic and Interfacing

To interface the DART (or the SIO) with the Z80, the signals are as follows:

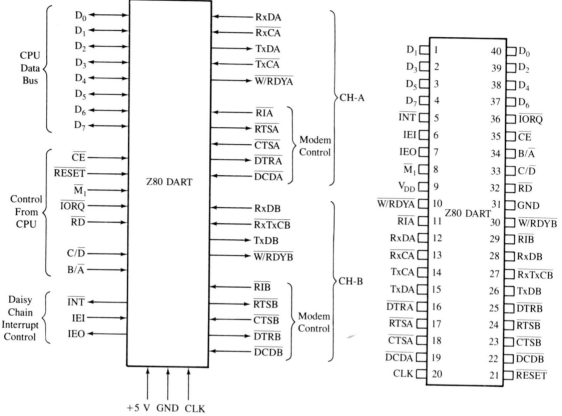

(b) Z80 DART Pin Functions

(c) Pin Assignments

FIGURE 15.17
(continued)

☐ D_0–D_7—Data Bus: This is a tri-state bidirectional data bus that transfers data and commands between the Z80 and the SIO.

☐ B/$\overline{A}$—Channel Select: This signal selects either channel A or channel B for communication. When it is logic 1, channel B is selected, and when it is logic 0, channel A is selected. Address line A_0 from the Z80 is generally connected to this signal.

☐ C/$\overline{D}$—Control or Data: This signal selects either the control register or the data register of the selected channel. When this signal is logic 1, the MPU communicates with the control register either to write a command or read the status. When this signal is logic 0, the MPU either writes a byte in the data register to transmit or reads a byte from the receiver. Address line A_1 from the Z80 is generally connected to this signal.

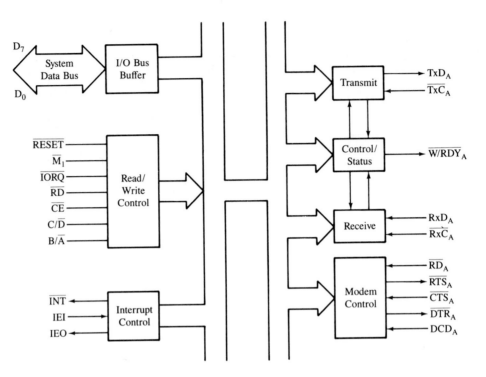

FIGURE 15.18
Z80 DART: Expanded Block Diagram of Channel A

- □ $\overline{CE}$—Chip Enable: When this signal goes low, it indicates that the SIO has been selected for communication. The decoded address bus is usually connected to this signal. The address lines connected to signals $\overline{CE}$, C/$\overline{D}$, and B/$\overline{A}$ determine the port addresses of the control register and the data register. Table 15.5 summarizes the active levels of these signals and the control signals.
- □ φ—System Clock: This is a single phase clock input from the system; it synchronizes the internal operations of the SIO.
- □ $\overline{RESET}$—Reset: This is an active low signal that disables all the SIO operations, including interrupts. After a reset, the control registers must be rewritten to transmit or receive.
- □ $\overline{IORQ}$ (I/O Request), $\overline{M_1}$ (Machine Cycle 1), and $\overline{RD}$ (Read): These are three active low signals that perform Read/Write/Interrupt Acknowledge operations as described below:

    1. *Read.* This operation is performed when $\overline{IORQ}$ and $\overline{RD}$ are active low and $\overline{M_1}$ is high. In this operation, the Z80 either receives a data byte or reads a status from the status register.

TABLE 15.5
Summary of Control Signals and Port Selection of Z80 SIO/DART

IORQ	RD	M₁	CE	C/D	B/A	Function and Port Selection
0	1	1	0	0	0	Z80 Selects Channel A for Data Transmission
			0	0	1	Z80 Selects Channel B for Data Transmission
			0	1	0	Z80 Writes Command in Channel A Control Register
			0	1	1	Z80 Writes Command in Channel B Control Register
0	0	1	0	0	0	Z80 Selects Channel A for Data Reception
			0	0	1	Z80 Selects Channel B for Data Reception
			0	1	0	Z80 Reads Channel A Status Register
			0	1	1	Z80 Reads Channel B Status Register
			1	X	X	SIO Is Not Selected
0	1	0				SIO acknowledges an interrupt and a vector address is placed on the data bus

2. *Write*. This operation is performed when $\overline{IORQ}$ is active low, but $\overline{RD}$ and M_1 are high; the SIO does not have a separate signal for the Write operation. In this operation, the Z80 either writes a command in the control register or transfers a byte for transmission.

3. *Interrupt Acknowledge*. The Z80 acknowledges an interrupt by asserting $\overline{IORQ}$ and $\overline{M_1}$ signals low, and the SIO places its interrupt vector on the data bus.

The control operations, the active level of the associated signals, and port selection are summarized in Table 15.5; Example 15.3 illustrates interfacing of the SIO with the Z80.

Determine the port addresses of the Z80 SIO control registers and data registers shown in Figure 15.19.

Example 15.3

According to Table 15.5, the SIO is selected when the $\overline{CE}$ signal goes low, and the $\overline{CE}$ goes low when the output line 0_0 of the decoder is asserted active low. By combining the logic levels of A_7–A_2 with those of A_1 and A_0, the port addresses range from 40_H to 43_H as shown.

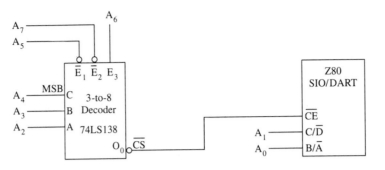

FIGURE 15.19
Interfacing Z80 SIO/DART

A_7	A_6	A_5	A_4	A_3	A_2	A_1	A_0		
						$C/\overline{D}$	$B/\overline{A}$		
0	1	0	0	0	0	0	0	$= 40_H$	Channel A data register
						0	1	$= 41_H$	Channel B data register
						1	0	$= 42_H$	Channel A control register
						1	1	$= 43_H$	Channel B control register

Decoder Enable   Decoder Input

15.5.3 Transmitter and Receiver Sections

When the MPU writes into the channel A data register, the byte is placed into the Transmit Data register of the transmitter section (Figure 15.20). The byte is properly framed by adding Start and Stop bits according to the instructions written into the control register during the initialization of the device. Then the framed byte is transmitted one bit at a time over the TxDA line by use of the shift register. The rate of transmission is determined by the transmitter clock and the scaling factor specified in the control register. The data transmission rate can be specified as 1, 1/16, 1/32, or 1/64 of the clock.

The receiver section has one 8-bit Receive Shift register and three buffer registers (Figure 15.20) arranged in the FIFO (first-in, first-out) format. The shift register receives bits over the RxDA line and converts the bits into a parallel word. This word is placed in the buffer register that can be read by the MPU. Three buffer registers can store three bytes, thus allowing the MPU sufficient time for an interrupt service if needed. The incoming data also go through the error logic section, which also has three registers. Status information associated with each byte and errors such as parity, framing error, and overrun are stored in Receive Error registers. The rate of reception is again determined by the receiver

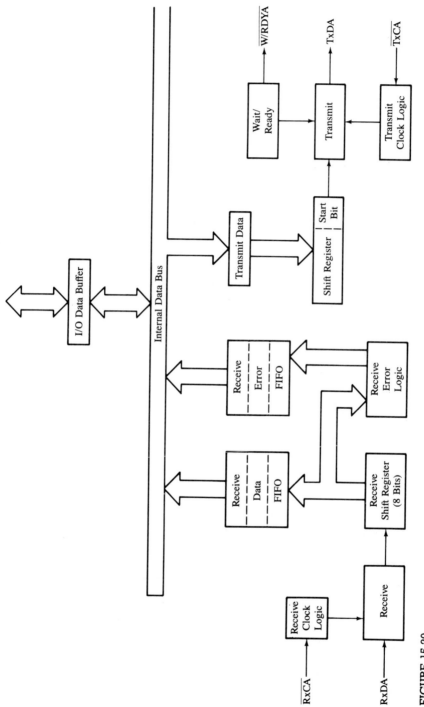

FIGURE 15.20

Z80 DART: Receive and Transmit Internal Block Diagram

SOURCE: Courtesy of Zilog, Inc.

clock and the scaling factor. The line called $\overline{\text{W/RDYA}}$ shown in Figure 15.20 synchronizes the data transfer (described later in more detail).

Although Figure 15.20 shows only the internal structure of Channel A of the DART, the discussion is equally valid for Channel B and the asynchronous section of the SIO. Five signals associated with this section are described below:

□ TxDA—Transmit Data: This is an output signal, and serial bits are transmitted on this line.
□ TxCA—Transmitter Clock: This is an input clock signal, and the clock frequency can be 1, 16, 32, or 64 times the transmission data rate. However, this scaling factor must be the same for both the transmitter and the receiver.
□ RxDA—Receive Data: Bits are received serially on this line.
□ RxCA—Receiver Clock: This is an input clock signal for the receiver, and the clock frequency can be 1, 16, 32, or 64 times the data rate.
□ W/RDYA—Wait/Ready: This is an output signal defined during the initialization of the device and used for two functions. When this line is defined as a Wait function, it has the characteristics of the open drain logic, and it synchronizes the data transfer between the device and the MPU by adding Wait states. When it is defined as a Ready function, it can be driven high or low, and it is used in conjunction with the DMA (Direct Memory Access) controller.

Channel B includes all the above signals except that it has only one clock signal used for both transmission and reception. The SIO has one additional signal called SYNC that is used in the synchronous communication.

15.5.4 Programming the SIO and DART

In the asynchronous format, the SIO and the DART can be set up to handle serial data transfer in three modes: polling, interrupt, and block transfer. However, prior to implementing data transfer, a series of commands must be issued to define various communication parameters such as number of bits in a character, number of Stop bits, and parity. These commands are issued using the **Write Registers** (WR) in the control section. Similarly, to synchronize the communication, the MPU needs to check the readiness of the peripheral, examine error conditions, and obtain information concerning the interrupt vector. The MPU performs these tasks by reading the status from **Read Registers** (RR). The DART has six Write Registers (WR0–WR5), shown in Figure 15.21, which are used to specify the communication parameters. It has three Read Registers (RR0–RR2), shown in Figure 15.22, which are used for status information. The SIO has two additional Write Registers (WR6–WR7) that are used only for synchronous communication. This type of architecture raises the question: How does the MPU write in these six (or eight in the SIO) registers and read three different status registers using one port address of the control register? This dilemma is resolved by using three bits (D_2–D_0) of the WR0 register as a pointer to the remaining registers; thus, each command issued through WR1–WR5 requires two bytes: one to the WR0 register to set up the pointer, and the other to write a command into the specified register.

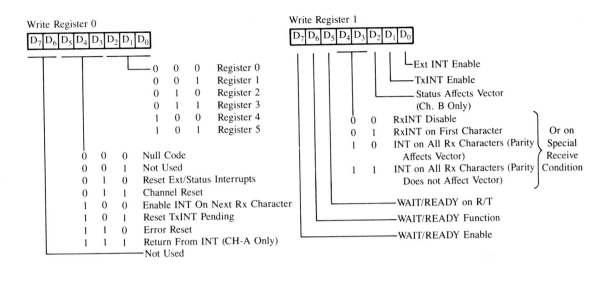

Write Register 0

| D7 | D6 | D5 | D4 | D3 | D2 | D1 | D0 |

0	0	0	Register 0
0	0	1	Register 1
0	1	0	Register 2
0	1	1	Register 3
1	0	0	Register 4
1	0	1	Register 5

0	0	0	Null Code
0	0	1	Not Used
0	1	0	Reset Ext/Status Interrupts
0	1	1	Channel Reset
1	0	0	Enable INT On Next Rx Character
1	0	1	Reset TxINT Pending
1	1	0	Error Reset
1	1	1	Return From INT (CH-A Only)

Not Used

Write Register 1

| D7 | D6 | D5 | D4 | D3 | D2 | D1 | D0 |

Ext INT Enable
TxINT Enable
Status Affects Vector (Ch. B Only)

0	0	RxINT Disable		Or on
0	1	RxINT on First Character		
1	0	INT on All Rx Characters (Parity Affects Vector)	}	Special Receive
1	1	INT on All Rx Characters (Parity Does not Affect Vector)		Condition

WAIT/READY on R/T
WAIT/READY Function
WAIT/READY Enable

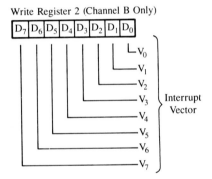

Write Register 2 (Channel B Only)

| D7 | D6 | D5 | D4 | D3 | D2 | D1 | D0 |

V0
V1
V2
V3   } Interrupt
V4   Vector
V5
V6
V7

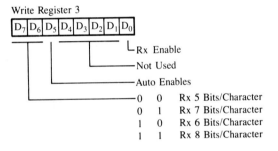

Write Register 3

| D7 | D6 | D5 | D4 | D3 | D2 | D1 | D0 |

Rx Enable
Not Used
Auto Enables

0	0	Rx 5 Bits/Character
0	1	Rx 7 Bits/Character
1	0	Rx 6 Bits/Character
1	1	Rx 8 Bits/Character

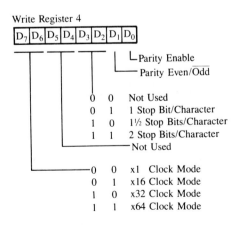

Write Register 4

| D7 | D6 | D5 | D4 | D3 | D2 | D1 | D0 |

Parity Enable
Parity Even/Odd

0	0	Not Used
0	1	1 Stop Bit/Character
1	0	1½ Stop Bits/Character
1	1	2 Stop Bits/Character

Not Used

0	0	x1 Clock Mode
0	1	x16 Clock Mode
1	0	x32 Clock Mode
1	1	x64 Clock Mode

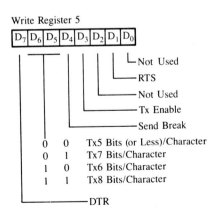

Write Register 5

| D7 | D6 | D5 | D4 | D3 | D2 | D1 | D0 |

Not Used
RTS
Not Used
Tx Enable
Send Break

0	0	Tx5 Bits (or Less)/Character
0	1	Tx7 Bits/Character
1	0	Tx6 Bits/Character
1	1	Tx8 Bits/Character

DTR

FIGURE 15.21
Z80 DART: Write Registers
SOURCE: Courtesy of Zilog, Inc.

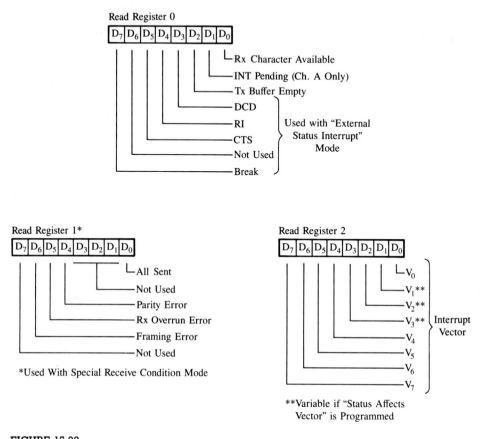

FIGURE 15.22
Z80 DART: Read Registers
SOURCE: Courtesy of Zilog, Inc.

The Read and Write operations are differentiated by the Read and Write control signals of the MPU.

Both channels A and B have identical architecture, except that register WR2 is included only in Channel B. When the device is set up to handle the interrupt mode, register WR2 is used to specify the low-order address of the interrupt vector, and this address can be used by both channels. Figure 15.21 shows bit definitions for Write Registers and Figure 15.22 shows the bit definitions of the Read (status) Registers. The functions of the Write Registers are briefly described here and illustrated in Examples 15.4 and 15.5. The Read (status) Registers are explained later.

WRITE REGISTERS

□ WR0 (Write Register 0): This is a special register; bits D_0–D_2 are used as pointers to the remaining registers and bits D_3–D_5 are used to issue initialization commands. Bits D_7–D_6 should be 00; they are used in Synchronous communication only.

☐ WR1 (Write Register 1): The bits in this register define various interrupt and Wait/Ready modes.

☐ WR2 (Write Register 2—Channel B only): This register is used to store the low-order address of the interrupt vector, and it can be used by the interrupts in both channels. The vector is automatically modified based on the status of bit D_2 in register WR1.

☐ WR3 (Write Register 3): The bits in this register define receiver parameters and enable the receiver.

☐ WR4 (Write Register 4): This register contains bits that define communication parameters such as Stop bits, parity, and baud multiplying factor.

☐ WR5 (Write Register 5): The bits in this register define transmitter parameters and enable the transmitter.

☐ WR6–WR7 (Write Registers 6–7): These registers are included in the SIO only and used for synchronous communication.

Draw a flowchart and give bit definitions to initialize the Z80 SIO or DART to meet the following specifications:

Example 15.4

1. Asynchronous transmission/receiver format without interrupts.
2. 7-bit character, two Stop bits, no parity, frequency multiplying factor = 16.

To initialize the SIO in the asynchronous mode, register WR0 is used to reset the device and as a pointer to other registers. The steps are as follows:

Solution

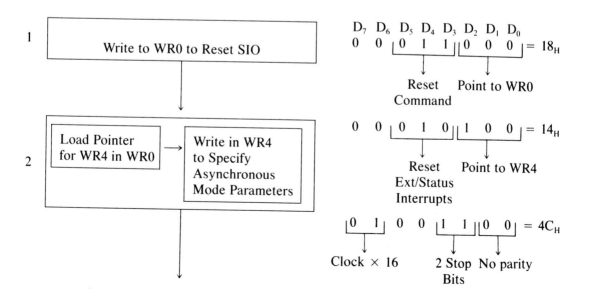

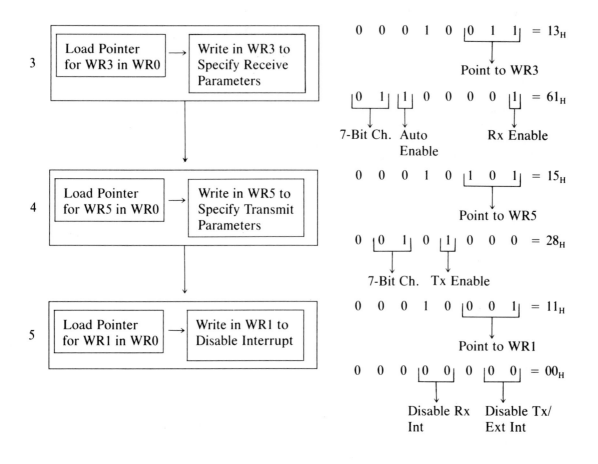

Example 15.5

Write a subroutine to initialize Channel A of the DART shown in Figure 15.19 to meet the specifications of Example 15.4.

Solution

As shown in Example 15.3, the Channel A control port address is 42_H. Referring to bit definitions in Example 15.4, we can write the instructions using register C as follows. However, the coding can be substantially reduced by using the instruction OTIR (see Assignment **29**).

```
DATAA     EQU 40H          ;Channel A data port address
CNTRLA    EQU 42H          ;Channel A control port address
DART:     LD C, CNTRLA     ;Load control port address into register C
          LD A, 18H        ;Reset byte
          OUT (C), A       ;Reset Channel A
          LD A, 14H        ;Pointer for WR4
          OUT (C), A
```

```
LD A, 4CH        ;Bit definitions for asynchronous communication
OUT (C), A       ;Specify parity, stop bits, clock multiplier
LD A, 13H        ;Pointer to WR3
OUT (C), A
LD A, 61H        ;Bit definitions for receiver
OUT (C), A       ;Enable receiver to receive 7-bit character
LD A, 15H        ;Point to WR5
OUT (C), A
LD A, 28H        ;Bit definition for transmitter
OUT (C), A       ;Enable transmitter to transmit 7-bit character
LD A, 11H        ;Point to WR1
OUT (C), A
LD A, 00H        ;Byte to disable interrupts
OUT (C), A       ;Disable interrupts
RET              ;Initialization complete
```

READ REGISTERS

The SIO (DART) has three registers (RR0, RR1, and RR2) that can be read by the MPU to obtain receiver/transmitter status information. Registers RR0 and RR1 are included in both channels; however, register RR2 is only in Channel B. The RR0 register can be read directly by accessing the control port; however, the remaining two registers have to be read by using the pointer bits in Write register WR0. Figure 15.22 shows bit definitions of the Read Registers. These registers are briefly described here and illustrated in the following examples.

☐ RR0 (Read Register 0): This register provides the status information of the receiver, transmitter, and the interrupts. Bit D_0 is set when a character is received, and bit D_2 is set when the transmitter buffer is empty.

☐ RR1 (Read Register 1): This register monitors errors in receiving data; bits in this register identify various types of the errors, such as parity, framing, and overrun. To read the information from this register, the pointer must be written in register WR0.

☐ RR2 (Read Register 2—Channel B only): The interrupt vector written in register WR2 of Channel B is available through this register for interrupts in both channels. If bit D_2 of Write Register WR1 is set, the vector address can be modified according to the interrupting source, and the modified address is returned to the MPU when the interrupt is acknowledged.

Assuming Channel A of the SIO or DART is initialized for asynchronous serial I/O with the polled mode, write a subroutine to receive a character and check for errors. The character should be stored in memory location INBUF, and if there are any errors, the contents of the status register RR1 should be stored in memory location ERRCHK.

Example 15.6

Solution   The availability of a character is indicated by bit D_0 in RR0. Therefore, in the polled mode, the program should continue to check bit D_0 until it is set.

```
READ:       IN A, (CNTRLA)        ;Read status register RR0
            BIT 0, A              ;Check bit D0
            JR Z, READ            ;Wait until character is available
            IN A, (PORTA)         ;Read character
            LD (INBUF), A         ;Store character
CHECK:      LD A, 01H             ;Load pointer for RR1
            OUT (CNTRLA), A       ;Select status register RR1
            IN A, (CNTRLA)        ;Read error flags in register RR1
            AND 01110000B         ;Mask all bits except D6, D5, D4
                                  ;These are error flags (refer to Figure
                                  ; 15.22)
            LD (ERRCHK), A        ;Store error status
            RET Z                 ;No errors
RESET:      LD A, 30H             ;Reset command
            OUT (CNTRLA), A       ;Read all error flags
            RET
```

Description   The first instruction (IN) of this subroutine places the contents of the status register RR0 in the accumulator by reading the control port of Channel A. To read register RR0 does not require a pointer in WR0. Bit D_0 of the register RR0 indicates the availability of a character. Thus, the routine continues to check bit D_0 until it is set. Once a character is available, it is stored in memory location INBUF.

If there are errors in the received character, bits D_6 (framing), D_5 (overrun), and D_4 (parity) of register RR1 are set. However, to read register RR1, the pointer needs to be loaded into Write Register WR0. The subroutine reads RR1, logically ANDs its contents with 01110000, and saves the result for further action in location ERRCHK. If there are no errors, error bits (D_6, D_5, and D_4) are reset, the Z flag of the Z80 is set, and the program returns on the Z flag. If there are errors, the error bits are reset by sending the reset instruction to the control port.

Example 15.7   Assuming the SIO (DART) Channel A is initialized for the polled I/O, write a subroutine to send a character stored in memory location OUTBUF.

Solution   The status of the transmitter section is indicated by bit D_2 in register RR0. Therefore, the subroutine should continue to check bit D_2 in RR0 until it is set, at which time it should transmit the character.

```
            TRNSMT
STATUS:     IN A, (CNTRLA)        ;Read register RR0
            BIT 2, A              ;Check transmitter buffer if it is empty
            JR Z, STATUS          ;Wait until buffer is empty
```

```
LD A, (OUTBUF)      ;Get character from memory
OUT (PORTA), A      ;Send the character
RET
```

15.5.5 SIO (DART) in the Interrupt Mode

The SIO has a powerful interrupt scheme that can respond quickly to various sources of interrupts. In the previous examples of data transmission and reception in the polled mode, we have seen that the MPU is kept occupied continuously in polling, even if there is no character to transmit or receive. In the interrupt mode, the SIO will interrupt the MPU only on a need basis—such as when it has received a character, when the transmitter is empty, or under some special error conditions. The MPU is thus free to perform other functions.

Figure 15.23 shows three sources of interrupts: transmit, receive, and external status. In transmission, when the buffer becomes empty and the SIO is ready for the next character, an interrupt is generated. The external status interrupt is generated whenever there is a transition in status lines and when transmission conditions such as Transmit Underrun and Break occur.

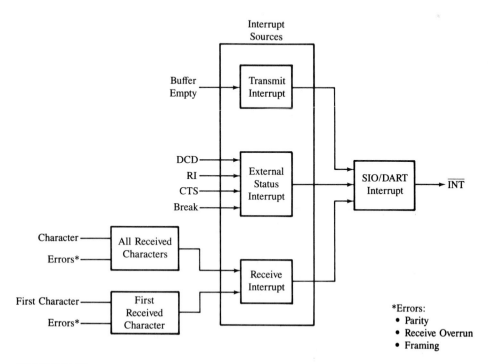

FIGURE 15.23
Z80 DART: Interrupt Structure

The receive interrupt is somewhat complex in that it has two categories: one for the first character received and the second for every character received. The second category is similar to the transmit interrupt; whenever a character is received, an interrupt is generated. The first category is used primarily for the block transfer. In this case, when the first character arrives, an interrupt is generated, and then no other interrupt is generated until the block transfer is completed or a higher priority source requests a service. The receive interrupt can also be generated when errors occur. Once an interrupt is generated, it is necessary to identify the source of the interrupt. Two procedures can be used: polling and modifying the interrupt vector. For both methods, an interrupt vector must be loaded into register WR2 in Channel B during the initialization. In the polling method, once an interrupt is acknowledged, the program control will be transferred to the vector location. Then the service routine will identify the source of the interrupt by checking the status registers RR0 and RR1. In the other method, the interrupt vector in register WR2 is modified according to the interrupting source, and eight different addresses can be generated, as shown in Table 15.6. The vectors shown in Table 15.6 are arranged according to their interrupt priorities, starting with the lowest priority 0; Channel B has lower priority than Channel A, and within each channel the interrupt generated by the receive errors (Special Receive Condition) has the highest priority. This is further illustrated in Example 15.8.

The Z80 SIO (DART) has three signals to handle the interrupts: one to generate an interrupt and the other two to set the priorities among various devices using the daisy chain scheme. The signals are as follows:

- $\overline{INT}$—Interrupt Request: This is an open drain active low signal, and it is generated to acknowledge the conditions previously discussed.

- IEI—Interrupt Enable In and IEO—Interrupt Enable Out: These signals are used to determine the priorities among devices in the system when multiple devices are connected in the interrupt driven mode. The functions of these

TABLE 15.6
Interrupt Vectors

	Type of Interrupt	D_7	D_6	D_5	D_4	D_3	D_2	D_1	D_0	Hex	Priority
Channel B:	External/Status Transition	0	0	0	0	0	0	1	0	= 02	0
	Transmitter Buffer Empty	0	0	0	0	0	0	0	0	= 00	1
	Received Character	0	0	0	0	0	1	0	0	= 04	2
	Special Receive Condition	0	0	0	0	0	1	1	0	= 06	3
Channel A:	External/Status Transition	0	0	0	0	1	0	1	0	= 0A	4
	Transmitter Buffer Empty	0	0	0	0	1	0	0	0	= 08	5
	Received Character	0	0	0	0	1	1	0	0	= 0C	6
	Special Receive Condition	0	0	0	0	1	1	1	0	= 0E	7

signals are identical to those of IEI and IEO signals in the Z80 PIO and CTC
described in the previous chapters.

Add the necessary instructions in the initialization subroutine SETUP in Example
15.4 to include the interrupt mode with the interrupt vector at 80_H. The vector
should be modified according to the interrupting source. Assuming the interrupt
register in the Z80 contains the address 20_H, specify the vector addresses for the
transmit interrupt in Channel A and the interrupt due to the parity error (refer to
Table 15.6).

**Example
15.8**

Referring to the subroutine DART in Example 15.4, we find that three commands
must be added to initialize the DART in the interrupt mode: one command in WR2
to specify the vector 80_H (Channel B), the second command to turn on bit D_2 in
WR1 (Channel B) to enable modification of the interrupt vector, and the third
command in WR1 to enable the interrupts. The second command is additional
here because we are using only Channel A, and the third command replaces the
last disable command in the previous routine. To load these commands, the register WR0 must be used as a pointer. The instructions are as follows:

Solution

```
LD A, 12H           ;Pointer to WR2
OUT (CNTRLB), A     ;Set up pointer to WR2
LD A, 80H           ;Low-order vector address
OUT (CNTRLB), A     ;Load vector into register WR2—Channel B
LD A, 11H           ;Point to WR1
OUT (CNTRLB), A
LD A, 04H           ;Bit D₂ = 1 (status affects vector)
OUT (CNTRLB), A     ;Set bit D₂ in Channel B
LD A, 12H           ;Byte to enable Tx, Rx (every received
                    ; character) and parity error interrupt
OUT (C), A          ;Enable interrupts
RET                 ;Initialization complete
```

By referring to Table 15.5 and using 20_H as the high-order address of the interrupt
vector, we can identify the memory locations where the pointers are stored for
various interrupts.

		D_3	D_2	D_1	
1. Transmitter Buffer Empty	1 0 0 0	1	0	0	0 = 20 88_H
2. Character Received	1 0 0 0	1	1	0	0 = 20 8C_H
3. Parity Error	1 0 0 0	1	1	1	0 = 20 8E_H

These vectors are situated two memory locations apart ($208A_H$ is not included in this problem); thus can 16-bit addresses of various service routines be
stored.

15.6 ILLUSTRATION: INTERFACING AN RS-232 TERMINAL USING DART (SIO) IN THE INTERRUPT MODE

The DART requirements for the interrupt-driven serial I/O have been discussed in the previous sections. Examples 15.6 and 15.7 illustrated how to receive and transmit a character using the polled mode, and Example 15.8 illustrated how to initialize the SIO for the interrupt mode. We will now use these concepts to interface an RS-232 terminal to a Z80 system using the DART in the interrupt mode.

The microprocessor views the ASCII terminal as two different peripherals: the keyboard as an input and the CRT as an output display. When a key is pressed, the DART receives a serial stream of bits that can be read by the microprocessor. However, to display that character on the screen, the same byte should be sent out as an output to the screen; these are two distinct processes. The following illustration shows how ASCII characters are received and displayed on the screen.

15.6.1 Problem Statement

1. Interface an ASCII terminal with the Z80 system using the DART in the interrupt mode. Use the same decoding logic as in Example 15.3 to assign port addresses 40_H to the Channel A data port and 42_H to the Channel A control port.
2. Initialize the DART for the interrupt mode to meet the following specifications: (a) asynchronous format, (b) seven-bit character with even parity, (c) transmit and receive frequency = 16 times baud, (d) interrupts should be generated on Rx (All Received Characters), Tx, and parity error.
3. Write a service routine to receive a character when a key is pressed.
4. Write a service routine to transmit (echo) the received character to the CRT screen.

15.6.2 Problem Analysis

1. Figure 15.24 shows the interfacing circuit using the DART in the interrupt mode. The decoding logic is the same as in Example 15.3 with Channel A port addresses PORTA = 40_H and CNTRLA = 42_H. In addition, $\overline{INT}$ of the DART is connected to the $\overline{INT}$ signal of the Z80, and the IEI line of the DART is tied high with the assumption there are no other devices in the system.
2. The specifications are the same as in Example 15.8, with the interrupt vector at location 80_H.
3. Main Program: This program is quite simple; it involves initializing the stack and the high-order interrupt vector and calling the initialization subroutine SETUP. To illustrate how characters are received or transmitted in the interrupt-driven mode, the program should have an endless loop. In a real-life example, the MPU would be free to perform other tasks.

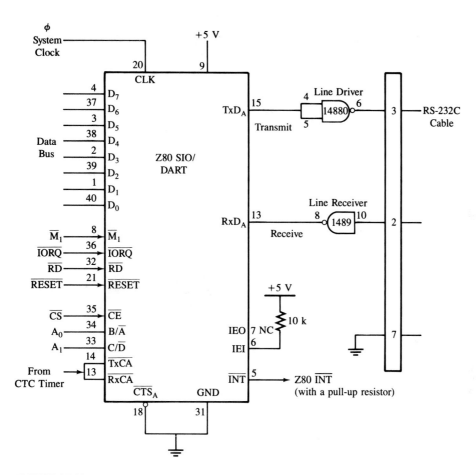

FIGURE 15.24

Interfacing an RS-232C Terminal with a Z80 System Using the DART in the Interrupt
Mode

PORTA	EQU 40H	;Channel A: data port address
CNTRLA	EQU 42H	;Channel A: control port address
STACK	EQU 2100H	;Stack address
SIO:	LD SP, STACK	;Initialize the stack
	IM 2	;Set up Z80 in interrupt Mode 2
	LD A, 20H	;High-order interrupt vector
	LD (I), A	;Load vector into interrupt register
	CALL SETUP	;Initialize DART as in Example 15.8
WAIT:	JR WAIT	;Wait here until an interrupt occurs

4. The following service routine receives a character when the receive interrupt occurs and transmits the same character to the CRT by checking the status of bit D_2 in register RR0.

```
ECHO:     EX AF, AF'        ;Save accumulator and flags
          PUSH BC           ;Save contents of BC
          LD C, PORTA       ;Load PORTA address into
                            ; register C
          IN B, (C)         ;Read received character in
                            ; register B
STATUS:   IN A, (CNTRLA)    ;Read status register RRO
          BIT 2, A          ;Is transmitter buffer empty?
          JR Z, STATUS      ;Wait until transmitter is ready
          OUT (C), B        ;Send character to CRT
          EX AF, AF'        ;Retrieve register contents
          POP BC
          EI                ;Enable interrupts
          RETI
```

SUMMARY

In this chapter, we discussed the technique of serial I/O for data communication, whereby one bit is transferred over one line rather than using eight data lines to transfer a byte. The serial I/O technique is necessary for certain types of equipment and media such as magnetic tapes and telephone lines. The rate of data transfer in serial I/O is determined by the time delay between two successive bits. Therefore, a host of issues such as error check and synchronization of data transfer between the transmitter and the receiver need to be resolved. The serial I/O data transfer can be implemented using software techniques; however, programmable devices called USART (Universal Synchronous/Asynchronous Receiver/Transmitter) are commonly used in industrial and commercial products. Two such devices, the Intel 8251A and the Z80 SIO (DART), are discussed with illustrations in this chapter. The basic concepts involved in serial I/O can be summarized as follows:

1. In serial I/O communication, a word is transmitted one bit at a time over a single line by converting a parallel word into a stream of serial bits. On the other hand, a word is received by converting a stream of bits into a parallel word.
2. Serial data communication can be either synchronous or asynchronous. The synchronous mode is used for high-speed and the asynchronous mode for low-speed data communications.

3. The MPU identifies a serial peripheral through a decoded address and an appropriate control signal. Data transfer can be implemented using such methods as polling (status check) and interrupt.

4. In software-controlled serial transmission, the MPU converts a parallel word into serial bits by using time delays and transmits one bit at a time over one data line of an output port.

5. In software-controlled serial reception, the MPU converts a serial word into a parallel word by using time delays and receives bits over one data line.

6. The Intel 8251A is a programmable serial I/O device known as a USART, which can perform all the functions of software techniques and is commonly used in synchronous and asynchronous data communication.

7. The Z80 SIO (Serial Input/Output Controller) and DART (Dual Asynchronous Receiver/Transmitter) are also commonly used in serial I/O communication.

DEFINITION OF TERMS

□ **ASCII** (American Standard Code for Information Interchange). A 7-bit alphanumeric code commonly used in computers.

□ **EBCDIC** (Extended Binary Coded Decimal Interchange Code). An 8-bit alphanumeric code used primarily in IBM large computers.

□ **Asynchronous Serial Data Transmission.** In this format, the transmitter is not synchronized with the receiver by the same master clock. A transmitted character includes information concerning the starting and ending of the character.

□ **Synchronous Serial Data Transmission.** In this format, the transmitter is synchronized with the receiver by a common clock.

□ **Simplex Transmission.** One-way data communication.

□ **Duplex Transmission.** Two-way data communication. Full duplex is simultaneous in both directions, and half duplex is one direction at a time.

□ **Baud** (Rate). The number of signal changes per second. In serial I/O, it is equal to bits per second, the rate of data transmission.

□ **Current Loop.** The transmission of serial data bits as current signals.

□ **RS-232C.** A data communications standard that defines voltage signals in reference to data terminal equipment and data communication equipment.

□ **RS-422A and -423A.** Data communication standards for high-speed data transmission.

□ **USART** (Universal Synchronous/Asynchronous Receiver/Transmitter). A programmable chip designed for synchronous/asynchronous serial data communication.

ASSIGNMENTS

1. Explain the difference between asynchronous and synchronous data transmission.
2. Explain the terms *odd* and *even parity.*
3. Calculate the bit time for 9,600 baud.
4. Sketch the serial output waveform for the ASCII character "A" when it is transmitted with 9,600 baud and even parity.
5. What is the Hex code necessary to transmit the ASCII character "H" with odd parity?
6. Sketch the serial output waveform for the ASCII sign " + " when it is transmitted with 2,400 baud and odd parity.
7. Explain the RS-232C serial I/O standard and specify the signals used in the minimum configuration.
8. Is a microcomputer connected as a DTE or DCE in the RS-232C standard serial I/O communication?
9. Show the RS-232C cable connections in the minimum configuration when a microcomputer and a printer are connected as DCEs.
10. In Figure 15.11, specify the control port and data port addresses if the address lines A_7 and A_0 are interchanged.
11. In Example 15.2 (Figure 15.11), change the mode word from CA_H to CB_H, and calculate the clock frequency for 1,200 baud.
12. In Example 15.2, change the mode word to meet the following specifications: 8-bit character, even parity, 1½ Stop bits, and 2,400 baud ($\overline{TxC} = 153.6$ kHz).
13. In Example 15.2, explain the consequences if the command word to enable the transmitter is changed to 51_H.
14. Write a program to transmit letters A to Z from the MPU to the terminal in Figure 15.14.
15. Write a subroutine to accept a letter from the CRT terminal (Figure 15.14).
16. In Figure 15.14, specify the command word to transmit and to receive characters.
17. Write a subroutine to check and identify an error in the received character by reading the status register (Figure 15.14).
18. In Figure 15.25, identify the addresses of the control and data ports (assume all "don't care" lines are at logic 0).
19. In Figure 15.25, if the following instructions are executed and the program is transferred to location CHECK, explain the possible reasons for such a transfer.

```
LD A, (8001H)      ;Read status register
AND 00111000B
JP NZ, CHECK
```

FIGURE 15.25
Schematic for Assignments 18–21

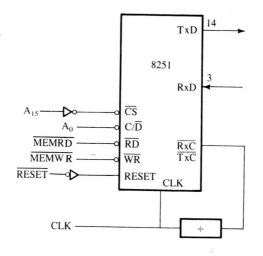

20. Write instructions to check a parity error when a character is received (Figure 15.25). If an error occurs, write a command word to disable the receiver, reset the error, and call the Error routine.

21. Specify the mode word and the command word for data communication having the following specifications (Figure 15.25): (a) asynchronous mode, (b) 1,200 baud (TxC = RxC = 76.8 kHz), (c) 8-bit character, (d) even parity, (e) 2 Stop bits.

22. Write an interrupt service routine to receive a character from the terminal and store the character in memory location INBUF.

23. How does the MPU write into the Z80 SIO without the WR signal pin on the SIO?

24. Specify the logic levels of the SIO control signals when the Z80 acknowledges an interrupt.

25. In Figure 15.19, identify the addresses of the control and the data ports if the address lines A_7 and A_0 are interchanged.

26. Write initialization instructions for the Z80 SIO to meet the following specifications: (a) asynchronous format to receive characters under program control, (b) 8-bit character with 2 Stop bits and even parity, (c) frequency multiplying factor 64.

27. Modify the instructions in the previous assignment to include the interrupt control and the low-order interrupt vector at 50_H that can be modified if an error occurs.

28. In assignment 27, specify the 16-bit address of the interrupt vector if the parity error occurs in Channel B and the Interrupt Register I contains 24_H.

29. Rewrite the initialization instructions in Example 15.5 using the instruction OTIR.

Advanced Topics in Memory and DMA Concepts

In Chapter 4, we discussed memory interfacing; however, to maintain clarity in our discussion, we avoided the details of memory access time and its effect on interfacing. Similarly, we did not discuss the need for Wait states in interfacing slow memory devices (peripherals) or the implementation of high-speed data transfer by giving control of system buses to external peripherals. We introduced the topic of dynamic memory, but we did not discuss its interfacing. In this chapter, we discuss these timing-related topics and how they affect interfacing and design processes.

We will begin by examining the memory access time in the context of the microprocessor execution time and determining the need for Wait states in interfacing slow memory devices. We will discuss the structure and the requirements of dynamic memory and illustrate the interfacing of a dynamic memory chip. Then we will examine the same memory-related topics from a design point of view and illustrate a

memory design using industrial practices. The chapter concludes with the discussion of high-speed data transfer using the Direct Memory Access (DMA) technique.

OBJECTIVES

□ Define memory access time and explain how it relates to the microprocessor machine cycles.

□ Determine the need for Wait states in interfacing slow memory devices and explain how to generate Wait states.

□ Explain the internal structure, interfacing requirements, and the need for refreshing dynamic memory.

□ Illustrate the interfacing of a 16K dynamic memory chip with the Z80.

□ Explain the need for data transfer using the Direct Memory Access technique and the functions of BUSRQ (Bus Request) and BUSAK (Bus Acknowledgment) signals of the Z80.

□ Explain the differences among the three modes of DMA data transfer: byte, burst, and continuous.

□ Explain the block diagram of the Z80 DMA controller and its interfacing with the Z80.

□ Explain the Bank Switching technique to extend memory addressing.

16.1 INTERFACING MEMORY USING WAIT STATES

In interfacing memory with the microprocessor, the interfacing circuit must satisfy the timing requirements of both the microprocessor and the memory chip. In Chapter 4, we assumed that memory response can match the execution speed of the microprocessor, but this assumption is invalid in some situations. Because of cost considerations, memory chips with slow response time are occasionally used in microprocessor-based systems. Therefore, it is necessary to synchronize the execution speed of the microprocessor with the response time of memory. This can be accomplished by using the Wait signal input to the Z80 microprocessor.

□ $\overline{\text{WAIT}}$ (Wait)—This is an active low signal, input to the Z80 as an external request from a slow peripheral (or memory), to indicate that the peripheral is not yet ready for data transfer. The Z80 samples the WAIT line at the falling edge of T_2 of each machine cycle, and if the WAIT line is low, it adds one T-state (T_W) as a Wait state to its machine cycle. Then it samples the T_W state and adds an additional Wait state if the WAIT signal is still low and continues to add Wait states until the WAIT signal goes high. During this time, the Z80 extends the time of control signals and preserves the contents of all the buses. Thus, the WAIT signal can be used to synchronize the response time of any type of peripheral.

To ascertain whether a given memory chip is too slow in comparison with the execution speed of the microprocessor and needs Wait states to synchronize the data transfer, we must examine the timing requirements of the microprocessor and the response time of the memory.

16.1.1 Z80 Machine Cycles and Memory Access Time

In Chapter 3, we examined three Z80 machine cycles: Opcode Fetch, Memory Read, and Memory Write. The Opcode Fetch machine cycle is shown here again in Figure 16.1 with precise timing for the Z80 with a 2.5 MHz clock. The read

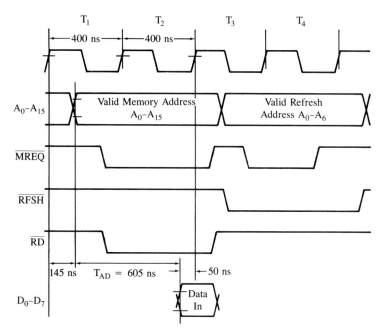

FIGURE 16.1
Z80 Opcode Fetch Machine Cycle
SOURCE: Adapted from *Memory Data Book and Designer's Guide*, p. x-40; courtesy of Mostek Corporation.

timing of the Opcode Fetch is the most restrictive because the microprocessor begins to read the data byte at the rising edge of T_3; in the Memory Read cycle, it reads the byte at the falling edge of T_3. If the memory chip can respond adequately in the Opcode Fetch cycle, we need not be concerned with the Memory Read cycle.

Figure 16.1 shows the time interval T_{AD}; this is the interval between the time the Z80 places the address on the address bus and the time it has to read the byte. In a 2.5 MHz system (400 ns clock period), the T_{AD} is 605 ns. This is calculated by subtracting the output address delay $T_{D(AD)}$ and the data set-up time T_{SD} on the data bus from the two clock periods (see Figure 16.1).

Allowable time interval for Z80 to read data after placing the address on the address bus	= 2 × Clock Period	— Address Delay — Data Set-Up Time

$$T_{AD} = (2 \times T) - T_{D(AD)} - T_{SD} \qquad \textbf{(Eq. 16.1)}$$
$$= 2 \times 400 \text{ ns} - 145 \text{ ns} - 50 \text{ ns}$$
$$= 605 \text{ ns*}$$

---

*These specifications are obtained from Z80 AC characteristics.

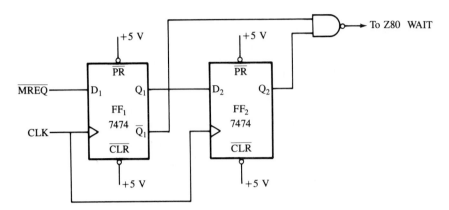

FIGURE 16.2
Generating One Wait State

The memory response is defined in terms of the memory access time T_{AC}; this is the delay between the time the memory address is placed on the address bus and the data byte is placed on the data bus. The memory access time plus the delay in the address decoding network must be less than T_{AD}; if it is more than T_{AD}, we must add Wait states.

16.1.2 Generating Wait States

In the definition of the WAIT signal, the only requirement to add Wait states is to keep the WAIT signal low when the Z80 samples it during the T_2 state. Figure 16.1 shows that the Memory Request ($\overline{MREQ}$) goes active after the falling edge of T_1. The $\overline{MREQ}$ signal can be used, after the delay of one clock period, to activate the WAIT signal, as shown in Figure 16.2.

Figure 16.2 shows that a WAIT signal can be generated by ANDing the outputs of the two edge-triggered flip-flops and using the $\overline{MREQ}$ as an input to the flip-flop FF_1. The $\overline{MREQ}$ stays high unless the microprocessor is accessing memory; therefore, we can safely assume that Q_2, the output of FF_2, is initially high. The $\overline{MREQ}$ goes low after the falling edge of T1 (Figure 16.1); thus, Q1 goes high in the next clock period at the rising edge of T_2 (the flip-flop is positive-edge-triggered) and generates the Wait signal, which should be connected to the WAIT pin of the Z80. Because $\overline{WAIT}$ is low at T_2, the Z80 extends the machine cycle by one clock period, T_W. At the next cycle, Q_2 goes low (Q_1 was low in the previous cycle), causing the WAIT signal to go inactive. The circuit shown in Figure 16.2 adds one Wait state to all memory access cycles in the system. To use the Wait state for a particular memory chip in the system, the input $\overline{MREQ}$ should be ANDed with the decoded address of the chip as shown in the next example.

**Example
16.1**   Figure 16.3 shows an interfacing circuit of the 2732 EPROM with a 4 MHz Z80A system; the circuit includes a Wait state circuit. The Z80A address delay is 110 ns

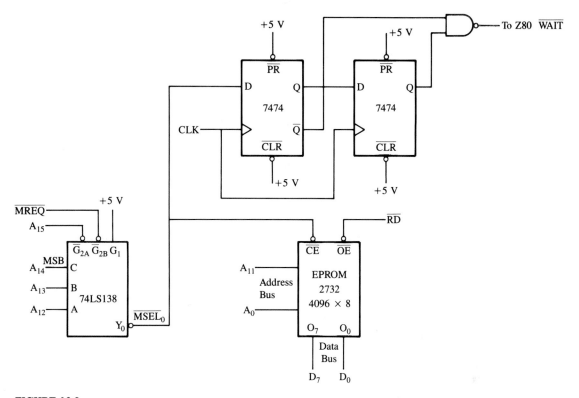

FIGURE 16.3
Interfacing EPROM 2732 with a Wait State

and data set-up time is 35 ns. The memory access time for the EPROM is given as 450 ns, and the delay in the decoder is 40 ns. Explain the timing, and calculate the number of Wait states required.

In this system, the clock period is 250 ns. In the Opcode Fetch cycle, the Z80 reads the data byte at the rising edge of the T_2 cycle. Therefore, the allowable microprocessor read time is (see Eq. 16.1)

Solution

$$T_{AD} = 2 \times 250 \text{ ns} - 110 \text{ ns} - 35 \text{ ns} = 355 \text{ ns}$$

The EPROM would require

$$\text{Memory Read Time} = \text{Memory Access Time} + \text{Address Decoding Delay}$$
$$= 450 \text{ ns} + 40 \text{ ns} = 490 \text{ ns}$$

These calculations show that the memory requires 490 ns and that the microprocessor, without the Wait states, would begin to read in 355 ns after placing the address on the bus. After adding one Wait state, the microprocessor read time is extended to 605 ns (355 ns + 250 ns). This leaves 115 ns (605 ns − 490 ns) as a safety margin for the memory read time.

      The interfacing circuit shown in Figure 16.3 is a combination of two circuits: Generating one Wait state (Figure 16.2) and the memory interfacing circuit. However, in this circuit, the input to the flip-flop of the Generating Wait State circuit is modified; the input is the gated signal of the $\overline{MREQ}$ and the decoded address from the 3-to-8 decoder. Thus, whenever the Z80 accesses the EPROM, this circuit will add one Wait state to the memory machine cycles without affecting the performance of other memory chips in the system.

16.2   INTERFACING DYNAMIC MEMORY

The dynamic Read/Write memory stores bit information in the form of a capacitive charge, and its internal structure differs from that of static memory. It is organized in the square matrix format of rows and columns, and its address lines are multiplexed. Therefore, to interface dynamic memory with the microprocessor, additional circuitry must be designed to address rows and columns separately. Furthermore, each memory cell needs to be refreshed at least every two milliseconds to retain the stored information. The circuitry necessary for refreshing the dynamic memory is built-in Z80 architecture; in other microprocessors, the refreshing is performed by external logic or LSI devices such as a Dynamic Memory Controller.

      In the following sections, we will examine the internal structure of dynamic memory and its timing requirements, and design an interfacing circuit.

16.2.1   Dynamic Memory: Structure and Addressing

The dynamic memory consists of MOS transistors, which store information as capacitive charge and are internally arranged in the matrix format. Figure 16.4(a) shows four such cells with two rows and two columns. Figure 16.4(b) shows the representation of 16 cells with four rows and four columns with 2-to-4 decoders and latches. Thus, two input lines R_1 and R_2 can identify four rows when strobe line $\overline{RAS}$ (Row Address Strobe) is active, and two lines C_1 and C_2 can identify four columns when the strobe line $\overline{CAS}$ (Column Address Strobe) is active. The lines R1, R2, C1, and C2 are connected together, and in turn connected to two address lines A_1 and A_0. Thus, with two address lines and two strobe lines, we can select any of the cells. For example, by sending address 11 and asserting the $\overline{RAS}$ line, the address 11 will be latched and row 3 will be selected, and if we follow that by sending the address 01 and asserting the $\overline{CAS}$ line, we select column 1. Therefore, by sending the address 01 11, we can select cell number 7. Of course, we need to know the timings of when to assert $\overline{RAS}$ and $\overline{CAS}$ strobes. After selecting the cell, if we want to write into the cell, the Write signal must be asserted.

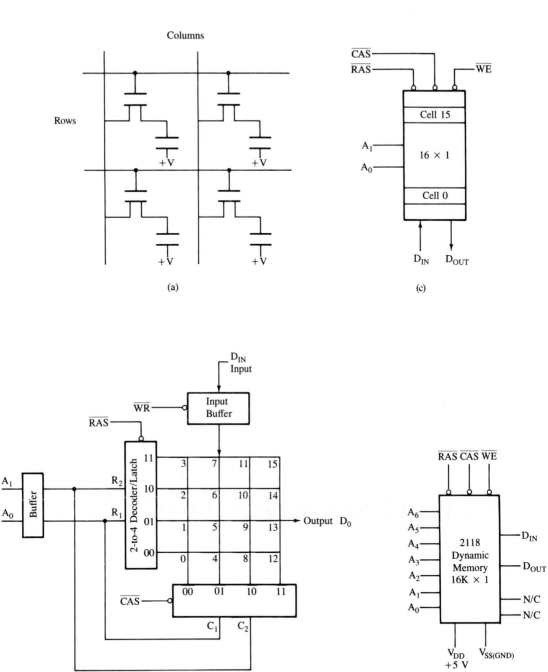

FIGURE 16.4

(a) Dynamic Memory Cells; (b) Dynamic Memory: Internal Structure; (c) Logic Symbol
for 16 × 1 Dynamic Memory; (d) Logic Symbol: Intel 2118 Dynamic Memory in a 16-pin
Package

The memory structure shown in Figure 16.4(b) has one input line and one output line; thus, we can write 16 bits or read 16 bits from this memory. This memory is represented by the logic symbol, shown in Figure 16.4(c) with two address lines, two strobe lines, one control signal $\overline{WE}$, one input line, and one output line; the size of this chip is 16×1. An 8-bit microprocessor such as the Z80 requires an 8-bit memory word; thus, we will need eight chips to have memory of 16 bytes. Figure 16.4(d) shows the logic symbol of the Intel 2118 family of $16,384 \times 1$ dynamic memory. To address 16K memory, we need 14 address lines, $A_{13}-A_0$—seven rows and seven columns; however, the chip shows only seven lines A_6-A_0. These lines are multiplexed; the low-order address A_6-A_0 is used for rows and the high-order address $A_{13}-A_7$ is used for columns.

To appreciate the complexities in interfacing this dynamic memory chip, let us first recall the steps for interfacing a static memory in relation to the Z80 Read/ Write operations. The Z80

1. Places a 16-bit address on the address bus
2. Sends the $\overline{MREQ}$ signal to indicate that the 16-bit address is on the address bus
3. Sends the control signal $\overline{RD}$ or $\overline{WR}$.

Therefore, to interface a static memory, the designer has to perform the following three steps:

1. Generate the $\overline{CS}$ signal by decoding the high-order bus and connect it to the $\overline{CE}$ pin of the memory chip.
2. Generate the $\overline{MEMRD}$ signal by ANDing $\overline{RD}$ and $\overline{MREQ}$ and connect it to the $\overline{RD}$ pin of the memory chip.
3. Generate the $\overline{MEMWR}$ signal by ANDing $\overline{WR}$ and $\overline{MREQ}$ and connect it to the $\overline{WR}$ pin of the memory chip.

In interfacing dynamic memory, the Z80 operations remain the same; it is the responsibility of the designer to generate the signals that are necessary for the dynamic memory chip. The steps and the issues involved are as follows:

1. Generate the $\overline{CS}$ signal to identify this chip among many memory chips in the system (However, there is no $\overline{CS}$ pin on the memory chip.)
2. Isolate the low-order address from the high-order address
3. Place the low-order address on the memory address lines and generate $\overline{RAS}$ (Row Address Strobe) to inform the memory that the row address is on the address lines
4. Switch from the low-order address to the high-order address and place the high-order address (column address) on the memory address lines
5. Generate the $\overline{CAS}$ (Column Address Strobe) to inform the memory that the high-order address is on the address lines
6. Use the $\overline{WR}$ signal to write into the memory or $\overline{RD}$ signal to read from memory (However, there is no $\overline{RD}$ pin on the memory chip.)

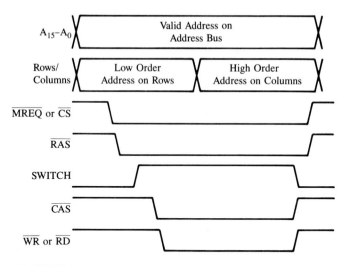

FIGURE 16.5
Timing Requirements to Read from or Write into Dynamic Memory

The timing diagram for the memory is shown in Figure 16.5. How to generate these signals is discussed in the next section.

16.2.2 Designing Circuits and Generating Timing Signals for Dynamic Memory

To generate timing signals shown in Figure 16.5, we will refer to the six steps listed above and use the memory chip 2118 as an illustration.

Step 1: *Generating the $\overline{CS}$ signal*

To address 16K memory, we need 14 address lines A_{13}–A_0; only two address lines A_{15}–A_{14} remain. We can use a 2-to-4 decoder or a simple two-input gate with an inverter as shown in Figure 16.6. The $\overline{CS}$ is generated when A_{15} is logic 1 and A_{14} is logic 0.

Step 2: *Isolating the low-order address from the high-order address*

This can be accomplished by using the 74LS157 multiplexer shown in Figure 16.7(a). The device has two control signals: SELECT and $\overline{STROBE}$, and the $\overline{STROBE}$ must be active (low) for the device to function. When the SELECT is low, the data on input lines 1A–4A are available on the output lines, and when the SELECT is high, the data on lines 1B–4B are available on the output lines.

To separate the low-order address from the high-order address, the low-order address lines can be connected to the A input lines of the multiplexer and the high-order address lines can be connected to the B input lines. The Intel 2118

FIGURE 16.6
Address Decoding to Generate
Chip Select Signal

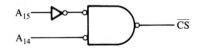

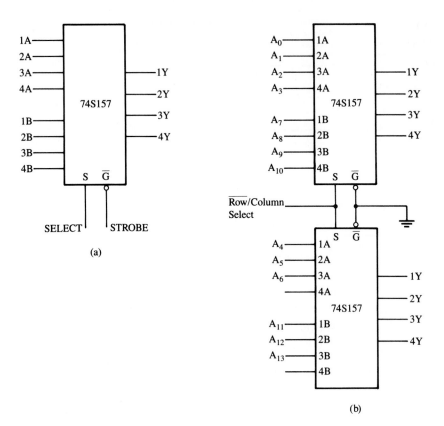

FIGURE 16.7
(a) Logic Symbol: 74S157 Multiplexer; (b) Z80 Address Lines to Multiplexer

memory chip has seven multiplexed address lines for 14-bit addresses; we therefore need to use two multiplexers as shown in Figure 16.7(b). When the SELECT is low, the address A_6–A_0 is placed on the output lines, and when the SELECT is high, the address A_{13}–A_7 is placed on the output lines.

Step 3: *Generating $\overline{RAS}$ (Row Address Strobe) and placing the low-order address on the memory address lines*

The $\overline{RAS}$ informs the memory that the row address is on the address lines. In the Z80, assertion of the $\overline{MREQ}$ (Memory Request) signal indicates that the 16-bit address is on the address bus. Therefore, the $\overline{MREQ}$ can be used as the $\overline{RAS}$ signal, and by keeping the SELECT low, the low-order address can be placed on the memory address lines. On the falling edge of the $\overline{RAS}$, the row address is latched by the memory.

Step 4: *Switching from the row address to the column address*

This is accomplished by asserting the SELECT line high. The multiplexer

FIGURE 16.8
Generating $\overline{\text{RAS}}$ and $\overline{\text{CAS}}$ Signals
Using a Delay Line

can be switched by using the $\overline{\text{MREQ}}$ signal with appropriate delay. This delay can be generated by using a delay line circuit as shown in Figure 16.8 or using propagation delays in logic gates. When the delay line, connected to the SELECT pin of the multiplexer, is asserted, the column address (A_{13}–A_7) is placed on the memory address lines.

Step 5: *Generating the $\overline{\text{CAS}}$ (Column Address Strobe) signal*

The $\overline{\text{CAS}}$ signal can be generated by delaying the $\overline{\text{MREQ}}$ signal as shown in Figure 16.8. When the $\overline{\text{CAS}}$ is asserted, the column address is latched by the memory chip.

Step 6: *Writing into or reading from a memory cell*

To write into a memory cell, three signals—$\overline{\text{RAS}}$, $\overline{\text{CAS}}$, and $\overline{\text{WR}}$—must be asserted. The $\overline{\text{WR}}$ signal can be asserted before the $\overline{\text{CAS}}$ signal (the early-write technique) or after the $\overline{\text{CAS}}$ signal. When these three signals are active, the data bit on the input line D_{IN} is latched into the internal register.

To read from a memory cell, the cell must be selected by asserting the $\overline{\text{RAS}}$ and $\overline{\text{CAS}}$ signals. After the selection of the cell, the Z80 can assert its $\overline{\text{RD}}$ signal to read from the cell; however, the memory chip does not have an $\overline{\text{RD}}$ pin. Therefore, the Read operation requires a buffer that can be enabled to read the data bit as shown in Figure 16.9.

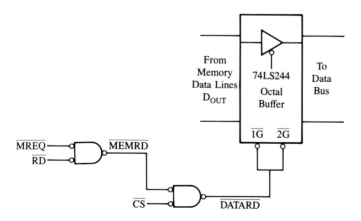

FIGURE 16.9
Output Port to Read from Dynamic Memory

16.2.3 Refreshing Dynamic Memory

As mentioned earlier, the bits are stored as capacitive charges in the dynamic memory cells and the charge leaks. Therefore, to retain information, the cells must be refreshed every 2 ms. A memory cell is automatically refreshed simply by accessing its row or by reading from or writing into the cell. However, there is no guarantee that each cell can be refreshed within a 2 ms period during the normal execution of a program. Therefore, additional circuitry must be used to refresh the cells in dynamic memory.

The commonly used technique to refresh dynamic memory is to place a row address on the memory address lines and assert the $\overline{RAS}$ signal without the $\overline{RD}$, $\overline{WR}$, or the $\overline{CAS}$ signals; this is called RAS-only refresh. The 2118 memory chip has seven rows with 128 cells that can be refreshed by using a 7-bit counter. The counter provides a 7-bit address, and by cycling the counter through 128 row addresses within 2 ms, the entire memory chip can be refreshed. The Z80 has a specially built register R that is used as a refresh counter and a signal called RFSH (Refresh).

Figure 16.1 shows the timing of the Z80 Opcode Fetch cycle. The time during T_3 and T_4, when the Z80 decodes the instruction internally and the address bus would otherwise be idle, is used in Z80-based systems for refreshing the dynamic memories. This process is called transparent refresh. During T_3, the $\overline{RFSH}$ signal goes low, indicating that the lower seven bits of the address bus contain a refresh address, and the $\overline{MREQ}$ is asserted low again. To latch the row address and refresh the cell, the $\overline{RAS}$ signal must be generated when the $\overline{RFSH}$ is active; this can be done by ANDing the $\overline{MREQ}$ and the $\overline{RFSH}$ signals. In addition, the $\overline{CAS}$ signal must be kept inactive during this period or the contents of the memory cell may be lost. The row address to refresh the cell is supplied by the contents of Refresh register R, and the address is incremented automatically after each Opcode Fetch cycle. The refresh process is automatic; the programmer can load an address into register R for testing purposes, but it is not necessary.

The refreshing technique discussed here can refresh 128 rows of a 16K dynamic memory. This technique is not, however, necessarily limited to 16K memory. If the system includes four 2118s (64K memory), the same refresh address can be used to refresh one row in each of the four memory chips if the $\overline{RAS}$ is generated without the Chip Select. We will combine the circuits discussed in this section in section 16.3, Illustration: Interfacing the 2118—16K R/W Dynamic Memory—with the Z80.

This refreshing technique is ideal in that it does not slow down the microprocessor operations. However, it has some limitations. It is based on the M_1 cycle's being executed at least 128 times within 2 ms. This may not be possible if the external Reset, Wait, and Hold signals are active more than 1 ms. Even if this technique can refresh several 16K memory chips, it cannot be used for a memory chip larger than 16K. Then, LSI devices such as Dynamic RAM Controllers are commonly used. These controllers not only refresh the dynamic memories but also provide such necessary timing signals as $\overline{RAS}$ and $\overline{CAS}$.

ILLUSTRATION: INTERFACING THE 2118—16K R/W DYNAMIC MEMORY—WITH THE Z80   16.3

This illustration is concerned with interfacing a 16K R/W dynamic memory with the Z80. The illustration synthesizes the concepts we discussed in the previous section.

16.3.1 Problem Statement

Design a circuit to interface the 2118—16K dynamic memory—with the Z80 for the memory map starting at 8000_H. Generate the necessary timing signals assuming the system clock is 2.5 MHz, and use the Z80 Refresh signal and register R to refresh the memory cells within 2 ms.

16.3.2 Problem Analysis

The interfacing of dynamic memory involves three aspects: assigning the memory map, generating timing signals, and refreshing memory cells. The steps are as follows:

1. Decode the high-order address lines to assign the map.
2. Generate $\overline{RAS}$, $\overline{CAS}$, and SELECT signals with appropriate delays.
3. Use the $\overline{RAS}$ signal to latch the row address, the SELECT signal to switch from the $\overline{RAS}$ to the $\overline{CAS}$ signal, and the $\overline{CAS}$ signal to latch the column address.
4. Use the Z80 $\overline{WR}$ signal to write into the selected cell.
5. Generate the Memory Read signal to enable a buffer as an input port.
6. Refresh the memory cell during T_3 and T_4 states of the Opcode Fetch cycle.

16.3.3 Interfacing Circuit and Its Operation

In this circuit design, the assignment of the memory map with the starting address 8000_H is easy. The 16K memory requires 14 address lines A_{13}–A_0 to address memory cells; thus, only two address lines, A_{15} and A_{14}, remain. These address lines can be decoded using either a simple gate and an inverter or a 2-to-4 decoder. Figure 16.10 shows that the $\overline{CS}$ signal is generated using the gate 74LS32 with an inverter. The memory map of this circuit ranges from 8000_H to $BFFF_H$ as shown.

A_{15}	A_{14}	A_{13}	A_{12}	A_{11}	A_{10}	A_9	A_8	A_7	A_6	A_5	A_4	A_3	A_2	A_1	A_0	
1	0	0	0	0	0	0	0	0	0	0	0	0	0	0	0	$= 8000_H$
Chip Select		1	1	1	1	1	1	1	1	1	1	1	1	1	1	$= BFFF_H$

Column Address   Row Address

GENERATING THE $\overline{RAS}$ SIGNAL

The $\overline{RAS}$ signal should be active when the row address is placed on the memory lines and when the $\overline{RFSH}$ signal is asserted to refresh the memory cells. However,

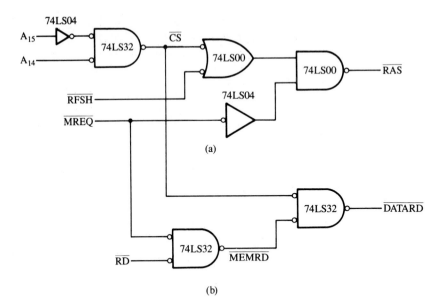

FIGURE 16.10
(a) Generating RAS Signal When CS or RFSH Is Active; (b) Generating MEMRD and DATARD to Read from Memory

the $\overline{\text{CS}}$ signal is not necessary for refreshing. Therefore, the $\overline{\text{CS}}$ and $\overline{\text{RFSH}}$ signals are logically ORed as shown in Figure 16.10. The $\overline{\text{RAS}}$ is generated by ANDing $\overline{\text{CS}}$ or $\overline{\text{RFSH}}$ with the $\overline{\text{MREQ}}$. The time delay in generating the $\overline{\text{RAS}}$ signal in relation to the $\overline{\text{MREQ}}$ will be 37 ns, the sum of the delays in 74LS04 and NAND gate. The delay in generating the $\overline{\text{CS}}$ is irrelevant because the address is placed on the address bus 300 ns before the $\overline{\text{MREQ}}$ is asserted.

CONNECTING THE ROW AND COLUMN ADDRESSES

Figure 16.11 shows that the row address lines A_6–A_0 are connected to A input and the column address lines A_{13}–A_7 are connected to B input of the two multiplexers 74S157. The seven output lines of the multiplexers are connected to the multiplexed address lines A_6–A_0 of the memory chip, and the eighth output line of the multiplexer is connected to the $\overline{\text{CAS}}$ signal of the memory chip. The input lines 4A and 4B of the second multiplexer are tied to +5 V and ground, respectively. When the SELECT is switched from low to high, the eighth output line goes from high to low (from +5 V to ground), and the $\overline{\text{CAS}}$ signal is asserted (active low). Figure 16.11 shows the details of only one memory chip, rather than eight chips, to avoid clutter.

PLACING THE ADDRESSES AND SWITCHING
FROM $\overline{\text{RAS}}$ TO $\overline{\text{CAS}}$

The SELECT signal of the multiplexer is controlled by the $\overline{\text{MREQ}}$ through the edge-triggered flip-flop 7474 (Figure 16.11). At the beginning of the Opcode Fetch

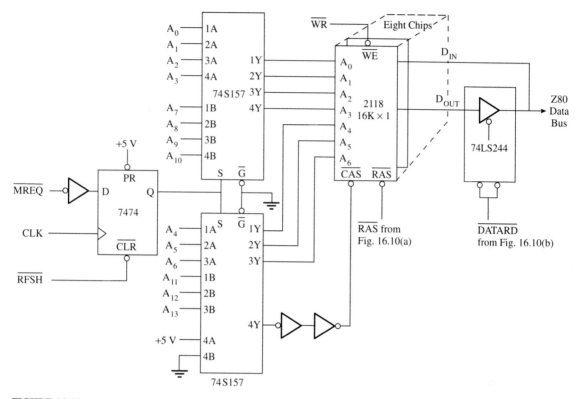

FIGURE 16.11

Interfacing Dynamic Memory

SOURCE: Adapted from *Memory Data Book and Designer's Guide*, p. x-45; courtesy of Mostek Corporation.

cycle, the $\overline{\text{MREQ}}$ is high and the output of the flip-flop is low. Thus, the SELECT signal is low, and the row address is placed on the output lines of the multiplexer. When the $\overline{\text{MREQ}}$ is asserted, the $\overline{\text{RAS}}$ is generated 37 ns later because of the delay in the inverter and the NAND gate (Figure 16.10), and the row address is latched by the memory. The $\overline{\text{MREQ}}$ also changes the input to the flip-flop; however, the output of the flip-flop changes on the rising edge of the clock T_2. When the output of the flip-flop goes high, the SELECT is switched from low to high, and the column address A_{13}–A_7 is placed on the address lines. The $\overline{\text{CAS}}$ is delayed by 37 ns by using two inverters, thus allowing sufficient time for the column address to settle. When the $\overline{\text{CAS}}$ is asserted, the column address is latched.

READING FROM AND WRITING DATA INTO MEMORY

The Memory Read signal is generated by ANDing $\overline{\text{CS}}$, $\overline{\text{MREQ}}$, and $\overline{\text{RD}}$ (Figure 16.10(b)); this is similar to generating the $\overline{\text{MEMRD}}$ signal for static R/W memory. However, this memory chip does not have an $\overline{\text{RD}}$ pin; therefore, the data bit is read by using the buffer 74LS244 as a memory-mapped input port. Figure 16.11

shows one input and one output data line; the other seven data lines are not shown here.

To write data into a selected cell, the $\overline{\text{WR}}$ signal, which is connected to the $\overline{\text{WE}}$ pin of the memory, must be asserted. The $\overline{\text{WR}}$ signal can also be asserted before the $\overline{\text{CAS}}$ signal (early-write); we have not used that technique in this illustration.

REFRESHING THE MEMORY CELL

During the T_3 state of the Opcode Fetch cycle, the $\overline{\text{RFSH}}$ is asserted and the address from the R register is placed on the address bus. The $\overline{\text{RAS}}$ signal is asserted again when the $\overline{\text{MREQ}}$ goes low, the row address is latched by the memory, and the cell is refreshed. However, the $\overline{\text{CAS}}$ is held inactive during the refresh by using the $\overline{\text{RFSH}}$ signal to reset the flip-flop. Thus, this operation is not confused with a Read or Write operation.

TIMING CALCULATIONS AND MICROPROCESSOR READ TIME

In section 16.1 we calculated that the Z80 with a 2.5 MHz clock begins to read data 450 ns after asserting the $\overline{\text{MREQ}}$. In dynamic memory, the sum of the memory access time and the delays in generating various signals must be less than the

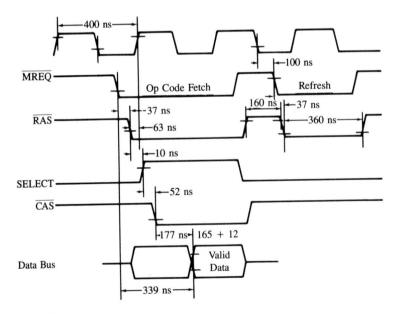

FIGURE 16.12

Timing: Dynamic Memory

SOURCE: Adapted from *Memory Data Book and Designer's Guide*, p. x-46; courtesy of Mostek Corporation.

microprocessor read time. In Figures 16.10 and 16.11, the delays in reference to $\overline{MREQ}$ can be calculated as follows:

1. $\overline{MREQ}$ to $\overline{RAS}$: Delay in 7404 and 7400   = 37 ns
2. $\overline{RAS}$ to SELECT: Rising clock + flip-flop delay   = 73 ns
3. SELECT to $\overline{CAS}$: Multiplexer and inverter delays   = 52 ns
4. $\overline{CAS}$ Access Time: = 165 ns
5. CAS to Octal Buffer: = 12 ns

Total Delay   339 ns

The timings are shown in Figure 16.12. The total delay is 339 ns, and the microprocessor would begin to read at 450 ns; thus, we have a 111 ns safety margin.

EXTENDING MEMORY ADDRESSING WITH THE BANK SWITCHING TECHNIQUE 16.4

The Z80 microprocessor is capable of addressing 64K memory with its 16-bit address bus. Most 8-bit processors with a 40-pin package are generally limited to 64K addressing capacity. However, in microprocessor-based product designs, situations arise where 64K memory is insufficient. For example, a microprocessor-based typewriter with a spelling checker capability would require memory larger than 64K. In such situations, the designer can extend the memory addressing capacity by using the technique called Bank Switching.

16.4.1 Bank Switching Concepts

The memory addressing can be viewed simply as a numbering scheme; a processor with 16-bit address lines can generate 64K (65,536) numbers and identify that many memory registers. To have additional numbers, either we should have additional address bits or we should group these registers into groups such as A, B, and C groups. The bank switching technique uses I/O address ports to classify various memory chips into different banks, and memory banks are made accessible to the microprocessor as necessary by using software instructions. Therefore, to implement this technique, we should have I/O ports to differentiate between various banks and a main memory where software instructions can reside to switch between various memory banks.

16.4.2 Interfacing Memory Using Bank Switching Circuit

Figure 16.13 shows a memory interfacing circuit with three 32K × 8 memory chips M_1, M_2, and M_3. Memory M_1 is interfaced as the main memory with the common memory addresses to all the banks, and M_2 and M_3 are interfaced as memory banks. Each memory chip requires 15 address lines (A_{14}–A_0) to select 32K registers. The address line A_{15} is used for selecting M_1 and memory banks 1 and 2.

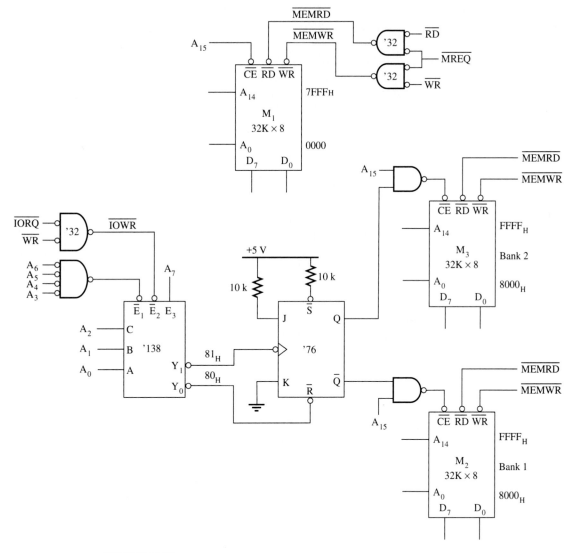

FIGURE 16.13
Bank Switching Circuit to Interface 96K Memory

The memory chip M_1 is selected when A_{15} is at logic 0. Therefore, the address range for this chip is from 0000 to $7FFF_H$. Memory chips M_2 and M_3 are selected when A_{15} is at logic 1; therefore, the addresses range from 8000_H to $FFFF_H$ for both chips. However, the selection also depends on the outputs Q and $\overline{Q}$ (of the edge-triggered J–K flip-flop), which are controlled by the outputs of the 3-to-8 decoder as explained below.

The decoder in Figure 16.13 serves as an output port; it is enabled when $\overline{\text{IORQ}}$ and $\overline{\text{WR}}$ are active and the address line A_7–A_3 are high. The output line Y_1 goes active when the input to the decoder is 0 0 1. Thus, the output instruction with the port address 81_H provides a clock pulse to the edge-triggered flip-flop that changes Q to logic 1 and $\overline{Q}$ to logic 0 state. These Q outputs select Bank 2 and deselect Bank 1. The output Y_0 of the decoder (with the port address 80_H) resets Q to logic 0 and sets $\overline{Q}$ to logic 1; thus, the system selects Bank 1 and deselects Bank 2. Therefore, when the system is turned on, the software in the main memory M_1 should execute the out instruction (port 80_H) to reset the flip-flop and select Bank 1, making 64K memory accessible to the microprocessor. When it is necessary to access Bank 2, the out instruction with the port address 81_H must be executed. By selecting Bank 1 (32K) and Bank 2 (32K) one at a time, 64K memory is always accessible to the processor, thus making the total memory in the system 96K.

DIRECT MEMORY ACCESS (DMA) AND THE Z80 DMA CONTROLLER 16.5

Direct Memory Access is a commonly used I/O technique for high-speed data transfer (for example, data transfer between system memory and a floppy disk). In polling and interrupt I/O, data transfer is relatively slow because each byte must be read and then written to its destination; thus, two instructions per byte are required. In DMA, the MPU releases the control of the buses to a device called a DMA controller. The controller manages data transfer between memory and a peripheral under its control, thus bypassing the MPU. Conceptually, this is an important I/O technique that requires two signals available on the Z80— BUSRQ (Bus Request) and $\overline{\text{BUSAK}}$ (Bus Acknowledge).

□ BUSRQ—Bus Request. This is an active low input signal to the Z80 from another device requesting the use of the address and the data buses, and control signals. After receiving the Bus Request, the MPU relinquishes the buses in the following machine cycle. All buses are tri-stated, so the Bus Acknowledge (BUSAK) signal is sent out. The MPU regains the control of the buses after the BUSRQ goes high.

□ BUSAK—Bus Acknowledge. This is an active low output signal indicating that the MPU has completed its current machine cycle and has relinquished control of the buses.

A DMA controller plays two roles in this type of data transfer: one as a peripheral to the Z80 and the other as a data transfer processor. The DMA controller uses the signals just discussed as if it were a peripheral requesting control of the buses from the MPU. The MPU communicates with the controller by using the Chip Select line, buses, and control signals. However, once the controller has gained control, it plays the role of a special-purpose processor for data transfer;

it uses the Z80 buses and the control signals to transfer data directly between memory and an I/O device. To perform this function the DMA controller must have the following:

1. Data bus
2. Address bus
3. Chip Enable and Read/Write control signals
4. Signals to communicate when it functions as a peripheral and as a processor.

Typically, the microprocessor accesses the DMA controller as an I/O device and writes the necessary initialization instructions in the DMA control registers. These instructions include the mode of data transfer (discussed later), the source and the destination addresses, and the number of bytes to be transferred. Figure 16.14 shows a block diagram of the DMA data transfer. When a peripheral is ready for data transfer, it sends the Ready signal to the DMA controller, and in turn, the DMA controller sends the Bus Request (BUSREQ) signal to the MPU. The MPU completes the execution of the present machine cycle, acknowledges the request by sending the Bus Acknowledge (BUSAK) signal, and releases the control of the buses to the DMA controller.

The DMA controller can transfer data either sequentially or simultaneously. In the **sequential transfer**, the Read cycle is followed by the Write cycle. In the **simultaneous transfer**, each byte is read from the source and written into the destination simultaneously; the Read and Write cycles are active at the same time. Figure 16.15 shows these two types of data transfer. In addition, for each type of data transfer, the DMA controller can be set up in one of three modes: *byte, burst,* and *continuous (block).* In the byte mode, the controller transfers one byte and releases the bus control back to the MPU. In the burst mode, the data transfer

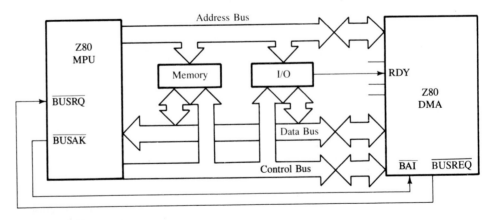

FIGURE 16.14
Block Diagram: DMA Data Transfer

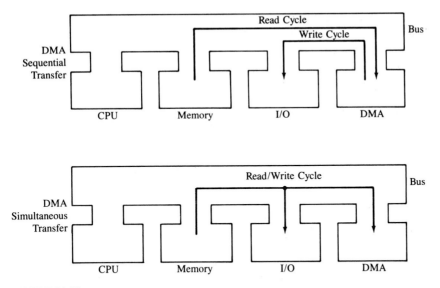

FIGURE 16.15
DMA Data Transfer: Sequential and Simultaneous
SOURCE: Courtesy of Zilog, Inc.

continues until the Ready goes inactive, and then the bus control is released. In the continuous transfer, the controller does not release control of the buses until the entire block of data transfer is completed.

The DMA data transfer has the highest priority in the system; no interrupt, not even the NMI (non-maskable interrupt), can be acknowledged during the DMA data transfer. One of the major disadvantages of the DMA process is that the refreshing of the dynamic memory is suspended during the data transfer; this suspension can be detrimental to the system, especially in the block mode. The process of DMA data transfer and the interfacing are discussed in the following sections in the context of the Z80 DMA controller.

16.5.1 Z80 DMA Controller

The Z80 DMA controller is a programmable device, capable of transferring a block of 64K bytes or searching for a particular 8-bit maskable byte. It can also combine data transfers with simultaneous search. The ability to search for a byte is generally not found in other controllers. Figure 16.16 shows the logic pinout of the device; it is similar to a processor and designed to be compatible with the Z80 control signals. It includes 16 address lines, eight data lines, control signals compatible with the Z80, interrupt control, and the signals to communicate with a peripheral and the MPU for the DMA data transfer. Some of these signals are bidirectional, and they perform different functions depending upon whether the DMA is in the peripheral mode or in the processor (master) mode. The signals

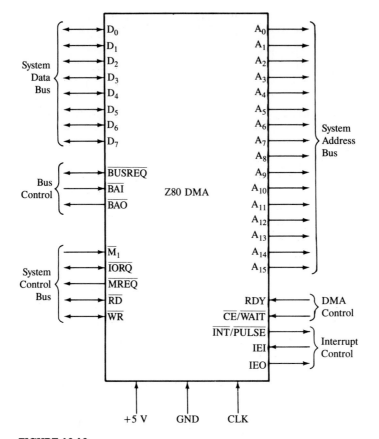

FIGURE 16.16
Z80 DMA: Logic Pinout
SOURCE: Courtesy of Zilog, Inc.

that perform some special functions or are unique to the DMA controller are described as follows.

□ $\overline{CE/WAIT}$—(Chip Enable and Wait): Generally, this is used as a Chip Enable signal through which the MPU can access the DMA as a peripheral and write instructions in the control register or read status registers. However, it can also be used as a Wait line. After the DMA receives the Bus Acknowledge ($\overline{BUSAK}$) signal and when it is in the processor mode, this line can be used as a Wait line by memory or I/O to slow down the speed of the DMA to match with memory or I/O.

□ $\overline{BAI}$—(Bus Acknowledge In): This is an active low input signal and is generally connected to the $\overline{BUSAK}$ signal of the Z80. When this signal is active, it indicates that the buses have been released by the MPU. In a multiple-DMA system, this signal is connected to the $\overline{\text{BAO}}$ (Bus Acknowledge Out) signal of the next higher priority DMA to form a daisy chain; the $\overline{\text{BAI}}$ of the highest priority is connected to the $\overline{\text{BUSAK}}$ of the Z80.

- $\square$ BAO—Bus Acknowledge Out: This is an active low signal and is used in a multiple-DMA system to form the daisy chain priority.
- $\square$ RDY—(Ready): This is an input signal and can be programmed as active low or high. When a peripheral is ready for data transfer, this signal goes active. When the DMA is in the processor mode, this signal controls the activities of the DMA.
- $\square$ IORQ, RD, and $\overline{\text{WR}}$—These are three bidirectional control signals. When the Z80 communicates with the DMA as a peripheral, these signals are input to the DMA. When the DMA functions as a processor, these signals are output signals and used to communicate with other memory or I/Os.
- $\square$ MREQ—This is an output signal used as a control signal to communicate with memory.
- $\square$ BUSREQ—(Bus Request): This is a bidirectional active low signal. As an output, it is connected to the $\overline{\text{BUSRQ}}$ of the Z80; it requests the use of the buses to the MPU. In a multiple-DMA system, it senses whether any other DMA is using the buses, and it refrains from requesting the buses until the other DMA operation is completed.

16.5.2 Interfacing the Z80 DMA Controller

The interfacing of the Z80 DMA is similar to that of any other peripheral. Figure 16.17 shows a schematic of interfacing the Z80 DMA with the Z80. The output line Y_1 of the decoder is connected to the $\overline{\text{CE/WAIT}}$ line of the DMA; thus, the DMA is assigned the port address $F9_H$. The Bus Request and Bus Acknowledge

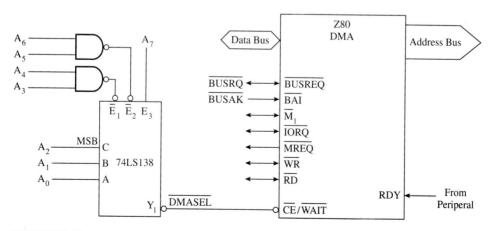

FIGURE 16.17
Interfacing DMA

signals of the Z80 are connected to the respective signals ($\overline{\text{BUSREQ}}$ and $\overline{\text{BAI}}$) of the DMA, and the RDY signal of the DMA is connected to a peripheral. The remaining control signals of the Z80 (M_1, $\overline{\text{RD}}$, $\overline{\text{WR}}$, $\overline{\text{IORQ}}$, and $\overline{\text{MREQ}}$) are connected to the respective control signals of the DMA; this is similar to interfacing any other programmable I/O. However, three control signals ($\overline{\text{RD}}$, $\overline{\text{WR}}$, $\overline{\text{IORQ}}$) of the DMA are bidirectional, and the $\overline{\text{MREQ}}$ is an output signal. When the DMA is in the peripheral mode, the Z80 communicates with the DMA using the $\overline{\text{RD}}$, $\overline{\text{WR}}$, and $\overline{\text{IORQ}}$. When the DMA is in the processor mode, the DMA can communicate with the system memory or I/O (such as a floppy disk controller) using all four control signals ($\overline{\text{IORQ}}$, $\overline{\text{MREQ}}$, $\overline{\text{RD}}$, and $\overline{\text{WR}}$).

16.5.3 Programming the DMA Controller

The Z80 DMA is a versatile device and offers many options; thus, it requires a series of instructions to program the device for given specifications. However, we will discuss only the important features of this device. Figure 16.18 shows the internal structure of the DMA, which includes two port addresses, one byte counter, control and status registers, and control logic.

    To program the DMA, we must write starting addresses of source and destination in Port A and Port B; either port can be used for source or destination. The addresses can be for memory or I/O; they can also be either fixed or variable, and if they are variable, they can be incremented or decremented. We must also specify the block length (the number of bytes to be transferred), type of operation (transfer, search, or search/transfer), and the mode of data transfer (byte, burst, or continuous).

    The Z80 DMA has 21 Write registers to write control words and seven Read

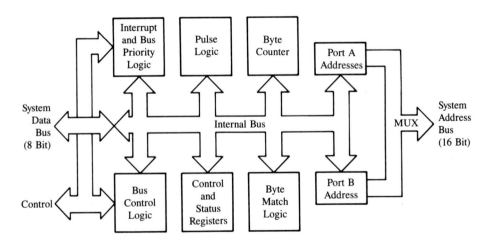

FIGURE 16.18
Z80 DMA Block Diagram
SOURCE: Courtesy of Zilog, Inc.

registers to read the status of an operation. The Write registers are organized in seven base register groups, and each group includes several control registers. The steps in writing control words into these registers are similar to those of writing into Z80 SIO registers; they involve writing to a base register and using the base register as a pointer to other registers. The Read registers provide status information of the DMA, including the number in the byte counter and addresses in

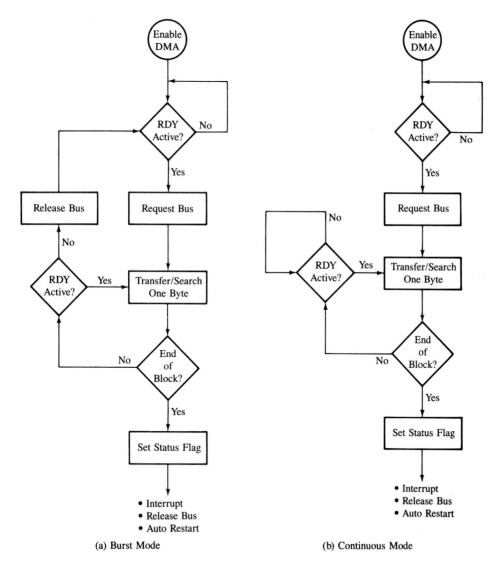

(a) Burst Mode (b) Continuous Mode

FIGURE 16.19

Flowchart: DMA Data Transfer in (a) Burst Mode and (b) Continuous Mode

SOURCE: Courtesy of Zilog, Inc.

Ports A and B. For the programming details of these registers, refer to the Technical Manual of the Z80 DMA included in the References.

16.5.4 Process of DMA Data Transfer

In a Z80 system, the DMA is normally connected as a peripheral, and control bytes must be written at the power-up initialization. Then the DMA begins to monitor the RDY line from the peripheral (such as a floppy disk controller, a printer, or an SIO). When the RDY line goes active, indicating that the peripheral is ready for data transfer, the DMA asserts the $\overline{\text{BUSREQ}}$. The Z80 MPU completes the present machine cycle, acknowledges the request by asserting the $\overline{\text{BUSAK}}$, which is connected to the $\overline{\text{BAI}}$ of the DMA, and releases the control of the buses. When the $\overline{\text{BAI}}$ signal goes low, the DMA assumes the role of the processor and begins the data transfer according to the specified mode. This can also be accomplished by generating an interrupt when the RDY goes active and then enabling the DMA data transfer.

If the DMA is set up in the byte mode, it transfers one byte and releases control of the buses to the MPU. The buses are requested again for each succeeding byte transfer. If the DMA is programmed in the burst mode, the DMA transfers a byte and checks the block length. If it is not the end of the block and the RDY is still active, the data transfer continues. When the RDY line goes inactive, the $\overline{\text{BUSREQ}}$ signal goes high, and the DMA releases bus control to the MPU.

If the DMA is programmed in the continuous (block) mode, the data transfer continues until the end of the block. During the transfer, if the RDY goes inactive, the DMA does not release the control of the buses; it waits until the RDY goes active again and continues the data transfer until the end of the block. Figure 16.19 shows two flowcharts, one for the burst mode and the other for the continuous (block) mode.

SUMMARY

In this chapter, we have discussed applications of two external request signals: Wait and Bus Request. The Wait signal is used to provide additional time to a slow peripheral so that data transfer is properly synchronized between the Z80 microprocessor and slow peripherals. On the other hand, the Bus Request is used to implement high-speed data transfer without the intervention of the microprocessor. In addition, interfacing of dynamic memory was illustrated. The important concepts discussed in this chapter can be summarized as follows.

□ The Z80 includes the "WAIT" signal, which can be used as an input from slow peripherals to add clock cycles in a given operation. The Z80 samples the WAIT line during T_2 of each machine cycle, and if it is asserted low, the

Z80 adds an additional clock period, thus providing extra time to slow peripherals.

☐ If memory access time is too slow in comparison with the execution speed of the microprocessor, the WAIT line can be used to synchronize the data transfer between the memory and the Z80.

☐ Dynamic memory stores a bit as a capacitive charge, which has a tendency to leak; therefore, all cells must be refreshed every two milliseconds.

☐ In a dynamic memory chip, the memory cells are organized in a square matrix format, and the row and the column address lines are multiplexed. Therefore, the row address must be placed on the memory address lines first, followed by the column address with an appropriate delay.

☐ Dynamic memory includes two signals, RAS (Row Address Strobe) and $\overline{\text{CAS}}$ (Column Address Strobe), which are used to latch the row address and the column address.

☐ The Z80 architecture includes a refresh register R that can be used as a 7-bit counter to refresh 128 rows every two milliseconds.

☐ Direct memory access (DMA) is a commonly used I/O technique for high-speed data transfer.

☐ The Z80 includes two signals—$\overline{\text{BUSRQ}}$ (Bus Request) and $\overline{\text{BUSAK}}$ (Bus Acknowledge)—which are used in the DMA data transfer.

☐ When the DMA controller sends the $\overline{\text{BUSREQ}}$ signal, the MPU acknowledges the request by asserting the $\overline{\text{BUSAK}}$ signal at the end of the machine cycle being executed and releases bus control to the DMA. The DMA uses the buses to transfer data, and then releases bus control back to the MPU.

☐ The DMA has three modes of data transfer: byte, burst, and block (continuous). In the byte mode, the DMA transfers one byte and releases the control back to the MPU. In the burst mode, the DMA continues to transfer data until the Ready signal of the DMA is inactive. In the block (continuous) mode, the DMA does not release control of the buses until the entire block of the data transfer is complete.

ASSIGNMENTS

1. Define the memory access time.
2. Explain the condition that must be satisfied to add a Wait state.
3. Explain the need to refresh the dynamic memory cells.
4. Explain why the refresh circuitry is unnecessary in static R/W memory.
5. Explain the DMA technique and the functions of the Z80 $\overline{\text{BUSRQ}}$ and $\overline{\text{BUSAK}}$ signals.
6. List the steps involved in the DMA controller's transfer of data using the $\overline{\text{BUSRQ}}$ and $\overline{\text{BUSAK}}$ signals.

7. In the DMA, what is the difference between the sequential and the simultaneous data transfer?

8. Explain the difference between the three modes of DMA data transfer: byte, burst, and block.

9. Calculate the time available for the Z80 to read data after an address is placed on the address bus in a 6 MHz system if the address delay is 90 ns and the data set-up time is 30 ns.

10. In Assignment **9**, can the memory chip with the access time 300 ns be used without a Wait state?

11. The Mostek MK4164 is a 64K memory chip. How many multiplexed address lines are necessary for this chip?

12. Figure 16.4(d) shows the logic pinout of the 16K memory chip, in which two pins are without any connections. If these two pins are used as address lines to design a new chip, what will be the memory size of this chip?

13. How does the MPU read data from the 2118 memory if the memory chip does not have the $\overline{RD}$ signal?

14. Specify the signals necessary to generate the $\overline{RAS}$ signal.

15. Explain how the $\overline{CAS}$ signal is generated in Figure 16.11.

16. In Figure 16.11, when the $\overline{RFSH}$ signal clears the flip-flop 7474, specify the logic levels of the signal STROBE (S) of the 74S157, the $\overline{CAS}$, and the contents of the memory address lines.

17. Write a subroutine to check bit D_0 of register B, and if D_0 is 1, select Bank 2. Otherwise, reset the flip-flop, and return to the calling program.

18. Explain the detrimental effect of the continuous (block) mode in DMA if the system includes dynamic memory.

Designing Microprocessor-Based Products

In Chapter 1, we began with an overview of microprocessor-based products and microcomputer systems. In subsequent chapters, we examined the architecture of the Z80 microprocessor and interfacing of memory and I/Os. An overview of the Z80 instruction set was given in Chapter 6, and Chapters 7 through 11 were devoted to the discussion of various programming techniques, applications of the Z80 instruction set, and familiarization with operating systems. Similarly, we examined processes of data transfer such as interrupts, serial I/O, and DMA using programmable devices. This chapter is concerned with integrating or synthesizing the concepts of the microprocessor architecture, software, and interfacing discussed previously by designing various sub-systems of microprocessor-based products, such as Z80 MPU, memory, scanned display, matrix keyboard, and IC tester. The chapter also includes troubleshooting techniques using an in-circuit emulator, a logic analyzer, and a signature analyzer.

OBJECTIVES

- ☐ Design modules (sub-systems) of microprocessor systems based on the Z80 microprocessor and Z80 family of programmable interfacing devices.
- ☐ Illustrate the interfacing of scanned display, and list the advantages.
- ☐ Illustrate the interfacing of a matrix keyboard using software.
- ☐ Illustrate the interfacing of a matrix keyboard using a keyboard encoder.

- ☐ Design an IC tester to illustrate the design process of a microprocessor-based product.
- ☐ List the primary features of an in-circuit emulator and explain its applications in troubleshooting microprocessor-based systems.
- ☐ Explain the functions of a logic analyzer and a signature analyzer as troubleshooting instruments.

17.1   DESIGNING MICROPROCESSOR-BASED SYSTEMS

A typical microprocessor-based system is shown in Figure 17.1. It includes three major sub-systems: processor, memory, and I/Os. Generally, it will have two types of memory devices: R/W memory and Read-Only memory (ROM, EPROM, etc.). The I/Os may include a wide variety of input–output devices depending upon the tasks the system is expected to perform. Typically, it may include a matrix keyboard, a scanned LED display, data converters, and devices under test (DUTs). The system may have a facility to communicate with a host computer

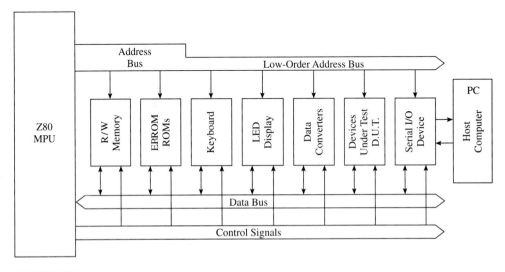

FIGURE 17.1

Block Diagram of a Microprocessor-Based System

such as a PC (Personal Computer) or minicomputer, or it could be an embedded system in a larger system.

To illustrate the design process, we will discuss the following sub-systems as specified.

- Input: Hex keyboard with minimum of 20 keys.
- Output: Six seven-segment LEDs for a display.
- Memory: 2732 (4096 × 8) and 2764 (8096 × 8) EPROMs.
  : 2K of R/W static memory—6116 (2048 × 8) or equivalent.
- Microprocessor: Z80.
- System frequency: 2 MHz.
- Suggested interfacing devices: Z80 PIOs, bus drivers, 3-to-8 decoders, key encoder, and segment and digit drivers.

The system should allow the user to enter and execute commands, and the buses should have enough driving capacity to interface with additional peripherals. The seven-segment LEDs should display various messages.

17.1.1   Sub-system Analysis

In analyzing the specifications of a microprocessor-based product it is essential to consider hardware and software simultaneously. Both are interrelated, and each will have an impact on the other. In this project we will explore various alternatives and tradeoffs between hardware and software. We will design various modules and leave the final decisions with the user.

Microprocessor   The system is designed around a general-purpose 8-bit microprocessor such as Z80. It requires additional circuitry to generate appropriate control and clock signals. It would also need bus drivers to support various I/O and memory devices.

Keyboard   The keyboard in this design is an input port with keys arranged in the matrix format. When a key is pressed, the processor should receive the binary equivalent of the key. This can be accomplished by two approaches: one is a software approach whereby a key closure is sensed, debounced, and identified, and the key code is obtained by using the software; the other is the hardware approach whereby all these key functions are performed through a programmable keyboard encoder.

The keys are divided into two groups: one group is for Hex digits from 0 to F, and the second is concerned with various functions. The software should be able to differentiate between these two groups and make appropriate decisions.

Display   This system includes a scanned display that can be implemented either through software or special integrated devices such as keyboard/display drivers. If the display is software driven, the microprocessor will have to scan the display at a given interval of a few milliseconds to keep the display visible. Figure 17.2

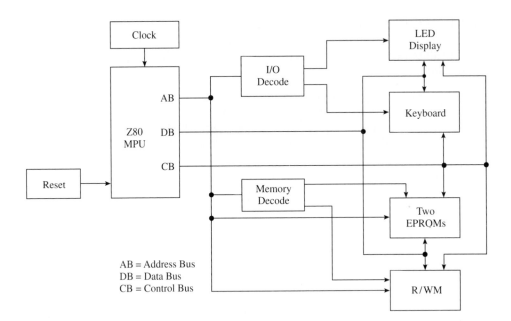

FIGURE 17.2
Block Diagram of a Microprocessor-Based System with Decoders

shows the block diagram of a microprocessor-based system with decoders, and we can divide the system design in the following sections:

1. Z80 MPU design
2. Memory design
3. Scanned display
4. Interfacing matrix keyboard

17.2   Z80 MPU DESIGN

The sub-systems of microprocessor-based products described in section 17.1 are designed around the Z80 microprocessor, and the MPU should provide necessary buses with appropriate driving capacity. The MPU design can be divided into the following segments:

1. Address bus
2. Data bus
3. Control signals
4. Frequency and power requirements
5. Externally triggered signals (Reset, Interrupts, etc.).

17.2.1 Address Bus

The Z80 has 16 address lines $A_{15}-A_0$; this is a unidirectional bus with driving current capacity of $I_{OH} = 250$ μa and sinking capacity I_{OL} of 1.8 mA. At this point, we do not know the total load on the address bus, but by examining the block diagram, we can make some reasonable estimates of the load on the address bus. Figure 17.2 shows that the address bus will drive two decode circuits (I/O and memory decoders) and three memory chips (CMOS 6116, EPROM 2732, and EPROM 2764). We can calculate the bus loading as follows (see Figure 17.3):

High-level input currents I_{IH}			Low-level input currents IP_{IL}	
Two Decoders =	20 μA × 2	= 40 μA	400 μA × 2	= 800 μA
R/W Memory		= 10 μA		= 10 μA
2732 EPROM		= 10 μA		= 10 μA
2764 EPROM		= 10 μA		= 10 μA
		70 μA		830 μA

By examining these load currents, we can conclude that the bus driver is unnecessary for the address bus; we can even add a few decode circuits or gates. However, this Z80 MPU is to be designed for a general-purpose microprocessor-based product; therefore, as a precaution we will use the 74LS244 as a bus driver to increase the driving capacity. The 74LS244 is an octal buffer/driver, capable of sourcing 15 mA and sinking 24 mA of current. Figure 17.4 shows two octal buffers for 16 address lines; the Enable lines of these buffers are active low, and they are permanently enabled. Thus, the Z80 address bus can drive additional devices (decoders, gates, etc.) without excessive loading.

17.2.2 Data Bus

The Z80 data bus has eight bidirectional lines with driving capacity similar to that of the address bus. Because the data bus is bidirectional, the loading on the bus

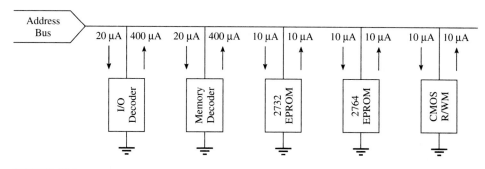

FIGURE 17.3
Loading on the Address Bus

varies considerably. When the Z80 is reading from memory, the memory chip that is enabled becomes the driving source and the microprocessor becomes the load; and when the Z80 is writing to an output port, the microprocessor is the source and the latches of the output port constitute the load. An octal latch, such as the 74LS363, requires a 400 μA input current at the low level logic; on the other hand, the 7475 requires 3 to 6 mA. Therefore, as a precaution, we will use a bidirectional buffer as a data bus driver.

Figure 17.4 shows the 74LS245 as an 8-bit bidirectional bus driver to increase the driving capacity of the data bus. The 74LS245 can sink 24 mA and source 15 mA of current. The 74LS245 has eight bidirectional data lines; the direction of the data flow is determined by the direction control line (DIR). Figure 17.4 shows that the bus driver is enabled by grounding the Enable (G) signal. The direction of the data flow is determined by connecting the $\overline{RD}$ signal from the Z80 to the DIR signal. When the Z80 is writing to peripherals, the $\overline{RD}$ is high and data flow from the Z80 to peripherals. When it is reading from peripherals, the $\overline{RD}$ is low and data flow toward the microprocessor (see Assignment 3).

17.2.3 Control Bus

The Z80 provides five active low signals—$\overline{M_1}$, $\overline{IORQ}$, $\overline{MREQ}$, $\overline{RD}$, and $\overline{WR}$—which can be combined to generate necessary control signals. The commonly used control signals are $\overline{IORD}$ (I/O Read), $\overline{IOWR}$ (I/O Write), $\overline{MEMRD}$ (Memory Read), $\overline{MEMWR}$ (Memory Write), and $\overline{INTA}$ (Interrupt Acknowledge); they can be generated by the logic combinations shown in Figure 17.5(a). However, in memory interfacing the $\overline{RD}$ and $\overline{WR}$ signals are generally connected to the memory chip directly and $\overline{MREQ}$ is combined with the address-decoding scheme. Figure 17.5(b) shows another scheme to generate the I/O control signals and the $\overline{INTA}$ signal by using a 3-to-8 decoder.

The driving capacity of these control signals is determined by the circuits used in generating them. If necessary, these control signals can be buffered by using the 74LS244 or the Hex drivers 74LS367. Generally, the circuits shown in Figure 17.5 will have sufficient drive so that buffers may not be needed.

17.2.4 Frequency and Power Requirements

The clock circuitry is of critical importance in designing Z80 systems. The Z80 does not have an oscillator circuit on its chip; therefore, a separate oscillator circuit needs to be built. The Z80 requires a single-phase TTL level clock with a maximum 30 nsec rise/fall time, and the voltage levels should be between (V_{CC} − 0.6 V) and 0.8 V. The Z80 microprocessor has four versions of the chip operating at different maximum frequencies: the Z80 operates at 2.5 MHz, the Z80A at 4 MHz, the Z80B at 6 MHz, and the Z80H at 8 MHz clock.

Figure 17.6(a) shows a typical oscillator circuit with two inverters and RC network; the 330 Ω pull-up resistor is necessary to obtain TTL voltage level within 0.6 V of V_{CC}. However, this type of circuit is somewhat unstable because of variances in the components. If the microprocessor is not operating at the specified

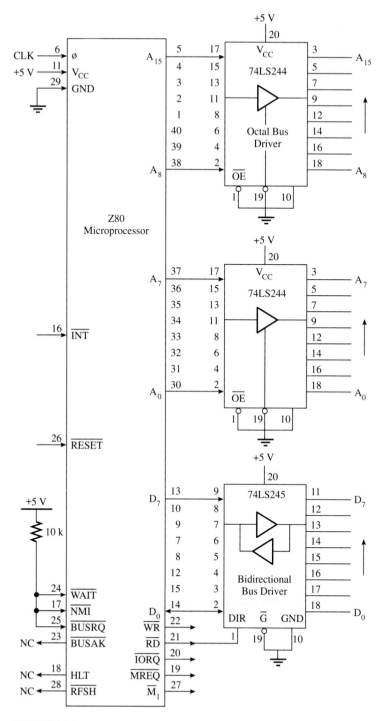

FIGURE 17.4
Z80 MPU with Bus Drivers

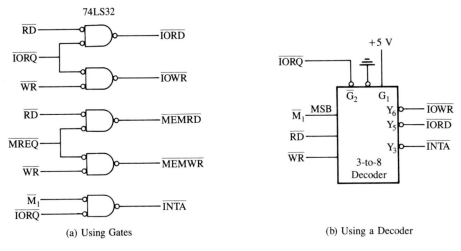

(a) Using Gates

(b) Using a Decoder

FIGURE 17.5
Generating Control Signals

maximum frequency, the circuit shown in Figure 17.6(a) can function very well. Figure 17.6(b) shows a circuit that is generally used in industrial products. The circuit uses a crystal to stabilize the frequency. The output of the oscillator circuit is fed to a flip-flop that divides the frequency in half; the flip-flop provides a 50 percent duty cycle for the clock. In addition to these circuits, several manufacturers (for example, the Motorola K1160 series) offer oscillator/driver circuits on a chip.

The Z80 and other components used in this system require one power supply with +5 V. The current requirement of the power supply is determined primarily by the display load and the peripherals of the system; the MPU and memory components of the system require less than 400 mA.

17.2.5 External Trigger Signals

As discussed in Chapter 3, the Z80 has provision for five external input signals: Reset ($\overline{\text{RESET}}$), Interrupt ($\overline{\text{INT}}$), Nonmaskable Interrupt ($\overline{\text{NMI}}$), Wait ($\overline{\text{WAIT}}$), and Bus Request ($\overline{\text{BUSRQ}}$). Of these five input signals, the $\overline{\text{RESET}}$ and the $\overline{\text{INT}}$ are used in this system, and the others are disabled by connecting them to +5 V (see Figure 17.4).

Reset Circuit   The $\overline{\text{RESET}}$ signal in the Z80 is active low; when this signal goes low, the system is reset. The reset forces the program counter to zero, disables the interrupt flip-flop, clears registers I and R, and sets the Z80 in the interrupt Mode 0.

The reset circuit shown in Figure 17.6(c) is an RC network with a time constant around 50 ms. When the reset key is pushed, the $\overline{\text{RESET}}$ goes low and slowly rises to +5 V, providing sufficient time for the MPU to reset the system; two inverters provide a sharp pulse. Some systems include a circuit called *power-*

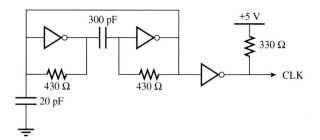

(a)

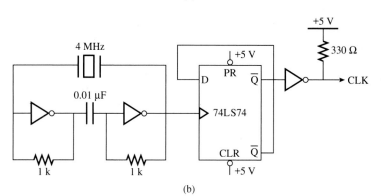

(b)

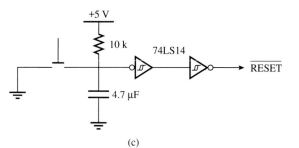

(c)

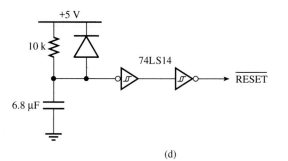

(d)

FIGURE 17.6

(a) RC Network Oscillator Circuit; (b) Oscillator with Crystal; (c) Manual Reset Circuit;
(d) Power-on Reset Circuit

on reset, as shown in Figure 17.6(d). As power is turned on, the voltage across the capacitor does not change instantaneously; therefore, the voltage at the junction of the resistor and the capacitor goes low and slowly rises to +5 V. This pulse can be used through two inverters as in Figure 17.6(c) to reset the system.

17.3 MEMORY DESIGN

In designing memory systems for microprocessor-based products, several critical issues must be considered at the beginning of the design cycle. These issues are:

1. Cost effectiveness
2. Ease of converting a product from the design to the production
3. Design flexibility and future upgrading

The first issue of cost effectiveness involves the unit price of the memory chips to be used in the system and the available space on the board (commonly known as the real estate of a printed circuit board). Ideally, the designer would like to use the minimum space and components with the lowest unit price, and at times, these requirements may conflict.

The first question to be considered is the need for R/W memory. This need is decided by two factors: stack and temporary data from the user. If the system software has subroutines, the stack pointer must be initialized to store return addresses in R/W memory whenever a subroutine is called. The R/W memory is also needed to store the contents of register pairs if PUSH and POP instructions are used in the programs. Similarly, if the system requires any temporary data from the user, the R/W memory is needed to store data. In general, most systems would require R/W memory.

After determining the need for R/W memory, the memory map must be divided between R/W memory and Read-Only-Memory; the distinction between these is based on the requirement of data retention. In the design stage, these requirements are generally not known; however, nowadays, compatible memory chips are available so that RAM, ROM, and EPROM can be interchanged in the same socket. The next decision concerning the R/W memory is to select either the static memory or the dynamic memory. For small systems with 8K or less memory, the static memory has a cost advantage. When memory size begins to approach 64K, the dynamic memory has a distinct price advantage in spite of the additional cost of the refresh circuitry. For the memory size between 8K and 32K, the integrated R/W memory (iRAM) appears to have a cost advantage. Similarly, for read-only-memory, we need to choose among masked ROM, PROM, and EPROM. In the design stage, the EPROM is the best choice until the system is completely developed and debugged. The masked ROM becomes cost effective only for large production quantities.

The remaining two issues of the ease of converting the product from the design to production and future expansion can be solved by using the Mostek's

BYTEWYDE concept, whereby a designer can use the 28-pin DIP socket that can accommodate compatible RAMs, ROMs, EPROMs, or E^2PROMs from memory size 1K $\times$ 8 to 32K $\times$ 8 as shown in Figure 17.7(a). This socket can accept a 24- or 28-pin memory chip; a 24-pin memory chip is inserted into the lower portion of the socket, leaving the top 4 pins unused. In this socket, out of the lower 24 pins, 21 pins are defined: ten address lines A_9–A_0, eight data lines D_0–D_7, the Chip Enable ($\overline{CE}$), the Output Enable ($\overline{OE}$), and the ground. The remaining pins are defined by using a jumper or left as no connections. Figure 17.7(b) shows how pins are connected for 1K $\times$ 8 and 8K $\times$ 8 memory chips. This BYTEWYDE concept provides flexibility during the design stage, ease in changing over from a laboratory design to a production unit, and future expandability.

After the general considerations discussed above, we need to examine how to mix different sizes of memory chips in a system; this is illustrated in the next example.

17.3.1 Memory Design: Problem Statement

Design a memory system using the following memory devices. The memory map of EPROM devices should begin at 0000, and the entire address range should be continuous. The R/W memory address should be placed at 4000_H or beyond. Illustrate the memory address decoding schemes using a 3-to-8 decoder and a 256 $\times$ 4 PROM.

1. EPROM-1: 2732 (4K $\times$ 8)
2. EPROM-2: 2764 (8K $\times$ 8)
3. One R/W memory: CMOS 6116 (2K $\times$ 8)

17.3.2 Design Considerations for Address Decoding

This design problem includes three memory chips: two EPROMs and one R/W memory. In memory design, we should be concerned about the size of the memory chips and their memory maps, future expandability, and the access time.

These three memory chips are of different sizes: 2K, 4K, and 8K; thus, they need 11, 12, and 13 address lines, respectively. If the system demands absolute decoding without wasting any space for foldback addresses, we may have to use more than one decoder or additional gates. If the system can tolerate foldback memory space, we can use just one 3-to-8 decoder and focus on the 8K memory chip for absolute decoding, and others can have multiple memory addresses (foldback space). However, in this problem, to illustrate different techniques, we will focus on the 4K EPROM memory chip.

The address decoding is largely influenced by the requirement that the address must begin at 0000. This requirement is necessary because when the Z80 processor is reset, the program counter is cleared and the program execution begins at this location. The 2732 memory chip has 4K registers; thus, it would require 12 address lines for the memory chip. The remaining four address lines A_{12}–A_{15} can be connected to the decoder, and all of them must be at logic 0 to place the beginning address at 0000. Figure 17.8 shows that the output Y_0 of the decoder

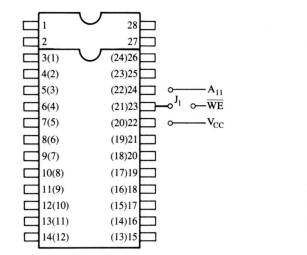

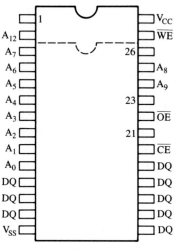

(a)

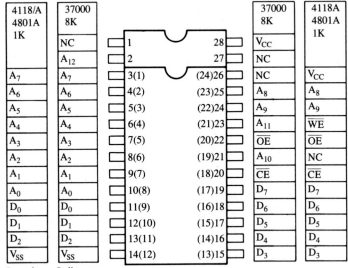

Parentheses Indicates
Pin Number of 24-Pin Packages

(b)

FIGURE 17.7

BYTEWYDE Concept: (a) 28-Pin Socket and Related Jumpers and (b) Used to Connect
8K and 1K Memory in a 28-Pin Socket

SOURCE: Courtesy of Mostek Corporation.

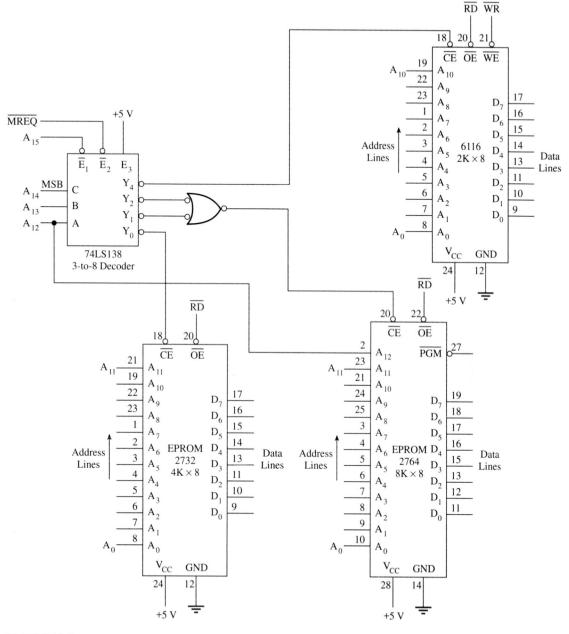

FIGURE 17.8
Memory Board Design

is connected to the $\overline{CE}$ signal of the 2732 memory chip. Now this decoder is set for a 4K memory block; thus, its eight output lines can decode 32K memory without any foldback space. However, it will generate foldback memory space for any chip smaller than 4K registers, and it cannot be used for memory chips larger than 4K without additional gates. Figure 17.8 shows a technique to use this decoder to interface the 2764 memory chip with 8K registers.

The next consideration is future expandability. The 2732 requires a 24-pin socket; however, its pinout is designed in such a way that it can use a 28-pin socket and be compatible with larger memory chips. By using a 28-pin socket with additional DIP switches, the system can be expanded to accommodate the 2764 (8K), 27128 (16K), and 27256 (32K) memory chips. However, this type of expansion cannot be easily accomplished by the decoding network shown in Figure 17.8; we will have to use a PROM for the decoding that can be reprogrammed to accommodate larger memory chips.

The last consideration is the memory access time and whether we need any Wait states in interfacing these memories. In the last decade, memory access time has improved considerably; memory devices with 200 to 250 ns are commonly available. If the clock frequency in our system is 2 MHz, we can conclude from the calculations shown in the last chapter that Wait states will be unnecessary in this system.

17.3.3   2732 EPROM Memory Map

Figure 17.8 shows the design of EPROM using the 2732 (4096×8) and the 74LS138 (3-to-8 decoder). The twelve address lines (A_{11}–A_0) of the MPU from the bus drivers are directly connected to pins A_{11}–A_0 of the 2732 to decode 4096 memory locations. The rest of the address lines (A_{15}–A_{12}) are decoded by the 74LS138; this provides a 4K decoding resolution for each output line of the decoder. The output Y_0 enables the memory chip; thus, the address of the memory chip will range from 0000 to $0FFF_H$ as shown below.

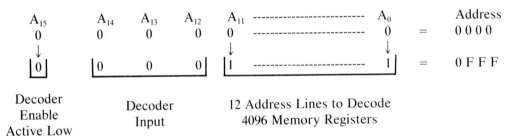

17.3.4   2764 EPROM Memory Map

The 2764 EPROM is an 8K chip and requires 13 address lines (A_0–A_{12}). However, the decoder is set to decode 4K memory size. Therefore, to address 8K memory locations, two output lines Y_2 and Y_1 are logically ORed and used for the Chip Enable ($\overline{CE}$) line of the memory chip. The address line A_{12} is connected to the decoder as well as to the memory chip. For Y_1 to select the memory chip, A_{12}

should be at logic 1. For Y_2 to select the memory chip, A_{12} should be at logic 0. By combining the address lines A_{11} to A_0 with the decoding lines, the memory map of the 2764 EPROM will range from 1000_H to $1FFF_H$ when A_{12} is 1 and from 2000_H to $2FFF_H$ when A_{11} is 0, as shown below.

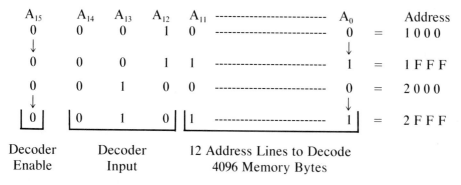

A_{15}	A_{14}	A_{13}	A_{12}	A_{11}	--------------------------	A_0		Address
0	0	0	1	0	--------------------------	0	=	1 0 0 0
↓						↓		
0	0	0	1	1	--------------------------	1	=	1 F F F
0	0	1	0	0	--------------------------	0	=	2 0 0 0
↓						↓		
0	0	1	0	1	--------------------------	1	=	2 F F F

Decoder Enable   Decoder Input   12 Address Lines to Decode 4096 Memory Bytes

17.3.5 6116 R/W Memory Map

The R/W memory (2K bytes) is designed with a 6116 (2048 × 8) memory chip. This chip requires eleven address lines A_{10}–A_0 to decode the 2048 memory locations; the address line A_{11} must be left "don't care." This chip is selected when the Y_4 line of the decoder goes low; thus, the memory map of this R/W memory ranges from 4000_H to $47FF_H$ when the "don't care" line A_{11} is assumed to be 0 and from 4800_H to $4FFF_H$ when A_{11} is assumed to be 1. By convention used in industry, the second address range is assumed to be foldback memory space.

A_{15}	A_{14}	A_{13}	A_{12}	A_{11}	A_{10}	------------------------	A_0	Address	
0	1	0	0	0	0	------------------------	0	= 4000_H	
↓							↓		
0	1	0	0	0	1	------------------------	1	= $47FF_H$	
0	1	0	0	1	0	------------------------	0	= 4800_H	Foldback Memory
↓							↓		
0	1	0	0	1	1	------------------------	1	= $4FFF_H$	Space

Y_4 active

Decoder Enable   Decoder Input   Don't Care   11 Address Lines to Decode 2048 Memory Bytes

17.3.6 Memory Design and BYTEWYDE Concept

Figure 17.9(a) shows the entire memory map, and Figure 17.9(b) shows how to connect different sizes of memory chips using the 28-pin package and the BYTEWYDE concept. For example, the 6116 (2K R/W) memory chip has a 24-pin package, and the 8K EPROM (2764) has a 28-pin package. To interface 2K R/W memory, pin 23 is connected to $\overline{\text{WE}}$. For 8K EPROM, pin 23 is connected to the address line A_{11}. These connections are made using the jumper.

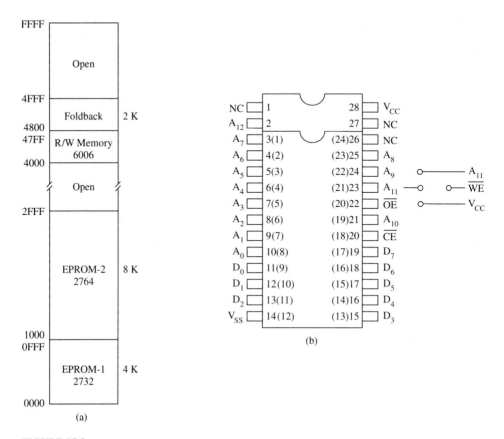

FIGURE 17.9
(a) Memory Map; (b) Using BYTEWYDE Concept

One of the drawbacks of this type of decoding technique is that it generates foldback memory addresses; thus, it wastes memory space and limits further expansion. However, in small systems this is not a serious problem. Another approach to avoid the foldback memory addresses is to use a separate decoder for each different size memory chip.

17.3.7 Address Decoding Using a PROM

Another technique, commonly used in industrial products, is to decode the address bus using a PROM. Figure 17.10 shows a PROM (256 × 4) with eight address lines and four data lines. We can connect each data line to the Chip Enable ($\overline{CE}$) signals of memory devices; thus, we can interface four memory devices. Now we can program the PROM in such a way that for a given range of the address, only one data line will go active (low), whereas others will stay high.

In this memory design problem, the smallest memory size is 2K, which requires 11 address lines; the remaining five address lines must be decoded. The PROM has eight address lines; we can connect the five address lines A_{15}–A_{11} to

FIGURE 17.10
Address Decoding Using a
PROM

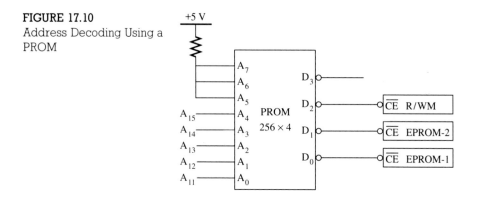

the address lines A_4–A_0 of the PROM, and the address lines A_7–A_5 of the PROM
can be tied high. The five address lines A_4–A_0 of the PROM can have 32 (2^5)
combinations, and we can determine the data output as shown in Table 17.1.

Table 17.1 shows that for the first 4K memory block of EPROM 2732, the
data line D_0 is active; others are high. Similarly, for the second 8K memory block

TABLE 17.1
PROM Decoding

A_7	A_6	A_5	A_4	A_3	A_2	A_1	A_0					
1	1	1	A_{15}	A_{14}	A_{13}	A_{12}	A_{11}	D_3	D_2	D_1	D_0	**Memory Addresses**
												2732 EPROM (4K)
			0	0	0	0	0	1	1	1	0	0 0 0 0
			0	0	0	0	1	1	1	1	0	0 F F F
												2764 EPROM (8K)
			0	0	0	1	0	1	1	0	1	1 0 0 0
			0	0	0	1	1	1	1	0	1	
			0	0	1	0	0	1	1	0	1	
			0	0	1	0	1	1	1	0	1	2 F F F
												Open
			0	0	1	1	0	1	1	1	1	3 0 0 0
			0	0	1	1	1	1	1	1	1	3 F F F
												6116 (2K)
			0	1	0	0	0	1	0	1	1	4 0 0 0
												4 7 F F
												Open
			0	1	0	0	1	1	1	1	1	4 8 0 0
			↓							↓		↓
			1	1	1	1	1	1	1	1	1	F F F F

of EPROM 2764, the data line D_1 is active; others are high. The PROM is decoded for 2K resolution; thus, every combination on A_4–A_0 of the PROM provides 2K memory map. Therefore, for 4K memory, we need D_0 to be active for two combinations. Similarly, D_1 is active for the next four combinations to provide 8K of memory map. For the next open memory space from 3000_H to $3FFFF_H$, all data lines are high. The R/W memory begins at 4000_H, and this is a 2K block accessed by the data line D_2.

The decoding technique using the PROM has two advantages: (1) It is programmable; therefore, the map can be altered or expanded by just reprogramming the PROM. (2) The entire memory space can be utilized without the foldback memory addresses.

17.4   DESIGNING SCANNED DISPLAYS

In Chapter 13, we discussed the interfacing of seven-segment displays with two approaches: one was software dependent based on the table look-up technique, and the other was hardware decoding. However, these approaches are expensive and use excessive current. Here, we will illustrate the scan technique using the Z80 PIO as the interfacing device.

17.4.1   Basic Concepts
The basic concepts in scanned display were discussed in section 13.5.8 (Figure 13.17). The display involves two output ports: one port is used to send seven-segment binary code, and the other port is used to turn seven-segment LEDs on or off in a sequence. The program repeats the sequence of code continuously; thus, the user can see a stable display.

17.4.2   Interfacing Circuit
Figure 17.11 shows the address-decoding network using the 74LS138 3-to-8 decoder. The address lines A_7–A_2 are connected to the decoder, and the remaining two address lines A_1 and A_0 will be connected directly to the Z80 PIO. The output lines of this decoder will be used for other displays and the matrix keyboard. The decode logic of the PIO is identical to that of Figure 13.5. The Z80 PIO is selected when the output line Y_0 of the decoder (Figure 17.11) is asserted. Therefore, the port addresses of the PIO (Figure 17.12) are as follows:

A_7	A_6	A_5	A_4	A_3	A_2	A_1	A_0	
1	0	0	0	0	0	0	0	$= 80_H$ Port A
						0	1	$= 81_H$ Port B
						1	0	$= 82_H$ Control Register A
						1	1	$= 83_H$ Control Register B

Decoder Enable Lines   Decoder Inputs

FIGURE 17.11
I/O Decoding Circuit

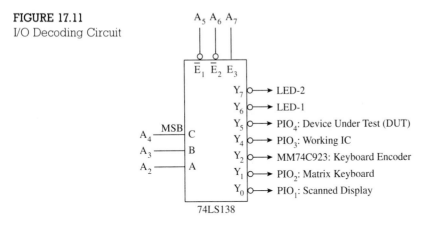

Figure 17.12 shows the schematic of a scanned display; it has six common cathode seven-segment LEDs, one Z80 PIO, and two drivers. Both ports of the PIO are set up as output ports: Port A with the address 80_H for segment codes and Port B with the address 81_H for digits to turn LEDs on or off. The SN 75491 and the SN 75492 are used as the segment code driver and the digit driver, respectively, to increase the current capacity in the circuit. These drivers are functionally equivalent to transistors and can be replaced by discrete transistors.

SN 75491—Segment Driver   The SN 75491 is a quad device that has four Darlington pair transistors in a package; to drive eight data lines, we need two devices, as shown in Figure 17.12. The SN 75491 can source or sink 50 mA current (approximately 12.5 mA/pair). Pin A, the base of the transistor, is connected to one of the data lines of the output port, and emitter E is connected to one of the LED segments.

SN 75492—Digit Driver   The SN 75492 has six Darlington pairs in a package and can sink 250 mA of total current. Each collector (pins 6Y–1Y) is connected to the common cathode of its respective LED, and the data lines from the port are connected to the base of the transistor to turn the LEDs on or off.

To display a digit, the seven-segment code for the digit is sent to Port A, and the corresponding cathode is turned on and off in sequence; the loop is repeated continuously.

17.4.3 Program
;The following program initializes the Z80 PIO Ports A and B as output ports
; and displays a constant message stored at memory location SYSRDY (System
; Ready). The message has six codes: uP-rdy (microprocessor ready). The
; code for the right-most letter "y" is stored at the first location SYSRDY,
; and the scanning begins at that location.

SEGMNT	EQU 80H	;Port address-Segment Driver
DIGIT	EQU 81H	;Port address-Digit Driver
PIO1A	EQU 82H	;Control Port A
PIO1B	EQU 83H	;Control Port B

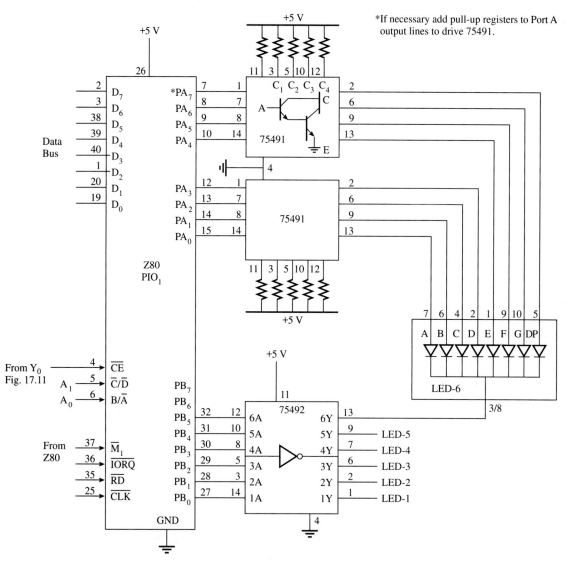

FIGURE 17.12
Schematic: Scanned Display

```
PIO1:      LD A, 00001111B      ;PIO control word 0FH for Mode 0
           OUT (PIO1A), A       ;Initialize Port A
           OUT (PIO1B), A       ;Initialize Port B
READY:     LD B, 00000001B      ;Initialize digit code
           LD C, 06             ;Initialize counter for six LEDs
           LD HL, SYSRDY        ;Use HL as memory pointer for
                                ; message
NEXT:      LD A, (HL)           ;Get segment code
           OUT (SEGMNT), A      ;Output segment code
           LD A, B              ;Get digit code
           OUT (DIGIT), A       ;Turn on one LED
           CALL DELAY1          ;Wait 1 millisecond
           XOR A                ;Code to turn off segments
           OUT (SEGMNT), A      ;Clear segments
           RLC B                ;Shift digit code to turn on next LED
           INC HL               ;Point to next code
           DEC C                ;Next LED count
           JR NZ, NEXT
           RET
SYSRDY:    DEFB 5EH, 50H,       ;Message codes
           DEFB 40H, 73H,       ;y d r–P u
               1CH
```

PROGRAM DESCRIPTION

This routine initializes Ports A and B of PIO1 as output ports by sending the word 00001111B ($0F_H$) to the control registers of Port A and Port B (see Figure 13.6 for the definition of the control word). The next instruction initializes the scan routine by placing the digit code 00000001 into register B; this code will turn on LED-1 (the first LED at the right). By rotating bit D_0 (logic 1) to the left, the next LED is turned on and the LED presently being displayed is turned off; thus, only one LED is on at a time. Register C is set up as a counter to scan six LEDs, and the HL register is used as a memory pointer to point to where the message is stored.

The scanning begins by sending the first code (the last letter "y" in the message) to Port A, and LED-1 is turned on by sending the digit code. This LED is kept on for approximately 1 ms by calling the delay routine, and the entire display is turned off by clearing the segment code; this eliminates the flicker and the ghost images. The segment codes are sent in a sequence as they are stored in memory, and the corresponding LED is turned on until the counter reaches zero. To keep the display on, the routine should be called repeatedly.

Comments   In the scanned display, the hardware is minimized. With two output ports, this scheme can scan eight LEDs. In addition, current consumption is considerably reduced. However, the major disadvantage is that the MPU is kept occupied in scanning the display continuously. To relieve the MPU from the continuous scanning task, the Intel 8279—programmable keyboard/display interface device—can be used.

Modifications   This scanned display is designed to display a fixed message stored at the location SYSRDY using six LEDs. In real life applications, display must change according to different tasks performed by the microprocessor. For example, in an IC Tester unit (discussed in section 17.6), messages could vary from an error message to a successful completion message. In addition, some messages may need less than six LEDs. To account for such situations, the scan routine must be changed. If a message requires less than six LEDs, the calling program must supply a parameter (number of LEDs to be scanned) for register C. To change a message, either the memory pointer in HL for SYSRDY must be supplied by the calling program or code in the SYSRDY memory locations must be changed before calling the scan routine.

17.5   INTERFACING A MATRIX KEYBOARD

A matrix keyboard is a commonly used input device when more than eight keys are necessary, rather than a row of keys as discussed in Chapter 13. A matrix keyboard reduces the number of connections, thus the number of interfacing devices required. For example, a keyboard with 20 keys, arranged in a 5×4 (five rows and four columns) matrix, requires nine lines from the microprocessor to make all the connections instead of twenty lines needed if the keys are connected in a linear format.

In interfacing a matrix keyboard, the major task is to identify which key is pressed and decode the key in terms of its binary value. This task can be accomplished through either software or hardware. In this section we explore both methods: first we discuss the basic concepts in interfacing a matrix keyboard, and then write subroutines to check, identify, and decode (interpret) the key pressed. Finally, we illustrate how these functions can be replaced by a hardware device, such as the National Semiconductor keyboard encoder MM74C923.

17.5.1 Basic Concepts

Figure 17.13 shows a matrix keyboard with 20 keys; the keyboard has five rows and four columns. The first sixteen keys in a sequence represent data 0 to F in Hex, and the remaining four will represent various functions such as Store and Execute; at present, they are identified as K_1, K_2, K_3, and K_4. The circuit includes two I/O ports: one output port and one input port. Rows are connected to the output port and columns to the input port. The columns and rows make contact only when a key is pressed; otherwise, they remain high ($+5$ V). When a key is pressed, the key must be identified by its column and the row, and the intersection

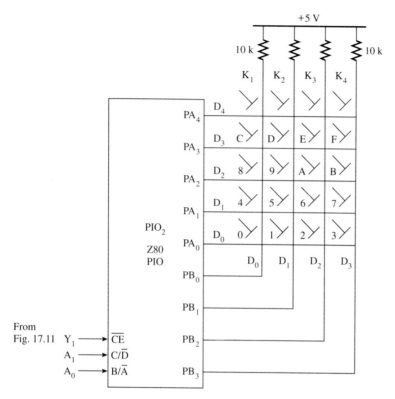

FIGURE 17.13
Interfacing a Matrix Keyboard

of the column and row must change from high to low. This can be accomplished as explained in the following steps.

1. Ground all the rows by sending logic 0 through the output port.
2. Check the columns by reading the input port. If no key is pressed, all columns remain high. Continue to repeat Steps **1** and **2** until the reading indicates a change.
3. When one of the keys is pressed, the corresponding column goes low; at that point, identify and decode the key.

17.5.2 Interfacing Circuit
Figure 17.13 shows an interfacing circuit of a 20-key matrix keyboard using a Z80 PIO, identified as PIO3. This circuit uses the decoding network of Figure 17.11; the output line Y_1 of the decoder is connected to the $\overline{CE}$ line of PIO2. Therefore, the port addresses of the PIO2 range from 84_H to 87_H as follows:

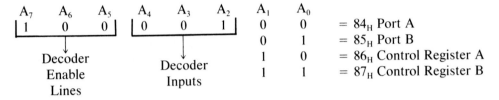

A_7	A_6	A_5	A_4	A_3	A_2	A_1	A_0	
1	0	0	0	0	1	0	0	$= 84_H$ Port A
						0	1	$= 85_H$ Port B
						1	0	$= 86_H$ Control Register A
						1	1	$= 87_H$ Control Register B

Decoder Enable Lines   Decoder Inputs

In Figure 17.13, the rows are connected to Port A, and the columns are connected to Port B; therefore, Port A should be initialized as an output port and Port B as an input port. To initialize the PIO2, the instructions are as follows:

```
PIO2A   EQU 86H            ;Port A control register
PIO2B   EQU 87H            ;Port B control register
PIO2:   LD A, 00001111B    ;Mode 0 control word (0FH)
        OUT (PIO2A), A     ;Initialize Port A as an output port
        LD A, 01001111B    ;Mode 1 control word (4FH)
        OUT (PIO2B), A     ;Initialize Port B as an input port
```

17.5.3 Program

The matrix keyboard routine is conceptually important because it illustrates how to set up relationships between hardware binary readings and expected codes. For example, when key "0" is pressed, the input reading at Port B will be 1 1 1 0 (D_3–D_0); however, the binary code for that key must be 0 0 0 0 0 0 0 0. This conversion is performed by the software routines, which are illustrated in this section. Similarly, when key "K_1" is pressed, the input reading will be the same as for the "0" key (1 1 1 0). The software routines will have to differentiate between data and function keys.

    This matrix keyboard problem can be divided into four steps (Figure 17.14).

Step 1: Check whether all keys are open.

    In this step, the program grounds all the rows by sending 0s to the output port. It reads the input port to check the key release, and debounces the key release by waiting for 10 ms. This step is necessary to avoid misinterpretation if a key is held for a long time.

Step 2: Check a key closure.

    In this step, the program checks for a key closure by reading the input port. If all keys are open, the input reading on data lines D_3–D_0 should be 1 1 1 1, and if one of the keys is closed, the reading will be less than 1 1 1 1. (Data lines D_7–D_4 are not connected; therefore, the data on these lines should be masked.)

Step 3: Identify the key.

    This is a somewhat complex procedure. Once a key closure is found, the key should be identified by grounding one row at a time and checking each column for zero. Figure 17.14 (Step 3) shows that two loops are set up: the outer loop grounds one row at a time, and the inner loop checks each column for zero.

Step 4: Find the binary key code for the key. The binary key code is identified through the counter procedure. For each row, the inner loop is repeated four times to check four columns, and for every column check, the counter is incremented. For five rows, the inner loop is repeated twenty times, and the counter is incremented from 0 to 13_H—thus maintaining the binary code in the counter. Once the key is identified, the code is transferred from the counter to the accumulator. The codes 0 to F are used for data keys and the remaining codes 10_H to 13_H are assigned various functions according to applications.

KEYBOARD SUBROUTINE

```
;This subroutine checks a key closure in the keyboard, identifies
; the key, and supplies the corresponding binary code in the
; accumulator. It does not modify any register contents.
;Input: None
;Output: Binary key code in the accumulator
;Calls DBONCE, a 10 ms delay subroutine
ROW          EQU 84H                      ;Port address for rows
COLUMN       EQU 85H                      ;Port address for
                                          ; columns
KYBORD:      PUSH BC                      ;Save registers
             PUSH DE
             XOR A                        ;Clear accumulator
             LD E, A                      ;Set up register E as
                                          ; binary code counter
                                          ; starting with code for
                                          ; key 0
             OUT (ROW), A                 ;Ground all rows
KYREL:       IN A, (COLUMN)               ;Read columns
             AND 0FH                      ;Mask data lines D₇–D₄
             CP 0FH                       ;Check for key release
             JR NZ, KYREL                 ;If previous key is not
                                          ; released, wait in loop
             CALL DBONCE                  ;Wait for 10 ms when
                                          ; key is released
KYCHK:       IN A, (COLUMN)               ;Read columns
             AND 0FH                      ;Mask data lines D₇–D₄
             CP 0FH                       ;Is any key closed?
             JR Z, KYCHK                  ;If not, wait in loop
             CALL DBONCE                  ;Wait for key debounce
             LD A, 01111111B              ;Load data byte to
                                          ; ground one row at a
                                          ; time
```

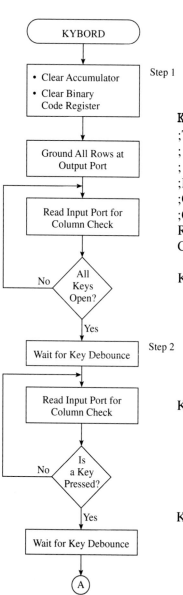

FIGURE 17.14
Flowchart: Matrix Keyboard Subroutine

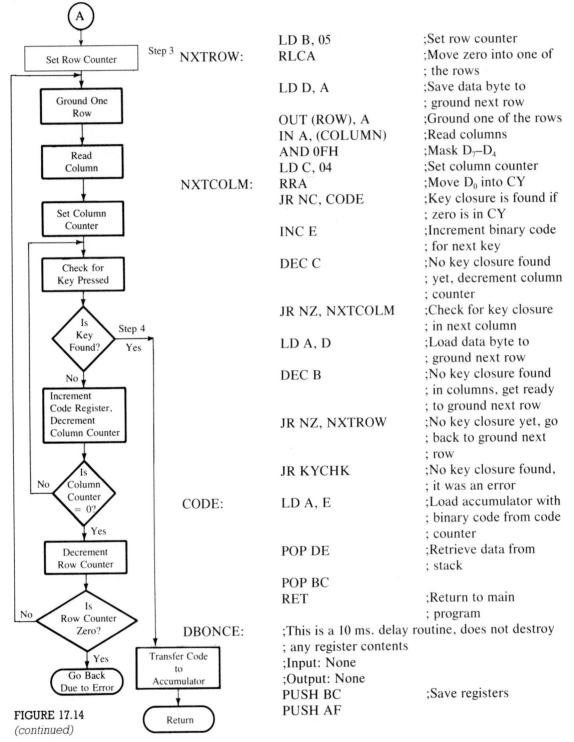

	LD B, 05	;Set row counter
NXTROW:	RLCA	;Move zero into one of ; the rows
	LD D, A	;Save data byte to ; ground next row
	OUT (ROW), A	;Ground one of the rows
	IN A, (COLUMN)	;Read columns
	AND 0FH	;Mask D_7–D_4
	LD C, 04	;Set column counter
NXTCOLM:	RRA	;Move D_0 into CY
	JR NC, CODE	;Key closure is found if ; zero is in CY
	INC E	;Increment binary code ; for next key
	DEC C	;No key closure found ; yet, decrement column ; counter
	JR NZ, NXTCOLM	;Check for key closure ; in next column
	LD A, D	;Load data byte to ; ground next row
	DEC B	;No key closure found ; in columns, get ready ; to ground next row
	JR NZ, NXTROW	;No key closure yet, go ; back to ground next ; row
	JR KYCHK	;No key closure found, ; it was an error
CODE:	LD A, E	;Load accumulator with ; binary code from code ; counter
	POP DE	;Retrieve data from ; stack
	POP BC	
	RET	;Return to main ; program
DBONCE:	;This is a 10 ms. delay routine, does not destroy ; any register contents	
	;Input: None	
	;Output: None	
	PUSH BC	;Save registers
	PUSH AF	

FIGURE 17.14
(continued)

```
          LD BC, COUNT        ;Load 10 ms delay
                              ; count
LOOP:     DEC BC              ;Repeat loop for delay
          LD A, C
          OR B                ;Set zero flag if BC = 0
          JR NZ, LOOP
          POP AF
          POP BC
          RET
```

PROGRAM DESCRIPTION

This keyboard routine saves register contents of the calling program and clears registers A and E. Register E is used as a binary code counter for the keys; it begins with the code of "0" key. The OUT instruction grounds all the rows, and the IN instruction reads the columns. The AND instruction masks the data on lines D_7–D_4 because they are not being used for this keyboard.

The next instruction, CP 0FH, checks whether the previous key pressed has been released; this is a precautionary step against someone holding a key for a long time. If all keys are open, D_3–D_0 will be high, the reading will be $0F_H$, and the Compare instruction will set the zero flag; otherwise, the routine stays in the loop KYREL until all keys are open. The subroutine DBONCE eliminates the key bounce by waiting for 10 ms.

Once all keys are open, the routine reads the columns to check for a key closure. If any of the keys is closed, one of the columns will be at logic 0, and the routine will skip the KYCHK loop. The DBONCE routine will debounce the key closure. At this point, a key closure is found, but the key is not identified. For example, if the reading on data lines D_3–D_0 is 1 1 1 0, any of the keys in Column 0 may have been pressed. Therefore, the next step is to identify the key.

To identify the key pressed, one row is grounded at a time, beginning at Row 0. The byte 0 1 1 1 1 1 1 1 ($7F_H$) is loaded into the accumulator and rotated left (RLCA) by one position; the byte is thus converted to 1 1 1 1 1 1 1 0. This byte is sent to Port A to ground Row 0. Then, Port B is read, and each column is checked for logic 0 by rotating the reading into the CY flag. Register C is set up to count four columns, and by rotating the byte to the left four times, each column is checked for logic 0 in the loop labelled as NXTCOLM. As each column is being checked, the code counter (Register E) is incremented at each iteration. For example, when Row 0 is grounded, four keys, 0 through 3, are checked, and the code counter is incremented from 00 to 03_H.

After checking the columns in Row 0, the program loops back to location NXTROW and grounds the next row by sending the code that was previously saved in register D. Register B is set up as a row counter to count five rows. For each row, the loop NXTCOLM is repeated four times; thus, all twenty keys are checked, and for each iteration the code counter is incremented. When columns are checked, each reading is rotated into the CY flag; the key closure is found and the key identified when CY is reset. The program jumps to location CODE. The routine copies the key code into the accumulator and returns to the calling program.

COMMENTS

If we were to use the scanned display (as specified) with the software-driven matrix keyboard, the keyboard subroutine would have to be coupled with the scanned display; otherwise, the display may go off. For example, when the subroutine is waiting for a key to be pressed, the scanned display cannot be refreshed by turning on and off digits in a sequence at a regular interval. Therefore, the program must alternate between refreshing the display and checking a keyboard to find a key pressed. Another approach is to interface the keyboard using the interrupt technique. In Figure 17.13, an interrupt can be generated by logically ORing all the input lines to PB_0–PB_3. In this approach, the program continues to scan the display until the interrupt signal is received. Then the program checks the keyboard, processes the key, and goes back to scanning the display.

17.5.4   Hardware Approaches to Interfacing
Matrix Keyboard and Scanned Display

The hardware approach reduces the software and allows the MPU to perform other tasks; however, it may increase the unit cost of the product. One of the approaches is to use a logic device, such as the National Semiconductor MM74C923 keyboard encoder. This keyboard encoder can sense a key closure, debounce the key, provide the binary code of the key, and generate an interrupt. Another approach is to use a programmable device, such as the Intel 8279 keyboard/display interface. This interface device performs two tasks: one task is to detect and encode a key (this is the same task as that of the National Semiconductor keyboard encoder), and the other is to refresh a scanned display. It is capable of displaying 16 bytes. The 8279 is a complex device and will not be discussed here. However, we will illustrate how to interface a matrix keyboard using the MM74C923 keyboard encoder.

MM74C923 KEYBOARD ENCODER

This is a 20-key encoder with four columns and five rows (Figure 17.15). The respective columns and rows of a matrix keyboard must be connected to the columns and rows of the encoder. The encoder includes Chip Select and Interrupt logic. The decoded address line (I/O Select) is connected to the $\overline{OE}$ pin of the encoder; it does not require a PIO or an input buffer. It has five output data lines that provide the binary code of a key closure from 00000 to 10011 (0–19). This is similar to the KYBORD routine providing a key code in the accumulator.

Figure 17.16 shows the schematic for interfacing a 20-key matrix keyboard using the encoder. The keyboard is assigned the port address by connecting the output Y_2 of the decoder from Figure 17.11. Thus, the keyboard can be accessed

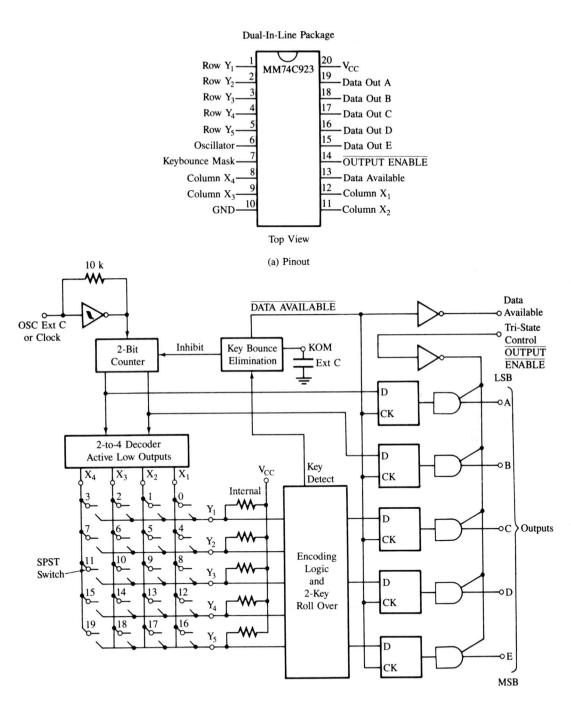

FIGURE 17.15

Keyboard Encoder MM74C923 (National Semiconductor): (a) Pinout; (b) Block Diagram

SOURCE: Reprinted with permission of National Semiconductor Corporation.

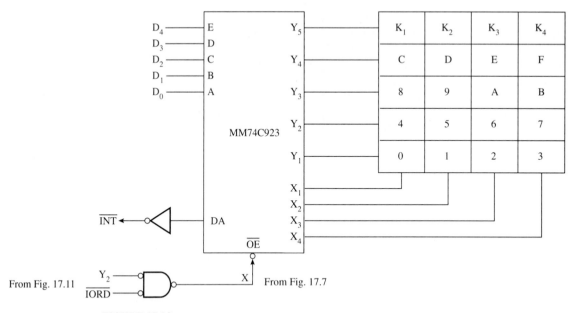

FIGURE 17.16
Interfacing 20-Key Matrix Keyboard Using the MM74C923

by any one of the port addresses 88_H to $8B_H$; the address lines A_1 and A_0 are left as "don't care."

When a key is pressed, the encoder debounces the key and checks again for a valid key. If a valid key is detected, the encoder generates an interrupt and places the binary code of the key into the internal latches, and the code can be read by enabling $\overline{OE}$. When the MPU acknowledges the interrupt and reads the binary code, the encoder turns off the interrupt. In this interfacing, the keyboard routine is reduced to a few instructions of a service routine, which reads the keyboard and stores the code in the input buffer. This technique reduces considerable software overhead for the MPU. Therefore, the MPU can continue to scan the display until an interrupt request is received. Then, it can process the key and go back to the scanned display routine.

17.6   DESIGN OF AN IC TESTER

Design a Z80-based microprocessor system to test 14- and 16-pin combinational logic circuits. The system should include the following components:

1. Input: Matrix keyboard
2. Output: Two seven-segment LEDs
3. Interfacing devices: Z80 PIOs.

The system should allow the user to test a 14- or a 16-pin combinational circuit. When the system is turned on, a sign-on message such as "GO" should be displayed. The IC Tester will have two test sockets, one for a working IC and the other for a Device Under Test (DUT). The user is expected to insert two ICs into test jigs and enter the given masking word for the DUT using the keyboard. The IC Tester will compare the outputs of the DUT with the outputs of the working unit for all possible input combinations. If they match, the tester will display PS (Pass); otherwise, it will display FL (Fail) at the seven-segment LEDs.

17.6.1 Basic Concepts of an IC Tester

A combinational logic IC is tested by verifying its truth table. To test the two-input NAND gate shown in Figure 17.17(a) requires four input signals (00, 01, 10, and 11), and we should be able to observe 1, 1, 1, and 0 as corresponding outputs. We can test this gate by using the microprocessor. The microprocessor requires two ports: one output port and one input port. The microprocessor outputs the necessary signals to the inputs of the gate and reads the output of the gate as inputs through its input port. Now, to verify the truth table of the gate, the microprocessor should be able to compare the outputs of the gate with the expected outputs. This can be accomplished in two ways. One is to store the expected output as a look-up table permanently in memory for a given gate and then, the microprocessor can compare its input readings with this table. The second approach is to test a working gate first, store its truth table in R/W memory, and then verify the outputs of the gate under test. The basic concept is the same: compare the outputs of the DUT with the known truth table. In the first method, we need to store the truth tables of various ICs permanently in ROM or EPROM

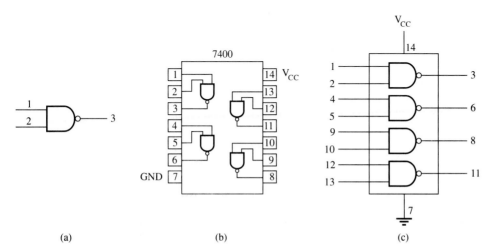

(a) (b) (c)

FIGURE 17.17
(a) NAND Gate; (b) 7400 NAND Gate Pinout; and (c) 8-Input/4-Output Configuration

and find a way to locate the appropriate table for a given IC. In the second method, the truth table is generated temporarily from a working IC, and the same type of IC is tested against the generated table. In this discussion, it is necessary to clarify the input/output terminology: the input to a logic gate is the output from the microprocessor, and the output of a gate becomes the input to the microprocessor.

The next question is how to test multiple devices in a package. Figure 17.17(b) shows the 14-pin package of 74LS00; it has four NAND gates. This package has eight input signals and four output signals. The easiest approach is to connect eight inputs of the gates to an output port and four outputs to an input port of the microprocessor. Even if this package has four gates, each gate requires four input combinations. Thus, by sending the four Hex bytes (00, 55, AA, FF), the outputs of the gates can be read as shown below. However, this approach cannot be generalized to test various types of ICs; as the device changes, connections will have to be changed.

Hex Input	Input Pins Necessary Input Combinations								Output Pins			
	13	12	10	9	5	4	2	1	11	8	6	3
00 =	0	0	0	0	0	0	0	0	1	1	1	1
55 =	0	1	0	1	0	1	0	1	1	1	1	1
AA =	1	0	1	0	1	0	1	0	1	1	1	1
FF =	1	1	1	1	1	1	1	1	0	0	0	0

Figure 17.17(c) suggests a generalized approach: view the package as an 8-input and 4-output pin device. We can set up an 8-bit counter to provide all possible input combinations to the gates and read the corresponding outputs. But this approach has a serious drawback: the 8-bit counter has 256 input combinations, and the 74LS00 needs only four as shown above. We need to find a way to eliminate the duplicate inputs. This can be accomplished by implementing the masking concept as discussed below.

Let us take an example of one NAND gate; it has two inputs (pins 1 and 2) and one output (pin 3). If we set up a 3-digit counter, it will have eight combinations including four duplications; however, there is no reason to send a signal to the output pin 3 and read the signals from pins 1 and 2.

If we examine eight inputs to pins 1 and 2, we find that input combinations **5 to 8** are duplicates of **1 to 4.** These inputs can be eliminated by using the masking bits (1 0 0): 1 for output pins and 0 for input pins. If the bits 1 0 0 are ANDed with the first four inputs, the results are zero (0 0 0), and if the same bits are ANDed with inputs 5 to 8, the results are non-zero (1 0 0). Therefore, to remove duplications, the inputs with the non-zero results after masking must be eliminated. Similarly, if the input readings to the microprocessor are masked by the same bits, the unnecessary output readings of pins 1 and 2 will be always zero.

	Output Pin 3	Input Pins 2	Input Pins 1	Expected Output at Pin 3
1.	0	0	0	1
2.	0	0	1	1
3.	0	1	0	1
4.	0	1	1	0
5.	1	0	0	1
6.	1	0	1	1
7.	1	1	0	1
8.	1	1	1	0

Now let us examine a masking word for an actual device. A 14-pin 74LS00 NAND gate will be connected in a 16-pin socket as shown in Figure 17.18. The power supply, ground, and no connection pins need no inputs and will be considered at logic 1 or as outputs. Therefore, the masking word for the 74LS00 will be as follows:

Socket Pins:	16	15	14	13	12	11	10	9	8	7	6	5	4	3	2	1
74LS00 Pins:	14	13	12	11	10	9	8	X	X	7	6	5	4	3	2	1
Logic Levels:	1	0	0	1	0	0	1	1	1	1	1	0	0	1	0	0

$$93_H \qquad\qquad E4_H$$

The designer must determine these masking words for each device to be tested and supply them to the user.

17.6.2 Hardware Design

To meet the specifications outlined earlier, we will use two PIOs: one for a working IC and the other for a device under test as shown in Figure 17.18. We can also design this tester by using only one PIO with some modifications in software. These PIOs are selected by the output lines Y_4 and Y_5 from Figure 17.11. Thus, the port addresses of the PIO_4 range from 90_H to 93_H and the port addresses of PIO_5 range from 94_H to 97_H, and both PIOs will be set up in I/O Bit Mode 3. To accommodate 14- and 16-pin ICs, pins A_7, A_6, and B_0 have jumpers to make ground connections.

Figure 17.19 shows the interfacing of two seven-segment LEDs using two latches 74LS373. These latches are selected by the output lines Y_6 and Y_7 of the decoder shown in Figure 17.11; thus, these output ports can be accessed with the addresses 98_H and 99_H, respectively. The messages in this project are two-letter fixed messages. This type of display will simplify the system program. Another alternative is to use the scanned display discussed in section 17.4.

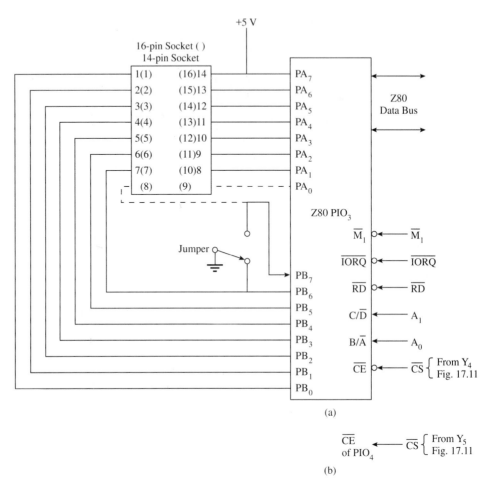

(a)

(b)

FIGURE 17.18

14- and 16-Pin Socket Connections to Z80 PIO Ports: (a) Working IC; (b) Identical Connections as in (a) to PIO$_4$

This project requires a keyboard to enter masking words for a given device and execute the program. To enter a masking word, the keyboard should have 16 keys to enter digits from 0 to F. The function keys can be limited to two keys: one to indicate that the next four keys will represent a masking word and the second to execute the program. The matrix keyboard discussed in section 17.5 can be used for this project. We will use key K_1 with code 10_H for the "Execute" function and key K_2 with code 11_H for the "Enter" function.

17.6.3   Designing Software Modules

The proposed system includes a matrix keyboard. Therefore, the main program primarily revolves around checking a key input by calling the KYBORD routines

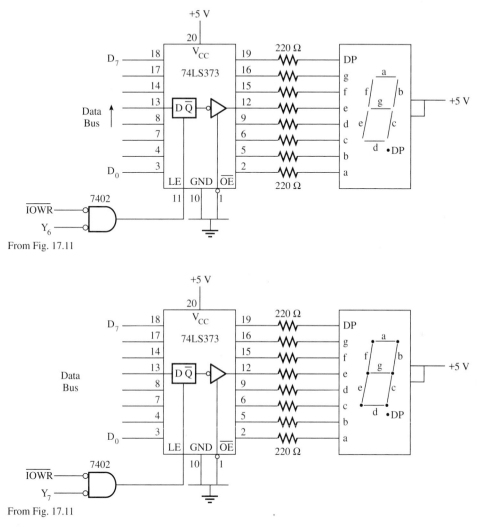

FIGURE 17.19
Interfacing Two Seven-Segment LEDs

shown in Figure 17.20. The primary task of the keyboard routine is to read and process the key pressed and perform the designated function of the key. We can divide the software design in the following modules:

1. Initialization: to initialize programmable devices such as PIOs
2. Display: to output the sign-on message and wait for a key to be pressed
3. Key Check and Masking Word: When a key is pressed, this module should read the key, check whether it is the ENTER key, and then accept the masking word for a DUT

FIGURE 17.20
Flowchart: Main Program

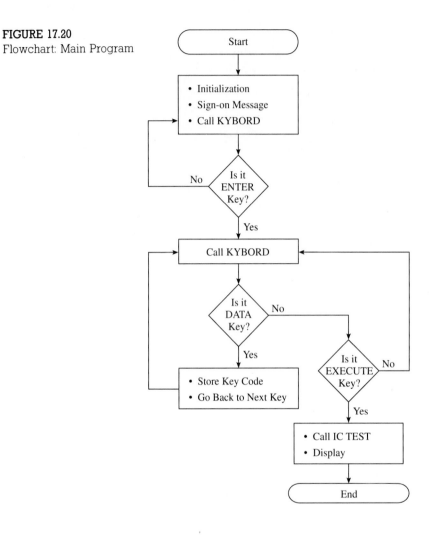

4. IC Test: This module should be executed when the "Execute" key is pressed; the module checks the working unit and tests the DUT. After the completion of the test, a result is displayed.
5. Final display.

INITIALIZATION

When a system is reset, the Z80 clears the program counter, and the program execution begins at location 0000_H. If the system includes several sources of interrupts, the initial memory locations (up to 0038_H, RST 38) can be used for Mode 0 interrupts. However, in this system, we have no interrupts; therefore, there is no compelling reason to save these Restart (RST) locations. The initialization program module can be written in the beginning segment of the 2732 EPROM.

This module must initialize the programmable devices (PIOs) and the stack pointer. The PIO ports for test units must be set up in I/O Bit Mode 3; however, their desired I/O characteristics are determined by the IC under test. The stack pointer is generally initialized at the top of the R/W memory.

DISPLAY

In this project, the messages are fixed and can be permanently stored in EPROM. These messages can be brought in the microprocessor by using memory pointers and displayed at the output ports.

KEYCHECK AND MASKING WORD

After the initialization and the sign-on message, the program calls for the KYBORD routine and expects the user to push the "Enter" key followed by the 16-bit mask word for a DUT. To enter the mask word, the user must press four Hex keys. Each key provides a four-digit code beginning with the most significant four digits (nibble) of a 16-bit mask word. These digits must be stored in a register-pair (such as DE) in a proper sequence. For example, the mask word for 74LS00 is $93E4_H$ (as discussed in section 17.7.1). The user is expected to push the keys in the sequence as 9, 3, E, and 4. The program should accept the first nibble, store it in the least significant position, and shift it to the left as the additional keys are pressed. If more than four keys are pressed, the first key must be discarded (see Example 11.4 in Chapter 11). Then the program waits for the "Execute" key as shown in Figure 17.20. When this key is pressed, the program jumps to ICTEST routine and checks and compares ICs as discussed below.

IC TEST

This routine is the backbone of this project and is based on the basic concepts discussed before. Figure 17.21 shows a flowchart of this routine, and the various steps in the routine are listed below.

1. Initialize 16 individual I/O lines of two PIOs: one for working unit and the other for device under test. For a masking byte, we used logic 0 for the input to the gates and logic 1 for the output of the gates. The input lines to the gates are the output lines of the PIO, and these lines are initialized as output lines by sending logic 0 to the control register of the PIO. Similarly, I/O lines are initialized as input lines by sending logic 1 to the PIO control register (refer to Figure 13.12(a): I/O Register Control Word). That means the I/O register control word to set up the PIO lines is the same as the mask word.
2. Set up a 16-bit counter to count from 0000 to $FFFF_H$.
3. Mask each count using the Mask word of the IC. If the result is zero, output the count to both units; otherwise, reject the count and go to the next count.
4. Read the outputs of both units and compare the readings. If the readings are the same, go to the next count, continue until the last count, and return to display the message PS (Pass).
5. Whenever readings differ, return immediately to the main program to display the message FL (Fail).

FIGURE 17.21
Flowchart: IC Test Subroutine

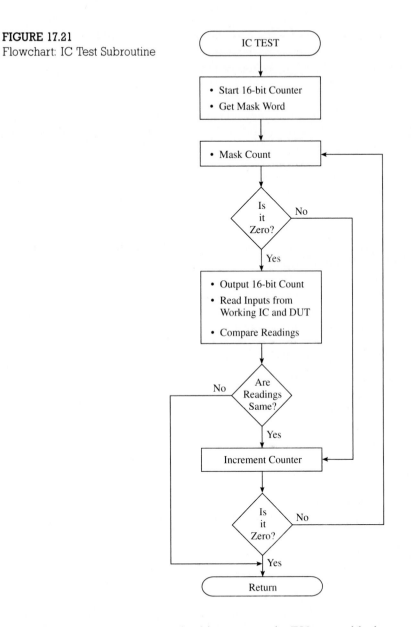

The next steps are to code this program in Z80 assembly language and to test it on prototype hardware, using such debugging tools as an in-circuit emulator and a logic analyzer (discussed later).

17.6.4   Trade-Off Between Hardware and Software

The IC Tester project discussed in this section can be used as a classroom project. It can be simplified or made more challenging depending on the objectives of the course. In general, we can simplify tasks by substituting hardware components for programs. However, the production cost will increase in relation to the components on the board. The trade-off between hardware and software is discussed here by examining various options for this IC Tester project.

Using One PIO   Assuming the availability of a single-board microcomputer, this project can be made as an interfacing project using one PIO. The keyboard of the microcomputer can be used to enter the masking word, and the results can be displayed using LEDs. If one PIO is used, a working IC and a DUT will have to be checked in two stages. In the first stage, the outputs of the working IC must be stored as a table in memory. Then, by inserting the DUT, its outputs can be compared with the table of the working IC. The program will have to be modified to add on an entire segment to perform the test in two stages.

Using Scanned Display   To make the programming aspect more challenging, the two-LED constant display can be replaced by a scanned display. The program will have to alternate between scanning the display and checking the keyboard. The program can be somewhat simplified if the keyboard is connected as an interrupting device. Then, the program will continue scanning until a keyboard interrupt is received.

Using Programmable Devices   The matrix keyboard and scanned display routines can be further simplified by using hardware. A 20-key encoder such as MM74C923 can be substituted for the matrix keyboard routine. This encoder checks for a key pressed, debounces the key, provides the equivalent binary code for the key, and generates an interrupt. This encoder performs the same functions as the keyboard subroutine. The program can be further simplified by using a keyboard/display programmable device such as Intel 8279. This device performs the functions of the encoder and scanning of the display. This relieves the processor from checking a key and scanning the display; thus, the processor is free to perform other functions in the system.

Decision Making   Now the question is, How does a designer make a decision among many options? Two of the primary criteria are cost and available space on the board. For large production units, cost is generally minimized and available space on the board is optimized by using less hardware and more software. This approach will cost more in development for writing and debugging the program and may require large memory. However, memory devices are less expensive, and the development cost is a one-time cost. On the other hand, for a particular unit, it may be cheaper to substitute hardware for software.

17.6.5   Prototype Building and Testing

Microprocessor-based products are hardly ever completely built and tested as complete systems during the initial stages of design. If a system is completely built, it is difficult to troubleshoot. Traditional approaches, such as signal injection and isolation of trouble spots, are ineffective for troubleshooting bus-oriented systems. Therefore, a system is built and tested in stages. Each subsystem, such as keyboard, displays, and memory, should be built and tested separately as an independent module. Now the question is, How do we test a module without building a system? An answer can be found in such everyday incidents as testing a light bulb or starting a car with a dead battery. The light bulb can be tested by plugging it into a working socket, and the car can be started with a jumper cable and another battery. There are two principles involved in these examples: (1) borrowing resources from a working system and (2) substitution. These principles can be used in testing each separate subsystem of a microprocessor-based product. What is needed is a working system that can create an environment similar to the complete prototype system and that is generous enough to share its resources with hardware modules to be built. Such a working system, called an in-circuit emulator, is described in section 17.7 and shown in Figure 17.22.

Assuming that such an in-circuit emulator is available, each subsystem of the single-board microcomputer can be built and tested one at a time. Similarly, as software modules are being written, they can be tested first on a software development system (discussed in Chapter 7). Finally, hardware and software can be integrated and tested using an in-circuit emulator.

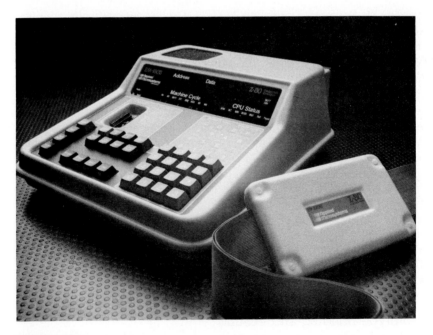

FIGURE 17.22
In-Circuit Emulator
SOURCE: Courtesy of Applied Microsystems

DEVELOPMENT AND TROUBLESHOOTING TOOLS 17.7

In bus-oriented systems, a constant flow of data changes logic states continuously. The flow of data is controlled by software instructions. Therefore, to examine what is happening inside the system, special instruments capable of capturing data in relation to instructions are required. Three such instruments—in-circuit emulator, logic state analyzer, and signature analyzer—are discussed briefly in the next sections.

17.7.1 In-Circuit Emulator

The in-circuit emulation technique has become an essential part of the design process for microprocessor-based products. In-circuit emulation is the execution of a prototype software program in prototype hardware under the control of a software development system. First, the microprocessor is removed from the prototype design board, and a 40-pin cable from an in-circuit emulator is plugged into the socket previously occupied by the microprocessor. The in-circuit emulator performs all the functions of the replaced microprocessor; in addition, it allows the prototype hardware to share all its resources, such as software, memory, and I/Os. It provides a window for looking into the dynamic, real-time operation of the prototype hardware. At present, a wide variety of in-circuit emulators is available, ranging from universal emulators with complete software development systems to stand-alone microprocessor units. Figure 17.22 shows a stand-alone in-circuit emulator (MT-180) designed by Applied Micro Systems.

Emulation Process   To test subsystems (such as I/O and memory) using an in-circuit emulator, the mninimum prototype hardware required is a 40-pin microprocessor socket (without the microprocessor), a power supply, and a system clock. All other resources can be borrowed from the in-circuit emulator. As more and more prototype hardware is built, fewer and fewer resources from the in-circuit emulator will be required. In the final stage, total software and hardware are integrated for testing. A hardware prototype can be viewed as a fetus growing in stages in the womb of an in-circuit emulator; until the fetus is fully developed and functioning independently, the in-circuit emulator provides the necessary environment and resources.

Features of the In-Circuit Emulator   An in-circuit emulator is a software/hardware troubleshooting instrument. It can be a stand-alone unit or part of a software development system. A small program can be entered directly into the emulator, or a program can be transferred into the emulator from a host computer system through an RS-232 serial link. Once a program is loaded, a user can interact with the emulator through its keyboard or a terminal. The emulator has its own software commands to perform various debugging functions. The main capabilities of an in-circuit emulator can be listed as follows:

☐ **Downloading:** Facilities to transfer programs between a software development system or a host computer and the in-circuit emulator.
☐ **Resource Sharing:** The in-circuit emulator allows the system being tested to share its memory and I/O ports. The memory and I/O ports of the in-circuit emulator can be assigned any addresses, which will avoid conflict with memory and I/O of the prototype; this is called memory and I/O mapping.
☐ **Debugging Tools:** Real-Time Trace
                        Breakpoints
                        Mnemonic Display
                        In-Line Assembly
                        Register Display/Modification
                        Disassembly

DEBUGGING TOOLS

The debugging tools listed are used in troubleshooting programs. Single-stepping and setting breakpoints have already been discussed in Chapters 7 and 8. The others are briefly described as follows.

Real-Time Trace   The in-circuit emulator has R/W memory used as a buffer to store the last several (128, for example) bus operations, and these can be displayed on the screen. This display is like a snapshot of all the bus operations in real time. The user can specify several requirements, such as a memory address and certain data conditions for recognizing an event, in order to trigger and display a trace. Similarly, a trace can be observed between two breakpoints or at a specified delay after a certain event. The real-time trace is a very valuable tool in debugging microprocessor-based products.

In-Line Assembly   This allows the user to change data or instructions while software is in the in-circuit emulator.

Disassembly   After instructions are changed in the in-circuit emulator, this facility can write mnemonics in software.

Register Display   This displays register contents after the execution of instructions.

17.7.2 Logic State Analyzer

The logic state analyzer, also known as the logic analyzer, is a multitrace digital oscilloscope specially designed to use with microprocessor-related products. In a multitrace scope, the timing relationships of several signals can be observed with respect to some triggering event or events. For example, a four-trace scope can show the timing relationships of four signals. In a microprocessor-related product the user is interested in observing digital signals on the address bus, the data bus, the control bus, and possibly on an external instrument, relative to a specified triggering event or events. Furthermore, data display should be in a conveniently readable format, such as Hex or binary. The logic analyzer performs these functions.

A typical logic analyzer designed primarily to work with microprocessors has a 40-pin probe plus an auxiliary probe to gather external information. It includes Read-Only Memory (ROM) to store instructions related to the analyzer, R/W buffer memory to store data from a product under test, a microprocessor to monitor data gathering, and a keyboard to specify operations and enter data in Hex or octal format. The analyzer can be triggered to gather information at a specified event related to the microprocessor in the product under test or in relation to an external word. The analyzer in a trace mode takes a snapshot of real-time information at a specific trigger, stores it in its buffer memory, and displays it on its CRT.

The in-circuit emulator is a very valuable tool in the initial stages of product development, and in later stages the logic analyzer can perform some of the troubleshooting functions.

17.7.3 Signature Analyzer

The signature analyzer is an instrument used in troubleshooting microprocessor products either in the field or during production. This instrument converts the complex serial data stream present at the intersections of logic circuits, called nodes, into a four-digit pattern called a signature. Conceptually, a signature is similar to a voltage level specified on the schematic of an analog product. To troubleshoot an analog product, voltages are measured at various locations until a mismatch is found between the measured reading and the specified reading to isolate the trouble. The signature analyzer is used in the same manner.

SUMMARY

In this chapter, the process of designing microprocessor-based products was illustrated by designing subsystems: the Z80 MPU, memory, and I/Os. Various techniques of interfacing the scanned display and the matrix keyboard, and the tradeoffs between hardware and software were discussed. Then, we used these subsystems in designing an IC Tester. In addition, debugging tools such as the in-circuit emulator, the logic analyzer, and the signature analyzer were introduced.

The design of the IC Tester integrates all the concepts of the microprocessor architecture, software, and interfacing discussed throughout this text. In this chapter, we discussed the necessary steps in designing hardware and software. The necessary software modules were illustrated with flowcharts; however, the coding of these modules is given as assignments.

ASSIGNMENTS

1. Draw a schematic to interface a 16-key matrix keyboard using one PIO port. Explain how the PIO should be initialized.
2. Draw a schematic to interface a 30-key matrix board and a six-LED scanned display using three PIO ports. Combine the matrix columns and the digit drivers, and explain why it is possible.
3. In Figure 17.4, redraw the schematic of the bidirectional bus driver as if the $\overline{WR}$ signal was to be connected to DIR. Explain the data flow and why this change might be preferred.
4. In a key monitor program, register C is used to save 4-bit codes of two data keys. Write a subroutine to insert a new 4-bit key code that is available in the accumulator; the new code must be inserted as a low-order nibble, and the most significant nibble in register C must be discarded.
5. Write instructions to unpack the data keys in **4** and place the codes in two different memory locations of the output buffer.
6. In a monitor program, register DE is used to save a 16-bit memory address. Write instructions to insert a 4-bit code of a new key in DE as a least significant nibble.
7. In **6,** unpack all the codes and store them in four memory locations in the output buffer.
8. In section 17.5, modify the matrix keyboard routine to accommodate 30 keys (six rows and five columns).
9. Modify the program in section 17.4.3 to display an error message as Err and blanks.
10. Write a subroutine to transfer a 16-bit address from register DE and a data byte from register C into the display buffer ($20FA_H$ to $20FF_H$); the least significant nibble of the memory address should be placed in location $20FA_H$ and the least significant nibble of the data byte in location $20FE_H$.
11. Write a Display subroutine that takes the unpacked memory address and the byte from the buffer, looks up the seven-segment code, sends the segment codes to the segment driver, and scans the digit code in a sequence to display the address and the byte.
12. Write the main program for the IC Tester illustrated in Figure 17.20.
13. Write the subroutine ICTEST illustrated in Figure 17.21.

Trends in Microprocessor Technology

The advent of the microprocessor is having an impact on industries as diversified as machine tools, chemical processes, medical instrumentation, and sophisticated guidance control. Some applications require simple timing and bit set/reset functions, while others require high-speed data processing capability. Therefore, different microprocessor families are being designed to meet these diversified requirements. In addition to general-purpose 8-bit microprocessors, microprocessor technology is evolving in various directions: (1) microcontrollers on single chips, also known as embedded controllers, geared toward dedicated applications; (2) the 16- and 32-bit microprocessors with general-purpose capability similar to mini- and mainframe computers; and (3) the integrated 8-bit and 16-bit chips, also known as embedded microprocessors.

This chapter includes brief descriptions of single-chip microcontrollers, 16-bit and 32-bit microprocessors, and integrated 8-bit and 16-bit chips; in addition, it examines recent trends in this fast-changing technology and their implications for industry.

18

OBJECTIVES

□ List the elements of a single-chip microcontroller and compare the characteristics of Zilog Z8 and Intel MCS-51 microcontrollers.

□ Describe important features of 16-bit microprocessors, and explain the concepts of memory segmentation, parallel processing, queueing, and coprocessing.

□ Compare the features of the Intel 8086, the Zilog Z8000, and the Motorola MC68000 16-bit microprocessors.

□ Explain the differences between the operating environments of single-user systems and multiuser systems.

□ Explain how 32-bit microprocessors differ from 16-bit microprocessors.

□ Explain the features of integrated chips, also known as embedded processors, such as Zilog Z280 and Toshiba HD64180.

18.1 SINGLE-CHIP MICROCONTROLLERS

Single-chip microcontrollers, also known as embedded controllers, are used primarily to perform dedicated functions. They are used as independent controllers in machines or dedicated to perform specialized functions in a larger system. Generally, they include all the essential elements of a computer on a single chip: MPU, R/W memory, ROM, and I/O lines. Examples of the single-chip microcontrollers are the Zilog Z8; the Intel MCS-48, MCS-51, and MCS-96 families; and the Motorola 68HC11.

Most of these microcontrollers have an 8-bit word size (except the MCS-96, with a 16-bit word size), at least 64 bytes of R/W memory, and 1K bytes of ROM. The range of I/O lines varies from 16 to 32 lines. However, most of these devices cannot be easily programmed in college laboratories except those with EPROM on the chip, such as the Intel 8748 and 8751. A variety of single-chip microcontrollers is available on the market to meet diversified industrial needs. To illustrate the trend, we will describe the Zilog Z8 and the Intel MCS-51.

18.1.1 Zilog Z8 Microcomputer

The Z8 microcomputer is a versatile and powerful 8-bit single-chip microcontroller, used primarily in dedicated control applications. The Z8 family includes three versions: the 40-pin with ROM, the 40-pin with EPROM, and the 64-pin version. They can operate with 8 MHz frequency.

Figure 18.1 shows the block diagram of the Z8 microcomputer. It includes four I/O ports (32 I/O lines), 2K ROM or EPROM, 128 bytes of R/W memory, two 8-bit timer/counters, and one serial I/O port (UART). It has 144 registers, including 124 general-purpose registers that can function as accumulators, address pointers, or index registers. It is capable of addressing 124K bytes of external memory. The Z8 has six interrupts, and each of the interrupts has a 16-bit vector that can point to its service routine. These interrupts can be prioritized through programming. The instruction set is quite powerful and especially suited for con-

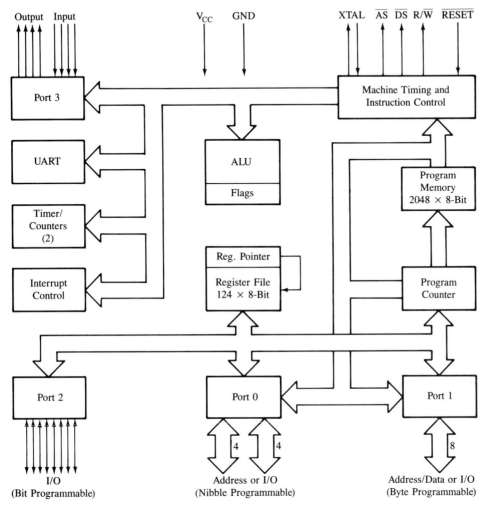

FIGURE 18.1
Z8 Block Diagram
SOURCE: Courtesy of Zilog, Inc.

trol applications. It has 46 instruction types that include bit manipulation, BCD operations, conditional and relative branching, and block transfer.

18.1.2 Intel MCS-51 Single-Chip Family

This is one of Intel's single-chip microcontroller families, at the high end of the single-chip device spectrum in terms of its capability and versatility. It is designed for use in sophisticated real-time instrumentation and industrial control. It can operate with a 12 MHz clock and has a very powerful instruction set.

Figure 18.2 shows the block diagram of the chip; its architecture is in many ways similar to the Zilog Z8 microcomputer. The 8051 is the core of all MCS-51 devices. It includes the following features:

1. 4K bytes of ROM or EPROM
2. 128 bytes of R/W memory
3. Four programmable I/O ports
4. Two 16-bit timer/event counters
5. A serial I/O port with a UART
6. Five interrupt lines: two for external signals and three for internal operations.

The 8051 is known as a *bit and byte processor*. The instruction set includes binary and BCD arithmetic operations, bit set/reset functions, and all logical functions. However, its real power comes from its ability to handle Boolean functions. On any addressable bit, the processor can perform such functions as Set, Clear, Complement, Jump If Set or Not Set, and Jump If Set Then Clear. It can also perform logical functions with two bits and place the result in the carry flag.

The 8051 can use its 32 I/O lines as 32 individual bits or as four 8-bit parallel ports. It can serve five interrupts: two external, two from the counters, and one from the serial I/O port. The chip includes two 16-bit counters, which can operate in three different modes, and a serial I/O port, which can operate in full duplex mode.

The MCS-51 family includes many devices (more than 10) with some variations. Some have 256 bytes of R/W memory, 8-bit I/O ports, and the capability of handling 19 interrupt sources with 11 interrupt vectors.

18.2 16- AND 32-BIT MICROPROCESSORS

The 16-bit microprocessor families are oriented primarily toward high-level languages. Their applications may overlap the high end of 8-bit microprocessor applications and may compete with the low end of minicomputers. They have powerful instruction sets and are capable of addressing megabytes of memory. Examples of widely used 16-bit microprocessors include Intel 8086/8088 and 80286, Zilog Z8001/8002, Digital Equipment LSI-11, Motorola 68000, and National Semiconductor NS16000. Apart from design concepts and instruction sets, a critical factor that decides the capability of the microprocessor is the number of pins available. One trend was to stay within the 40-pin package size and take advantage of existing production and testing facilities. The 40-pin package either limits the size of the memory that can be addressed or necessitates multiplexing of several functions. Intel, Zilog (for Z8002), and Digital Equipment stayed initially with the 40-pin package. Another trend is to go beyond the 40-pin limit, either to a 48-pin size or to a 64-pin size. National Semiconductor (for NS16000) and Zilog (for Z8001) have chosen the 48-pin size package. Motorola and Texas Instruments

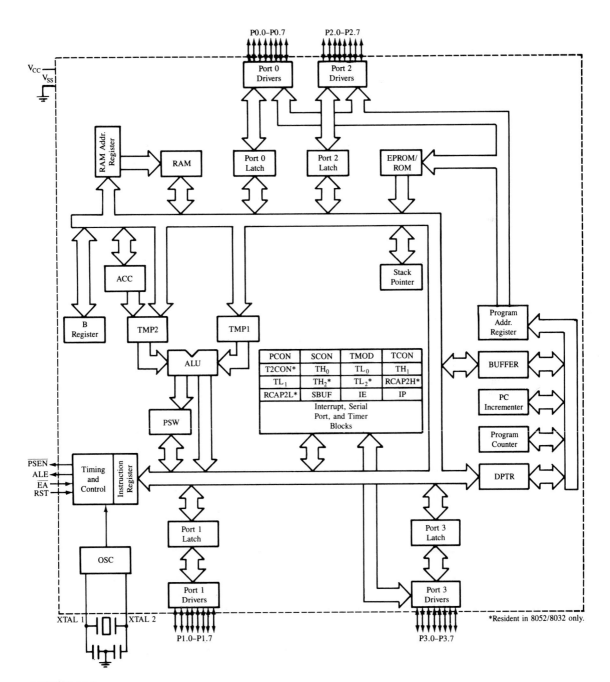

FIGURE 18.2

MCS-51 Architectural Block Diagram

SOURCE: Courtesy of Intel Corporation.

have selected the 64-pin size package. The primary objectives of these 16-bit microprocessors can be summarized as follows:

1. Increase memory-addressing capacity.
2. Increase execution speed.
3. Provide a powerful instruction set.
4. Facilitate programming in high-level languages.

These objectives can be met by using various design concepts. To illustrate differences in design philosophies, the next two sections will briefly describe three 16-bit microprocessors: Intel 8086/8088, Zilog Z8001/Z8002, and Motorola MC68000.

18.2.1   Intel 8086/8088

This is a 16-bit microprocessor housed in a 40-pin package and capable of addressing 1 megabyte of memory. Various versions of this chip can operate with clock frequencies from 5 to 10 MHz. Figure 18.3 shows internal registers; the shaded portions of the figure are identical with the 8085/8080A registers. This microprocessor includes fourteen 16-bit registers, of which the top four registers (AX, BX, CX, and DX) are used as general-purpose accumulators. These four can also be used as 8-bit registers. The next four 16-bit registers are used primarily as memory pointers and index registers; they hold part of a 20-bit memory address, as described under **Memory Segmentation.** They can also be used as general-purpose registers. The next four 16-bit registers are used to specify a segment of the 1-megabyte memory. The last two registers are similar to the program counter and flag register in the 8085/8080A, but they have four additional flags.

The 8088 is functionally similar to the 8086, except that it has an 8-bit data bus. Its internal architecture and instruction set are essentially identical with those of the 8086. The only difference is that a 16-bit data word must be transferred in two segments in the 8088. The 8088 can be viewed as an 8-bit microprocessor with the execution power of a 16-bit microprocessor. The next few paragraphs describe the features of the 8086 architecture that meet the objectives described.

MEMORY SEGMENTATION

To increase the memory addressing capacity, the concept of memory segmentation is employed in this device. This concept involves combining the addresses from two 16-bit registers to form a 20-bit effective address. A segment register provides a base address, and another register supplies an offset address. For example, to fetch an instruction from the 256th location on page 0, the address can be formed as follows:

1. Define the memory segment by loading 1000_H into the Code Segment Register.
2. The Instruction Pointer should hold $00FF_H$ as the offset.
3. The processor shifts the address in the Code Segment Register by four bits to

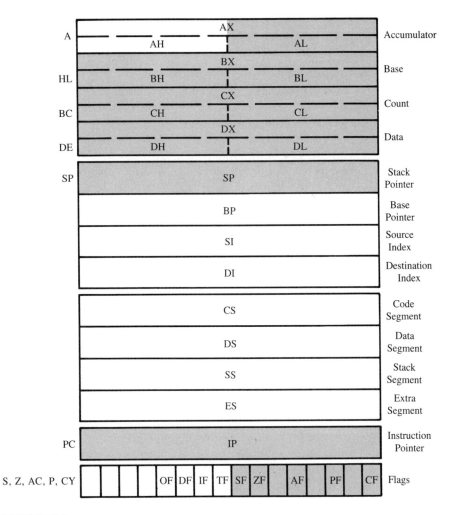

FIGURE 18.3

The 8086 Programming Registers

SOURCE: Reprinted by permission of Intel Corporation, copyright 1981.

the left and adds the content of the Instruction Pointer to form the 20-bit address:

$$
\begin{aligned}
\text{Code Segment:} &\quad 1\,0\,0\,0 \\
\text{Instruction Pointer:} &\quad\;\; 0\,0\,F\,F \\
\text{Effective Address:} &\quad 1\,0\,0\,F\,F
\end{aligned}
$$

The same address can be obtained by redefining the address in the Code Segment Register and using an appropriate count from the Instruction Pointer. By having four segment registers, the 1-megabyte memory space can be conveniently divided into different sections such as program, data, and stack.

SIMULTANEOUS PROCESSING

The 8086 includes two processors called Execution Unit and Bus Interface Unit, as shown in Figure 18.4. They speed up execution by employing the concept of dividing work between two processors and processing it simultaneously. The execution process in the 8086 is similar to that of the Z80: fetch, decode, and execute. However, in the 8-bit processor, the buses are idle during the execution cycle. This idle time is avoided in the 8086 by assigning execution to the Execution Unit and fetching to the Bus Interface Unit. When an instruction is being executed, the Bus Interface Unit fetches instructions and places them on the queue, as shown in Figure 18.4; this is also known as *pipelining* the instructions.

COPROCESSING

The 8086 family of microprocessors is also designed to implement the concept of coprocessing. Basically, coprocessing involves partitioning specialized tasks such as mathematical calculations, input/output, and graphics functions among other processors called coprocessors. In addition to the 8086 family (80286, 386, and 486 are described later), Intel has designed a series of special function processors such as I/O Processors (82586, 82258, and 82380), Numeric Processors (8087, 80287, and 80387), and Graphics Processors (82716 and 82786).

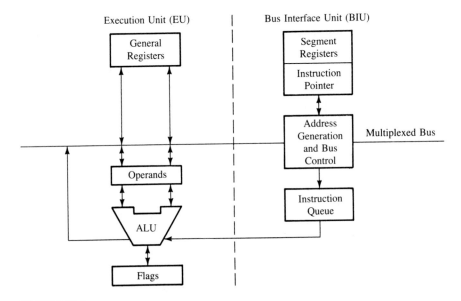

FIGURE 18.4

Execution and Bus Interface Units (EU and BIU) of the 8086

SOURCE: Reprinted by permission of Intel Corporation, copyright 1981.

These coprocessors are compatible with the 8086 family in the master-slave relationship. They are designed with additional instructions and can be assigned dedicated functions to increase the overall execution speed in large systems. For example, numeric-intensive applications are assigned to the numeric processors mentioned above. These coprocessors extend the base architecture of the microprocessor by adding eight 80-bit registers and approximately 70 instructions. These coprocessors can improve the performance of floating point calculations with 80-bit precision up to 100 times over the calculations performed through software subroutines. This is one illustration of hardware-software trade-off among newer processors.

INSTRUCTION SET
The 8086 has a large instruction set, consisting of 135 basic instruction types, that can operate on individual bits, bytes, 16-bit words, and 32-bit double words. The set includes such instructions as multiply, divide, and bit and string manipulation.

MODULAR PROGRAMMING
In addition to the powerful instruction set, the chip design is oriented toward modular programming, which is highly desirable for high-level languages. The memory-segmentation concept facilitates programming of independent modules that can communicate with each other as well as share common data.

18.2.2   Zilog Z8000
The Zilog Z8000 is a 16-bit microprocessor with two versions—Z8001 and Z8002. The Z8002 is a 40-pin device capable of addressing 64K non-segmented memory. The Z8001 is a 48-pin device, almost identical to the Z8002 but capable of directly addressing eight megabytes of memory. Like the 8086, it can also use the concept of segmented memory. But unlike the 8086, it requires an additional device called the Memory Management Unit, and the memory addressing can be extended to 48 megabytes.

The overall architectural philosophy of the Z8000 is similar to that of the 8086. The Z8000 is a register-oriented microprocessor; the Z8002 version has twenty-one 16-bit registers, of which 16 are general-purpose registers (Figure 18.5). Any of these general-purpose registers, with the exception of the register R_0, can be used as an accumulator, index register, memory pointer, or stack pointer. This is unlike the 8086, in which most registers have designated functions. In addition to 16 general-purpose registers, the Z8000 includes five registers: program counter, flag register, status pointer, instruction register, and refresh counter. To speed up the execution, it uses the prefetched pipeline technique and has a powerful interrupt structure. One of the unique features of the Z8000 is that it provides a refresh counter to refresh dynamic memory. It can operate in either the system or normal mode. The system mode permits privileged operations, thereby facilitating multi-user systems.

The Z8000 has a very powerful instruction set of 110 instruction types; it has seven addressing modes and can operate on a bit, byte, 16-bit word, 32-bit

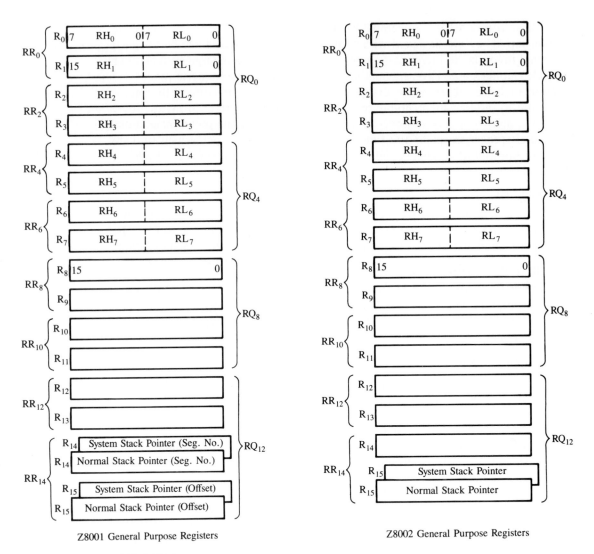

Z8001 General Purpose Registers   Z8002 General Purpose Registers

FIGURE 18.5
Z8001/Z8002 General-Purpose Registers
SOURCE: Courtesy of Zilog, Inc.

long word, and 64-bit quad word. The instruction set includes instructions such as multiply/divide, block transfer, and string manipulations.

18.2.3   Motorola MC68000

This is a 16-bit microprocessor with a 32-bit internal architecture housed in a 64-pin package. It is capable of addressing 16 megabytes of memory, and the clock frequency ranges from 4 to 10 MHz for different versions of the chip. The recent versions of this family of microprocessors (MC68020 and MC68030) include a 32-bit data bus.

Figure 18.6 shows the internal architecture of the device. It includes seventeen 32-bit, general-purpose registers; a 32-bit program counter; and a 16-bit status register. The general-purpose registers are divided into three groups: eight data registers, seven address registers, and two stack pointers. The contents of the data registers can be accessed as bytes, 16-bit words, or 32-bit words, and the contents of the address registers can be accessed as 16-bit or 32-bit addresses. The 68000 can operate in two different modes: the user mode and the supervisor mode. The supervisor mode is designed primarily for operating systems; in this mode, some privileged system control instructions can be used. Some of its other features can be described as follows.

NONSEGMENTED MEMORY

To increase the memory addressing capacity, Motorola has increased the number of pins in its package. The chip is designed with 23 separate lines to address eight megawords (16 megabytes). Similarly, its program counter is 32 bits long; however, only the low-order 24 bits are necessary to address the entire memory map.

FIGURE 18.6
Programming Registers of the 68000

SOURCE: Courtesy of Motorola, Inc.

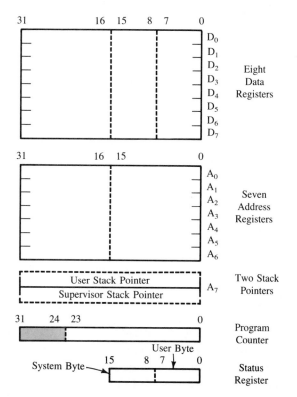

INSTRUCTION SET

The 68000 has one of the most powerful and simple instruction sets. It includes 56 basic instructions and can operate on five different types of data: bit, byte, BCD, 16-bit word, and 32-bit word. It has only memory-mapped I/O but includes 14 memory addressing modes. To cite one example of its powerful set, its MOV instruction can transfer data from any source to any destination. It includes such instructions as Multiply and Divide and special instructions to deal with numbers longer than 32 bits. Its orientation toward high-level languages comes primarily from its instruction set.

ASYNCHRONOUS AND SYNCHRONOUS CONTROL LINES

The 68000 has a special way of handling slow and fast peripherals. It has two sets of control signals, called asynchronous and synchronous signals. Communication with asynchronous peripherals is handled through the control lines called Upper Data Strobe (UDS), Lower Data Strobe (LDS), and Data Acknowledge (DACK). The DACK signal is similar to a handshake line; until the signal DACK is received, the bus cycle is not terminated. The 68000 family offers some synchronous peripherals, and communication with these peripherals is handled through the control signals called Valid Peripheral Address (VPA), Valid Memory Address (VMA), and Enable (E).

18.2.4 Intel 80286

The Intel 80286 is a 16-bit microprocessor, an extended version of the 8086. One of the critical barriers among the Intel's earlier microprocessors was the 40-pin package. Once that barrier was broken, it became easier to address large memory. The 80286 microprocessor is housed in a 68-pin package. It is designed using the concepts of prefetched pipeline structure, parallel processing, and memory management.

The 80286 has a different architectural philosophy from that of the 8086. It has eliminated the multiplexing of the buses; it has a linear address bus with 24 address lines that can address 16 megabytes of memory directly. It can also support a memory management unit, and through the memory management unit it can address 1 gigabyte of memory, also known as virtual memory. The processor includes various built-in mechanisms that can protect system software from user programs, protect users' programs, and restrict access to some regions of memory. The 80286 is designed for a multi-user system in an environment similar to that of minicomputers and mainframe computers; its architectural philosophy is closer to the Intel's 80386 32-bit microprocessor, which is described in the next section.

18.2.5 32-Bit Microprocessors

At the high end of the microprocessor range, 32-bit microprocessors are now available; examples include the Intel 80386 and 486, Zilog Z80000, National Semiconductor NS32032, and Motorola MC68020 and MC68030. We are interested not in discussing the details of these microprocessors but in exploring trends in the microprocessor technology. These microprocessors are not merely more of the same, except bigger and faster; they offer some unique features unavailable in 16-bit microprocessors. The applications and the environments in which they operate are far different from those of the 8-bit microprocessors and the 16-bit microprocessors. It appears that two trends are evolving: one is multi-user, multi-tasking, time-sharing environments, and the other is distributed processing interconnected with networks. As soon as we move away from the single-user system, the demands on these microprocessors change dramatically; the environment is more like that of minicomputers or mainframe computers. These microprocessors should not be viewed as programmable logic devices.

In a single-user system, the user has unlimited access to all aspects of the system. The user need not be concerned with sharing the time or the resources of the system but can schedule various tasks according to his or her convenience. The user has access to the operating system, can tamper with the system to include some personal conveniences, or in the process can lock up the system. However, the multi-user system cannot afford to provide the luxuries of unlimited access to all users. Some of the requirements of the multi-user system are as follows:

1. Higher speed of execution
2. Ability to handle different types of tasks efficiently
3. Large memory space that can be shared by multiple users
4. Appropriate memory allocations and the management of memory access
5. Data security and data access
6. Limited and selected access to part of the system
7. Resource (printer, hard disk, etc.) sharing and management

Some of these requirements must be managed by a multi-user operating system, and some should be facilitated by the architectural design of the microprocessors. The 32-bit microprocessors are designed to work in this type of environment. Some of the important features of the Intel 80386 and 80486 and the Zilog Z80000 are described in this section as representative samples of 32-bit microprocessor technology.

The 80386 is a 32-bit microprocessor with a nonmultiplexed 32-bit address bus, and its various versions can operate at from 16 to 20 MHz clock. It is capable of addressing 4 gigabytes of physical memory, and through its memory management unit, it can address 64 terabytes (2^{46}) of memory. The 80386 has 32-bit registers, and it is upward software compatible with the 8086. The execution of instructions is highly pipelined, and it is designed to operate in a multi-user and multitasking environment. It has the protection mechanism that is necessary for this type of environment.

The 80486 is a very recent 32-bit microprocessor, an improved version of the 80386 and available in 25- and 33-MHz versions. It is essentially similar to the 80386 but includes a math coprocessor and an internal 8K-byte cache memory. It executes many instructions in one clock period rather than two clock periods used by the 80386; therefore, it is significantly faster in execution of instructions than the 80386. The cache memory also helps to speed up the execution. The 8K cache memory is essentially a high-speed memory on the microprocessor chip. External memory chips tend to be slower in response to high-speed microprocessors. To speed up the information transfer between the processor and memory, frequently used data and instructions are copied into cache memory from the main memory. Whenever the microprocessor requests information, it checks whether it is in the cache memory. If it is in the cache memory, it does not need to access the main memory. If it is not in the cache memory, the processor accesses the main memory as well as copies a block of data into cache memory and expects to use that block of data in subsequent read operations. Normally, it works because the processor is a sequential machine; it goes from lower memory addresses to higher memory addresses in a sequence.

The Z80000 is also a 32-bit microprocessor with architecture similar to that of the 80386. It can directly address 4 gigabytes of memory, and it can extend the memory addressing capacity similar to the 80386 by using the built-in memory management unit. It is designed to operate in two primary modes—system and normal—supported by separate stacks. The normal mode is for user programs, and the system mode is used for some of the critical functions of an operating system, such as protecting the operating system from user access.

In summary, these 32-bit microprocessors are oriented toward high-level languages. They can address a large memory space, execute instructions with high speed, and perform arithmetic operations with high precision. These microprocessors suggest a trend toward replacing software functions with hardware. They are designed to perform the functions normally found in mainframe computers.

18.3 HIGH-INTEGRATION 8- AND 16-BIT MICROPROCESSORS

In general-purpose microprocessors, one of the trends seems to be toward integrated devices that reduce the chip count; these devices are known as integrated MPUs. Examples of such devices are Hitachi HD64180, Zilog Z280, and Intel 80186/188; these are described briefly here to indicate the trend.

18.3.1 Hitachi HD64180

This is an 8-bit, high-integration CMOS microprocessor in a 64-pin package, designed for applications with low power consumption, and it can operate with a 6 MHz clock. It includes a clock generator, an interrupt controller, and a memory management unit (MMU) as support devices for the microprocessor (Figure 18.7). It has 19 address lines that can address 512K bytes of physical memory, and the MMU translates internal 64K logical addressing into appropriate physical ad-

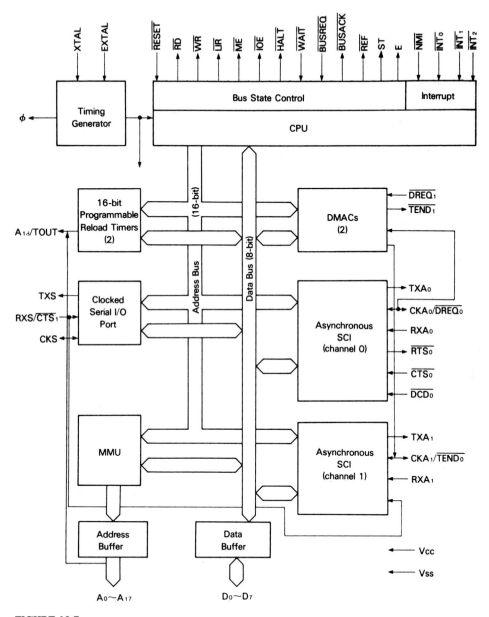

FIGURE 18.7

Block Diagram: HD64180

SOURCE: Courtesy of Hitachi America, Ltd., Semiconductor & I.C. Division.

dressing. The interrupt controller is capable of handling four external and eight internal interrupting sources.

Figure 18.7 also shows that the HD64180 includes four I/O-related devices: DMA controller (DMAC—two channels), asynchronous serial communication interface (ASCI—two channels), clocked serial I/O port (CSI/O), and programmable reload timer (PRT—two channels). The DMAC has two channels that support high-speed data transfer of 64K bytes per channel anywhere in the physical space of 512K bytes of memory. The ASCI has two separate channels for full-duplex communication, and the CSI/O provides half-duplex communication; it is used primarily for simple high-speed connection between microcomputers. Similarly, the timer has two channels with 16-bit counters, and one of the channels can be used for waveform generation.

The instruction set of the HD64180 is upward compatible with the Z80 instruction set. The HD64180 has seven additional instructions, including 8-bit Multiply and Sleep. The Sleep instruction reduces the power consumption to 19 mW. One of the powerful features of this device is that the Opcode Fetch cycle of an instruction consists of three T-states versus four T-states in the Z80, resulting in faster program execution.

18.3.2 Zilog Z280

This is a 16-bit, high-integration CMOS microprocessor in a 68-pin package, and it can operate with a 12.5 MHz clock. It includes a clock generator, refresh address generator, 256 bytes of on-chip memory, and a memory management unit (MMU) as support devices for the microprocessor operations (Figure 18.8). The MMU enables the microprocessor to address 16M bytes of memory, and the refresh address generator provides a 10-bit address that is used in refreshing dynamic memory. The on-chip memory allows programs to run significantly faster by reducing the number of external bus accesses.

Figure 18.8 also shows that the Z280 includes four I/O-related devices: DMA (four channels), Universal Asynchronous Receiver/Transmitter (UART), and Counter/Timer (three channels). The DMA has four channels that can transfer data between any two ports (source and destination), including memory-to-I/O, I/O-to-memory, memory-to-memory, and I/O-to-I/O. The UART is capable of handling any full-duplex asynchronous data communication. Similarly, the Z280 has three channels of Timer/Counter with 16-bit time constant; these can be used for event counting, interrupt and interval timing, and general clock generation.

The Z280 can operate in either user or system mode, and each has separate stacks. System mode is intended for the functions of an operating system, and user mode is intended for application programs. Thus, the sensitive and critical functions of the operating system are protected from user interference. The instruction set of the Z280 retains compatibility with that of the Z80 and includes additional instructions such as 8- and 16-bit signed and unsigned multiply and divide. It has a powerful interrupt structure that has four modes of operation; the first three modes are similar to those of the Z80.

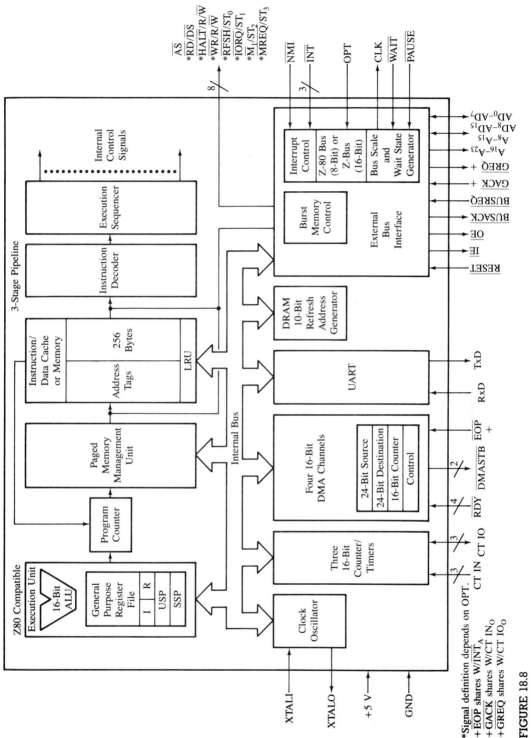

FIGURE 18.8

Block Diagram: Z280

SOURCE: Courtesy of Zilog, Inc.

*Signal definition depends on OPT.
+EOP shares W/$\overline{\text{INT}}_A$
+GACK shares W/CT IN_O
+GREQ shares W/CT IO_O

18.3.3   Intel 80186/80188

The Intel 80186 is classified as a high-integration embedded controller or a microprocessor. It is a 16-bit microprocessor, an extended version of the 8086. It is an integrated device designed to reduce the chip count, rather than to increase the memory addressing capacity; it combines 15 to 20 of the most common 8086 system components. It has multiplexed address and data buses, and the additional lines of the 68-pin package are used to include devices such as a clock generator, interrupt controller, timers, DMA controller, and a chip select unit. The 80188 is similar to the 80186 except that it has an 8-bit external data path; it is an integrated version of 8088. Similarly, Zilog also has 16-bit embedded processors. These devices suggest a trend toward high integration, combining many functions on a chip and reducing the chip count.

18.4   TECHNOLOGY TRENDS

The Intel 8008, superseded by the Intel 8080A, was the first 8-bit microprocessor. Just about the same time (1974), Motorola brought out the MC6800 as an improvement over the first 8008, but with substantially different architecture. Within a few years, Zilog designed the Z80, and Intel came up with the 8085 as an improvement over the 8080A. Both are upward machine-language compatible with the 8080A. Within a few years, Motorola introduced the MC6809, a vastly improved version of the MC6800. These 8-bit microprocessors were discussed briefly in Chapter 3. Now the qustion is, What is the role of these general-purpose 8-bit microprocessors in the fast-changing microprocessor technology?

Along with the development of general-purpose 8-bit microprocessors, the single-chip microcontrollers began to assume a major role in the area of dedicated functions. Examination of two examples discussed in section 18.1 shows that the single-chip microcontroller plays a vital role in control applications and is an important segment of microprocessor technology. These devices are designed for special purpose applications, and the circuitry on the chip varies according to the objectives. Applications range from bit set/reset functions to processing high-speed analog signals.

At the other end of the application spectrum, 16- and 32-bit microprocessors have begun to dominate the microcomputer industry. The 8086 and the Z8002 have employed several new architectural concepts, such as memory segmentation, parallel processing, queuing, and coprocessing. In addition, the Motorola MC68000 and the Zilog Z8001 broke the barrier of the 40-pin package. These processors are oriented toward high-level languages and will perform some functions of mini- and mainframe computers. Recent microprocessors, such as Intel 80286, -386, and -486 and Zilog Z80000, have begun to accept the challenges of multi-user and multitasking environments.

Figure 18.9 shows the progression in development of Intel microprocessor families from 8- to 32-bit. Recent 32-bit processors are housed in larger packages and are significantly faster and more efficient than the 8-bit processors; the clock frequency has increased from 2.2 to 33 MHz, and the package size has increased from 40 to 132 pins. The earlier 8-bit processors are capable of addressing 64K bytes of memory, and now, 32-bit processors can address 4 gigabytes of memory.

Now the question is, Will these general-purpose 8-bit microprocessors disappear from the scene because of the competition from sophisticated, high-speed, and powerful 16- and 32-bit microprocessors? We think not. Recent worldwide sales figures indicate that 8-bit processor chips (general-purpose and microcontrollers) account for about 85 percent of the total market. The 16- and 32-bit microprocessors are used primarily in computers; on the other hand, 8-bit processors are used in a variety of applications such as appliances, instrumentation, and

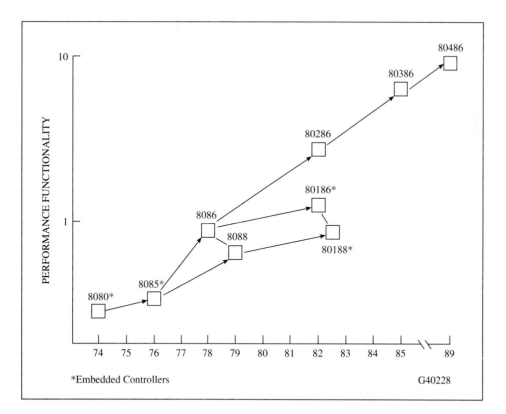

FIGURE 18.9

Evolution of Intel Microprocessor Families (Adapted)

SOURCE: Courtesy of Intel Corporation.

process control. Each group has captured its own share of applications. This is similar to the automobile industry; there is room for subcompacts as well as luxury sports cars.

The 16- and 32-bit microprocessors are too powerful to perform the functions of general-purpose 8-bit microprocessors; therefore, they are less likely to replace 8-bit processors. Competition for the general-purpose 8-bit microprocessors will come from the other direction: the single-chip microcontrollers. However, the single-chip microcontrollers do not lend themselves as suitable learning vehicles, and the 16- and 32-bit microprocessors are too complex and cumbersome to introduce basic concepts.

But it appears that some of the 8-bit microprocessors have begun to reassert their presence in the form of superintegrated processors in industrial applications. Figure 18.10 shows the evolution of the Z80 processor. In earlier years, most of

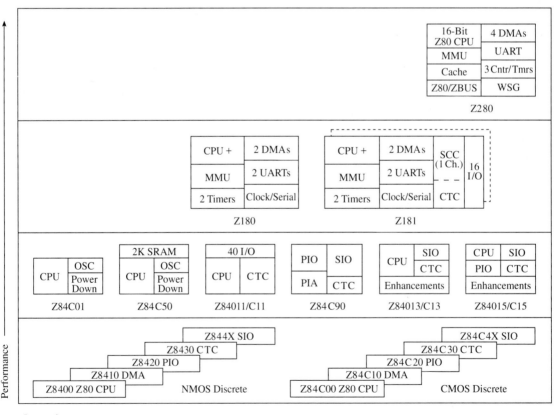

FIGURE 18.10
Z80 Product Evolution
SOURCE: Courtesy of Zilog, Inc.

the peripheral devices were discrete, as shown in Figure 18.10. Now the trend is toward the integration of the microprocessor and its peripheral devices on one chip as typified by the Z280. In addition, Figure 18.10 shows several versions of the Z80 with various combinations of peripheral chips to meet the diversified needs of the marketplace. It seems that the demand for 8-bit processors is increasing and likely to continue growing.

SUMMARY

In this chapter, various microprocessors—from 8- to 32-bit—and single-chip microcontrollers were discussed, compared, and contrasted in terms of their characteristics and applications. Future trends in microprocessor technology were suggested.

Single-chip microcontrollers and their various applications were discussed in section 18.1. These microcontrollers are specially designed for specific applications, and their characteristics differ according to their areas of applications.

Microprocessors with 16- and 32-bit words were discussed in section 18.2. These are designed to facilitate the use of high-level languages and are expected to compete with functions of minicomputers and mainframe computers. New architectural concepts such as memory segmentation, parallel processing, and queueing were employed in designing some of these processors, and some are designed with a pin package larger than 40. In general-purpose microprocessors, Z80 and 80186 type microprocessors have begun to appear in the form of integrated devices that include a microprocessor, memory management unit, DMA controllers, UARTs, and timers on one chip.

Z80 Instruction Set

Appendix A describes each Z80 instruction fully in terms of its operation and the operand, including details such as number of bytes, machine cycles, T-states, Hex code, and affected flags. The instructions appear in alphabetical order and are illustrated with examples.

The following abbreviations and symbols are used in the description of the instruction set.

r = Z80 Registers
rp = Register Pair
rx = Index Registers
r' = Z80 Alternate Registers
m = Memory Location
r_s = Register Source
r_d = Register Destination
$(\ )$ = Contents of
d = 7-bit Displacement (Expressed in 2's Complement for Backward Displacement)
b = Bit from 0 to 7
MC = Machine Cycles
1 = Flag Set
0 = Flag Reset
$\checkmark$ = Flag Affected
[Blank] = No Effect On Flag
$?$ = Flag Indeterminate

Flags
  S = Sign
  Z = Zero
  H = Half-Carry
P/V = Parity/Overflow
  N = Add/Subtract
  C = Carry (In the description of an
      instruction, the abbreviation CY
      is used instead of C to avoid
      confusion with register C.)

cc = Flag Condition Code
  P = Plus
  M = Minus
  Z = Zero
NZ = No Zero
PE = Parity Even
PO = Parity Odd
  C = Carry
NC = No Carry

ADC A, r: ADD REGISTER TO ACCUMULATOR WITH CARRY
ADC A, 8-BIT: ADD 8-BIT TO ACCUMULATOR WITH CARRY

Opcode	Operand	Bytes	MC /T-States	Hex Codes						
ADC	r	1	1 /4	A	B	C	D	E	H	L
				8F	88	89	8A	8B	8C	8D
	8-Bit	2	2 /7(4,3)	CE 8-Bit						

Description   The contents of the operand (register or 8-bit data) and the carry flag CY are added to the contents of the accumulator and the result is placed in the accumulator.

	S	Z		H		P/V	N	C
Flags	√	√		√		√	0	√

Example   The register BC contains 2498_H and the register DE contains $54A1_H$. Add (BC) and (DE) and store the result in BC.

Step 1: Copy (B) into A and add (D) using ADD instruction.

$(C) \rightarrow$ (A): 98_H
      (E): $A1_H$
      (A): $1/39_H$

Step 2: Save the sum (39_H) in register C.

Step 3: Copy (B) into A and add (D) using the ADC instruction to account for the carry from the previous sum.

$(B) \rightarrow$ (A): 24_H
      (D): 54_H
    Carry: $\underline{\quad 1 \quad}$
      79_H

Step 4: Save the sum (79_H) in B. The ADC instruction resets the previous CY flag.

Comments   The instruction is generally used in 16-bit addition or multi-byte number; the carry generated by bit D_7 is added to bit D_0 of the next addition. This instruction should not be used to account for carries generated in summing 8-bit numbers.

ADC A, (HL)   : ADD THE CONTENTS OF MEMORY AND CARRY TO
ACCUMULATOR
ADC A, (IX + d):
ADC A, (IY + d):

Opcode	Operand	Bytes	MC /T-States	Hex Codes
ADC	A, (HL)	1	2 /7(4,3)	8E
ADC	A, (IX + d)	3	5 /19(4,4,3,5,3)	DD 8E d
	A, (IY + d)			FD 8E d

Description   The contents of memory specified by the operand (HL, IX + d, or IY + d) and the carry flag are added to the contents of the accumulator.

Flags

S	Z	H	P/V	N	C
√	√	√	√	0	√

ADC HL, rp: ADD REGISTER PAIR TO HL WITH CARRY

Opcode	Operand	Bytes	MC /T-States	Hex Codes
ADC	HL, rp	2	2 /15(4,4,4,3)	BC DE HL SP
				ED 4A 5A 6A 7A

Description   The contents of the operand (BC, DE, HL, or SP) and the carry flag are added to the contents of the HL register and the result is stored in the HL register.

Flags

S	Z	H	P/V	N	C
√	√	?	√	0	√

Example   The HL register contains 8200_H, the DE register contains $F850_H$, and the carry flag CY is set. Add the contents of HL and DE with carry.

Mnemonics: ADC HL, DE   Hex Code: ED 5A

Addition with Carry

(DE):	1111	1000	0101	0000	($F850_H$)
(HL):	1000	0010	0000	0000	(8200_H)
CY :				1	
1/0111	1010	0101	0001	($7A51_H$)

Register Contents After Instruction

		S Z H V N C	
A	X	0 0 0 1 0 1	F
D	F8	50	E
H	7A	51	L

ADD A, r: ADD REGISTER TO ACCUMULATOR

Opcode	Operand	Bytes	MC /T-States	Hex Codes
ADD	A, r	1	1 /4	A B C D E H L
				87 80 81 82 83 84 85

Description   The contents of the register are added to the contents of the accumulator, and the result is stored in the accumulator.

Flags

S	Z		H		P/V	N	C
√	√		√		√	0	√

Example   Register B has 51_H and the accumulator has 47_H. Add (B) to (A).

Mnemonics: ADD A, B   Hex Code: 80

Addition

(B)	0101	0001	(51_H)
(A)	0100	0111	(47_H)
(A)	1001	1000	(98_H)

Register Contents After Execution

		S Z H V N C	
A	98	1 0 0 0 0 0	F
B	51	X	C

ADD A, 8-BIT: ADD 8-BIT TO ACCUMULATOR

Opcode	Operand	Bytes	MC /T-States	Hex Code
ADD	8-Bit	2	2 /7(4,3)	C6 8-Bit

Description   The operand byte (8-bit data) is added to the contents of the accumulator, and the result is placed in the accumulator.

Flags

S	Z		H		P/V	N	C
√	√		√		√	0	√

Example   The accumulator contains $4A_H$. Add the data byte 59_H to the contents of the accumulator.

Mnemonics: ADD A, 59H   Hex Codes: C6 59

Addition

(A)	0100	1010	($4A_H$)
8-bit	0101	1001	(59_H)
	1010	0011	($A3_H$)

Register Contents After Execution

		S Z H V N C
A	A3	1 0 1 1 0 0

ADD A, (HL) : ADD CONTENTS OF MEMORY TO
                  ACCUMULATOR
ADD A, (IX + d):
ADD A, (IY + d):

Opcode	Operand	Bytes	MC /T-States	Hex Codes
ADD	A, (HL)	1	2 /7(4,3)	86
ADD	A, (IX + d)	3	5 /19(4,4,3,5,3)	DD 86 d
	A, (IX + d)			FD 86 d

Description   The contents of the accumulator are added to the contents of memory location shown by the address in HL registers, and the result is stored in the accumulator. When the operand is an index register, the memory address is calculated by adding the index register and the displacement byte d.

Flags

S	Z	H	P/V	N	C
√	√	√	√	0	√

Example   The accumulator contains the byte 76_H, and the HL pair contains 2050_H. Add the byte $A2_H$ which is stored in memory location 2050_H to the contents of the accumulator.

Mnemonics: ADD A, (HL)   Hex Code:86

Addition

(A) 0111 0110   (76_H)
(2050)Mem 1010 0010   ($A2_H$)
     1 0001 1000
CY

Register Contents After Execution

		S	Z	H		V	N	C	
A	18	0	0	0		0	0	1	F
H	20			50					L

Example   Use the index register IX as a memory pointer in Example A to add the contents of the accumulator and memory location 2050_H. Assume that the index register IX contains 2035_H. The displacement byte d ($1B_H$) is calculated by subtracting the index address 2035_H from the memory address 2050_H.

Mnemonics: ADD A, (IX + 1B)   Hex Code: DD 86 1B

ADD HL, rp: ADD REGISTER PAIR TO HL

Opcode	Operand	Bytes	MC /T-States	Hex Codes
ADD	HL, rp	1	3 /11(4,4,3)	BC DE HL SP
				09 19 29 39

Description   The contents of the specified register rp (BC, DE, HL, or SP) are added to the contents of HL and the result is placed in HL.

Flags

S Z   H   P/V N C

| | | √ | | 0 | √ |

$C = 1$ if bit D_{15} generates carry; otherwise it is reset.
$H = 1$ if bit D_{11} generates carry; otherwise it is reset.

Example   The HL register contains 2900_H and the DE register contains $F895_H$. Add (HL) and (DE).

Mnemonics: ADD HL, DE   Hex Code: 19

Addition

(HL):	0010 1001 0000 0000	(2900_H)	
(DE):	1111 1000 1001 0101	($F895_H$)	
(HL):	1/0010 0001 1001 0101	(2195_H)	
	CY = 1, H = 1		

Register Contents
After Instruction

D	F8	95	E
H	21	95	L

ADD IX, rp: ADD REGISTER PAIR TO INDEX REGISTER
ADD IY, rp:

Opcode	Operand	Bytes	MC /T-States	Hex Codes
ADD	IX, rp	2	4 /15(4,4,4,3)	

	BC	DE	IX/IY	SP
IX: DD	09	19	29	39
IY: FD	09	19	29	39

Description   The contents of the specified register pair rp are added to the contents of the index register and the result is placed in the index register.

1. This is a 2-byte instruction. The first byte specifies the index register (IX or IY), and the second byte specifies the register pair to be added to the index register.
2. This instruction cannot add (HL) to an index register or add (IX) and (IY). If the second byte is 29_H, the contents of the index register specified adds to its own contents.

Flags

S Z   H   P/V N C

| | | ? | | 0 | √ |

AND r: LOGICALLY AND REGISTER WITH ACCUMULATOR

Opcode	Operand	Bytes	MC /T-States	Hex Codes
AND	r	1	1 /4	

A	B	C	D	E	H	L
A7	A0	A1	A2	A3	A4	A5

Description   The contents of the specified register are ANDed with the contents of the accumulator and the result is placed in the accumulator.

Flags

S	Z		H		P/V	N	C
√	√		1		√	0	0

Example   The contents of the accumulator and register B are 54_H and 82_H respectively. Logically AND (B) with (A) and show the flags and the contents of each register after ANDing.

Mnemonics: AND B   Hex Code: A0

Logical AND	Register Contents After Instruction

(A)	1 0 0 0 0 0 1 0	(82_H)
(B)	0 1 0 1 0 1 0 0	(54_H)
(A)	0 0 0 0 0 0 0 0	(00_H)

		S Z H P N C	
A	00	0 1 1 1 0 0	F
B	54	X	C

AND 8-BIT: LOGICALLY AND 8-BIT WITH ACCUMULATOR

Opcode	Operand	Bytes	MC /T-States	Hex Codes
AND	8-Bit	2	2 /7(4,3)	E6 8-Bit

Description   The contents of the operand (8-bit data) are logically ANDed with the contents of the accumulator and the result is placed in the accumulator.

Flags

S	Z		H		P/V	N	C
√	√		1		√	0	0

Example   The accumulator contains $A3_H$. AND byte 97_H with (A).

Mnemonics: AND 97H   Hex Code: E6   97

Logical AND	Register Contents After Instruction

(A) :	1 0 1 0 0 0 1 1	$(A3_H)$
(Data):	1 0 0 1 0 1 1 1	(97_H)
(A) :	1 0 0 0 0 0 1 1	(83_H)

		S Z H P N C	
A	83	1 0 0 0 0 0	F

AND (HL)   : LOGICALLY AND CONTENTS OF MEMORY
WITH ACCUMULATOR
AND (IX + d):
AND (IY + d):

Opcode	Operand	Bytes	MC /T-States	Hex Codes
AND	(HL)	1	2 /7(4,3)	A6
AND	(IX + d)	3	5 /19	DD A6 d
	(IY + d)		(4,4,3,5,3)	FD A6 d

Description   The contents of memory are ANDed with the contents of the accumulator. The memory address is specified by the contents of the HL register or an index register with a displacement byte d.

	S	Z		H		P/V	N	C
Flags	√	√		1		√	0	0

Example   Write mnemonics to AND the contents of memory location 2070_H with the contents of the accumulator, assuming index register IY contains address 2000_H.

Mnemonics: AND (IY + 70H)   Hex Code: FD   A6   70

BIT b, r: TEST BIT IN REGISTER

Opcode	Operand	Bytes	MC /T-States	Hex Codes
BIT	b, r	2	2 /8(4,4)	Source Register

	(Bit)	A	B	C	D	E	H	L
CB (7)		7F	78	79	7A	7B	7C	7D
CB (6)		77	70	71	72	73	74	75
CB (5)		6F	68	69	6A	6B	6C	6D
CB (4)		67	60	61	62	63	64	65
CB (3)		5F	58	59	5A	5B	5C	5D
CB (2)		57	50	51	52	53	54	55
CB (1)		4F	48	49	4A	4B	4C	4D
CB (0)		47	40	41	42	43	44	45

Description   This instruction tests the specified bit in a given register r and sets the Z flag if bit is zero; otherwise, Z flag is reset. The register r can be any one of the registers: A, B, C, D, E, H, L.

	S	Z		H		P/V	N	C
Flags	?	√				?	0	

Example   Register B has 1000 0111(87_H). Test bit D_3.

Mnemonics: BIT 3, B   Hex Code: CB   58

This instruction tests bit D_3 and sets the Z flag because $D_3 = 0$.

BIT b, (HL)   : TEST BIT IN MEMORY LOCATION
BIT b, (IX + d):
BIT b, (IY + d):

Opcode	Operand	Bytes	MC /T-States	Hex Codes

				(BIT)	7	6	5	4	3	2	1	0
BIT	b, (HL)	2	3 /12(4,4,4,)	CB [7E	76	6E	66	5E	56	4E	46]
BIT	b, (IX + d)	4	5 /20	DD CB d [7E	76	6E	66	5E	56	4E	46]
BIT	b, (IY + d)		(4,4,3,5,4)	FD CB d [7E	76	6E	66	5E	56	4E	46]

Description   This instruction tests the bit in the specified memory location and sets Z flag if the bit is zero. The memory location is specified by the contents of HL or index registers (plus displacement).

	S	Z	H	P/V	N	C
Flags	?	√	1	?	0	

CALL 16-BIT: CALL SUBROUTINE SPECIFIED BY OPERAND

Opcode	Operand	Bytes	MC /T-States	Hex Code
CALL	16-Bit	3	5 /17(4,3,4,3,3)	CD 16-bit

Description   The program execution is transferred to the subroutine address specified by the operand. Before the transfer, the address of the opcode following the CALL (the contents of the program counter) is stored on the stack. The sequence of events is described in the example below. This instruction should be accompanied by one of the return (RET or conditional RET) instructions in the subroutine.

Flags   No flags are affected.

Example   Write the instruction to call the subroutine located at memory location 2050_H. Explain how the contents of the program counter are stored on the stack if the stack pointer is at location 2099_H.

Instruction: CALL 2050H   Hex Code: CD   50   20

As an example, this machine code can be stored as follows:

Memory Address	Hex Code	Mnemonics
2010	CD	CALL 2050H
2011	50	
2012	20	

Make a note of the difference between writing a 16-bit address as mnemonics and machine code. In the code, the low-order byte (50_H) is entered first, followed by the high-order byte (20_H). However, in mnemonics the bytes are shown in the proper sequence. If an assembler is used to obtain the codes, it will automatically reverse the sequence of the mnemonics.

When the last machine code (20_H), located at 2012_H, is fetched by the microprocessor, the program counter holds the address 2013_H. This address is placed on the stack as follows.

1. Stack pointer is decremented to 2098_H and the MSB is stored.
2. Stack pointer is decremented to 2097_H and the LSB is stored.
3. Call address (2050_H) is temporarily stored in internal registers and placed on the bus for the fetch cycle.

	2097	13
↑	2098	20
SP	2099	XX

CALL cc, 16-BIT: CALL SUBROUTINE IF CONDITION IS TRUE

Opcode	Operand	Bytes	MC /T-States
CALL	cc, 16-Bit	3	5 /17(4,3,4,3,3); If condition is true
			3 /10(4,3,3) ; If condition is false

Condition Flags	NZ	Z	NC	C	PO	PE	P	M
Hex Codes	C4	CC	D4	DC	E4	EC	F4	FC

Description   The program execution is transferred to the subroutine address specified by the 16-bit of the operand if the flag condition is true. If the condition is false, the program continues without calling the subroutine.

Flags   No flags are affected.

Example   Write two conditional Call instructions: one with Carry set (C) and the other with Zero flag not set (NZ).

	Instructions:	1) CALL C, 2050H	Hex Codes:	DC	50	20
		2) CALL NZ, 2070H		C4	70	20

CCF: COMPLEMENT CARRY FLAG

Opcode	Operand	Bytes	MC /T-States	Hex Code
CCF		1	1 /4	3F

Description   The Carry flag is complemented.

	S	Z	H	P/V	N	C
Flags			?		0	√

CP r   : COMPARE REGISTER WITH ACCUMULATOR
CP 8-Bit: COMPARE 8-BIT DATA WITH ACCUMULATOR

Opcode	Operand	Bytes	MC /T-States	Hex Codes						
CP	r	1	1 /4	A	B	C	D	E	H	L
				BF	B8	B9	BA	BB	BC	BD
CP	8-bit	2	2 /7(4,3)	FE 8-bit						

Description   The operand is compared with the accumulator by subtracting the contents of the operand from the contents of the accumulator. None of the contents are altered and the comparison is shown by setting the flags as follows:

☐ If (A) < (r /8-bit): Carry flag is set and Zero flag is reset.
☐ If (A) = (r /8-bit): Zero flag is set and Carry flag is reset.
☐ If (A) > (r /8-bit): Carry and Zero flags are reset.

Flags   In addition to C and Z, the other flags are also modified to reflect the result of the operation.

S	Z		H		P/V	N	C
√	√		√		√	1	√

Example   Register B contains data byte 62_H and the accumulator contains data byte 57_H. Compare (B) with (A).

Mnemonics: CP   B   Hex Code: B8

Register Contents
Before Instruction

Register Contents
After Instruction

S Z H V N C

A	57	X	X	F
B	62	X	X	C

A	57	1 0 0 0 1 1	F
B	62	X X	C

☐ No contents are changed.
☐ Carry flag is set because (A) < (B).
☐ Other flags are also modified as shown.

CP (HL)   : COMPARE MEMORY CONTENTS WITH
              ACCUMULATOR
CP (IX + d):
CP (IY + d):

Opcode	Operand	Bytes	MC /T-States	Hex Codes		
CP	(HL)	1	2 /7(4,3)	BE		
CP	(IX + d)	3	5 /19(4,4,3,5,3)	DD	BE	8-bit
CP	(IY + d)			FD	BE	8-bit

Description   The memory is compared with the accumulator by subtracting the contents of the memory from the contents of the accumulator. None of the contents are altered and the comparison is shown by setting the flags as follows. The memory address is specified by the contents of the HL register or index register.

☐ If (A) < (M): Carry flag is set and Zero flag is reset.
☐ If (A) = (M): Zero flag is set and Carry flag is reset.
☐ If (A) > (M): Carry and Zero flags are reset.

Flags   In addition to CY and Z, the other flags are also modified to reflect the result of the operation.

S	Z		H		P/V	N	C
√	√		√		√	1	√

Example   The memory location 2050$_H$ contains 64$_H$, the accumulator contains 64$_H$, and the HL register holds the address 2050$_H$. Write the instruction to compare the contents of the accumulator with the contents of the memory location 2050H and show the status of the flags.

Mnemonics: CP (HL)   Hex Code: BE

Register Contents
Before Instruction

Memory Contents

Register Contents
After Instruction

A	64	X X	F
H	20	50	L

204F	XX
2050	64

S Z H V N C

A	64	0 1 0 0 1 0 F
H	20	50 L

☐ No contents are changed.
☐ Zero flag is set because (A) = (M).
☐ Other flags are also modified as shown.

CPD: COMPARE MEMORY WITH ACCUMULATOR, AND
DECREMENT MEMORY ADDRESS AND BYTE COUNTER

Opcode	Operand	Bytes	MC /T-States	Hex Code
CPD		2	4 /16(4,4,3,5)	ED A9

Description   The contents of the memory location addressed by the HL register are compared with the contents of the accumulator, and the flags are set as follows without altering the contents. The HL and BC registers are decremented. Register BC can be used as a byte counter.

□ If (A) < (M): Sign flag is set and Zero flag is reset.
□ If (A) = (M): Zero flag is set and Sign flag is reset.
□ If (A) > (M): Sign and Zero flags are reset.

Flags   In addition to S and Z, the other flags are also modified to reflect the result of the operation.

S	Z		H		P/V	N	C	
√	√		√		0/1	1		

P/V = 0 if BC = 0
    = 1 if BC ≠ 0

CPDR: COMPARE MEMORY WITH ACCUMULATOR, AND
DECREMENT MEMORY ADDRESS AND BYTE COUNTER UNTIL
CONTENTS ARE EQUAL OR COUNTER IS ZERO

Opcode	Bytes	MC /T-States		Hex Code
CPDR	2	5 /21(4,4,3,5,5)	if BC ≠ 0 and (A) ≠ (HL)	ED B9
		4 /16(4,4,3,5)	if BC = 0 or (A) = (HL)	

Description   The contents of the memory location addressed by the HL register are compared with the contents of the accumulator, and HL and BC registers are decremented. The instruction is repeated until either BC = 0 or (A) = (HL). Register BC is used as a byte counter.

Flags

S	Z		H		P/V	N	C	
√	√		√		0/1	1		

Z = 1 if (A) = (HL)   P/V = 0 if BC = 0
                             = 1 if BC ≠ 0

Example   The contents of the registers are (A) = $9F_H$, BC = $000F_H$, and (HL) = 2099_H. The memory location 2090_H has the byte 9F. Specify the contents of the registers after the execution of the instruction CPDR.

Instruction: CPDR   Hex Code: ED   B9

The instruction begins its search from the location 2099_H, and it will be repeated ten times until the memory location 2090_H, where (A) = (HL). The contents of the registers at the end of the search will be as follows:

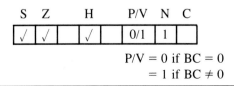

		S	Z	H	P/V	N	C	
A	9F	0	1	1	1	1	0	F
B	00			05				C
H	20			8F				L

CPI: COMPARE MEMORY WITH ACCUMULATOR,
INCREMENT MEMORY ADDRESS, AND DECREMENT BYTE
COUNTER

Opcode	Operand	Bytes	MC /T-States	Hex Code
CPI		2	4 /16(4,4,3,5)	ED A1

Description The contents of the memory location addressed by the HL register are compared with the contents of the accumulator, and the flags are set as follows without altering the contents. The HL register is incremented and the BC register is decremented. Register BC can be used as a byte counter.

☐ If (A) < (M): Sign flag is set and Zero flag is reset.
☐ If (A) = (M): Zero flag is set and Sign flag is reset.
☐ If (A) > (M): Sign and Zero flags are reset.

Flags In addition to S and Z, the other flags are also modified to reflect the result of the operation.

S	Z		H		P/V	N	C
√	√		√		0/1	1	

P/V = 0 if BC = 0
    = 1 if BC ≠ 0

CPIR: COMPARE MEMORY WITH ACCUMULATOR,
INCREMENT MEMORY ADDRESS, AND DECREMENT BYTE
COUNTER UNTIL CONTENTS ARE EQUAL OR COUNTER IS
ZERO

Opcode	Bytes	MC /T-States		Hex Code
CPIR	2	5 /21(4,4,3,5,5)	if BC ≠ 0 and (A) (HL)	ED B1
		4 /16(4,4,3,5)	if BC = 0 or (A) = (HL)	

Description The contents of the memory location addressed by the HL register are compared with the contents of the accumulator, and the HL register is incremented and the BC register decremented. The instruction is repeated until either BC = 0 or (A) = (HL). Register BC is used as a byte counter.

Flags

S	Z		H		P/V	N	C
√	√		√		0/1	1	

Z = 1 if (A) = (HL)   P/V = 0 if BC = 0
                          = 1 if BC ≠ 0

Example The contents of the registers are (A) = 9F$_H$, BC = 000F$_H$, and (HL) = 2090$_H$. None of the memory locations between 2090$_H$ and 209F$_H$ has the byte 9F. Specify the contents of the registers after the execution of the instruction CPIR.

Instruction: CPIR   Hex Code: ED B1

The instruction begins its search from the location 2090$_H$, and it will be repeated fifteen times until the byte counter BC is zero. The contents of the registers at the end of the search will be as follows:

		S Z H PNC		
A	9F	0 0 1	F	S and H flags will be determined
B	00	00	C	by the last comparison.
H	20	A0	L	

CPL: COMPLEMENT ACCUMULATOR

Opcode	Operand	Bytes	MC /T-States	Hex Code
CPL		1	1 /4	2F

Description The contents of the accumulator are complemented (inverted or 1's complement).

	S	Z	H	P/V	N	C
Flags			1		1	

Example The accumulator has 89$_H$. Show the contents after the execution of the instruction CPL.

Mnemonics: CPL   Hex Code: 2F

Before Instruction	After Instruction
A 1 0 0 0 1 0 0 1 (89$_H$)	A 0 1 1 1 0 1 1 0 (76$_H$)

DAA: DECIMAL ADJUST ACCUMULATOR

Opcode	Operand	Bytes	MC /T-States	Hex Code
DAA		1	1 /4	27

Description If this instruction is used after an addition or subtraction of two BCD numbers, the result is adjusted for BCD values. This instruction uses the Half Carry (H) flag internally to convert the binary result into BCD values shown as follows.

After an addition of two BCD numbers

1. If the value of the low-order four bits (D_3–D_0) in the accumulator is greater than 9 or if H flag is set, the instruction adjusts the low-order bits by adding 06 (0 1 1 0) to D_3–D_0.

2. If the value of the high-order bits (D_7–D_4) is greater than 9 or if CY flag is set, the instruction adjusts the high-order bits by adding 60 (0 1 1 0) to D_7–D_4.

After a subtraction of two BCD numbers, the above procedure is also valid, except the instruction adds 2's complement of 06 or 60 to the respective group of digits.

S	Z		H		P/V		N	C

Flags

(With check marks under S, Z, H, P/V, C)

Example   The accumulator contains 85_{BCD} and register B contains 68_{BCD}. Add the two numbers and adjust the result for the BCD value.

```
Mnemonics:  ADD  B     Hex Code:  80
            DAA                    27
       (A)  1 0 0 0  0 1 0 1      (85)BCD
       (B) +0 1 1 0  1 0 0 0      (68)BCD
            1 1 1 0  1 1 0 1      (153)BCD
```

The binary sum is ED_H, and the values of both low- and high-order four bits are higher than 9 (1 0 0 1). The instruction adds 6 (0 1 1 0) to both groups as shown below:

```
       (A)  1 1 1 0  1 1 0 1      (ED)
           +0 1 1 0  0 1 1 0      (66)
          1 0 1 0 1  0 0 1 1      1 53BCD
          CY
```

The accumulator contains 53 and the CY flag is set to indicate that the sum is larger than eight bits. The program should keep track of the carry; otherwise it may be altered by subsequent instructions.

Example   The accumulator contains 97_{BCD} and register B contains 39_{BCD}. Subtract (B) from (A) and adjust the result for decimal numbers.

```
Mnemonics:  SUB B     Hex Codes:  90
            DAA                    27
```

The subtraction is performed in 2's complement as follows:

```
       (A)  1 0 0 1  0 1 1 1      97
     + (B)  1 1 0 0  0 1 1 1      2's Comp. (39)
          1 0 1 0 1  1 1 1 0  →  5EH
```

After the subtraction, the low-order byte is larger than (1 0 0 1). The instruction adjusts the result by adding 2's complement of 06 (1 1 1 1 1 0 1 0) as shown.

$$
\begin{array}{llll}
\text{(A)} & 0\ 1\ 0\ 1\ \ 1\ 1\ 1\ 0 & & \text{5E} \\
+ & 1\ 1\ 1\ 1\ \ 1\ 0\ 1\ 0 & & \text{2's Comp. (06)} \\
\hline
1 & 0\ 1\ 0\ 1\ \ 1\ 0\ 0\ 0 & \to 58_{BCD}
\end{array}
$$

DEC r   : DECREMENT REGISTER CONTENTS
DEC (HL)   : DECREMENT MEMORY CONTENTS
DEC (IX + d):
DEC (IY + d):

Opcode	Operand	Bytes	MC /T-States	Hex Codes
				A B C D E H L
DEC	r	1	1 /4	3D 05 0D 15 1D 25 2D
DEC	(HL)	1	3 /11(4,4,3)	35
DEC	(IX + d)	3	6 /23(4,4,3,5,4,3)	DD 35 d
DEC	(IY + d)			FD 35 d

Description   The contents of the designated register/memory location are decremented by 1. If the operand is a memory location, it is specified by the contents of HL or index registers.

	S	Z	H	P/V	N	C
Flags	√	√		√		√	1	

DEC rp: DECREMENT REGISTER PAIR OR INDEX REGISTER
DEC rx:

Opcode	Operand	Bytes	MC /T-States	Hex Codes
				BC DE HL SP
DEC	rp	1	1 /6	0B 1B 2B 3B
DEC	IX	2	2 /10(4,6)	DD 2B
DEC	IY			FD 2B

Description   The contents of the specified register are decremented by 1; the contents are viewed as a 16-bit number.

Flags   No flags are affected.

Example   Register HL contains 2000$_H$. Specify the contents of the entire register after the instruction DEC HL.

Mnemonics: DEC   HL   Hex Code: 2B

The contents of the HL register will be 1FFF$_H$.

DI: DISABLE INTERRUPTS

Opcode	Operand	Bytes	MC /T-States	Hex Code
DI		1	1 /4	F3

Description   This instruction resets the interrupt enable flip-flops (IFF1 and IFF2) and disables maskable interrupts.

Flags   No flags are affected.

DJNZ d: JUMP RELATIVE IF B IS NOT ZERO

Opcode	Operand	Bytes	MC /T-States	Hex Code
DJNZ	d	2	3 /13(5,3,5) if B≠0	10 d
			2 /8(5,3) if B = 0	

Description   Register B is decremented, and if B≠0, the program execution is transferred to the memory location by adding displacement byte to the program counter +2.

Flags   No flags are affected.

EI: ENABLE INTERRUPTS

Opcode	Operand	Bytes	MC /T-States	Hex Code
EI		1	1 /4	FB

Description   This instruction sets the interrupt enable flip-flops (IFF1 and IFF2) to logic 1 and enables the maskable interrupts.

Flags   No flags are affected.

Comments   After the system reset or the acknowledgment of an interrupt, the interrupt enable flip-flops are reset, thus disabling the interrupts. This instruction must be executed to reenable the maskable interrupts.

EX AF, AF': EXCHANGE ACCUMULATOR AND FLAGS WITH ALTERNATE ACCUMULATOR AND FLAGS

Opcode	Operand	Bytes	MC /T-States	Hex Code
EX	AF, AF'	1	1 /4	08

Description   The contents of the accumulator and the flag register are exchanged with their respective alternate registers.

Flags   All flags are affected.

EX DE, HL: EXCHANGE HL AND DE REGISTERS

Opcode	Operand	Bytes	MC /T-States	Hex Code
EX	DE, HL	1	1 /4	EB

Description   The contents of register H are exchanged with the contents of register D, and the contents of register L are exchanged with the contents of register E.

Flags   No flags are affected.

EX (SP), HL: EXCHANGE CONTENTS OF REGISTERS WITH TOP OF STACK
EX (SP), IX:
EX (SP), IY:

Opcode	Operand	Bytes	MC /T-States	Hex Code
EX	(SP), HL	1	5 /19(4,3,4,3,5)	E3
EX	(SP), IX	2	6 /23(4,4,3,4,3,5)	DD E3
EX	(SP), IY			FD E3

Description   The contents of the low-order register (L or the low-order byte of an index register) are exchanged with the contents of the memory location pointed to by the stack pointer. The contents of the high-order register or the high-order byte of an index register are exchanged with the contents of the next memory (stack) location (SP + 1).

Flags   No flags are affected.

Example   The contents of registers and stack location are as follows:

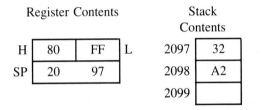

After the execution of the instruction EX (SP), HL, the contents of registers and stack locations will be as follows:

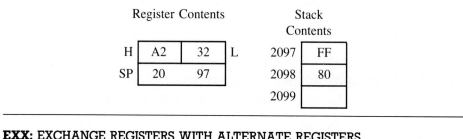

EXX: EXCHANGE REGISTERS WITH ALTERNATE REGISTERS

Opcode	Operand	Bytes	MC /T-States	Hex Code
EXX		1	1 /4	D9

Description The contents of the general-purpose registers BC, DE, and HL are exchanged with the contents of their respective alternate registers BC′, DE′ and HL′.

Flags No flags are affected.

HALT: SUSPEND OPERATIONS

Opcode	Operand	Bytes	MC /T-States	Hex Code
HALT		1	1 /4	76

Description This instruction suspends (halts) all operations, and the microprocessor waits until an interrupt or the reset is received. During the halt, the microprocessor continues to execute NOP instruction to maintain memory refresh cycles.

Flags No flags are affected.

IM 0: SET UP INTERRUPT MODE 0

Opcode	Operand	Bytes	MC /T-States	Hex Code
IM	0	2	2 /8(4,4)	ED 46

Description This instruction sets up the microprocessor in Interrupt Mode 0. In this mode, the interrupting device can insert any instruction onto the data bus to restart the MPU execution; the first byte must be inserted during the interrupt acknowledge cycle.

Flags No flags are affected.

IM 1: SET UP INTERRUPT MODE 1

Opcode	Operand	Bytes	MC /T-States	Hex Code
IM	1	2	2 /8(4,4)	ED 56

Description This instruction sets up the microprocessor in Interrupt Mode 1. In this mode, the MPU responds to an interrupt by executing the restart at location 0038$_H$.

Flags No flags are affected.

IM 2: SET UP INTERRUPT MODE 2

Opcode	Operand	Bytes	MC /T-States	Hex Code
IM	2	2	2 /8(4,4)	ED 5E

Description This instruction sets up the microprocessor in Interrupt Mode 2. In this mode, the MPU responds to an interrupt by executing an indirect call to the specified 16-bit address of a memory location. The low-order 8-bit address is supplied by the interrupting device, and the high-order address is supplied by the contents of the interrupt vector register I.

Flags No flags are affected.

IN A, (8-BIT): INPUT DATA TO ACCUMULATOR FROM A PORT
WITH 8-BIT ADDRESS

Opcode	Operand	Bytes	MC /T-States	Hex Code
IN	8-bit	2	3 /11(4,3,4)	DB 8-bit

Description The contents of the input port specified in the operand are read and placed in the accumulator.

Flags No flags are affected.

IN r, (C): INPUT DATA TO REGISTER FROM A PORT WITH
ADDRESS IN C

Opcode	Operand	Bytes	MC /T-States	Hex Codes						
IN	r, (C)	2	3 /12(4,4,4)	A	B	C	D	E	H	L
				ED 78	40	48	50	58	60	68

Description The contents of the input port with the address in register C are read and placed in the specified register.

	S	Z	H	P/V	N	C
Flags	√	√		√		√	0	

INC r: INCREMENT REGISTER

Opcode	Operand	Bytes	MC /T-States	Hex Codes
INC	r	1	1 /4	A B C D E H L
				3C 04 0C 14 1C 24 2C

Description   The contents of the specified register are incremented by 1.

Flags

	S	Z		H		P/V	N	C
	√	√		√		√	0	

Example   The accumulator contains FF_H. Specify the contents of the accumulator and the status of CY and Z flags after the INC instruction.

Mnemonics: INC   A   Hex Code: 3C

$$(A) = \quad 1\ 1\ 1\ 1 \quad 1\ 1\ 1\ 1$$
$$+0\ 0\ 0\ 0 \quad 0\ 0\ 0\ 1$$
$$(A) = 1\ 0\ 0\ 0\ 0 \quad 0\ 0\ 0\ 0$$

After the byte FF has been incremented, the sum should be 00 with carry. However, the INC instruction does not set the CY flag even though it affects all other flags. If ADD instruction is used, the accumulator contents will be 00 with the CY flag set.

INC rp: INCREMENT REGISTER PAIR OR INDEX REGISTER
INC rx:

Opcode	Operand	Bytes	MC /T-States	Hex Codes			
				BC	DE	HL	SP
INC	rp	1	1 /6	03	13	23	33
INC	IX	2	2 /10(4,6)	DD	23		
INC	IY			FD	23		

Description   The contents of the specified register pair or the index register are incremented by 1.

Flags   No flags are affected.

INC (HL):   INCREMENT MEMORY CONTENTS
INC (IX + d):
INC (IY + d):

Opcode	Operand	Bytes	MC /T-States	Hex Codes		
INC	(HL)	1	3 /11(4,4,3)		34	
INC	(IX + d)	3	6 /23(4,4,3,5,4,3)	DD	34	d
INC	(IY + d)			FD	34	d

Description The contents of the specified memory are incremented by 1. The memory location is specified either by the contents of HL register or the contents of an index register plus the displacement.

Flags

S	Z		H		P/V	N	C	
√	√		√		√	0		

Example The memory register at 2040_H contains the byte FF_H. The index register IX holds the address 2050_H. Write the instruction to increment the contents of the memory register and specify the status of the flags.

Mnemonics: INC (IX + F0H)   Hex Codes: DD   34   F0

The displacement is calculated by taking 2's complement of 10_H, the difference between 2050_H and 2040_H. After the execution of the instruction, the memory contents will be 00. The flag status will be as follows:

S	Z		H		V	N	C	
0	1		1		0	0		

Note: This instruction does not affect the C flag.

IND: INPUT DATA TO MEMORY AND DECREMENT BYTE COUNTER AND MEMORY POINTER

Opcode	Operand	Bytes	MC /T-States	Hex Code
IND		2	4 /16(4,5,3,4)	ED AA

Description This instruction reads the input port specified by the contents of register C, and the reading is stored in the memory location specified by the contents of register HL. Register B is used as a byte counter, and both B and HL are decremented by one.

Flags

S	Z		H		P/V	N	C	
?	0/1		?		?	1		

Z = 1 if B = 0
  = 0 if B≠0

INDR: INPUT DATA TO MEMORY AND DECREMENT MEMORY POINTER AND BYTE COUNTER UNTIL BYTE COUNTER IS ZERO

Opcode	Operand	Bytes	MC /T-States	Hex Code
INDR		2	5 /21(4,5,3,4,5) if B≠0	ED BA
			4 /16(4,5,3,4) if B = 0	

Description This instruction reads the input port specified by the contents of register C, and the reading is stored in the memory location specified by the contents of register HL. Register B is used as a byte counter, both B and HL are decremented by one, and the instruction is repeated until B = 0.

	S	Z		H		P/V	N	C	
Flags	?	1		?		?	1		

Example The contents of the registers are HL = 2070_H and BC = 0401_H. Show the contents of memory locations and registers after the execution of the instruction INDR.

Instruction: INDR   Hex Code: ED BA

The instruction reads the data at the input port 01_H four times until register B = 0 and stores the data in memory starting from 2070_H. The contents of registers and the memory locations are as follows:

Register Contents Before Instruction			Memory Contents		Register Contents After Instruction		
B	04	01	C	206C		B	00	01	C
H	20	70	L	206D	BYTE4	H	20	6C	L
				206E	BYTE3			
				206F	BYTE2			
				2070	BYTE1			

INI: INPUT DATA TO MEMORY, DECREMENT BYTE
COUNTER, AND INCREMENT MEMORY POINTER

Opcode	Operand	Bytes	MC /T-States	Hex Code
INI		2	4 /16(4,5,3,4)	ED A2

Description This instruction reads the input port specified by the contents of register C, and the reading is stored in the memory location specified by the contents of register HL. The contents of register B are decremented and those of register HL are incremented by one.

	S	Z		H		P/V	N	C	
Flags	?	0/1		?		?	1		

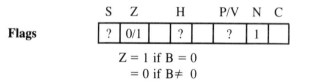

Z = 1 if B = 0
= 0 if B ≠ 0

INIR: INPUT DATA TO MEMORY, INCREMENT MEMORY
POINTER, AND DECREMENT BYTE COUNTER UNTIL BYTE
COUNTER IS ZERO

Opcode	Operand	Bytes	MC /T-States	Hex Code
INIR		2	5 /21(4,5,3,4,5) if B≠0	ED B2
			4 /16(4,5,3,4) if B = 0	

Description   This instruction reads the input port specified by the contents of register C, and the reading is stored in the memory location specified by the contents of register HL. The contents of register B are decremented and those of register HL are incremented by one. Register B is used as a byte counter, and the instruction is repeated until B = 0.

Flags

S	Z	H	P/V	N	C	
?	1	?		?	1	

Example   The contents of the registers are HL = 2070$_H$ and BC = 0407$_H$. Show the contents of memory locations and registers after the execution of the instruction INIR.

Instruction: INIR   Hex Code: ED   B2

The instruction reads the data at the input port 07$_H$ four times until register B = 0 and stores the data in memory starting from 2070$_H$. The contents of registers and the memory locations are as follows:

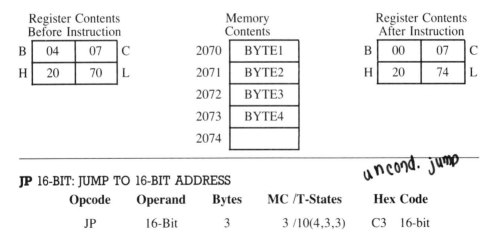

Register Contents Before Instruction

B	04	07	C
H	20	70	L

Memory Contents

2070	BYTE1
2071	BYTE2
2072	BYTE3
2073	BYTE4
2074	

Register Contents After Instruction

B	00	07	C
H	20	74	L

uncond. jump

JP 16-BIT: JUMP TO 16-BIT ADDRESS

Opcode	Operand	Bytes	MC /T-States	Hex Code
JP	16-Bit	3	3 /10(4,3,3)	C3 16-bit

Description   The program execution is transferred to the memory location specified by the 16-bit address. This is a 3-byte instruction; the second byte specifies the low-order byte and the third byte specifies the high-order byte of the 16-bit address.

Flags   No flags are affected.

Example   Write the instruction at location 2010_H to transfer the program sequence to location 2050_H.

Instruction: JP   2050H   Hex Code: C3   50   20

This machine code can be stored as follows:

Memory Address	Hex Code	Mnemonics
2010	C3	JP 2050H
2011	50	
2012	20	

Make a note of the difference between writing a 16-bit address as mnemonics and machine code. In the code, the low-order byte (50) is entered first, followed by the high-order byte (20). However, in mnemonics the bytes are shown in the proper sequence. If an assembler is used to obtain the codes, it will automatically reverse the sequence of the machine codes.

JP cc, 16-BIT: JUMP TO 16-BIT ADDRESS IF CONDITION IS TRUE

Opcode	Operand	Bytes	MC /T-States	Hex Codes
JP	cc, 16-Bit	3	3 /10(4,3,3)	NZ Z NC C PO PE P M C2 CA D2 DA E2 EA F2 FA

Description   The program execution is transferred to the address specified by the 16-bit of the operand if the flag condition is true. If the condition is false, the program continues to the next memory location.

Flags   No flags are affected.

Example   Write two conditional Jump instructions: one with Carry set (C) and the other when the Zero flag is not set (NZ).

Instructions: 1) JP C, 2050H   Hex Codes: DA 50 20
2) JP NZ, 2070H   C2 70 20

JP (HL): JUMP TO MEMORY LOCATION SPECIFIED BY HL OR INDEX REGISTERS
JP (IX):
JP (IY):

Opcode	Operand	Bytes	MC /T-States	Hex Codes
JP	(HL)	1	1 /4	E9
JP	(IX)	2	2 /8(4,4)	DD E9
JP	(IY)			FD E9

Description   The program execution is transferred to the memory location specified by the contents of the HL register or the index register.

Flags   No flags are affected.

JR: JUMP RELATIVE EQUAL TO DISPLACEMENT

Opcode	Operand	Bytes	MC /T-States	Hex Codes	
JR	d	2	3 /12(4,3,5)	18	d

Description   The program execution is transferred to the memory location specified by the sum of the present program counter and the displacement byte. The value of a displacement byte can be positive for a forward jump or in 2's complement for a backward jump. The total range of the jump is -126 to $+129$; this accounts for the additional two memory locations due to the instruction Jump Relative.

Flags   No flags are affected.

Example   Write the instruction at location 2010 to transfer the program sequence to location 2050_H.

Instruction: JR 3EH   Hex Code: 18 3E

This machine code can be stored as follows:

Memory Address	Hex Code	Mnemonics
2010	18	JR 3EH
2011	3E	
2012		

When the instruction Jump Relative located at 2010_H is executed, the program counter contains 2012_H. By adding $3E_H$ to 2012_H, the program counter contains 2050_H; thus, the program is transferred to the location 2050_H. Therefore, to calculate the displacement byte for a forward jump, the value obtained by subtracting the instruction location (2010_H) from the jump location (2050_H) should be reduced by two. On the other hand, two should be added to the displacement byte in 2's complement for a backward jump as shown in the following example.

Example   Write the instruction at location 2010_H to transfer the program sequence to location 2000H.

Instruction: JR EEH   Hex Code: 18 EE

This machine code can be stored as follows:

Memory Address	Hex Code	Mnemonics
2010	18	JR EEH
2011	EE	
2012		

The displacement byte is calculated as follows:

$$(PC) = 2\ 0\ 1\ 2\ _H$$
$$\text{Jump Location} = 2\ 0\ 0\ 0\ _H$$

$$1\ 2\ _H = 0\ 0\ 0\ 1\ 0\ 0\ 1\ 0$$
$$\text{2's Complement of } 12_H = 1\ 1\ 1\ 0\ 1\ 1\ 1\ 0 \quad (EE_H)$$

JR cc, d: JUMP RELATIVE EQUAL TO DISPLACEMENT IF FLAG CONDITION IS TRUE

Opcode	Operand	Bytes	MC /T-States	Hex Codes			
JR	cc, d	2	3 /12(4,3,5)	NZ	Z	NC	C
			If condition is true				
			2 /7(4,3)	20	28	30	38
			If condition is false				

Description   The program execution is transferred to the memory location specified by the sum of the present program counter and the displacement byte if the condition is true. The value of a displacement byte can be positive for a forward jump or in 2's complement for a backward jump. The total range of the jump is -126 to $+129$; this accounts for the additional two memory locations due to the instruction Jump Relative.

Note: There are no conditional relative jump instructions based on other flags.

Flags   No flags are affected.

Example   Write the instruction at location 2010_H to transfer the program sequence to location 2000_H if Carry is set.

Instruction: JR   C,   EEH   Hex Code: 38   EE

This machine code can be stored as follows:

Memory Address	Hex Code	Mnemonics
2010	38	JR C, EEH
2011	EE	
2012		

For the calculation of the displacement byte, see the example in the previous instruction.

LD r_d, r_s: COPY SOURCE REGISTER INTO DESTINATION REGISTER

Opcode	Operand	Bytes	MC /T-States	Hex Codes
LD	r_d, r_s	1	1 /4	Source Register

Destination Register		A	B	C	D	E	H	L
	A	7F	78	79	7A	7B	7C	7D
	B	47	40	41	42	43	44	45
	C	4F	48	49	4A	4B	4C	4D
	D	57	50	51	52	53	54	55
	E	5F	58	59	5A	5B	5C	5D
	H	67	60	61	62	63	64	65
	L	6F	68	69	6A	6B	6C	6D

Description The contents of the source register r_s are copied into the destination register r_d. The letters r_s and r_d represent any of the registers A, B, C, D, E, H, and L.

Flags No flags are affected.

Example Register B contains 72_H and register C contains $9F_H$. Transfer the contents of register B to register C.

Mnemonics: LD C, B   Hex Code: 48

Note that the first operand C specifies the destination register and the second operand B specifies the source register.

Register Contents Before Instruction		Register Contents After Instruction	
B	72	9F	C

Register Contents After Instruction			
B	72	72	C

LD r, 8-BIT: LOAD REGISTER r WITH 8-BIT DATA

Opcode	Operand	Bytes	MC /T-States	Hex Codes

				A	B	C	D	E	H	L	
LD	r, 8-Bit	2	2 /7(4,3)	[3E	06	0E	16	1E	26	2E]	8-bit

Description The second byte (8-bit data) is loaded into the specified register r. Register r can be any of the registers A, B, C, D, E, H, or L.

Flags No flags are affected.

Example   Load 92_H into register B.

Mnemonics: LD   B,   92H   Hex Code: 06   92

LD r, (HL):   COPY CONTENTS OF MEMORY INTO REGISTER
LD r, (IX + d):
LD r, (IY + d):

Opcode	Operand	Bytes	MC /T-States	Hex Codes						
LD	r, (HL)	1	2 /7(4,3)	A	B	C	D	E	H	L
				7E	46	4E	56	5E	66	6E
LD	r, (IX + d)	3	5 /19	DD [7E 46 4E 56 5E 66 6E] d						
	r, (IY + d)		(4,4,3,5,3)	FD [7E 46 4E 56 5E 66 6E] d						

Description   The contents of the memory location indicated by the HL register or by one of the index registers (plus displacement) is copied into the specified register r. Register r can be any one of the registers A, B, C, D, E, H, or L.

Flags   No flags are affected.

Example   Assume the contents of register HL are 20_H and 50_H, respectively. The byte $9F_H$ is stored in memory location 2050_H. Copy the contents of the memory location 2050_H into register D.

Mnemonics: LD   D,   (HL)   Hex Code: 56

	Register Contents Before Instruction			Memory Contents		Register Contents After Instruction		
D	XX	XX	E		D	9F	XX	E
H	20	50	L	2050 9F	H	20	50	L

Example   Assume the index register IX has 2040_H. Copy the contents of memory location 2050_H into register D as in the previous example.

Mnemonics: LD   D,   (IX + 10H)   Hex Code: DD   56   10

This instruction adds the displacement byte 10_H to the contents of the index register (2040_H) and points to location 2050_H. Then it copies the contents of 2050_H into register D.

LD (HL), r   : COPY CONTENTS OF REGISTER INTO MEMORY
LD (IX + d), r:
LD (IY + d), r:

Opcode	Operand	Bytes	MC /T-States	Hex Codes

				A B C D E H L
LD	(HL), r	1	2 /7(4,3)	77 70 71 72 73 74 75
LD	(IX + d), r	3	5 /19	DD [77 70 71 72 73 74 75] d
	(IY + d), r		(4,4,3,5,3)	FD [77 70 71 72 73 74 75] d

Description The contents of register r are copied into the memory location specified by either the contents of the HL register pair or one of the index registers (plus displacement). Register r represents any one of the registers A, B, C, D, E, H, or L.

Flags No flags are affected.

Example Register B contains 98_H and the register pair HL contains 2065_H. Copy the contents of register B into memory location 2065_H.

Mnemonics: LD   (HL), B   Hex Code: 70

This instruction copies the contents of register B (98H) into memory location 2065H.

LD (HL), 8-BIT   : LOAD 8-BIT INTO MEMORY
LD (IX + d), 8-BIT:
LD (IY + d), 8-BIT:

Opcode	Operand	Bytes	MC /T-States	Hex Codes
LD	(HL), 8-Bit	2	3 /10(4,3,3)	36 8-bit
LD	(IX + d), 8-Bit	4	5 /19(4,4,3,5,3)	DD 36 d 8-bit
	(IY + d), 8-Bit			FD 36 d 8-bit

Description The 8-bit data are loaded into the specified memory location. The address of the memory location is specified by the contents of register pair HL or by one of the index registers (plus displacement).

Flags No flags are affected.

Example Assume the contents of register pair HL are 20_H and 50_H, respectively. Load the byte 97_H into memory location 2050_H.

Mnemonics: LD   (HL),   97H   Hex Code: 36   97

This instruction loads 97_H into memory location 2050_H.

Example Explain the data transfer in the following instruction if the index register IY holds the contents 2060_H.

Instruction: LD   (IY + 0FH),   00H   Hex Code: FD   36   0F   00

This instruction adds the displacement byte $0F_H$ to the contents of the index register IY (2060_H) and specifies the memory location $206F_H$, then clears that location by loading 00_H.

LD A, (16-BIT): COPY MEMORY CONTENTS INTO ACCUMULATOR
LD A, (BC)   :
LD A, (DE)   :

Opcode	Operand	Bytes	MC /T-States	Hex Codes
LD	A, (16-Bit)	3	4 /13(4,3,3,3)	3A 16-bit
LD	A, (BC)	1	2 /7(4,3)	0A
	A, (DE)			1A

Description   The contents of the specified memory location are copied into the accumulator. The memory location is specified either directly by 16-bit address or by the contents of BC or DE registers.

Flags   No flags are affected.

Example   The register BC contains 2050_H and the byte $F8_H$ is stored in memory location 2050_H. Copy the byte into the accumulator.

Mnemonics: LD A, (BC)   Hex Code: 0A

This instruction copies the contents, $F8_H$, of the memory location 2050_H into the accumulator.

Example   Write the instruction to copy the byte from the memory location 2050_H into the accumulator.

Instruction: LD A, (2050H)   Hex Code: 3A 50 20

Note that the 16-bit address is entered in the reversed order: the low-order byte (50_H) first, followed by the high-order byte (20_H).

LD (16-BIT), A: COPY ACCUMULATOR CONTENTS INTO MEMORY
LD (BC), A   :
LD (DE), A   :

Opcode	Operand	Bytes	MC /T-States	Hex Codes
LD	(16-Bit), A	3	4 /13(4,3,3,3)	32 16-bit
LD	(BC), A	1	2 /7(4,3)	02
LD	(DE),A			12

Description   The contents of the accumulator are copied into the specified memory location. The memory location is specified either directly by a 16-bit address or by the contents of BC or DE registers.

Flags   No flags are affected.

Example   Write instructions to copy the contents of the accumulator into memory location 2050$_H$ by using the direct addressing and the indirect addressing methods.

Direct Addressing: LD   (2050H),   A   Hex Code: 32   50   20

Indirect   : To use the DE pair as a memory pointer, the address 2050$_H$
Addressing : must be loaded into the DE register. Then the following instruction can be used:

LD   (DE),   A   Hex Code: 12

LD A, I: COPY INTERRUPT VECTOR REGISTER INTO ACCUMULATOR
LD A, R: COPY MEMORY REFRESH REGISTER INTO ACCUMULATOR

Opcode	Operand	Bytes	MC /T-States	Hex Codes
LD	A, I	2	2 /9(4,5)	ED 57
LD	A, R	2	2 /9(4,5)	ED 5F

Description   The first instruction copies the contents of the interrupt vector register and the second instruction copies the contents of the memory refresh register into the accumulator.

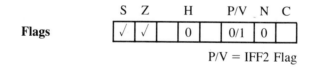

Flags

S	Z	H	P/V	N	C
√	√	0	0/1	0	

P/V = IFF2 Flag

LD I, A: COPY ACCUMULATOR INTO INTERRUPT VECTOR REGISTER
LD R, A: COPY ACCUMULATOR INTO MEMORY REFRESH REGISTER

Opcode	Operand	Bytes	MC /T-States	Hex Codes
LD	I, A	2	2 /9(4,5)	ED 47
LD	R, A	2	2 /9(4,5)	ED 4F

Description   The instructions copy the contents of the accumulator into the interrupt vector register and the memory refresh register, respectively.

Flags   No flags are affected.

LD rp, 16-BIT: LOAD 16-BIT INTO REGISTER PAIR
LD IX, 16-BIT: LOAD 16-BIT INTO INDEX REGISTER
LD IY, 16-BIT:

Opcode	Operand	Bytes	MC /T-States	Hex Codes				
				BC	DE	HL	SP	
LD	rp, 16-Bit	3	3 /10(4,3,3)	01	11	21	31	16-bit
LD	IX, 16-bit	4	4 /14(4,4,3,3)	DD	21	16-bit		
LD	IY, 16-bit			FD	21	16-bit		

Description   16-bit data are loaded into the specified register pair or index register. The 16-bit data are entered low-order byte first, followed by the high-order byte.

Flags   No flags are affected.

Example   Write instructions to load 2050_H into register BC and 4000_H into index register IY.

Instructions: LD   BC,   2050H   Hex Code: 01   50   20

LD   IY,   4000H   FD   21   00   40

Note the order of 16-bit data: low-order byte first, followed by the high-order byte.

LD rp, (16-BIT): LOAD CONTENTS OF TWO MEMORY
LD rx, (16-BIT): LOCATIONS INTO REGISTER PAIR OR INDEX
LD HL, (16-BIT): REGISTER

Opcode	Operand	Bytes	MC /T-States	Hex Codes				
				BC	DE	HL	SP	
LD	rp, (16-Bit)	4	6 /20(4,4,3,3,3,3)	ED [4B	5B	6B	7B]	16-bit
LD	IX, (16-bit)			DD	2A	16-bit		
LD	IY, (16-bit)			FD	2A	16-bit		
LD	HL, (16-bit)	3	5 /16	2A	16-bit			

Description   The instruction copies the contents of the memory location specified by the 16-bit address into low-order register and then copies the contents of the next memory location into high-order register.

Flags   No flags are affected.

Example   The memory locations 2050_H and 2051_H contain the data bytes 19_H and 86_H respectively. Copy the memory contents into BC and IX registers.

Instruction: LD   BC,   (2050H)   Hex Code: ED   4B   50   20

Memory Contents

2050 | 19
2051 | 86

Register Contents After Instruction

B | 86 | 19 | C

Instruction: LD IX, (2050H)   Hex Code: DD 2A 50 20

Memory
Contents

| 2050 | 19 |
| 2051 | 86 |

Register Contents
After Instruction

IX | 86 | 19 |

LD (16-BIT), rp: LOAD CONTENTS OF REGISTER PAIR OR INDEX REGISTER INTO TWO CONSECUTIVE MEMORY LOCATIONS
LD (16-BIT), XY:
LD (16-BIT), HL:

Opcode	Operand	Bytes	MC /T-States	Hex Codes
				BC DE HL SP
LD	(16-Bit), rp	4	6 /20(4,4,3,3,3,3)	ED [43 53 63 73] 16-bit
LD	(16-bit), IX			DD 22 16-bit
LD	(16-bit), IY			FD 22 16-bit
LD	(16-bit), HL	3	5 /16	22 16-bit

Description   The instruction copies the contents of the low-order register into memory location specified by the 16-bit address and copies the contents of the high-order register into the next memory location.

Flags   No flags are affected.

Example   The BC register contains data $408F_H$. Copy the register contents into memory locations 2050_H and 2051_H.

Instruction: LD (2050H), BC   Hex Code: ED 43 50 20

Register Contents
Before Instruction

B | 40 | 8F | C

Memory Contents
After Instruction

| 8F | 2050 |
| 40 | 2051 |

LD SP, HL: COPY HL OR INDEX REGISTER INTO STACK POINTER
LD SP, IX:
LD SP, IY:

Opcode	Operand	Bytes	MC /T-States	Hex Codes
LD	SP, HL	1	1 /6	F9
LD	SP, IX	2	2 /10(4,6)	DD F9
LD	SP, IY			FD F9

Description   The instruction copies the contents of the HL register or an index register into the stack pointer.

Flags   No flags are affected.

Example   The HL register contains 2050_H. Specify the contents of the stack pointer after executing the following instruction.

Instruction: LD SP, HL   Hex Code: F9

After the execution of the above instruction, both the stack pointer and the HL register will have 2050_H. The contents of the source are not destroyed.

LDD: COPY DATA FROM SOURCE MEMORY TO
DESTINATION MEMORY, AND DECREMENT MEMORY
POINTERS AND COUNTER

Opcode	Operand	Bytes	MC /T-States	Hex Codes
LDD		1	4 /16(4,4,3,5)	ED A8

Description   The contents of the memory location addressed by the HL register are copied into the memory location addressed by the DE register. Then registers BC, DE, and HL are decremented. In this instruction, HL functions as a source memory pointer, DE as a destination memory pointer, and BC as a counter.

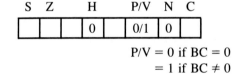

Flags

P/V = 0 if BC = 0
    = 1 if BC ≠ 0

Example   The memory locations 2070_H, 2071_H, and 2072_H contain 97_H, $4F_H$, and $7A_H$, respectively. The contents of the registers are HL = 2072_H, DE = 2045_H, and BC = $01FF_H$. Show the contents of memory locations and registers after the execution of the instruction LDD.

Instruction: LDD   Hex Code: ED A8

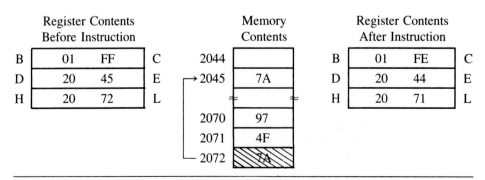

LDDR: COPY DATA FROM SOURCE MEMORY TO
        DESTINATION MEMORY, AND DECREMENT MEMORY
        POINTERS AND COUNTER UNTIL COUNTER IS ZERO

Opcode	Operand	Bytes	MC /T-States	Hex Codes
LDDR		2	5 /21(4,4,3,5,5) if BC ≠ 0	ED B8
			4 /16(4,4,3,5) if BC = 0	

Description   The contents of the memory location addressed by the HL register are
copied into the memory location addressed by the DE register. Then registers BC, DE, and
HL are decremented, and the copying process is continued until BC = 0. In this instruction, HL functions as a source memory pointer, DE as a destination memory pointer, and
BC as a counter.

Flags

	S	Z	H	P/V	N	C
			0		0	0	

Example   The memory locations 2071_H and 2072_H contain 97_H and $4F_H$, respectively.
The contents of the registers are HL = 2072_H, DE = 2045_H, and BC = 0002_H. Show the
contents of memory locations and registers after the execution of the instruction
LDDR.

Instruction: LDDR   Hex Code: ED B8

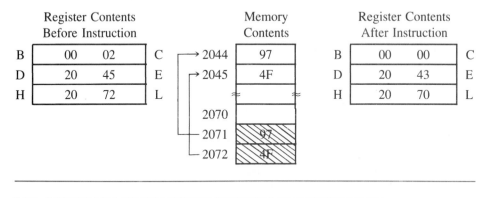

LDI: COPY DATA FROM SOURCE MEMORY TO DESTINATION
       MEMORY, INCREMENT MEMORY POINTERS, AND
       DECREMENT COUNTER

Opcode	Operand	Bytes	MC /T-States	Hex Codes
LDI		2	4 /16(4,4,3,5)	ED A0

Description   The contents of the memory location addressed by the HL register are
copied into the memory location addressed by the DE register. Then DE and HL are
incremented and BC is decremented. In this instruction, HL functions as a source memory
pointer, DE as a destination memory pointer, and BC as a counter.

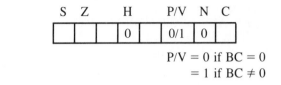

$$P/V = 0 \text{ if } BC = 0$$
$$= 1 \text{ if } BC \neq 0$$

Example   The memory locations 2070_H, 2071_H, and 2072_H contain 97_H, $4F_H$, and $7A_H$, respectively. The contents of the registers are HL = 2070_H, DE = 2045_H, and BC = $01FF_H$. Show the contents of memory locations and registers after the execution of the instruction LDI.

Instruction: LDI   Hex Code: ED A0

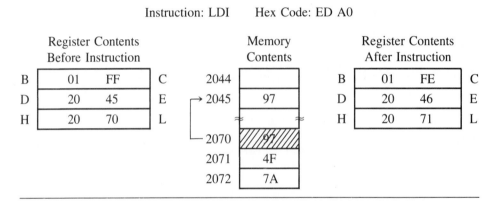

LDIR: COPY DATA FROM SOURCE MEMORY TO
       DESTINATION MEMORY, INCREMENT MEMORY
       POINTERS, AND DECREMENT COUNTER UNTIL IT IS
       ZERO

Opcode	Operand	Bytes	MC /T-States	Hex Codes
LDIR		2	5 /21(4,4,3,5,5) if BC ≠ 0	ED B0
			4 /16(4,4,3,5) if BC = 0	

Description   The contents of the memory location addressed by the HL register are copied into the memory location addressed by the DE register. Then registers DE and HL are incremented and BC is decremented. and the copying process is continued until BC = 0. In this instruction, HL functions as a source memory pointer, DE as a destination memory pointer, and BC as a counter.

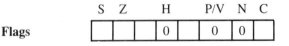

Example   The memory locations 2070_H, 2071_H, and 2072_H contain 97_H, $8A_H$, $4F_H$, respectively. The contents of the registers are HL = 2070_H, DE = 2045_H, and BC = 0003_H. Show the contents of memory locations and registers after the execution of the instruction LDIR.

Instruction: LDIR   Hex Code: ED B0

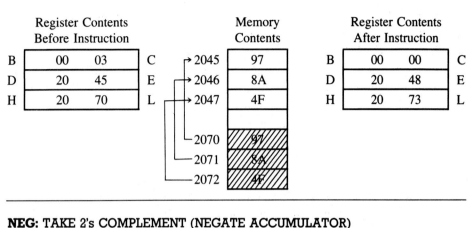

	Register Contents Before Instruction				Memory Contents			Register Contents After Instruction		
B	00	03	C	2045	97		B	00	00	C
D	20	45	E	2046	8A		D	20	48	E
H	20	70	L	2047	4F		H	20	73	L
				2070	97					
				2071	8A					
				2072	4F					

NEG: TAKE 2's COMPLEMENT (NEGATE ACCUMULATOR)

Opcode	Operand	Bytes	MC /T-States	Hex Code
NEG		2	2 /8 (4, 4)	ED 44

Description   The instruction converts the accumulator contents into 2's complement by subtracting the contents from 0.

Flags

S	Z		H		P/V	N	C
√	√		√		√	1	√

Example   The accumulator holds 97_H. Specify the contents of the accumulator and explain the S and CY flags after the execution of NEG instruction.

Mnemonics: NEG   Hex Code: ED 44

Before Instruction: (A) = 1 0 0 1 0 1 1 1 (97_H)
After Instruction : (A) = 0 1 1 0 1 0 0 1 (69_H)
Flags : S = 0, CY = 1

The Sign flag is reset because $D_7 = 0$, and the Carry flag is set because the larger number 97_H is subtracted from 00. However, the result does not mean that 69_H is a negative number; it depends upon the interpretation of 97_H. The appropriate interpretation is that 97_H and 69_H are 2's complements of each other.

NOP: NO OPERATION

Opcode	Operand	Bytes	MC /T-States	Hex Code
NOP		1	1 /4	00

Description   No operation is performed. The instruction is fetched and decoded; however, no operation is executed.

Flags   No flags are affected.

Comments   The instruction is used to increase time delays or delete and insert instructions while troubleshooting.

OR r   : LOGICALLY OR REGISTER, 8-BIT, OR MEMORY WITH
              ACCUMULATOR
OR 8-Bit:
OR (m)   :

Opcode	Operand	Bytes	MC /T-States	Hex Codes						
OR	r	1	1 /4	A	B	C	D	E	H	L
				B7	B0	B1	B2	B3	B4	B5
OR	8-bit	2	2 /7(4,3)	F6 d						
OR	(HL)	1	2 /7(4,3)	B6						
OR	(IX + d)	3	5 /19(4,4,3,5,3)	DD B6 d						
	(IY + d)			FD B6 d						

Description   The contents of a register or memory or an 8-bit word are ORed with the contents of the accumulator. The memory address is specified by the contents of the HL register or an index register with a displacement byte d.

	S	Z		H		P/V	N	C
Flags	√	√		0		√	0	0

Example   The contents of the accumulator and register B are 54_H and 82_H respectively. Logically OR (B) with (A) and show the flags and the contents of each register after ORing.

Mnemonics: OR   B   Hex Code: B0

Logical OR   Register Contents After Instruction

(A)	1 0 0 0	0 0 1 0	(82_H)			S Z	H	P N C
(B)	0 1 0 1	0 1 0 0	(54_H)	A	D6	1 0	0	0 0 0	F
(A)	1 1 0 1	0 1 1 0	$(D6_H)$	B	54		X		C

Example   Write mnemonics to OR the contents of memory location 2070_H with the contents of the accumulator assuming index register IY contains address 2000_H.

Mnemonics: OR   (IY + 70H)   Hex Code: FD   B6   70

OUT (8-Bit), A: OUTPUT DATA FROM ACCUMULATOR TO
                 PORT WITH 8-BIT ADDRESS

Opcode	Operand	Bytes	MC /T-States	Hex Code
OUT	8-Bit	2	3 /11(4,3,4)	D3 8-bit

Description   The contents of the accumulator are copied into the I/O port specified by the 8-bit address.

Flags   No flags are affected.

OUT (C), r: OUTPUT DATA FROM REGISTER r TO THE PORT
          WITH ADDRESS IN C

Opcode	Operand	Bytes	MC /T-States	Hex Codes
OUT	(C), r	2	3 /12 (4,4,4)	A B C D E H L
				ED 79 41 49 51 59 61 69

Description   The contents of register r are copied into the I/O port specified by the address in register C.

Flags   No flags are affected.

OUTD: OUTPUT DATA FROM MEMORY AND DECREMENT
         BYTE COUNTER AND MEMORY POINTER

Opcode	Operand	Bytes	MC /T-States	Hex Code
OUTD		2	4 /16(4,5,3,4)	ED AB

Description   This instruction copies data from the memory location specified by the contents of register HL into the output port specified by register C. Register B is used as a byte counter, and both B and HL are decremented by one.

	S	Z	H	P/V	N	C
Flags	?	0/1	?		?	1	

OTDR: OUTPUT DATA FROM MEMORY AND DECREMENT
         MEMORY POINTER AND BYTE COUNTER UNTIL BYTE
         COUNTER IS ZERO

Opcode	Operand	Bytes	MC /T-States	Hex Code
OTDR		2	5 /21(4,5,3,4,5)	ED BB
			if B≠0	
			4 /16(4,5,3,4)	
			if B=0	

Description   This instruction copies data from the memory location specified by the contents of register HL into the output port specified by register C. Register B is used as a byte counter, and both B and HL are decremented by one; the instruction is repeated until B = 0.

	S	Z	H	P/V	N	C
Flags	?	1	?		?	1	

Example   The contents of the registers are HL = 2070$_H$ and BC = 0401$_H$. Show the contents of memory locations and registers after the execution of the instruction OTDR.

Instruction: OTDR   Hex Code: ED   BB

The instruction copies data starting from memory 2070$_H$ to the output port 01$_H$ four times until register B = 0. Assuming the port 01$_H$ is a printer, the four bytes will be printed. The contents of registers at the end of the instruction are as follows:

	Register Contents Before Instruction				Register Contents After Instruction		
B	04	01	C	B	00	01	C
H	20	70	L	H	20	6C	L

OUTI: OUTPUT DATA FROM MEMORY, DECREMENT BYTE
        COUNTER, AND INCREMENT MEMORY POINTER

Opcode	Operand	Bytes	MC /T-States	Hex Code
OUTI		2	4 /16(4,5,3,4)	ED A3

Description   This instruction copies data from the memory location specified by the contents of register HL into the output port specified by register C. The contents of register B are decremented and those of register HL are incremented by one.

	S	Z	H	P/V	N	C	
Flags	?	0/1	?	?	1		

OTIR: OUTPUT DATA FROM MEMORY, INCREMENT
        MEMORY POINTER, AND DECREMENT BYTE COUNTER
        UNTIL BYTE COUNTER IS ZERO

Opcode	Operand	Bytes	MC /T-States	Hex Code
OTIR		2	5 /21(4,5,3,4,5) if B≠0	ED B3
			4 /16(4,5,3,4) if B = 0	

Description   This instruction copies data from the memory location specified by the contents of register HL into the output port specified by register C. The contents of register B are decremented and those of register HL are incremented by one. The instruction is repeated until B = 0.

Flags

S	Z	H	P/V	N	C
?	1		?		?	1	

Example The contents of the registers are HL = 2070$_H$ and BC = 0407$_H$. Show the contents of memory locations and registers after the execution of the instruction OTIR.

Instruction: OTIR   Hex Code: ED   B3

The instruction copies data starting from memory location 2070$_H$ into output port 07$_H$. The instruction is repeated four times until B = 0, and every time data is taken from the next memory location by incrementing HL. The contents of registers are as follows:

Register Contents
Before Instruction

B | 04 | 07 | C
H | 20 | 70 | L

Register Contents
After Instruction

B | 00 | 07 | C
H | 20 | 74 | L

POP rp: PLACE STACK CONTENTS INTO REGISTER PAIR OR
        INDEX REGISTER
POP rx:

Opcode	Operand	Bytes	MC /T-States	Hex Codes			
				BC	DE	HL	AF
POP	rp	1	3 /10(4,3,3)	C1	D1	E1	F1
POP	IX	2	4 /14(4,4,3,3)		DD	E1	
POP	IY				FD	E1	

Description The contents at the top of the stack indicated by the address in the stack pointer are copied into the low-order register (C, E, L, or F) or as a low-order byte into an index register and the stack pointer is incremented by one. Again, the contents of the top of the stack (after incrementing the stack pointer) are copied into the high-order register or as a high-order byte into an index register. The stack pointer is incremented by one to indicate the new top of the stack.

Flags No flags are affected.

Example Assume the stack pointer contains 2090$_H$, data byte 50$_H$ is stored in location 2090$_H$ and 80$_H$ is stored in location 2091$_H$. Transfer the contents of the top two stack locations into HL registers.

Mnemonics: POP   HL   Hex Code: E1

Register Contents Before Instruction			Stack Contents		Register Contents After Instruction		
H	XX	XX	L	2090	50	H	80
SP	2090			2091	80	SP	2092

(In the After Instruction block: H | 80 | 50 | L, SP | 2092)

PUSH rp: COPY REGISTER PAIR OR INDEX REGISTER ON
STACK
PUSH rx:

Opcode	Operand	Bytes	MC /T-States	Hex Codes
				BC DE HL AF
PUSH	rp	1	3 /10(4,3,3)	C5 D5 E5 F5
PUSH	IX	2	4 /14(4,4,3,3)	DD E5
PUSH	IY			FD E5

Description   The contents of the specified register pair or index register are copied into the stack locations as follows. First, the stack pointer is decremented by one and the contents of the high-order register (B, D, H, A) or high-order byte of the index register are copied into the memory location indicated by the stack pointer. The stack pointer is decremented again and the contents of the low-order register (C, E, L, F) or the low-order byte of the index register are copied into that location.

Flags   No flags are affected.

Example   Assume that the stack pointer contains 2099_H, register H contains 40_H, and register L contains $F8_H$. Save the contents of HL on the stack.

Mnemonics: PUSH   HL   Hex Code: E5

Register Contents Before Instruction			Stack Contents		Register Contents After Instruction		
H	40	F8	L	2097	F8	H	40
SP	2099			2098	40	SP	2097
				2099	XX		

(After Instruction: H | 40 | F8 | L, SP | 2097)

RES b, r: RESET BIT IN A REGISTER OR IN MEMORY
RES b, (m):

Opcode	Operand	Bytes	MC /T-States	Hex Codes
RES	b, r	2	2 /8(4,4)	*Register*

(Bit)	A	B	C	D	E	H	L
CB (0)	87	80	81	82	83	84	85
CB (1)	8F	88	89	8A	8B	8C	8D
CB (2)	97	90	91	92	93	94	95

CB (3)	9F	98	99	9A	9B	9C	9D
CB (4)	A7	A0	A1	A2	A3	A4	A5
CB (5)	AF	A8	A9	AA	AB	AC	AD
CB (6)	B7	B0	B1	B2	B3	B4	B5
CB (7)	BF	B8	B9	BA	BB	BC	BD

Bit

		0	1	2	3	4	5	6	7
RES	b, (HL)	2	4 /15 (4,4,4,3)	CB	[86 8E 96 9E A6 AE B6 BE]
RES	b, (IX + d)	4	6/23 (4,4,3,5,4,3)	DD CB d [86 8E 96 9E A6 AE B6 BE]
RES	b, (IY + d)			FD CB d [86 8E 96 9E A6 AE B6 BE]

Description The specified bit is reset in a register or in memory. The values of b (0–7) correspond to bits D_0–D_7.

Flags No flags are affected.

Example Write instructions to reset bit 3 in register A and bit 0 in memory 2055_H. Assume that registers HL are already loaded with the address 2055_H.

Mnemonics	Hex Code
RES 3, A	CB 9F
RES 0, (HL)	CB 86

RET: RETURN FROM SUBROUTINE UNCONDITIONALLY

Opcode	Operand	Bytes	MC /T-States	Hex Code
RET		1	3 /10(4,3,3)	C9

Description The program execution is transferred from the subroutine to the calling program. The two bytes from the top of the stack are copied into the program counter and the program execution begins at the new address. The instruction is equivalent to POP Program Counter.

Flags No flags are affected.

Example Assume that the stack pointer contains 2095_H. Explain the effect of the RET instruction if the contents of the stack location are as follows:

2095	50
2096	20

After instruction RET, the contents of the top two stack locations are copied into the program counter, and the program execution is transferred to location 2050_H. The stack pointer is incremented to location 2097_H.

RET cc: RETURN FROM SUBROUTINE IF CONDITION IS TRUE

Opcode	Operand	Bytes	MC /T-States	
RET	cc	1	3 /11(5,3,3) ;	If condition is true
			1 /5 ;	If condition is false

	NZ	Z	NC	C	PO	PE	P	M
Condition Flags	NZ	Z	NC	C	PO	PE	P	M
Hex Codes	C0	C8	D0	D8	E0	E8	F0	F8

Description The program execution is transferred from the subroutine to the calling program if the flag condition is true. If the condition is false, the program continues to the next memory location.

Flags No flags are affected.

RETI: RETURN FROM INTERRUPT

Opcode	Operand	Bytes	MC /T-States	Hex Code
RETI		2	4 /14(4,4,3,3)	ED 4D

Description The instruction copies the contents of the top two stack locations into the program counter, and the program execution is transferred to the address stored on the stack; this execution is similar to that of a RET instruction.

This instruction is used at the end of a maskable interrupt service routine. In addition to transferring the program execution to the interrupted program, it indicates to a Z80 family I/O device that it is the end of the service routine.

Flags No flags are affected.

RETN: RETURN FROM NONMASKABLE INTERRUPT

Opcode	Operand	Bytes	MC /T-States	Hex Code
RETN		2	4 /14(4,4,3,3)	ED 45

Description The instruction copies the contents of the top two stack locations into the program counter and the program execution is transferred to the address stored on the stack; this execution is similar to that of a RET instruction.

This instruction is used at the end of the nonmaskable interrupt service routine. In addition to transferring the program execution to the interrupted program, it restores the status of the maskable interrupts by copying the state of IFF2 (Interrupt Flip-flop 2) into IFF1 (Interrupt Flip-flop 1).

RLA: ROTATE ACCUMULATOR LEFT THROUGH CARRY

Opcode	Operand	Bytes	MC /T-States	Hex Code
RLA		1	1 /4	17

Description Each bit in the accumulator is rotated left by one position through the Carry flag. Bit D_7 is placed into the CY position and the CY flag is placed into bit D_0.

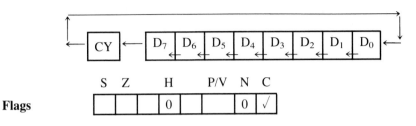

Flags

S	Z	H	P/V	N	C
		0		0	√

The CY flag is modified according to bit D_7.

Example The accumulator contains $A7_H$ and the CY flag is reset. Show the contents of the accumulator and the CY flag after the execution of the instruction RLA.

Mnemonics: RLA   Hex Code: 17

Accumulator Contents
Before Instruction

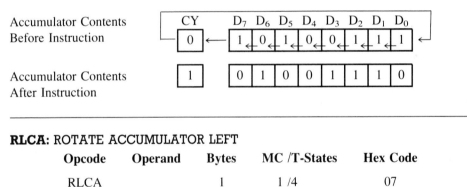

Accumulator Contents
After Instruction

RLCA: ROTATE ACCUMULATOR LEFT

Opcode	Operand	Bytes	MC /T-States	Hex Code
RLCA		1	1 /4	07

Description Each bit in the accumulator is rotated left by one position. Bit D_7 is placed into the position of bit D_0 and the CY flag is modified according to bit D_7.

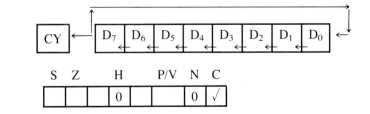

Flags

S	Z	H	P/V	N	C
		0		0	√

Example The accumulator contains $A7_H$ and the CY flag is reset. Show the contents of the accumulator and the CY flag after the execution of the instruction RLCA.

Mnemonics: RLCA   Hex Code: 07

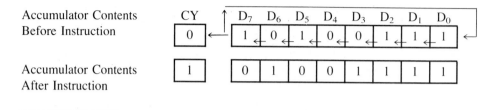

RL r: ROTATE EACH BIT LEFT IN REGISTER OR MEMORY THROUGH CARRY
RL (m):

Opcode	Operand	Bytes	MC /T-States	Hex Codes							
					A	B	C	D	E	H	L
RL	r	2	2 /8(4,4)	CB 17	10	11	12	13	14	15
RL	(HL)	2	4 /15(4,4,4,3)	CB 16							
RL	(IX + d)	4	6 /23(4,4,3,5,4,3)	DD CB	d	16					
RLC	(IY + d)			FD CB	d	16					

Description Each bit in the specified register or memory is rotated left by one position through carry. Bit D_7 is placed into the CY flag and the CY flag is placed into bit D_0. The memory address is specified using either HL or an index register.

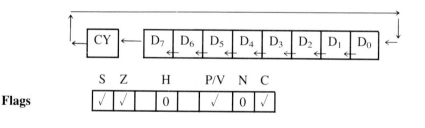

Flags

S	Z	H	P/V	N	C
√	√	0	√	0	√

RLC r: ROTATE EACH BIT LEFT IN REGISTER OR MEMORY
RLC (m):

Opcode	Operand	Bytes	MC /T-States	Hex Codes							
					A	B	C	D	E	H	L
RLC	r	2	2 /8(4,4)	CB	07	00	01	02	03	04	05
RLC	(HL)	2	4 /15(4,4,4,3)			CB	06				
RLC	(IX + d)	4	6 /23(4,4,3,5,4,3)	DD	CB	d	06				
RLC	(IY + d)			FD	CB	d	06				

Description Each bit in the specified register or memory is rotated left by one position. Bit D_7 is placed into the position of bit D_0 and the CY flag is modified according to bit D_7. The memory address is specified using either HL or an index register.

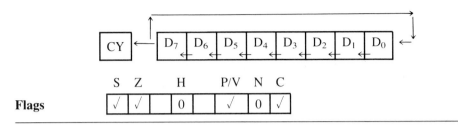

S Z H P/V N C

Flags | √ | √ | | 0 | | √ | 0 | √ |

RLD: ROTATE LEFT BCD DIGIT BETWEEN ACCUMULATOR AND MEMORY

Opcode	Operand	Bytes	MC /T-States	Hex Code
RLD		2	5 /18(4,4,3,4,3)	ED 6F

Description The instruction shifts 4-bit digits between memory and the accumulator as shown below. The four low-order bits (D_3–D_0) in the memory location indicated by HL register are shifted left, bits D_7–D_4 are copied into the low-order bits of the accumulator, and bits D_3–D_0 of the accumulator are copied into bits D_3–D_0 of the memory.

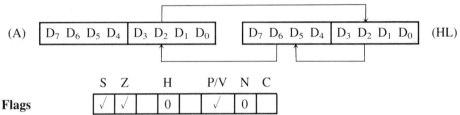

S Z H P/V N C

Flags | √ | √ | | 0 | | √ | 0 | |

Example The accumulator contains 67_H and the memory location 2050_H contains 92_H. If the HL register holds the address 2050_H, show the contents of the memory location and the accumulator after the execution of the instruction RLD.

Mnemonics: RLD   Hex Code: ED   6F

Contents Before Instruction   A | 6 | 7 | | 9 | 2 | 2050

Contents After Instruction   A | 6 | 9 | | 2 | 7 | 2050

RRA: ROTATE ACCUMULATOR RIGHT THROUGH CARRY

Opcode	Operand	Bytes	MC /T-States	Hex Code
RRA		1	1 /4	1F

Description Each bit in the accumulator is rotated right by one position through the Carry flag. Bit D_0 is placed into the CY position, and the CY flag is placed into bit D_7.

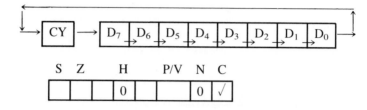

S   Z   H   P/V   N   C

Flags

The CY flag is modified according to bit D_0.

Example   The accumulator contains $A7_H$ and the CY flag is reset. Show the contents of the accumulator and the CY flag after the execution of the instruction RRA.

Mnemonics: RRA   Hex Code: 1F

Accumulator Contents
Before Instruction

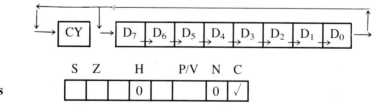

Accumulator Contents
After Instruction

RRCA: ROTATE ACCUMULATOR RIGHT

Opcode	Operand	Bytes	MC /T-States	Hex Code
RRCA		1	1 /4	0F

Description   Each bit in the accumulator is rotated right by one position. Bit D_0 is placed in the position of bit D_7 and the CY flag is also modified according to bit D_0.

S   Z   H   P/V   N   C

Flags

Example   The accumulator contains $A7_H$ and the CY flag is reset. Show the contents of the accumulator and the CY flag after the execution of the instruction RRCA.

Mnemonics: RRCA   Hex Code: 0F

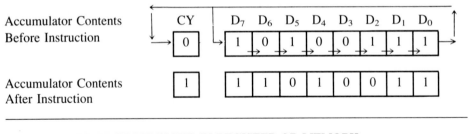

Accumulator Contents Before Instruction

Accumulator Contents After Instruction

RR r: ROTATE EACH BIT RIGHT IN REGISTER OR MEMORY THROUGH CARRY
RR (m):

Opcode	Operand	Bytes	MC /T-States	Hex Codes
				A B C D E H L
RR	r	2	2 /8(4,4)	CB 1F 18 19 1A 1B 1C 1D
RR	(HL)	2	4 /15(4,4,4,3)	CB 1E
RR	(IX + d)	4	6 /23 (4,4,3,5,4,3)	DD CB d 1E
RR	(IY + d)			FD CB d 1E

Description Each bit in the specified register or memory is rotated right by one position through carry. Bit D_0 is placed into the CY flag and the CY flag is placed into bit D_7. The memory address is specified using either HL or an index register.

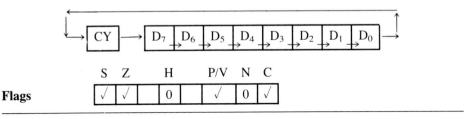

S	Z	H	P/V	N	C
√	√	0	√	0	√

Flags

RRC r: ROTATE EACH BIT RIGHT IN REGISTER OR MEMORY
RRC (m):

Opcode	Operand	Bytes	MC /T-States	Hex Codes
				A B C D E H L
RRC	r	2	2 /8(4,4)	CB 0F 08 09 0A 0B 0C 0D
RRC	(HL)	2	4 /15(4,4,4,3)	CB 0E
RRC	(IX + d)	4	6 /23 (4,4,3,5,4,3)	DD CB d 0E
RRC	(IY + d)			FD CB d 0E

Description   Each bit in the specified register or memory is rotated right by one position. Bit D_0 is placed into the position of bit D_7, and the CY flag is modified according to bit D_0. The memory address is specified using either HL or an index register.

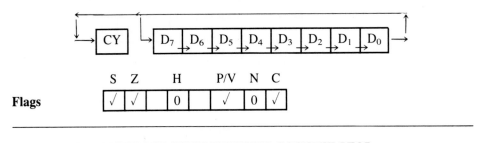

Flags

S	Z		H		P/V	N	C
√	√		0		√	0	√

RRD: ROTATE RIGHT BCD DIGIT BETWEEN ACCUMULATOR AND MEMORY

Opcode	Operand	Bytes	MC /T-States	Hex Code
RRD		2	5 /18(4,4,3,4,3)	ED 67

Description   The instruction shifts 4-bit digits between memory and the accumulator as shown below. The four high-order bits (D_7–D_4) in the memory location indicated by HL are shifted right, bits D_3–D_0 are copied into low-order bits of the accumulator, and bits D_3–D_0 of the accumulator are copied into bits D_7–D_4 of the memory.

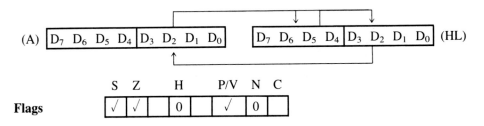

Flags

S	Z		H		P/V	N	C
√	√		0		√	0	

Example   The accumulator contains 67_H and the memory location 2050_H contains 92_H. If the HL register holds the address 2050_H, show the contents of the memory location and the accumulator after the execution of the instruction RRD.

Mnemonics: RRD   Hex Code: ED 67

Contents Before Instruction   A | 6 | 7 | | 9 | 2 | 2050

Contents After Instruction   A | 6 | 2 | | 7 | 9 | 2050

RST: RESTART

Opcode	Operand	Bytes	MC /T-States	Hex Codes
RST	00H to 38H	1	3 /11(5,3,3)	As shown below

Opcode/Operand	Restart Address (Hex)	Hex Code
RST 00H	0000	C7
RST 08H	0008	CF
RST 10H	0010	D7
RST 18H	0018	DF
RST 20H	0020	E7
RST 28H	0028	EF
RST 30H	0030	F7
RST 38H	0038	FF

Description   The RST instructions are 1-byte call instructions to one of eight memory locations on page 0. The instructions are generally used in conjunction with interrupts and inserted using external hardware. These instructions are also used in a program as software instructions to set up breakpoints or to transfer program execution to one of the eight memory locations.

Flags   No flags are affected.

SBC A, r: SUBTRACT REGISTER AND BORROW FROM ACCUMULATOR
SBC A, 8-BIT: SUBTRACT 8-BIT AND BORROW FROM ACCUMULATOR
SBC A, (m):   SUBTRACT MEMORY AND BORROW FROM ACCUMULATOR

Opcode	Operand	Bytes	MC /T-States	Hex Codes
				A B C D E H L
SBC	A, r	1	1 /4	9F 98 99 9A 9B 9C 9D
SBC	A, 8-Bit	2	2 /7(4,3)	DE 8-Bit
SBC	A, (HL)	1	2 /7(4,3)	9E
SBC	A, (IX + d)	3	5 /19(4,4,3,5,3)	DD 9E d
SBC	A, (IY + d)			FD 9E d

Description   The contents of the operand (register, 8-bit data, memory) and the Carry flag CY (as borrow) are subtracted from the contents of the accumulator, and the result is placed in the accumulator.

	S	Z		H		P/V	N	C
Flags	√	√		√		√	1	√

Example The register BC contains 7498_H and the register DE contains $19A1_H$. Subtract (DE) from (BC) and store the result in BC.

Step 1: Copy (C) into A and subtract (E) using SUB instruction. The Z80 performs this subtraction in 2's complement.

$$
\begin{array}{rl}
(B) \rightarrow & (A): \quad 98_H \\
& -(E): \quad A1_H \\
\hline
& (A): \; 1/F7_H
\end{array}
$$

Step 2: Save the result $F7_H$ in register C.

Step 3: Copy (B) into A and subtract (D) using SBC instruction to account for the borrow of the previous result. The Z80 performs this subtraction in 2's complement.

$$
\begin{array}{rl}
(B) \rightarrow & (A): \quad 74_H \\
& (D): \quad 19_H \\
& Borrow: \quad 1 \\
\hline
& \quad 5A_H
\end{array}
$$

Step 4: Save the result ($5A_H$) in B. The SBC instruction resets the previous CY flag.

Comments The instruction is generally used in 16-bit subtraction or multi-byte subtraction; the borrow generated by D_7 is subtracted from bit D_8 in the next subtraction. This instruction should not be used to account for carries (borrows) generated in subtracting 8-bit numbers.

SBC HL, rp: SUBTRACT REGISTER PAIR AND BORROW FROM HL

Opcode	Operand	Bytes	MC /T-States	Hex Codes
				BC DE HL SP
SBC	HL, rp	2	4 /15(4,4,4,3)	ED 42 52 62 72

Description The contents of the operand (BC, DE, HL, or SP) and the Carry flag (as borrow) are subtracted from the contents of the HL register, and the result is stored in the HL register.

	S	Z		H		P/V	N	C
Flags	√	√		?		√	1	√

Example The HL register contains $F850_H$, the DE register contains 8200_H, and the Carry flag CY is set. Subtract the contents of DE from HL with borrow.

Mnemonics: SBC HL, DE   Hex Code: ED 52

Subtraction with Borrow

$$
\begin{array}{ll}
(HL): 1111 \quad 1000 \quad 0101 \quad 0000 & (F850_H) \\
(DE): 1000 \quad 0010 \quad 0000 \quad 0000 & (8200_H) \\
CY : \qquad\qquad\qquad\qquad\qquad\qquad 1 \\
\hline
0/0111 \quad 0110 \quad 0100 \quad 1111 & (764F_H)
\end{array}
$$

Register Contents After Instruction

D	82	00	E
H	76	4F	L

SCF: SET CARRY FLAG

Opcode	Operand	Bytes	MC /T-States	Hex Code
SCF		1	1 /4	37

Description   The Carry flag (C) is set to 1.

Flags

	S	Z		H		P/V	N	C
				0			0	1

SET b, r: SET BIT IN REGISTER OR MEMORY
SET b, (m):

Opcode	Operand	Bytes	MC /T-States	Hex Codes
SET	b, r	2	4 /8(4,4)	*Register*

	Register					
(Bit)	A	B	C	D	E	H	L
CB (0)	C7	C0	C1	C2	C3	C4	C5
(1)	CF	C8	C9	CA	CB	CC	CD
(2)	D7	D0	D1	D2	D3	D4	D5
(3)	DF	D8	D9	DA	DB	DC	DD
(4)	E7	E0	E1	E2	E3	E4	E5
(5)	EF	E8	E9	EA	EF	EC	ED
(6)	F7	F0	F1	F2	F3	F4	F5
(7)	FF	F8	F9	FA	FB	FC	FD

Bit

0	1	2	3	4	5	6	7

Opcode	Operand	Bytes	MC /T-States	Hex Codes
SET	b, (HL)	2	4 /15 (4,4,4,3)	[CB C6 CE D6 DE E6 EE F6 FE]
SET	b, (IX + d)	4	6/23 (4,4,3,5,4,3)	DD CB d [C6 CE D6 DE E6 EE F6 FE]
SET	b, (IY + d)	4		FD CB d [C6 CE D6 DE E6 EE F6 FE]

Description   The specified bit is set in a register or in memory. The values of b (0–7) correspond to bits D_0–D_7.

Flags   No flags are affected.

Example   Write instructions to set bit 6 in register A and bit 0 in memory 2055_H. Assume that HL is already loaded with the address 2055_H.

Mnemonics	Hex Code
SET 6, A	CB F7
SET 0, (HL)	CB C6

SLA r: ARITHMETIC SHIFT LEFT IN REGISTER OR MEMORY
SLA (m):

Opcode	Operand	Bytes	MC /T-States	Hex Codes									
						A	B	C	D	E	H	L	
SLA	r	2	2 /8(4,4)	CB	27	20	21	22	23	24	25		
SLA	(HL)	2	4 /15 (4,4,4,3)	CB	26								
SLA	(IX + d)	4	6 /23 (4,4,3,5,4,3)	DD	CB	d	16						
SLA	(IY + d)			FD	CB	d	16						

Description Each bit in the specified register or memory is arithmetically shifted left by one position. Bit D_7 is placed into the CY flag and 0 is placed into bit D_0. The memory address is specified using either HL or an index register.

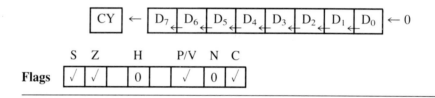

	S	Z		H		P/V	N	C
Flags	√	√		0		√	0	√

SRA r: ARITHMETIC SHIFT RIGHT IN REGISTER OR MEMORY
SRA (m):

Opcode	Operand	Bytes	MC /T-States	Hex Codes									
						A	B	C	D	E	H	L	
SRA	r	2	2 /8(4,4)	CB	2F	28	29	2A	2B	2C	2D		
SRA	(HL)	2	4 /15 (4,4,4,3)	CB	2E								
SRA	(IX + d)	4	6 /23 (4,4,3,5,4,3)	DD	CB	d	2E						
SRA	(IY + d)			FD	CB	d	2E						

Description Each bit in the specified register or memory is arithmetically shifted right by one position. Bit D_0 is placed into the CY flag and bit D_7 remains unchanged. The memory address is specified using either HL or an index register.

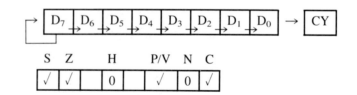

	S	Z		H		P/V	N	C
Flags	√	√		0		√	0	√

SRL r: LOGICAL SHIFT RIGHT IN REGISTER OR MEMORY
SRL (m):

Opcode	Operand	Bytes	MC /T-States	Hex Codes
				A B C D E H L
SRL	r	2	2 /8(4,4)	CB 3F 38 39 3A 3B 3C 3D
SRL	(HL)	2	4 /15(4,4,4,3)	CB 3E
SRL	(IX + d)	4	6 /23 (4,4,3,5,4,3)	DD CB d 3E
SRL	(IY + d)			FD CB d 3E

Description Each bit in the specified register or memory is logically shifted right by one position. Bit D_0 is placed into the CY flag and 0 is placed into bit D_7. The memory address is specified using either HL or an index register.

$$0 \rightarrow \boxed{D_7 \mid D_6 \mid D_5 \mid D_4 \mid D_3 \mid D_2 \mid D_1 \mid D_0} \rightarrow \boxed{CY}$$

	S	Z	H	P/V	N	C
Flags	√	√	0	√	0	√

SUB r: SUBTRACT REGISTER FROM ACCUMULATOR
SUB 8-BIT: SUBTRACT 8-BIT FROM ACCUMULATOR
SUB (m):   SUBTRACT MEMORY FROM ACCUMULATOR

Opcode	Operand	Bytes	MC /T-States	Hex Codes
				A B C D E H L
SUB	r	1	1 /4	97 90 91 92 93 94 95
SUB	8-Bit	2	2 /7(4,3)	D6 8-Bit
SUB	(HL)	1	2 /7(4,3)	96
SUB	(IX + d)	3	5 /19(4,4,3,5,3)	DD 96 d
	(IY + d)			FD 96 d

Description The contents of the operand (register, 8-bit, or memory) are subtracted from the contents of the accumulator, and the result is stored in the accumulator.

	S	Z	H	P/V	N	C
Flags	√	√	√	√	1	√

Example Register B has 47_H and the accumulator has 61_H. Subtract (B) from (A).

Mnemonics: SUB B   Hex Code: 90

Subtraction   Register Contents After Execution

(A)   0 1 1 0 0 0 0 1   (61$_H$)

    +

(B)   1 0 1 1 1 0 0 1   (2's comp.
                                of 47$_H$)

(A) 1 0 0 0 1 1 0 1 0   Complement
   CY   CY

CY   0 0 0 1 1 0 1 0   (1A$_H$)

		S	Z	H		V	N	C	
A	1A	0	0	1		0	1	0	F
B	47				X				C

Example   The accumulator contains the byte 76$_H$, and the HL pair contains 2050$_H$. Subtract the byte A7$_H$ which is stored in memory location 2050$_H$ from the contents of the accumulator.

Mnemonics: SUB (HL)   Hex Code: 96

Subtraction   Register Contents After Execution

(A)   0 1 1 1 0 1 1 0   (76$_H$)

    +

2050 (Mem) 0 1 0 1 1 0 0 1   (2's comp.
                                of A7$_H$)

        1 1 0 0 1 1 1 1   (Complement CY)

   1   1 1 0 0 1 1 1 1   CF

CY

		S	Z	H		V	N	C	
A	CF	1	0	1		1	1	1	
H	20			50					L

XOR r: EXCLUSIVELY OR REGISTER, 8-BIT, OR
              MEMORY WITH ACCUMULATOR
XOR 8-bit:
XOR (m):

Opcode	Operand	Bytes	MC /T-States	Hex Codes						
				A	B	C	D	E	H	L
XOR	r	1	1 /4	AF	A8	A9	AA	AB	AC	AD
XOR	8-Bit	2	2 /7(4,3)	EE 8-bit						
XOR	(HL)	1	2 /7(4,3)	AE						
XOR	(IX + d)	3	5 /19(4,4,3,5,3)	DD AE d						
	(IY + d)			F D AE d						

Description   The contents of register, memory, or an 8-bit are exclusively ORed with the contents of the accumulator. The memory address is specified by the contents of the HL register or an index register with a displacement byte d.

Flags

	S	Z		H		P/V	N	C
	√	√		0		√	0	0

Example The contents of the accumulator and register B are 54_H and 96_H respectively. Exclusively OR (B) with (A) and show the flags and the contents of each register after the operation.

Mnemonics: XOR B   Hex Code: A8

Exclusive OR

(A) 1 0 0 1 0 1 1 0 (96_H)
(B) 0 1 0 1 0 1 0 0 (54_H)
_____
(A) 1 1 0 0 0 0 1 0 ($C2_H$)

Register Contents After Instruction

		S Z H P N C
A	C2	1 0 0 0 0 0
B	54	X C

Example Write mnemonics to exclusive OR the contents of memory location 2070_H with the contents of the accumulator assuming index register IY contains address 2000_H.

Mnemonics: XOR (IY + 70H)   Hex Code: FD   AE   70

Number Systems

Computers communicate and operate in binary digits 0 and 1; on the other hand, human beings generally use the decimal system with ten digits, from 0–9. Other number systems are also used, such as octal with eight digits, from 0–7, and hexadecimal (Hex) system with digits from 0–15. In the hexadecimal system, digits 10 through 15 are designated as A through F, respectively, to avoid confusion with the decimal numbers 10 to 15.

A positional scheme is usually used to represent a number in any of the number systems. This means that each digit will have its value according to its position in a number. The number of digits in a position is also referred to as the base. For example, the binary system has base 2, the decimal system has base 10, and the hexadecimal system has base 16.

B.1 NUMBER CONVERSION

A number in any base system can be represented in a generalized format as follows:

$$N = A_n B^n + A_{n-1} B^{n-1} + \ldots + A_1 B^1 + A_0 B^0$$
$$N = \text{number}, B = \text{base}, A = \text{any digit in that base}$$

For example, number 154 can be represented in various number systems as follows:

Decimal: $154 = 1 \times 10^2 + 5 \times 10^1 + 4 \times 10^0 = 154$

Octal: $232 = 2 \times 8^2 + 3 \times 8^1 + 2 \times 8^0$

$$= \quad 128 \quad + \quad 24 \quad + \quad 2 \quad = 154$$

Hexadecimal: $9A = \qquad 9 \times 16^1 + A \times 16^0$

$$= \qquad 144 + 10 \qquad = 154$$

Binary: $10011010 = 1 \times 2^7 + 0 \times 2^6 + 0 \times 2^5 + 1 \times 2^4 +$
$$1 \times 2^3 + 0 \times 2^2 + 1 \times 2^1 + 0 \times 2^0$$
$$= 128 \qquad + 0 \qquad + 0 \qquad + 16 \qquad + 8$$
$$+ 0 \qquad + 2 \qquad + 0 = 154$$

The above example also shows how to convert a given number in any system into its decimal equivalent.

CONVERSION TABLE: DECIMAL, HEXADECIMAL, BINARY, AND OCTAL

Decimal	Hex	Binary	Octal
0	0	0000	00
1	1	0001	01
2	2	0010	02
3	3	0011	03
4	4	0100	04
5	5	0101	05
6	6	0110	06
7	7	0111	07
8	8	1000	10
9	9	1001	11
10	A	1010	12
11	B	1011	13
12	C	1100	14
13	D	1101	15
14	E	1110	16
15	F	1111	17

HOW TO CONVERT A NUMBER FROM BINARY INTO HEXADECIMAL AND OCTAL

Example

Convert the binary number 1 0 0 1 1 0 1 0 into its Hex and octal equivalents.

Hexadecimal

Step 1: Starting from the right (LSB) arrange the binary digits in groups of four.

    1 0 0 1   1 0 1 0

Step 2: Convert each group into its equivalent Hex number.

    9 A

Octal

Step 1: Starting from the right (LSB) arrange the binary digits in groups of three.

    1 0   0 1 1   0 1 0

Step 2: Convert each group into its equivalent octal number.

    2 3 2

2'S COMPLEMENT AND ARITHMETIC OPERATIONS   B.2

The Z80 microprocessor performs the subtraction of two binary numbers using the 2's complement method. In digital logic circuits, it is easier to design a circuit to add numbers than to design a circuit to subtract numbers. The 2's complement of a binary number is equivalent to its negative number; thus, by adding the complement of the subtrahend (the number to be subtracted) to the minuend, a subtraction can be performed. The method of 2's complement is explained below with examples from the decimal number system.

DECIMAL SUBTRACTION

Subtract the following two decimal numbers using the borrow method and the 10's complement method: $(52 - 23)$

Example B.1

Borrow Method

$$\text{Minuend: } 52 = 5 \times 10 + 2$$
$$\text{Subtrahend: } 23 = 2 \times 10 + 3$$

Step 1: To subtract 3 from 2, 10 must be borrowed from the second place of the minuend.

$$52 = 4 \times 10 + 12$$

Step 2: The subtraction of the digits in the first place and the second place is as follows.

$$
\begin{array}{r}
52 = 4 \times 10 + 12 \\
-23 = \underline{2 \times 10 + 3} \\
2 \times 10 + 9 = 29
\end{array}
$$

**10's
Complement
Method**

Step 1: Find 9's complement of the subtrahend (23), meaning subtract each digit of the subtrahend from 9.

$$9\text{'s complement of 23:} \quad \begin{array}{r} 9\ 9 \\ -2\ 3 \\ \hline 7\ 6 \end{array}$$

Step 2: Add 1 to the 9's complement to find the 10's complement of the subtrahend.

$$10\text{'s complement of 23:} \quad \begin{array}{r} 76 \\ +\ 1 \\ \hline 77 \end{array}$$

The reason for finding the 9's complement is to demonstrate a similar procedure to find the 2's complement of a binary number. However, in reality, the 10's complement of 23 is equivalent to subtracting 23 from 100.

Step 3: Add 10's complement of the subtrahend (77) to the minuend (52) to subtract 23 from 52.

$$\begin{array}{r} 10\text{'s complement of 23:} \quad 77 \\ \text{Minuend:}\ +\ 52 \\ \hline 1\ \ 29 = 29\ \text{(By dropping the most significant digit)} \end{array}$$

The elimination of the most significant bit is equivalent to subtracting 100 from the sum. This is necessary to compensate for the 100 that was added to find the 10's complement of 23.

**Example
B.2**

Perform the subtraction of the following two numbers using the borrow method and the 10's complement method: $23 - 52$.

Borrow Method

$$\begin{array}{l} \text{Minuend: 2}\ \ 3 \\ \text{Subtrahend: 5}\ \ 2 \end{array}$$

Step 1: The subtraction of the digits in the first place results in: $3 - 2 = 1$.

Step 2: To subtract the digits in the second place, a borrow is required from the third place. Assuming the borrow is available from the third place, the digit 5 can be subtracted from 2 as follows:

$$\begin{array}{r} 1\ 2 \\ -\ \ \ 5 \\ \hline \bar{1}\ 7\ \text{(the nonexistent borrow is shown with the bar)} \end{array}$$

$$\begin{array}{r} \text{Result:}\quad 23 \\ -\ 52 \\ \hline \bar{1}\ 71 \end{array}$$

The same result is obtained with the 10's complement method, as shown below.

Step 1: Find the 9's complement of the subtrahend (52).

$$\begin{array}{r} 9\text{'s complement of 52:} \quad 9\ 9 \\ -5\ 2 \\ \hline 4\ 7 \end{array}$$

Step 2: Add 1 to the 9's complement to find 10's complement: $47 + 1 = 48$

Step 3: Add the 10's complement of the subtrahend to the minuend.

$$\begin{array}{r} 10\text{'s complement of 52:} \quad 48 \\ \text{Minuend:} \quad \underline{23} \\ 71 \ (\text{this is negative 29, expressed in 10's complement}) \end{array}$$

By examining these two examples, the following conclusions can be drawn, and these conclusions can be used for any number system.

1. The complement of a number is its equivalent negative number.
2. A number can be subtracted by using its complement.
3. The sum of a number and its complement results in 0 if the most significant digit of the sum is ignored.
4. When the subtrahend is larger than the minuend, the result of the 10's complement method is negative, and it is expressed in terms of 10's complement. The same result can be obtained by borrowing a digit from the most significant position.

PROCEDURE TO FIND 2'S COMPLEMENT OF A BINARY NUMBER

Step 1: Find 1's complement. This amounts to replacing 0 by 1 and 1 by 0.

Step 2: To find 2's complement, add 1 to the 1's complement. This is similar to the procedure of 10's complement.

Find the 2's complement of the binary number:

$$0\ 0\ 0\ 1 \quad 1\ 1\ 0\ 0 \quad (1C_H \text{ or } 28_{10})$$

Step 1: Find 1's complement, meaning replace 0 with 1 and 1 with 0.

$$\begin{array}{rl} \text{1's complement} = & 1\ 1\ 1\ 0 \quad 0\ 0\ 1\ 1 \end{array}$$

Step 2: Add 1

$$\begin{array}{rl} + & \qquad\qquad\qquad\quad 1 \\ \hline \text{2's complement} = & 1\ 1\ 1\ 0 \quad 0\ 1\ 0\ 0 \end{array}$$

By examining the result of the example, the following rule can be stated to find the 2's complement of a binary number, instead of the above procedure of the 1's complement.

Rule 1: Start at the LSB of a given number, and check all the bits to the left. Keep all the bits as they are up to and including the least significant 1.
Rule 2: After the first 1, replace all 0's with 1's and 1's with 0's.

These rules can be applied to the given binary number ($1C_H$) as illustrated below:

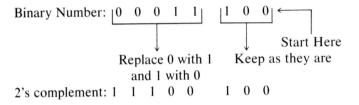

Binary Number: |0   0   0   1   1| |1   0   0| ←

Replace 0 with 1   Keep as they are   Start Here
and 1 with 0

2's complement: 1   1   1   0   0   1   0   0

The 2's complement of the number can be verified by adding the complement to the original number as follows, and the sum should be 0:

Binary Number: 0 0 0 1   1 1 0 0
2's Complement: 1 1 1 0   0 1 0 0
                 1 0 0 0 0   0 0 0 0 (ignore the MSB)

BINARY SUBTRACTION USING 2'S COMPLEMENT
Binary subtraction can be performed by using the 2's complement method, and if the result is negative, it is expressed in terms of 2's complement.

Example B.4

Subtract 32_H (0011 0010) from 45_H (0100 0101).

Subtrahend: 32_H = 0 0 1 1   0 0 1 0

2's complement of 32_H =   1 1 0 0   1 1 1 0
                                                    +
Minuend: 45_H = 0 1 0 0   0 1 0 1
CY: = 1   1   1
1   0 0 0 1   0 0 1 1 = 13_H
CY

The last step is to complement the carry (9th bit). This will indicate that the result is $+13_H$.

Example B.5

Subtract 45_H (0100 0100) from 32_H (0011 0010).

Subtrahend: 45_H = 0 1 0 0   0 1 0 1
2's complement of 45_H = 1 0 1 1   1 0 1 1

$$\overset{+}{\text{Minuend: } 32_H} = 0\ 0\ 1\ 1\quad 0\ 0\ 1\ 0$$
$$CY = \underline{1\ 1\quad1}$$
$$1\ 1\ 1\ 0\quad 1\ 1\ 0\ 1 = ED_H$$

The result is negative and it is expressed in 2's complement. This can be verified by taking the 2's complement of the result; the 2's complement of the result should be 13_H as in Example 4. In this subtraction, the 9th bit is zero. The processor sets the 9th bit indicating a borrow; thus, it is a negative result.

$$\text{Result } ED_H = 1\ 1\ 1\ 0\quad 1\ 1\ 0\ 1$$
$$\text{2's complement of } ED_H = 0\ 0\ 0\ 1\quad 0\ 0\ 1\ 1 = 13_H$$

SIGNED NUMBERS

To perform the arithmetic operations with signed numbers (positive and negative), the sign must be indicated as well as the magnitude of the number. In 8-bit microprocessors, bit D_7 is used to indicate the sign of a number; 0 in D_7 indicates a positive number and 1 indicates a negative number. Bit D_7 can be used to indicate the sign of a number because:

1. The Z80 performs the subtraction of two numbers using 2's complement and, if the result is negative, it saves (shows) the result in the form of 2's complement.
2. 2's complements of all the 7-bit numbers have 1 in D_7.

When a programmer uses bit D_7 to indicate the sign of a number, the magnitude of the number can be represented by seven bits (D_6–D_0). For example, number 74_H is represented with sign as follows:

	D_7	D_6	D_5	D_4	D_3	D_2	D_1	D_0	
$+74_H =$	0	1	1	1	0	1	0	0	
$-74_H =$	1	0	0	0	1	1	0	0	(2's complement of 74_H)
	sign				magnitude				

However, the microprocessor cannot differentiate between a positive number and a negative number. For example, in the above illustration, -74_H can be interpreted as the unsigned positive number $8C_H$ or the bit pattern. It is the responsibility of the programmer to provide the necessary interpretation.

SUBTRACTION PROCESS IN THE Z80 MICROPROCESSOR

The Z80 performs the following operations when it subtracts (SUB) two binary numbers:

Step 1: Finds 1's complement of the subtrahend.

Step 2: Finds 2's complement of the subtrahend by adding 1 to the result of Step 1.

Step 3: Adds the 2's complement of the subtrahend to the minuend.

Step 4: Complements the CY flag.

    These steps are internal to the microprocessor and invisible to the user; only the result is available to the user.

Example B.6

Show the internal steps performed by the microprocessor to subtract the following unsigned numbers:

a. $FA_H - 62_H$

b. $62_H - FA_H$

a. Minuend: $FA_H = 1\ 1\ 1\ 1$ $1\ 0\ 1\ 0$

   Subtrahend: $62_H\ = 0\ 1\ 1\ 0$ $0\ 0\ 1\ 0$

Step 1: 1's complement of $62_H =$ $1\ 0\ 0\ 1$ $1\ 1\ 0\ 1$

Step 2: Add 1 $+$ 1

        2's complement of $62_H =$ $1\ 0\ 0\ 1$ $1\ 1\ 1\ 0$

Step 3: Add minuend (FA_H) $+1\ 1\ 1\ 1$ $1\ 0\ 1\ 0$

                           1 $1\ 0\ 0\ 1$ $1\ 0\ 0\ 0$

Step 4: Complement CY 0 $1\ 0\ 0\ 1$ $1\ 0\ 0\ 0$

        Result: 0 $1\ 0\ 0\ 1$ $1\ 0\ 0\ 0$ $= 98_H$

        Flags: $CY = 0, S = 1, Z = 0, V = 0$

b. Minuend: $62_H\ = 0\ 1\ 1\ 0$ $0\ 0\ 1\ 0$

   Subtrahend: $FA_H = 1\ 1\ 1\ 1$ $1\ 0\ 1\ 0$

Step 1: 1's complement of $FA_H =$ $0\ 0\ 0\ 0$ $0\ 1\ 0\ 1$

Step 2: Add 1 $+$ 1

        2's complement of $FA_H =$ $0\ 0\ 0\ 0$ $0\ 1\ 1\ 0$

Step 3: Add minuend (62_H) $+0\ 1\ 1\ 0$ $0\ 0\ 1\ 0$

                           0 $0\ 1\ 1\ 0$ $1\ 0\ 0\ 0$

Step 4: Complement CY 1 $0\ 1\ 1\ 0$ $1\ 0\ 0\ 0$

        Result: 1 $0\ 1\ 1\ 0$ $1\ 0\ 0\ 0$ $= 68_H\ (CY = 1)$

        Flags: $CY = 1, S = 0, Z = 0, V = 0$

This result is negative and expressed in 2's complement of the magnitude.

Results

a. $FA_H - 62_H = 98_H$ (positive), $CY = 0, S = 1$

b. $62_H - FA_H = 68_H$ (negative), $CY = 1, S = 0$

These results and associated flags appear to be confusing. In Example B.6a, the result is positive but the sign flag indicates that it is negative. On the other hand, in Example B.6b, the result is negative but the sign flag indicates that it is positive. This confusion can be explained as follows:

1. This subtraction is concerned with the unsigned numbers; therefore, the sign flag is irrelevant. In signed arithmetic, the number FA_H is invalid because it is an 8-bit number.
2. The programmer can check whether the result indicates the true magnitude by checking the CY flag. If CY is reset, the result is positive, and if CY is set, the result is expressed in 2's complement.

In Example B.6a, assume that the numbers are signed numbers, and interpret the result.

Minuend: FA_H

This is a negative number because $D_7 = 1$; therefore, this must be represented in 2's complement. The magnitude of the number can be found by taking the 2's complement of FA_H:

$$FA_H = 1\ 1\ 1\ 1\quad 1\ 0\ 1\ 0$$
$$\text{2's complement of } FA_H = 0\ 0\ 0\ 0\quad 0\ 1\ 1\ 0$$
$$= 06_H \text{ (magnitude)}$$

Subtrahend: 62_H (This is a positive number because $D_7 = 0$.)

The problem given in 6a can be represented as follows:

$$FA_H - 62_H = (-06_H) - (+62_H)$$
$$= -68_H$$

The final result is -68_H, which will be in the form of its 2's complement:

$$-68_H = -(0\ 1\ 1\ 0\quad 1\ 0\ 0\ 0)$$
$$\text{2's complement of } 68_H = 1\ 0\ 0\ 1\quad 1\ 0\ 0\ 0$$
$$= 98_H$$

The final answer is the same as before; however, it will be interpreted as a negative number with the magnitude of 68_H. When signed numbers are used in arithmetic operations, the sign flag will indicate the proper sign of the result.

Add the following two positive numbers and interpret the sign flag: $+41_H$, $+54_H$.

$$41_H = 0\ 1\ 0\ 0\quad 0\ 0\ 0\ 1$$
$$+$$
$$\underline{54_H = 0\ 1\ 0\ 1\quad 0\ 1\ 0\ 0}$$
$$95_H = 1\ 0\ 0\ 1\quad 0\ 1\ 0\ 1 \quad S = 1, CY = 0, Z = 0, V = 1$$

This is an addition of two positive numbers. The sign flag indicates that the sum is negative. However, the overflow (P/V = 1) flag indicates that there is an overflow; therefore, the sum is inaccurate if these are signed numbers. If this had been the sum of two unsigned numbers, the sign flag would have no significance.

B.3 MODULO-2 ARITHMETIC

Modulo-2 arithmetic is binary addition (or subtraction) without carries. There are no negative numbers, and the result can be either 0 or 1. An addition or subtraction of two numbers in Modulo-2 is similar to exclusive-ORing two logic functions as shown, and the results are the same.

$$
\begin{array}{r}
1\ 0\ 1\ 0 \\
+\ 1\ 1\ 1\ 0 \\
\hline
0\ 1\ 0\ 0
\end{array}
\qquad
\begin{array}{r}
1\ 0\ 1\ 0 \\
-\ 1\ 1\ 1\ 0 \\
\hline
0\ 1\ 0\ 0
\end{array}
$$

Similarly, a division of two polynomials can be performed as follows. The example is from the Cyclic Redundancy Check (CRC—Section 15.1.3).
The modified polynomial for data bits 1000 1010: $x^{10} + x^8 + x^4$
The generator polynomial: $x^4 + 1$

$$
\begin{array}{r}
x^6 + x^4 + x^2 \\
\hline
x^4 + 1 \,\big)\ x^{10} + x^8 + x^4 \\
\end{array}
$$

$$x^{10} \qquad\quad + x^6 \quad \rightarrow \text{ By multiplying } (x^4 + 1)(x^6)$$

$$x^8 + x^6 + x^4 \quad \rightarrow \text{ In Modulo-2, subtraction is the same as addition}$$

$$x^8 \qquad\quad + x^4 \quad \rightarrow \text{ By multiplying } (x^4 + 1)(x^4)$$

$$x^6$$

$$x^6 + x^2 \quad \rightarrow \text{ By multiplying } (x^4 + 1)(x^2)$$

$$x^2 \quad \rightarrow \text{ Remainder}$$

American Standard Code for Information Interchange: ASCII Codes

Graphic or Control		ASCII (Hexadecimal)
NUL	Null	00
SOH	Start of Heading	01
STX	Start of Text	02
ETX	End of Text	03
EOT	End of Transmission	04
ENQ	Enquiry	05
ACK	Acknowledge	06
BEL	Bell	07
BS	Backspace	08
HT	Horizontal Tabulation	09
LF	Line Feed	0A
VT	Vertical Tabulation	0B
FF	Form Feed	0C
CR	Carriage Return	0D
SO	Shift Out	0E
SI	Shift In	0F
DLE	Data Link Escape	10
DC1	Device Control 1	11
DC2	Device Control 2	12
DC3	Device Control 3	13
DC4	Device Control 4	14
NAK	Negative Acknowledge	15
SYN	Synchronous Idle	16
ETB	End of Transmission Block	17
CAN	Cancel	18
EM	End of Medium	19
SUB	Substitute	1A
ESC	Escape	1B

Graphic or Control		ASCII (Hexadecimal)
FS	File Separator	1C
GS	Group Separator	1D
RS	Record Separator	1E
US	Unit Separator	1F
SP	Space	20
!		21
"		22
#		23
$		24
%		25

Graphic or Control	ASCII (Hexadecimal)	Graphic or Control	ASCII (Hexadecimal)
&	26	S	53
'	27	T	54
(	28	U	55
)	29	V	56
*	2A	W	57
+	2B	X	58
,	2C	Y	59
—	2D	Z	5A
.	2E	[	5B
/	2F	\	5C
0	30	]	5D
1	31	∧	5E
2	32	—	5F
3	33	`	60
4	34	a	61
5	35	b	62
6	36	c	63
7	37	d	64
8	38	e	65
9	39	f	66
:	3A	g	67
;	3B	h	68
<	3C	i	69
=	3D	j	6A
>	3E	k	6B
?	3F	l	6C
@	40	m	6D
A	41	n	6E
B	42	o	6F
C	43	p	70
D	44	q	71
E	45	r	72
F	46	s	73
G	47	t	74
H	48	u	75
I	49	v	76
J	4A	w	77
K	4B	x	78
L	4C	y	79
M	4D	z	7A
N	4E	{	7B
O	4F	|	7C
P	50	}	7D
Q	51	~	7E
R	52	DEL Delete	7F

Logic Symbols and Pin Configuration of Selected Logic and Display Devices

THE OR GATE AS THE NEGATIVE NAND GATE

The OR gate is normally represented as shown in Figure D.1(a). The truth table in Figure D.1(c) shows that when any one of the inputs is high, the output is high; when both inputs are low, the output is low. In applications where the output required is active high, the symbol in Figure D.1(a) accurately represents the signal states. However, in some applications, the output required is *active low* when

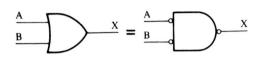

Inputs		Output
A	B	X
High	High	High
High	Low	High
Low	High	High
Low	Low	Low

(a) OR Gate   (b) Negative NAND Gate   (c) Truth Table for Two-Input OR Gate

FIGURE D.1
OR Gate Logic Symbols and Truth Table

both inputs are low. For example, in Figure 3.9(a), the control signal $\overline{\text{MEMWR}}$ is generated when both inputs $\overline{\text{MREQ}}$ and $\overline{\text{WR}}$ are low. Therefore, it is preferable to represent the active states by the Negative NAND gate as shown in Figure D.1(b). Physically, the gate in Figure D.1(a) is the same as the gate in D.1(b); both are OR gates. However, they will be interpreted differently. In Figure D.1(a), the gate function should be read as follows: when input A *or* input B is high, the output goes high. In Figure D.1(b), the gate function should be read as follows: when input A *and* input B are low, the output goes low.

THE AND GATE AS THE NEGATIVE NOR GATE

The AND gate shown in Figure D.2(a) should be read as follows: when input A *and* input B are high, the output goes high. However, the equivalent gate shown in Figure D.2(b) should be read as follows: when input A *or* input B is low, the output goes low.

THE NOR GATE AS THE NEGATIVE AND GATE

The NOR gate in Figure D.2(c) should read as follows: when input A *or* input B is high, the output goes low. However, its equivalent gate shown in Figure D.2(d) should be read as follows: when input A *and* input B are low, the output goes high. Figure 5.4 shows the NOR gate (74LS02) connected as the Negative AND

FIGURE D.2
Logic Gates and Their Equivalent Symbols

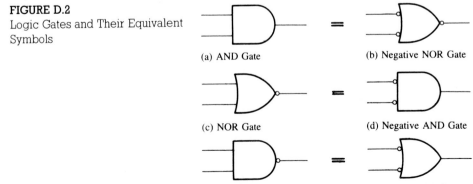

(a) AND Gate   (b) Negative NOR Gate

(c) NOR Gate   (d) Negative AND Gate

(e) NAND Gate   (f) Negative OR Gate

gate. It suggests that when the signal I/O write ($\overline{\text{IOWR}}$) and the decoded address pulse are low, the output goes high and enables the flip-flop.

THE NAND GATE AS THE NEGATIVE OR GATE

Figure D.2(e) shows the normal representation of the NAND gate and Figure D.2(f) shows its equivalent as the Negative OR gate.

INVERTERS AND BUBBLE MATCHING

When the inverter is represented by its symbol, the bubble can be shown either in the front or in the back depending upon the active level of the input signal. For example, in Figure 2.10 the inverters to the 8-input NAND gate are shown with bubbles at the back. The bubble suggests that address lines A_{15}–A_8 should be at logic 0 to cause the output of the gate to go active low.

SUMMARY

A logic gate can be represented with different symbols. However, the symbol should be selected based on the active level of the signals. If the active level of the signals is represented, it is easy to interpret the gate function and it facilitates troubleshooting.

D.2   SELECTED LOGIC AND DISPLAY DEVICES: PIN CONFIGURATION AND LOGIC SYMBOLS

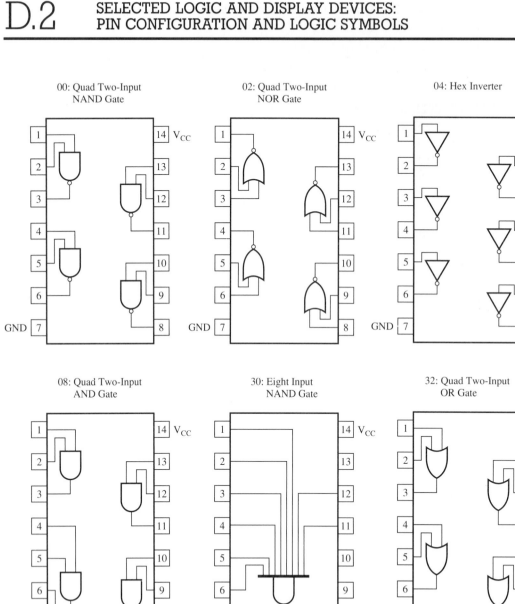

00: Quad Two-Input
NAND Gate

02: Quad Two-Input
NOR Gate

04: Hex Inverter

08: Quad Two-Input
AND Gate

30: Eight Input
NAND Gate

32: Quad Two-Input
OR Gate

74: DUAL D-TYPE POSITIVE EDGE-TRIGGERED FLIP-FLOP

Description   This is a positive edge-triggered flip-flop with Set and Reset inputs and complementary outputs (Q and $\overline{Q}$).

Information at D input is transferred to Q output on the positive edge (Low-to-High) of the clock pulse (CP). Set (S) and Reset (R) are asynchronous active low inputs and operate independently of the clock; S input sets Q to logic 1 and R resets Q to logic 0.

Pin Configuration   Logic Symbol

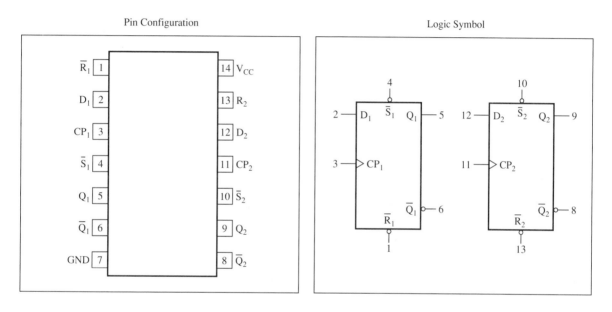

75: 4-BIT BISTABLE LATCH

Description   '75 is a level sensitive 4-bit latch; each pair of bits is controlled by High Enable input E. It also has complementary outputs (Q and $\overline{Q}$).

Information at D input is transferred to Q output when E is High, and Q follows D input as long as E is High. When E goes Low, D input is latched at the output and remains latched until E goes High again.

Pin Configuration   Logic Symbol

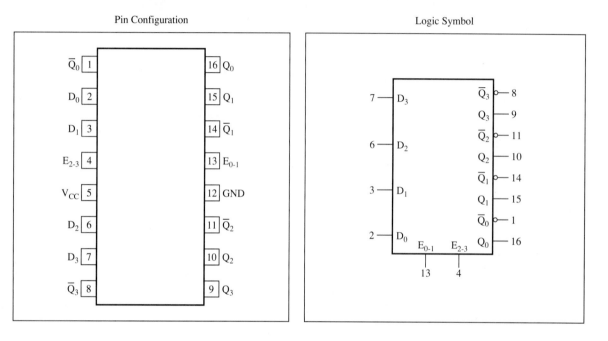

76: DUAL JK FLIP-FLOP

Description '76 is a dual JK flip-flop with J, K, Clock, Set, and Reset inputs for each flip-flop. JK information is loaded into the master when the Clock is high and transferred to the slave on the High-to-Low Clock transition.

'LS76 is a negative edge-triggered flip-flop.

Pin Configuration · Logic Symbol

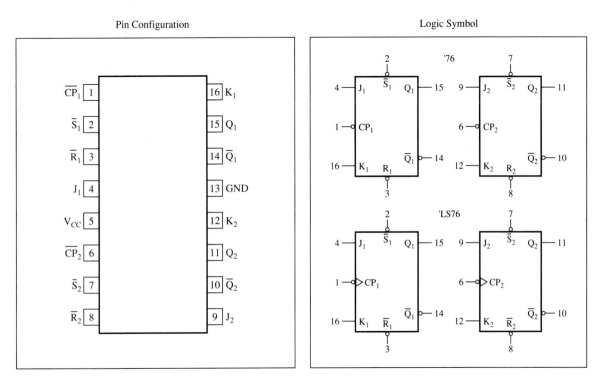

138: 3-TO-8 DECODER/DEMULTIPLEXER*

Description   '138 has three binary weighted inputs (C, B, A or A_2, A_1, A_0) and eight mutually exclusive active Low outputs. It has three enable inputs, two active Low, and one active High; all three must be enabled to obtain an output.

When '138 is enabled, one of the output signals goes active Low corresponding to the decimal equivalent of the input. When it is not enabled, all output signals remain High.

Pin Configuration   Logic Symbol

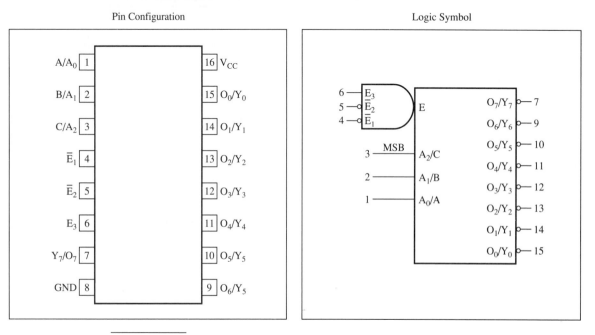

*Note: Pin configuration shows notations commonly used by various manufacturers.

139: 2-TO-4 DECODER/DEMULTIPLEXER

Description   '139 is a dual 2-to-4 decoder with two binary weighted inputs (B, A or A_1, A_0) and one active Low enable input. When it is enabled, one of four output signals, corresponding to the decimal equivalent of the input, goes active Low. When it is not enabled, all output signals remain High.

Pin Configuration   Logic Symbol

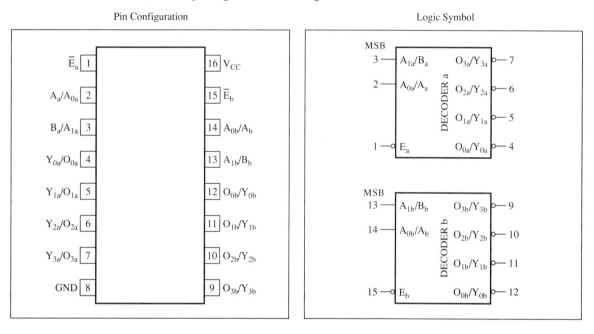

148: 8-INPUT PRIORITY ENCODER

Description   '148 has eight active Low inputs ($\bar{I}_7$ to $\bar{I}_0$), one enable input, and three active Low outputs. When it is enabled, the output provides the binary equivalent of the active input. If multiple inputs go active simultaneously, the input with the highest priority is encoded on the output; other inputs are ignored. $\bar{I}_7$ has the highest priority, and $\bar{I}_0$ has the lowest priority.

Pin Configuration   Logic Symbol

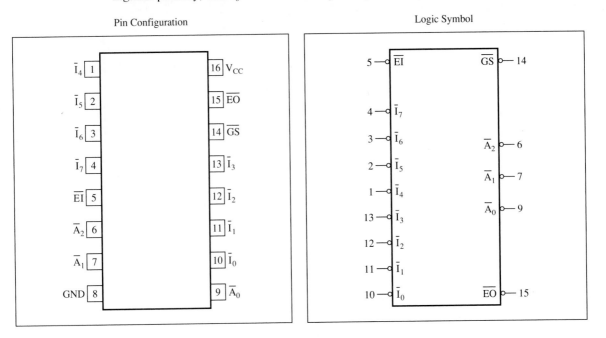

244: OCTAL BUFFER

Pin Configuration   Logic Symbol

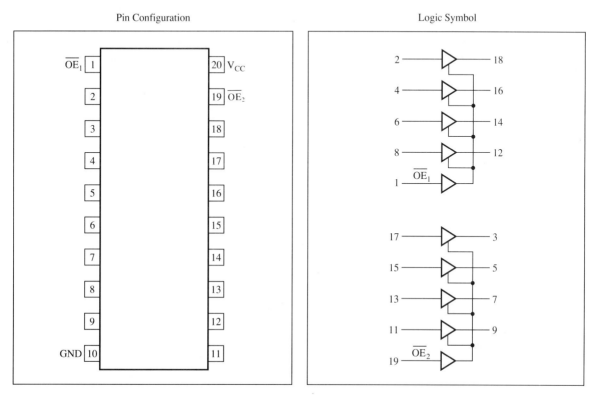

245: OCTAL TRANSCEIVER (BIDIRECTIONAL BUFFER)

Description   '245 is a bidirectional buffer with $\overline{E}$ (Enable) and DIR as two control inputs. $\overline{E}$ is active Low, and it enables the buffer. DIR determines the direction of the data flow; if it is High, data flow from A to B and if it is low, data flow from B to A.

Pin Configuration   Logic Symbol

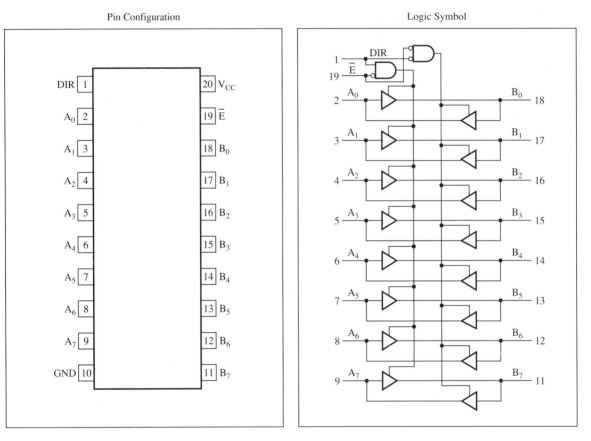

373: OCTAL TRANSPARENT LATCH

Description   '373 is an octal transparent latch followed by tri-state output buffers. The data from D inputs are transferred to Q outputs when the latch enable (LE) signal is High and are latched when LE goes from High to Low. When $\overline{OE}$ goes Low, latched data appear on the outputs; otherwise, the outputs remain in high impedance.

Pin Configuration   Logic Symbol

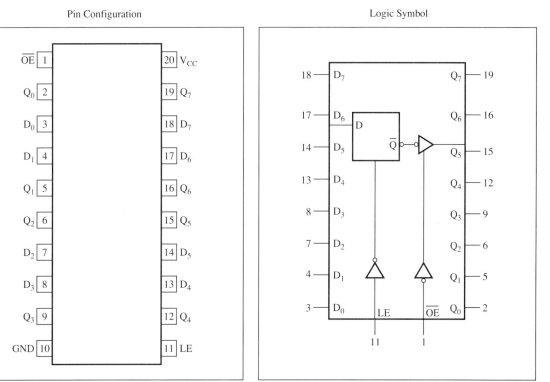

SEVEN-SEGMENT NUMERIC DISPLAY: (10-PIN PACKAGE)

Pin Configuration
(Front View)   Common Anode   Common Cathode

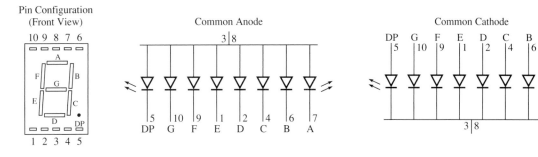

Data Converters

The microprocessor is a logic device; it processes digital signals that are binary and discontinuous. On the other hand, the real-world physical quantities such as temperature and pressure are continuous. These are represented by equivalent electrical quantities called analog signals. Even though an analog signal may represent a real physical parameter with accuracy, it is difficult to process or store the analog signal for later use without introducing considerable error. Therefore, in microprocessor-based industrial products, it is necessary to translate an analog signal into a digital signal. The electronic circuit that translates an analog signal into a digital signal is called an analog-to-digital (A/D) converter (ADC). Similarly, a digital signal needs to be translated into an analog signal to represent a physical quantity (e.g., to regulate a machine). This translator is called a digital-to-analog (D/A) converter (DAC). Both A/D and D/A are also known as data converters and are now available as integrated circuits.

E.1 DIGITAL-TO-ANALOG (D/A) CONVERTERS

Digital-to-Analog converters can be broadly classified in two categories: **current output** and **voltage output.** The current output DAC, as the name suggests, provides current as the output signal. The voltage output DAC internally converts the current signal into the voltage signal. The voltage output DAC is slower than the current output DAC because of the delay in converting the current signal into the voltage signal. However, in many applications, it is necessary to convert current into voltage by using an external operational amplifier.

D/A converters are available as **integrated circuits.** Some are specially designed to be compatible with the microprocessor. Typical applications include digital voltmeters, peak detectors, panel meters, programmable gain and attenuation, and stepping motor drive.

E.1.1 Basic Concepts

Figure E.1(a) shows a block diagram of a 3-bit D/A converter; it has three digital input lines (D_2, D_1, and D_0) and one output line for the analog signal. The three input lines can assume eight ($2^3 = 8$) input combinations from 000 to 111, D_2 being the most significant bit (MSB) and D_0 being the least significant bit (LSB). If the

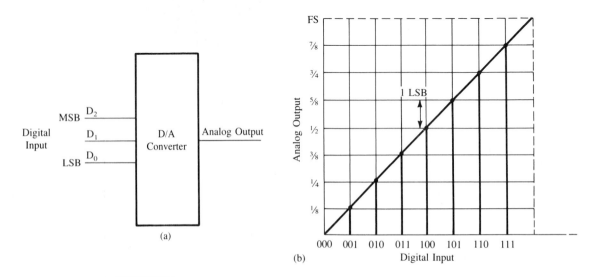

FIGURE E.1

A 3-Bit D/A Converter: (a) Block Diagram and (b) Digital Input versus Analog Output

input ranges from 0 to 1 V, it can be divided into eight equal parts ($\frac{1}{8}$ V); each successive input is $\frac{1}{8}$ V higher than the previous combination, as shown in Figure E.1(b).

The following points can be summarized from the graph:

1. The 3-bit D/A converter has eight possible combinations. If a converter has n input lines, it can have 2^n input combinations.
2. If the full-scale analog voltage is 1 V, the smallest unit or the LSB (001_2) is equivalent to $\frac{1}{2^n}$ of 1 V. This is defined as resolution. In this example, the LSB = $\frac{1}{8}$ V.
3. The MSB represents half of the full-scale value. In this example, the MSB (100_2) = $\frac{1}{2}$ V.
4. For the maximum input signal (111_2), the output signal is equal to the value of the full-scale input signal minus the value of the 1 LSB input signal. In this example, the maximum input signal (111_2) represents $\frac{7}{8}$ V.

Calculate the values of the LSB, MSB, and full-scale output for an 8-bit DAC for the 0 to 10 V range.

Example E.1

1. LSB = $\frac{1}{2^8}$ = $\frac{1}{256}$
   For 10 V, LSB = 10 V/256 = 39 mV
2. MSB = $\frac{1}{2}$ full scale = 5 V
3. Full-Scale Output = (Full-Scale Value − 1 LSB)
   $$= 10\ V - 0.039\ V$$
   $$= 9.961\ V$$

Solution

E.1.2 D/A Converter Circuits

Input signals representing appropriate binary values can be simulated by an operational amplifier with a summing network, as shown in Figure E.2.

The input resistors R_1, R_2, and R_3 are selected in binary weighted proportion; each has double the value of the previous resistor. If all three inputs are 1 V, the total output current is

FIGURE E.2
Summing Amplifier with Binary Weighted Input Resistors

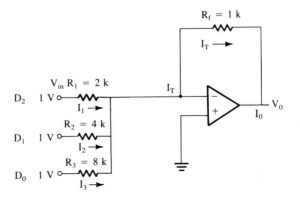

$$I_O = I_T = I_1 + I_2 + I_3$$

$$= \frac{V_{in}}{R_1} + \frac{V_{in}}{R_2} + \frac{V_{in}}{R_3} = \frac{V_{in}}{1\text{ k}}\left(\frac{1}{2} + \frac{1}{4} + \frac{1}{8}\right)$$

$$= \frac{V_{in}}{1\text{ k}}\left(\frac{7}{8}\right) = \frac{V_{in}}{1\text{ k}}\frac{(\text{Digital Input})_{10}}{2^n}$$

where Digital Input is expressed in decimal equivalent and n is the number of digital inputs.

The voltage output is

$$V_O = -R_f I_T$$
$$= -(1\text{ k})(0.875\text{ mA})$$
$$= -0.875\text{ V}$$
$$= |\tfrac{7}{8}\text{ V}|$$

This example shows that for the input $= 111_2$, the output is equal to either $\tfrac{7}{8}$ mA or $\tfrac{7}{8}$ V, representing the D/A conversion process.

Now we can redraw Figure E.2 as shown in Figure E.3(a), where input voltage V_{in} is replaced by V_{Ref}, which can be turned on or off by the switches. The output current I_O can be generalized for any number of bits as

$$I_O = \frac{V_{Ref}}{R}\left(\frac{A_1}{2} + \frac{A_2}{4} + \ldots + \frac{A_n}{2^n}\right)$$

$$= \frac{V_{Ref}}{R}\frac{(\text{Digital Input})_{10}}{2^n}$$

where A_1 to A_n can be zero or one.

Figure E.3(b) illustrates the transitorized switch for input D_0; when bit D_0 is

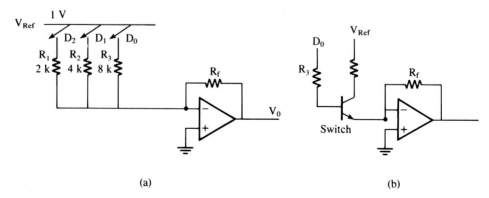

(a)   (b)

FIGURE E.3
(a) Simulated D/A Converter and (b) Transistor Switch to Turn On/Off Bit D_0

high, it will drive the transistor into saturation, and the current is determined by the resistor R_3 with appropriate binary weighting. When bit D_0 is low, the transistor is turned off. The switching speed of the transistor, shown in Figure E.3(b), determines the settling time of a D/A converter, which is defined as the time necessary for the output to stabilize within $\pm \frac{1}{2}$ LSB of its final value. The accuracy of the output depends on the tolerance of resistor values, and it is generally specified in terms of relative accuracy (also known as linearity)—the difference between the actual output and the expected fraction for a given digital input. The accuracy of the converter is also specified in terms of monotonicity, which guarantees that analog output increases in magnitude with increasing digital code. Most commercial D/A converters are specified as monotonic; this limits the output error within $\pm \frac{1}{2}$ LSB at each digital input.

The following points can be inferred from the above example:

1. A D/A converter circuit requires three elements: resistor network with appropriate weighting, switches, and a reference source.
2. The output can be a current signal or converted into a voltage signal using an operational amplifier.
3. The time required for conversion, called settling time, depends on the response time of the switches and the output amplifier (for a voltage output DAC).

R/2R LADDER NETWORK

One major drawback of designing a DAC as shown in Figure E.3 is the requirement for various precision resistors. The R/2R ladder network shown in Figure E.4 uses only two resistor values. The resistors are connected in such a way that for any number of inputs, the total current I_T is in binary proportion. The R/2R ladder network (or a similar network called an inverted ladder) is used commonly in designing integrated D/A converters.

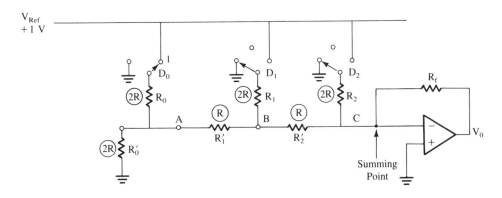

◯ = Values of resistors

FIGURE E.4
R/2R Ladder Network

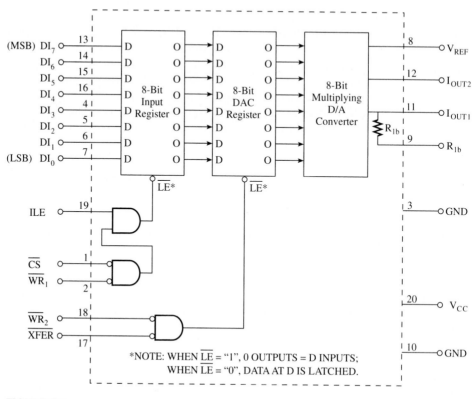

FIGURE E.5
DAC0830 Functional Diagram

MICROPROCESSOR-COMPATIBLE D/A CONVERTERS

To interface a data converter with the microprocessor, an external latch is necessary to build an I/O port. However, in response to the growing need for interfacing data converters with the microprocessor, specially designed microprocessor-compatible D/A converters are now available. These data converters include a latch and control signals such as Chip Select ($\overline{\text{CS}}$) and Write ($\overline{\text{WR}}$) on the converter chip, thus eliminating the need for an I/O port. Figure E.5 shows the functional diagram of the National Semiconductor DAC0830 8-bit microprocessor-compatible D/A converter.

This converter has two internal 8-bit registers; this allows it to output a voltage corresponding to one digital word while holding the next digital word. It has also two output current signals I_{OUT1} and I_{OUT2}. The current I_{OUT1} is directly proportional to the digital input, and the current I_{OUT2} is proportional to the complement of the digital input. For simple applications, where two registers and I_{OUT2} are unnecessary, the interfacing can be done by using $\overline{\text{CS}}$ and $\overline{\text{WR}}_1$ and by connecting $\overline{\text{XFER}}$, $\overline{\text{WR}}_2$, and I_{OUT2} to ground and ILE to +5 V.

ANALOG-TO-DIGITAL (A/D) CONVERTERS E.2

The A/D conversion is a quantizing process whereby an analog signal is represented by equivalent binary states. Analog-to-Digital converters can be classified into two general groups based on the conversion technique. One technique involves comparing a given analog signal with the internally generated equivalent signal. This group includes successive-approximation, counter, and flash-type converters. The second technique involves changing an analog signal into time or frequency and comparing these new parameters to known values. This group includes integrator converters and voltage-to-frequency converters. The trade-off between the two techniques is based on accuracy versus speed. The successive-approximation and the flash type are faster but generally less accurate than the integrator and the voltage-to-frequency type converters.

The basic concepts of the most commonly used A/D converters—the successive-approximation and the integrator—are discussed in this section. The successive-approximation A/D converters are used in applications such as data loggers and instrumentation, where conversion speed is important. On the other hand, integrating-type converters are used in applications such as digital meters, panel meters, and monitoring systems, where the conversion accuracy is critical.

E.2.1 Basic Concepts

Figure E.6(a) shows a block diagram of a 3-bit A/D converter. It has one input line for an analog signal and three output lines for digital signals. Figure E.6(b) shows the graph of the analog input voltage (0 to 1 V) and the corresponding digital output signal. It shows eight (2^3) discrete output states from 000_2 to 111_2, each step being $\frac{1}{8}$ V apart. This is defined as the resolution of the converter. The LSB, the MSB, and the full-scale output are calculated the same way as in D/A converters.

In A/D conversion, another critical parameter is **conversion time.** This is defined as the total time required to convert an analog signal into its digital output and is determined by the conversion technique used and by the propagation delay in various circuits.

E.2.2 Successive-Approximation A/D Converter

Figure E.7(a) shows the block diagram of a successive approximation A/D converter. It includes three major elements: the D/A converter, the successive approximation register (SAR), and the comparator. The conversion technique involves comparing the output of the D/A converter V_O with the analog input signal V_{in}. The digital input to the DAC is generated using the successive-approximation method (explained below). When the DAC output matches the analog signal, the input to the DAC is the equivalent digital signal.

The successive-approximation method of generating input to the DAC is similar to weighing an unknown material (e.g., less than 1 gram) on a chemical balance with a set of such fractional weights as $\frac{1}{2}$ g, $\frac{1}{4}$ g, $\frac{1}{8}$ g, etc. The weighing

FIGURE E.6

A 3-Bit A/D Converter: (a) Block
Diagram and (b) Analog Input
versus Digital Output

SOURCE: Analog Devices, Inc., *Integrated Circuit Converters, Data Acquisition Systems, and Analog Signal Conditioning Components* (Norwood, Mass.: Author, 1979), p. I-18.

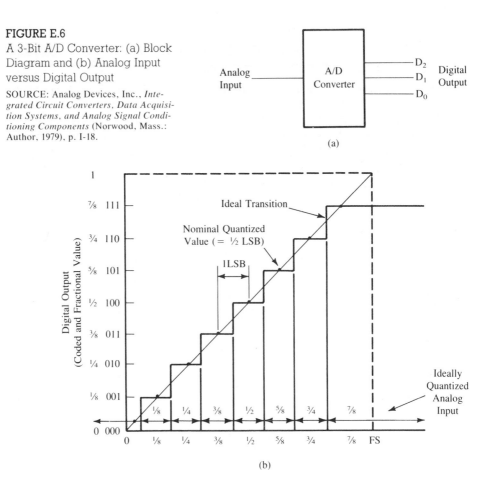

(a)

(b)

procedure begins with the heaviest weight (½ g), and subsequent weights (in decreasing order) are added until the balance is tipped. The weight that tips the balance is removed, and the process is continued until the smallest weight is used. In the case of a 4-bit A/D converter, bit D_3 is turned on first and the output of the DAC is compared with an analog signal. If the comparator changes the state, indicating that the output generated by D_3 is larger than the analog signal, bit D_3 is turned off in the SAR and bit D_2 is turned on. The process continues until the input reaches bit D_0. Figure E.7(b) illustrates a 4-bit conversion process. When bit D_3 is turned on, the output exceeds the analog signal and, therefore, bit D_3 is turned off. When the next three successive bits are turned on, the output becomes approximately equal to the analog signal.

INTERFACING 8-BIT A/D CONVERTERS

As an integrated circuit, the A/D converter includes all three elements—SAR, DAC, and comparator—on a chip (Figure E.8). In addition, it has a tri-state output buffer. Typically, it has two control lines, START (or CONVERT) and DATA

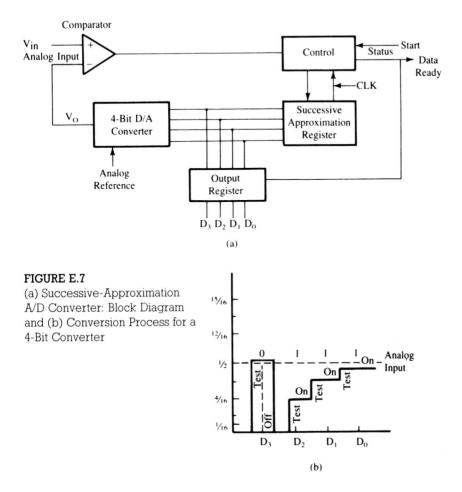

FIGURE E.7
(a) Successive-Approximation
A/D Converter: Block Diagram
and (b) Conversion Process for a
4-Bit Converter

READY (or BUSY); they are TTL-compatible and can be active low or high depending upon the design.

A pulse to the START pin begins the conversion process and disables the tri-state output buffer. At the end of the conversion period, DATA READY becomes active and the digital output is made available at the output buffer. To interface an A/D converter with the microprocessor, the microprocessor should

1. Send a pulse to the START pin. This can be derived from a control signal such as Write ($\overline{WR}$).
2. Wait until the end of the conversion. The end of the conversion period can be verified either by status checking (polling) or by using the interrupt.
3. Read the digital signal at an input port.

A microprocessor-compatible A/D converter, such as National Semiconductor ADC0801, has the necessary control signals built into it. (Data sheets for the ADC0801 are found at the end of this appendix.) A conversion is started by as-

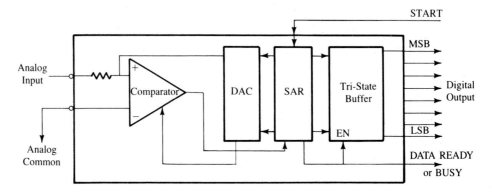

FIGURE E.8
Block Diagram of a Typical Successive-Approximation A/D Converter as an Integrated Circuit

serting $\overline{\text{CS}}$ and $\overline{\text{WR}}$ signals. At the end of the conversion, the converter generates an $\overline{\text{INTR}}$ (similar to DATA READY in Figure E.8) signal. This signal can be used to interrupt the processor to indicate that the data byte is ready and can be read. The processor reads the byte by asserting the $\overline{\text{RD}}$ signal and can start the next conversion if necessary.

E.2.3   Integrating A/D Converters

Integrating A/D converters use an indirect conversion method. An analog signal is converted into a proportional time period, which is then measured using a digital counter. Several variations of this technique are used. The most commonly known—the dual-slope conversion method—is described below.

DUAL-SLOPE A/D CONVERTERS

Figure E.9(a) is a block diagram of a typical dual-slope converter. It includes an integrator, comparator, counter, control logic, and a reference voltage. The conversion process follows three steps:

1. The switch S_1 connects the analog voltage V_{in} for a fixed count, shown in Figure E.9(b) as period T_1. During this period, the capacitor is charged with the current I_C, resulting in a linear ramp at the integrator output.
2. After the period T_1, the control logic switches the integrator input to the reference voltage V_{Ref} of the opposite polarity of the voltage V_{in}, and the counter is reset.
3. The counter starts counting again from zero as the capacitor begins to discharge with the current I_D for the period T_2. This results in a ramp with the opposite slope, and the counter is stopped when the ramp crosses the zero level. The counter reading is the equivalent digital signal for the analog input voltage V_{in}.

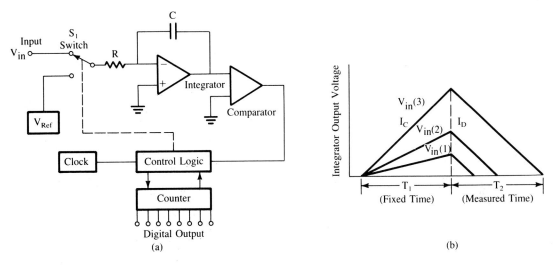

FIGURE E.9
Dual-Slope A/D Converter: (a) Block Diagram and (b) Conversion Process

In Figure E.9(b), the total charge in the capacitor while charging and discharging must be equal. Therefore

$$I_C T_1 = I_D T_2$$
$$V_{in} T_1 = V_{Ref} T_2 \ (I_C \text{ and } I_D \text{ are proportional to } V_{in} \text{ and } V_{Ref}, \text{ respectively})$$
$$T_2 = \frac{V_{in}}{V_{Ref}} \times T_1$$

Because T_1 and V_{Ref} are constant, the counter output for period T_2 is proportional to the analog input voltage V_{in}. The output voltage of the integrator reaches the final value proportional to the magnitude of the input voltage; see Figure E.9(b). However, the slope during the capacitor discharge is constant; thus, the higher voltage takes a longer period.

The characteristics of the integrating A/D converter can be summarized as follows:

1. The conversion accuracy is high.
2. The conversion speed is slow.
3. The noise-rejection level is high.

Interfacing an integrator-type converter with the microprocessor involves considerations similar to those involved in interfacing a successive-approximation converter.

![National Semiconductor]

DAC0830/DAC0831/DAC0832 8-Bit μP Compatible, Double-Buffered D to A Converters

General Description

The DAC0830 is an advanced CMOS/Si-Cr 8-bit multiplying DAC designed to interface directly with the 8080, 8048, 8085, Z80®, and other popular microprocessors. A deposited silicon-chromium R-2R resistor ladder network divides the reference current and provides the circuit with excellent temperature tracking characteristics (0.05% of Full Scale Range maximum linearity error over temperature). The circuit uses CMOS current switches and control logic to achieve low power consumption and low output leakage current errors. Special circuitry provides TTL logic input voltage level compatibility.

Double buffering allows these DACs to output a voltage corresponding to one digital word while holding the next digital word. This permits the simultaneous updating of any number of DACs.

The DAC0830 series are the 8-bit members of a family of microprocessor-compatible DACs (MICRO-DAC™). For applications demanding higher resolution, the DAC1000 series (10-bits) and the DAC1208 and DAC1230 (12-bits) are available alternatives.

Features

- Double-buffered, single-buffered or flow-through digital data inputs
- Easy interchange and pin-compatible with 12-bit DAC1230 series
- Direct interface to all popular microprocessors
- Linearity specified with zero and full scale adjust only— NOT BEST STRAIGHT LINE FIT.
- Works with ±10V reference-full 4-quadrant multiplication
- Can be used in the voltage switching mode
- Logic inputs which meet TTL voltage level specs (1.4V logic threshold)
- Operates "STAND ALONE" (without μP) if desired
- Available in 20-pin small-outline or molded chip carrier package

Key Specifications

- Current settling time   1 μs
- Resolution   8 bits
- Linearity   8, 9, or 10 bits
  (guaranteed over temp.)
- Gain Tempco   0.0002% FS/°C
- Low power dissipation   20 mW
- Single power supply   5 to 15 V_{DC}

Typical Application

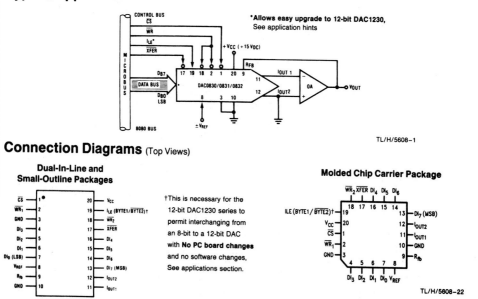

TL/H/5608–1

Connection Diagrams (Top Views)

Dual-In-Line and Small-Outline Packages

$\overline{CS}$	1	20 — V_{CC}
$\overline{WR}_1$	2	19 — I_{LE} (BYTE1/$\overline{BYTE2}$)†
GND	3	18 — $\overline{WR}_2$
DI_3	4	17 — $\overline{XFER}$
DI_2	5	16 — DI_4
DI_1	6	15 — DI_5
DI_0 (LSB)	7	14 — DI_6
V_{REF}	8	13 — DI_7 (MSB)
R_{fb}	9	12 — I_{OUT2}
GND	10	11 — I_{OUT1}

†This is necessary for the 12-bit DAC1230 series to permit interchanging from an 8-bit to a 12-bit DAC with **No PC board changes** and no software changes. See applications section.

TL/H/5608–21

Molded Chip Carrier Package

TL/H/5608–22

Absolute Maximum Ratings (Notes 1 & 2)

If Military/Aerospace specified devices are required, please contact the National Semiconductor Sales Office/Distributors for availability and specifications.

Supply Voltage (V_{CC})	17 V_{DC}
Voltage at Any Digital Input	V_{CC} to GND
Voltage at V_{REF} Input	$\pm 25V$
Storage Temperature Range	$-65°C$ to $+150°C$
Package Dissipation at $T_A = 25°C$ (Note 3)	500 mW
DC Voltage Applied to I_{OUT1} or I_{OUT2} (Note 4)	-100 mV to V_{CC}
ESD Susceptability (Note 14)	800V

Lead Temperature (soldering, 10 sec.)

Dual-In-Line Package (plastic)	260°C
Dual-In-Line Package (ceramic)	300°C
Surface Mount Package	
Vapor Phase (60 sec.)	215°C
Infrared (15 sec.)	220°C

Operating Conditions

Temperature Range	$T_{MIN} \leq T_A \leq T_{MAX}$
Part numbers with 'LCN' suffix	0°C to $+70°C$
Part numbers with 'LCWM' suffix	0°C to $+70°C$
Part numbers with 'LCV' suffix	0°C to $+70°C$
Part numbers with 'LCJ' suffix	$-40°C$ to $+85°C$
Part numbers with 'LJ' suffix	$-55°C$ to $+125°C$
Voltage at Any Digital Input	V_{CC} to GND

Electrical Characteristics

$V_{REF} = 10.000\ V_{DC}$ unless otherwise noted. **Boldface limits apply over temperature, $T_{MIN} \leq T_A \leq T_{MAX}$.** For all other limits $T_A = 25°C$.

Parameter		Conditions	See Note	$V_{CC} = 4.75\ V_{DC}$ $V_{CC} = 15.75\ V_{DC}$		$V_{CC} = 5\ V_{DC} \pm 5\%$ $V_{CC} = 12\ V_{DC} \pm 5\%$ to 15 $V_{DC} \pm 5\%$	Limit Units
				Typ (Note 12)	Tested Limit (Note 5)	Design Limit (Note 6)	
CONVERTER CHARACTERISTICS							
Resolution				8	8	**8**	bits
Linearity Error Max		Zero and full scale adjusted $-10V \leq V_{REF} \leq +10V$	4, 8				% FSR
DAC0830LJ & LCJ					**0.05**	**0.05**	% FSR
DAC0832LJ & LCJ					**0.2**	**0.2**	% FSR
DAC0830LCN, LCWM & LCV					0.05	**0.05**	% FSR
DAC0831LCN					0.1	**0.1**	% FSR
DAC0832LCN, LCWM & LCV					0.2	**0.2**	% FSR
Differential Nonlinearity Max		Zero and full scale adjusted $-10V \leq V_{REF} \leq +10V$	4, 8				% FSR
DAC0830LJ & LCJ					**0.1**	**0.1**	% FSR
DAC0832LJ & LCJ					**0.4**	**0.4**	% FSR
DAC0830LCN, LCWM & LCV					0.1	**0.1**	% FSR
DAC0831LCN					0.2	**0.2**	% FSR
DAC0832LCN, LCWM & LCV					0.4	**0.4**	% FSR
Monotonicity		$-10V \leq V_{REF}$ $\leq +10V$ LJ & LCJ	4		**8**	**8**	bits
		LCN, LCWM & LCV			8	**8**	bits
Gain Error Max		Using Internal R_{fb} $-10V \leq V_{REF} \leq +10V$	7	± 0.2	± 1	± 1	% FS
Gain Error Tempco Max		Using internal R_{fb}		**0.0002**		**0.0006**	% FS/°C
Power Supply Rejection		All digital inputs latched high $V_{CC} = 14.5V$ to 15.5V		0.0002	0.0025		% FSR/V
		11.5V to 12.5V		0.0006			
		4.5V to 5.5V		0.013	0.015		
Reference Input	Max			**15**	**20**	**20**	$k\Omega$
	Min			**15**	**10**	**10**	$k\Omega$
Output Feedthrough Error		$V_{REF} = 20$ Vp-p, f = 100 kHz All data inputs latched low		3			mVp-p

Electrical Characteristics

$V_{REF} = 10.000\ V_{DC}$ unless otherwise noted. **Boldface limits apply over temperature, $T_{MIN} \leq T_A \leq T_{MAX}$.** For all other limits $T_A = 25°C$. (Continued)

Parameter		Conditions		See Note	$V_{CC} = 4.75\ V_{DC}$ $V_{CC} = 15.75\ V_{DC}$		$V_{CC} = 5\ V_{DC} \pm 5\%$ $V_{CC} = 12\ V_{DC} \pm 5\%$ to 15 $V_{DC} \pm 5\%$	Limit Units
					Typ (Note 12)	Tested Limit (Note 5)	Design Limit (Note 6)	
CONVERTER CHARACTERISTICS (Continued)								
Output Leakage Current Max	I_{OUT1}	All data inputs latched low	LJ & LCJ LCN, LCWM & LCV	10		**100** 50	**100** **100**	nA
	I_{OUT2}	All data inputs latched high	LJ & LCJ LCN, LCWM & LCV			**100** 50	**100** **100**	nA
Output Capacitance	I_{OUT1} I_{OUT2}	All data inputs latched low			45 115			pF
	I_{OUT1} I_{OUT2}	All data inputs latched high			130 30			pF
DIGITAL AND DC CHARACTERISTICS								
Digital Input Voltages	Max	Logic Low	LJ 4.75V LJ 15.75V LCJ 4.75V LCJ 15.75V LCN, LCWM, LCV			**0.6** **0.8** **0.7** **0.8** 0.95	0.8	V_{DC}
	Min	Logic High	LJ & LCJ LCN, LCWM, LCV			**2.0** 1.9	**2.0** **2.0**	V_{DC}
Digital Input Currents	Max	Digital inputs <0.8V	LJ & LCJ LCN, LCWM, LCV		−50	**−200** −160	**−200** **−200**	µA µA
		Digital inputs >2.0V	LJ & LCJ LCN, LCWM, LCV		0.1	**+10** +8	**+10** **+10**	µA
Supply Current Drain	Max		LJ & LCJ LCN, LCWM, LCV		1.2	**3.5** 1.7	**3.5** **2.0**	mA

682

Electrical Characteristics V_{REF} = 10.000 V_{DC} unless otherwise noted. **Boldface limits apply over temperature, $T_{MIN} \leq T_A \leq T_{MAX}$.** For all other limits T_A = 25°C. (Continued)

Symbol	Parameter	Conditions	See Note	V_{CC} = 15.75 V_{DC}			V_{CC} = 12 $V_{DC} \pm 5\%$ to 15 $V_{DC} \pm 5\%$	V_{CC} = 4.75 V_{DC}			V_{CC} = 5 V_{DC} $\pm 5\%$	Limit Units
				Typ (Note 12)	Tested Limit (Note 5)	Design Limit (Note 6)	Design Limit (Note 6)	Typ (Note 12)	Tested Limit (Note 5)	Design Limit (Note 6)	Design Limit (Note 6)	
AC CHARACTERISTICS												
t_s	Current Setting Time	V_{IL} = 0V, V_{IH} = 5V		1.0				1.0				µs
t_W	Write and XFER Pulse Width Min	V_{IL} = 0V, V_{IH} = 5V	11 9	100	250 **320**	**320**		375	600 **900**	**900**		
t_{DS}	Data Setup Time Min	V_{IL} = 0V, V_{IH} = 5V	9	100	250 **320**	**320**		375	600 **900**	**900**		
t_{DH}	Data Hold Time Min	V_{IL} = 0V, V_{IH} = 5V	9		30 **30**				50 **50**			ns
t_{CS}	Control Setup Time Min	V_{IL} = 0V, V_{IH} = 5V	9	110	250 **320**	**320**		600	900 **1100**	**1100**		
t_{CH}	Control Hold Time Min	V_{IL} = 0V, V_{IH} = 5V	9	0	0 **0**	**10**		0	0 **0**			

Note 1: Absolute Maximum Ratings indicate limits beyond which damage to the device may occur. DC and AC electrical specifications do not apply when operating the device beyond its specified operating conditions.

Note 2: All voltages are measured with respect to GND, unless otherwise specified.

Note 3: The maximum power dissipation must be derated at elevated temperatures and is dictated by T_{JMAX}, θ_{JA}, and the ambient temperature, T_A. The maximum allowable power dissipation at any temperature is $P_D = (T_{JMAX} - T_A)/\theta_{JA}$ or the number given in the Absolute Maximum Ratings, whichever is lower. For this device, T_{JMAX} = 125°C (plastic) or 150°C (ceramic), and the typical junction-to-ambient thermal resistance of the J package when board mounted is 80°C/W. For the N package, this number increases to 100°C/W and for the V package this number is 120°C/W.

Note 4: For current switching applications, both I_{OUT1} and I_{OUT2} must go to ground or the "Virtual Ground" of an operational amplifier. The linearity error is degraded by approximately $V_{OS} \div V_{REF}$. For example, if V_{REF} = 10V then a 1 mV offset, V_{OS}, on I_{OUT1} or I_{OUT2} will introduce an additional 0.01% linearity error.

Note 5: Tested limits are guaranteed to National's AOQL (Average Outgoing Quality Level).

Note 6: Guaranteed, but not 100% production tested. These limits are not used to calculate outgoing quality levels.

Note 7: Guaranteed at V_{REF} = ± 10 V_{DC} and V_{REF} = ± 1 V_{DC}.

Note 8: The unit "FSR" stands for "Full Scale Range." "Linearity Error" and "Power Supply Rejection" specs are based on this unit to eliminate dependence on a particular V_{REF} value and to indicate the true performance of the part. The "Linearity Error" specification of the DAC0830 is "0.05% of FSR (MAX)". This guarantees that after performing a zero and full scale adjustment (see Sections 2.5 and 2.6), the plot of the 256 analog voltage outputs will each be within 0.05% $\times V_{REF}$ of a straight line which passes through zero and full scale.

Note 9: Boldface tested limits apply to the LJ and LCJ suffix parts only.

Note 10: A 100nA leakage current with R_{fb} = 20k and V_{REF} = 10V corresponds to a zero error of $(100 \times 10^{-9} \times 20 \times 10^3) \times 100/10$ which is 0.02% of FS.

Note 11: The entire write pulse must occur within the valid data interval for the specified t_W, t_{DS}, t_{DH}, and t_s to apply.

Note 12: Typicals are at 25°C and represent most likely parametric norm.

Note 13: Human body model, 100 pF discharged through a 1.5 kΩ resistor.

Switching Waveform

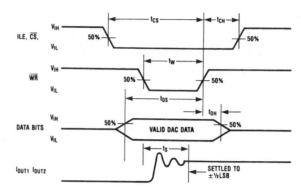

ILE, $\overline{CS}$,

$\overline{WR}$

DATA BITS

I_{OUT1} I_{OUT2}

VALID DAC DATA

SETTLED TO
$\pm\frac{1}{2}$LSB

TL/H/5608–2

Definition of Package Pinouts

Control Signals (All control signals level actuated)

$\overline{CS}$: **Chip Select** (active low). The $\overline{CS}$ in combination with ILE will enable $\overline{WR}_1$.

ILE: **Input Latch Enable** (active high). The ILE in combination with $\overline{CS}$ enables $\overline{WR}_1$.

$\overline{WR}_1$: **Write 1.** The active low $\overline{WR}_1$ is used to load the digital input data bits (DI) into the input latch. The data in the input latch is latched when $\overline{WR}_1$ is high. To update the input latch—$\overline{CS}$ and $\overline{WR}_1$ must be low while ILE is high.

$\overline{WR}_2$: **Write 2** (active low). This signal, in combination with $\overline{XFER}$, causes the 8-bit data which is available in the input latch to transfer to the DAC register.

$\overline{XFER}$: **Transfer control signal** (active low). The $\overline{XFER}$ will enable $\overline{WR}_2$.

Other Pin Functions

DI_0–DI_7: **Digital Inputs.** DI_0 is the least significant bit (LSB) and DI_7 is the most significant bit (MSB).

I_{OUT1}: **DAC Current Output 1.** I_{OUT1} is a maximum for a digital code of all 1's in the DAC register, and is zero for all 0's in DAC register.

I_{OUT2}: **DAC Current Output 2.** I_{OUT2} is a constant minus I_{OUT1}, or $I_{OUT1} + I_{OUT2} = $ constant (I full scale for a fixed reference voltage).

R_{fb}: **Feedback Resistor.** The feedback resistor is provided on the IC chip for use as the shunt feedback resistor for the external op amp which is used to provide an output voltage for the DAC. This on-chip resistor should always be used (not an external resistor) since it matches the resistors which are used in the on-chip R-2R ladder and tracks these resistors over temperature.

V_{REF}: **Reference Voltage Input.** This input connects an external precision voltage source to the internal R-2R ladder. V_{REF} can be selected over the range of $+10$ to $-10V$. This is also the analog voltage input for a 4-quadrant multiplying DAC application.

V_{CC}: **Digital Supply Voltage.** This is the power supply pin for the part. V_{CC} can be from $+5$ to $+15V_{DC}$. Operation is optimum for $+15V_{DC}$.

GND: The pin 10 voltage must be at the same ground potential as I_{OUT1} and I_{OUT2} for current switching applications. Any difference of potential (V_{OS} pin 10) will result in a linearity change of

$$\frac{V_{OS} \text{ pin 10}}{3V_{REF}}$$

For example, if $V_{REF} = 10V$ and pin 10 is 9mV offset from I_{OUT1} and I_{OUT2} the linearity change will be 0.03%.

Pin 3 can be offset $\pm100mV$ with no linearity change, but the logic input threshold will shift.

![National Semiconductor Corporation]

ADC0801, ADC0802, ADC0803, ADC0804, ADC0805 8-Bit μP Compatible A/D Converters

General Description

The ADC0801, ADC0802, ADC0803, ADC0804 and ADC0805 are CMOS 8-bit successive approximation A/D converters that use a differential potentiometric ladder—similar to the 256R products. These converters are designed to allow operation with the NSC800 and INS8080A derivative control bus with TRI-STATE® output latches directly driving the data bus. These A/Ds appear like memory locations or I/O ports to the microprocessor and no interfacing logic is needed.

Differential analog voltage inputs allow increasing the common-mode rejection and offsetting the analog zero input voltage value. In addition, the voltage reference input can be adjusted to allow encoding any smaller analog voltage span to the full 8 bits of resolution.

Features

- Compatible with 8080 μP derivatives—no interfacing logic needed - access time - 135 ns
- Easy interface to all microprocessors, or operates "stand alone"
- Differential analog voltage inputs
- Logic inputs and outputs meet both MOS and TTL voltage level specifications
- Works with 2.5V (LM336) voltage reference
- On-chip clock generator
- 0V to 5V analog input voltage range with single 5V supply
- No zero adjust required
- 0.3″ standard width 20-pin DIP package
- 20-pin molded chip carrier or small outline package
- Operates ratiometrically or with 5 V_{DC}, 2.5 V_{DC}, or analog span adjusted voltage reference

Key Specifications

- Resolution   8 bits
- Total error   ± 1/4 LSB, ± 1/2 LSB and ± 1 LSB
- Conversion time   100 μs

Typical Applications

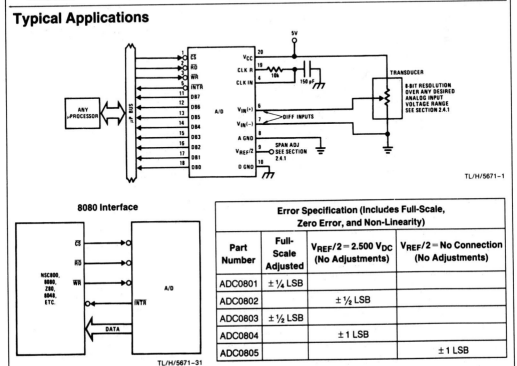

TL/H/5671-1

8080 Interface

TL/H/5671-31

Part Number	Error Specification (Includes Full-Scale, Zero Error, and Non-Linearity)		
	Full-Scale Adjusted	$V_{REF}/2 = 2.500\ V_{DC}$ (No Adjustments)	$V_{REF}/2 = $ No Connection (No Adjustments)
ADC0801	± 1/4 LSB		
ADC0802		± 1/2 LSB	
ADC0803	± 1/2 LSB		
ADC0804		± 1 LSB	
ADC0805			± 1 LSB

Absolute Maximum Ratings (Notes 1 & 2)

If Military/Aerospace specified devices are required, contact the National Semiconductor Sales Office/Distributors for availability and specifications.

Supply Voltage (V_{CC}) (Note 3)	6.5V
Voltage	
Logic Control Inputs	-0.3V to $+18$V
At Other Input and Outputs	-0.3V to ($V_{CC}+0.3$V)
Lead Temp. (Soldering, 10 seconds)	
Dual-In-Line Package (plastic)	260°C
Dual-In-Line Package (ceramic)	300°C
Surface Mount Package	
Vapor Phase (60 seconds)	215°C
Infrared (15 seconds)	220°C

Storage Temperature Range	-65°C to $+150$°C
Package Dissipation at $T_A = 25$°C	875 mW
ESD Susceptibility (Note 10)	800V

Operating Ratings (Notes 1 & 2)

Temperature Range	$T_{MIN} \leq T_A \leq T_{MAX}$
ADC0801/02LJ	-55°C $\leq T_A \leq +125$°C
ADC0801/02/03/04LCJ	-40°C $\leq T_A \leq +85$°C
ADC0801/02/03/05LCN	-40°C $\leq T_A \leq +85$°C
ADC0804LCN	0°C $\leq T_A \leq +70$°C
ADC0802/03/04LCV	0°C $\leq T_A \leq +70$°C
ADC0802/03/04LCWM	0°C $\leq T_A \leq +70$°C
Range of V_{CC}	4.5 V_{DC} to 6.3 V_{DC}

Electrical Characteristics

The following specifications apply for $V_{CC} = 5$ V_{DC}, $T_{MIN} \leq T_A \leq T_{MAX}$ and $f_{CLK} = 640$ kHz unless otherwise specified.

Parameter	Conditions	Min	Typ	Max	Units
ADC0801: Total Adjusted Error (Note 8)	With Full-Scale Adj. (See Section 2.5.2)			$\pm\frac{1}{4}$	LSB
ADC0802: Total Unadjusted Error (Note 8)	$V_{REF}/2 = 2.500$ V_{DC}			$\pm\frac{1}{2}$	LSB
ADC0803: Total Adjusted Error (Note 8)	With Full-Scale Adj. (See Section 2.5.2)			$\pm\frac{1}{2}$	LSB
ADC0804: Total Unadjusted Error (Note 8)	$V_{REF}/2 = 2.500$ V_{DC}			±1	LSB
ADC0805: Total Unadjusted Error (Note 8)	$V_{REF}/2$-No Connection			±1	LSB
$V_{REF}/2$ Input Resistance (Pin 9)	ADC0801/02/03/05 ADC0804 (Note 9)	2.5 0.75	8.0 1.1		kΩ kΩ
Analog Input Voltage Range	(Note 4) V(+) or V(−)	Gnd−0.05		$V_{CC}+0.05$	V_{DC}
DC Common-Mode Error	Over Analog Input Voltage Range		$\pm\frac{1}{16}$	$\pm\frac{1}{8}$	LSB
Power Supply Sensitivity	$V_{CC} = 5$ $V_{DC} \pm10\%$ Over Allowed $V_{IN}(+)$ and $V_{IN}(-)$ Voltage Range (Note 4)		$\pm\frac{1}{16}$	$\pm\frac{1}{8}$	LSB

AC Electrical Characteristics

The following specifications apply for $V_{CC} = 5$ V_{DC} and $T_A = 25$°C unless otherwise specified.

Symbol	Parameter	Conditions	Min	Typ	Max	Units
T_C	Conversion Time	$f_{CLK} = 640$ kHz (Note 6)	103		114	μs
T_C	Conversion Time	(Note 5, 6)	66		73	$1/f_{CLK}$
f_{CLK}	Clock Frequency Clock Duty Cycle	$V_{CC} = 5$V, (Note 5) (Note 5)	100 40	640	1460 60	kHz %
CR	Conversion Rate in Free-Running Mode	$\overline{INTR}$ tied to $\overline{WR}$ with $\overline{CS} = 0$ V_{DC}, $f_{CLK} = 640$ kHz	8770		9708	conv/s
$t_{W(\overline{WR})L}$	Width of $\overline{WR}$ Input (Start Pulse Width)	$\overline{CS} = 0$ V_{DC} (Note 7)	100			ns
t_{ACC}	Access Time (Delay from Falling Edge of $\overline{RD}$ to Output Data Valid)	$C_L = 100$ pF		135	200	ns
t_{1H}, t_{0H}	TRI-STATE Control (Delay from Rising Edge of $\overline{RD}$ to Hi-Z State)	$C_L = 10$ pF, $R_L = 10$k (See TRI-STATE Test Circuits)		125	200	ns
t_{WI}, t_{RI}	Delay from Falling Edge of $\overline{WR}$ or $\overline{RD}$ to Reset of $\overline{INTR}$			300	450	ns
C_{IN}	Input Capacitance of Logic Control Inputs			5	7.5	pF
C_{OUT}	TRI-STATE Output Capacitance (Data Buffers)			5	7.5	pF
CONTROL INPUTS [Note: CLK IN (Pin 4) is the input of a Schmitt trigger circuit and is therefore specified separately]						
V_{IN} (1)	Logical "1" Input Voltage (Except Pin 4 CLK IN)	$V_{CC} = 5.25$ V_{DC}	2.0		15	V_{DC}

AC Electrical Characteristics (Continued)

The following specifications apply for $V_{CC} = 5V_{DC}$ and $T_{MIN} \leq T_A \leq T_{MAX}$, unless otherwise specified.

Symbol	Parameter	Conditions	Min	Typ	Max	Units
CONTROL INPUTS [Note: CLK IN (Pin 4) is the input of a Schmitt trigger circuit and is therefore specified separately]						
$V_{IN}(0)$	Logical "0" Input Voltage (Except Pin 4 CLK IN)	$V_{CC} = 4.75\ V_{DC}$			0.8	V_{DC}
$I_{IN}(1)$	Logical "1" Input Current (All Inputs)	$V_{IN} = 5\ V_{DC}$		0.005	1	μA_{DC}
$I_{IN}(0)$	Logical "0" Input Current (All Inputs)	$V_{IN} = 0\ V_{DC}$	-1	-0.005		μA_{DC}
CLOCK IN AND CLOCK R						
V_T+	CLK IN (Pin 4) Positive Going Threshold Voltage		2.7	3.1	3.5	V_{DC}
V_T-	CLK IN (Pin 4) Negative Going Threshold Voltage		1.5	1.8	2.1	V_{DC}
V_H	CLK IN (Pin 4) Hysteresis $(V_T+) - (V_T-)$		0.6	1.3	2.0	V_{DC}
$V_{OUT}(0)$	Logical "0" CLK R Output Voltage	$I_O = 360\ \mu A$ $V_{CC} = 4.75\ V_{DC}$			0.4	V_{DC}
$V_{OUT}(1)$	Logical "1" CLK R Output Voltage	$I_O = -360\ \mu A$ $V_{CC} = 4.75\ V_{DC}$	2.4			V_{DC}
DATA OUTPUTS AND $\overline{INTR}$						
$V_{OUT}(0)$	Logical "0" Output Voltage Data Outputs $\overline{INTR}$ Output	$I_{OUT} = 1.6\ mA, V_{CC} = 4.75\ V_{DC}$ $I_{OUT} = 1.0\ mA, V_{CC} = 4.75\ V_{DC}$			0.4 0.4	V_{DC} V_{DC}
$V_{OUT}(1)$	Logical "1" Output Voltage	$I_O = -360\ \mu A, V_{CC} = 4.75\ V_{DC}$	2.4			V_{DC}
$V_{OUT}(1)$	Logical "1" Output Voltage	$I_O = -10\ \mu A, V_{CC} = 4.75\ V_{DC}$	4.5			V_{DC}
I_{OUT}	TRI-STATE Disabled Output Leakage (All Data Buffers)	$V_{OUT} = 0\ V_{DC}$ $V_{OUT} = 5\ V_{DC}$	-3		3	μA_{DC} μA_{DC}
I_{SOURCE}		V_{OUT} Short to Gnd, $T_A = 25°C$	4.5	6		mA_{DC}
I_{SINK}		V_{OUT} Short to V_{CC}, $T_A = 25°C$	9.0	16		mA_{DC}
POWER SUPPLY						
I_{CC}	Supply Current (Includes Ladder Current)	$f_{CLK} = 640\ kHz$, $V_{REF}/2 = NC, T_A = 25°C$ and $\overline{CS} = 5V$				
	ADC0801/02/03/04LCJ/05			1.1	1.8	mA
	ADC0804LCN/LCV/LCWM			1.9	2.5	mA

Note 1: Absolute Maximum Ratings indicate limits beyond which damage to the device may occur. DC and AC electrical specifications do not apply when operating the device beyond its specified operating conditions.

Note 2: All voltages are measured with respect to Gnd, unless otherwise specified. The separate A Gnd point should always be wired to the D Gnd.

Note 3: A zener diode exists, internally, from V_{CC} to Gnd and has a typical breakdown voltage of 7 V_{DC}.

Note 4: For $V_{IN}(-) \geq V_{IN}(+)$ the digital output code will be 0000 0000. Two on-chip diodes are tied to each analog input (see block diagram) which will forward conduct for analog input voltages one diode drop below ground or one diode drop greater than the V_{CC} supply. Be careful, during testing at low V_{CC} levels (4.5V), as high level analog inputs (5V) can cause this input diode to conduct–especially at elevated temperatures, and cause errors for analog inputs near full-scale. The spec allows 50 mV forward bias of either diode. This means that as long as the analog V_{IN} does not exceed the supply voltage by more than 50 mV, the output code will be correct. To achieve an absolute 0 V_{DC} to 5 V_{DC} input voltage range will therefore require a minimum supply voltage of 4.950 V_{DC} over temperature variations, initial tolerance and loading.

Note 5: Accuracy is guaranteed at $f_{CLK} = 640$ kHz. At higher clock frequencies accuracy can degrade. For lower clock frequencies, the duty cycle limits can be extended so long as the minimum clock high time interval or minimum clock low time interval is no less than 275 ns.

Note 6: With an asynchronous start pulse, up to 8 clock periods may be required before the internal clock phases are proper to start the conversion process. The start request is internally latched, see *Figure 2* and section 2.0.

Note 7: The $\overline{CS}$ input is assumed to bracket the $\overline{WR}$ strobe input and therefore timing is dependent on the $\overline{WR}$ pulse width. An arbitrarily wide pulse width will hold the converter in a reset mode and the start of conversion is initiated by the low to high transition of the $\overline{WR}$ pulse (see timing diagrams).

Note 8: None of these A/Ds requires a zero adjust (see section 2.5.1). To obtain zero code at other analog input voltages see section 2.5 and *Figure 5*.

Note 9: The $V_{REF}/2$ pin is the center point of a two resistor divider connected from V_{CC} to ground. Each resistor is 2.2k, except for the ADC0804LCJ where each resistor is 16k. Total ladder input resistance is the sum of the two equal resistors.

Note 10: Human body model, 100 pF discharged through a 1.5 kΩ resistor.

Typical Performance Characteristics

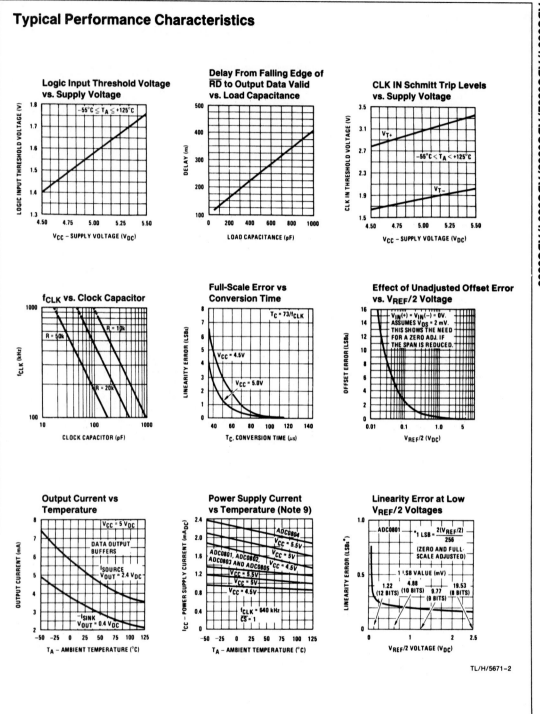

TL/H/5671–2

Z80 Instructional Summary

Key:

 n = 8-bit number   ( ) = contents as a pointer to memory or I/O
nn = 16-bit number
 d = 7-bit displacement (express in 2's complement for backward displacement)
 e = 7-bit displacement in reference to program counter (express in 2's complement for backward displacement)
Shading indicates instructions seldom used in simple programs.

Mnemonic		Hex	Mnemonic		Hex	Mnemonic		Hex
ADC	A,A	8F	CALL	C,nn	DC 16-bit	HALT		76
ADC	A,B	88	CALL	M,nn	FC 16-bit	IM	0	ED 46
ADC	A,C	89	CALL	NC,nn	D4 16-bit	IM	1	ED 56
ADC	A,D	8A	CALL	NZ,nn	C4 16-bit	IM	2	ED 5E
ADC	A,E	8B	CALL	P,nn	F4 16-bit	IN	A,(n)	DB 8-bit
ADC	A,H	8C	CALL	PE,nn	EC 16-bit	IN	A,(C)	ED 78
ADC	A,L	8D	CALL	PO,nn	E4 16-bit	IN	B,(C)	ED 40
ADC	A,n	CE 8-bit	CALL	Z,nn	CC 16-bit	IN	C,(C)	ED 48
ADC	A,(HL)	8E	CCF		3F	IN	D,(C)	ED 50
ADC	A,(IX+d)	DD 8E d	CP	A	BF	IN	E,(C)	ED 58
ADC	A,(IY+d)	FD 8E d	CP	B	B8	IN	F,(C)	ED 70
ADC	HL,BC	ED 4A	CP	C	B9	IN	H,(C)	ED 60
ADC	HL,DE	ED 5A	CP	D	BA	IN	L,(C)	ED 68
ADC	HL,HL	ED 6A	CP	E	BB	INC	A	3C
ADC	HL,SP	ED 7A	CP	H	BC	INC	B	04
ADD	A,A	87	CP	L	BD	INC	BC	03
ADD	A,B	80	CP	n	FE 8-bit	INC	C	0C
ADD	A,C	81	CP	(HL)	BE	INC	D	14
ADD	A,D	82	CP	(IX+d)	DD BE d	INC	DE	13
ADD	A,E	83	CP	(IY+d)	FD BE d	INC	E	1C
ADD	A,H	84	CPD		ED A9	INC	H	24
ADD	A,L	85	CPDR		ED B9	INC	HL	23
ADD	A,n	C6 8-bit	CPI		ED A1	INC	IX	DD 23
ADD	A,(HL)	86	CPIR		ED B1	INC	IY	FD 23
ADD	A,(IX+d)	DD 86 d	CPL		2F	INC	L	2C
ADD	A,(IY+d)	FD 86 d	DAA		27	INC	SP	33
ADD	HL,BC	09	DEC	A	3D	INC	(HL)	34
ADD	HL,DE	19	DEC	B	05	INC	(IX+d)	DD 34 d
ADD	HL,HL	29	DEC	BC	0B	INC	(IY+d)	FD 34 d
ADD	HL,SP	39	DEC	C	0D	IND		ED AA
ADD	IX,BC	DD 09	DEC	D	15	INDR		ED BA
ADD	IX,DE	DD 19	DEC	DE	1B	INI		ED A2
ADD	IX,IX	DD 29	DEC	E	1D	INIR		ED B2
ADD	IX,SP	DD 39	DEC	H	25	JP	nn	C3 16-bit
ADD	IY,BC	FD 09	DEC	HL	2B	JP	(HL)	E9
ADD	IY,DE	FD 19	DEC	IX	DD 2B	JP	(IX)	DD E9
ADD	IY,IY	FD 29	DEC	IY	FD 2B	JP	(IY)	FD E9
ADD	IY,SP	FD 39	DEC	L	2D	JP	C,nn	DA 16-bit
AND	A	A7	DEC	SP	3B	JP	M,nn	FA 16-bit
AND	B	A0	DEC	(HL)	35	JP	NC,nn	D2 16-bit
AND	C	A1	DEC	(IX+d)	DD 35 d	JP	NZ,nn	C2 16-bit
AND	D	A2	DEC	(IY+d)	FD 35 d	JP	P,nn	F2 16-bit
AND	E	A3	DI		F3	JP	PE,nn	EA 16-bit
AND	H	A4	DJNZ	e	10 e	JP	PO,nn	E2 16-bit
AND	L	A5	EI		FB	JP	Z,nn	CA 16-bit
AND	n	E6 8-bit	EX	(SP),HL	E3	JR	C,e	38 e
AND	(HL)	A6	EX	(SP),IX	DD E3	JR	NC,e	30 e
AND	(IX+d)	DD A6 d	EX	(SP),IY	FD E3	JR	NZ,e	20 e
AND	(IY+d)	FD A6 d	EX	AF,AF'	08	JR	Z,e	28 e
BIT	b,s	see pp. 568–69	EX	DE,HL	EB	JR	e	18 e
CALL	nn	CD 16-bit	EXX		D9	LD	A,A	7F
						LD	A,B	78

Mnemonic		Hex	Mnemonic		Hex	Mnemonic		Hex
LD	A,C	79	LD	E,A	5F	LD	(HL),D	72
LD	A,D	7A	LD	E,B	58	LD	(HL),E	73
LD	A,E	7B	LD	E,C	59	LD	(HL),H	74
LD	A,H	7C	LD	E,D	5A	LD	(HL),L	75
LD	A,I	ED 57	LD	E,E	5B	LD	(HL),n	36 8-bit
LD	A,L	7D	LD	E,H	5C	LD	(IX+d),A	DD 77 d
LD	A,n	3E 8-bit	LD	E,L	5D	LD	(IX+d),B	DD 70 d
LD	A,R	ED 5F	LD	E,n	1E 8-bit	LD	(IX+d),C	DD 71 d
LD	A,(BC)	0A	LD	E,(HL)	5E	LD	(IX+d),D	DD 72 d
LD	A,(DE)	1A	LD	E,(IX+d)	DD 5E d	LD	(IX+d),E	DD 73 d
LD	A,(HL)	7E	LD	E,(IY+d)	FD 5E d	LD	(IX+d),H	DD 74 d
LD	A,(IX+d)	DD 7E d	LD	H,A	67	LD	(IX+d),L	DD 75 d
LD	A,(IY+d)	FD 7E d	LD	H,B	60	LD	(IX+d),n	DD 36 d 8-bit
LD	A,(nn)	3A 16-bit	LD	H,C	61	LD	(IY+d),A	FD 77 d
LD	B,A	47	LD	H,D	62	LD	(IY+d),B	FD 70 d
LD	B,B	40	LD	H,E	63	LD	(IY+d),C	FD 71 d
LD	B,C	41	LD	H,H	64	LD	(IY+d),D	FD 72 d
LD	B,D	42	LD	H,L	65	LD	(IY+d),E	FD 73 d
LD	B,E	43	LD	H,n	26 8-bit	LD	(IY+d),H	FD 74 d
LD	B,H	44	LD	H,(HL)	66	LD	(IY+d),L	FD 75 d
LD	B,L	45	LD	H,(IX+d)	DD 66 d	LD	(IY+d),n	FD 36 d 8-bit
LD	B,n	06 8-bit	LD	H,(IY+d)	FD 66 d	LD	(nn),A	32 16-bit
LD	B,(HL)	46	LD	HL,nn	21 16-bit	LD	(nn),BC	ED 43 16-bit
LD	B,(IX+d)	DD 46 d	LD	HL,(nn)	2A 16-bit	LD	(nn),DE	ED 53 16-bit
LD	B,(IY+d)	FD 46 d	LD	I,A	ED 47	LD	(nn),HL	22 16-bit
LD	BC,nn	01 16-bit	LD	IX,nn	DD 21 16-bit	LD	(nn),IX	DD 22 16-bit
LD	BC,(nn)	ED 4B 16-bit	LD	IX,(nn)	DD 2A 16-bit	LD	(nn),IY	FD 22 16-bit
LD	C,A	4F	LD	IY,nn	FD 21 16-bit	LD	(nn),SP	ED 73 16-bit
LD	C,B	48	LD	IY,(nn)	FD 2A 16-bit	LDD		ED A8
LD	C,C	49	LD	L,A	6F	LDDR		ED B8
LD	C,D	4A	LD	L,B	68	LDI		ED A0
LD	C,E	4B	LD	L,C	69	LDIR		ED B0
LD	C,H	4C	LD	L,D	6A	NEG		ED 44
LD	C,L	4D	LD	L,E	6B	NOP		00
LD	C,n	0E 8-bit	LD	L,H	6C	OR	A	B7
LD	C,(HL)	4E	LD	L,L	6D	OR	B	B0
LD	C,(IX+d)	DD 4E d	LD	L,n	2E 8-bit	OR	C	B1
LD	C,(IY+d)	FD 4E d	LD	L,(HL)	6E	OR	D	B2
LD	D,A	57	LD	L,(IX+d)	DD 6E d	OR	E	B3
LD	D,B	50	LD	L,(IY+d)	FD 6E d	OR	H	B4
LD	D,C	51	LD	R,A	ED 4F	OR	L	B5
LD	D,D	52	LD	SP,HL	F9	OR	n	F6 8-bit
LD	D,E	53	LD	SP,IX	DD F9	OR	(HL)	B6
LD	D,H	54	LD	SP,IY	FD F9	OR	(IX+d)	DD B6 d
LD	D,L	55	LD	SP,nn	31 16-bit	OR	(IY+d)	FD B6 d
LD	D,n	16 8-bit	LD	SP,(nn)	ED 7B 16-bit	OTDR		ED BB
LD	D,(HL)	56	LD	(BC),A	02	OTIR		ED B3
LD	D,(IX+d)	DD 56 d	LD	(DE),A	12	OUT	(C),A	ED 79
LD	D,(IY+d)	FD 56 d	LD	(HL),A	77	OUT	(C),B	ED 41
LD	DE,nn	11 16-bit	LD	(HL),B	70	OUT	(C),C	ED 49
LD	DE,(nn)	ED 5B 16-bit	LD	(HL),C	71	OUT	(C),D	ED 51

*Z80 Assembler Dictionary. Copyright 1986 by CAMI Research Inc.

Mnemonic		Hex	Mnemonic		Hex	Mnemonic		Hex
OUT	(C),E	ED 59	RLCA		07	SLA	B	CB 20
OUT	(C),H	ED 61	RLD		ED 6F	SLA	C	CB 21
OUT	(C),L	ED 69	RR	A	CB 1F	SLA	D	CB 22
OUT	(n),A	D3 8-bit	RR	B	CB 18	SLA	E	CB 23
OUTD		ED AB	RR	C	CB 19	SLA	H	CB 24
OUTI		ED A3	RR	D	CB 1A	SLA	L	CB 25
POP	AF	F1	RR	E	CB 1B	SLA	(HL)	CB 26
POP	BC	C1	RR	H	CB 1C	SLA	(IX+d)	DD CB d 26
POP	DE	D1	RR	L	CB 1D	SLA	(IY+d)	FD CB d 26
POP	HL	E1	RR	(HL)	CB 1E	SRA	A	CB 2F
POP	IX	DD E1	RR	(IX+d)	DD CB d 1E	SRA	B	CB 28
POP	IY	FD E1	RR	(IY+d)	FD CB d 1E	SRA	C	CB 29
PUSH	AF	F5	RRA		1F	SRA	D	CB 2A
PUSH	BC	C5	RRC	A	CB 0F	SRA	E	CB 2B
PUSH	DE	D5	RRC	B	CB 08	SRA	H	CB 2C
PUSH	HL	E5	RRC	C	CB 09	SRA	L	CB 2D
PUSH	IX	DD E5	RRC	D	CB 0A	SRA	(HL)	CB 2E
PUSH	IY	FD E5	RRC	E	CB 0B	SRA	(IX+d)	DD CB d 2E
RES	b,s	see pp. 604–5	RRC	H	CB 0C	SRA	(IY+d)	FD CB d 2E
RET		C9	RRC	L	CB 0D	SRL	A	CB 3F
RET	C	D8	RRC	(HL)	CB 0E	SRL	B	CB 38
RET	M	F8	RRC	(IX+d)	DD CB d 0E	SRL	C	CB 39
RET	NC	D0	RRC	(IY+d)	FD CB d 0E	SRL	D	CB 3A
RET	NZ	C0	RRCA		0F	SRL	E	CB 3B
RET	P	F0	RRD		ED 67	SRL	H	CB 3C
RET	PE	E8	RST	00H	C7	SRL	L	CB 3D
RET	PO	E0	RST	08H	CF	SRL	(HL)	CB 3E
RET	Z	C8	RST	10H	D7	SRL	(IX+d)	DD CB d 3E
RETI		ED 4D	RST	18H	DF	SRL	(IY+d)	FD CB d 3E
RETN		ED 45	RST	20H	E7	SUB	A	97
RL	A	CB 17	RST	28H	EF	SUB	B	90
RL	B	CB 10	RST	30H	F7	SUB	C	91
RL	C	CB 11	RST	38H	FF	SUB	D	92
RL	D	CB 12	SBC	A,A	9F	SUB	E	93
RL	E	CB 13	SBC	A,B	98	SUB	H	94
RL	H	CB 14	SBC	A,C	99	SUB	L	95
RL	L	CB 15	SBC	A,D	9A	SUB	n	D6 8-bit
RL	(HL)	CB 16	SBC	A,E	9B	SUB	(HL)	96
RL	(IX+d)	DD CB d 16	SBC	A,H	9C	SUB	(IX+d)	DD 96 d
RL	(IY+d)	FD CB d 16	SBC	A,L	9D	SUB	(IY+d)	FD 96 d
RLA		17	SBC	A,n	DE 8-bit	XOR	A	AF
RLC	A	CB 07	SBC	A,(HL)	9E	XOR	B	A8
RLC	B	CB 00	SBC	A,(IX+d)	DD 9E d	XOR	C	A9
RLC	C	CB 01	SBC	A,(IY+d)	FD 9E d	XOR	D	AA
RLC	D	CB 02	SBC	HL,BC	ED 42	XOR	E	AB
RLC	E	CB 03	SBC	HL,DE	ED 52	XOR	H	AC
RLC	H	CB 04	SBC	HL,HL	ED 62	XOR	L	AD
RLC	L	CB 05	SBC	HL,SP	ED 72	XOR	n	EE 8-bit
RLC	(HL)	CB 06	SCF		37	XOR	(HL)	AE
RLC	(IX+d)	DD CB d 06	SET	b,s	see p. 615	XOR	(IX+d)	DD AE d
RLC	(IY+d)	FD CB d 06	SLA	A	CB 27	XOR	(IY+d)	FD AE d

*Z80 Assembler Dictionary. Copyright 1986 by CAMI Research Inc.

SUMMARY OF FLAG OPERATION

Instructions	D₇ S	Z	H		P/V	N	D₀ C	Comments
ADD A, s; ADC A, s	‡	‡	X	‡	X	V	0	‡	8-bit add or add with carry.
SUB s; SBC A, s; CP s; NEG	‡	‡	X	‡	X	V	1	‡	8-bit subtract, subtract with carry, compare and negate accumulator.
AND s	‡	‡	X	1	X	P	0	0	Logical operation.
OR s, XOR s	‡	‡	X	0	X	P	0	•	Logical operation.
INC s	‡	‡	X	‡	X	V	0	•	8-bit increment.
DEC s	‡	‡	X	‡	X	V	1	•	8-bit decrement.
ADD DD, ss	•	•	X	X	X	•	0	‡	16-bit add.
ADC HL, ss	‡	‡	X	X	X	V	0	‡	16-bit add with carry.
SBC HL, ss	‡	‡	X	X	X	V	1	‡	16-bit subtract with carry.
RLA; RLCA; RRA; RRCA	•	•	X	0	X	•	0	‡	Rotate accumulator.
RL m; RLC m; RR m; RRC m; SLA m; SRA m; SRL m	‡	‡	X	0	X	P	0	‡	Rotate and shift locations.
RLD; RRD	‡	‡	X	0	X	P	0	•	Rotate digit left and right.
DAA	‡	‡	X	‡	X	P	•	‡	Decimal adjust accumulator.
CPL	•	•	X	1	X	•	1	•	Complement accumulator.
SCF	•	•	X	0	X	•	0	1	Set carry.
CCF	•	•	X	X	X	•	0	‡	Complement carry.
IN r (C)	‡	‡	X	0	X	P	0	•	Input register indirect.
INI; IND; OUTI; OUTD	X	‡	X	X	X	X	1	•	Block input and output. Z = 1 if B ≠ 0, otherwise Z = 0.
INIR; INDR; OTIR; OTDR	X	1	X	X	X	X	1	•	Block input and output. Z = 1 if B ≠ 0, otherwise Z = 0.
LDI; LDD	X	X	X	0	X	‡	0	•	Block transfer instructions. P/V = 1 if BC ≠ 0, otherwise P/V = 0.
LDIR; LDDR	X	X	X	0	X	0	0	•	Block transfer instructions. P/V = 1 if BC ≠ 0, otherwise P/V = 0.
CPI; CPIR; CPD; CPDR	X	‡	X	X	X	‡	1	•	Block search instructions. Z = 1 if A = (HL), otherwise Z = 0. P/V = 1 if BC ≠ 0, otherwise P/V = 0.
LD A; I, LD A, R	‡	‡	X	0	X	IFF	0	•	IFF, the content of the interrupt enable flip-flop, (IFF₂), is copied into the P/V flag.
BIT b, s	X	‡	X	1	X	X	0	•	The state of bit b of location s is copied into the Z flag.

SYMBOLIC NOTATION

Symbol	Operation
S	Sign flag. S = 1 if the MSB of the result is 1.
Z	Zero flag. Z = 1 if the result of the operation is 0.
P/V	Parity or overflow flag. Parity (P) and overflow (V) share the same flag. Logical operations affect this flag with the parity of the result while arithmetic operations affect this flag with the overflow of the result. If P/V holds parity: P/V = 1 if the result of the operation is even; P/V = 0 if result is odd. If P/V holds overflow, P/V = 1 if the result of the operation produced an overflow. If P/V does not hold overflow, P/V = 0.
H*	Half-carry flag. H = 1 if the add or subtract operation produced a carry into, or borrow from, bit 4 of the accumulator.
N*	Add/Subtract flag. N = 1 if the previous operation was a subtract.
C	Carry/Link flag. C = 1 if the operation produced a carry from the MSB of the operand or result.

Symbol	Operation
‡	The flag is affected according to the result of the operation.
•	The flag is unchanged by the operation.
0	The flag is reset by the operation.
1	The flag is set by the operation.
X	The flag is indeterminate.
V	P/V flag affected according to the overflow result of the operation.
P	P/V flag affected according to the parity result of the operation.
r	Any one o the CPU registers A, B, C, D, E, H, L.
s	Any 8-bit location for all the addressing modes allowed for the particular instruction.
ss	Any 16-bit location for all the addressing modes allowed for that instruction.
ii	Any one of the two index registers IX or IY.
R	Refresh counter.
n	8-bit value in range < 0, 255 >.
nn	16-bit value in range < 0, 65535 >.

*H and N flags are used in conjunction with the decimal adjust instruction (DAA) to properly correct the result into packed BCD format following addition or subtraction using operands with packed BCD format.

Index